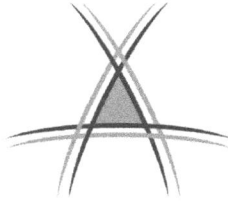

ASCENT®
CENTER FOR TECHNICAL KNOWLEDGE

Creo Parametric 10.0
Sheet Metal Design

Learning Guide
1ˢᵗ Edition

ASCENT - Center for Technical Knowledge®
Creo Parametric 10.0
Sheet Metal Design
1st Edition

Prepared and produced by:

ASCENT Center for Technical Knowledge
630 Peter Jefferson Parkway, Suite 175
Charlottesville, VA 22911

866-527-2368
www.ASCENTed.com

Lead Contributor: Mark Potrzebowski

ASCENT - Center for Technical Knowledge (a division of Rand Worldwide Inc.) is a leading developer of professional learning materials and knowledge products for engineering software applications. ASCENT specializes in designing targeted content that facilitates application-based learning with hands-on software experience. For over 25 years, ASCENT has helped users become more productive through tailored custom learning solutions.

We welcome any comments you may have regarding this guide, or any of our products. To contact us please email: feedback@ASCENTed.com.

Contents

Preface vii

In This Guide ix

Practice Files xi

Chapter 1: Introduction to Sheet Metal Modeling   1-1

1.1   **Sheet Metal Environment**.. 1-2

1.2   **Display of Sheet Metal Parts**... 1-3

1.3   **Parameters**... 1-4

1.4   **Orienting a Sheet Metal Part**... 1-5

1.5   **Developed Length of Sheet Metal Bends**........................ 1-6

1.6   **Designing in Sheetmetal Mode** 1-7
     Sheetmetal Mode 1-7
     Assembly Mode 1-10
     Convert Parts...1-10

Chapter 2: Primary Walls   2-1

2.1   **Primary Walls** 2-2
     Extruded..2-2
     Planar..2-6
     Revolved..2-7
     Blended 2-7
     Offset 2-8

2.2   **Capturing Design Intent in Sketcher** 2-9

Practice 2a: Primary Extruded Unattached Wall............................ 2-12

Practice 2b: Primary Planar Unattached Wall 2-17

Practice 2c: Create an Extruded Bracket 2-20

Practice 2d: Create an Unattached Revolved Wall......................... 2-23

Practice 2e: Create an Offset Wall... 2-25

Practice 2f: Create the Project Part 2-28

Chapter Review Questions 2-29

Chapter 3: Secondary Walls   3-1

3.1   **Selecting an Attachment Edge** 3-2

3.2   **Flat Wall** 3-6

3.3   **Flange Wall** 3-12

3.4   **Twisted Wall** 3-21
        Offset 3-23
        Symmetrical 3-25

3.5   **Extended Wall** 3-27

3.6   **Unattached Walls** 3-29
        Merging Walls 3-30

3.7   **Wall Section Reuse** 3-32

3.8   **Bend Relief** 3-33
        No Relief 3-33
        Rip Relief 3-33
        Stretch Relief 3-35
        Rectangular Relief 3-36
        Obround Relief 3-37
        Relief on Both Sides 3-39

Practice 3a: Secondary Walls 3-40

Practice 3b: Unattached Wall 3-48

Practice 3c: Flange Walls I 3-55

Practice 3d: Flange Walls II 3-59

Practice 3e: Add Walls to the Project Part 3-65

Practice 3f: Extrude and Reuse 3-69

Practice 3g: Twist Walls 3-80

Chapter Review Questions 3-89

Chapter 4: Regular Unbends, Bend Backs, and Extruded Cuts   4-1

4.1   **Unbending Sheet Metal Geometry** 4-2

4.2   **Bending Back Unbent Geometry** 4-4

4.3   **Solid and Sheet Metal Cuts** 4-6

4.4   **Creating a Cut Requiring Unbend and Bend Back Features** 4-12

Practice 4a: Create a Sheet Metal Cut 4-16

Practice 4b: Projected Curve and a Cut 4-21

Practice 4c: Additional Sheet Metal Cuts 4-27

Chapter Review Questions 4-30

Chapter 5: Notches and Punches 5-1

5.1 **Corner Relief** 5-2
 Corner Relief Types 5-6
 Corner Relief Options 5-10

5.2 **Introduction to Notches and Punches** 5-12

5.3 **Creating Notch and Punch UDFs** 5-14

5.4 **Placing Notch or Punch UDFs** 5-18

Practice 5a: Create Corner Reliefs 5-24

Practice 5b: Create a Notch for Bend Relief I 5-32

Practice 5c: Create a Punch Feature 5-41

Practice 5d: Create a Notch for Bend Relief II 5-45

Chapter Review Questions 5-59

Chapter 6: Bend Features 6-1

6.1 **Bend Features** 6-2
 Bend 6-2
 Edge Bend 6-4
 Planar Bend 6-5

6.2 **Creating a Bend Feature** 6-6
 Transition 6-6
 Bend Relief 6-6
 Bend Line 6-9
 Bend Surface 6-10
 Bend Line References 6-10
 Sketched Bend Line 6-11
 Bend Placement 6-11
 Transitions 6-12
 Relief 6-12

6.3 **Position of the Bend Line** 6-14

6.4 **Bend Line Adjustment** 6-17

6.5 **Bend Line Notes** 6-20
 Bend Note Orientation 6-22
 Best Practices for Bend Features 6-23

Practice 6a: Bend Flat Geometry 6-24

Practice 6b: Create a Bend Line Adjustment 6-42

Practice 6c: Edge Bends 6-50

Chapter Review Questions 6-55

Chapter 7: Unbending Complex Geometry — 7-1

7.1	**Ruled and Non-Ruled Geometry**	7-2
	Ruled Geometry	7-2
	Non-Ruled Geometry	7-3
7.2	**Unbending Non-Ruled Geometry**	7-4
7.3	**Split Area Feature**	7-6
7.4	**Cross-Section Driven Unbends**	7-7
7.5	**Rip Features**	7-9
	Sketch Rip	7-10
	Edge Rip	7-10
	Surface Rip	7-11
	Rip Connect	7-11
	Practice 7a: Deform Surfaces	7-12
	Practice 7b: Cross-Section Driven Unbend	7-15
	Practice 7c: Rip Features and Deformation Control	7-20
	Practice 7d: Split Area Feature	7-25
	Chapter Review Questions	7-31

Chapter 8: Sheet Metal Forms — 8-1

8.1	**Introduction to Form Features**	8-2
	Die	8-2
	Punch	8-2
8.2	**Placing a Punch or Die Form Feature**	8-4
	Dependency Options	8-8
	Assembly Considerations	8-8
	Radius Considerations	8-9
	Bending	8-10
8.3	**Flattening Form Geometry**	8-11
8.4	**Flat Patterns**	8-13
8.5	**Flattened Representation**	8-15
8.6	**Unstamp Edges Feature**	8-17
8.7	**Form Feature Restrictions**	8-19
	Practice 8a: Punch Form	8-20
	Practice 8b: Die Form	8-25
	Practice 8c: Flatten Form Geometry	8-34
	Practice 8d: Flat Patterns	8-39
	Chapter Review Questions	8-46

Chapter 9: Documenting a Sheet Metal Part   9-1

9.1   **Flat States** 9-2

9.2   **Creating Flat States** 9-3

9.3   **Opening Flat State Instances** 9-6

9.4   **Adding a Flat State Instance to a Drawing** 9-7
     Deformed Areas 9-8

9.5   **Documenting the Bend Order** 9-10

Practice 9a: Sheet Metal Drawing 9-13

Practice 9b: Bend Tables in Drawings 9-27

Chapter Review Questions 9-28

Chapter 10: Converting Solid Parts   10-1

10.1   **Converting Solid Parts** 10-2

10.2   **Conversion Feature** 10-4
     Edge Rip 10-4
     Rip Connect... 10-6
     Edge Bends 10-7
     Corner Relief 10-7

10.3   **Additional Conversion Options** 10-9

Practice 10a: Convert a Solid Part 10-13

Practice 10b: Conversion Feature 10-19

Practice 10c: Convert Walls with Non-Uniform Thickness 10-27

Chapter Review Questions 10-35

Chapter 11: Sheet Metal Setup   11-1

11.1   **Calculating the Developed Length** 11-2

11.2   **Y-Factor and the Default Formula**................................ 11-3

11.3   **Bend Tables**... 11-5

11.4   **Sheet Metal Parameters and Relations** 11-9

11.5   **Default Fixed Geometry**... 11-14

Practice 11a: Calculate Developed Length........................ 11-15

Practice 11b: Sheet Metal Parameters and Relations 11-23

Chapter Review Questions 11-35

Chapter 12: Investigating a Sheet Metal Part   12-1

12.1 Investigation Tools 12-2

12.2 Sheet Metal Reports 12-3
    Text Reports 12-6

12.3 Design Rules 12-7
    Design Check 12-8

Practice 12a: Sheet Metal Information Tools 12-9

Chapter Review Questions 12-15

Preface

The *Creo Parametric 10.0: Sheet Metal Design* guide enables you to use your introductory modeling skills to create sheet metal models, including walls, bends, notches, and form features. On completion of this guide, you will have acquired the skills to confidently manipulate sheet metal geometry, adjust bend developed lengths, and convert solid parts.

Topics Covered

- The sheet metal environment
- Primary and secondary walls
- Bend relief
- Corner relief
- Regular unbends, back bends, and cuts
- Notches and punches
- Bend features
- Unbending complex geometry
- Sheet metal forms
- Documenting a sheet metal part
- Converting solid parts
- Sheet metal setup
- Investigating a sheet metal part

Prerequisites

- Access to the Creo Parametric 10.0 software. The practices and files included with this guide might not be compatible with prior versions. Practice files included with this guide are compatible with the commercial version of the software, but not the student edition.

- Completion of the *Creo Parametric: Introduction to Solid Modeling* guide, or similar levels of prior experience using the Creo Parametric software.

Note on Software Setup

This guide assumes a standard installation of the software using the default preferences during installation. Lectures and practices use the standard software templates and default options for the Content Libraries.

This guide was developed against Creo Parametric 10.0, Build 10.0.3.0.

Note on Learning Guide Content

ASCENT's learning guides are intended to teach the technical aspects of using the software and do not focus on professional design principles and standards. The exercises aim to demonstrate the capabilities and flexibility of the software, rather than following specific design codes or standards, which can vary between regions.

Lead Contributor: Mark Potrzebowski

Mark has been a trainer and curriculum developer in the PLM industry for over 14 years, with experience on multiple CAD systems, including Pro/ENGINEER, Creo Parametric, Inventor, and CATIA. Trained in Instructional Design, Mark uses his skills to develop instructor-led and web-based training products. Before joining ASCENT, Mark worked as a Technical Trainer with a focus on CATIA, Creo, and PLM systems. He holds a Bachelors degree in Computer Graphics Technology from Purdue University, West Lafayette, Indiana.

Mark Potrzebowski has been the Lead Contributor for *Creo Parametric: Sheet Metal Design* since 2021.

In This Guide

The following highlights the key features of this guide.

Feature	Description
Practice Files	The Practice Files page includes a link to the practice files and instructions on how to download and install them. The practice files are required to complete the practices in this guide.
Chapters	A chapter consists of the following: Learning Objectives, Instructional Content, Practices, and Chapter Review Questions.
	• **Learning Objectives** define the skills you can acquire by learning the content provided in the chapter.
	• **Instructional Content**, which begins right after Learning Objectives, refers to the descriptive and procedural information related to various topics. Each main topic introduces a product feature, discusses various aspects of that feature, and provides step-by-step procedures on how to use that feature. Where relevant, examples, figures, helpful hints, and notes are provided.
	• **Practice** for a topic follows the instructional content. Practices enable you to use the software to perform a hands-on review of a topic. It is required that you download the practice files (using the link found on the Practice Files page) prior to starting the first practice.
	• **Chapter Review Questions**, located close to the end of a chapter, enable you to test your knowledge of the key concepts discussed in the chapter.

Practice Files

To download the practice files for this guide, use the following steps:

1. Type the URL *exactly as shown below* into the address bar of your Internet browser to access the Course File Download page.

    Note: If you are using the ebook, you do not have to type the URL. Instead, you can access the page by clicking the URL below.

    ## https://www.ascented.com/getfile/id/jaculatrixPF

    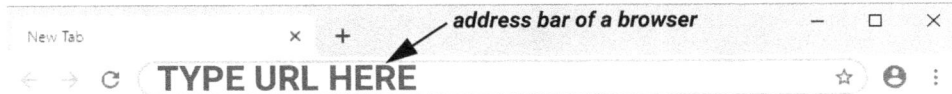

2. On the Course File Download page, click the **DOWNLOAD NOW** button, as shown below, to download the .ZIP file that contains the practice files.

3. Once the download is complete, unzip the file and extract its contents.

    The recommended practice files folder location is:
    C:\Creo Parametric Sheet Metal Design Practice Files

    Note: It is recommended that you do not change the location of the practice files folder. Doing so may cause errors when completing the practices.

Stay Informed!

To receive information about upcoming events, promotional offers, and complimentary webcasts, visit:

www.ASCENTed.com/updates

Introduction to Sheet Metal Modeling

The Creo Parametric sheet metal tools enable you to create thin-walled parts that can be bent and flattened to form the final geometry. This chapter provides an overview of the sheet metal environment and workflow.

Learning Objectives

- Understand the benefits of using the Creo Parametric sheet metal environment to design sheet metal models.
- Identify the similarities in generating a sheet metal part and a solid part.
- Identify the color scheme when creating a sheet metal part in Creo Parametric.
- Identify parameters that can be specified when a sheet metal part is created.
- Understand how sheet metal parts are oriented using the commands that are also used in part mode.
- Gain a general understanding of the formula that Creo Parametric uses to compensate for the stretching and compression that occurs in areas that are bent.
- Understand the overall workflow that is used to create a sheet metal model using feature-based and top-down design techniques.
- Identify the method that can be used to convert a solid part into a sheet metal part.

1.1 Sheet Metal Environment

Working in Sheetmetal mode to design sheet metal parts enables you to efficiently and effectively capture design intent. Sheetmetal mode also enables you to design components for the following uses:

- Design a model within the context of an assembly so that all 3D information is present.

- Create features specific to the sheet metal modeling process.

- Create different instances of the model to use at different times, such as for design and documentation.

- Extract information and establish controls that are beneficial to the manufacturing process.

- Generate reports and other information to document the design of the sheet metal part.

The process of creating a sheet metal model is similar to the process of creating a solid part in the following ways:

- Individual features (e.g., walls, bends, notches, bend back, and forms) are created in sequence and reference one another, resulting in parent/child relationships.

- Sketching references are established when creating certain types of walls, just as they are for protrusions and cuts.

- Depth options are specified in Sheetmetal mode.

  Note: It is important to consider design intent in Sheetmetal mode and not necessarily the order in which the part would be bent during manufacturing.

Parent/child references and design intent are equally important in Sheetmetal mode and solid part creation. You must carefully consider feature type and order of creation.

1.2 Display of Sheet Metal Parts

Geometry created in Sheetmetal mode has a specific color scheme; one side of the model is green and the other side is white, as shown in Figure 1–1.

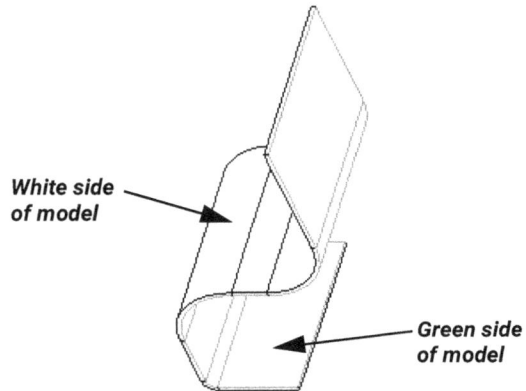

White side of model

Green side of model

Figure 1–1

When modeling a sheet metal part, remember that it always has a constant wall thickness. The green side of the model is used as the driving side. The white surface is then offset by a distance that is equal to the material thickness. Typically, references and geometry are generated based on the green side of the model.

1.3 Parameters

A default material thickness can be set for a sheet metal part. Once a sheet metal part has been created, select **Model Intent>Parameters**. The Parameters dialog box lists the **SMT_THICKNESS** parameter, as shown in Figure 1–2. When you create sheet metal features they use this value by default.

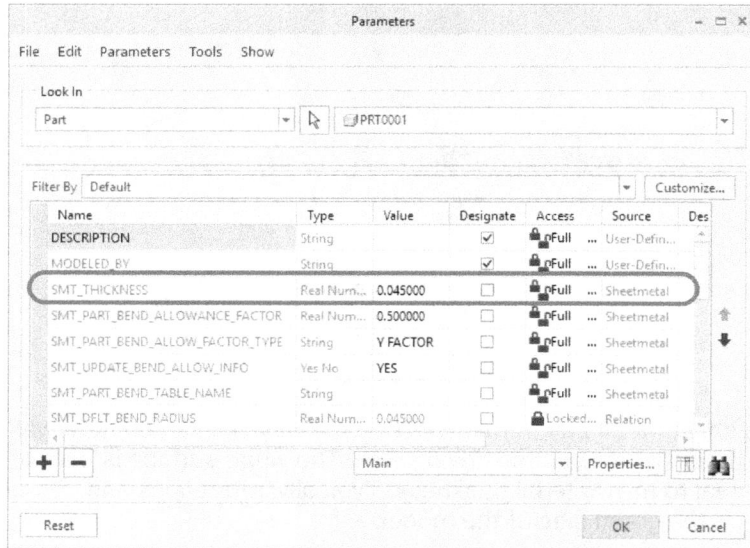

Figure 1–2

When the first wall is created, the parameter value entered in the Parameters dialog box is automatically assigned in the *Thickness* field in the dashboard, as shown in Figure 1–3.

Figure 1–3

1.4 Orienting a Sheet Metal Part

Models are oriented in Sheetmetal mode similar to how parts are oriented in Part mode. You can pan, zoom, and spin a model using the same options. You can also display the model in a 2D orientation using the Orientation dialog box (⚒ (Reorient)) and selecting two planar surfaces to face Front, Back, Top, Bottom, Left, or Right. When displaying a 2D orientation in Sheetmetal mode, the first viewing reference selected must be a planar face or datum plane, as shown in Figure 1–4. The second reference can be a planar surface or an edge.

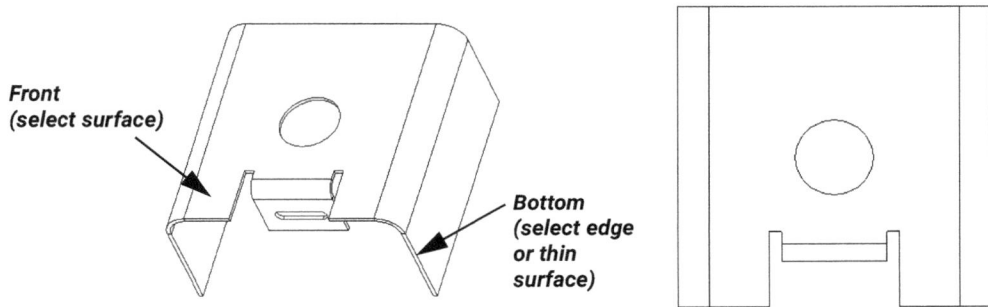

Figure 1–4

Note: Use 🔳 (Pick From List) (shortcut menu) when selecting edges and surfaces for orientation to ensure that the intended reference is selected.

1.5 Developed Length of Sheet Metal Bends

One of the primary methods for manipulating sheet metal is bending (forming). Stretching and compression occur in some areas when the part is bent. As a result, material thickness on the part can vary.

Creo Parametric compensates for this by using a formula that considers material thickness, bend radius, bend angle, and other properties. This formula locates a neutral bend line and measures its length to determine the developed length of the bend. With this technique, Sheetmetal mode captures your design intent when creating the model in the bent (formed) condition. You can then create a flat instance of the model to be used for manufacturing, as shown in Figure 1–5.

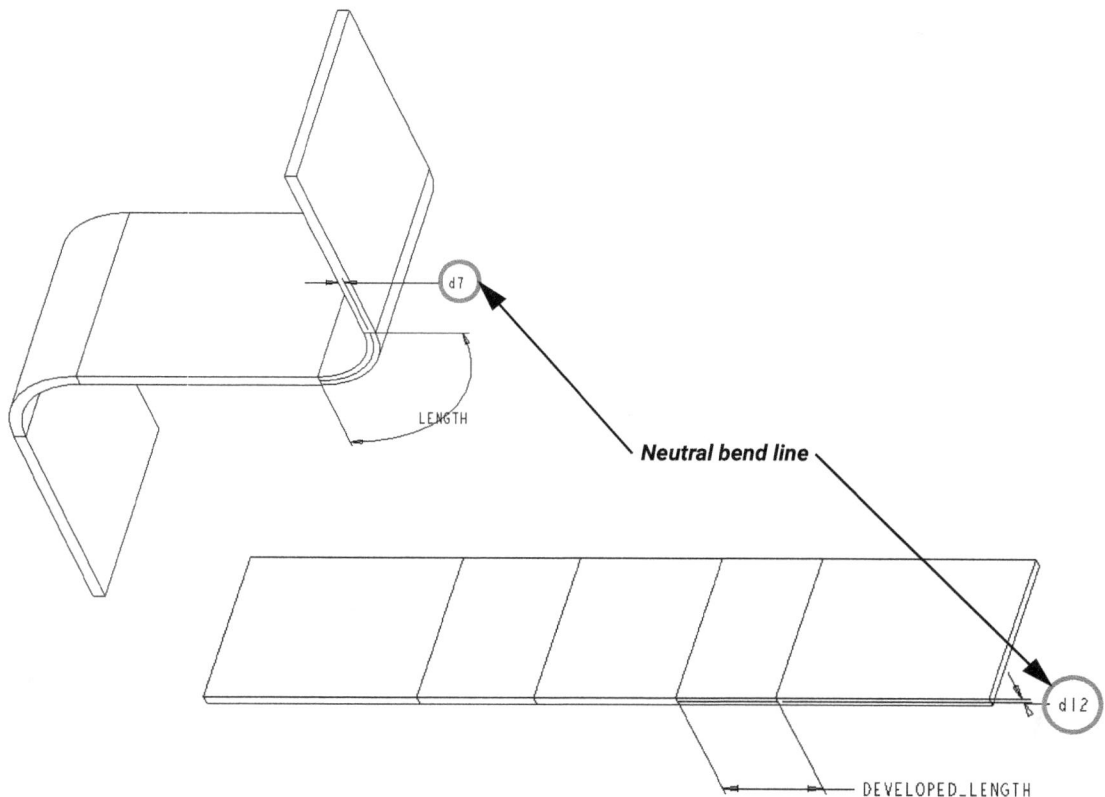

Figure 1–5

Note: The calculation of the developed length can also be defined in a bend table. A bend table includes information about the bend radius, sequence, and angle.

1.6 Designing in Sheetmetal Mode

Sheetmetal Mode

A common way of creating sheet metal parts in Creo Parametric is to build them using feature-based techniques, similar to those used when building a solid part.

How To: Create a Part in Sheetmetal Mode

1. Open a template or create default datum planes in a new model, as shown in Figure 1−6.

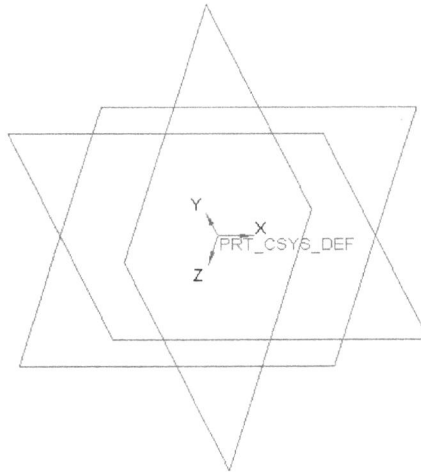

Figure 1−6

2. Create any required reference geometry.
3. Create the primary wall feature, as shown in Figure 1−7.

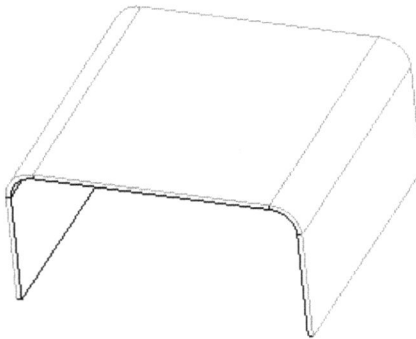

Figure 1−7

4. Create additional walls, as shown in Figure 1–8.

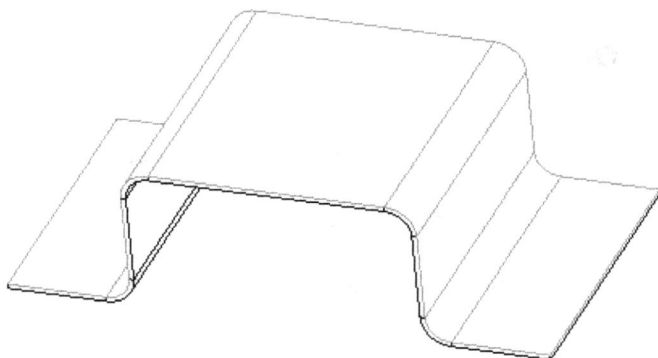

Figure 1–8

5. Apply a bend relief, as shown in Figure 1–9.

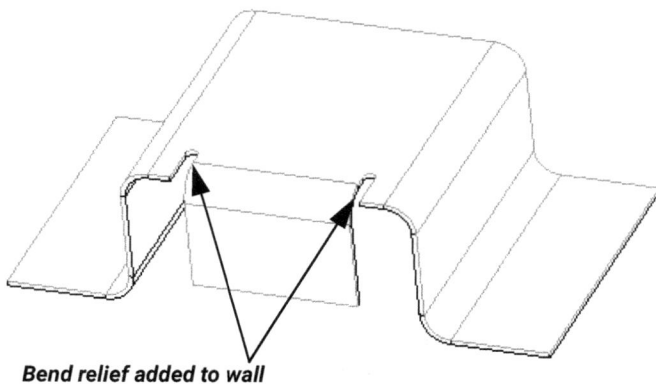

Bend relief added to wall

Figure 1–9

6. Create notches, punches, and cuts, as shown in Figure 1–10.

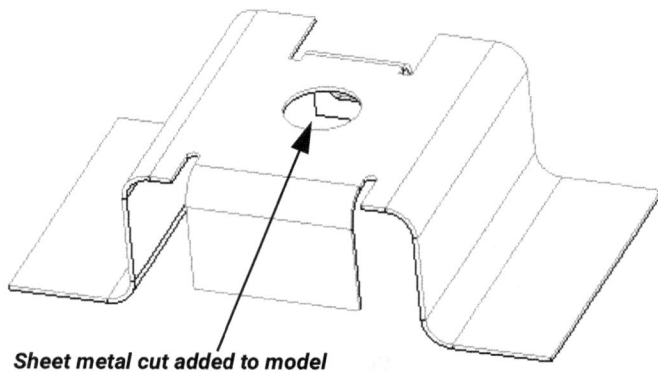

Sheet metal cut added to model

Figure 1–10

7. Create forms as shown in Figure 1–11. In this example they are used to stiffen the opening in the part.

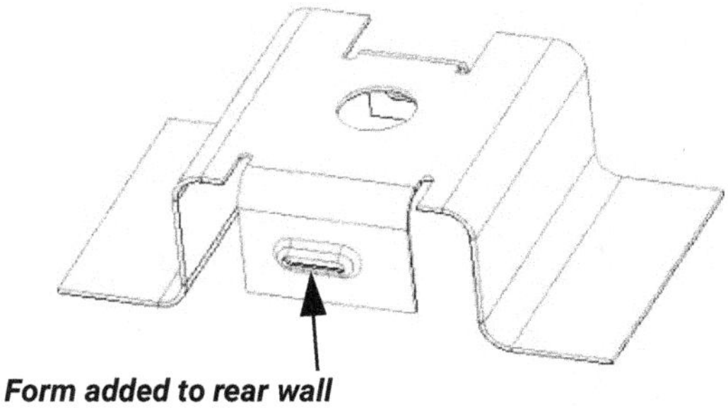

Form added to rear wall

Figure 1–11

8. Create a flat state to facilitate documentation, as shown in Figure 1–12.

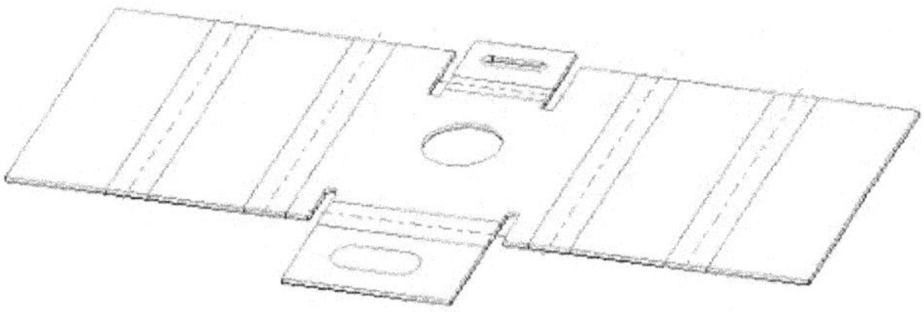

Figure 1–12

9. Create a detail drawing including bend information to document the design, as shown in Figure 1–13.

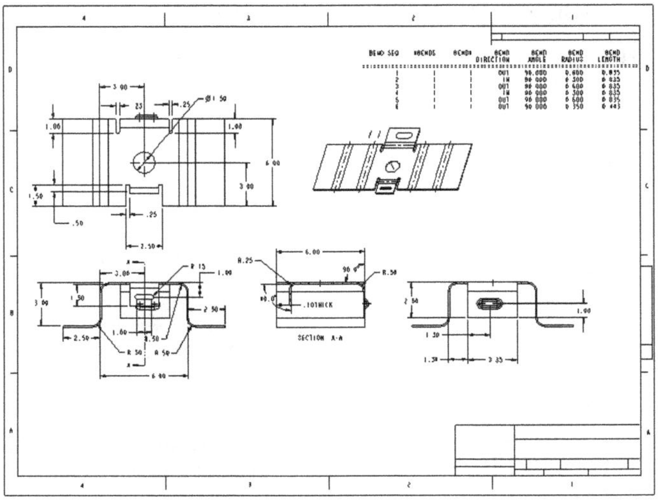

Figure 1–13

Assembly Mode

If you use top-down design principles, working with an assembly could be more beneficial. Sheet metal parts created within the context of an assembly model often act as supporting structures for principle components in a larger assembly.

How To: Create a Sheet Metal Part in Assembly Mode

1. Assemble all of the required components relative to each other or to a default reference.
2. Create the required sheet metal components with appropriate parent/child references.
3. Add any remaining components.
4. Apply an appropriate bend table to the sheet metal part so that it has correct clearance with the surrounding components.
5. Define a bend order table in Sheetmetal mode to generate the bend sequence for the part.
6. Create a flat state to display fully formed and flattened instances of the part on a drawing.
7. Create a detail drawing, including bend information.

Convert Parts

You can also create a sheet metal model by converting a solid part.

How To: Convert a Solid Part to Sheet Metal

1. Open the part and select **Operations>Convert to Sheetmetal** in the *Model* tab. Based on the type of part, click ↳ (Driving Surface) or ▢ (Shell).

   Note: You can work with the part in Sheetmetal mode once it has been converted.

2. Add relief as required.
3. Add any required additional features.

Figure 1–14 shows an example of a converted part.

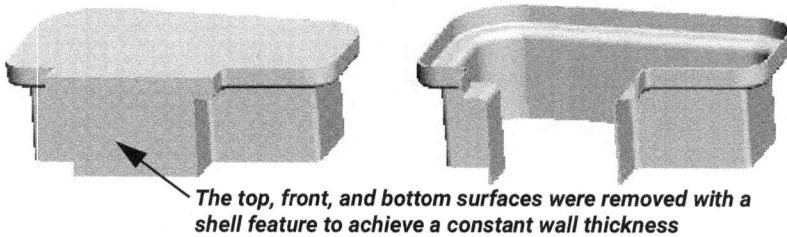

The top, front, and bottom surfaces were removed with a shell feature to achieve a constant wall thickness

Figure 1–14

Primary Walls

In this chapter, you will learn about the various tools available for creating the first or primary wall in a sheet metal model. You can include bend geometry in the sketched wall profile.

Learning Objectives

- Understand the difference between primary and secondary sheet metal walls.
- Learn the different types of primary walls available.
- Learn the process of creating a primary extruded wall in sheet metal using the appropriate tools.
- Learn to include the bend geometry in the sketched section to accurately describe the profile of the wall.
- Learn to thicken the wall and create a mold line to accurately describe the profile of the wall.

2.1 Primary Walls

Sheetmetal mode contains two types of walls: primary and secondary. The primary wall is the first wall that is created in the sheet metal model. It only references default datum planes or other reference geometry, and forms the foundation on which all other wall features are built. This is considered an unattached wall.

The primary wall is similar to the base feature in a solid part. Both the base feature of a solid model and the primary wall of a sheet metal model represent the basic shape of the object.

In Sheetmetal mode (similar to other Creo Parametric modes) it is good practice to begin the creation of a model with three default datum planes. The next feature is generally the primary (unattached) wall feature.

Figure 2–1 shows the types of primary walls available in the *Sheetmetal* tab for creation.

Figure 2–1

The following types of primary (unattached) walls are the most common: Extruded, Planar, Blended, Revolved, and Offset.

Extruded

The **Extrude** tool enables you to create an unattached extruded wall feature. You can use this tool to create a first wall and a secondary unattached wall. Click (Extrude) in the *Sheetmetal* tab to create an extruded wall. Select a sketching plane to open the *Sketch* tab. You can also right-click, select (Define Internal Sketch), and select a sketching plan and orientation plane.

Alternatively, you can select the sketching plane and click ⬦ (Extrude) in the mini toolbar, as shown in Figure 2−2.

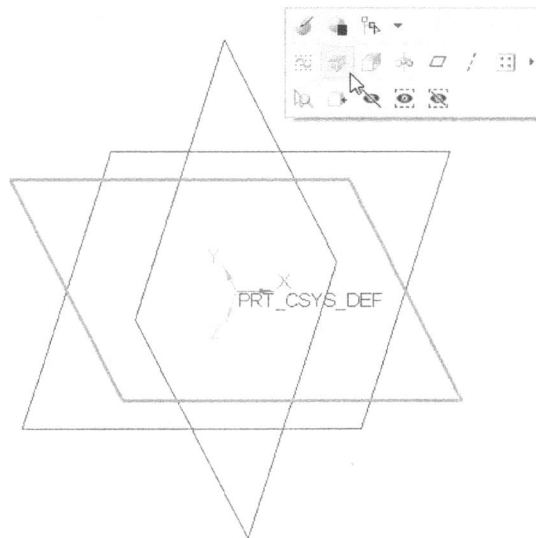

Figure 2−2

For an extruded wall, the cross-section is sketched using the *Sketch* tab. Sketch the section for the wall and add the required dimensions, as shown in Figure 2−3. The section represents the green (driving) side of the wall.

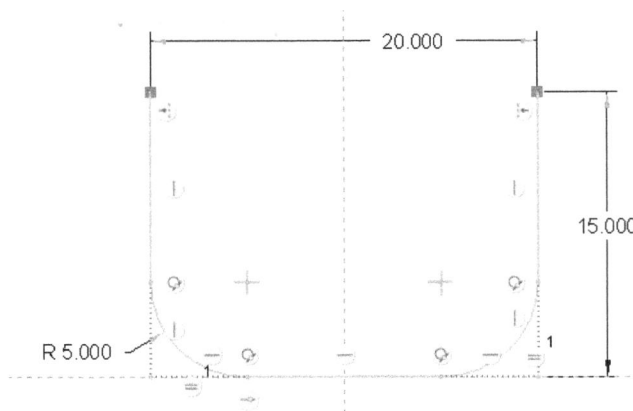

Figure 2−3

Extruded walls are generally sketched as open sections. Once the sketch is finished, you can define the wall depth and wall thickness in the appropriate *Extrude* dashboard fields, as shown in Figure 2–4.

Wall depth   **Wall thickness**

Figure 2–4

The model displays as shown in Figure 2–5.

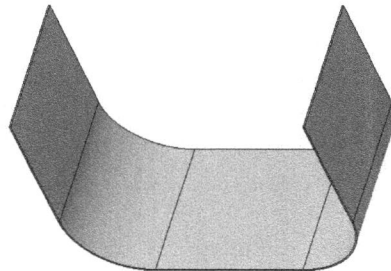

Figure 2–5

Thicken

To add a dimension related to the white (offset) side of the wall, in the *Sketch* tab, select **Setup>Feature Tools>Thicken**. A dotted offset line displays in the section, as shown in Figure 2–6. You can select elements of this line to create the required dimensions. The **Thicken** option does not work if the section contains sharp corners.

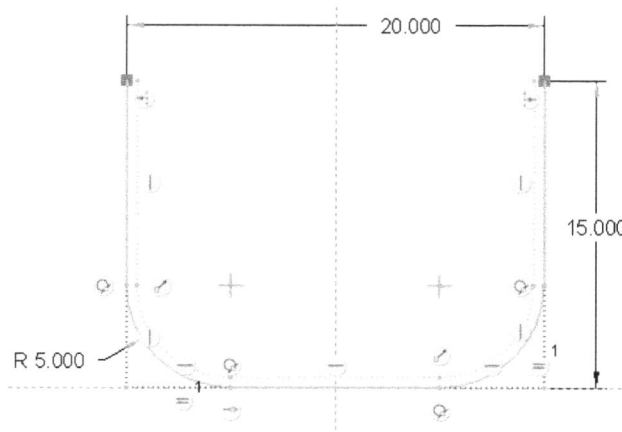

Figure 2–6

Add Bends to Sharp Edges

When you sketch an extruded wall, you can include bends in the section, or you can leave them as sharp corners and convert them to bends using the **Add bends on sharp edges** option in the Options panel in the dashboard, as shown in Figure 2–7.

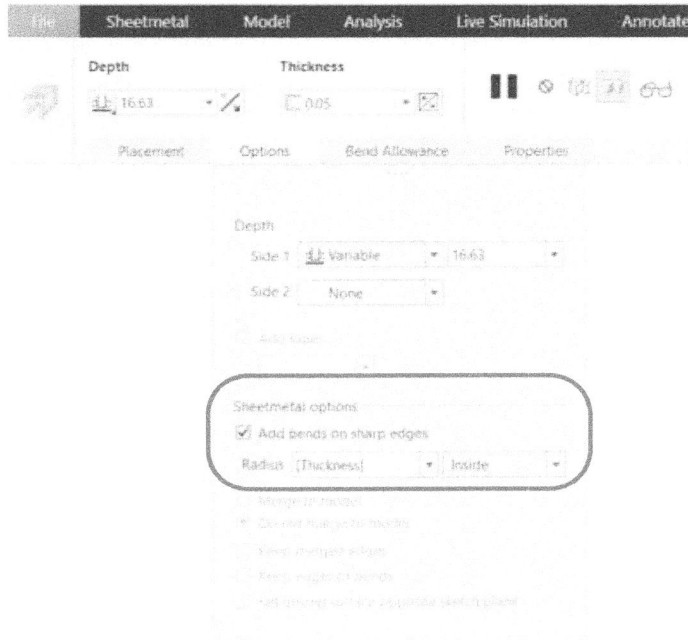

Figure 2–7

*Note: The **Add bends on sharp edges** option is set by default.*

The **Add bends on sharp edges** option causes one radius to be applied to all sharp corners in the section. You can apply it to the inside or outside radius. Radius values can be specified based on the thickness, double the thickness, or a user-defined value. The automatic conversion of sharps to bends does not include sharp edges connected to existing geometry, it only affects the entities sketched in the current feature's section.

Planar

The **Planar** tool enables you to create an unattached planar wall feature. You can use this tool to create a first wall and a secondary wall. Click ✐ (Planar) in the *Sheetmetal* tab to create a planar wall.

A planar wall is created by sketching its outline, as shown in Figure 2-8.

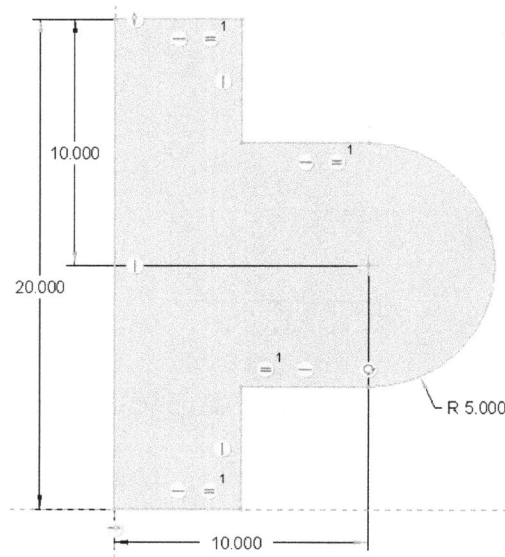

Figure 2-8

The flat wall has thickness (depth) applied to it as the final step, as shown in Figure 2-9.

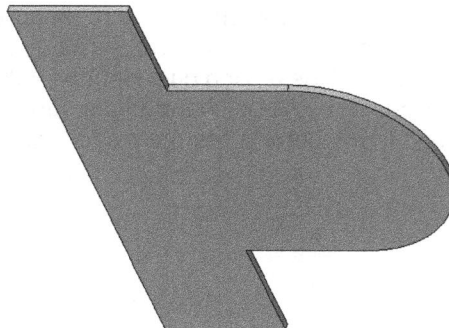

Figure 2-9

Revolved

A revolved wall has a sketched cross-section and is rotated about a centerline, as shown in Figure 2–10. Select **Walls>** ⬚ (Revolve) in the *Sheetmetal* tab to create a revolved wall.

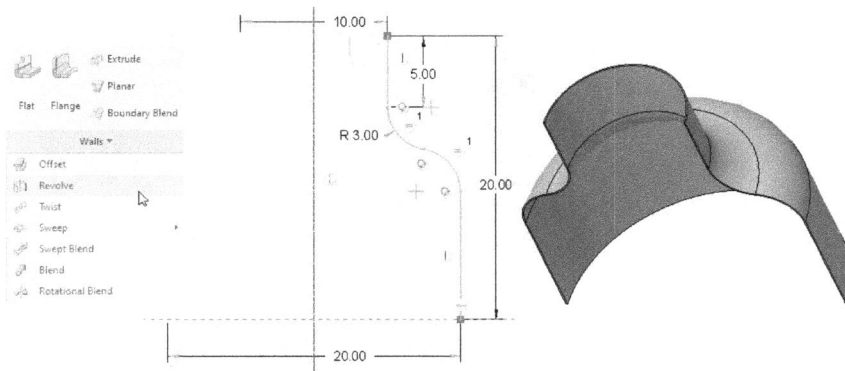

Figure 2–10

Blended

The cross-sections of a blended wall are sketched, as shown in Figure 2–11. Parallel, rotational, and general blend characteristics are all options when creating this type of wall. Select **Walls> Blend** in the *Sheetmetal* tab to create a blended wall.

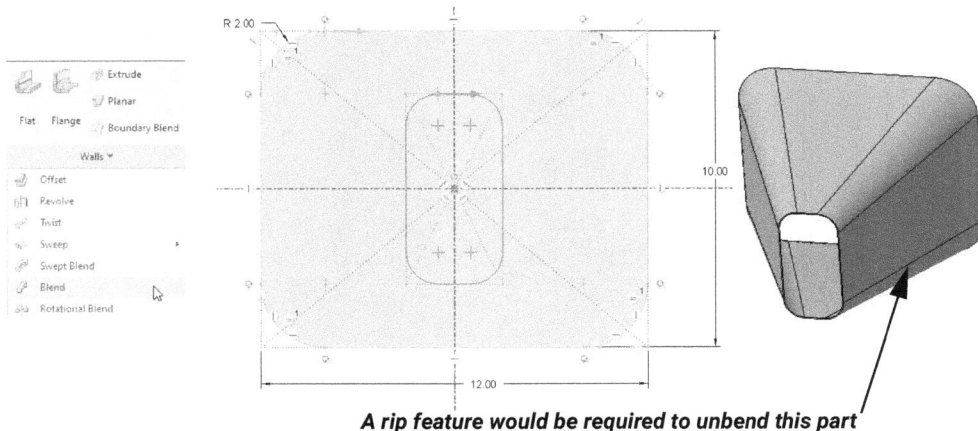

A rip feature would be required to unbend this part

Figure 2–11

Offset

An offset sheet metal wall is created by offsetting from an existing surface, as shown in Figure 2–12. Click ⬙ (Offset) in the *Walls* group in the *Sheetmetal* tab to create an offset wall.

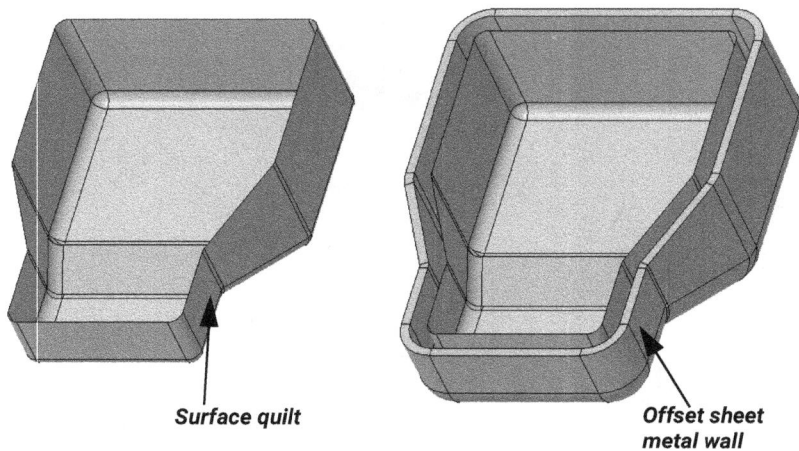

Surface quilt

Offset sheet metal wall

Figure 2–12

2.2 Capturing Design Intent in Sketcher

Bend geometry can be included in the sketch when extruded and revolved walls are created. This enables you to accurately describe the profile of the wall. However, this also means you must account for the material thickness in the sketch. Sheet metal bends are generally dimensioned according to the inside bend radius in the part, as shown in Figure 2–13. It is valuable to include the bend geometry in the sketch when there are multiple bends with different radius values.

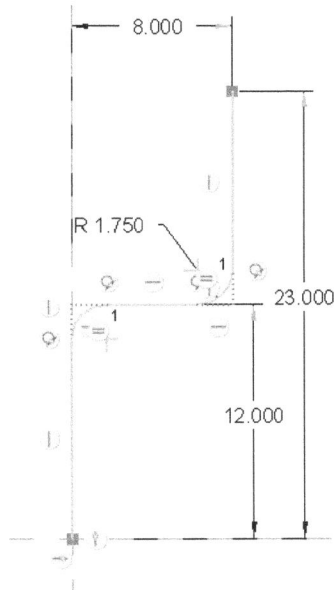

Figure 2–13

Using the **Add bends on sharp edges** option in the Options panel of the feature's dashboard applies the same value for all bends.

The **Thicken** option in the *Sketch* tab enables you to offset the material thickness and dimension the inside radii on the wall, as shown in Figure 2–14.

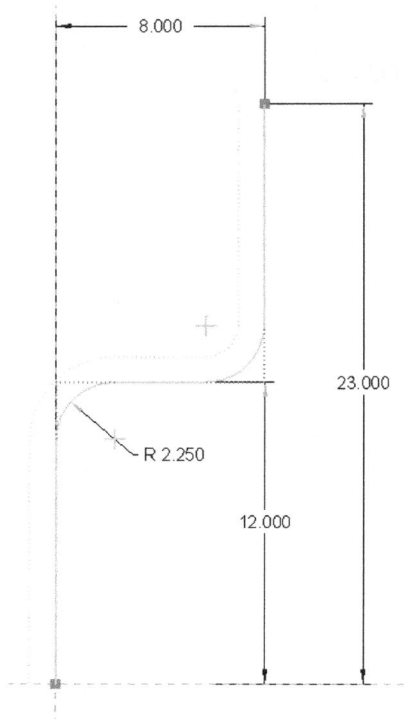

Figure 2–14

Note: *Constraints are toggled off for clarity.*

When modeling in Sheetmetal mode, you might need to dimension a wall to the mold line. The mold line is the theoretical intersection of the flat wall extensions. Use Sketcher centerlines and points to define the intersection of the flat wall extensions to create the dimensioning scheme. Instead of dimensioning to the tangency points on the wall, add dimensions from the end points of the wall profile to the Sketcher points.

An example of how you can dimension to the mold line is shown in Figure 2–15. Note the application of material thickness and the resulting dimensioning scheme.

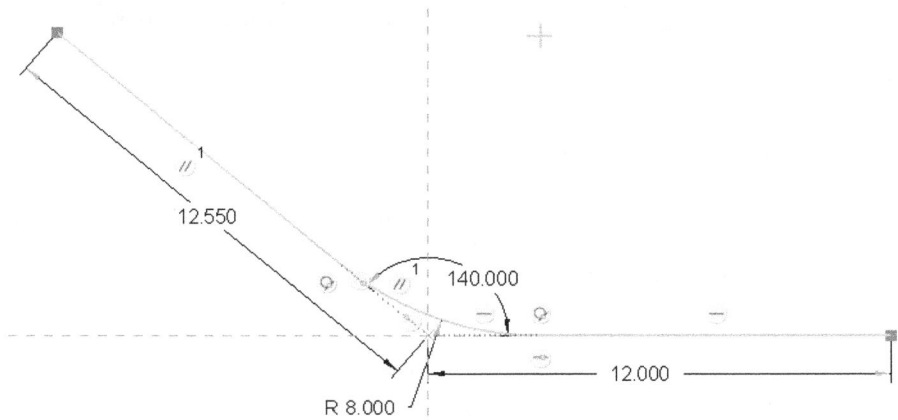

A Sketcher point is placed at the intersection of the two centerlines

Figure 2–15

Practice 2a
Primary Extruded Unattached Wall

Practice Objective

*   Create a primary extruded unattached wall.

In this practice, you will create the primary extruded unattached wall shown in Figure 2–16. The primary wall is the first wall that is created in the sheet metal model. It only references the default datum planes or other reference geometry and forms the foundation on which all other wall features are built.

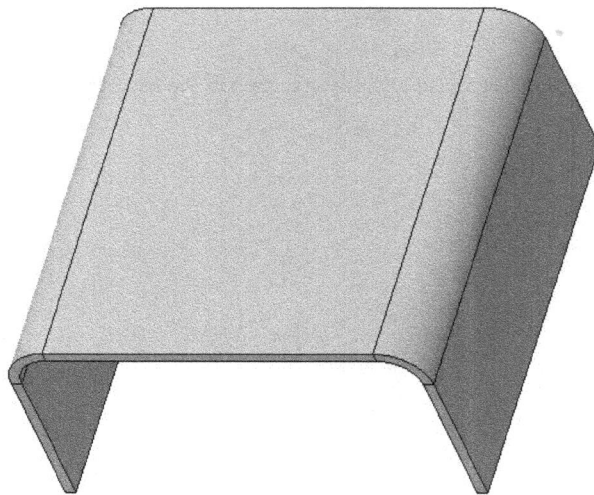

Figure 2–16

Task 1: Create a new sheet metal part.

1. Set the working directory to the *Unattached_Extruded_Wall* folder.
2. Create a new part file and select the **Sheetmetal** Sub-type option in the New dialog box. Ensure that the **Use default template** option is selected.

3. Set the File name to **support**, as shown in Figure 2–17.

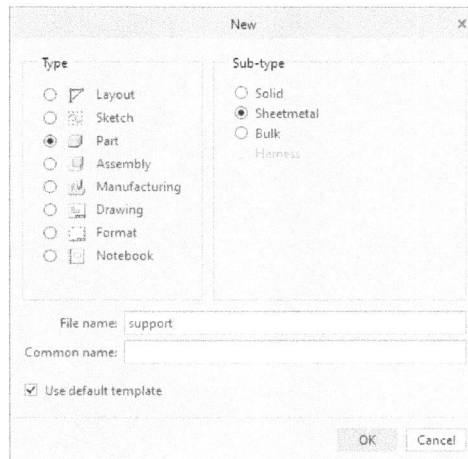

Figure 2–17

4. Click **OK**

5. Set the model display as follows:

   - ⚙ *(Datum Display Filters)*: None

   - ➤ *(Spin Center)*: Off

   - ⬛ *(Display Style)*: ⬛ (Shading With Edges)

Task 2: Create an extruded wall on datum plane FRONT.

1. In the Model Tree, select datum plane **FRONT.** This will be the sketching plane.

2. Click 📐 (Extrude) in the mini toolbar, as shown in Figure 2–18.

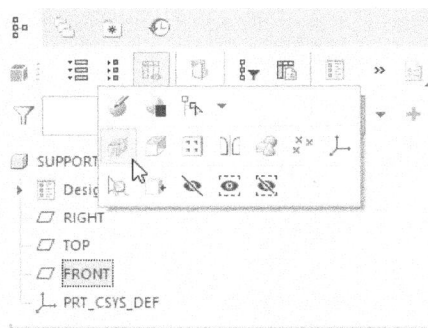

Figure 2–18

3. The *Sketch* tab opens. Click ⚏ (Sketch View).

4. Create the sketch shown in Figure 2–19.

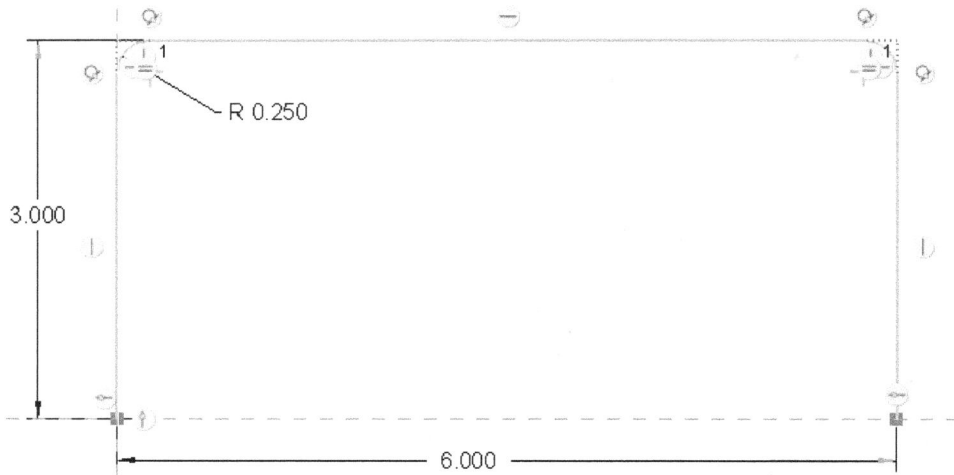

R 0.250

3.000

6.000

Figure 2–19

Task 3: Add the material thickness to the profile.

Sheet metal bends are generally dimensioned according to the inside bend radius in the part. The **Thicken** option enables you to offset the material thickness and dimension the inside radii on the wall.

1. In the *Sketch* tab, click **Setup>Feature Tools>Thicken**.

2. Verify that the arrow points toward the interior of the section. If required select **Flip** in the menu manager (located on the right side of the Creo Parametric window) to flip the arrow direction.

3. Select **Okay**.

4. The **0.15** *Offset* value is listed in the message area (entered in Task 2). Press <Enter>. The dotted line displays, offset from the existing section.

5. Delete the *.25* radius dimension.

6. Add a radius dimension to the dotted arc.

7. Set the radius to **0.5**. The sketch updates, as shown in Figure 2–20.

Figure 2–20

8. Click ✓ (OK) to complete the sketch.

9. In the *Extrude dashboard*, set the blind wall depth to **6** and the wall thickness to **0.15**, as shown in Figure 2–21.

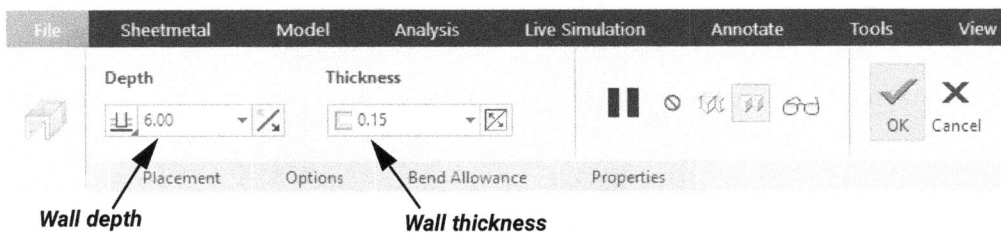

Figure 2–21

10. Verify that the arrow points toward the interior of the model, as shown in Figure 2-22. If required, click on the arrow to flip its direction.

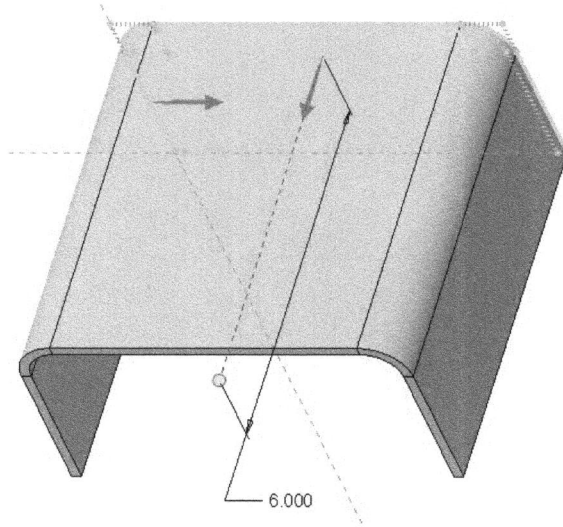

Figure 2-22

Note: You may have to zoom in to see the model.

11. Complete the feature. The completed wall feature displays as shown in Figure 2-23.

Figure 2-23

Note: The green side should be on the outside of the model when it is finished.

12. Save the part and erase it from memory.

End of practice

Practice 2b
Primary Planar Unattached Wall

Practice Objective

* Create a primary planar unattached wall.

In this practice, you will create the primary planar unattached wall shown on the left in Figure 2-24. This wall can be used as base geometry for the bracket part shown on the right in Figure 2-24. The primary wall is the first wall that is created in the sheet metal model. It only references the default datum planes or other reference geometry, and forms the foundation on which all other wall features are built.

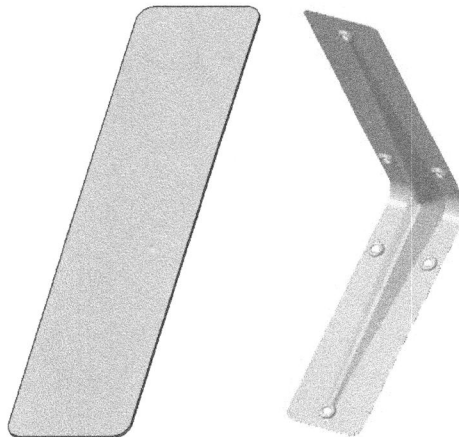

Figure 2-24

Task 1: Create a new sheet metal part.

1. Set the working directory to the *Unattached_Planar_Wall* folder.
2. Create a new part file and select **Sheetmetal** in the New dialog box. Verify that **Use default template** is selected.
3. Set the part name to **bracket** and click **OK**.
4. Set the model display as follows:

    * *(Datum Display Filters)*: None

    * *(Spin Center)*: Off

    * *(Display Style)*: (Shading With Edges)

Task 2: Create a planar wall on datum plane TOP.

A planar wall is created by sketching its outline. In this task, you will create a flat wall by sketching on datum plane **TOP**.

1. In the Walls panel in the ribbon, click ✏ (Planar) to create a unattached planar wall. The *Planar* dashboard displays, as shown in Figure 2–25.

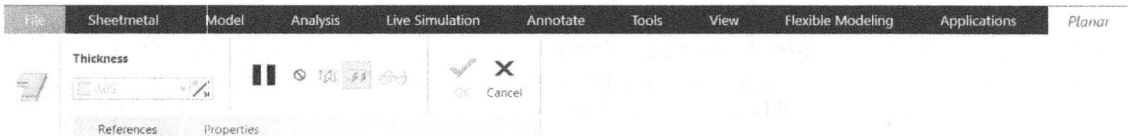

Figure 2–25

2. In the Model Tree, select datum plane **TOP** as the sketching plane.

3. The *Sketch* tab opens. Click ✏ (Sketch View) and sketch the section as shown in Figure 2–26.

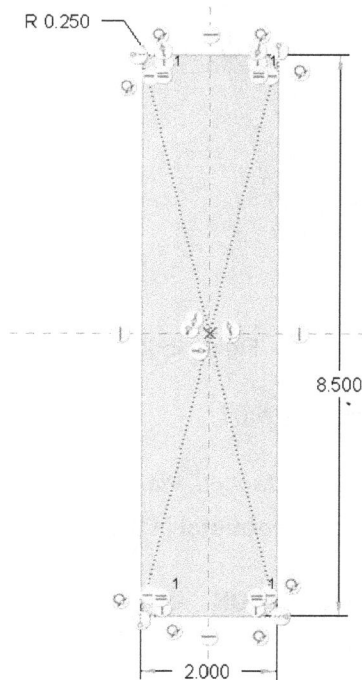

Figure 2–26

Note: Use a ▱ (Center Rectangle) to aid in the sketching process.

4. Complete the section.

Task 3: Complete the wall feature.

1. In the *Planar* dashboard, set the wall *Thickness* to **0.04**, as shown in Figure 2–27.

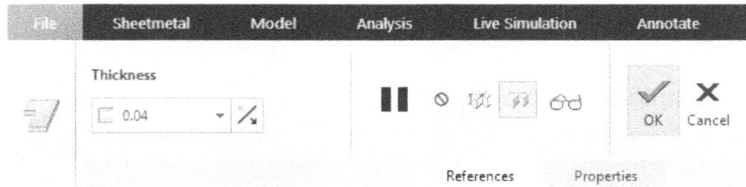

Figure 2–27

2. Complete the feature. The completed wall displays as shown in Figure 2–28.

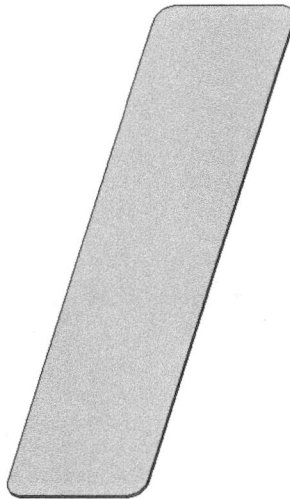

Figure 2–28

3. Save the part and erase it from memory.

End of practice

Practice 2c
Create an Extruded Bracket

Practice Objectives

- Create a primary extruded unattached wall.
- Convert sharp corners to bends.

In this practice, you will create the primary extruded unattached wall shown in Figure 2–29. The primary wall is the first wall that is created in the sheet metal model. It only references the default datum planes or other reference geometry, and forms the foundation on which all other wall features are built.

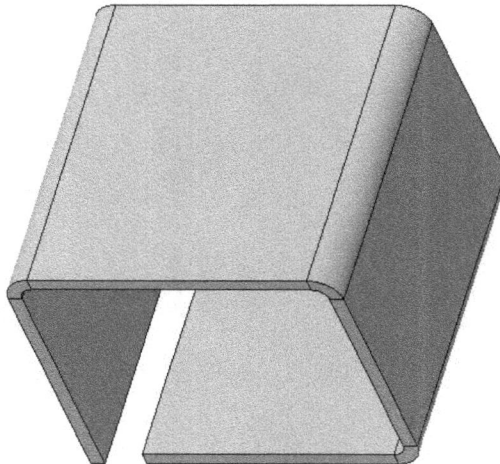

Figure 2–29

Task 1: Create a new sheet metal part.

1. Set the working directory to the *Sheetmetal_Extruded_Bracket* folder.
2. Create a new part file and select the **Sheetmetal** Sub-type option in the New dialog box. Use the default template.
3. Set the part name to **Extrude** and click **OK**.
4. Set the model display as follows:

    - *(Datum Display Filters)*: None
    - *(Spin Center)*: Off
    - *(Display Style)*: ⬜ (Shading With Edges)

Task 2: Create an extruded wall on datum plane FRONT.

1. In the Model Tree, select datum plane **FRONT**.

2. Click ◈ (Extrude) in the mini toolbar to start the creation of the wall.

3. Click ◈ (Sketch View).

4. Sketch and dimension the section shown in Figure 2-30.

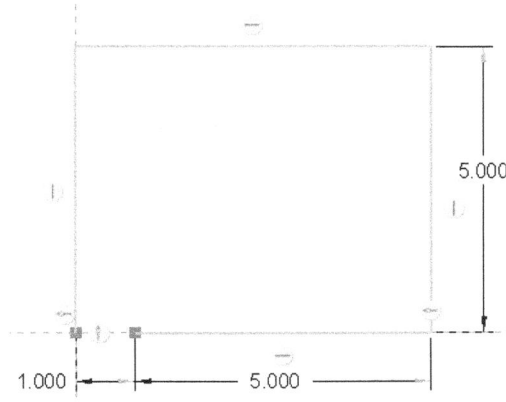

Figure 2-30

5. Complete the sketch.

6. Set the *Depth value* to **6** and the *Thickness* to **0.25**. The geometry preview displays as shown in Figure 2-31. Note the automatic addition of radii on the sharp corners.

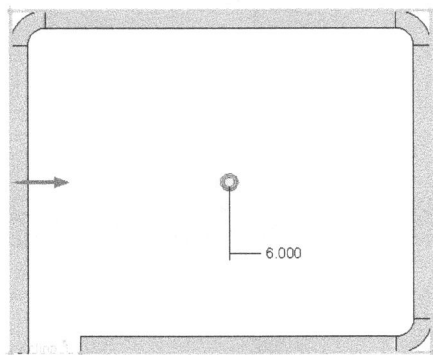

Figure 2-31

7. Ensure that the arrow points toward the interior of the model. If required, click on the arrow to flip its direction.

8. Open the Options panel in the *Extrude* dashboard.

9. Note that the **Add bends on sharp edges** option is selected, which causes one radius to be applied to all sharp corners in the section. Select **Thickness** in the Radius drop-down list, if required, as shown in Figure 2–32.

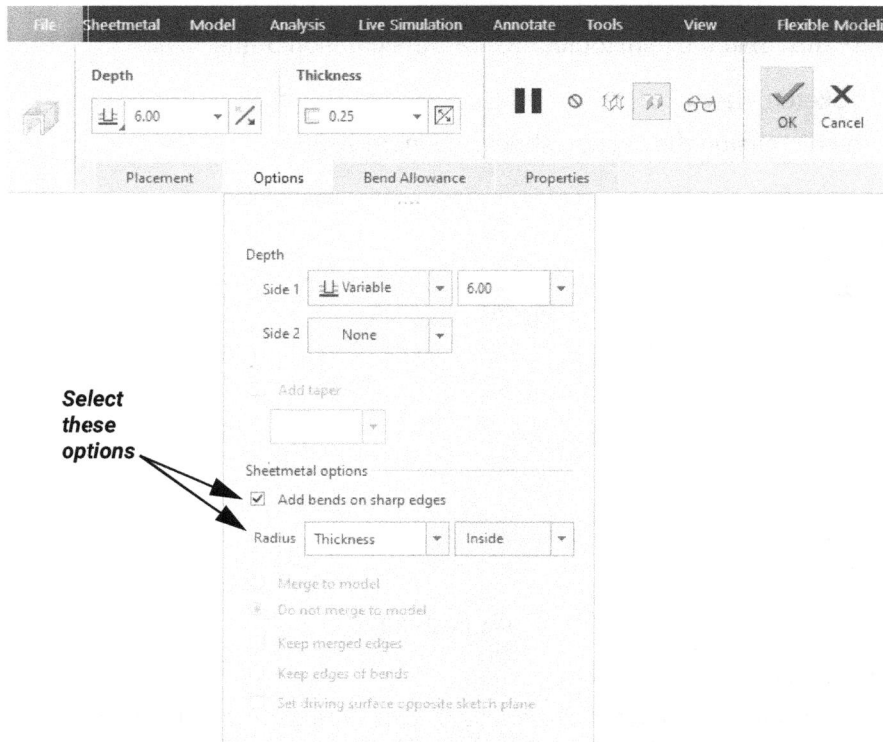

Figure 2–32

Note: The green side should be on the outside of the model when it is finished.

10. Complete the feature.

11. Save the part and erase it from memory.

End of practice

Practice 2d
Create an Unattached Revolved Wall

Practice Objective

- Create a revolved wall.

In this practice, you will create a revolved wall as the primary wall of a sheet metal part.

1. Set the working directory to the *Unattached_Revolved_Wall* folder.

2. Click ☐ (New), select **Sheetmetal** as the sub-type, and then enter **revolved_wall** as the filename.

3. Set the model display as follows:

   - ⚹ (Datum Display Filters): None

   - ⚹ (Spin Center): Off

   - ◰ (Display Style): ▱ (Shading With Edges)

4. Select **Walls>Revolve** in the *Sheetmetal* tab to create a revolved wall.

5. In the Model Tree, select datum plane **FRONT** as the sketching plane.

6. Sketch the section for the revolved wall as shown in Figure 2−33. Remember to create a centerline from the *Sketching* group for the axis of revolution.

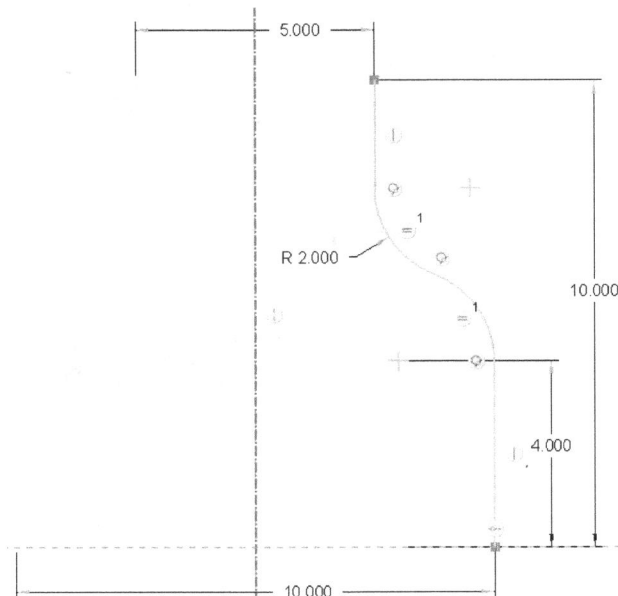

Figure 2−33

7. Click ✓ (OK) to complete the sketch.

8. Set the *Thickness* of the sheet metal wall to **0.25.**

9. Set the *Angle* of revolution to **180**. The *Revolve* dashboard displays as shown in Figure 2−34.

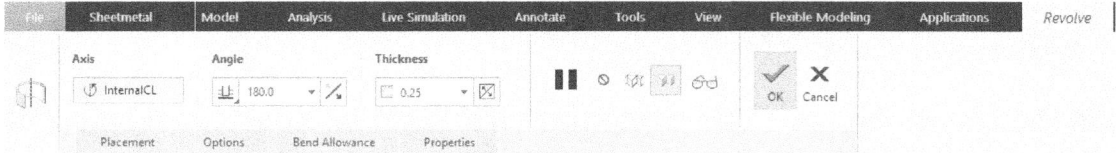

Figure 2−34

10. Click ✓ (OK) in the *Revolve* dashboard. The completed feature is shown in Figure 2−35.

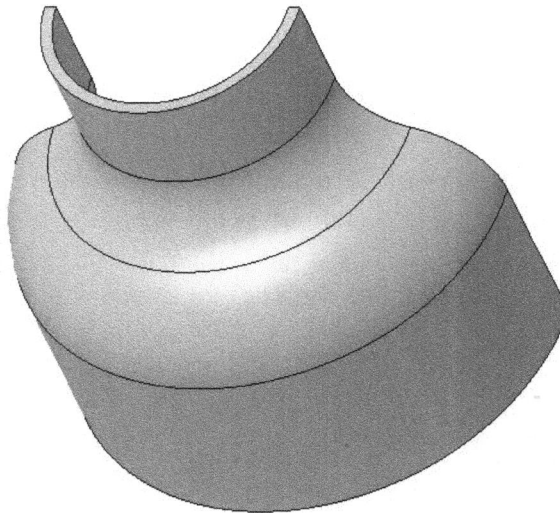

Figure 2−35

11. Save the part and erase it from memory.

End of practice

Practice 2e
Create an Offset Wall

Practice Objective

* Create an offset wall.

In this practice, you will create a sheet metal wall by offsetting from a surface quilt.

1. Set the working directory to the *Offset_Wall* folder.

2. Open **oil_pan.prt**.

3. Set the model display as follows:

   * ⚒ *(Datum Display Filters)*: None

   * ➤ *(Spin Center)*: Off

   * ▦ *(Display Style)*: 🗇 (Shading With Edges)

4. Using the investigate options in the *Tools* tab, examine how the model was constructed. In the Model Tree, the part consists of a surface and some round features, as shown in Figure 2–36.

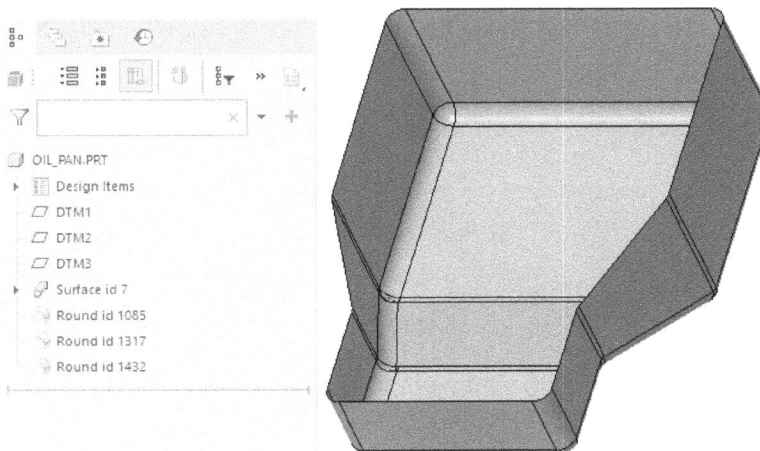

Figure 2–36

5. You must use the sheet metal application to create the wall feature. If required, select the *Model* tab.

6. Select **Operations>Convert to Sheetmetal**.

7. Click ✔ (OK) to complete the feature.

8. In the *Wall* group of the *Sheetmetal* tab, click ⬧ (Offset) to create an offset wall.

9. Set the selection filter to **Quilt**.

10. Select the surface shown in Figure 2−37 to use as a reference for the offset wall.

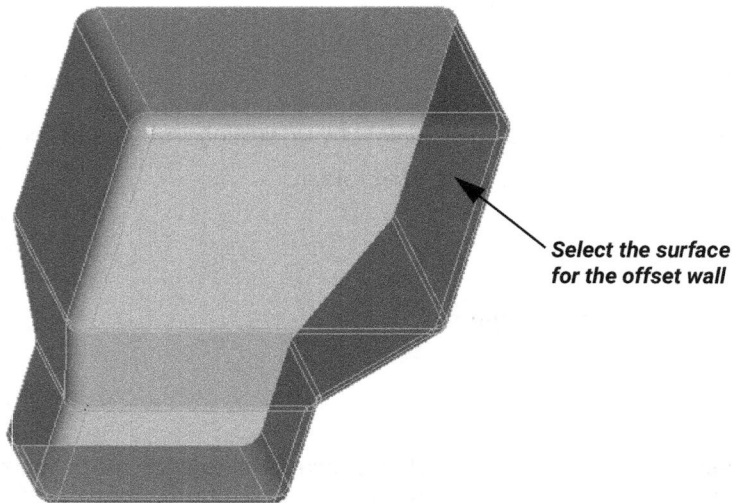

Select the surface for the offset wall

Figure 2−37

11. Set the material *Thickness* to **2** and *Offset* distance away from the surface to **10**, as shown in Figure 2−38.

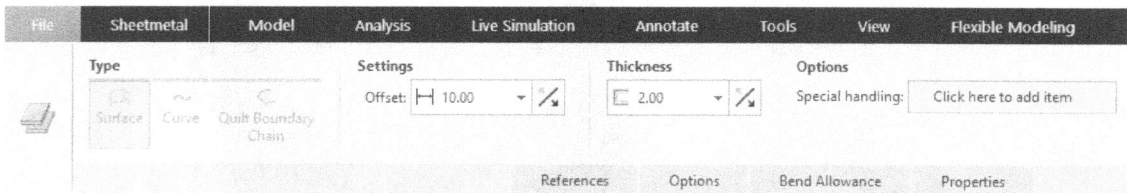

Figure 2−38

12. Verify that the creation direction points outward from the model. Click ⬧ (Change Thickness Direction), if required.

13. Click ✓ (OK) to complete the feature.

14. The offset wall and original surface display as shown in Figure 2–39.

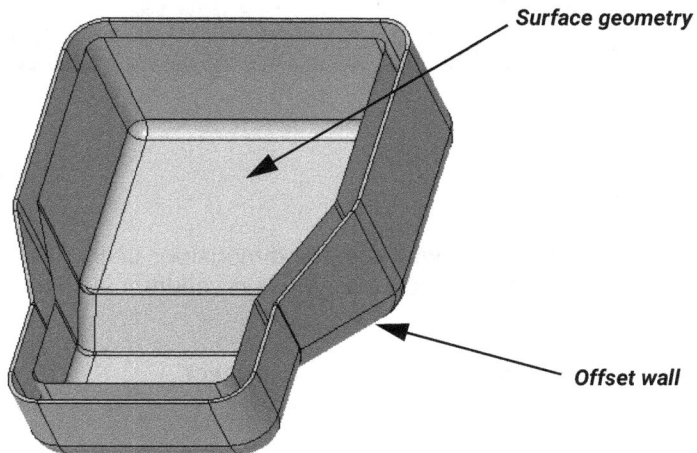

Figure 2–39

15. In the Model Tree, select **Surface id 7** and click ✎ (Hide) in the mini toolbar. The finished wall displays as shown in Figure 2–40.

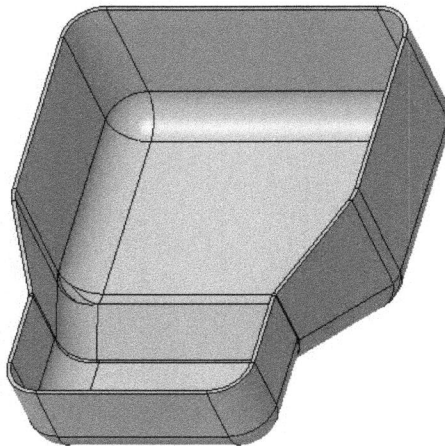

Figure 2–40

16. Save the model and erase it from memory.

End of practice

Practice 2f
Create the Project Part

Practice Objective

- Create an extruded primary wall.

In this practice, you will create a primary wall with the dimensions shown below. This part will be used in several practices later in this course as you learn additional sheet metal features.

1. Set the working directory to the *Project_Part* folder.

2. Create a new sheet metal part and set the name to **project**.

3. Set the model display as follows:

   - ⊹ *(Datum Display Filters)*: None

   - ⤞ *(Spin Center)*: Off

   - ⬚ *(Display Style)*: ⬚ (Shading With Edges)

4. Create the extruded primary wall feature, as shown in Figure 2–41. Verify that the inside radii of the two bends are equal.

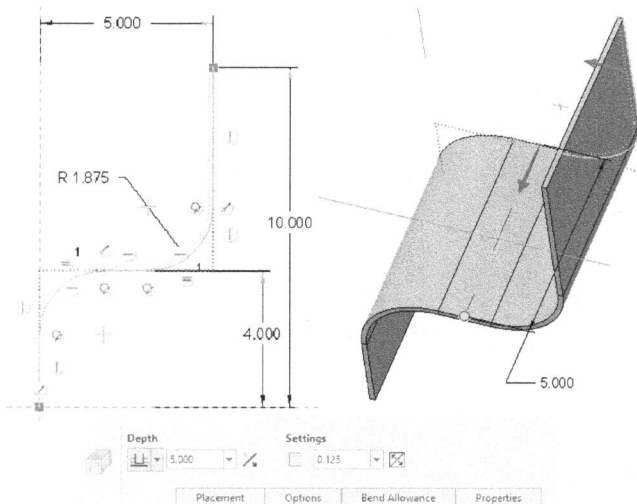

Figure 2–41

5. Save the part and erase it from memory.

End of practice

Chapter Review Questions

1. The first wall that is created in the sheet metal model only references default datum planes or other reference geometry.

    a. True

    b. False

2. Which tool(s) enables you to create an unattached planar wall feature. You can use this tool to create a first wall and a secondary wall. (Select all that apply.)

    a. Extrude

    b. Planar

    c. Flange

    d. Flat

3. The **Thicken** option does not work if the section contains sharp corners.

    a. True

    b. False

4. When you sketch an extruded wall, you cannot include bends in the section.

    a. True

    b. False

5. Using the **Add bends on sharp edges** option in the Options panel in the feature's dashboard applies the same value for all bends.

    a. True

    b. False

Answers: 1a, 2ab, 3a, 4b, 5a

Secondary Walls

Like solid models, sheet metal models are built by adding features. Once the first wall is created, you can add additional walls that are attached to one another. The walls can take various forms, such as flat, flange, or twist.

Learning Objectives

- Learn to create a secondary wall and consider the attachment edge that is selected.
- Learn to create a flat wall by sketching an outline or selecting a predefined shape in the tab.
- Learn to create a flange wall by sketching or selecting a cross-section to sweep along an attachment edge.
- Learn the creation sequence to create a twisted wall and the additional options available.
- Use the general steps and extended wall option to close any gaps between sheet metal walls.
- Create additional unattached walls to work on different regions of a sheet metal model.
- Reuse a section to create an additional flat or flange sheet metal wall.
- Recognize the bend relief geometry that can be used in a sheet metal model.

3.1 Selecting an Attachment Edge

Just as secondary solid features are built by referencing the base feature, secondary walls are built by attaching them to the primary wall, as shown in Figure 3–1. By attaching the wall to an existing edge, you establish a parent/child relationship between the primary wall and the wall you are creating. Carefully consider the edge references to avoid having to redefine them later.

The type of wall being created and options selected during creation determine the available preselected shapes or sketching orientation for user-defined shapes.

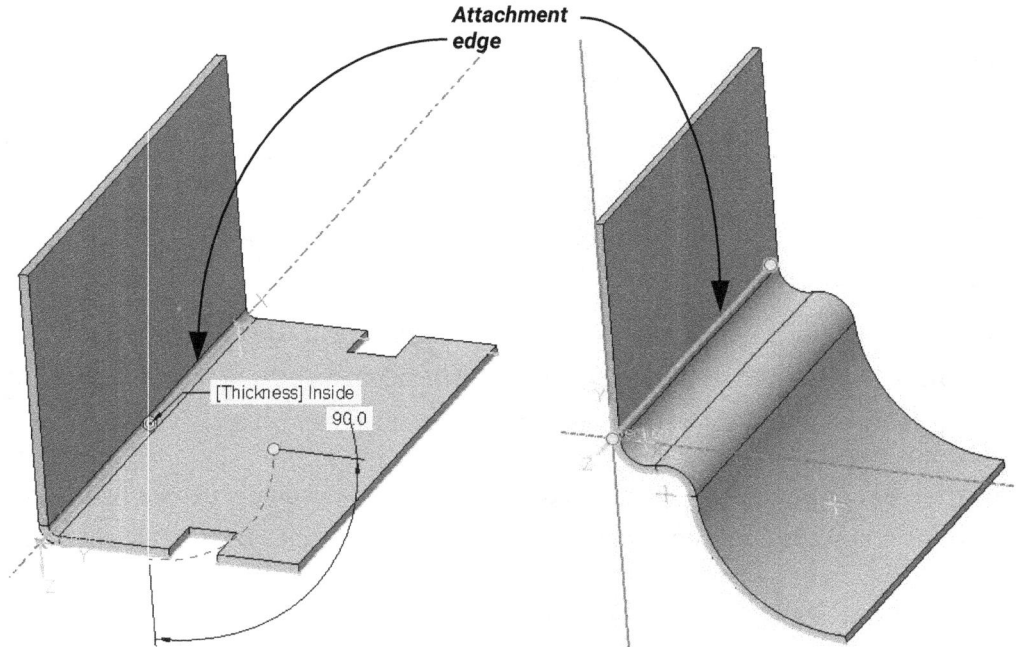

Attachment edge

[Thickness] Inside
90.0

Figure 3–1

Note: Remember to use 🔳 (Pick From List) to ensure that you are selecting the required attachment edge.

Creating a secondary wall with bends can change the length of the wall to which it is attached. Consider the example shown in Figure 3–2. The overall length of the part might increase depending on the selection of the attachment edge. In either case, the length of the original wall decreases by the value of the bend radius R or by the sum of the bend radius R and the material thickness T.

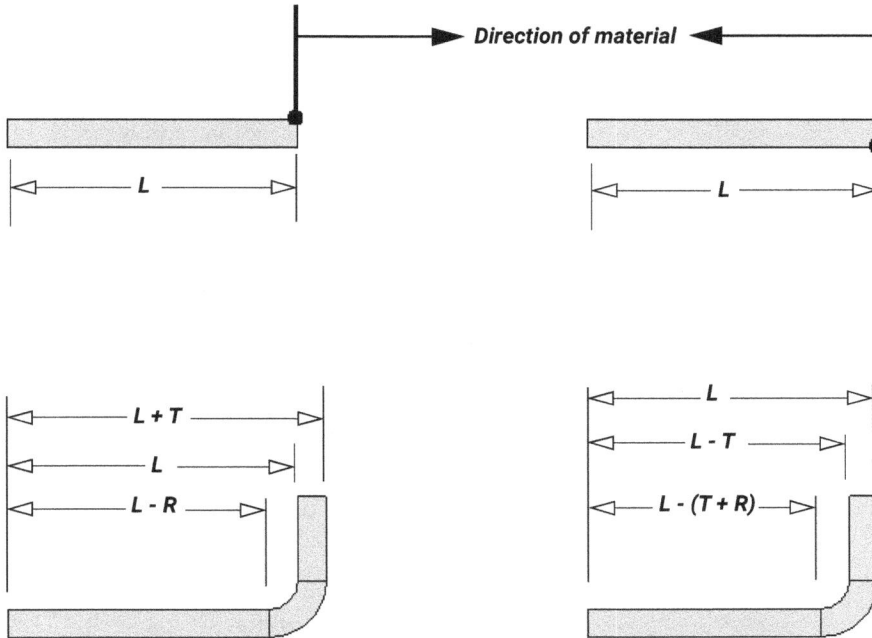

Figure 3–2

When creating a secondary wall, ⤢ (Change Thickness Direction) in the dashboard can be used to flip the direction of material so that you can control the resulting length of the original wall, as shown in the top images in Figure 3–2.

For further control, several offset options are available in Bend Position panel in the dashboard or from the mini toolbar. Click on the screen to open the mini toolbar, then hover over any of the options for a description of how the offset works, as shown in Figure 3–3.

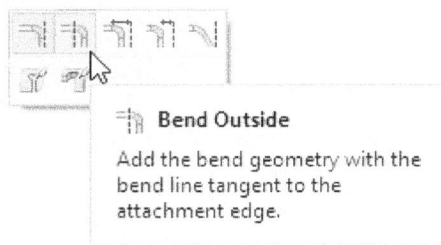

Figure 3–3

Option	Description	Example
(Profile on Edge)	Add bend geometry and keep the new wall profile aligned with the attachment edge.	
(Bend Outside)	Add bend geometry and make the bend line tangent to the attachment edge.	
(Offset from Bend Start)	Add bend geometry and measure the offset from the attachment edge to the bend start.	

Option	Description	Example
(Offset from Bend Apex)	Add bend geometry and measure the offset from the attachment edge to the bend apex.	
(Constrained)	Add bend geometry and keep the new wall profile within the boundary of the attachment edge.	

Options used to determine the radius of the bend are accessible in the tab, as shown in Figure 3–4. You can select any of the values displayed in the drop-down list or enter a new value.

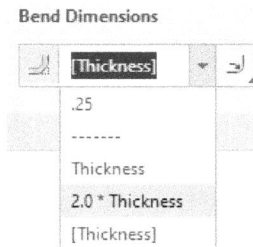

Figure 3–4

3.2 Flat Wall

To create a flat wall, you can sketch its outline or select from a predefined shape, as shown in Figure 3–5.

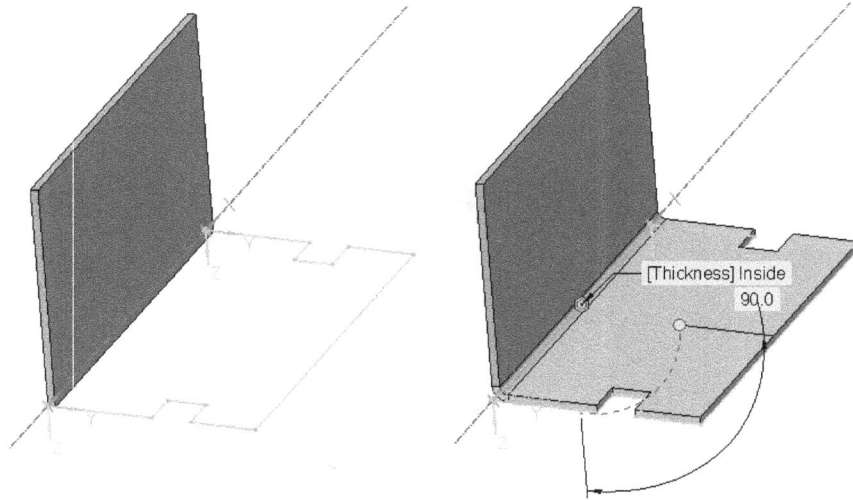

[Thickness] Inside
90.0

Figure 3–5

How To: Create a Flat Wall

1. Click (Flat) in the *Sheetmetal* tab. The *Flat* dashboard displays, as shown in Figure 3–6.

Figure 3–6

2. Select one or more edges to place the flat wall. You can select the edges using one of the following methods:

- **One by One:** Enables you to select one or more adjacent edges. It does not matter whether selected edges form a tangent chain or not. To start adding edges to the first selected edge, press and hold <Shift>. You can select adjacent edges on both ends of the current chain. The selected edge is added to the current chain. To remove the selected edge from the chain, select it again. You can only remove the outer edges.

- **Tangent chain:** Enables you to select a tangent edge chain. Select the first edge, press and hold <Shift>, and hover the cursor over any non-adjacent tangent edge. The tangent chain is prehighlighted on the model and a message displays in the message area. Select the edge to select the complete tangent chain.

- **Surface loop chain:** Enables you to select edges that belong to a surface. Select the first edge, press and hold <Shift>, and hover the cursor over the surface that is shared by the first selected edge. Creo Parametric highlights the first possible edge chain and displays the corresponding message in the message area. If the highlighted edge chain is not the one you want to use, right-click to display another possible edge chain. When the correct edge chain is highlighted, select it. Using this method you can select all surface edges or the from-to subset of surface edges.

- To remove a selected edge chain, release <Shift>, right-click, and select **Clear**. You can also open the Placement panel, as shown in Figure 3−7. Right-click on the *Placement* collector and select **Remove**.

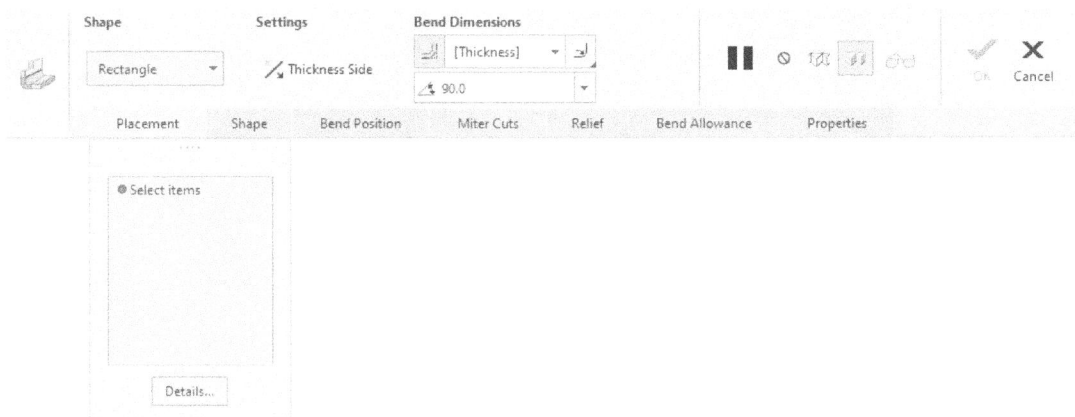

Figure 3−7

Note: If only selecting one edge, you can select the edge first, then click ⬚ (Flat) in the mini toolbar.

Selecting only one edge for the flat wall displays on the model, as shown in Figure 3–8.

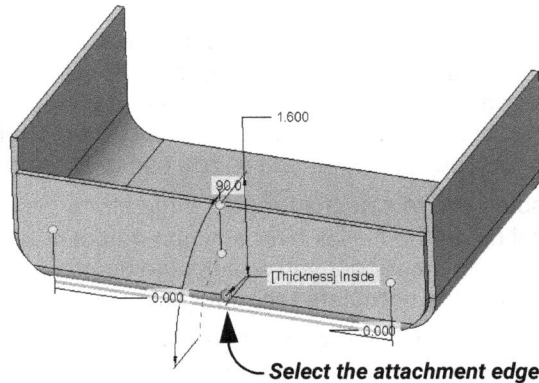

1.600

90.0

[Thickness] Inside

0.000

0.000

Select the attachment edge

Figure 3–8

The attachment edge can be changed at any time by clicking **Placement** in the *Flat* dashboard to open the Placement panel. To clear the reference, select the *Placement* collector so that it displays in yellow, right-click and select **Remove**.

3. Four predefined shapes and one user-defined option are available when creating flat walls. By default, a rectangular flat wall is created on the placement edge.

    The shape can be changed by selecting another option in the Shape drop-down list in the dashboard, as shown in Figure 3–9.

Shape	Settings	Bend Dimensions					
Rectangle	Thickness Side	[Thickness]					OK Cancel
Rectangle		90.0					
Trapezoid	Shape	Bend Position	Miter Cuts	Relief	Bend Allowance	Properties	
L							
T							
User Defined							

Figure 3–9

Figure 3–10 shows the predefined shapes.

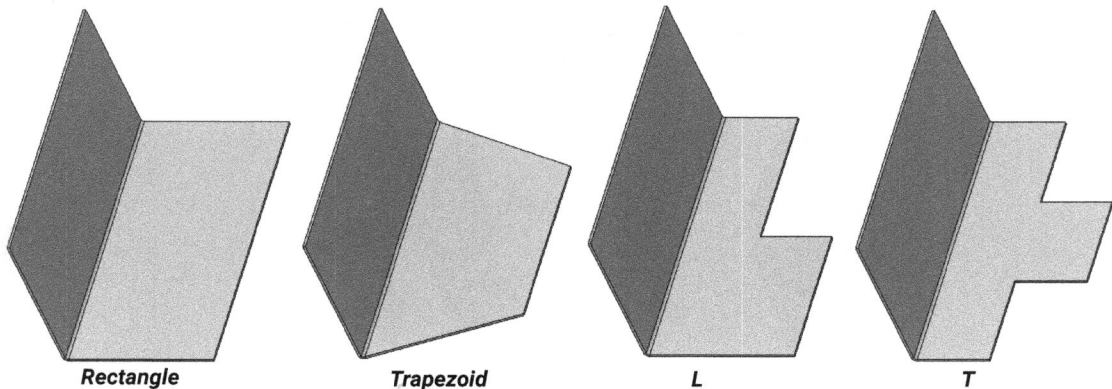

Rectangle   **Trapezoid**   **L**   **T**

Figure 3–10

4. To make dimensional changes to any of the predefined flat wall types, open the Shape panel and click ⊕ (Section Preview). Double-click on the dimension to modify. Figure 3–11 shows an example of the Shape panel for the predefined rectangular shape.

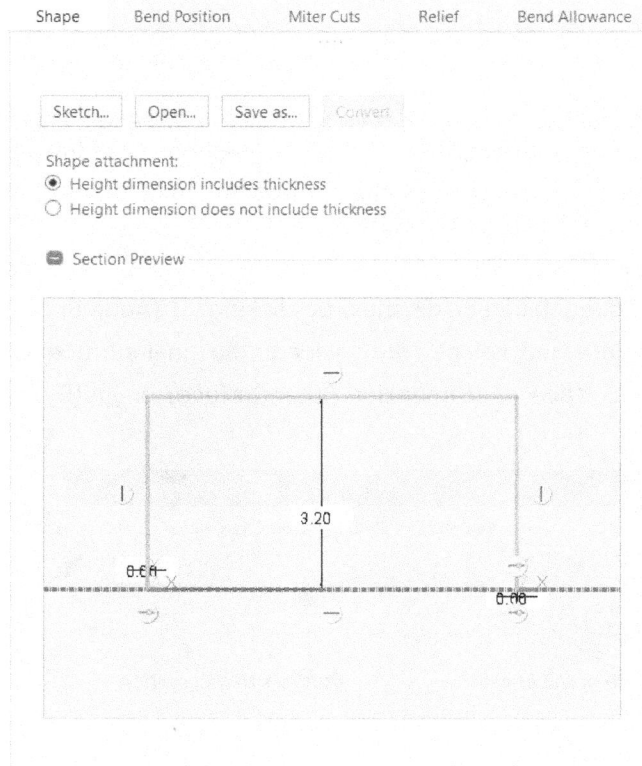

Figure 3–11

The user-defined option enables you to sketch a section. To sketch the section, click **Sketch** in the Shape panel. Sketch the outline of the wall so that the end points are coincident with the linear attachment edge. The outline of the wall can include the entire attachment edge as shown on the left in Figure 3–12, or a segment of it, as shown on the right in Figure 3–12.

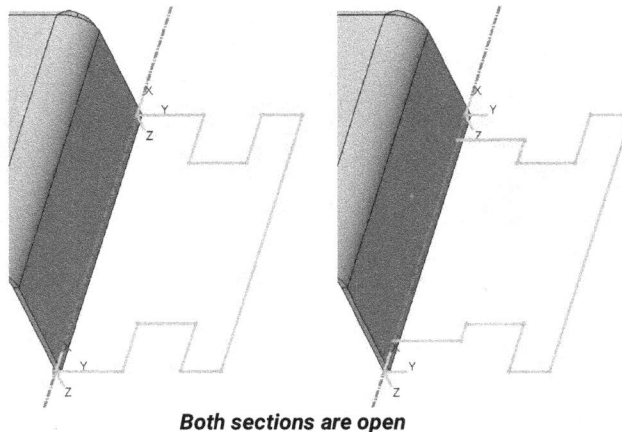

Both sections are open

Figure 3–12

*Note: The predefined shapes can also be used as a starting point for sketching and you can customize the sketch further by clicking **Sketch** in the Shape panel.*

5. To change the angle of the flat wall relative to the reference edge, enter a value in the *Angle* field. The default value is **90 degrees**. To flip the direction of the flat wall, enter a negative value (i.e., **-90**). The ⟋ (Change Thickness Direction) option is used to change the thickness and is applied in the opposite direction.

   The remaining options in the dashboard control the bend at the attachment edge. By default, a bend is added. It can be disabled by clicking ⌐ (Adds Bend), as shown in Figure 3–13. When enabled, you can dimension to the inner surface ⌐ (Dimension Inner Surface), the outer surface ⌐ (Dimension Outer Surface), or ⌐₀ (By Parameter). You can also enter a value.

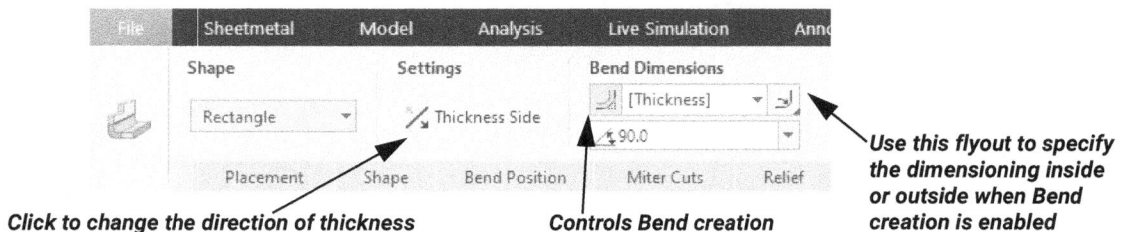

Click to change the direction of thickness   *Controls Bend creation*   *Use this flyout to specify the dimensioning inside or outside when Bend creation is enabled*

Figure 3–13

6. To control the wall location relative to the attachment edge, use the Bend Position panel or mini toolbar.

7. You can define the type of relief for both sides or each individual side using the options in the Relief panel. The type of relief is selected in the drop-down list in this panel, as shown in Figure 3–14.

Figure 3–14

8. Click ✓ (OK) to finish.

3.3 Flange Wall

A flange wall is created by sweeping a cross-section along an attachment edge as shown in Figure 3–15. You can place the flange wall on straight, arched, or swept edges.

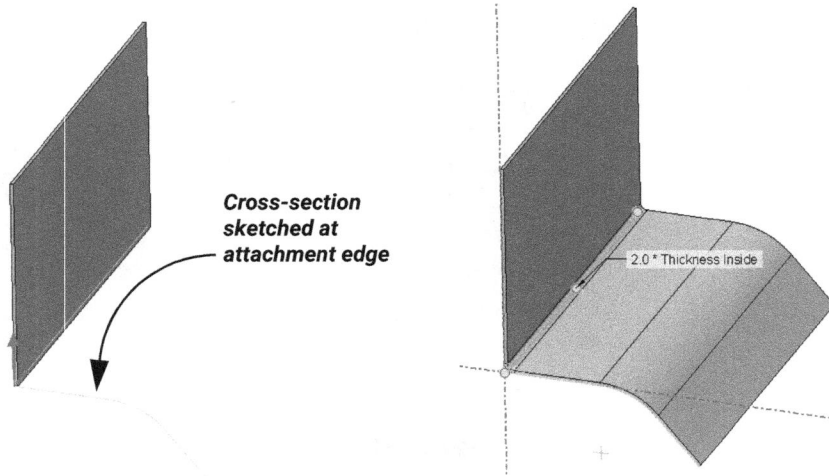

Cross-section sketched at attachment edge

2.0 * Thickness Inside

Figure 3–15

To create a flange wall, click ![Flange icon] (Flange) in the *Sheetmetal* tab. The *Flange* dashboard displays, as shown in Figure 3–16.

Figure 3–16

Select one or more edges to place the flange wall. You can select multiple edges using one of the following methods:

*   One by one

*   Point or Tangent chain

*   Surface loop chain

> **Note:** *If only selecting one edge, you can select the edge first, then click ![Flange icon] (Flange) in the mini toolbar.*

To remove a selected edge chain, release <Shift>, right-click, and select **Clear**. You can also open the Placement panel, as shown in Figure 3–17, select the *Placement* collector, right-click, and select **Remove**.

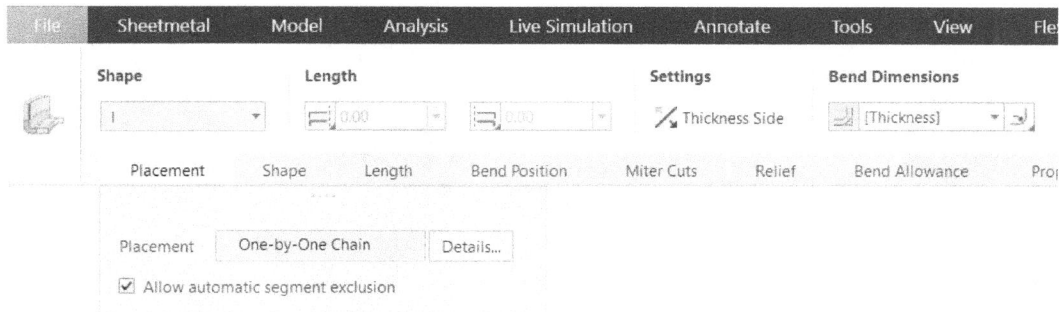

Figure 3–17

- **The Allow automatic segment exclusion** option in the Placement panel enables you to remove small arcs from the selected edge chain. Figure 3–18 shows the effect of this option

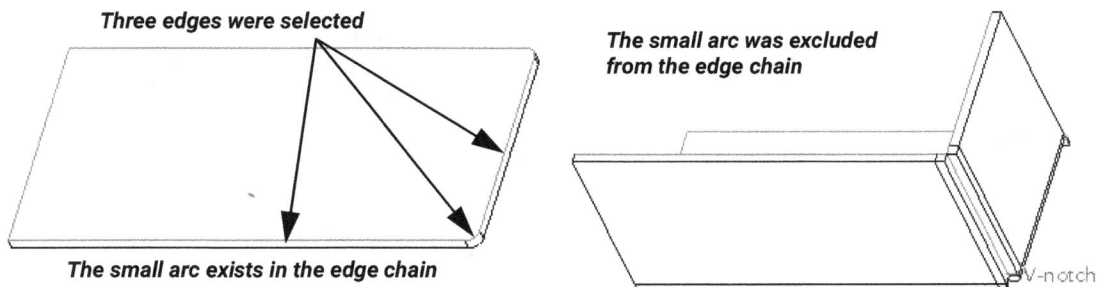

Figure 3–18

Eight predefined and one user-defined options are available when creating flange walls. Figure 3–19 shows the nine predefined shapes.

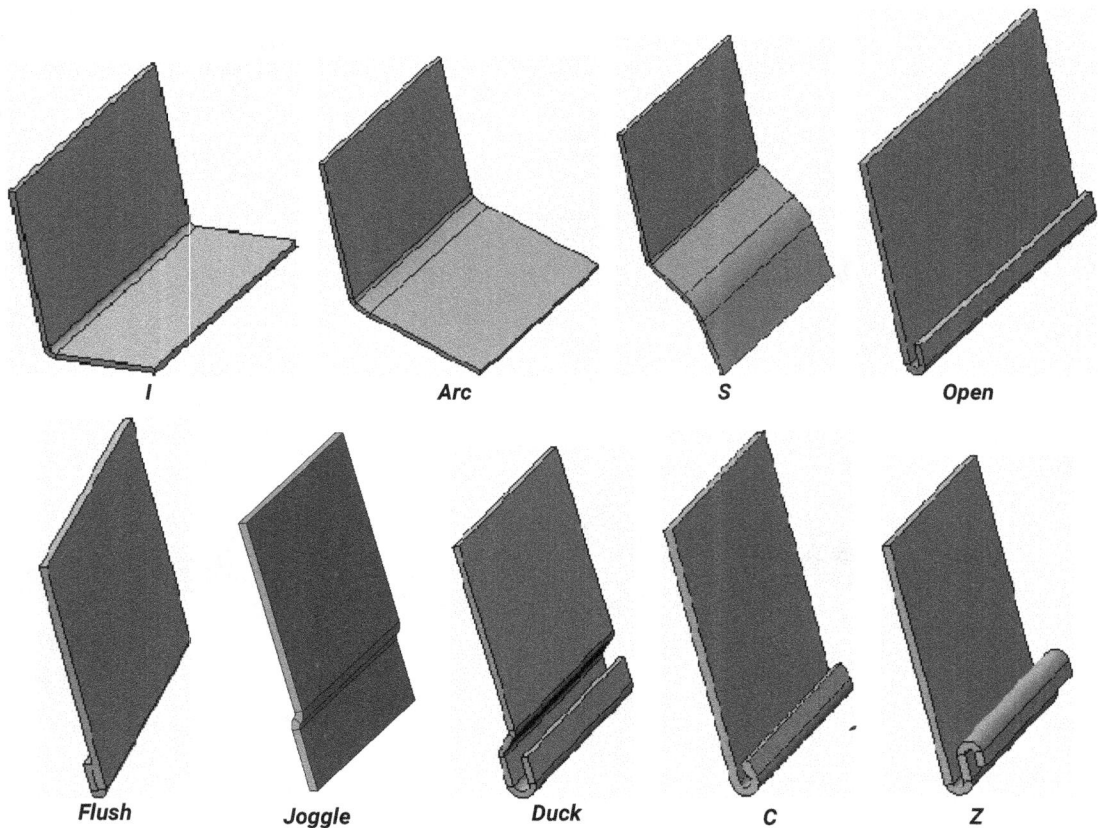

Figure 3–19

By default, an I flange wall is created on the placement edge. The shape can be changed by selecting another option in the Shape drop-down list in the dashboard, as shown in Figure 3-20.

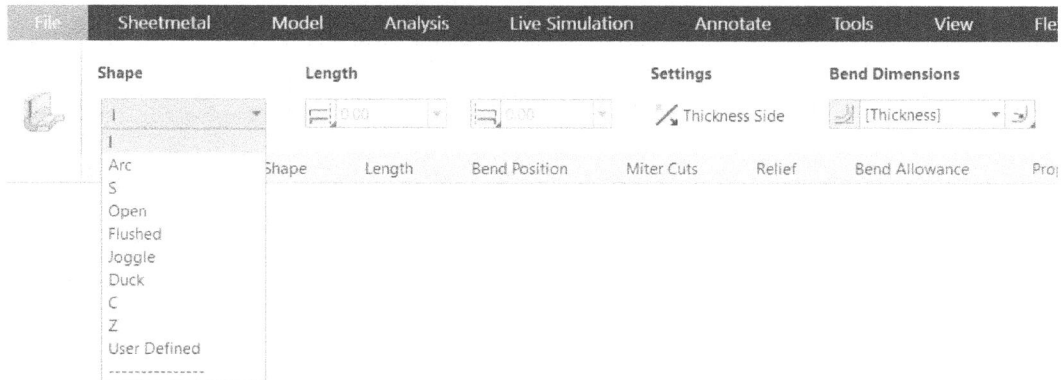

Figure 3-20

To make dimensional changes to any of the predefined flange wall types, open the Profile panel and modify the dimensions.

- **User Defined:** Enables you to sketch your own section. To sketch the section, click **Sketch** in the Shape panel. You can accept the default sketch plane that is automatically created at the end point of the edge or you can select another Sketcher reference, as shown in Figure 3-21. Sketch the section of the flange wall so that one of the end points of the section touches the attachment edge.

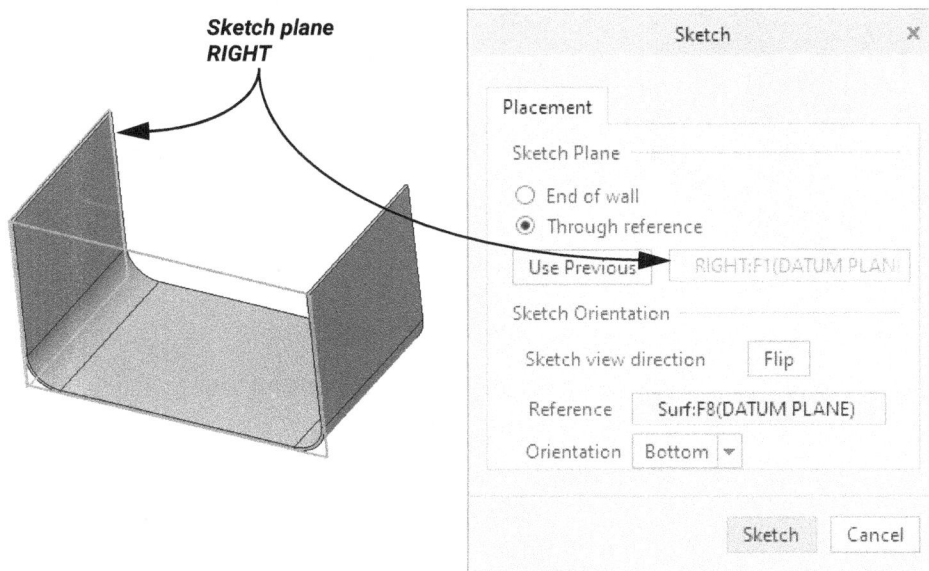

Figure 3-21

- The length options for the first and second end of the chain, which define if or how the wall is extended past each end of the reference edge, can be defined using the two flyouts shown in Figure 3-22. These options are also tied to the Length panel.

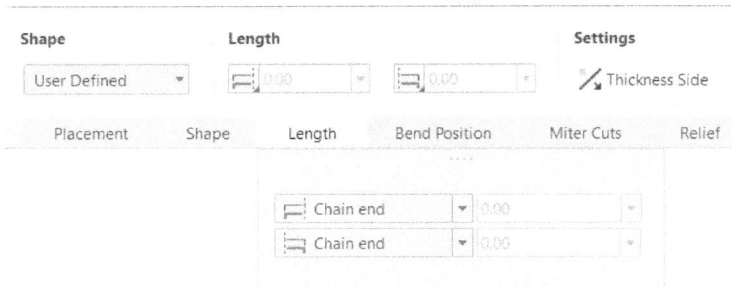

Figure 3-22

- The default option 🗗 (Chain end) or 🗗 (Chain end) terminates the wall at the end of the edge reference for the first direction and/or second direction respectively. An example is shown on the left in Figure 3-23.

- 🗗 (Blind) or 🗗 (Blind): Enables you to enter a value to determine the length of the wall as shown on the right in Figure 3-23.

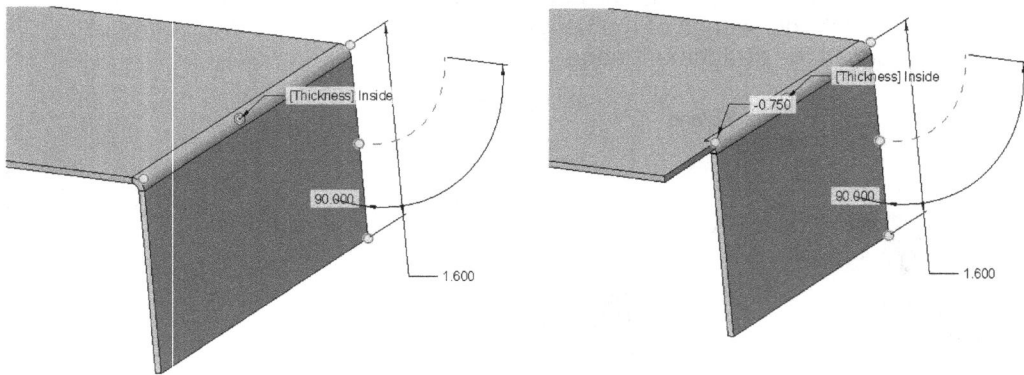

Figure 3-23

- 🗗 (To selected) or 🗗 (To selected): Enables you to extend the wall to a selected reference.

To change the thickness so that it is applied in the opposite direction, click ✕ (Change Thickness Direction) in the dashboard, as shown in Figure 3–24.

Use this flyout to specify the dimensioning surface when Bend creation is enabled

Settings

Bend Dimensions

✕ Thickness Side

⬛ [Thickness]   ▼ ⬛

Click to change the direction of thickness

Enables Bend creation

Figure 3–24

By default, a bend is added if the **User Defined, I**, **Arc**, or **S** predefined flange shapes are selected. They can be used to control the bend at the attachment edge. It can be disabled by

clicking ⬛ (Adds Bend). When enabled, you can dimension to the inner surface using

⬛ (Dimension Inner Surface), or to the outer surface using ⬛ (Dimension Outer Surface). In addition, you can enter a value for the radius.

To control the flange wall location relative to the attachment edge, use the Bend Position panel or mini toolbar.

The *Corner Treatment* panel enables you to modify the shape of adjacent walls, as shown in Figure 3–25.

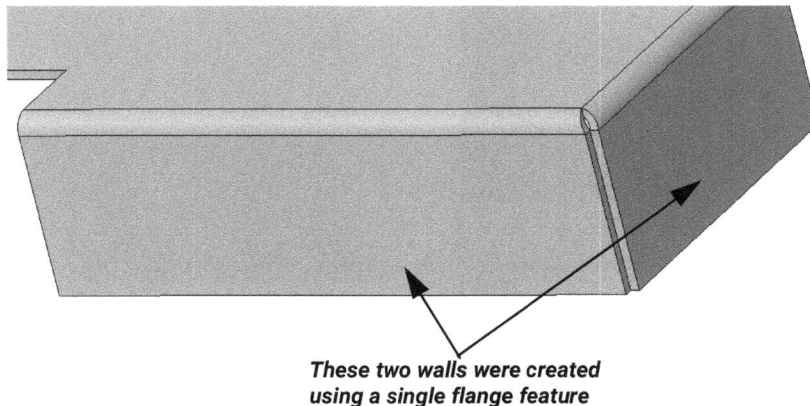

These two walls were created using a single flange feature

Figure 3–25

The available options are shown in Figure 3–26. The **Open** option is set by default.

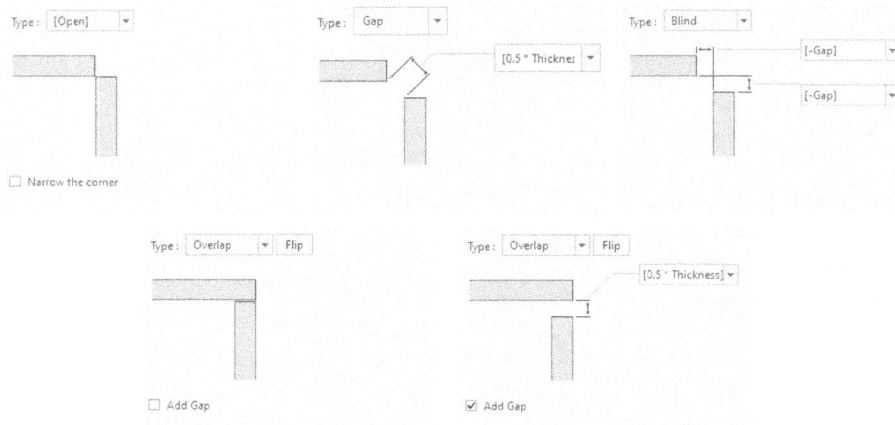

Figure 3–26

- With the **Open** edge treatment, you can use the **Narrow the corner** option to close the corner completely, as shown in Figure 3–27.

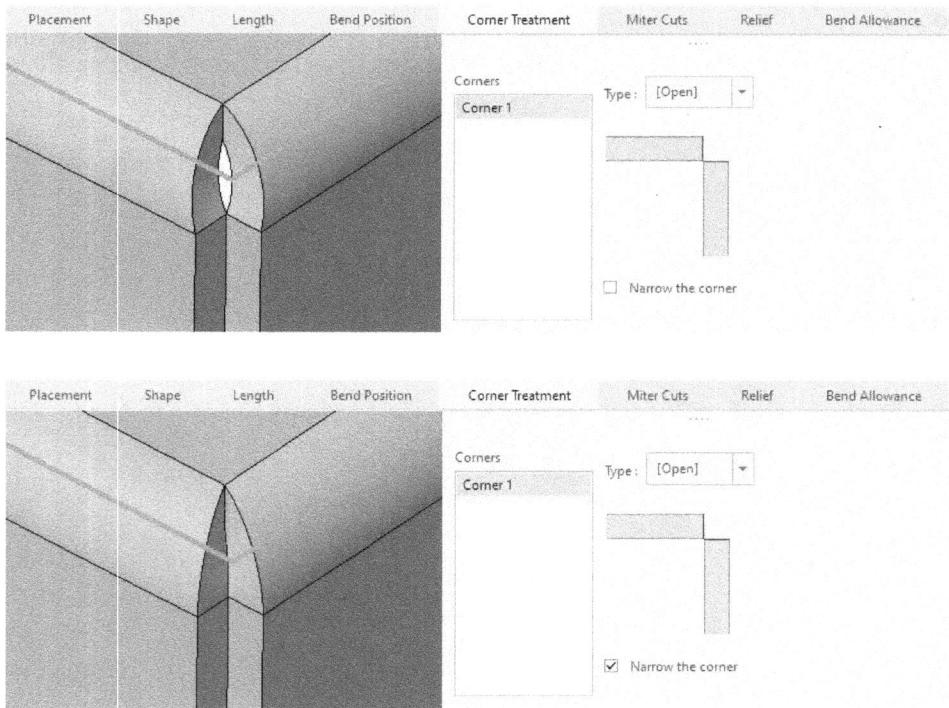

Figure 3–27

- The *Miter Cuts* panel enables you to add a miter cut between two walls, as shown in Figure 3-28, which are defined by a tangent edge chain.

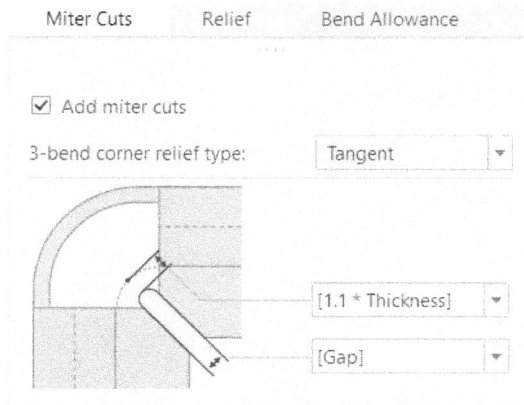

Figure 3-28

Figure 3-29 shows examples of miter cuts created on a model.

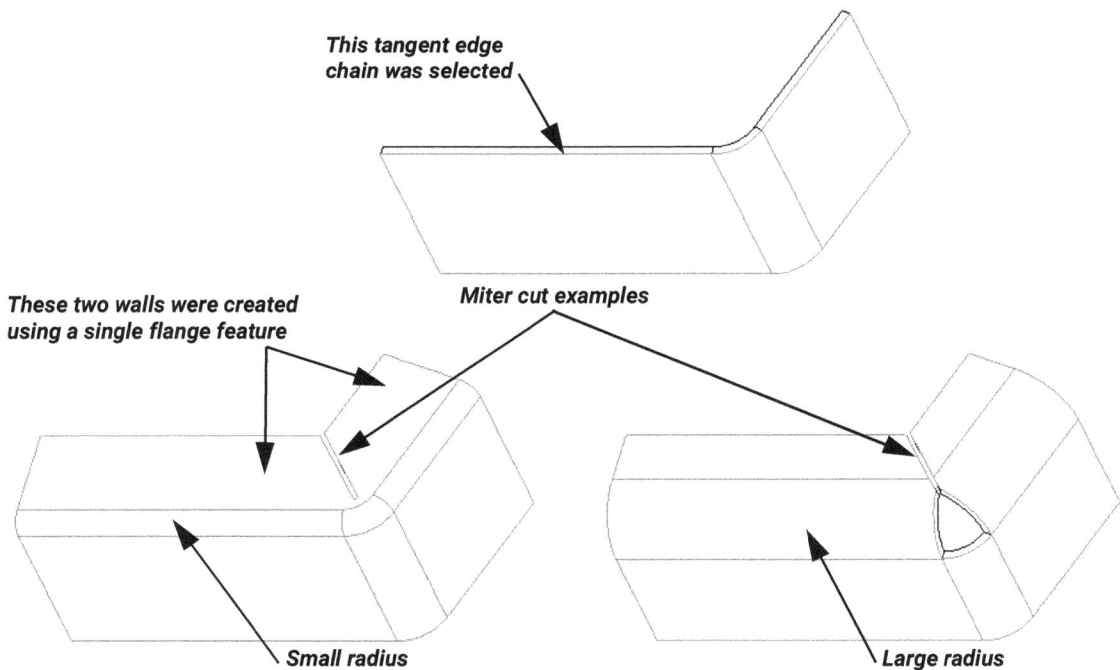

Figure 3-29

- The *Relief* panel enables you to define the bend and corner relief. The bend relief can be defined for both sides or each individual side. Select the type of bend relief in the drop-down list shown in Figure 3–30.

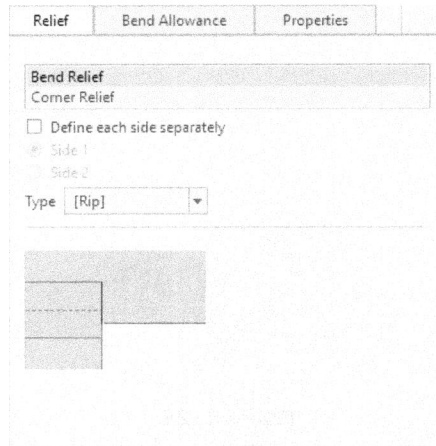

Figure 3–30

- Select the type of corner relief in the drop-down list shown in Figure 3–31.

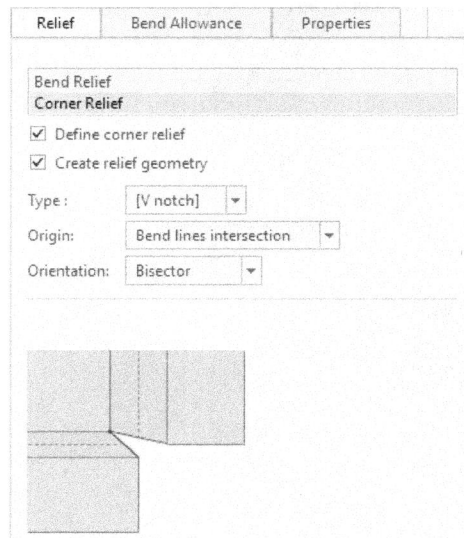

Figure 3–31

Click ✔ (OK) to complete the feature.

3.4 Twisted Wall

A twisted wall acts as an extension to a straight edge on an existing planar wall. The twisted wall can be rectangular or trapezoidal in shape. Once you complete the wall, an axis is created through the center of the twist, perpendicular to the attachment edge. Figure 3-32 shows a twisted wall and the resulting dimensions.

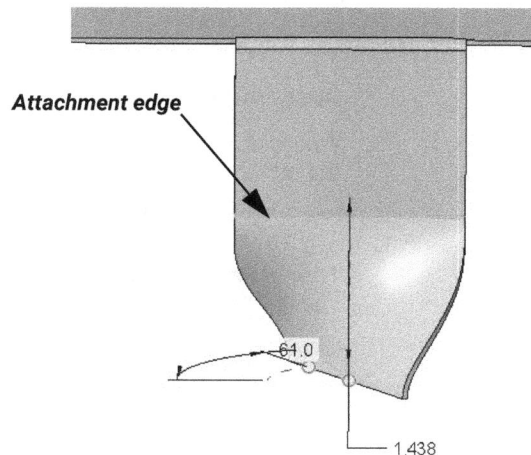

Figure 3-32

To create a twisted wall, expand the **Walls** group and select (Twist), as shown in Figure 3-33.

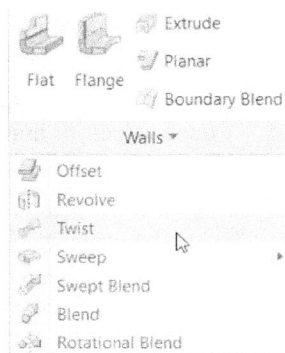

Figure 3-33

The *Twist* dashboard opens, as shown in Figure 3-34.

Figure 3-34

The options available in the dashboard are as follows:

Option	Description
(Offset)	Wall width is calculated using offset dimensions from the attachment edge.
(Up to end)	Use edge end for first direction.
(Blind)	Trim or extend in first direction from edge end by a specified value.
(Up to end)	Use edge end for second direction.
(Blind)	Trim or extend in second direction from edge end by a specified value.
(Symmetrical)	Width is calculated and centered from the twist axis by a width dimension.
(Twist Axis)	Sets a datum point as the twist axis location.
(Modify End Side Width)	Enables end wall width modification.
8.00 (Length)	Enter wall length value, select from a list of recently used values, or drag handle to set value.
61.0 (Angle)	Enter twisting angle value, select from a list of recently used values, or drag handle to set value.

Offset

Select an attachment edge to place the twisted wall. By default, ⬚ (Offset) is active. The first end side and second end side are, by default, set to ⊟ (Up to end) and ⊟ (Up to end) respectively, as shown in Figure 3–35.

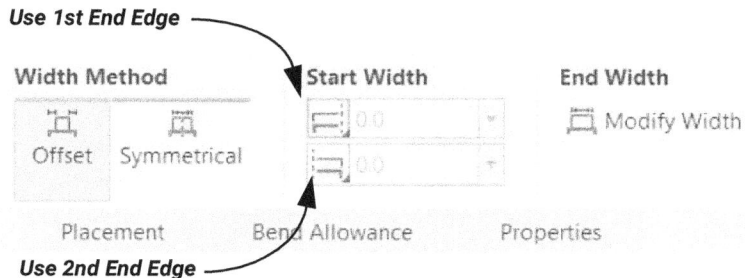

Figure 3–35

That means the wall will extend the full width of the attachment wall, as show in Figure 3–36.

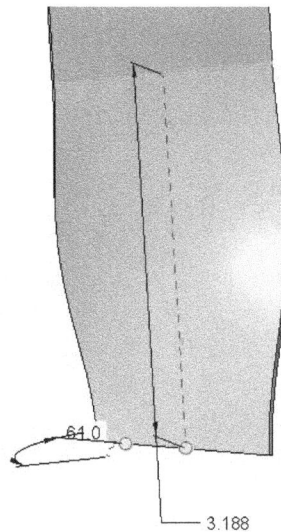

Figure 3–36

You can offset the twist wall from either edge by changing the end condition to ⬚ (Blind) or ⬚ (Blind) for the first and/or second edge respectively. Once selected, you can edit the offset distance or use the drag handles, as shown in Figure 3–37. The offset can be positive or negative.

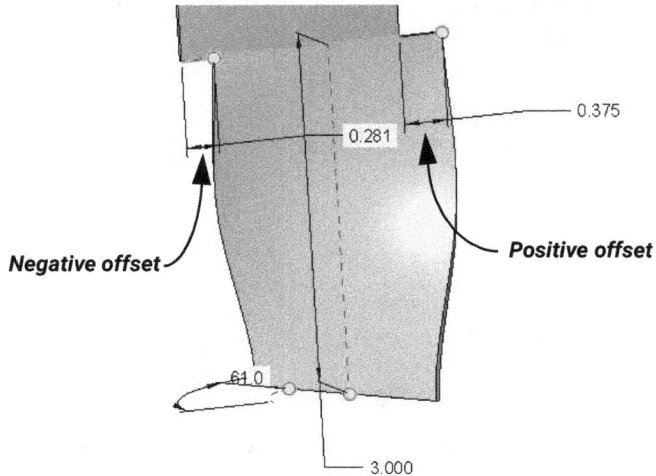

Figure 3–37

You can use the ⬚ (Modify Width) option to adjust the width at the end of the twist wall, such that it either tapers in or flares out. The value is symmetric about the center axis of the wall, as shown in Figure 3–38.

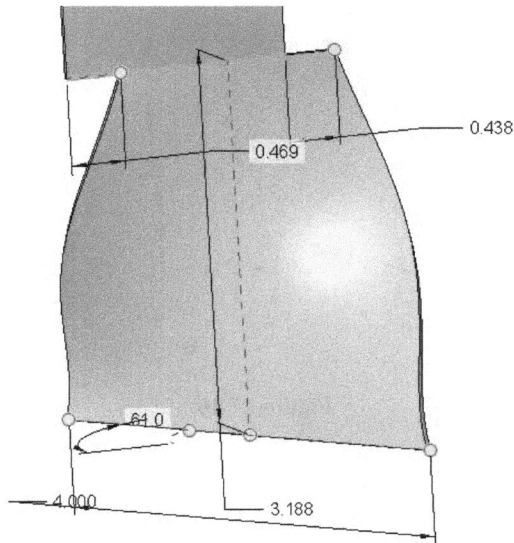

Figure 3–38

Symmetrical

Alternatively, if you want the twist wall to be symmetric about an axis running through the center of the attachment wall, you can apply the ⊞ (Symmetrical) option. You can adjust the width by dragging the handles or entering a value, but the overall width is driven by a single value, symmetric about the twist axis, as shown in Figure 3−39.

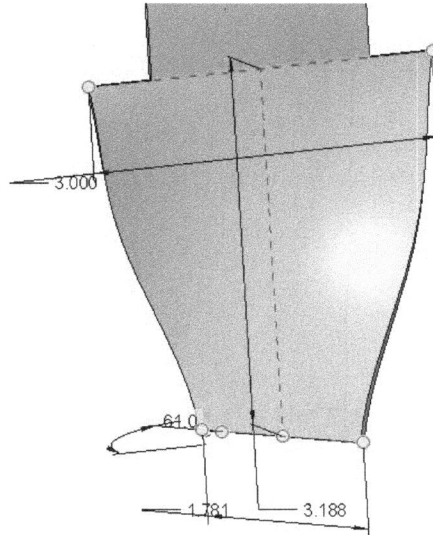

Figure 3−39

You can also use the ⊞ (Symmetrical) option, in conjunction with ⊡ (Set Twist Axis) to select a datum point to locate the twist axis on the attachment wall, as shown in Figure 3−40.

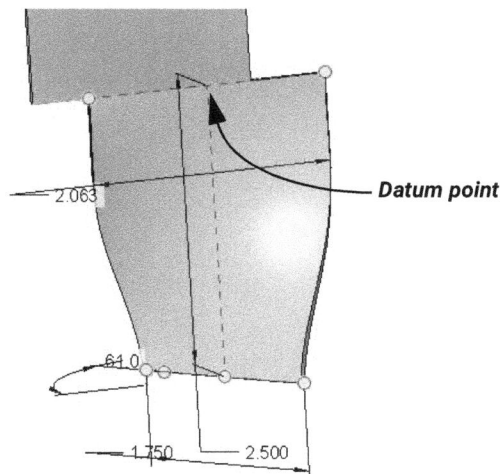

Figure 3−40

The developed length, or the length of the flattened geometry, is equal to the length of the wall by default. In other words, deformation of the metal as it is twisted is considered negligible. You can define a developed length by expanding the Bend Allowance panel, and entering a value in the *Wall length in unbent state* field. The dimensions, including the developed length, are shown in Figure 3–41.

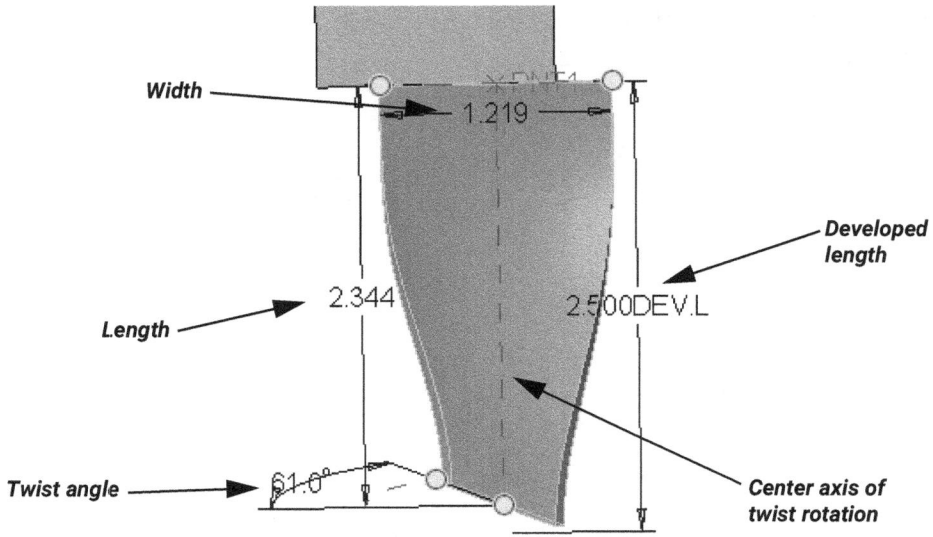

Figure 3–41

3.5 Extended Wall

An extended wall can be used to close gaps. The wall is extended a specified distance or up to a planar surface. Consider the example in Figure 3−42. The gap is closed by extending the wall on the right to the inside surface of the wall on the left.

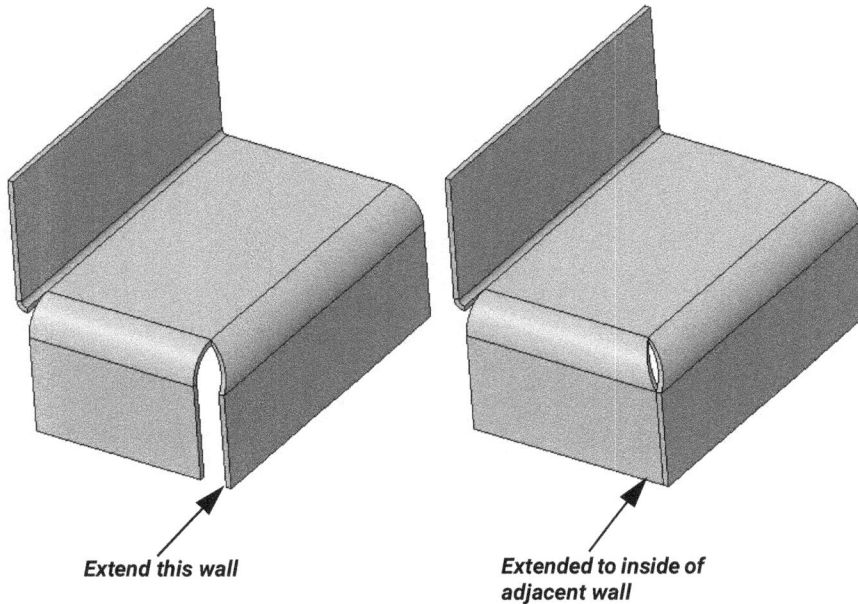

Extend this wall

Extended to inside of adjacent wall

Figure 3−42

How To: Create an Extended Wall

1. Select the straight edge of the wall to extend.

2. Click (Extend) in the Editing group in the *Sheetmetal* tab. The *Extend* dashboard opens, as shown in Figure 3−43.

Figure 3−43

3. Enter a depth for the extended wall and select one of the following options in the *Extend* dashboard:

- Click (Along Original Surface) to extend the wall by value.

- Click (Up to Intersecting) to extend the wall to intersect with a reference plane.

- Click (Up to Plane) to extent the wall to a reference plane.

4. Click (OK) to complete the feature.

3.6 Unattached Walls

Some secondary walls can be created without connecting them to the geometry of the rest of the part, as shown in Figure 3-44. These walls are known as unattached walls.

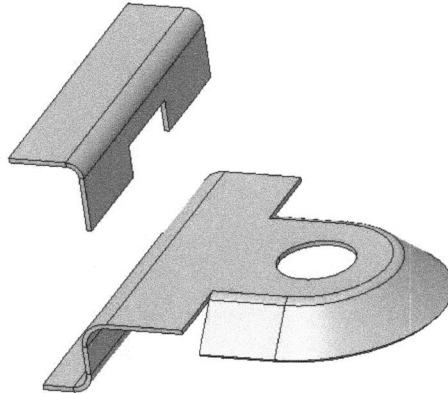

Figure 3-44

Unattached walls enable you to work on different regions of a sheet metal model. The following types of walls can be created as unattached: Planar, Extrude, Revolve, Blend, and Sweep.

A wall can then be added between the unattached sections, as shown in Figure 3-45.

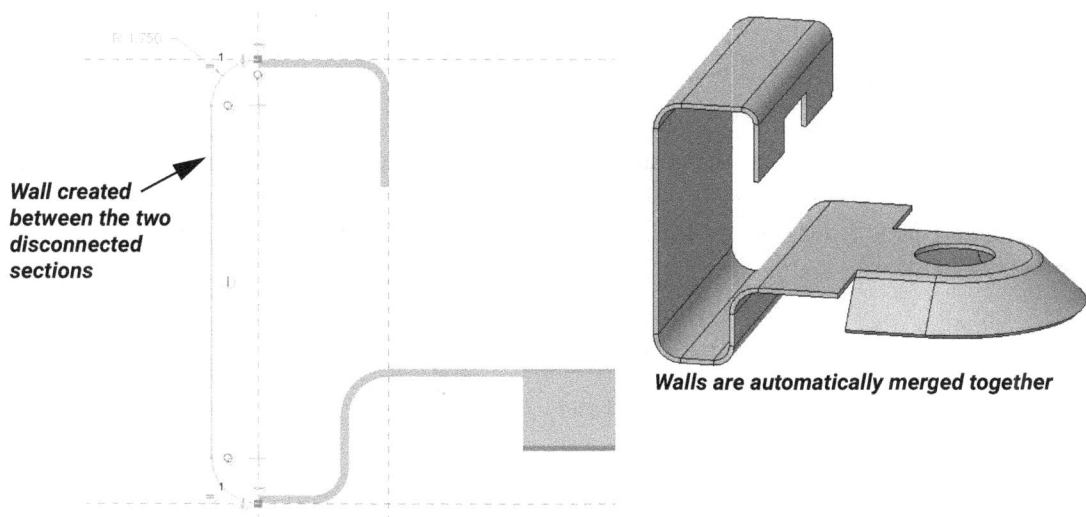

Wall created between the two disconnected sections

Walls are automatically merged together

Figure 3-45

The **Merge to model** option in the Options panel is automatically selected, as shown in Figure 3–46.

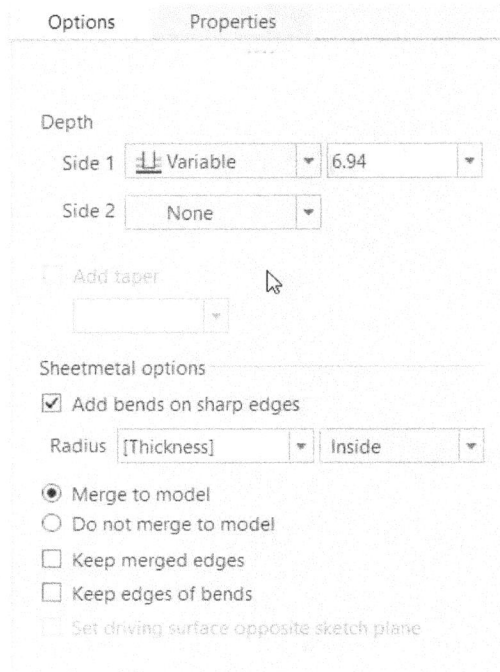

Figure 3–46

Merging Walls

If the **Do not merge to model** option is selected, the resulting wall will be treated as unattached. For example, if the extruded walls in Figure 3–45 were created using the **Do not merge to model option**, you can click ⬚ (Merge Walls) in the Editing group. The *Merge* dashboard opens, as shown in Figure 3–47.

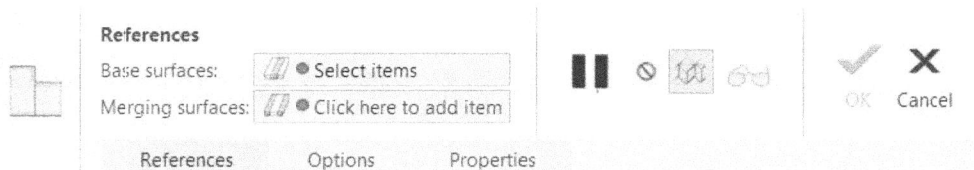

Figure 3–47

Select a surface on the base wall that contacts the wall you want to merge, then select the adjacent surface on the merge wall, as shown in Figure 3–48.

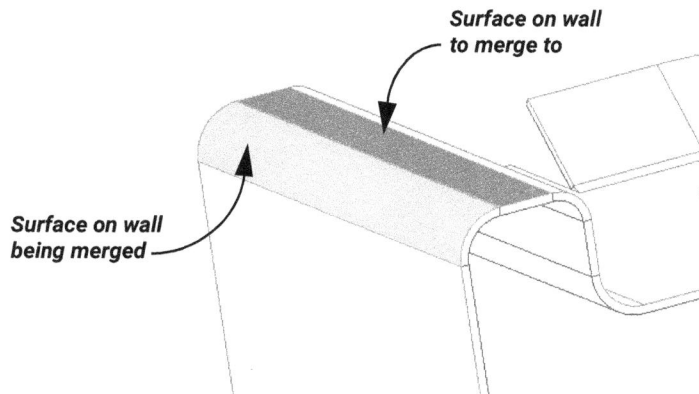

Figure 3–48

You can make multiple merges at the same time, provided, for each surface on the unattached wall, you have a corresponding surface on the model to merge to, as shown in Figure 3–49.

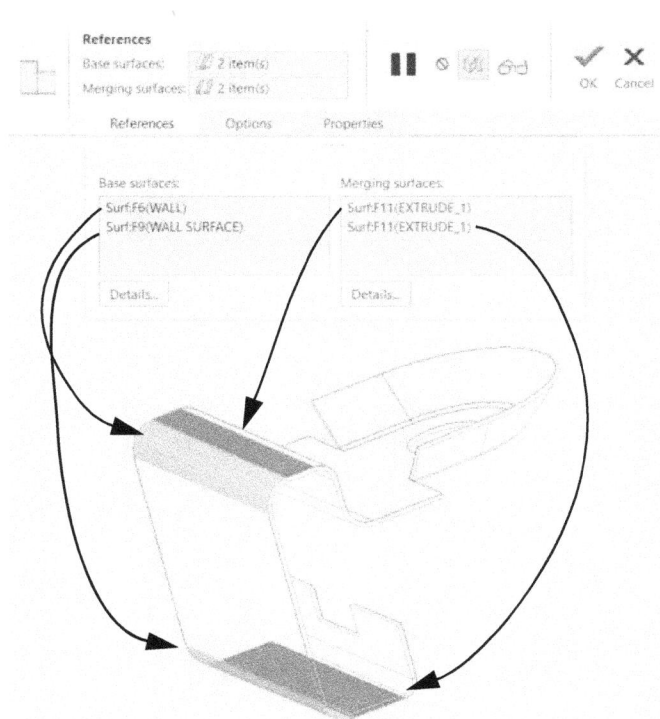

Figure 3–49

3.7 Wall Section Reuse

A flat and flange wall section can be saved and reused. Once created, a wall's section (.SEC) can be saved using **Save As** in the Shape panel for flat and flange walls. These user-defined wall sections can be retrieved for future use in other flat and flange walls by clicking **Open**. The tab shown in Figure 3–50 displays the Shape panel for flat walls.

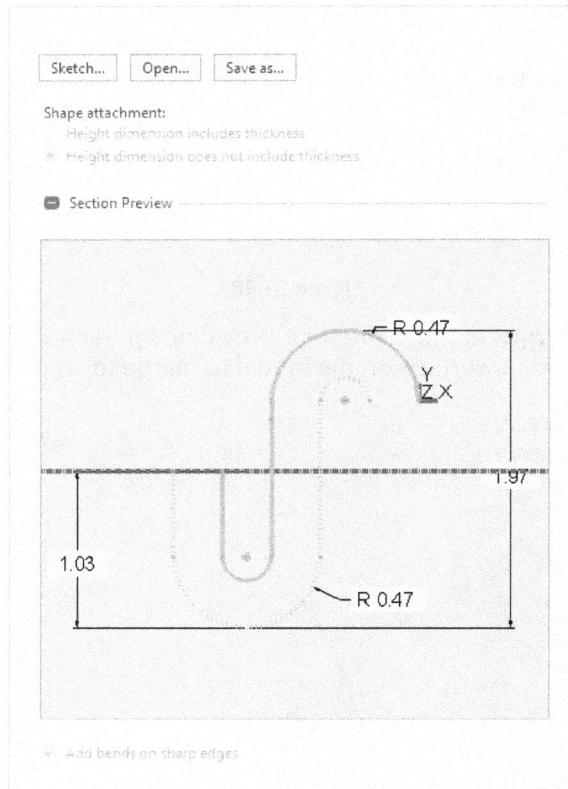

Figure 3–50

3.8 Bend Relief

In certain cases, especially when creating partial flat or flange walls, you need to add a bend relief to the ends of the secondary wall. This enables Creo Parametric to reshape or remove a specific portion of the primary wall so that the secondary wall can be created. You can add a bend relief to one or both ends of the wall using the Relief panel in the tab. The following types of bend relief can be added to a model: **No relief**, **Stretch**, **Rip**, **Rectangular**, and **Obround**.

No Relief

The **No relief** option can be selected if a relief is not required at an end of a wall, as shown in Figure 3–51. If a wall requires relief and this option is selected, the wall cannot be created.

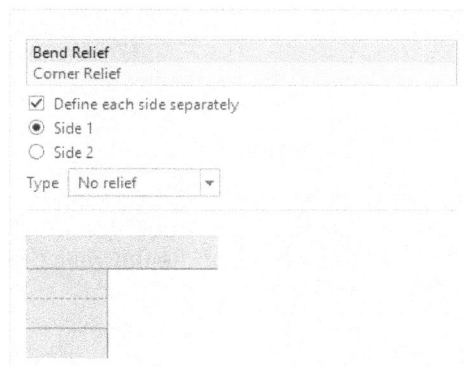

Figure 3–51

Rip Relief

The **Rip** option, shown in Figure 3–52, creates a cut in the primary wall.

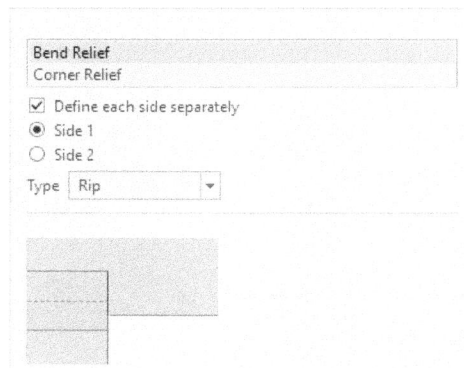

Figure 3–52

The cut is applied at the secondary wall attachment points normal to the attachment edge and back to the tangent line that defines the bend area. This relief results in a zero-volume cut in the metal, as shown in Figure 3–53.

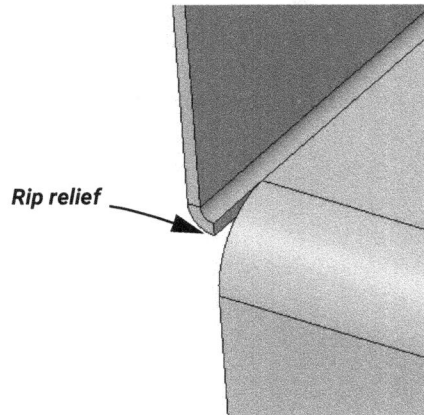

Rip relief

Figure 3–53

When sketching a flat wall, you can sketch beyond the boundaries of the attachment edge and align them to an existing wall. When using this technique, you must apply rip relief along the attachment edge at one or both of the end points of the flat wall. Creo Parametric automatically miters the corner, as shown in Figure 3–54.

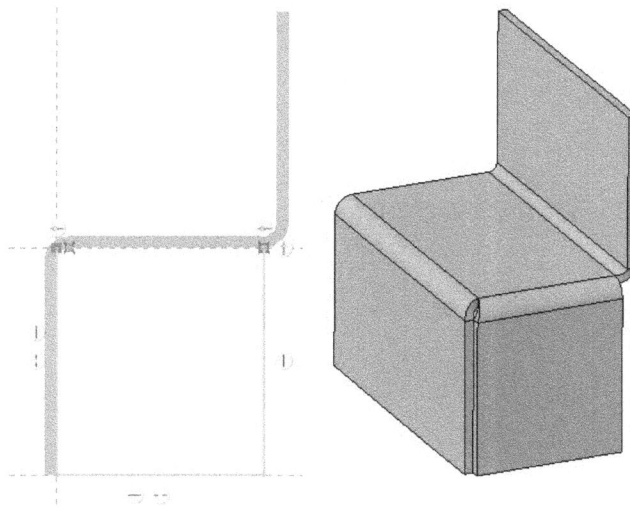

Figure 3–54

Stretch Relief

When the **Stretch** option is selected, as shown in Figure 3–55, the secondary wall is attached to the primary wall by stretching the wall at the attachment points.

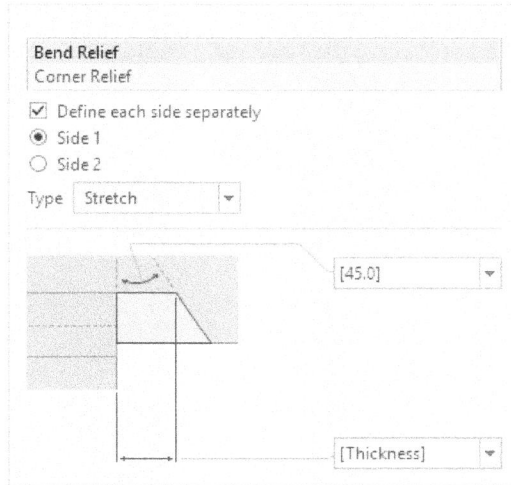

Figure 3–55

You must specify an offset distance and an angle for this relief type, as shown in Figure 3–56.

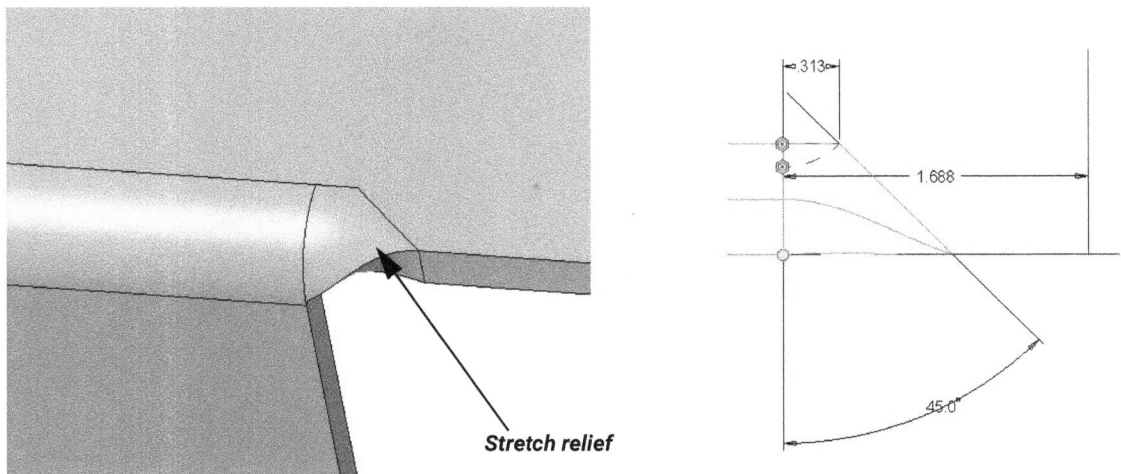

Stretch relief

Figure 3–56

Rectangular Relief

The **Rectangular** option, shown in Figure 3–57, creates a rectangular-shaped cut at the attachment points of the secondary wall using a specified depth and width, as shown in Figure 3–58. The width is defined by selecting **Thickness**, **2 * Thickness**, **[Thickness]** (uses the **SMT_DFLT_BEND_ REL_WIDTH** parameter), or by using an entered value. The depth of the rectangular relief is defined by selecting **Up To Bend** (creates the bend relief up to the bend boundary), **[Up To Bend]** (uses the **SMT_DFLT_BEND_REL_ DEPTH_TYPE** parameter), or by using an entered value.

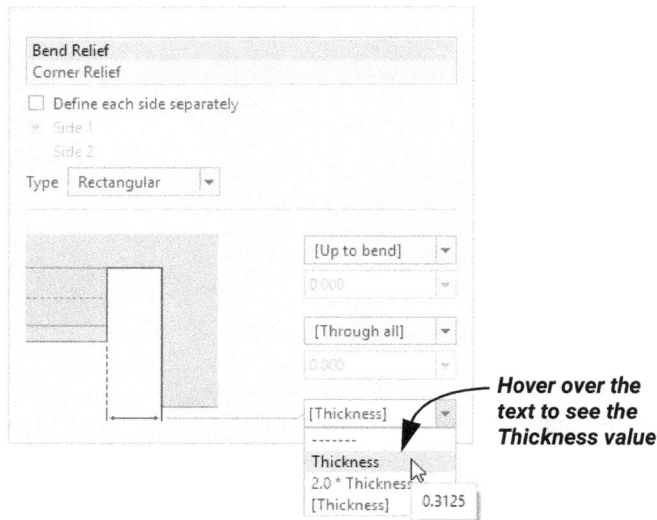

Figure 3–57

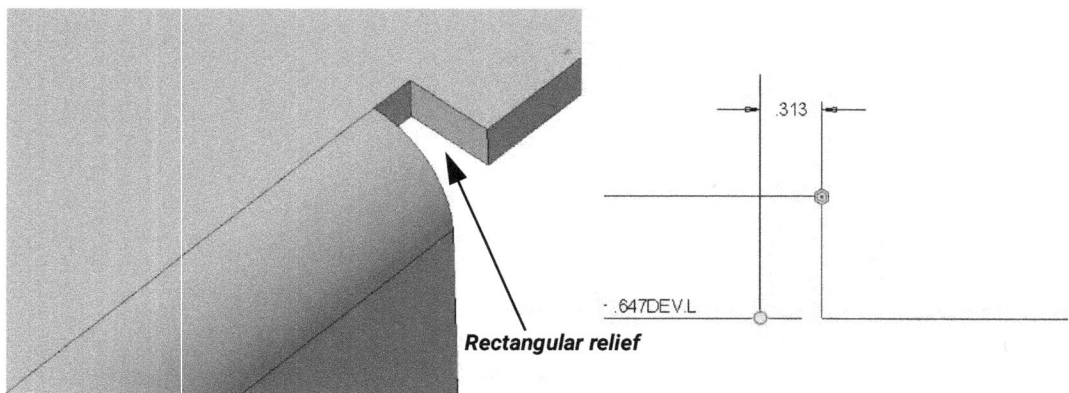

Figure 3–58

Obround Relief

The **Obround** option, shown in Figure 3–59, creates an obround cut at the attachment points of the secondary wall.

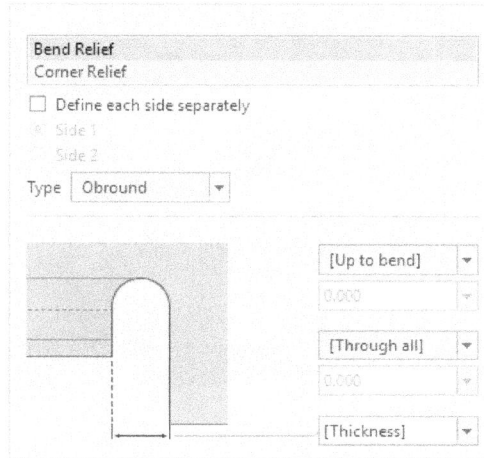

Figure 3–59

You must define the width and depth of the cut, as shown in Figure 3–60. The width is defined by selecting **Thickness**, **2 * Thickness**, **[Thickness]** (uses the **SMT_DFLT_BEND_ REL_WIDTH** parameter), or by using an entered value. The depth of obround relief is defined by selecting **Up To Bend** (creates the bend relief up to the bend boundary), **Tan To Bend** (creates the bend relief tangent to the side of the bend boundary), **[Up To Bend]** (uses the **SMT_DFLT_BEND_ REL_DEPTH_TYPE** parameter), or by using the **Blind** option and entering a value.

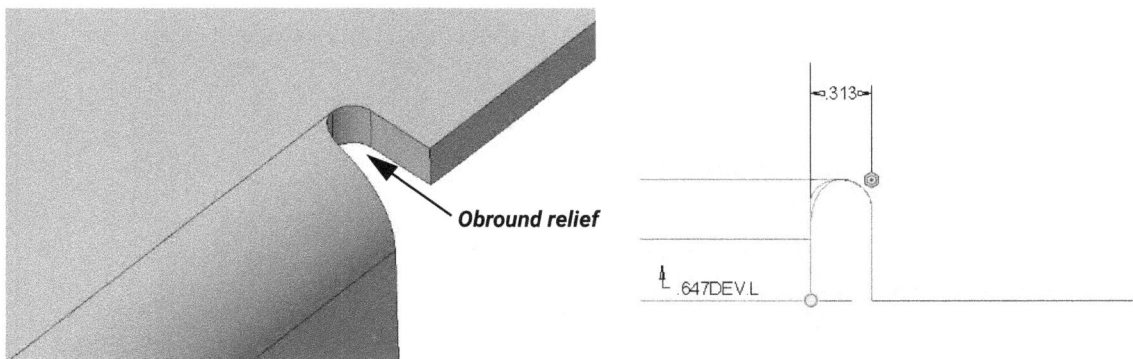

Figure 3–60

When creating or modifying bend relief with rectangular or oblong shapes, you can control the length of shape. There are three options for controlling the length, as shown in Figure 3-61.

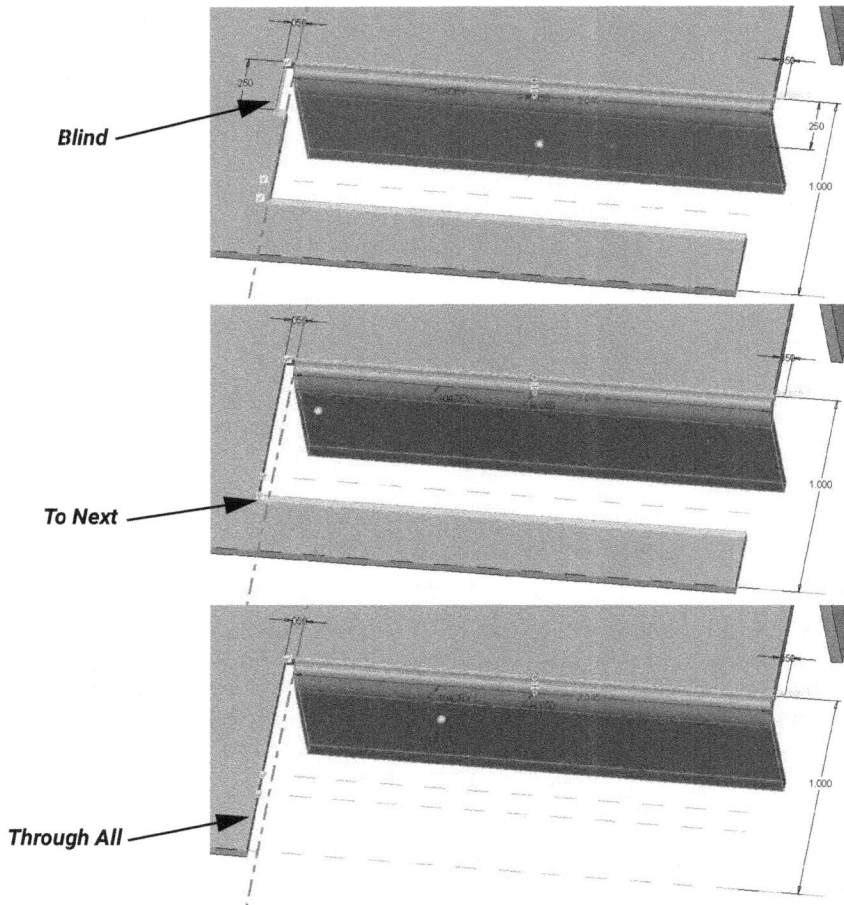

Figure 3-61

To control the relief length, expand the relief panel and select the option from the Length drop-down list, as shown in Figure 3−62.

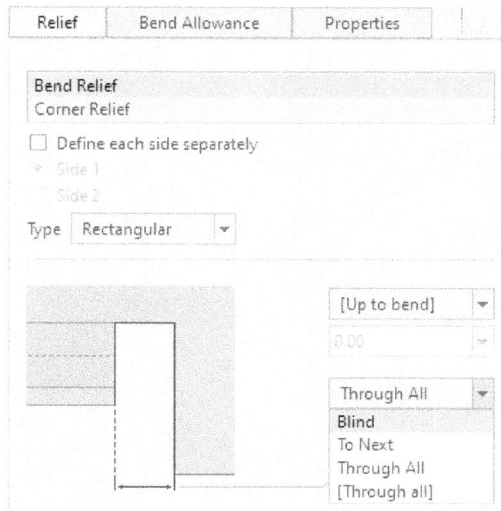

Figure 3−62

Relief on Both Sides

You can define the type of relief for both sides or each side individually by selecting the **Define each side separately** option in the Relief panel. The relief can be different types, as shown in Figure 3−63.

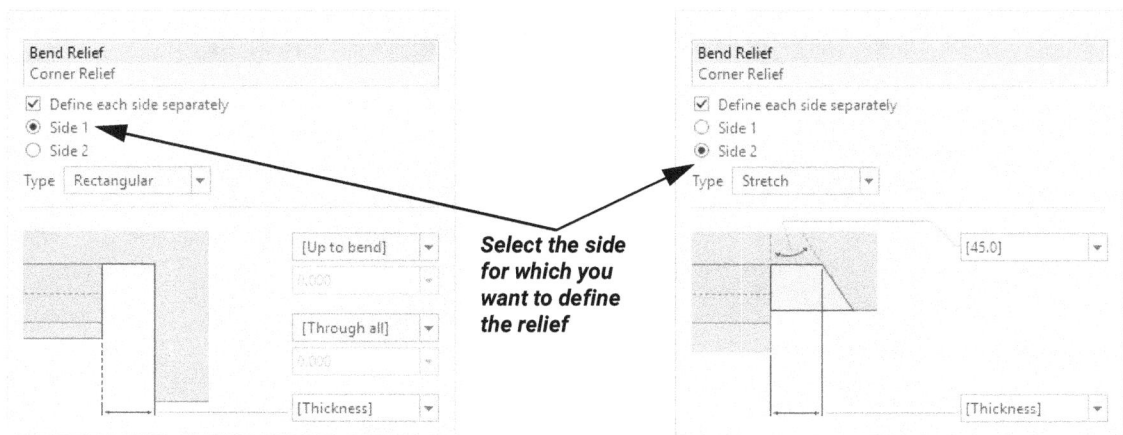

Figure 3−63

Practice 3a
Secondary Walls

Practice Objectives

- Create a secondary flange wall and a secondary flat wall.
- Create an obround relief.

In this practice, you will create several secondary walls on the support part, as shown in Figure 3–64.

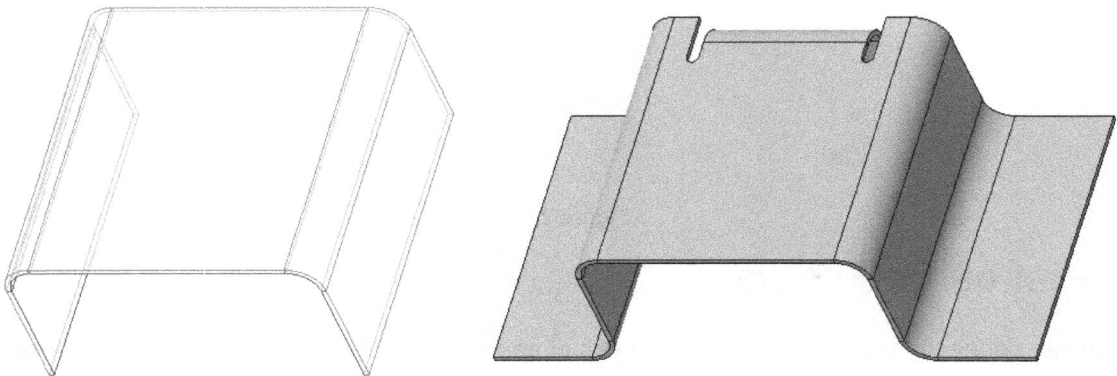

Figure 3–64

Task 1: Open a part and create a flange wall with a predefined shape.

Design Considerations

When you build sheet metal geometry, the first solid feature you create is a primary wall. After that you can add secondary walls, reliefs, and other geometry. In this task you will create the secondary flange wall using one of the available predefined shapes. You will also use the **Copy** functionality to copy the wall you create to another edge in the part.

1. Set the working directory to the *Secondary_Walls a* folder.

2. Open **02_support.prt**.

3. Set the model display as follows:

    - ⚡ *(Datum Display Filters)*: None

    - ⟩∘ *(Spin Center)*: Off

    - ▢ *(Display Style)*: ▢ (Shading With Edges)

4. Select the outside edge as the attachment edge and click ⬚ (Flange) in the mini toolbar to create a flange wall, as shown in Figure 3–65.

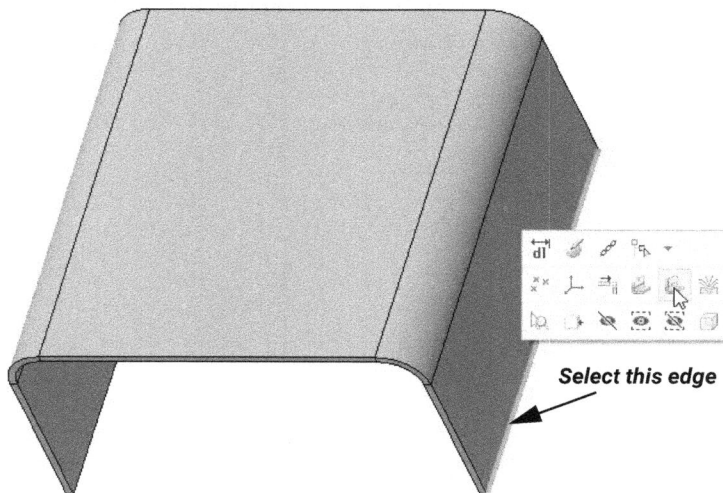

Figure 3–65

5. Accept the **I** shaped wall in the Wall type drop-down list in the *Flange* dashboard.

6. Set the display to ⬚ (Hidden Line). The model preview updates as shown in Figure 3–66.

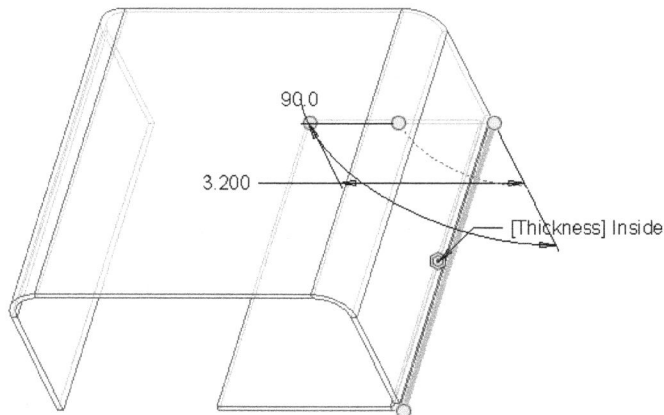

Figure 3–66

7. Expand the **Shape** panel in the *Flange* dashboard and click ⊕ (Section Preview) to view the sketch the system is using for the wall.

8. Set the *Angle* to **-90 or 270** and the *Length* to **2.5**, as shown in Figure 3–67.

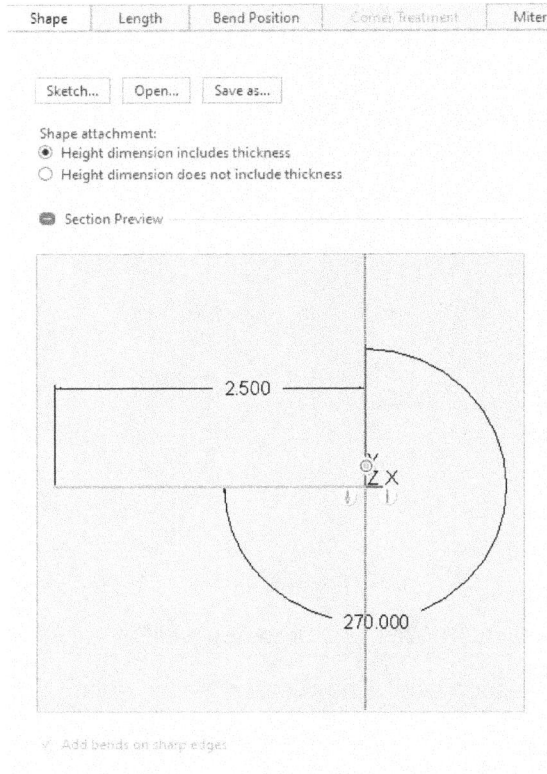

Shape	Length	Bend Position	Corner Treatment	Miter

Sketch...   Open...   Save as...

Shape attachment:
◉ Height dimension includes thickness
○ Height dimension does not include thickness

◉ Section Preview

2.500

Z X

270.000

☑ Add bends on sharp edges

Figure 3–67

Note: *You can edit the dimensions in the Shape panel, and you can Pan and Zoom the sketch as needed.*

9. Click ⤵ (Inside), if necessary, from the flyout, as shown in Figure 3–68.

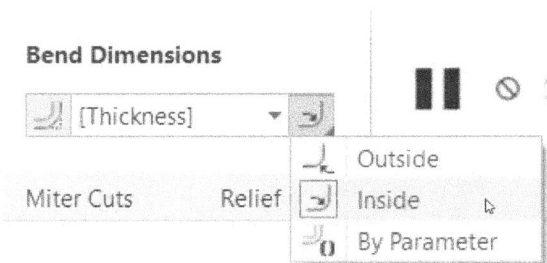

Bend Dimensions

⤵ [Thickness] ▾ ⤵

Miter Cuts   Relief | ⤵ Inside

⌐ Outside
⤵ Inside
⤵₀ By Parameter

Figure 3–68

10. In the *Flange* dashboard, or directly on the model, set the bend *Radius* to **0.5,** as shown in Figure 3–69.

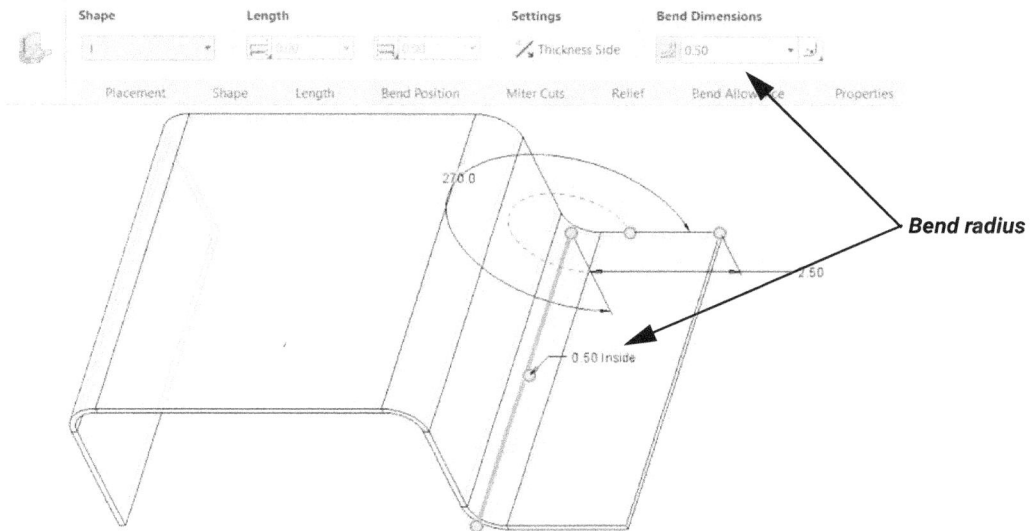

Figure 3–69

Note: ⤴ *(Dimension Inner Surface) applies the radius value to the inside of the bend.*

11. Click ✔ (OK).

12. Set the display to ▱ (Shading With Edges). The part displays as shown in Figure 3–70.

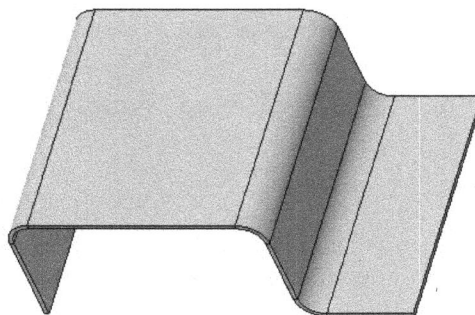

Figure 3–70

13. Create a similar wall on the opposite side of the part, as shown in Figure 3–71. Instead of creating a new wall feature and changing the required options, use the **Copy** and **Paste** tools.

- Set the selection filter to **Feature**.
- Select the wall that you just created.
- Click ▣ (Copy) and click ▣ (Paste).
- The *Flange dashboard* opens and the only selection that is required is the attachment edge. Select the attachment edge (ensure that you select the outside edge).
- Click ✓ (OK). All the other options are copied from the previous feature.

Note: You can also select the wall and press <Ctrl>+<C> and <Ctrl>+<V> to copy and paste the wall.

14. Set the selection filter back to **Geometry**.

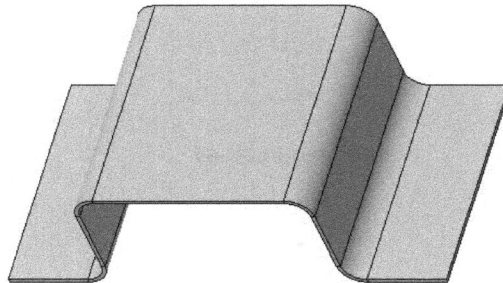

Figure 3–71

Note: The two secondary walls could have been created as part of the original primary wall. They are created separately to accommodate a possible future design change.

Task 2: Create a flat wall with a user-defined shape.

Design Considerations

In this task, you will create another secondary wall. You will sketch the shape of this wall instead of using the existing predefined shapes. To create this wall, you need to add reliefs at both ends of the wall.

1. Select the edge shown in Figure 3–72 and click 🦫 (Flat) in the mini toolbar to create a flat wall.

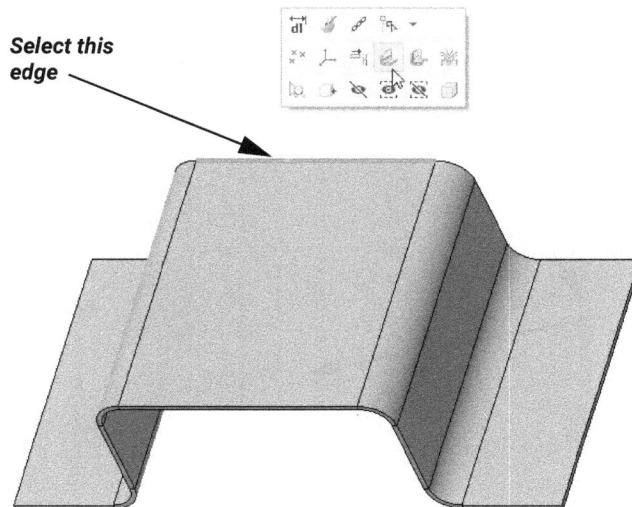

Figure 3–72

2. In the *Flat* dashboard, click **Shape** and click ⊕ (Section Preview). The Shape panel displays as shown in Figure 3–73.

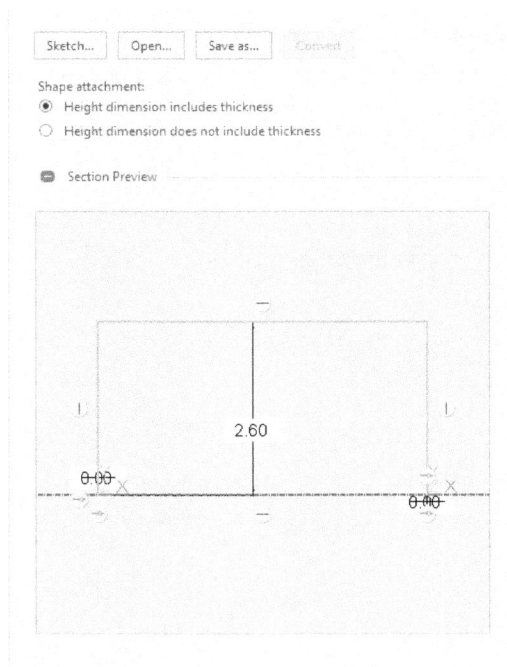

Figure 3–73

3. To obtain the required dimensioning scheme for this wall, click **Sketch** to manually edit the sketch. The *Sketch* tab opens.

4. Click 🖳 (Sketch View).

5. Change the dimensioning scheme as shown in Figure 3–74.

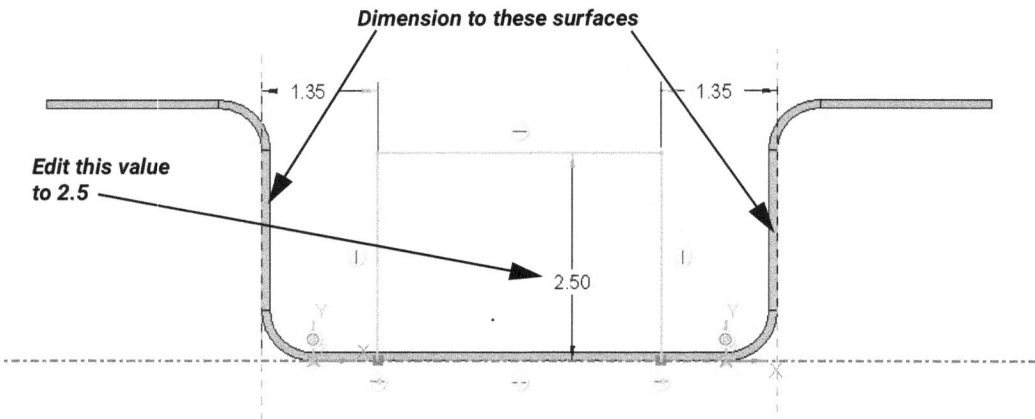

Figure 3–74

6. Click ✓ (OK) to complete the sketch and return to the *Flat* dashboard.

7. Press <Ctrl>+<D> to return to the default orientation.

8. Click **Relief** and select **Obround** in the Type drop-down list.

9. Modify the Obround relief's *Depth* to **Blind**. Change the depth to **0.5** and the width to **0.25**, as shown in Figure 3–75.

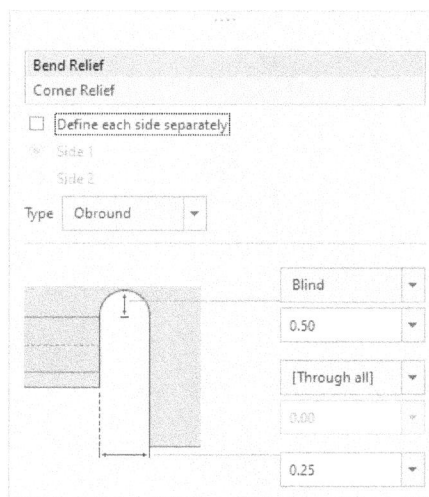

Figure 3–75

10. Set the Bend Dimension *Radius* to **0.5** in the *Flat* dashboard or directly on the model.

11. Click ✓ (OK). The completed part displays as shown in Figure 3–76.

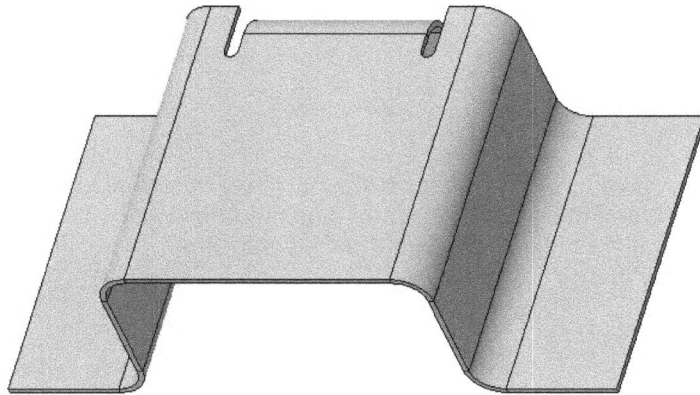

Figure 3–76

12. Save the part and erase it from memory.

End of practice

Practice 3b
Unattached Wall

Practice Objective

- Create and merge unattached walls.

In this practice, you will work with the sheet metal part that was used in an assembly. Note the space requirements, one of the walls of this part was created in Assembly mode as an unattached wall. You will create a second unattached wall and merge both with the base geometry, as shown in Figure 3–77.

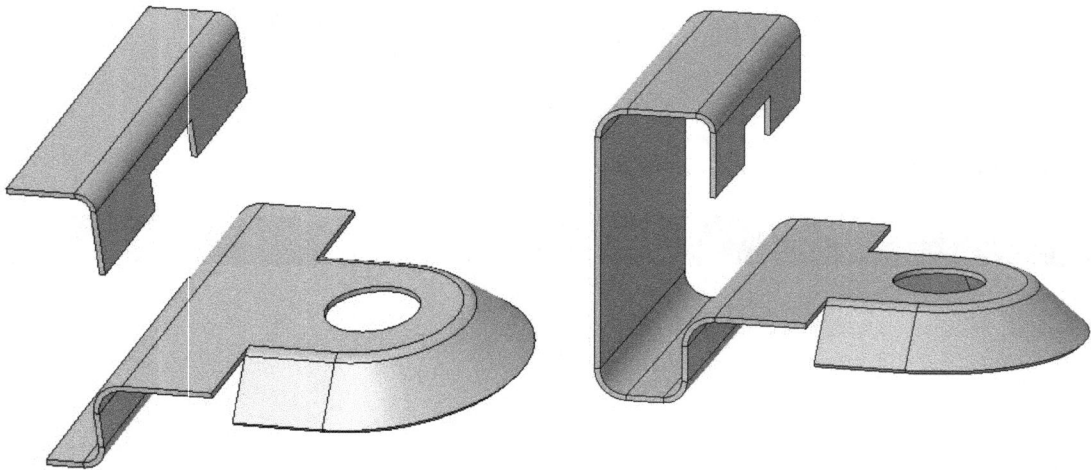

Figure 3–77

Task 1: Open a part file and examine how it was created.

1. Set the working directory to the *Unattached_Wall* folder.
2. Open **cover.prt** part.
3. Set the model display as follows:

- *⚡ (Datum Display Filters)*: None
- *➣ (Spin Center)*: Off
- *▢ (Display Style)*: ▢ (Shading With Edges)

4. Examine the Model Tree. It contains an unattached wall, as shown in Figure 3–78.

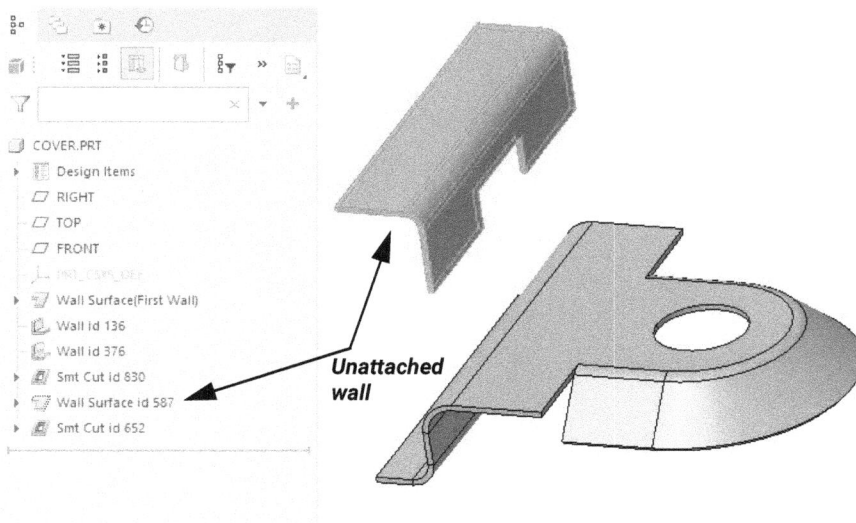

Figure 3–78

Task 2: Create a second wall.

Design Considerations

In this task, you will create an extruded wall by sketching its shape. This wall should join the existing unattached wall and the base geometry of the part.

1. Click (Extrude) in the *Sheetmetal* tab. The *Extrude* dashboard displays, as shown in Figure 3–79.

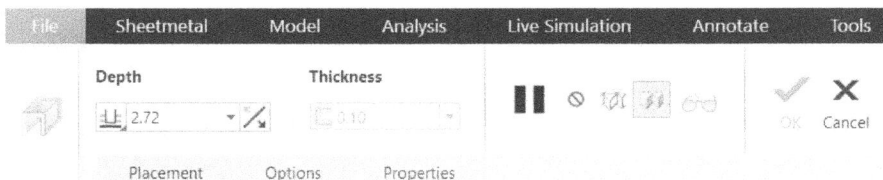

Figure 3–79

2. In the Model Tree, select datum plane **TOP**. It will be used as the sketching plane. The *Sketch* tab is now active.

    Note: You can also click and select *(Define Internal Sketch) and select datum plane* **TOP** *as the sketching plane.*

3. Click (Sketch View).

4. Sketch the section shown in Figure 3−80. Ensure that the arcs are tangent to the adjacent walls.

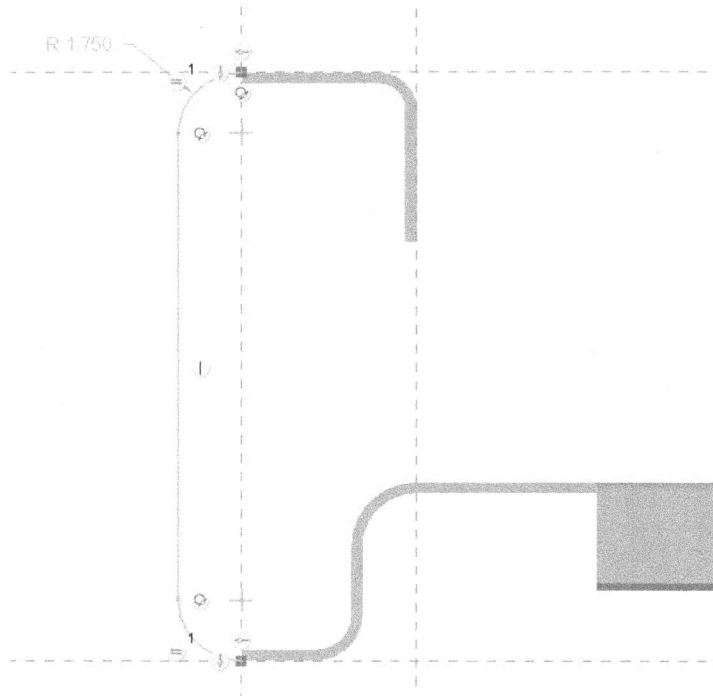

R 1.750

Figure 3−80

5. Edit the dimensioning scheme to match that shown in Figure 3-81. Creo Parametric will thicken this wall to the same value as the existing walls.

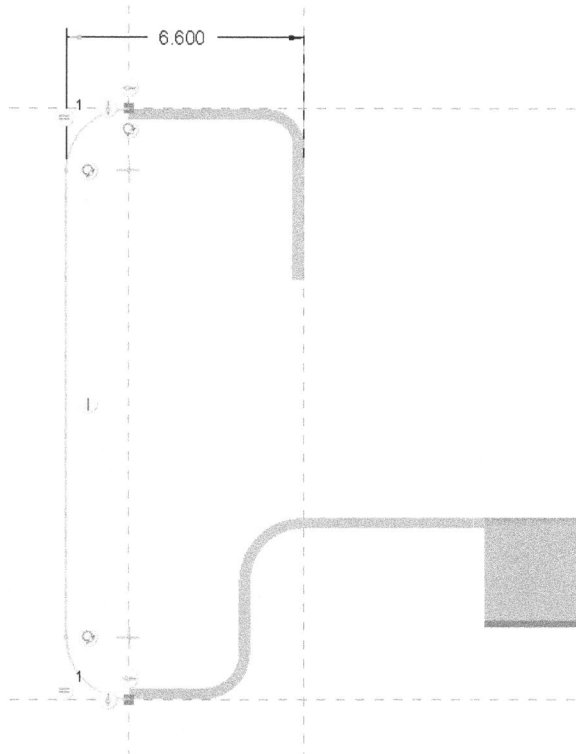

Figure 3-81

6. Complete the sketch.

7. Ensure that the thickness arrow points toward the interior of the model. If required, click on the arrow to flip its direction.

    Note: You cannot enter the wall thickness. Creo Parametric uses the value defined for the first wall.

8. Right-click the depth drag handle and select **To Reference**, as shown in Figure 3−82. Select the top surface as the surface to extrude to, as shown in Figure 3−83.

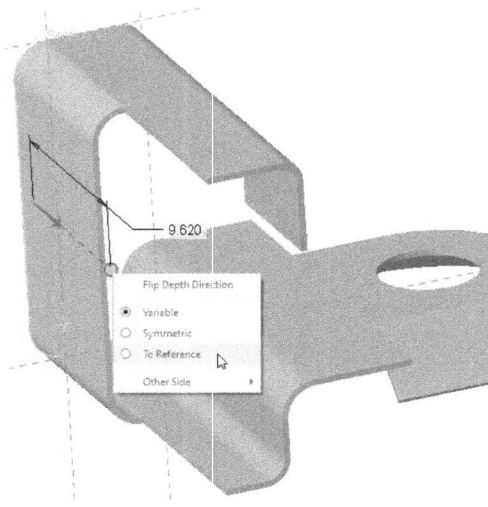

Figure 3−82

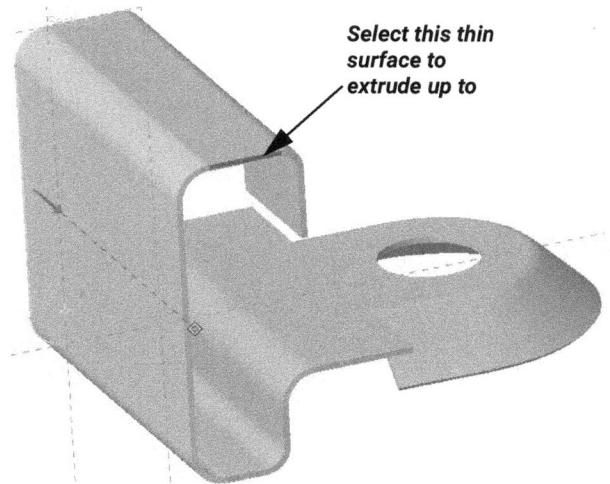

Select this thin surface to extrude up to

Figure 3−83

9. Expand the Options panel in the *Extrude* dashboard. Note that **Merge to model** is selected, as shown in Figure 3−84. To be able to flatten a sheet metal part, you must make the geometry of the unattached walls and geometry of the base feature continuous.

Figure 3−84

10. Click ✔ (OK) in the *Extrude* dashboard. The cover part displays as shown in Figure 3−85.

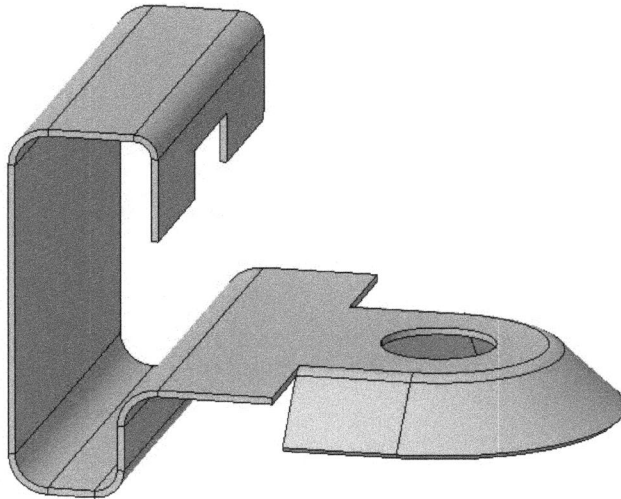

Figure 3−85

Task 3: Unbend the part.

In this task, you will check whether the merge commands were successful by unbending the part. If the part flattens successfully, the merge has been created correctly.

1. In the *Sheetmetal* tab, click ⬚ (Unbend).

> **Note:** *Unbend is covered in detail in a later chapter.*

2. Select the surface shown in Figure 3−86 as the surface to remain fixed, if required.

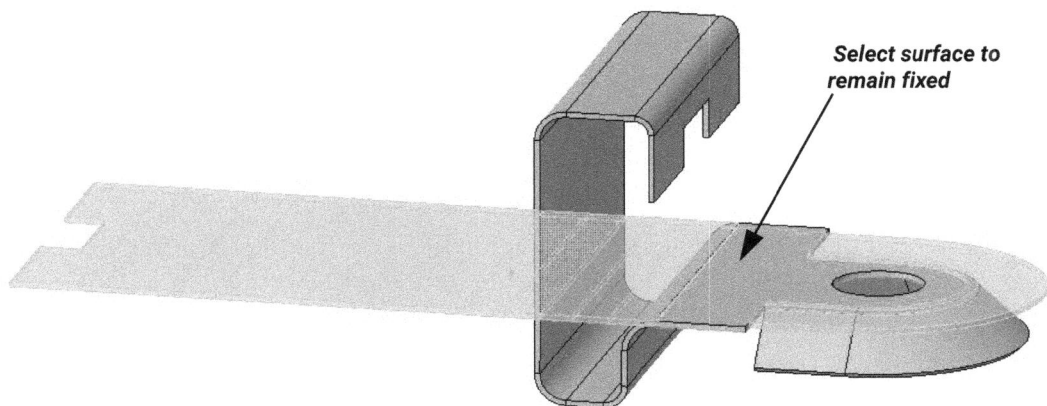

Select surface to
remain fixed

Figure 3−86

3. Click ✓ (OK) in the *Unbend* dashboard. The model displays as shown in Figure 3−87.

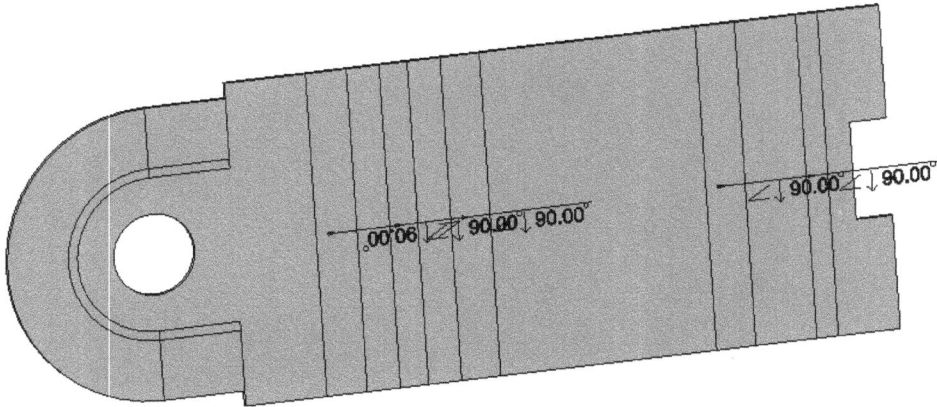

Figure 3−87

4. Delete the unbend feature.
5. Save the part and erase it from memory.

End of practice

Practice 3c
Flange Walls I

Practice Objective

* Create a flange wall using the predefined Z profile.

The Flange feature enables you to create secondary walls quickly and easily using a set of predefined profiles. You can also define your own profile. In this practice, you will create the flange wall shown in Figure 3–88.

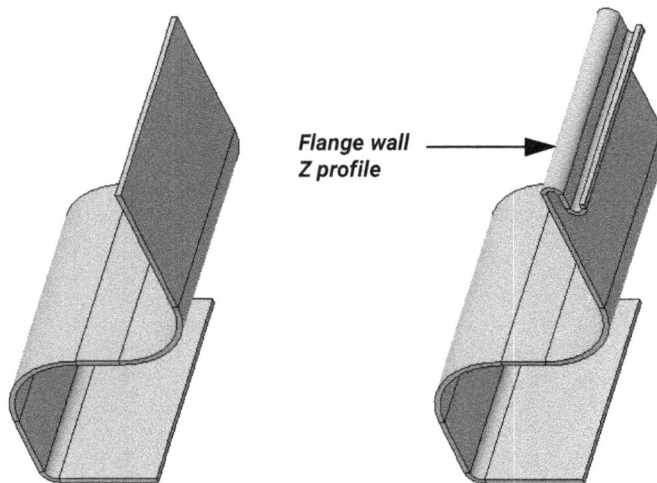

Flange wall Z profile

Figure 3–88

Design Considerations

In this task, you will create the secondary flange wall using one of the available predefined shapes.

1. Set the working directory to the *Flange_Walls_I* folder.
2. Open **clip.prt**.
3. Set the model display as follows:
   * ⚙ *(Datum Display Filters)*: None
   * ⚙ *(Spin Center)*: Off
   * ⚙ *(Display Style)*: ⬜ (Shading With Edges)

4. Select the edge shown in Figure 3–89 as the attachment edge and click ⬛ (Flange) in the mini toolbar.

Select this edge as the attachment edge

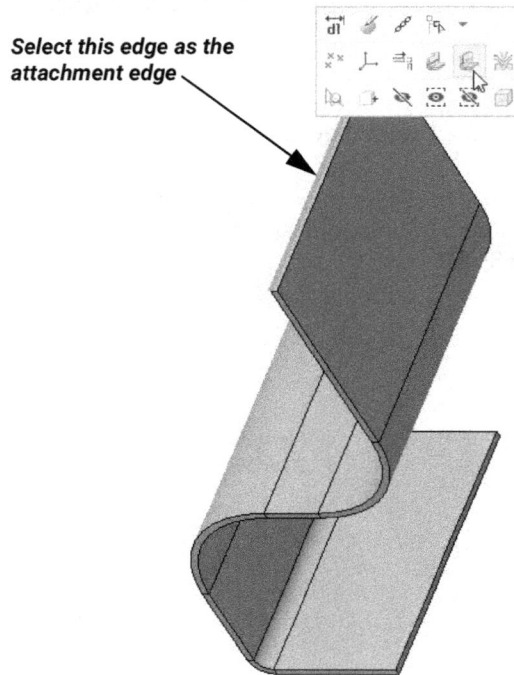

Figure 3–89

5. Select the **Z** profile in the drop-down list, as shown in Figure 3–90.

Figure 3–90

6. The system displays the geometry preview, as shown in Figure 3–91.

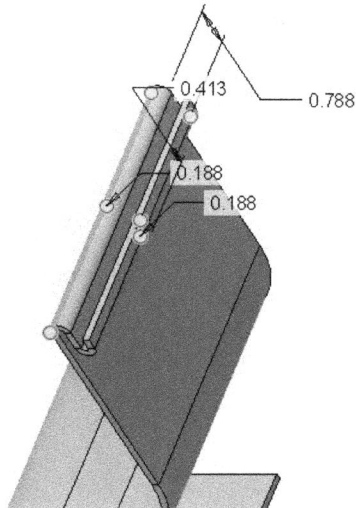

Figure 3–91

7. In the Shape panel, enter the dimension values shown in Figure 3–92. Press <Enter> after each dimension modification.

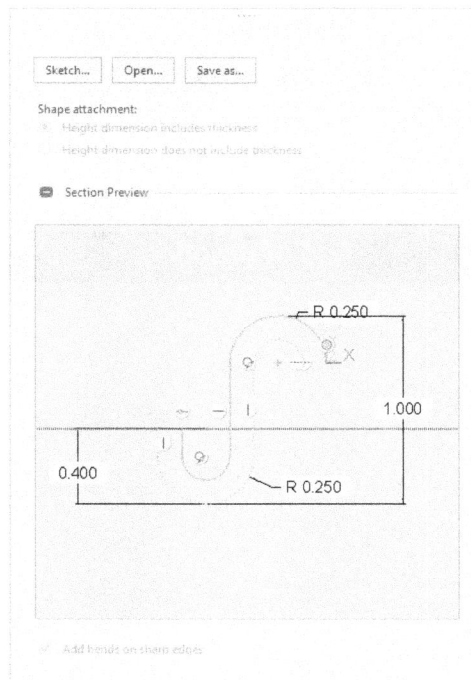

Figure 3–92

Note: *You can also modify the values directly in the model.*

8. Click ✓ (OK) to complete the feature. The completed feature displays as shown in Figure 3–93.

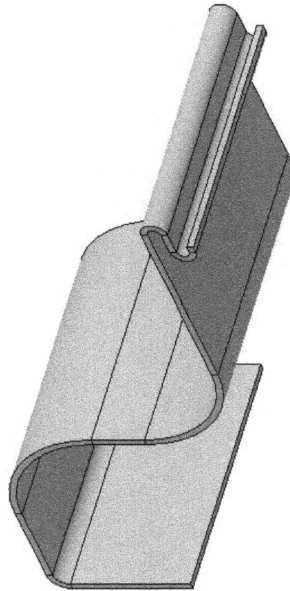

Figure 3–93

Note: *Dimensions can be modified, as with any other feature.*

9. Save the part and erase it from memory.

End of practice

Practice 3d
Flange Walls II

Practice Objective

* Create a flange wall.

Flange features enable you to create secondary walls quickly and easily using a set of predefined profiles. In this practice, you will create the flange wall shown in Figure 3−94.

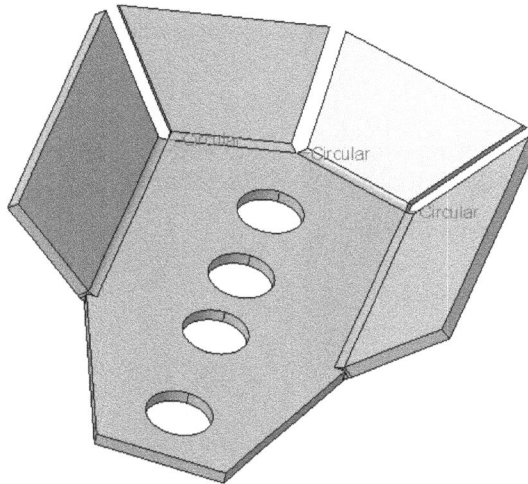

Figure 3−94

Task 1: Open a part file and create a flange wall.

In this task, you will create secondary walls using the Flange feature. You will select multiple edges using the loop chain method.

1. Set the working directory to the *Flange_Walls_II* folder.

2. Open **flanged_part.prt**.

3. Set the model display as follows:

   * ⁙ *(Datum Display Filters)*: None

   * ⤳ *(Spin Center)*: Off

   * ⬚ *(Display Style)*: ⬚ (Shading With Edges)

4. Select the bottom edge shown in Figure 3−95.

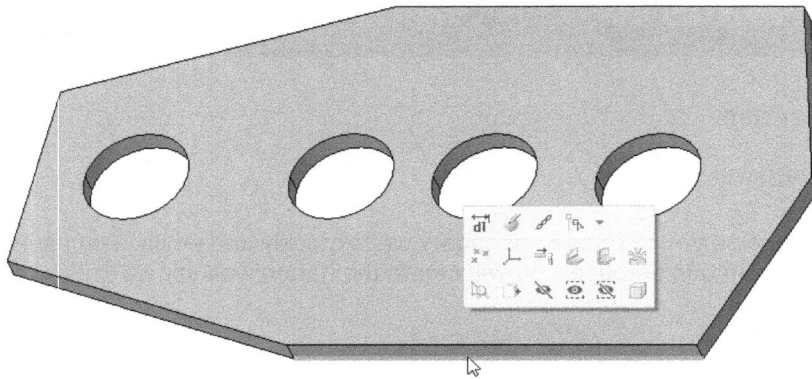

Figure 3−95

5. Hold <Shift> and hover the cursor over the edge shown in Figure 3−96. Right-click several times until the chain of edges shown highlights. Select the edge, then release <Shift> and click ⬚ (Flange) in the mini toolbar.

Select this edge

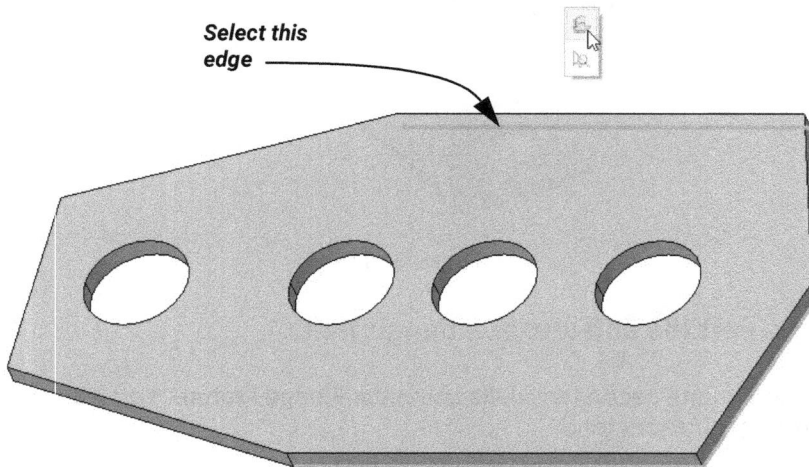

Figure 3−96

6. Edit the angle to **45** and the length to **1.00**, as shown in Figure 3–97.

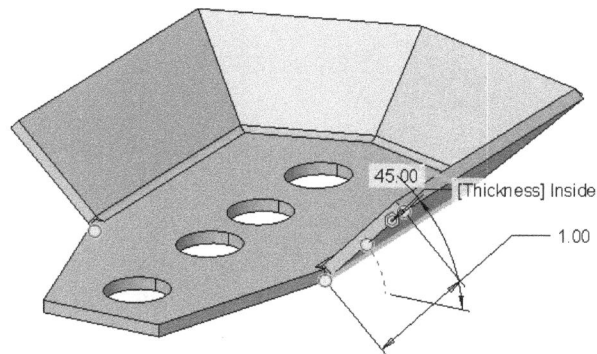

Figure 3–97

7. Define the *Corner Treatment* as **Gap** for all **three** corners and set each gap to **0.125**, as shown in Figure 3–98.

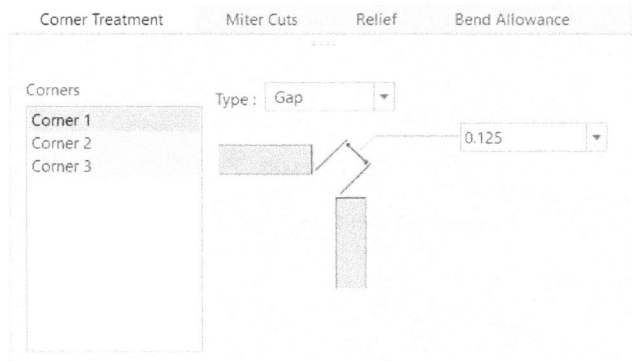

Figure 3–98

8. Select the Relief panel.

   Note: Corner Relief is covered in detail in a later chapter.

9. Select **Corner Relief**, remove the checkmark next to **Create relief geometry**, and select **Circular** from the Type drop-down list**.**

10. Select **Bend lines intersection** from the Origin drop-down list. Select **2.0*Thickness** for the parameter, as shown in Figure 3–99.

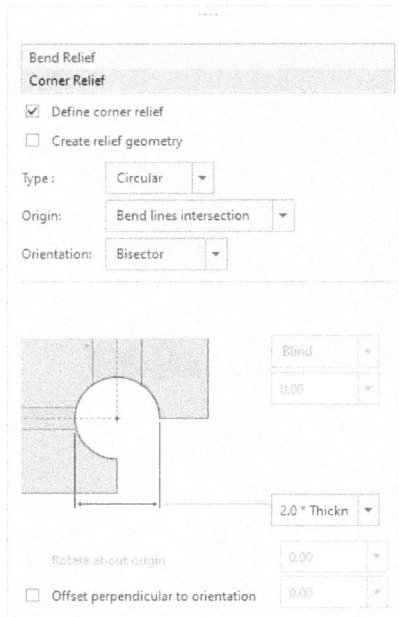

Figure 3–99

11. Complete the flange wall. The part displays as shown in Figure 3–100.

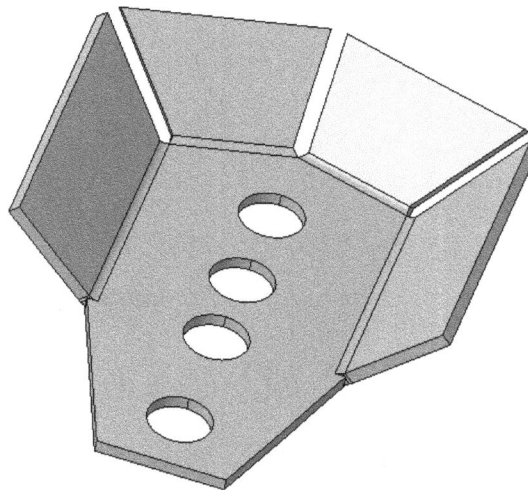

Figure 3–100

Task 2: Change the Thickness parameter.

1. In the *Sheetmetal* tab, select **Model Intent>**[ ] (Parameters). Set the **SMT_THICKNESS** parameter to **0.063**, as shown in Figure 3–101.

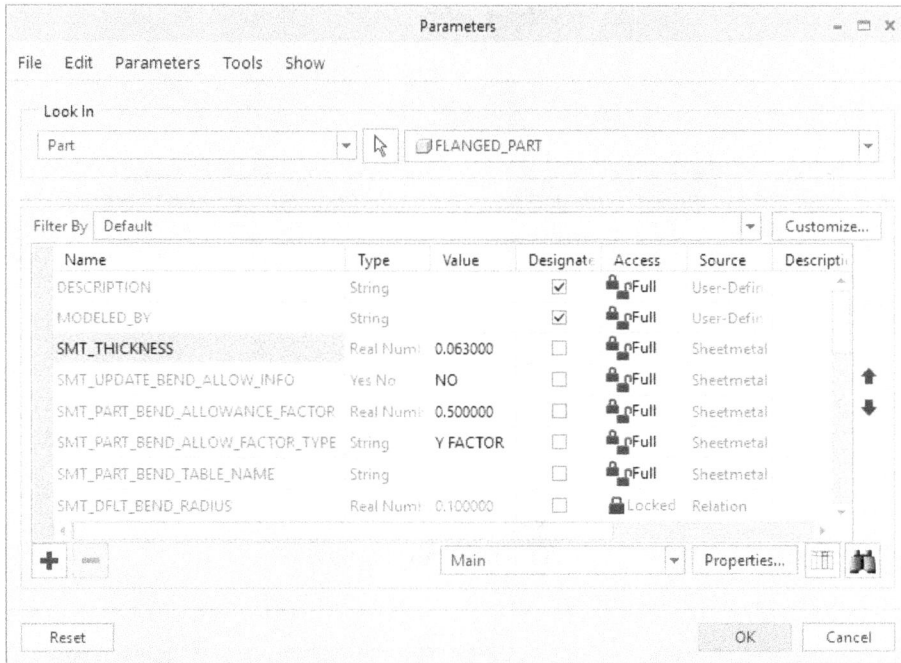

Figure 3–101

2. Click **OK**. Regenerate the part. The wall thickness of the part updates with the new value.

3. In the In-graphics toolbar, expand ⛐ (Annotation Display Filters) and click ⛐ (Corner Relief Notes). The model updates as shown in Figure 3–102.

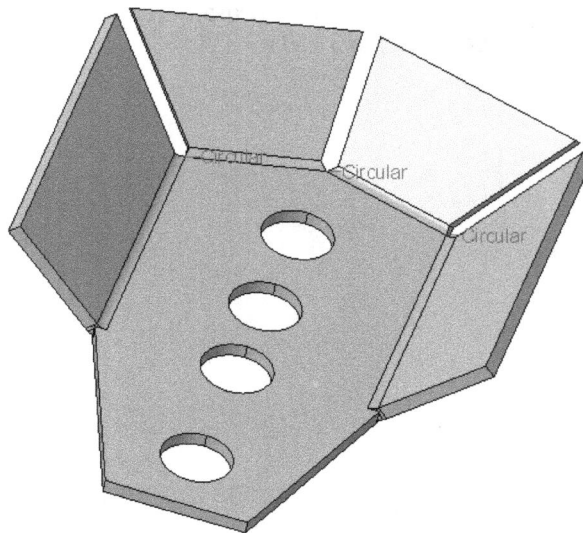

Figure 3–102

4. Click ⛐ (Corner Relief Notes) to toggle off their display.
5. Save the part and erase it from memory.

End of practice

Practice 3e
Add Walls to the Project Part

Practice Objective

- Add secondary walls.

In this practice, you will continue to add features to the project part. You will create additional walls, as shown in Figure 3–103. This part will be used again in the practices in this guide.

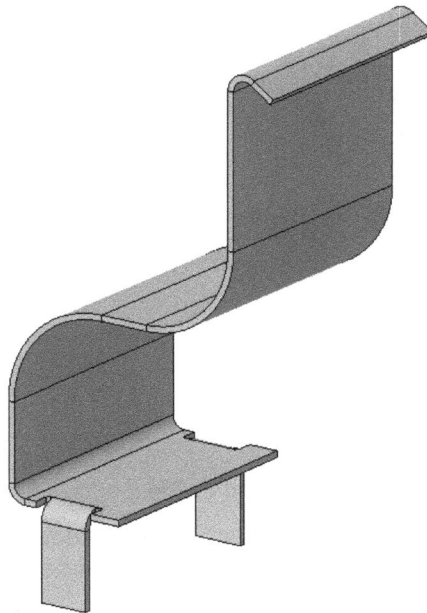

Figure 3–103

1. Set the working directory to the *Adding_Walls* folder.
2. Open **sheetmetal_project_ex2.prt**
3. Set the model display as follows:

   - *(Datum Display Filters)*: None
   - *(Spin Center)*: Off
   - *(Display Style)*: (Shading With Edges)

4. Create a flange wall. Use the inside radius for the radius dimension. The completed wall displays as shown in Figure 3−104.

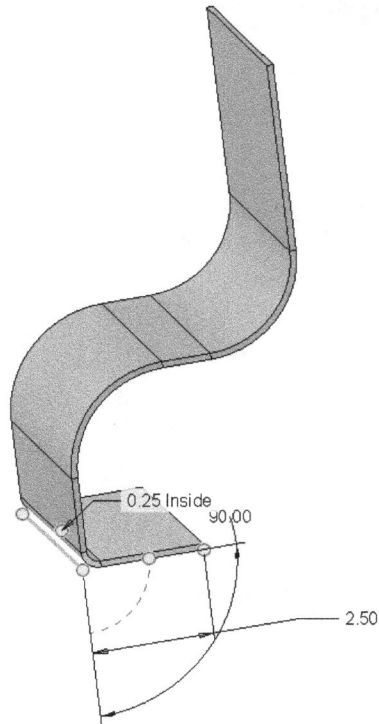

Figure 3−104

5. Create a flat wall on the other end of the part. Use the edge shown in Figure 3−105 as the attachment edge. Use the inside radius for the radius dimension. The model displays as shown in Figure 3−105.

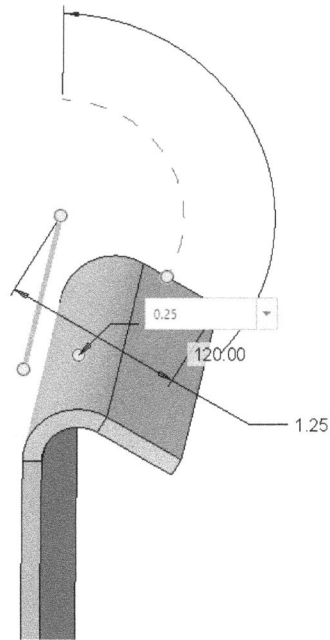

Figure 3–105

6. Create a partial wall, as shown in Figure 3–106. Select the upper edge and use the following parameters:

   • Use a Flat wall.

   • Use Sketcher functionality to obtain the required dimensions.

   • Ensure that the inside radius is used.

   • Apply an obround bend relief with the depth set to **Tangent to bend**.

   • The dimensions required for the wall are shown in Figure 3–106.

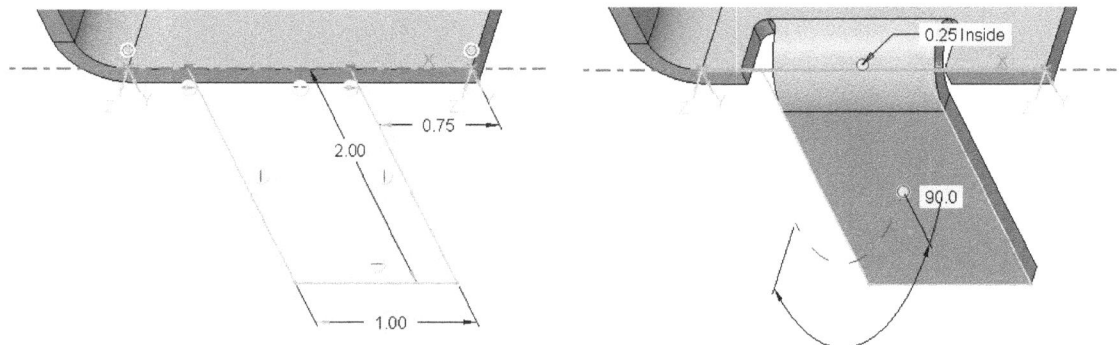

Figure 3–106

7. Create a similar wall on the opposite side of the part using the **Copy** tool. The completed part is shown in Figure 3−107.

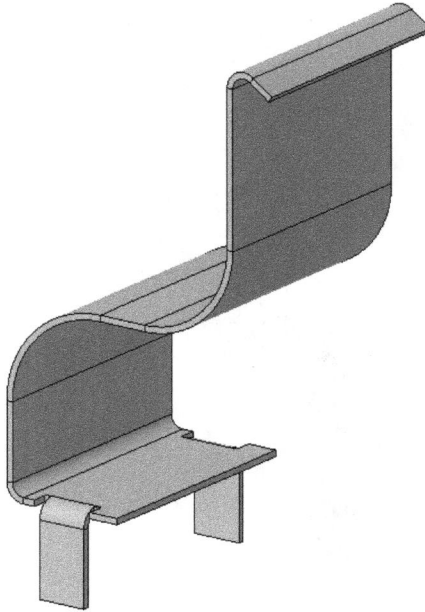

Figure 3−107

8. Save the part and erase it from memory.

End of practice

Practice 3f
Extrude and Reuse

Practice Objectives

- Create an extruded cut.
- Reuse a sketched section.

In this practice, you will create an extruded primary wall and a secondary extrude feature that is a sheet metal class cut. You will also create a flange wall by sketching the profile, saving the profile, and using it in a different sheet metal part. The resulting part is shown in Figure 3–108.

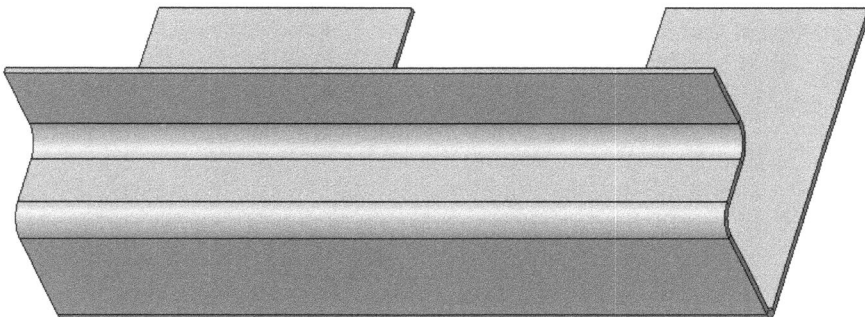

Figure 3–108

Task 1: Create a sheet metal part.

1. Set the working directory to the *Extrude_Reuse* folder.
2. Create a new sheet metal part and set the *Name* to **HOLDER**.
3. Set the model display as follows:

    - ⅍ *(Datum Display Filters)*: None
    - ⅟ *(Spin Center)*: Off
    - ⬜ *(Display Style)*: ⬛ (Shading With Edges)

4. In the *Sheetmetal* tab, expand **Model Intent** and select [ ] (Parameters).

5. Set the sheet metal *Thickness* parameter to **0.25**, as shown in Figure 3–109.

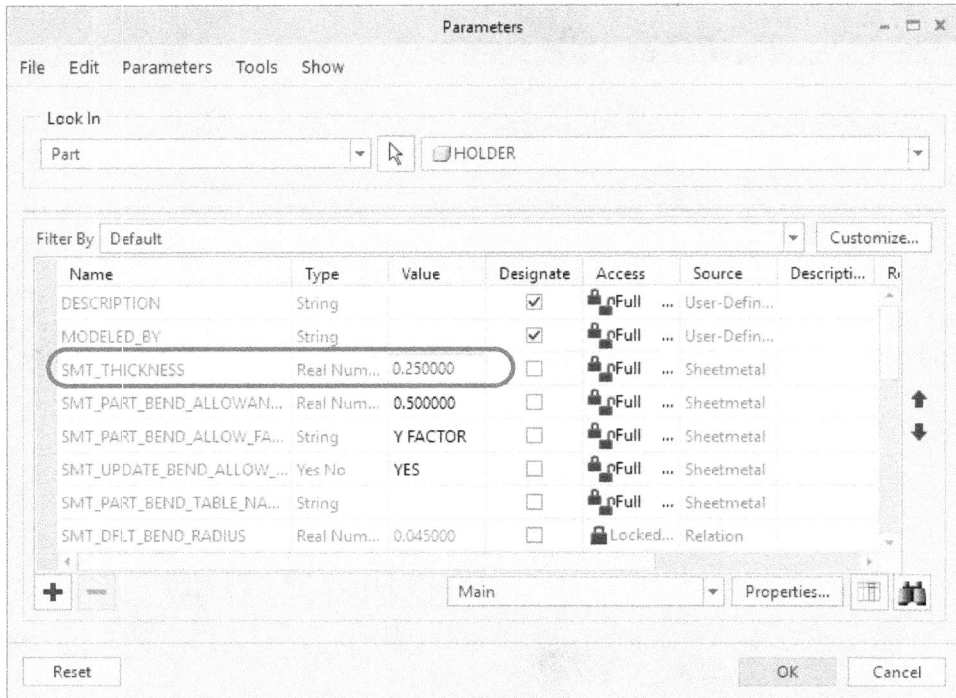

Figure 3–109

Task 2: Create an extruded primary wall.

1. In the Model Tree, select datum plane **FRONT** and click ✐ (Extrude) as the sketching plane.

2. Click ⌕ (Sketch View).

3. Create the sketch shown in Figure 3–110 using two lines and a circular fillet.

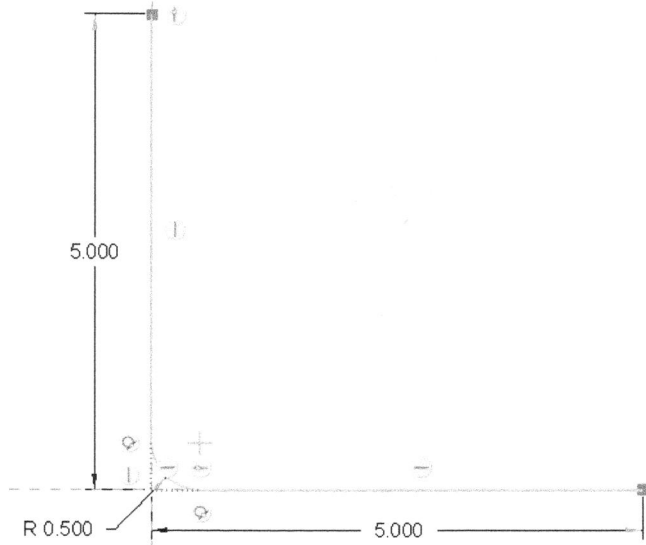

5.000

R 0.500

5.000

Figure 3–110

4. Complete the sketch and set the symmetrical *Depth* value to **10**, as shown in Figure 3–111.

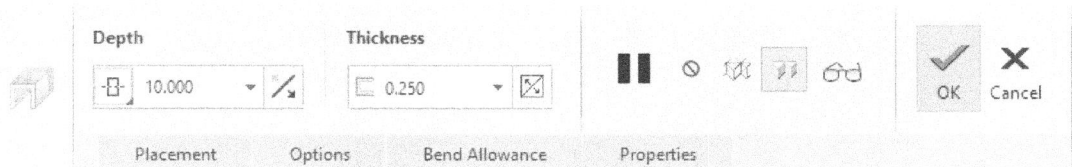

Depth		Thickness								OK	Cancel
10.000		0.250									

| Placement | Options | Bend Allowance | Properties |

Figure 3–111

5. Complete the extrude. The extruded primary wall displays as shown in Figure 3–112.

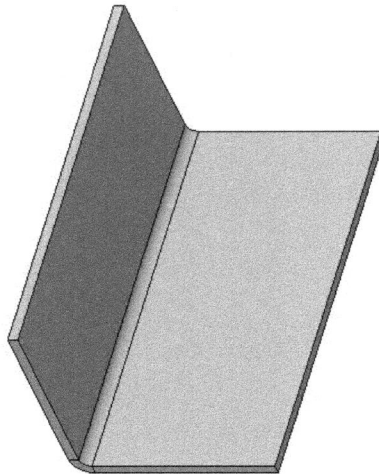

Figure 3–112

Task 3: Create a flange wall.

1. Select the edge shown in Figure 3–113 and click 🖫 (Flange) in the mini toolbar.

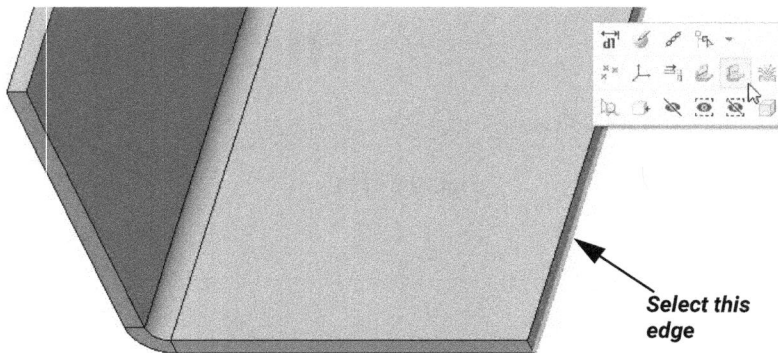

Select this edge

Figure 3–113

2. The wall previews as shown in Figure 3–114.

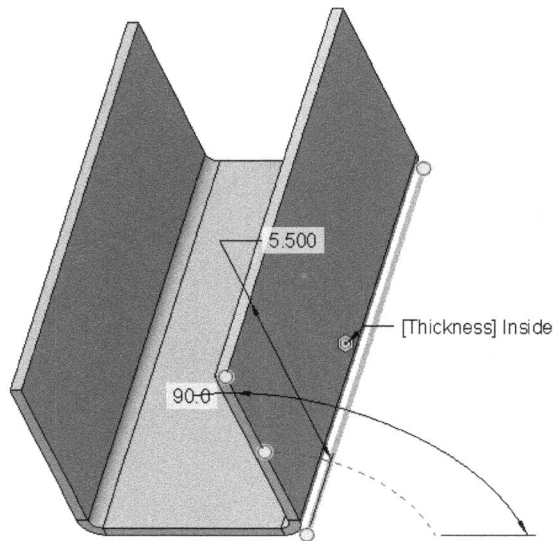

Figure 3–114

3. Open the Shape panel and click **Sketch**. The Sketch dialog box opens as shown in Figure 3–115.

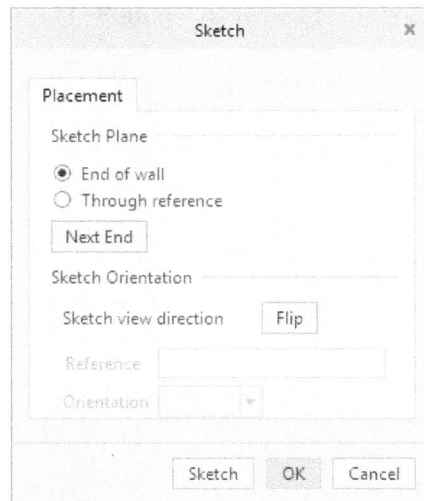

Figure 3–115

4. Click **Sketch** in the Sketch dialog box.

5. In the *Sketch* tab, delete the default section (the line), as shown in Figure 3–116.

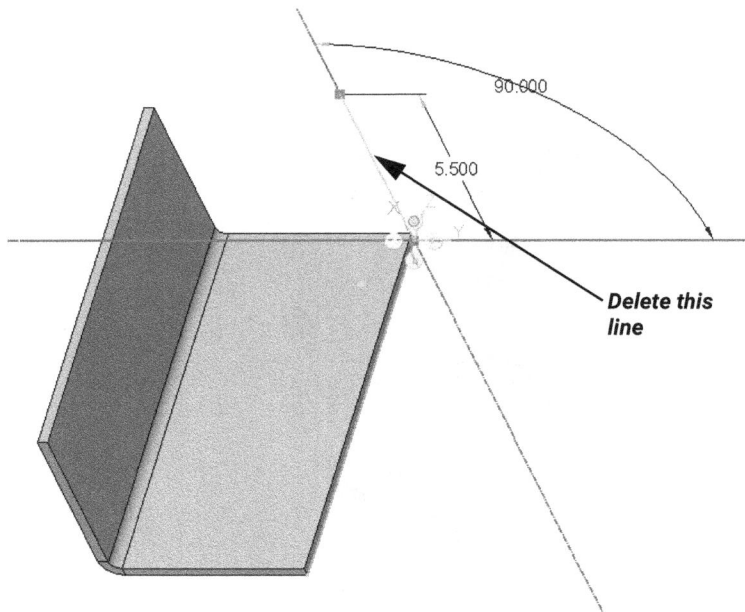

Figure 3–116

6. Click 🖳 (Sketch View) to orient the sketch to the sketched view.

7. Create and dimension the sketch as shown in Figure 3–117, using three lines and two fillets.

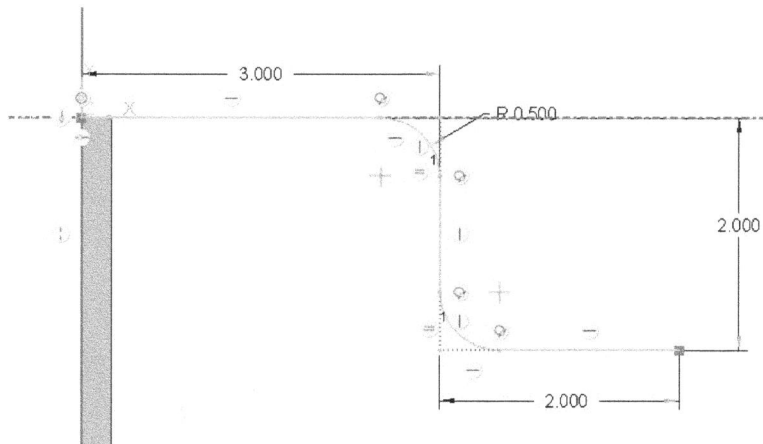

Figure 3–117

8. Complete the sketch and specify an inside *Radius* of **2.0 * Thickness Inside**, as shown in Figure 3–118.

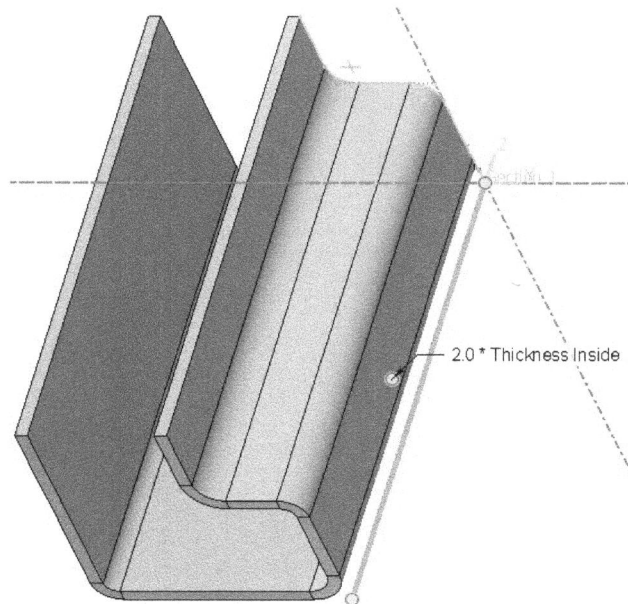

2.0 * Thickness Inside

Figure 3–118

9. Complete the flange wall. The part displays as shown in Figure 3–119.

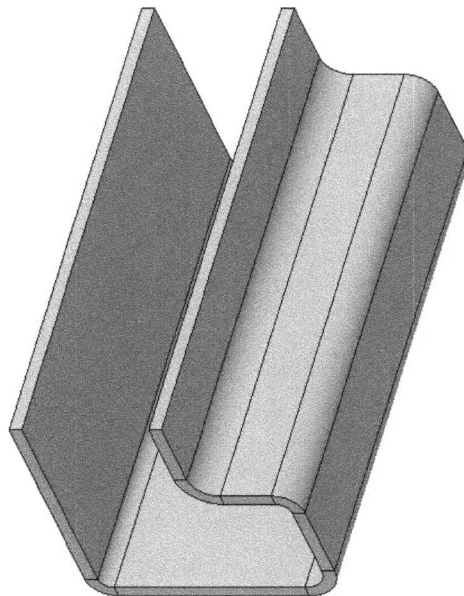

Figure 3–119

Task 4: Create an extruded cut.

1. Select the surface shown in Figure 3–120 and click ⬛ (Extruded Cut) in the mini toolbar.

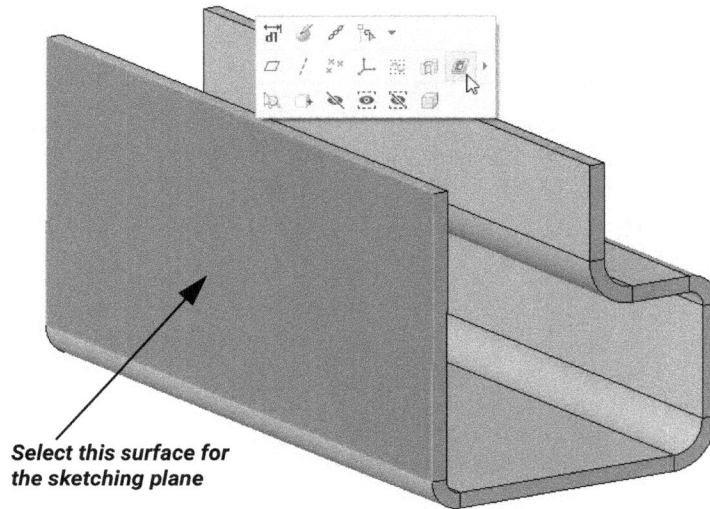

Select this surface for the sketching plane

Figure 3–120

2. Click ⬛ (Sketch View).
3. Right-click and select **References**.
4. In the Model Tree, select datum plane **FRONT**.
5. Click **Close** in the References dialog box.
6. Create and dimension the sketch as shown in Figure 3–121.

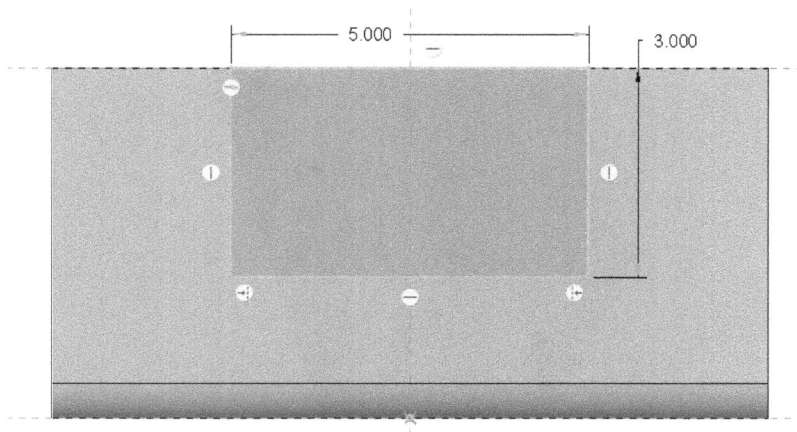

Figure 3–121

7. Extrude the cut through all. The complete cut displays as shown in Figure 3-122.

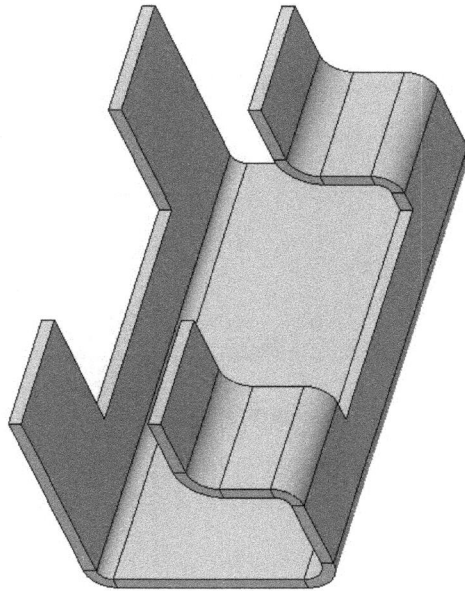

Figure 3-122

8. Save the part.

Task 5: Save a profile.

1. Edit the definition of the flange wall.
2. Open the Shape panel and click **Save as** to save the profile.
3. Set the *Name* to **interface**.
4. Click ✕ (Cancel Feature) in the dashboard.
5. Save the part and erase it from memory.

Task 6: Reuse a saved profile.

1. Open the **holder_wall.prt.**
2. Create a flange wall on the edge, as shown in Figure 3-123.

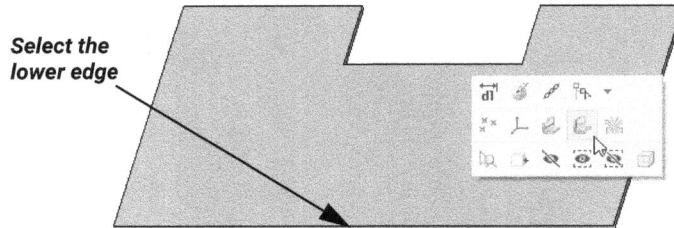

**Select the
lower edge**

Figure 3-123

- The default profile is shown in Figure 3-124.

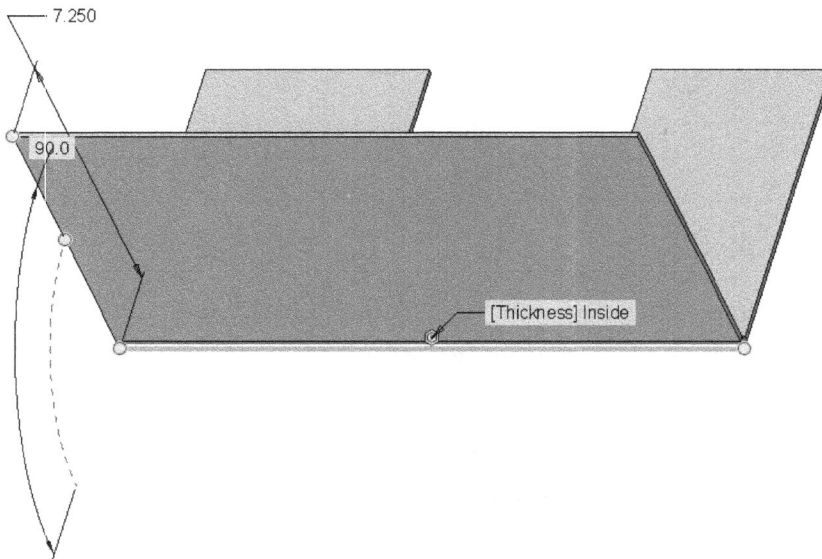

7.250

90.0

[Thickness] Inside

Figure 3-124

3. Open the Shape panel and click **Open**. Select **interface.sec**. The profile previews as shown in Figure 3−125.

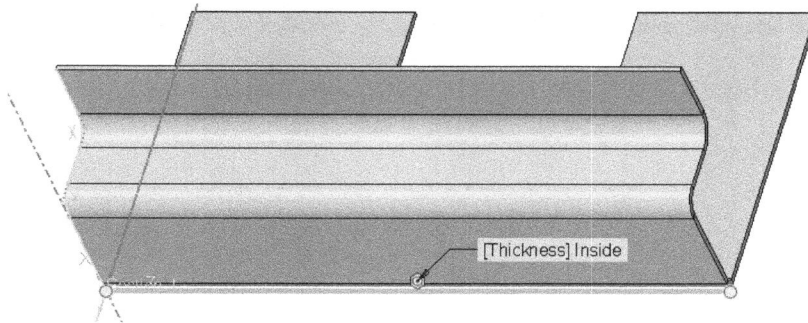

[Thickness] Inside

Figure 3−125

4. Complete the flange. The part is shown in Figure 3−126.

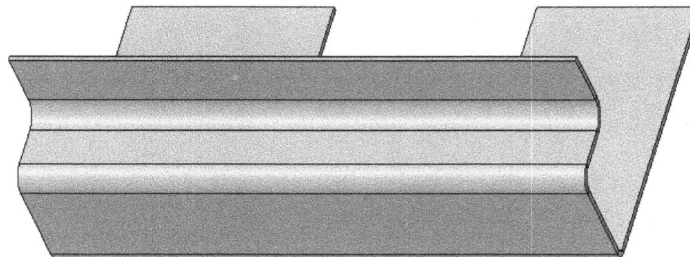

Figure 3−126

5. Save the part and erase it from memory.

End of practice

Practice 3g
Twist Walls

Practice Objective

* Create a twist wall.

In this practice, you will add a twist wall to a sheet metal model.

Task 1: Open the flat_pattern.prt model.

1. Set the working directory to the *Twist_Wall* folder.
2. Open **twist_wall.prt**.
3. Set the model display as follows:

    * ⋏. *(Datum Display Filters)*: All Off

    * ⪢ *(Spin Center)*: Off

    * ⬛. *(Display Style)*: ⬛ (Shading With Edges)

    The model displays as shown in Figure 3–127.

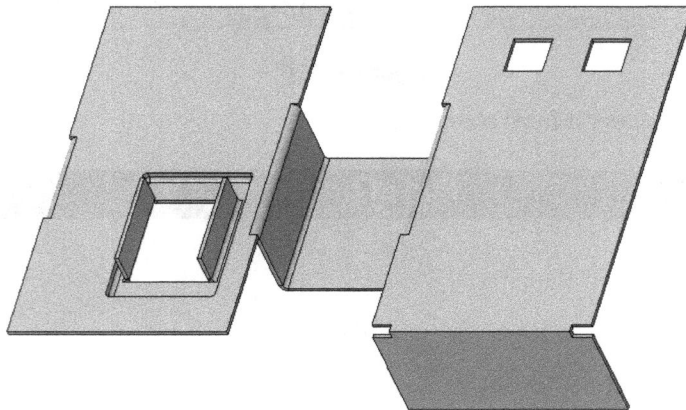

Figure 3–127

Task 2: Add a Twist wall to one of the Flange walls.

1. In the In-graphics toolbar, expand ▦ (Saved Orientations), scroll to the bottom of the list of saved orientations, and select **TWIST** to reorient the model.

2. Select the edge shown in Figure 3−128.

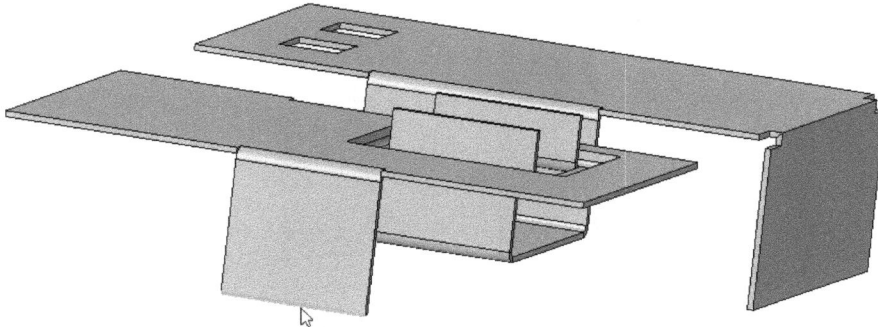

Figure 3−128

3. In the *Sheetmetal* tab in the ribbon, expand the Walls group and select ✎ (Twist). The preview displays as shown in Figure 3−129.

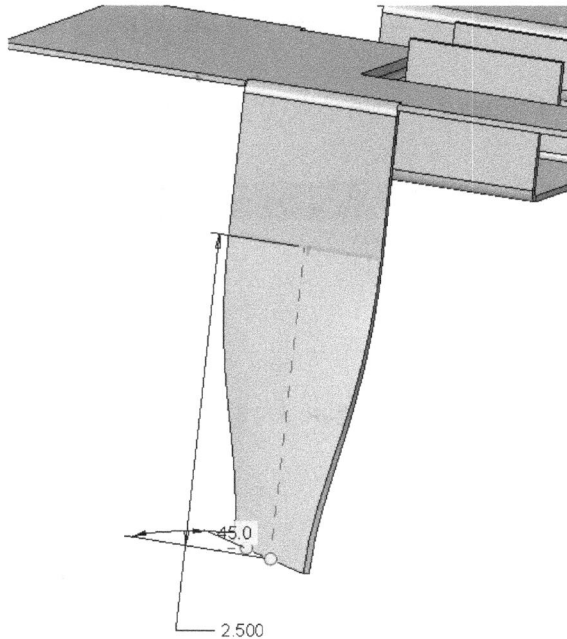

Figure 3−129

4. Drag the rotation handle to **60°** and the length handle to **1.5**, as shown in Figure 3−130.

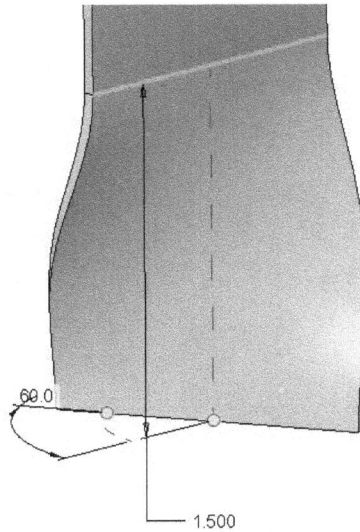

Figure 3−130

Note: The width of the twist wall matches the width of the attachment edge.

Task 3: Offset the edges of the wall from the attachment edge.

1. In the *Twist* dashboard, expand ⊏ (Up to end) and select ⊏ (Blind), as shown in Figure 3−131.

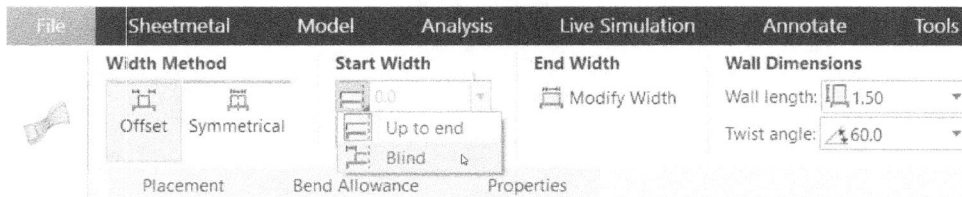

Figure 3−131

2. Drag the handle or edit the dimension to **-0.25**, as shown in Figure 3−132.

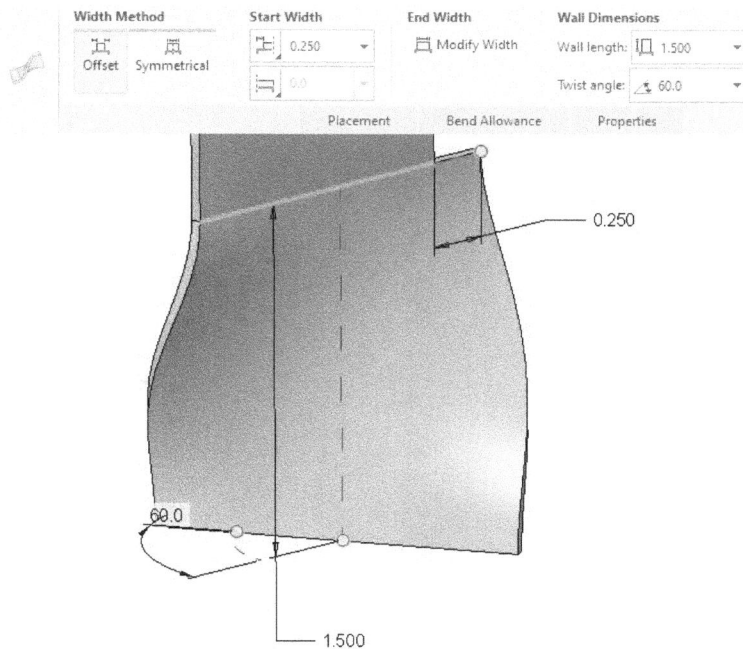

Figure 3−132

Note: When modifying values, a positive offset extends the twist surface inward, while a negative offset extends it outward.

3. Expand (Up to end) and select (Blind), as shown in Figure 3−133.

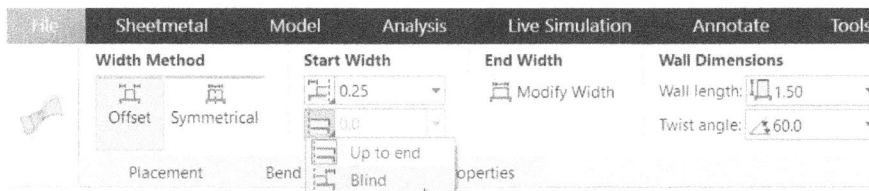

Figure 3−133

4. Drag the handle or edit the dimension to **0.1**, as shown in Figure 3−134.

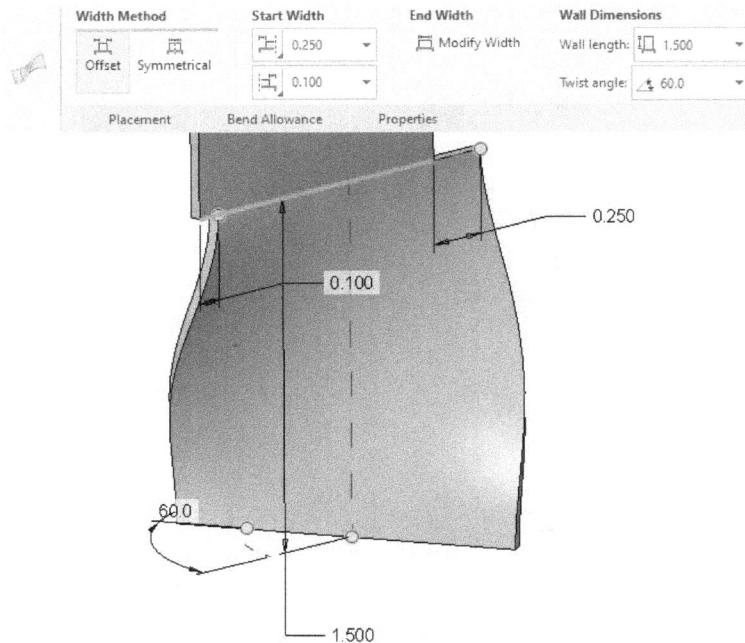

Figure 3−134

Task 4: Edit the width of the free end of the twist wall.

1. In the *Twist* dashboard, click ⬚ (Modify Width).

2. Spin the model to the orientation shown in Figure 3−135 and note the addition of the drag handles on the outer edges of the free end.

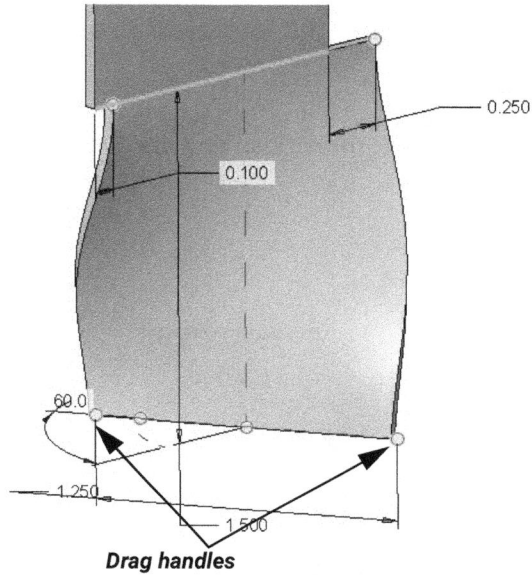

Drag handles

Figure 3–135

3. Edit the width of the free end to **0.75**, as shown in Figure 3–136.

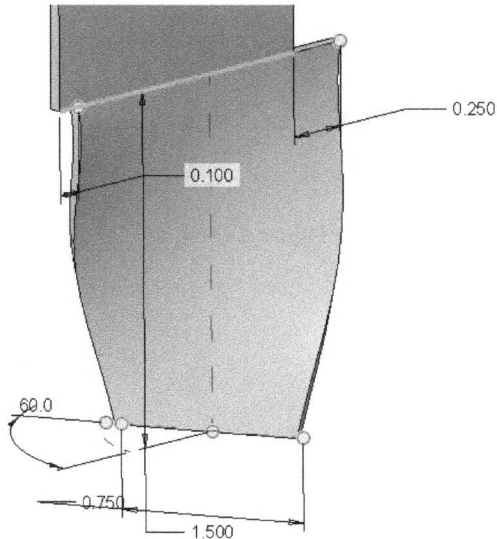

Figure 3–136

Note: If you use the drag handles, it does not matter which one you drag. The width will always be symmetric about the twist axis.

Task 5: Use a datum point to locate the center of the twist wall on the attachment edge.

1. In the *Twist* dashboard, click ⊞ (Symmetrical) and the twist wall updates as shown in Figure 3–137.

Figure 3–137

Note: There are two drag handles. Moving either handle will update the width symmetrically about the twist axis.

2. Drag one of the handles or edit the width to **2.00**, as shown in Figure 3–138.

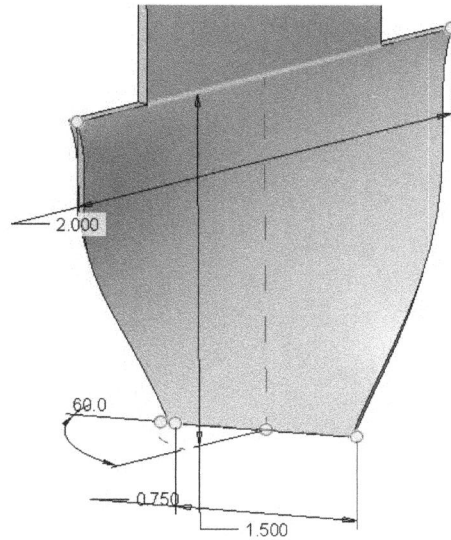

Figure 3–138

3. In the In-graphics toolbar, enable ⁺⁺⊙ (Point Display).

4. In the dashboard, click 🔳 (Set Twist Axis).

5. Select the datum point shown in Figure 3–139.

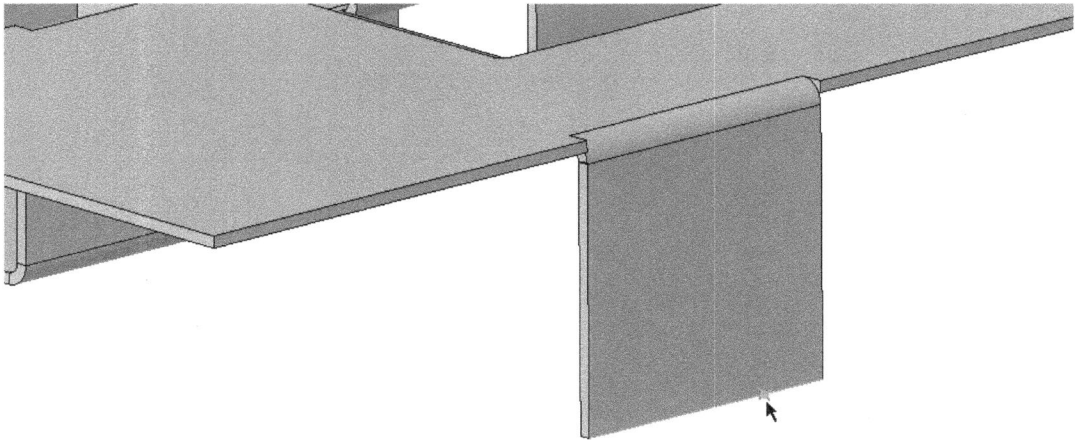

Figure 3–139

6. The twist wall updates as shown in Figure 3–140.

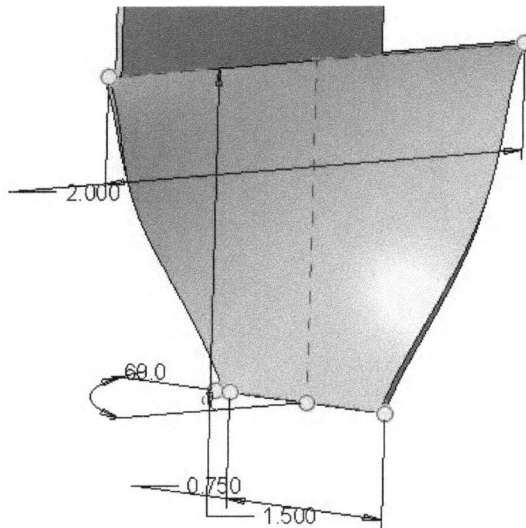

Figure 3–140

Note: The width is still symmetric about the twist axis, which has been shifted to the point.

7. Click ✔ (OK) to complete the twist wall.

8. In the In-graphics toolbar, disable ✕̽̽ (Point Display). The model displays as shown in Figure 3–141.

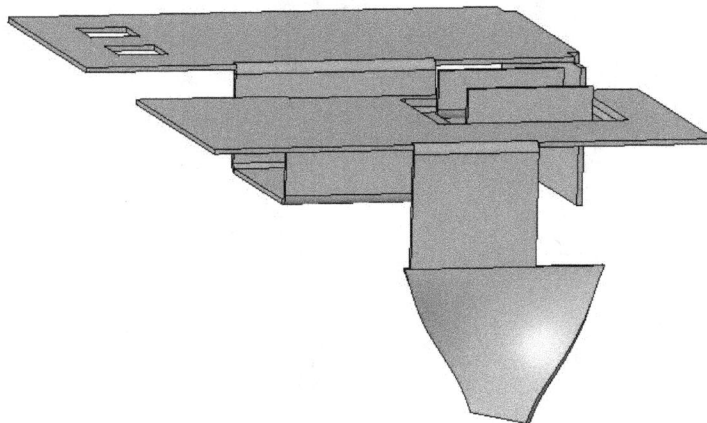

Figure 3–141

9. Save the part and erase it from memory.

End of practice

Chapter Review Questions

1. Creating a secondary wall with bends does not change the length of the wall to which it is attached.

   a. True

   b. False

2. What type of wall is created by sweeping a cross-section along an attachment edge?

   a. Flat

   b. Flange

   c. Twist

   d. Extend

3. The bend relief can be defined for both sides or each individual side.

   a. True

   b. False

4. What type of wall can be used to close gaps?

   a. Flat

   b. Flange

   c. Twist

   d. Extend

5. Which of the following types of walls can be created as unattached? (Select all that apply.)

   a. Planar

   b. Extrude

   c. Revolve

   d. Twist

6. If an unattached wall is separate from the rest of the model, you must create walls to bridge the gap.

   a. True

   b. False

7. Which of the following are bend relief types that can be added to a model? (Select all that apply.)

a. No Relief

b. Stretch

c. Rip

d. Rectangular

e. Obround

Regular Unbends, Bend Backs, and Extruded Cuts

You can bend existing walls to form the final geometry. In addition, you can return bent geometry to its flat state and create cuts in sheet metal parts. This chapter discusses the implications of where and when cuts can be made.

Learning Objectives

- Learn why creating a bend is required.
- Learn how bends are created using default surfaces or by picking a fixed surface.
- Return the unbent geometry back to the bent condition and, if required, leave the contours unbent.
- Learn how to create a sheet metal cut using the **Extruded Cut** command.
- Understand the sequence of events for a cut that must take place to achieve the required result.
- Understand the sequence required for creating a sheet metal cut requiring the use of unbend and bend back features.

4.1 Unbending Sheet Metal Geometry

It is often necessary to unbend sheet metal geometry to create other features or to test whether or not geometry can be developed (i.e., flattened). The simplest form of unbend feature is the regular unbend. It enables you to flatten ruled bends, as shown in Figure 4-1.

Ruled geometry only exhibits curvature in one direction

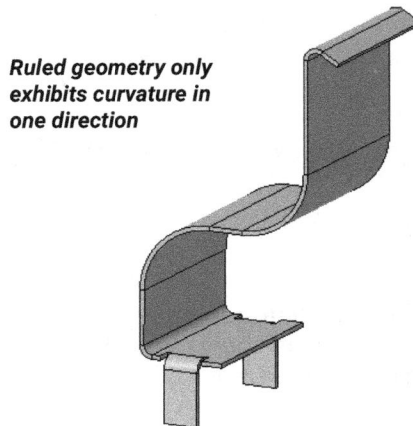

Figure 4-1

When creating a regular unbend feature, you can flatten all bends, or you can flatten individual bends, as shown in Figure 4-2.

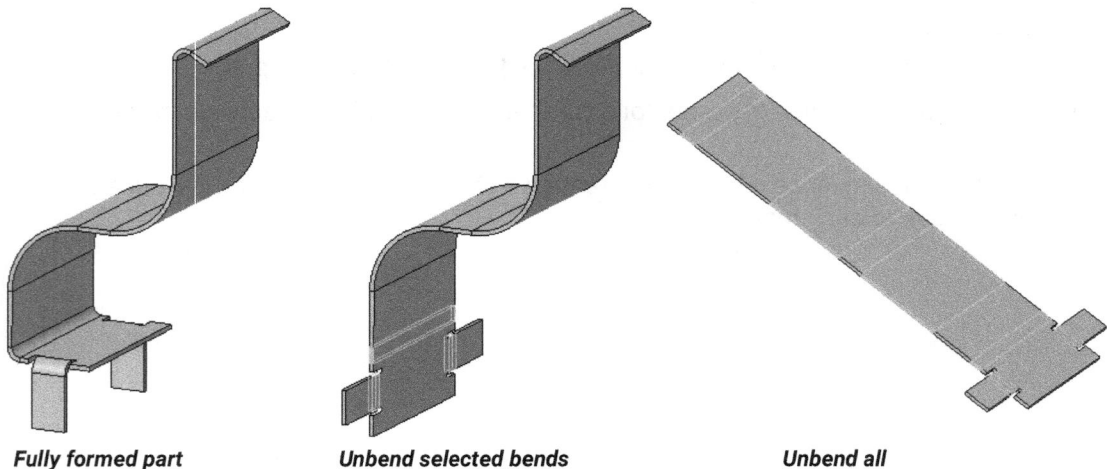

Fully formed part   *Unbend selected bends*   *Unbend all*

Figure 4-2

Creo Parametric picks a surface to remain fixed by default, however a different surface can also be selected to remain fixed. Try to select the same edge or surface for every unbend to maintain a consistent default orientation.

How To: Create an Unbend Feature

1. Start the creation of the unbend feature. Click ⬏ (Unbend) in the *Sheetmetal* tab, as shown in Figure 4–3.

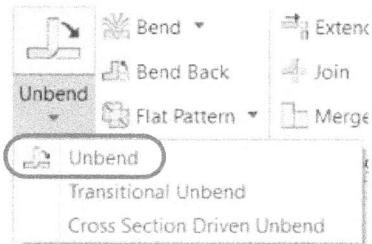

Figure 4–3

2. By default, ⬏ (Select Automatically) is selected in the *Unbend* dashboard, which means that a fixed surface is selected by the system. If required, click ⬏ (Select Manually) to select a different fixed surface. Select the References panel, remove the default fixed surface, and select a new fixed surface, as shown in Figure 4–4. You can also right-click and select **Remove** to remove the default fixed surface.

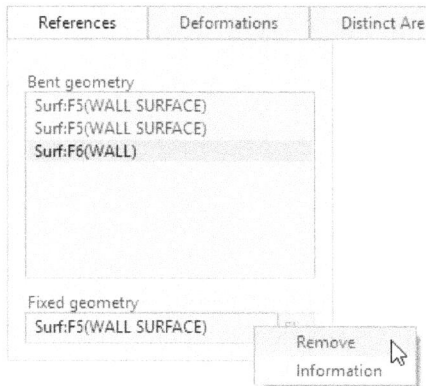

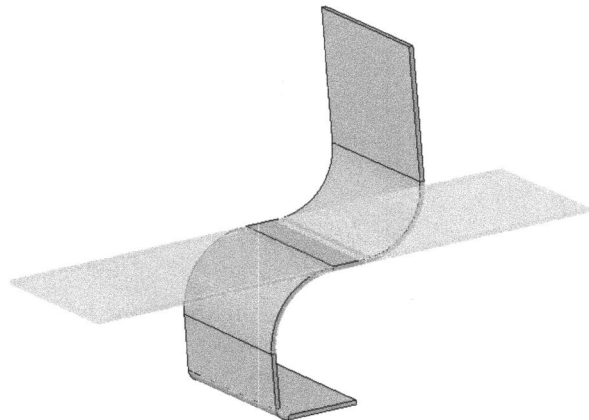

Figure 4–4

3. Complete the feature.

4.2 Bending Back Unbent Geometry

To return unbent sheet metal geometry to the bent condition, you can create a bend back feature. As with the unbend feature, you can accept the default fixed surface or click ⬚ (Select Manually), to remove the default fixed surface and select a new fixed surface. You can bend back all unbent geometry or bend back selected unbent geometry using the Bend Control panel in the *Bend Back* dashboard, as shown in Figure 4–5.

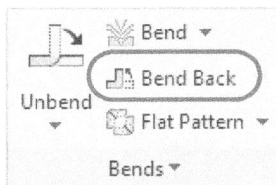

Figure 4–5

Contours that intersect a bend area can be left unbent, as shown in the example in Figure 4–6.

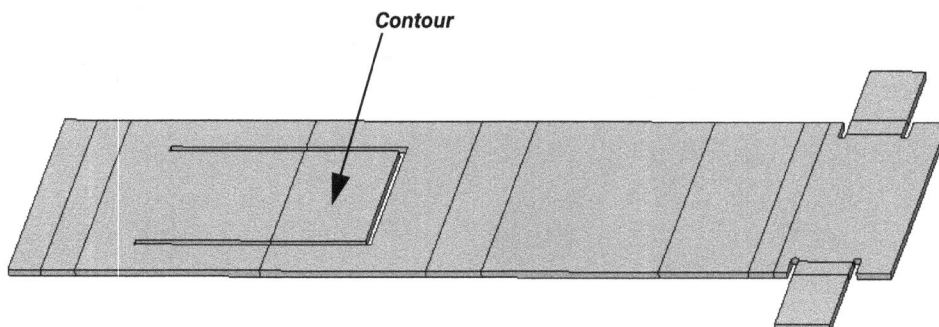

Figure 4–6

A cut has left an isolated contour in one of the bends. When the flattened bend is bent back you can select the contours that you want to remain unbent. If this isolated contour is selected, the resulting bend displays as shown in Figure 4–7.

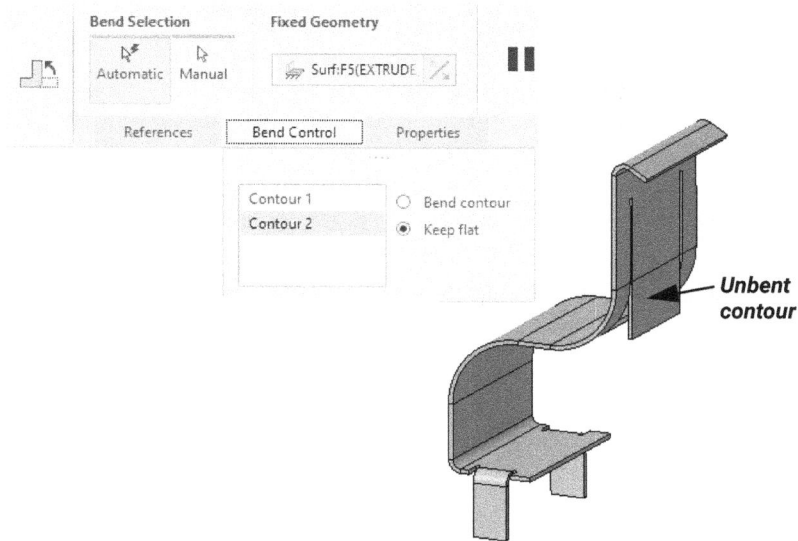

Figure 4–7

Avoid having an unbend feature followed by a bend back feature in your Model Tree. You can click ⚎ (Flat Pattern Preview) in the In-graphics toolbar or the *View* tab to preview the flat state of the model, as shown in Figure 4–8. Click ⚎ (Flat Pattern Preview) to remove to preview window.

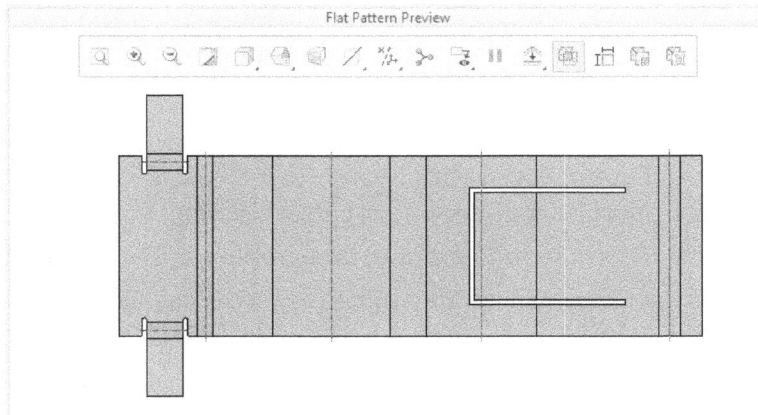

Figure 4–8

If you create an unbend feature to display the flattened geometry, delete the feature when you are finished. Consecutive unbend and bend back features result in unnecessarily increased regeneration times.

4.3 Solid and Sheet Metal Cuts

When you create a cut in Sheetmetal mode, you can create a solid cut or a sheet metal cut. Solid cuts and sheet metal cuts are created using the **Extruded Cut** tool that is also used to create an unattached extruded wall.

How To: Create a Solid or Sheet Metal Cut

1. Select a wall and click ▱ (Extruded Cut) in the mini toolbar.

2. Sketch the cut geometry, then click ✔ (OK).The *Extruded Cut* dashboard displays, as shown in Figure 4−9.

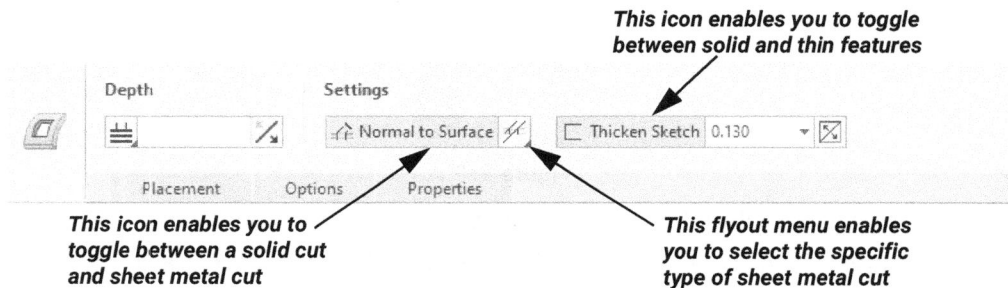

This icon enables you to toggle between solid and thin features

This icon enables you to toggle between a solid cut and sheet metal cut

This flyout menu enables you to select the specific type of sheet metal cut

Figure 4−9

3. Cuts can be created as a solid or a thin. If required, click ▢ (Thicken Sketch). When ▢ (Thicken Sketch) is selected, an additional field displays in the dashboard enabling you to enter the feature's thickness.

    Note: You can also click and select ▢ (Thicken Sketch) *in the mini toolbar.*

4. You can toggle between solid and sheet metal cuts by clicking ⌲ (Normal To Surface) in the dashboard. When ⌲ (Normal To Surface) is depressed, a sheet metal cut is created.

5. When creating a sheet metal cut, use the flyout menu in the dashboard to define how the geometry is constructed. The flyout options are described as follows:

Icon	Description
⫽	Enables you to extrude the sheet metal cut normal to both the green Driving and Offset surfaces.
⫻	Enables you to extrude the sheet metal cut normal to the Driving surface.
⫽	Enables you to extrude a sheet metal cut normal to the Offset surface.

In the part shown in Figure 4–10, the section of a cut is about to be extruded on a sheet metal part.

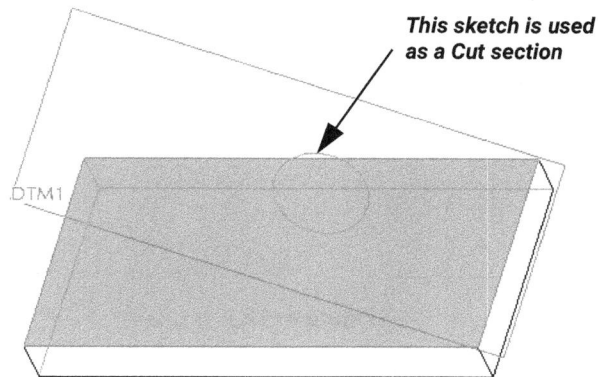

This sketch is used as a Cut section

Figure 4–10

Note: The shaded surface represents the green (driving) surface of a sheet metal part.

If ⌂ (Normal To Surface) is not enabled, a solid cut is created. The solid cut is extruded normal to the sketching plane, as shown in Figure 4–11.

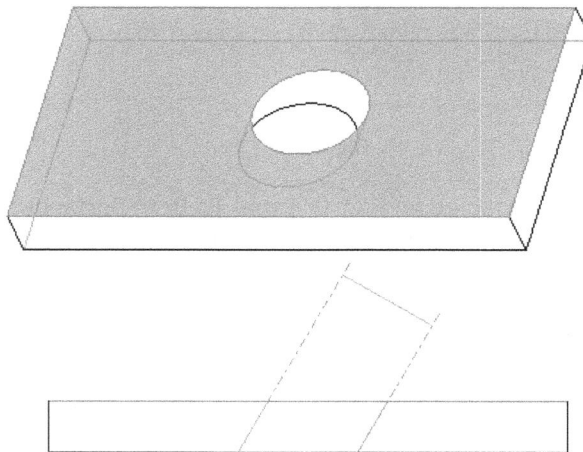

Figure 4–11

If ⌐ (Normal To Surface) is enabled and ⫽ (Normal To Driving Surface) is selected in the flyout, a sheet metal cut is created, with the green surface selected as the driving surface. The section of the cut is projected onto the green surface and extruded normal to it, as shown in Figure 4–12.

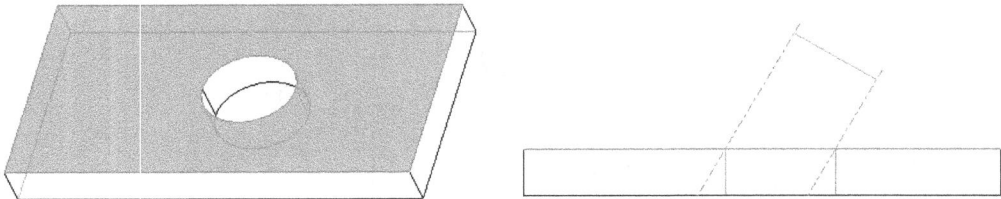

Figure 4–12

If ⌐ (Normal To Surface) is enabled and ⫽ (Normal To Offset Surface) is selected in the flyout, the sheet metal cut is created with the white surface selected as the driving surface. The section of the cut is projected onto the white surface and extruded normal to it, as shown in Figure 4–13.

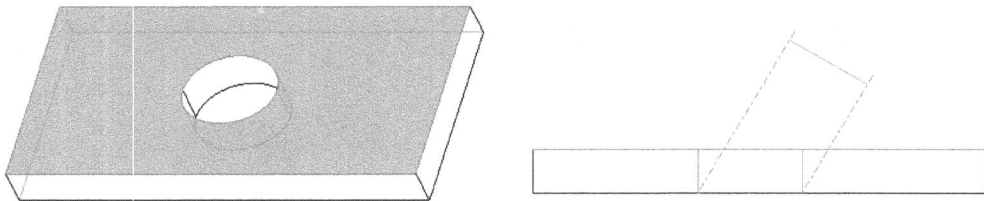

Figure 4–13

If ⌐ (Normal To Surface) is enabled and ⫽ (Normal To Both Surfaces) in the flyout is selected, then both surfaces are selected as the driving surfaces. The result is shown in Figure 4–14. The section of the cut is projected onto both surfaces and extruded normal to both of them. The cut created using this option enables you to assemble a component at an angle to a sheet metal part.

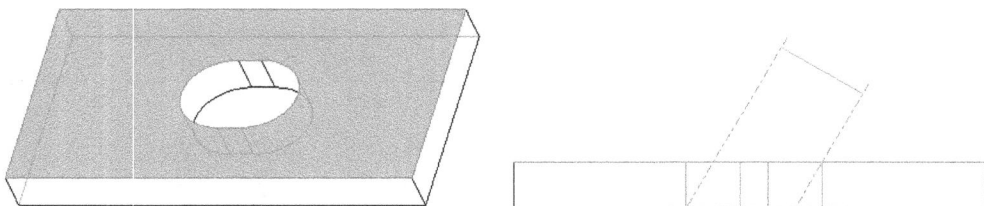

Figure 4–14

6. Click ✔ (OK) to complete the feature.

Cuts Using Datum Curves

When you create a cut that must follow the contour of the sheet metal wall, use a projected datum curve as the reference for your cut. Generally, it is more intuitive to capture your design intent in the bent condition rather than in the flat condition. You can create a datum curve that traces the profile of the cut in the bent condition, and then unbend the model to create the sheet metal cut feature to remove the material. This is particularly useful when dealing with walls that have irregular shapes.

If you create a projected datum curve as the reference for the cut and select the **Follow surface** option in the Reference panel, the projected datum curve follows the sheet metal wall when you unbend and bend back the model, as shown in Figure 4–15.

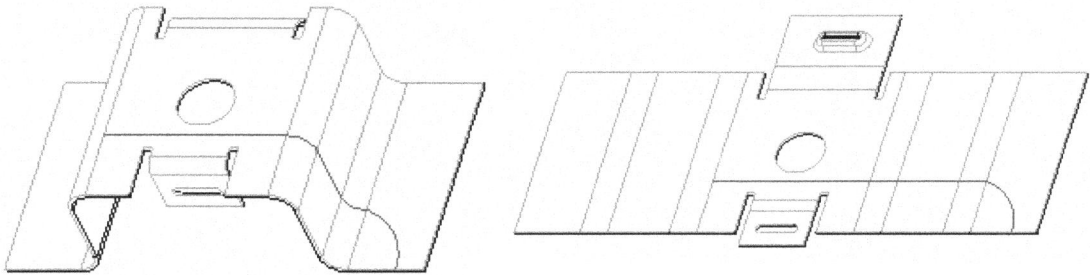

Figure 4–15

> Note: Select **Editing>Project** to create a projected datum curve.

If the **Follow surface** option is not selected, the projected datum curve stays in the location where it was originally projected. It is not affected by unbends and bend backs. The projected curve created in the bent state does not follow the surfaces when the part is unbent, as shown in Figure 4–16.

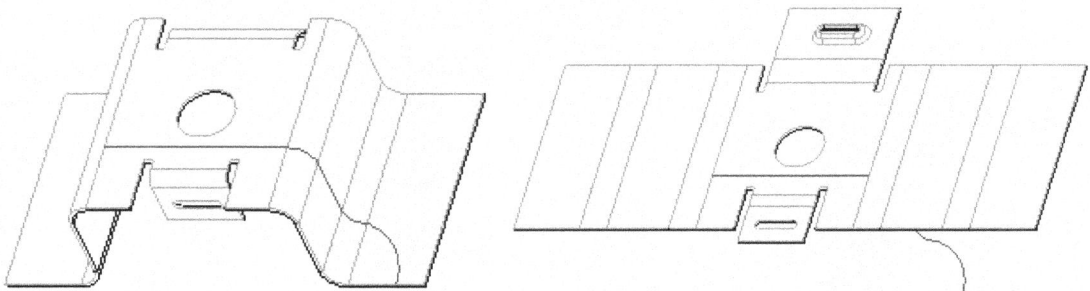

Figure 4–16

Coordinate Systems

A coordinate system placed on the surface of a sheet metal wall stays on the wall surface after bend and unbend operations have been performed on the wall. The orientation of the coordinate system follows the wall orientation. The coordinate system **CSO** is placed on the surface of the wall in the bent state, as shown in Figure 4–17.

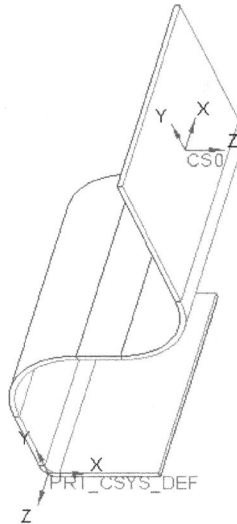

Figure 4–17

When the model is unbent, the **CSO** follows the orientation of the surface on which it is placed, as shown in Figure 4–18. the default coordinate system, **PRT_CSYS_DEF** remains in fixed.

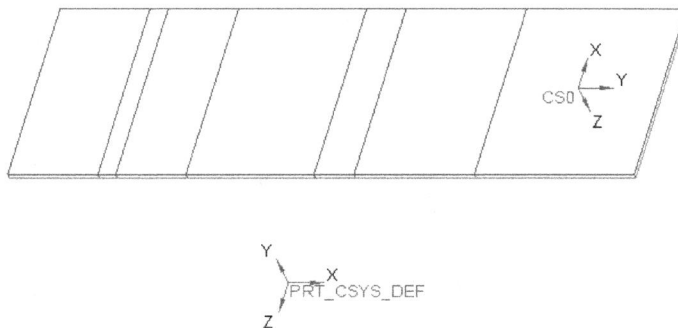

Figure 4–18

Dimension Scheme and Feature Order

If you create a sheet metal cut before bending the geometry, the location of the dimension scheme for the cut could be different than expected. Consider the example shown in Figure 4–19.

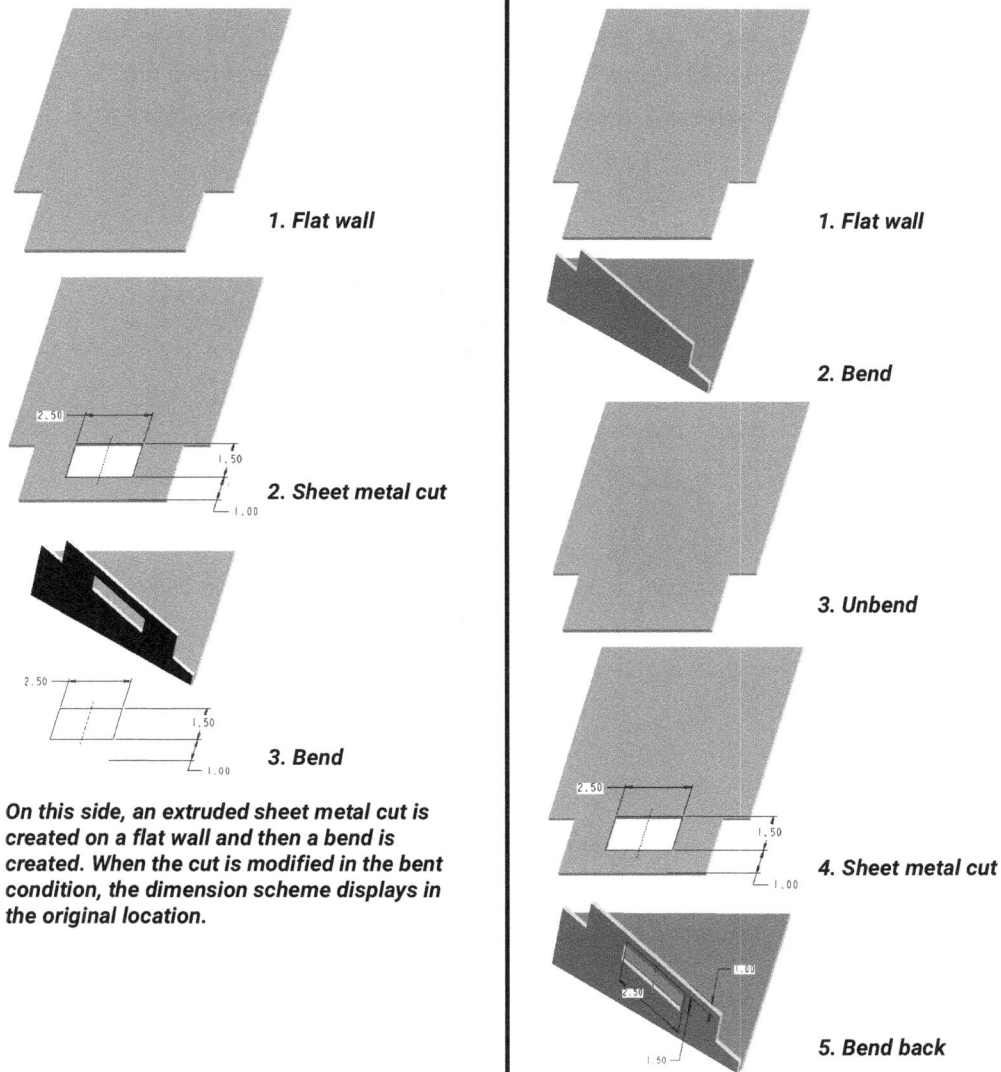

1. Flat wall

2. Sheet metal cut

3. Bend

On this side, an extruded sheet metal cut is created on a flat wall and then a bend is created. When the cut is modified in the bent condition, the dimension scheme displays in the original location.

1. Flat wall

2. Bend

3. Unbend

4. Sheet metal cut

5. Bend back

On this side, the bend and unbend features are created before the cut. The cut is still created in the unbent condition, but when the part is bent back, the dimension scheme for the cut follows the geometry.

Figure 4–19

4.4 Creating a Cut Requiring Unbend and Bend Back Features

How To: Create a Sheet Metal Cut Using the Unbend and Bend Back Features

1. Start the creation of the unbend feature. Click ⬚ (Unbend) in the *Sheetmetal* tab.

2. By default Creo Parametric selects a default fixed surface as shown in Figure 4–20.

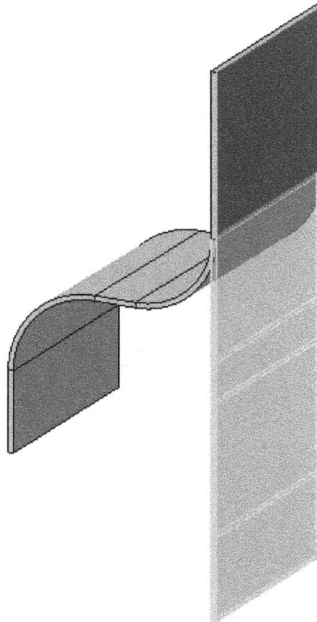

Figure 4–20

3. If required, enable ⬚ (Select Manual), remove the default fixed surface, and select a new surface to remain fixed, as shown in Figure 4–21.

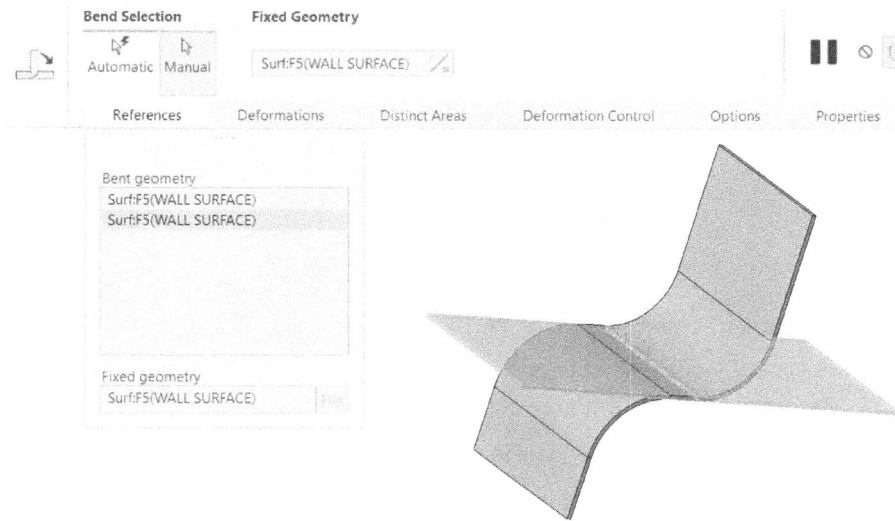

Figure 4–21

*Note: You can also right-click and select **Clear** to remove the default fixed surface.*

4. Complete the feature.

5. Select the surface shown in Figure 4–22 and click ⬛ (Extruded Cut) in the mini toolbar.

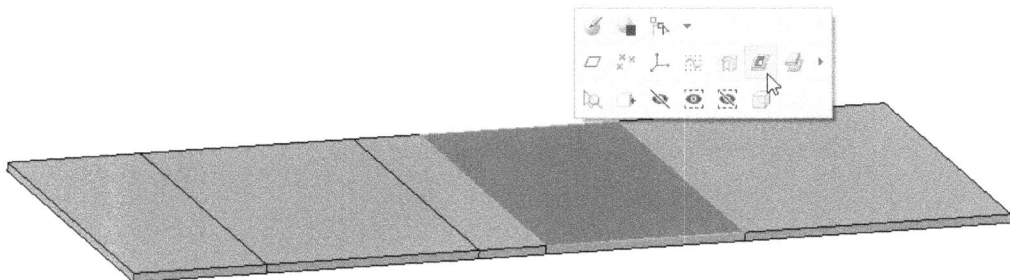

Figure 4–22

6. Sketch the profile of the cut as shown in Figure 4–23.

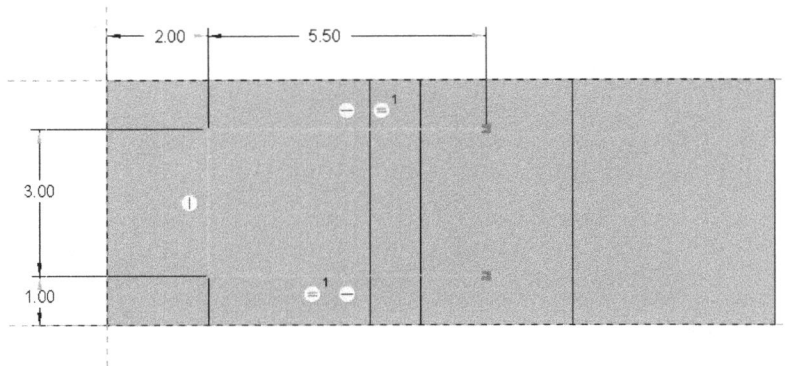

Figure 4–23

7. Ensure that ⊏ (Thicken Sketch) is selected.

8. Specify the cut thickness.

9. Specify the material to be removed and select the depth option.

10. Finish the feature.

11. Create the bend back feature. Click 🗗 (Bend Back) in the *Sheetmetal* tab.

12. Accept or select the surface to remain fixed.

13. Select any contours that should remain unbent by selecting the Bend Control panel and selecting **Keep flat**, as shown in Figure 4–24.

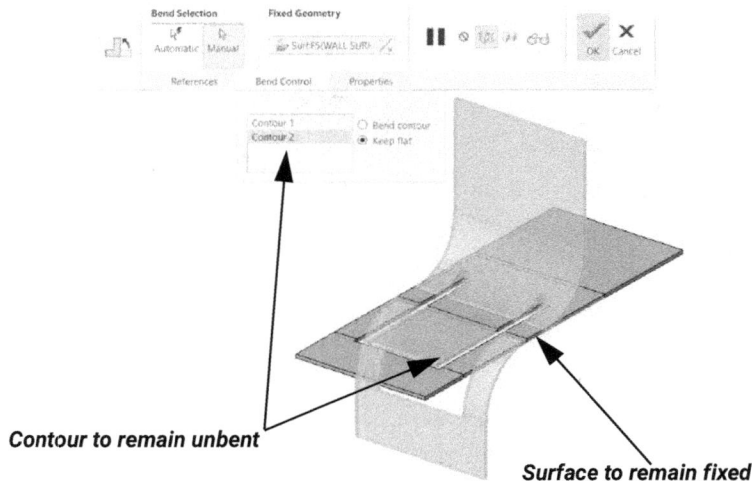

Figure 4–24

14. Complete the feature, as shown in Figure 4–25.

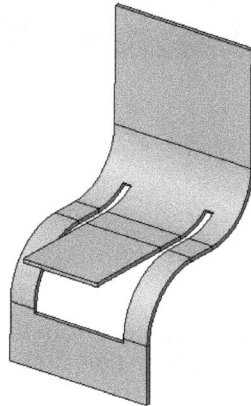

Figure 4–25

Practice 4a
Create a Sheet Metal Cut

Practice Objectives

- Unbend a sheet metal part.
- Create a cut in the unbent condition.
- Bend back a sheet metal part.

In some situations, it is difficult to remove material from the sheet metal part in its bent state. In that case, it is recommended that you unbend a part first, create a cut, and then bend the geometry back. In this practice, you will create the sheet metal cut shown in Figure 4–26. Creating the cut will require you to unbend the part first.

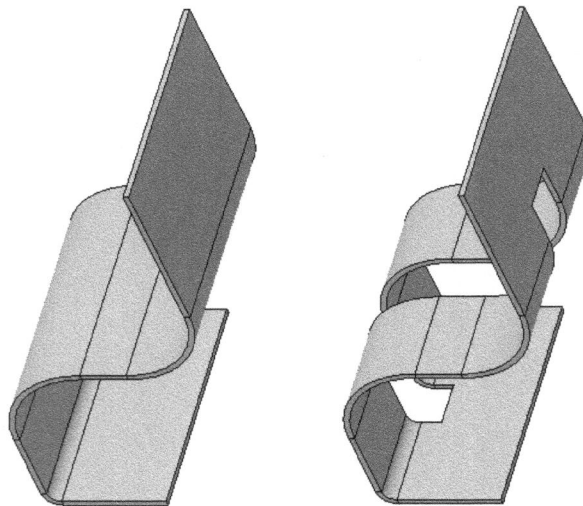

Figure 4–26

Task 1: Open and unbend a part.

Design Considerations

In this task, you will manipulate a part that was created in its fully formed state. To be able to create a cut in the flat condition of the part, you will unbend a part using the **Unbend** option.

1. Set the working directory to the *Sheetmetal_Cut* folder.

2. Open **hanger.prt**.

3. Set the model display as follows:

- *⅔* *(Datum Display Filters)*: None

- *⅔* *(Spin Center)*: Off

- *⅃* *(Display Style)*: ⬜ (Shading With Edges)

4. In the *Sheetmetal* tab of the ribbon, click ⬚ (Unbend).

5. A fixed surface is automatically selected in the *Unbend* dashboard and highlighted in the model, as shown in Figure 4–27.

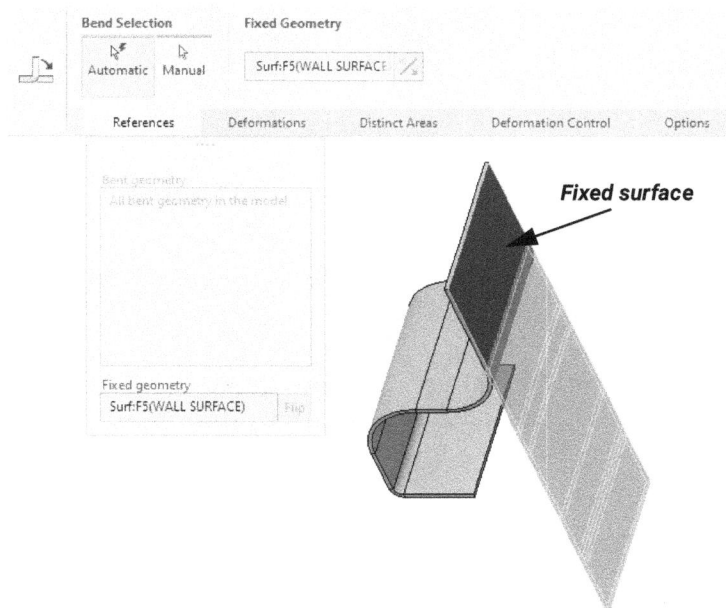

Figure 4–27

6. Click ⬚ (References Selected Manual) in the *Unbend* dashboard.

7. Right-click the **Fixed Geometry** collector in the *Unbend* dashboard and select **Remove**, as shown in Figure 4–28.

Figure 4–28

8. Select the surface shown in Figure 4–29.

Figure 4–29

9. Click ✔ (OK) to complete the unbend feature. The finished unbent part is shown in Figure 4–30.

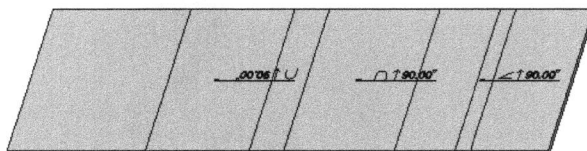

Figure 4–30

Task 2: Create the sheet metal cut in the unbent condition.

1. In the In-graphics toolbar, expand 🗐 (Annotation Display) and select 🗐 (Bend Notes) to remove bend notes from display.

2. Select the surface shown in Figure 4–31 and click 🗐 (Extruded Cut) in the mini toolbar.

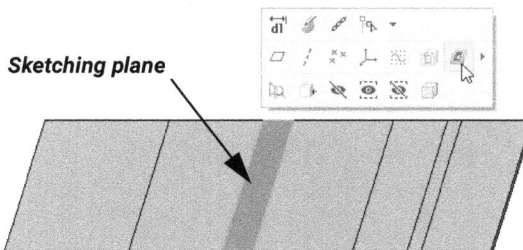

Figure 4–31

3. Sketch the section shown in Figure 4–32.

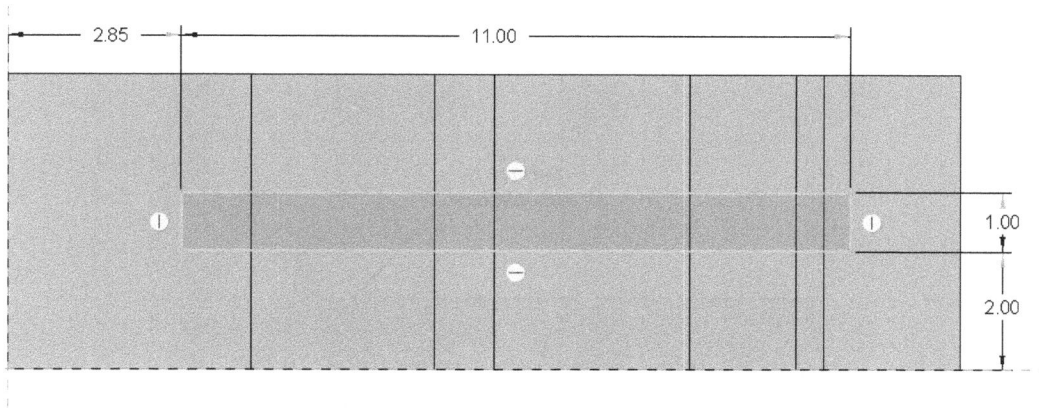

Figure 4–32

4. Complete the sketch and ensure the arrow points to remove the material inside the cut section.

5. Click ⫴ ⫶ (Through All) to define depth of the cut and complete the feature. The cut displays as shown in Figure 4–33.

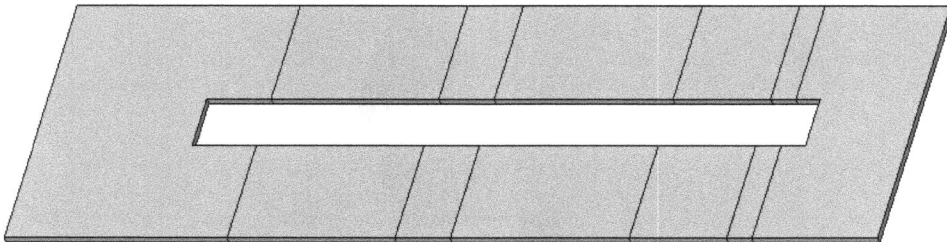

Figure 4–33

Task 3: Return the part to its bent condition.

1. In the *Sheetmetal* tab, click 🗒 (Bend Back).

2. Accept the surface to remain fixed, as shown in Figure 4–34. The selected surface should be the one used to create the unbend feature.

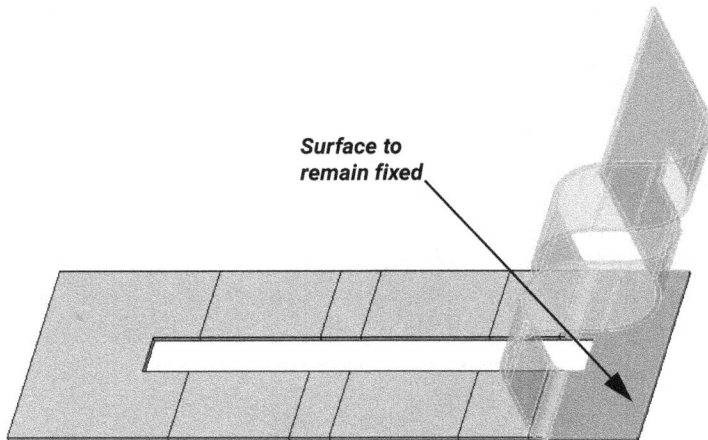

Surface to remain fixed

Figure 4–34

3. Click ✔ (OK) to complete the unbend feature. The part displays as shown in Figure 4–35.

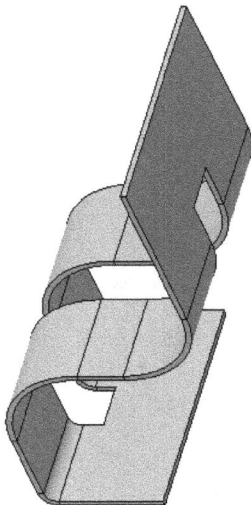

Figure 4–35

4. Save the part and erase it from memory.

End of practice

Practice 4b
Projected Curve and a Cut

Practice Objectives

- Project a datum curve that follows the part surfaces during unbending and bending back.
- Create a sheet metal cut that references a projected datum curve.

In this practice, you will project a curve onto the model in the bent condition and unbend the part. You will then use the projected datum curve as a reference for a cut and return the model to the bent condition, as shown in Figure 4–36.

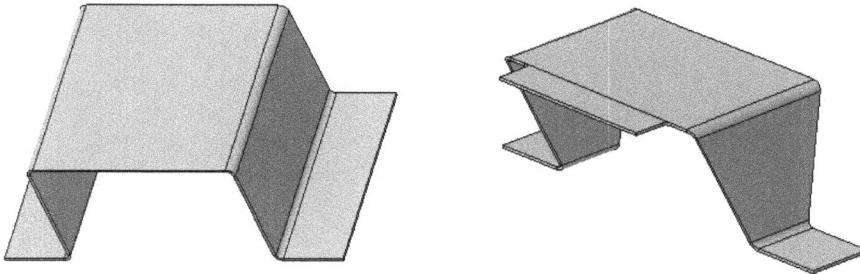

Figure 4–36

Task 1: Open a part and create a projected datum curve.

Design Considerations

The use of a projected datum curve following the sheet metal geometry in the process of building complex sheet metal geometry is very valuable. It enables you to create requested geometry easily and quickly. You can create a cut in the unbent condition of the part and know exactly how it will display after you bend back the part. In this task, you will create a projected datum curve to use as a reference for a cut feature. The curve is created using the **Follow Surf** option while the part is in the bent condition.

1. Set the working directory to the *Sheetmetal_Curve_Cut* folder.
2. Open **curve_cut.prt**.
3. Set the model display as follows:

   - ⬚ *(Datum Display Filters)*: None
   - ⬚ *(Spin Center)*: Off
   - ⬚ *(Display Style)*: ⬚ (Shading With Edges)

4. Select **Editing>Project** to create a datum curve. The *Projected dashboard* displays.

5. Open the References panel.

6. Select **Project a sketch** in the drop-down list to sketch the outline of the projected datum curve, and ensure that the **Follow surface** option is selected as shown in Figure 4–37.

Figure 4–37

7. Click **Define** next to the *Sketch* collector to define the Sketcher references.

8. Select the surface shown in Figure 4–38 as the sketching plane.

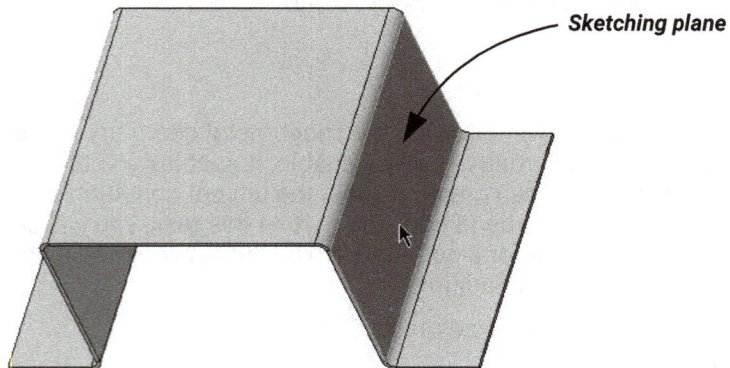

Figure 4–38

9. In the Model Tree, select datum plane **FRONT** to face Bottom.

10. Keep the direction of feature creation and click **Sketch**.

11. Sketch the section shown in Figure 4–39.

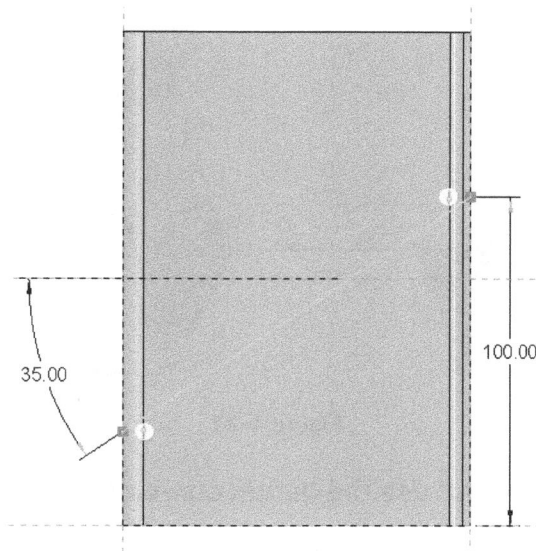

Figure 4–39

12. Complete the sketch and set the model to the default orientation.

13. You are prompted to select surfaces onto which to project the curves. Use <Ctrl> to select the surfaces shown in Figure 4–40.

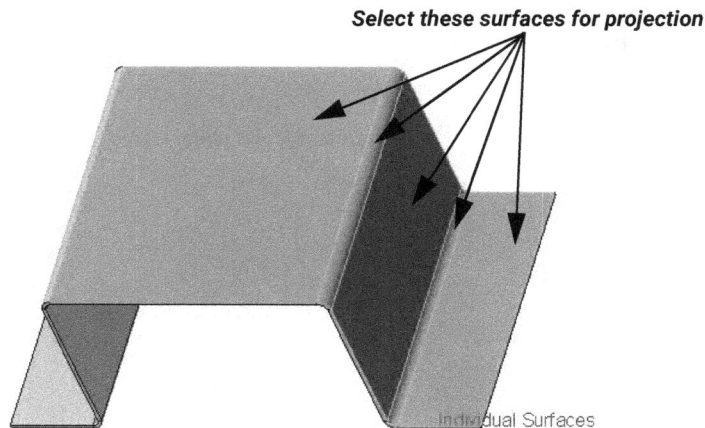

Select these surfaces for projection

Individual Surfaces

Figure 4–40

14. Keep **Along direction** selected as the **Projection Direction** option in the dashboard.

15. Select in the *Direction* reference collector in the dashboard, and select the same surface used as the sketching plane.

16. Complete the feature. The curve should display as shown in Figure 4–41.

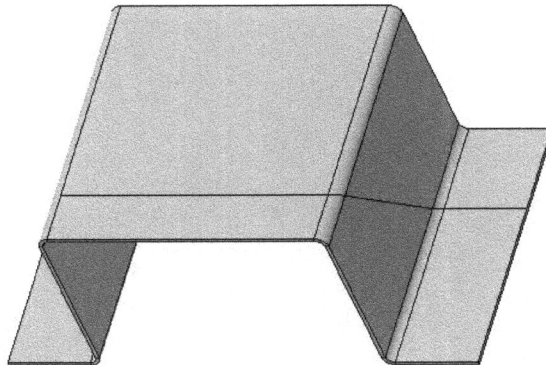

Figure 4–41

Task 2: Unbend the part and use the datum curve as a reference for a sheet metal cut.

Design Considerations

In this task, you will create a cut using the datum curve as a reference. To be able to create the required cut, you must first unbend the part. You will use the **Project** and **Trim** options to copy the curve into Sketcher mode.

1. Click ⬐ (Unbend) in the *Sheetmetal* tab.

2. Maintain the fixed surface shown in Figure 4–42.

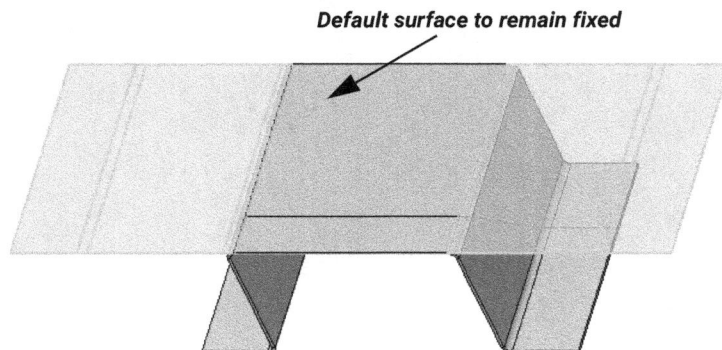

Default surface to remain fixed

Figure 4–42

3. Click ✓ (OK) to complete the unbend feature. The projected datum curve follows the surfaces in the unbent condition.

4. Select the surface shown in Figure 4–43 and click ⬜ (Extruded Cut) in the mini toolbar.

Sketching plane

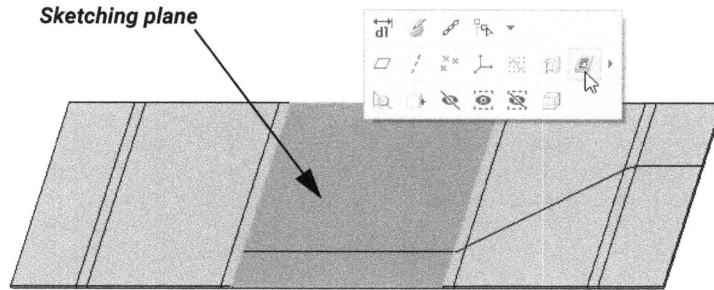

Figure 4–43

5. Sketch the section shown in Figure 4–44. Click ⬜ (Project) and press <Shift> to copy the datum curve into the sketch. Trim the entities as required.

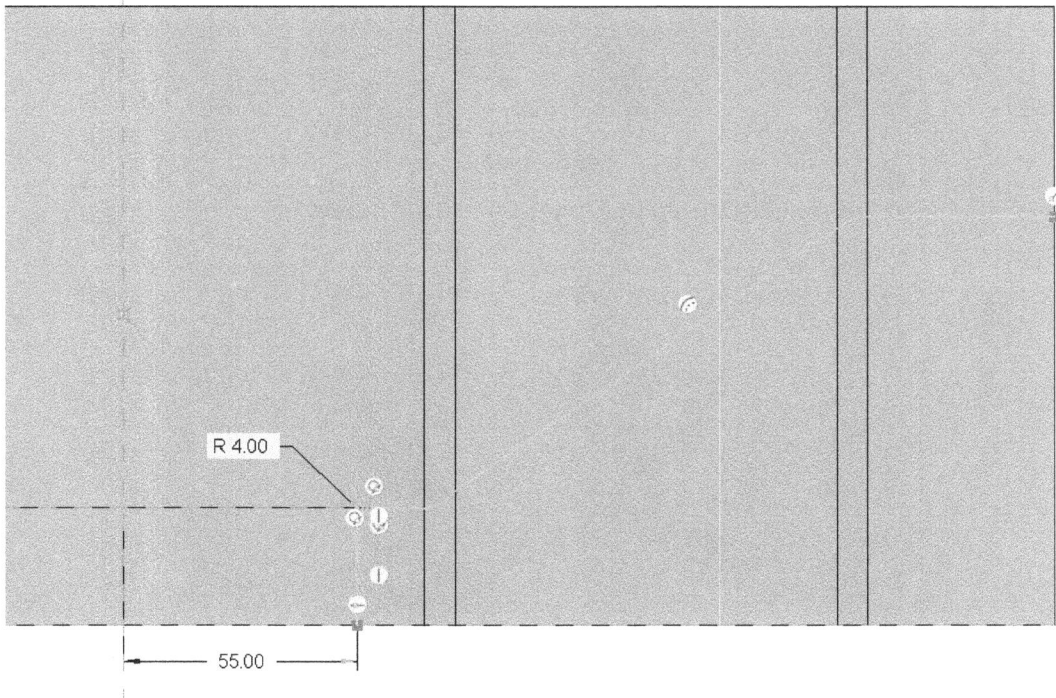

R 4.00

55.00

Figure 4–44

6. Complete the sketch and click ⫤ ⫥ (Through All) to define the depth of the cut. The completed cut displays as shown in Figure 4–45.

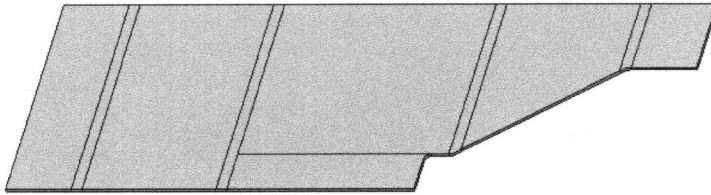

Figure 4–45

7. Select **Extruded Cut 1** in the Model Tree and click ⫲⫳ (Mirror).

8. Select datum plane **RIGHT** as the mirroring plane and complete the feature. The part displays as shown in Figure 4–46.

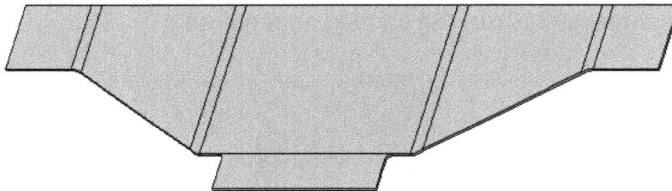

Figure 4–46

9. Click 📐 (Bend Back) in the *Sheetmetal* tab to bend back the part.

10. Accept the default fixed surface.

11. The part displays as shown in Figure 4–47.

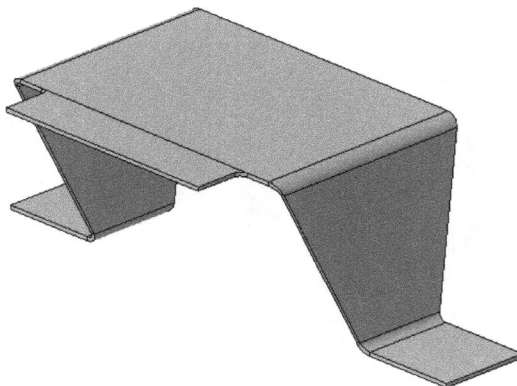

Figure 4–47

12. Save the part and erase it from memory.

End of practice

Practice 4c
Additional Sheet Metal Cuts

Practice Objective

- Create a sheet metal cut.

In this practice, you will create a thin sheet metal cut feature on the project part created in a previous practice, as shown in Figure 4–48. Note the methods of unbending the model and creating cuts introduced in this chapter.

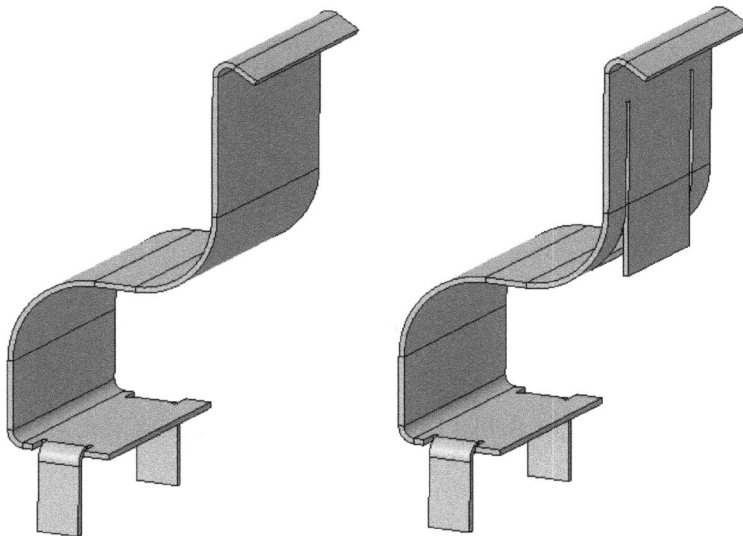

Figure 4–48

Design Considerations

The design intent of the part requires that a cut be created that removes material from the bend of the sheet metal part. To accomplish that, you will create a thin cut in the unbent condition of the part and then bend back the part by selecting surfaces to bend.

1. Set the Working Directory to the *Additional_SM_Cuts folder*.

2. Open **project_ex3.prt**.

3. Set the model display as follows:

   - ⚞ *(Datum Display Filters)*: None

   - ⚟ *(Spin Center)*: Off

   - ⬛ *(Display Style)*: ⬜ (Shading With Edges)

4. Press <Ctrl>+<D> to ensure that the part is in the default orientation.

5. Unbend the entire part.

6. Click ⬛ (Extruded Cut).

7. In the dashboard, click ⬜ (Thicken Sketch) to create a thin sheet metal cut using the dimension scheme shown in Figure 4–49. Set the thickness of the cut to **0.125**.

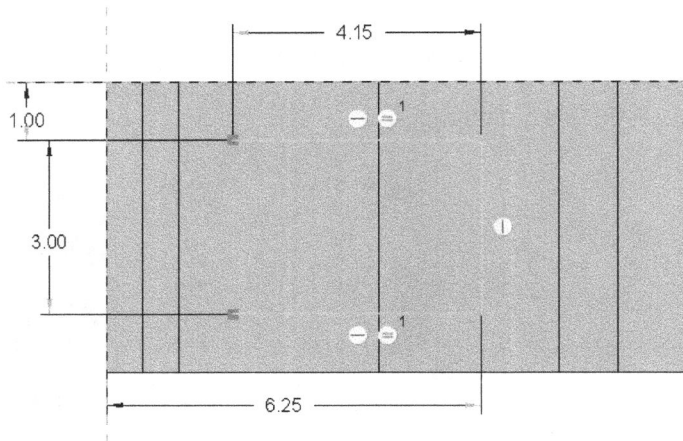

Figure 4–49

8. Click ⬛ (Bend Back).

9. Select the Bend Control panel. Select **Contour 1** and select **Keep flat,** as shown in Figure 4–50.

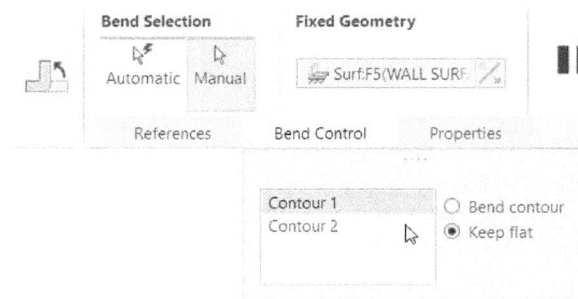

Figure 4–50

*Note: If the wrong bend is flat, you may need to use **Contour 2** instead of **Contour 1**.*

10. Click ✓ (OK). The completed part displays as shown in Figure 4−51.

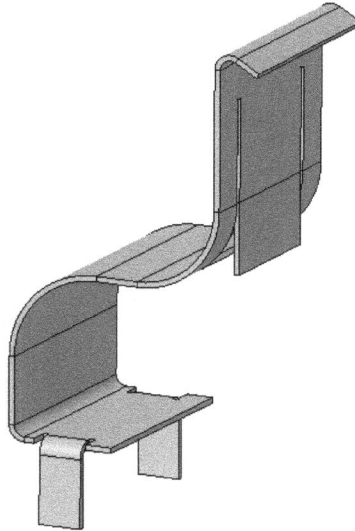

Figure 4−51

11. Save the part and erase it from memory.

End of practice

Chapter Review Questions

1. Which of the following methods should be used to investigate the flat state of the geometry, to avoid having an unbend feature followed by a bend back feature?

    a. Click ⬚ in the *Sheetmetal* tab and leave the model flat.

    b. Click ⬚ in the In-graphics toolbar or *View* tab to view the flattened model.

    c. Click ⬚ in the *Sheetmetal* tab.

    d. It is acceptable to have consecutive unbend and bend-back features.

2. What can you use to create a cut that must follow the contour of the sheet metal wall, using a projected datum curve as the reference for your cut?

    a. Extrude

    b. Flange

    c. Project

    d. This cannot be achieved with these options.

3. A coordinate system placed on the surface of a sheet metal wall stays on the wall surface after the **Bend** and **Unbend** operations have been performed on the wall.

    a. True

    b. False

4. When creating an unbend feature, you can manually select a fixed surface instead of using the one that is automatically selected by Creo Parametric.

    a. True

    b. False

Answers: 1b, 2c, 3a, 4a

Notches and Punches

In this chapter, you will learn how to add relief to corners and edges to avoid unwanted deformation that can occur when sheet metal parts are bent.

Learning Objectives

- Identify the many different methods of creating a corner relief in the sheet metal model.
- Learn to create a corner relief feature using the many types available in the *Corner Relief* dashboard.
- Understand the geometry and the differences between notch and punch features.
- Learn the general steps and options when creating a notch or punch in conjunction with creating a user-defined feature (UDF).

5.1 Corner Relief

Corner relief is used to prevent unwanted deformations. There are many ways to create a corner relief:

- Define the corner relief as a feature.

- Define the corner relief as part of a flange feature.

- Create a default corner relief automatically while unbending by selecting **File>Prepare>Model Properties**. Select **change** beside Relief, as shown in Figure 5–1.

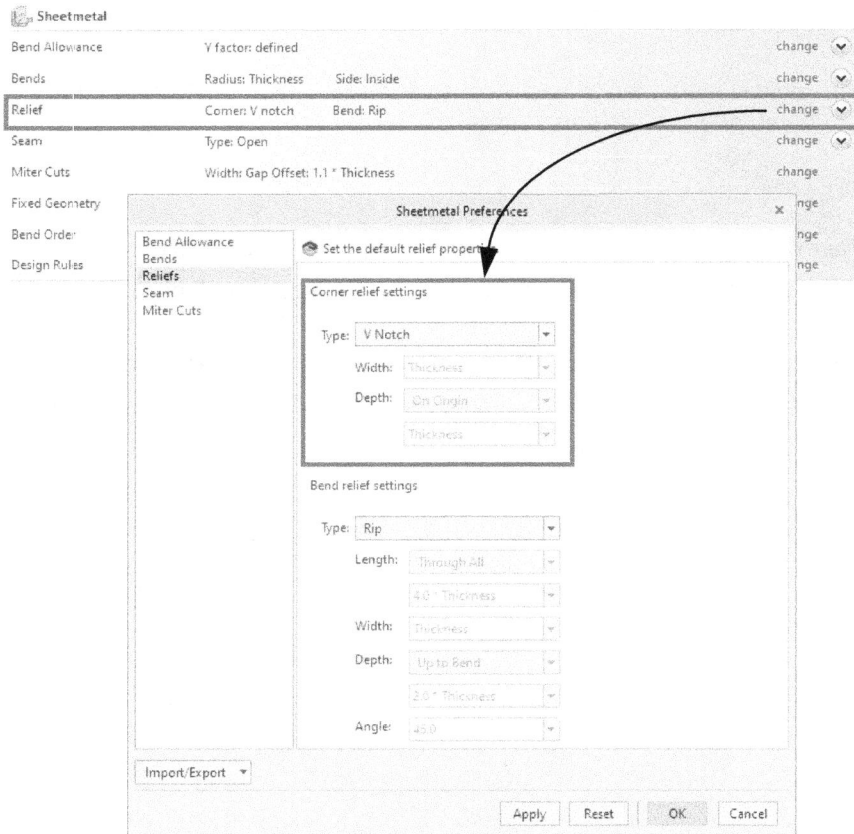

Figure 5–1

- Define a default relief for corners in the model using sheet metal parameters as shown in Figure 5–2. In the *Sheetmetal* tab, select **Model Intent>Parameters**.

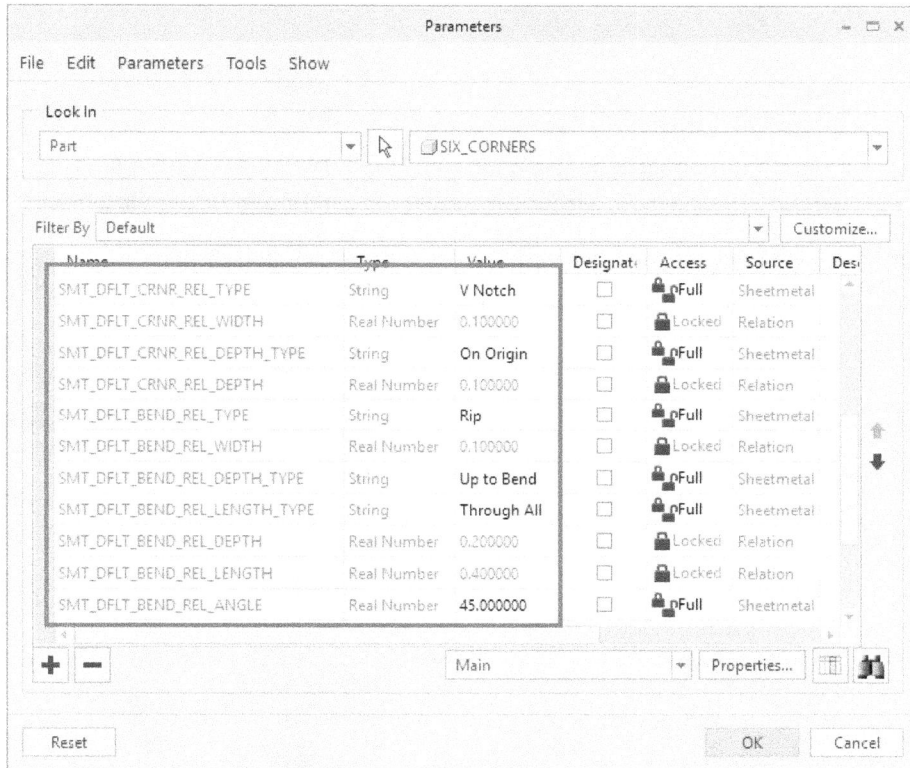

Figure 5–2

- Define the corner relief in the conversion feature when converting a solid part into a sheet metal part.

How To: Create a Corner Relief Feature

1. To apply a corner relief you must have at least one ripped edge in the model.

   The corner relief is only displayed when the geometry is in its unbent state. A 3D note can then be displayed to indicate the type of relief.

   Expand 🗂 (Annotation Display Filters) and click 🖉 (Corner Relief Notes) in the In-graphics toolbar to toggle the note display of corner relief notes on and off.

   Note: *You can also select the View tab and click 🖉 (Corner Relief Notes) to toggle bend relief notes on and off.*

2. Click 🔧 (Corner Relief) in the *Sheetmetal* tab to add the corner relief. The *Corner Relief* dashboard opens as shown in Figure 5–3.

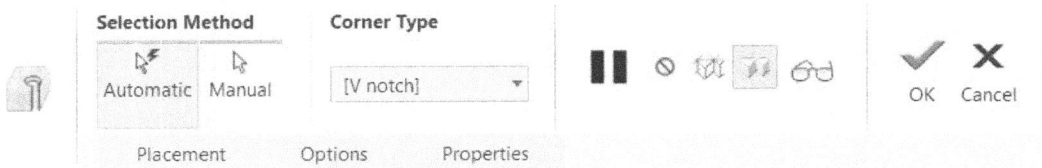

Figure 5–3

The corner relief notes display on the model as shown in Figure 5–4.

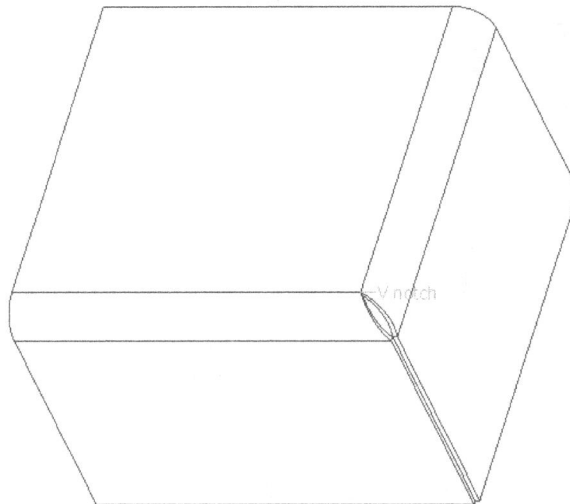

Figure 5–4

3. By default, Creo Parametric selects all of the 3D notes. To manually select the notes, click ⟑ (Select Manually) or right-click and change *Automatic Selection* to **Manual Selection** and then select the corresponding 3D note(s).

Once the notes have been selected, click, and select the relief type from the mini toolbar, as shown in Figure 5–5. You can also select the type in the *Corner Relief* dashboard, as shown in Figure 5–5.

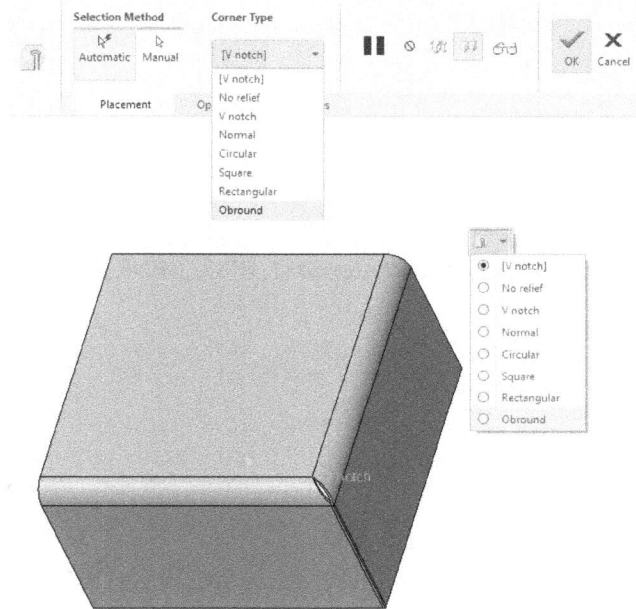

Figure 5–5

4. Use the Placement panel to enter the dimensional values for the selected relief, as shown in Figure 5–6.

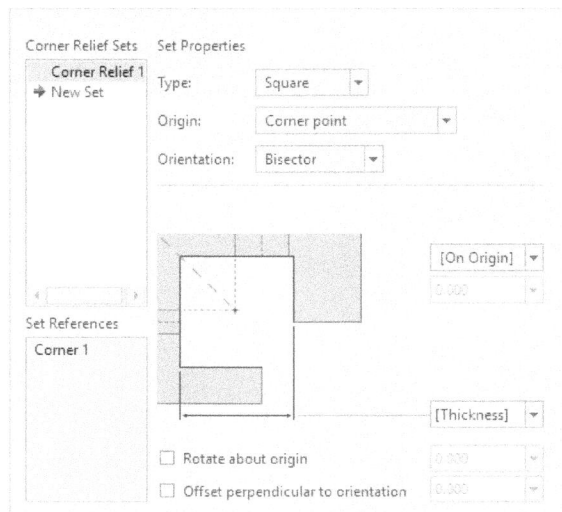

Figure 5–6

5. Once you have selected the Corner relief type, and set any related options, click ✓ (OK) to complete the feature.

- In some instances, the corner relief feature does not create the required geometry. You might need to flatten the model and use a sheet metal cut, or use a user-defined feature (UDF).

Corner Relief Types

There are seven types of corner relief:

- **[V notch]** (SMT_DFLT_CRNR_REL_TYPE) or manually selected **V Notch:** Generates a corner relief specified in the sheet metal parameter SMT_DFLT_CRNR_REL_TYPE, as shown in Figure 5-7.

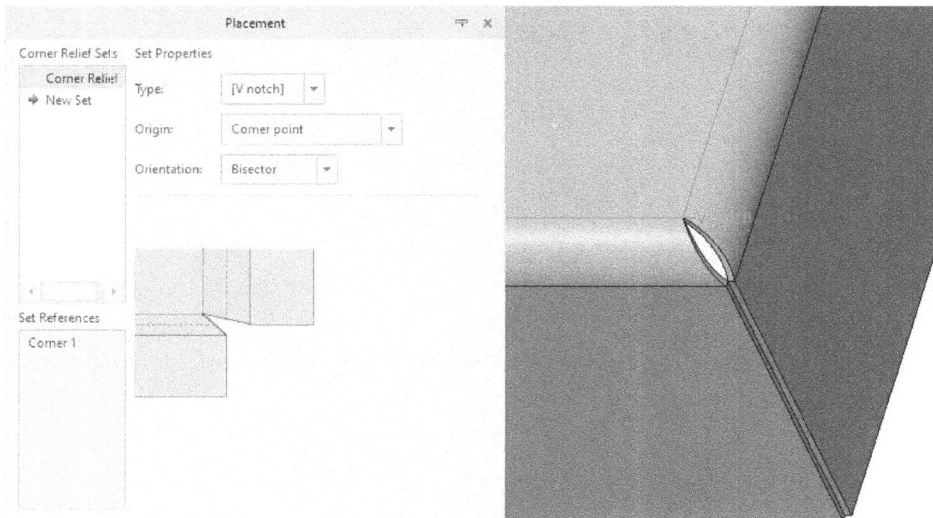

Figure 5-7

- **No relief:** Retains the default V-notch characteristic when formed, as shown in Figure 5–8.

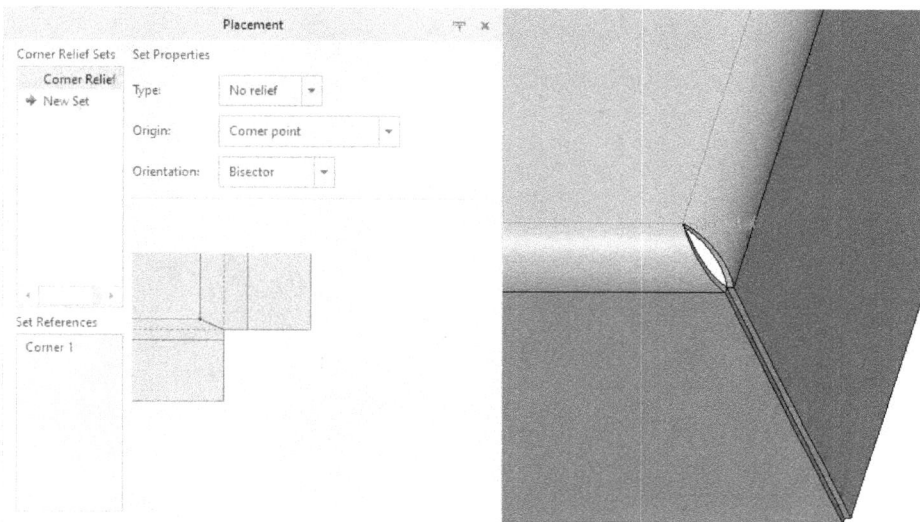

Figure 5–8

- **Normal:** A cut from the corner, up to and normal to the bend end, as shown in Figure 5–9.

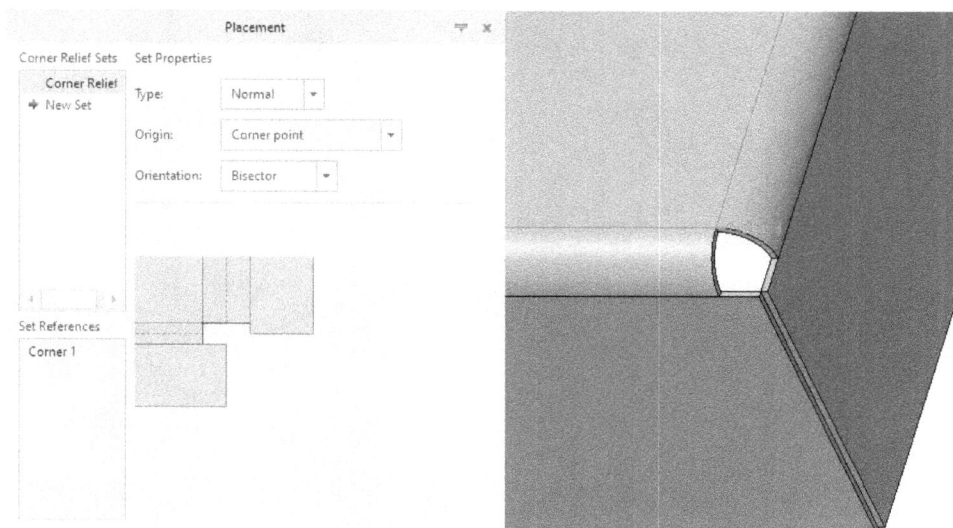

Figure 5–9

- **Circular:** A circular section is removed, as shown in Figure 5–10.

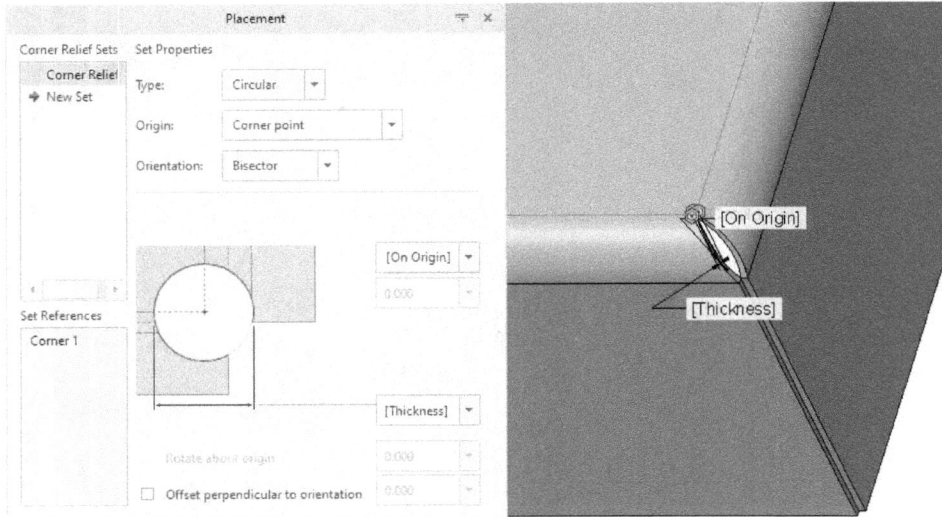

Figure 5–10

- **Square:** A rectangular section is removed. cut concentric with the relief anchor point. The section diagonal is parallel to the relief orientation reference, as shown in Figure 5–11.

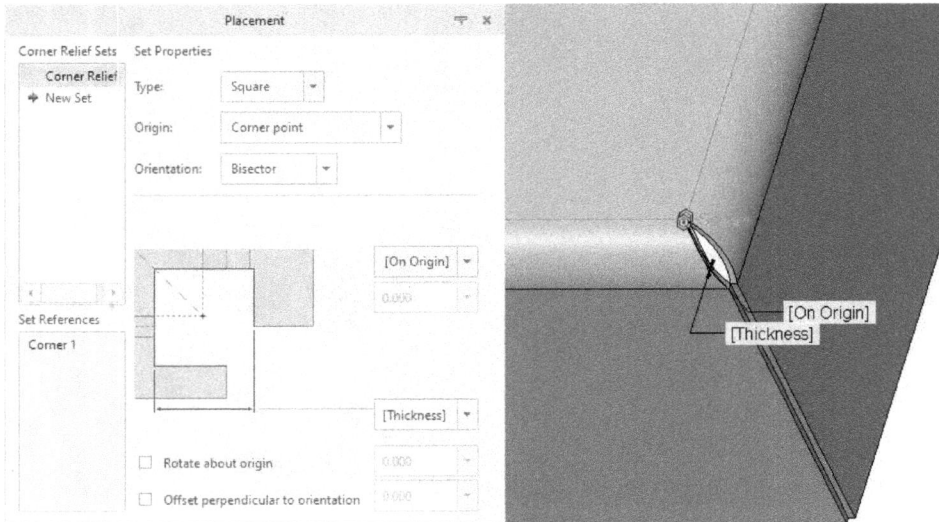

Figure 5–11

- **Rectangular:** A rectangular section is removed, as shown in Figure 5–12.

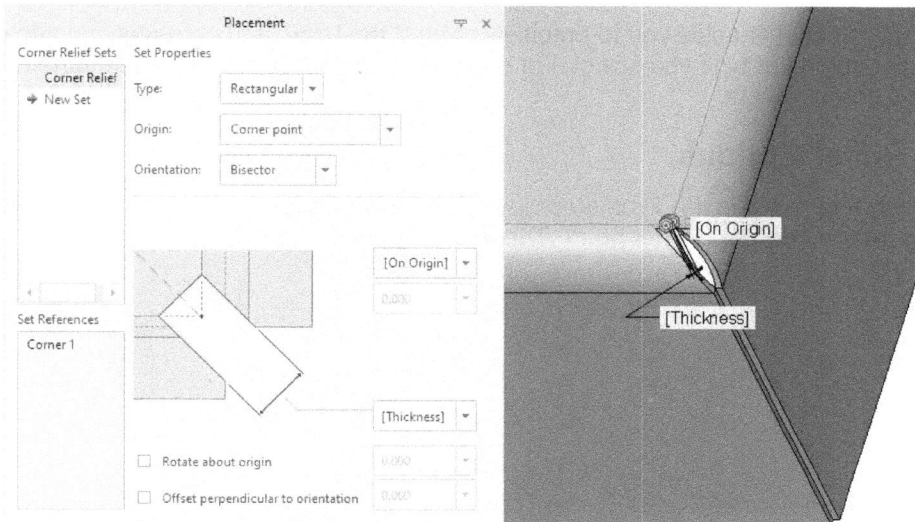

Figure 5–12

- **Obround:** An obround section is removed, as shown in Figure 5–13.

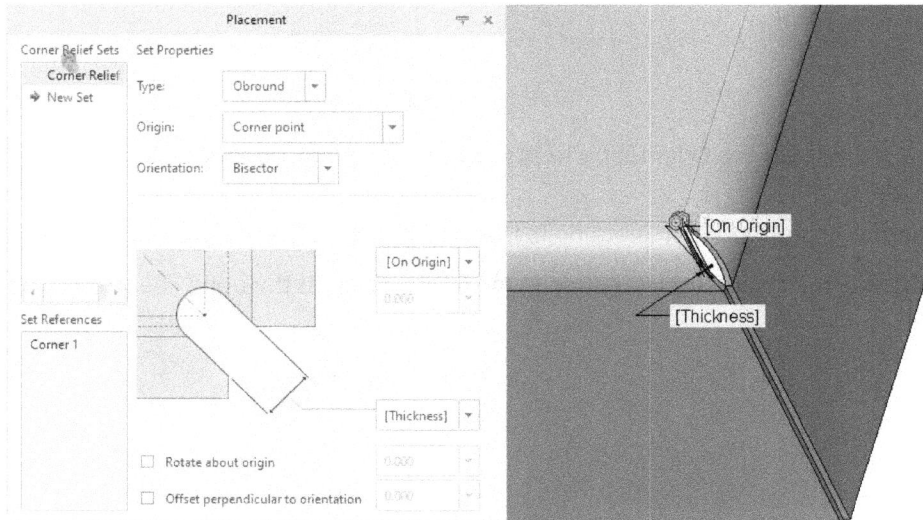

Figure 5–13

Corner Relief Options

The Placement panel enables you to precisely control the relief, and contains specific settings depending on the relief type you select. For example, consider the following options for **Square** and **Normal** corner reliefs.

Square Relief Options

To apply a square relief, in the Type drop-down list, select **Square**. You can set the Origin to **Bend lines intersection** or **Corner point**. The resulting geometry differs, as shown in Figure 5–14.

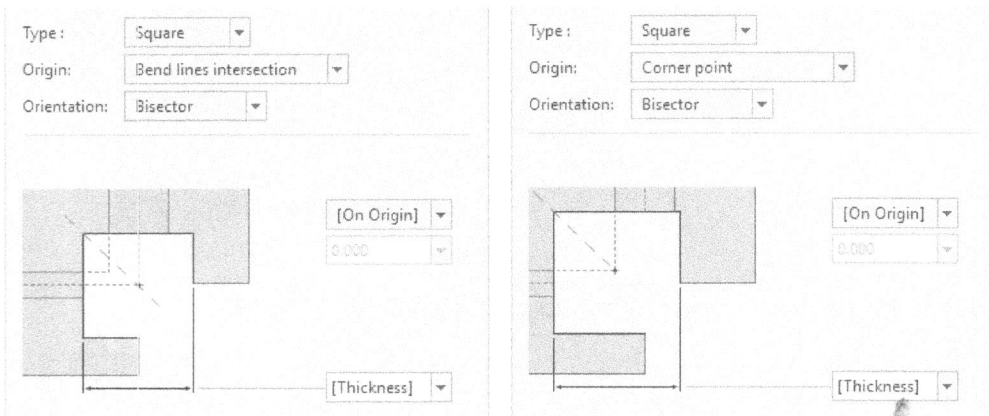

Figure 5–14

In addition, you can set the Orientation to **Bisector** or **Diagonal**, updating the geometry as shown in Figure 5–15.

- For **Bisector**, the orientation direction is the bisector of the bend edges at the corner point.

- For **Diagonal**, the orientation direction is the intersection of the bend lines and corner point.

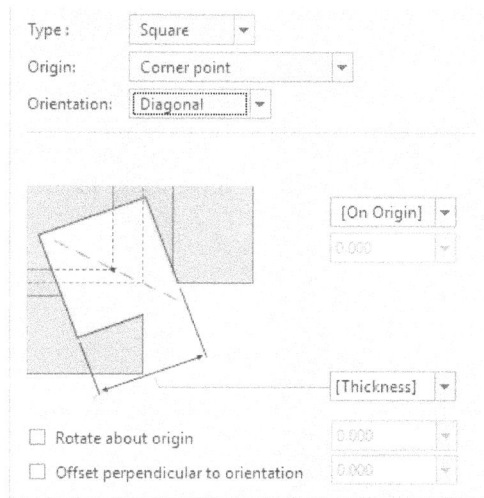

Figure 5−15

Normal Relief Options

To apply a normal relief, in the Type drop-down list, select **Normal**. For a **Normal** corner relief, you can edit the **Origin** and **Orientation**, as shown in Figure 5−16.

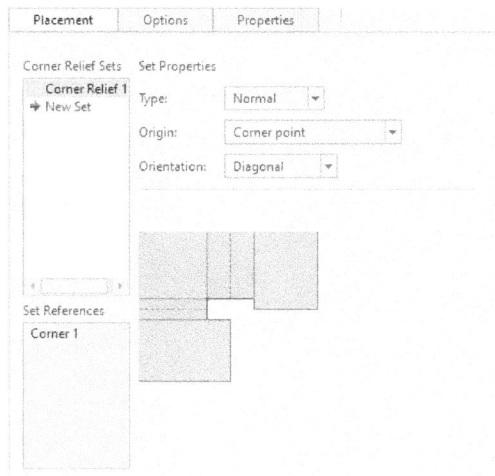

Figure 5−16

Similar to the Square relief, you can set the Origin to **Corner point** or **Bend lines intersection**, and the Orientation to **Bisector** or **Diagonal**.

5.2 Introduction to Notches and Punches

Notch and punch features are created in a sheet metal model using sheet metal cuts and user-defined features (UDFs) to create geometry. Notch features are often used for bend relief at corners, since obround and rectangular reliefs cannot cross the bend geometry of another wall. Punches tend to be closed-profile shapes that remove material, usually in a template format. Figure 5−17 shows an example of a notch and punch feature.

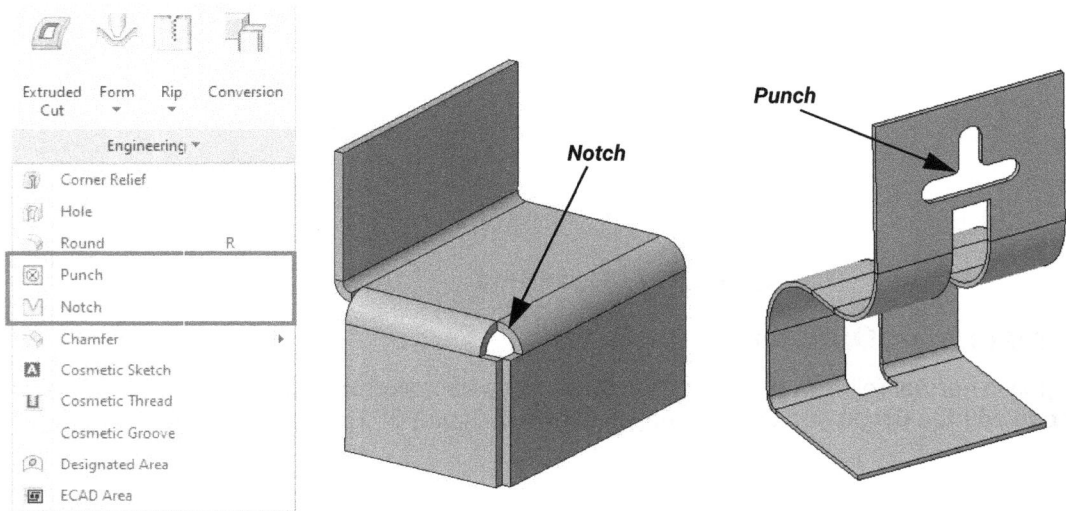

Figure 5−17

Notches and punches are made with specific tools. Creo Parametric enables you to create notch and punch UDFs with unique geometry that can be reused on different models. When creating a notch or punch UDF, you are prompted to define the following items:

* A coordinate system to locate tooling.

* A specific tool ID for fabrication purposes.

* A single sheet metal cut feature.

The part shown on the left in Figure 5–18 contains a sheet metal cut. It was used in a notch UDF and placed on the part shown on the right. The cut remains normal to the sheet metal surfaces in the bend area.

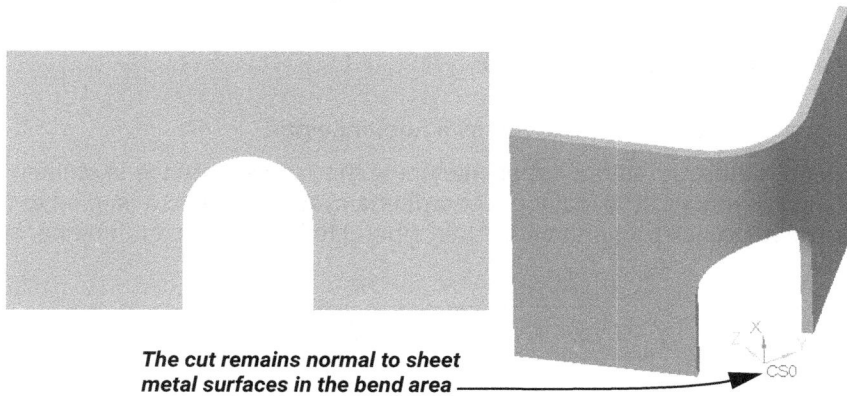

The cut remains normal to sheet metal surfaces in the bend area

Figure 5–18

5.3 Creating Notch and Punch UDFs

Notches and punches are created in conjunction with UDFs. UDFs enable the geometry to be created once and then reused as required in other models.

How To: Create a Notch or Punch UDF

1. Create a simple sheet metal part to act as a reference part.

    Create a sheet metal cut feature. When sketching the profile, note the sketching and dimensioning references, and include a coordinate system. If the cut is used to relieve a bend area, the reference part should contain a bend to be used as a reference, as shown in Figure 5–19.

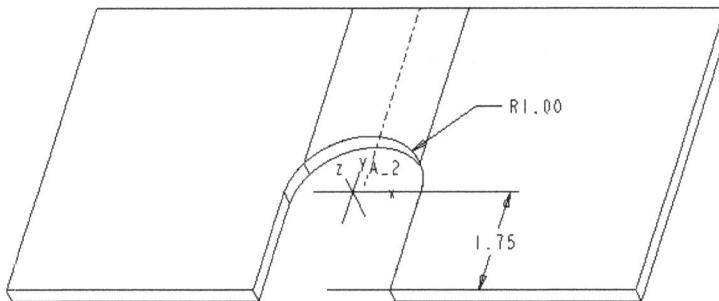

Figure 5–19

Note: Use relations to capture design intent and to minimize and control variability in future use.

2. Select the *Tools* tab and click ⬚ (UDF Library)>**Create** to start the creation of a UDF. Specify a name for the UDF. Creo Parametric saves the file as **<udf_name>.gph**.

3. When creating a UDF, you have two options: **Subordinate** and **Stand Alone**.

    *   **Stand Alone**: Copies the UDF geometry from the reference part to the .GPH file. This enables you to discard the reference part when you are finished. If the option is selected, click **Yes** or **No** in the message window to specify whether or not to create a reference model. By including the reference part, the system saves a copy of it with the name **<udf_name>.prt**. This reference information is available when you place the UDF in another part. For a Stand Alone UDF a reference model is not required, but it can be helpful in placing the UDF.

    *   A **Subordinate** UDF obtains values directly from the original model. To place a subordinate UDF, verify that the original model used to create the UDF file is easily identified in a search path or in the working directory. Subordinate UDFs automatically generate a reference model.

    Note: A complex reference part increases the file size. Therefore, if you plan to create a reference model, keep the reference part as simple as possible.

4. Once you have defined the type of UDF you are prompted to select the feature(s) you want to include in it. Select the cut feature in the Model Tree or directly on the model, as shown in Figure 5–20.

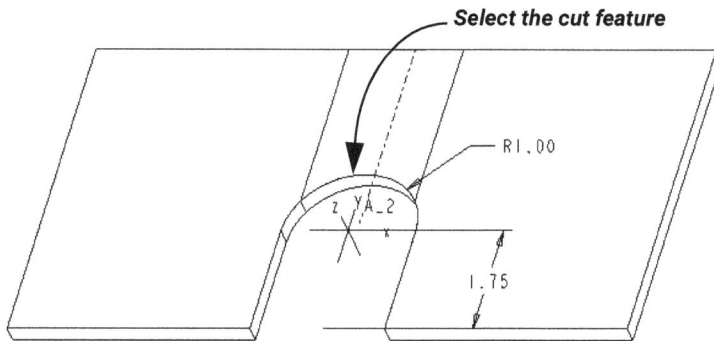

Figure 5–20

5. Once selected, select **Done>Done/Return** to continue.

6. Creo Parametric prompts you whether you are defining the UDF for a punch or notch feature. Click **Yes** and enter a name for the tool used to create the notch or punch on the actual sheet metal part as shown in Figure 5–21.

Figure 5–21

7. Define symmetry for the tool relative to the coordinate system in the cut feature using the **SYMMETRY** menu. Select the appropriate option as shown in Figure 5–22.

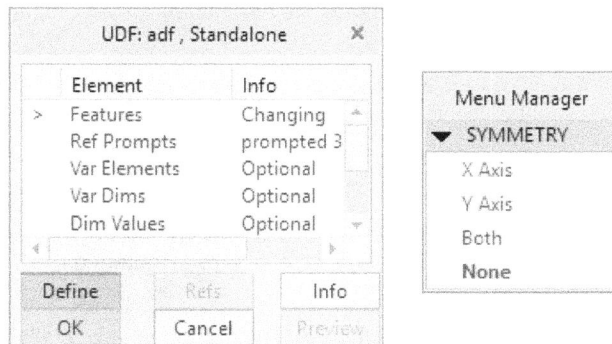

Figure 5–22

8. Creo Parametric then prompts you for information about the external references required to place the UDF, as shown in Figure 5-23.

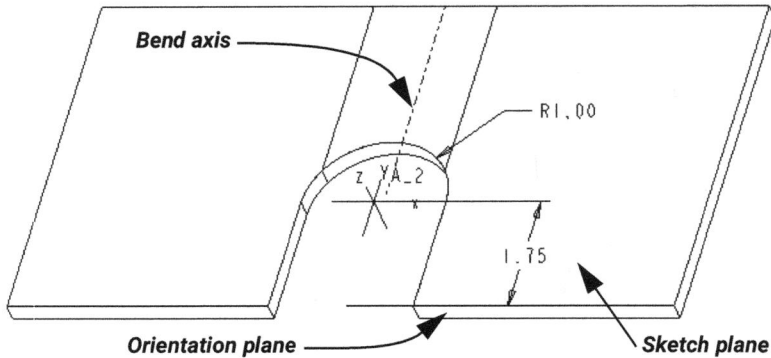

Figure 5-23

*Note: UDF attributes can be changed after the UDF has been placed on a part. Select the UDF feature, right-click, and select **Edit Definition**.*

9. Enter a reference prompt for Creo Parametric to use to prompt you for appropriate references when placing the UDF on another part.

10. Optional elements can be used to further define the UDF. Double-click on any element in the dialog box to define it. These elements are described as follows:

Element	Description
Var Elements	Specifies any feature element in the UDF as variable. For example, the depth of a cut can be variable. When the UDF is placed, the cut can be specified as **Thru All** in one situation and **Blind** in another.
Var Dims	Specifies dimensions of any feature in the UDF as variable. When placing the UDF, the prompts for the dimension values display in the message window.
Dim Values	Modifies the values of invariable dimensions on the UDF. This option is only available for standalone UDFs.
Var Parameters	Specifies parameters in the UDF as variable. When placing the UDF, the prompts for the dimension values display in the message window.
Family Table	Creates a family table that is stored with the UDF. When placing the UDF, the **INSTANCES** menu displays and an instance must be selected before placement.
Units	Sets the UDF's length units. This option is only available for standalone UDFs.

Element	Description
Pro/Program	Creates a program in the UDF that is copied to the program of the part during placement. The program is executed after the UDF has been placed. This option is only available with subordinate UDFs.
Ext Symbols	Defines relations involving symbols (dimensions and parameters) to be variable in the UDF. For example, a dimension has a relation d2=width, where width is a parameter. The width parameter can be added to the UDF and the relation can be maintained.

11. Click **OK** in the UDF dialog box and select **Done/Return** in the **UDF** menu.

5.4 Placing Notch or Punch UDFs

How To: Place a Notch or Punch a UDF

1. Select **Engineering>Notch** (for a notch) or **Engineering>Punch** (for a punch) in the *Sheetmetal* tab. Select the appropriate UDF file in the Open dialog box.

   The Insert User-Defined Feature dialog box opens, as shown in Figure 5–24.

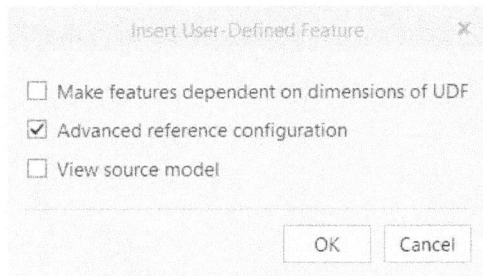

Figure 5–24

Note: Use an unbend feature to flatten the model, if required.

2. To display the reference part while placing the UDF, select the **View source model** option. With the option selected, the reference part displays in a sub-window, as shown in Figure 5–25.

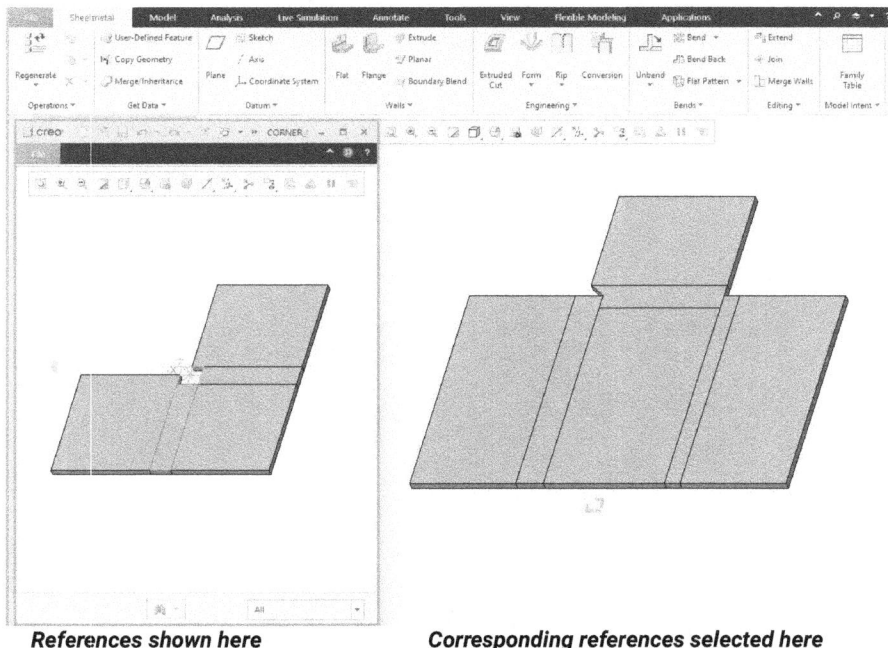

References shown here   *Corresponding references selected here*

Figure 5–25

- The *Placement* tab in the User Defined Feature Placement dialog box lists all of the references for the original features as shown in Figure 5–26. This enables you to review the original references used to place the features that form the UDF and select the appropriate references in the current model.

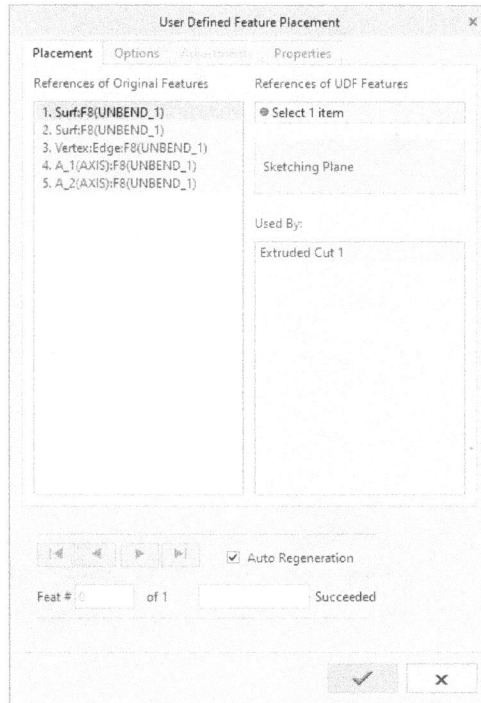

Figure 5–26

If you select to retrieve the reference part, then once an item is selected in the dialog box, the original reference on the reference part highlights as well. This can be useful for placing the UDF on the current part.

For example, to place the cut shown previously in Figure 5–25, select the corresponding placement references, similar to those in Figure 5–27.

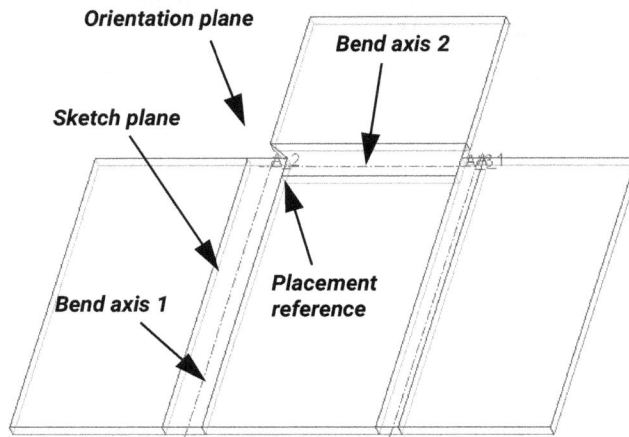

Figure 5–27

Note: *The entity type selected as a reference must be similar to the entity type used during the initial creation of the feature.*

- The *Options* tab shown in Figure 5–28, enables you to specify the UDF scaling, how non-variable UDF dimensions are dealt with, and whether feature redefinition is possible after UDF has been placed.

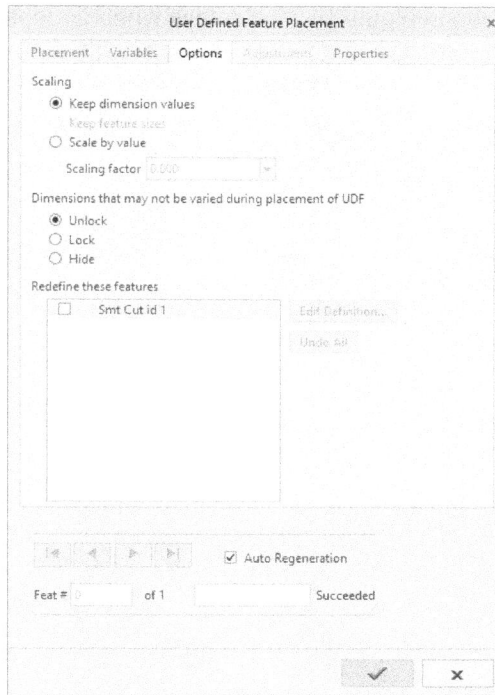

Figure 5–28

Note: Displaying non-variable dimensions is determined by design intent.

The options available for *Scaling* and for non-variable dimensions are as follows:

Option	Description
Scaling Options	
Keep dimension values	Maintains the dimensional values regardless of differences in the units between the UDF and target model.
Keep feature size	Maintains the size of the original UDF by re-scaling all dimensional values. It is only available when the UDF and target model have different units.
Scale by value	Enables you to enter a scale value for all dimensions. It disregards any varying units in the UDF and target model.
Non-Variable Dimension Options	
Unlock	Displays the invariable dimensions so that the values can be modified. It is only available if the UDF was created as independent.
Lock	Displays the invariable dimensions so that the values are read-only and cannot be modified.
Hide	Prevents the display of invariable dimensions.

- The *Variables* tab shown in Figure 5–29 displays when dimensions have been specified as variable during UDF creation. It enables you to modify dimensional values according to your needs. If no dimensions were specified as variable, the tab is not available.

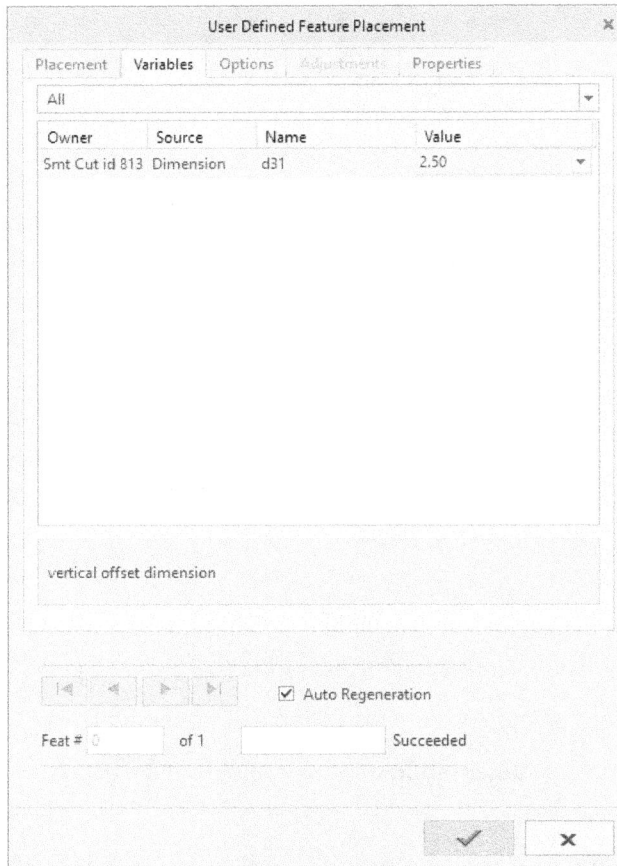

Figure 5–29

3. Click ✔ (OK) to complete the feature. The model in Figure 5–30 has two notches.

   - During manufacturing, notches are created before bends. In Creo Parametric, you create the walls and bends in the bent condition firs to enable you to incorporate design intent. You then create notches in the unbent condition. It is easier to design in the bent condition and then unbend than it is to design in the flat or unbent condition.

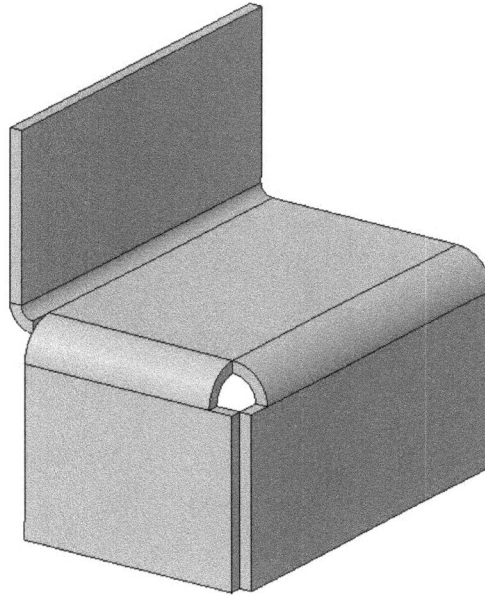

Figure 5–30

Practice 5a
Create Corner Reliefs

Practice Objective

- Create corner reliefs.

In this practice, you will create six different corner reliefs, as shown in Figure 5–31.

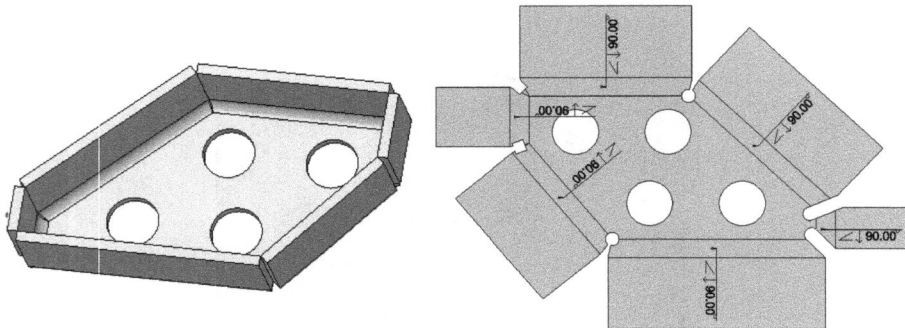

Figure 5–31

Task 1: Open the reference part.

1. Set the working directory to the *Corner_Relief* folder.
2. Open **six_corners.prt**.
3. Set the model display as follows:
   - *(Datum Display Filters)*: None
   - *(Spin Center)*: Off
   - *(Display Style)*: (Shading With Edges)

Task 2: Define corner reliefs.

Design Considerations

In this task, you will create corner reliefs to control the sheet metal behavior. You will create six ripped edges and use the Corner Relief feature to create corner reliefs. The corner relief is only displayed as geometry in the unbend state of the model. The type of corner relief is only displayed as a 3D note in the bend state.

1. Expand ⬚ (Annotation Display Filters) in the Graphics toolbar and ensure that ⬚ (Corner Relief Notes) is enabled.

   Note: You can also select the View tab and click ⬚ (Corner Relief Notes) in the Show group.

2. Click ⬚ (Corner Relief) in the Engineering group in the *Sheetmetal* tab. The *Corner Relief* dashboard opens, as shown in Figure 5–32.

Figure 5–32

3. The 3D notes of the corner relief are now displayed.

4. Right-click anywhere in the graphics area and select **Manual Selection**, as shown in Figure 5–33.

Figure 5–33

   Note: You can also click ⬚ (Select Manually) in the Corner Relief dashboard.

5. Hold <Ctrl> and select the two 3D notes shown in Figure 5–34.

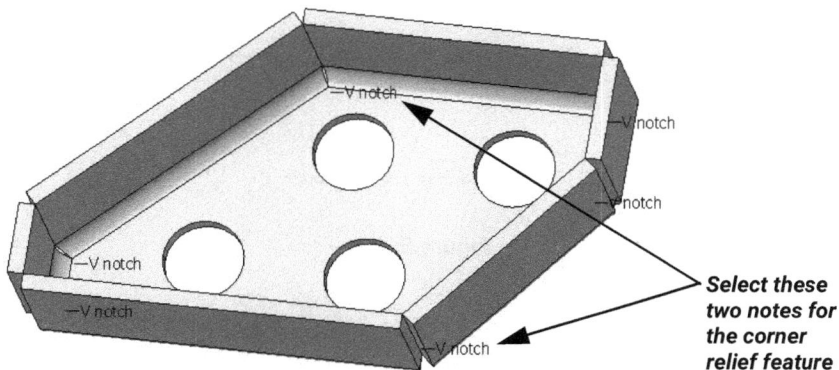

Figure 5–34

6. Click on the screen and expand ⬚ (Corner Relief Type) in the mini toolbar.

7. Select **Circular**, as shown in Figure 5-35.

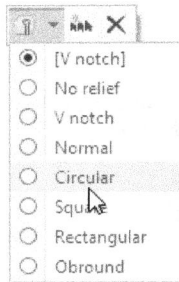

Figure 5-35

8. Select the Placement panel and set the *Width* to **0.15**, as shown in Figure 5-36.

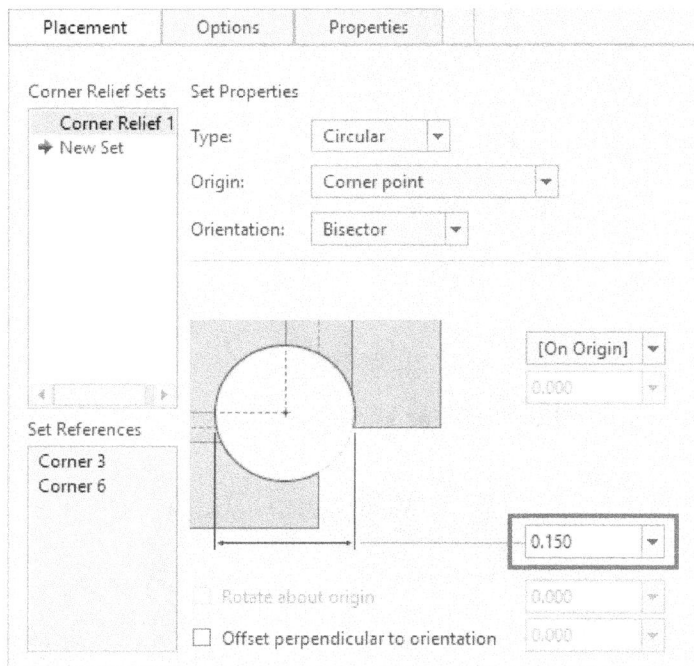

Figure 5-36

9. Complete the feature. The model displays as shown in Figure 5–37.

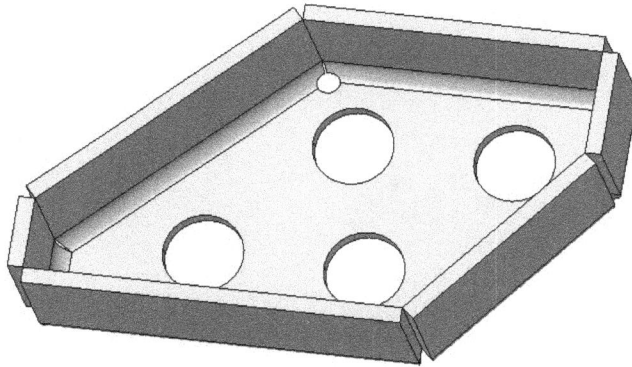

Figure 5–37

Task 3: Create obround reliefs on the third and fourth corners.

1. Click ⊡ (Corner Relief).
2. Right-click and select **Manual Selection**.
3. Select the two 3D notes shown in Figure 5–38.

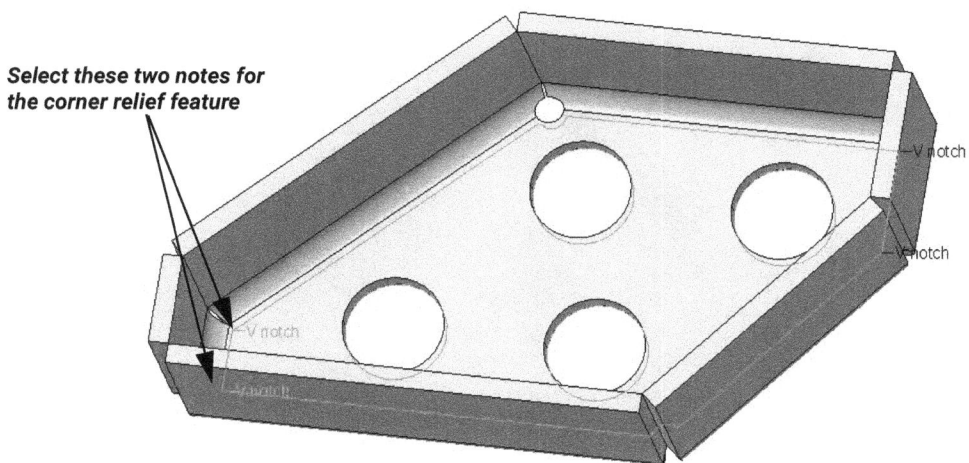

Select these two notes for the corner relief feature

Figure 5–38

4. Click on the screen and expand ⊡ (Corner Relief Type) in the mini toolbar and select **Obround.**
5. Select the Placement panel and set the *Width* of the obround corner relief to **0.15**.

6. Select **Blind** from the drop-down list, as shown in Figure 5–39 and set the *Distance* from the tangent point to the intersection of the bend centerlines to **0.15**.

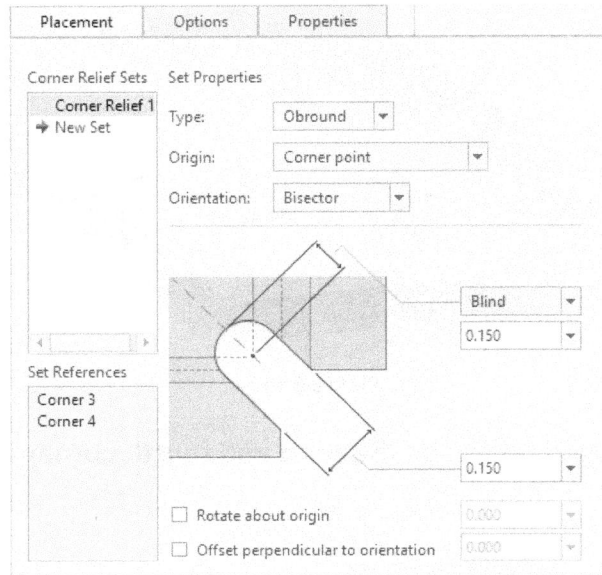

Figure 5–39

7. Complete the feature. The relief is added as shown in Figure 5–40.

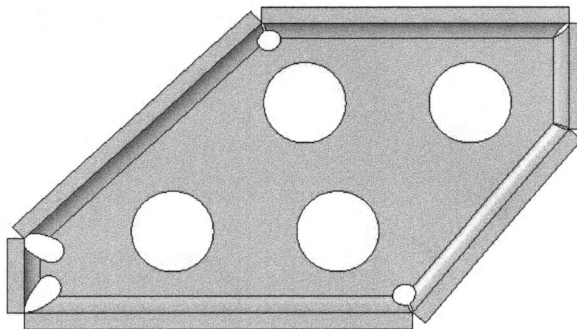

Figure 5–40

Task 4: Add a corner relief to the final two corners.

1. Click ⬚ (Corner Relief).

2. The 3D notes for the corner relief are displayed. Right-click and select **Manual Selection**. Select both 3D notes shown in Figure 5–41.

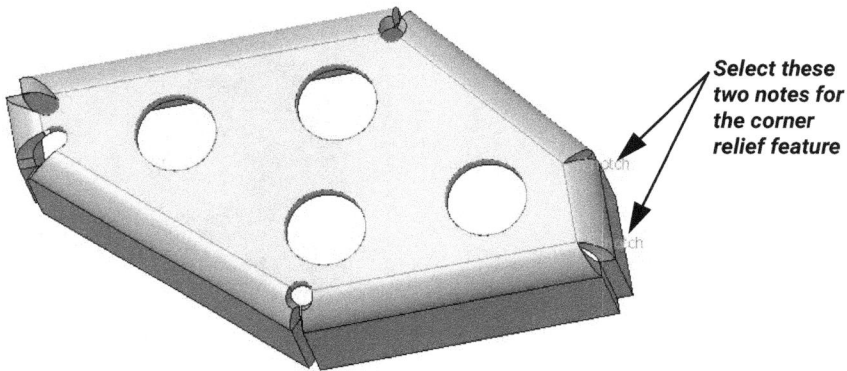

Select these two notes for the corner relief feature

Figure 5–41

3. Click on the screen and expand ⬚ (Corner Relief Type) in the mini toolbar and select **Square**.

4. A preview of the relief displays as shown in Figure 5–42.

   - Note that the drag handles are disabled because the depth is driven by the sheet metal thickness parameter.

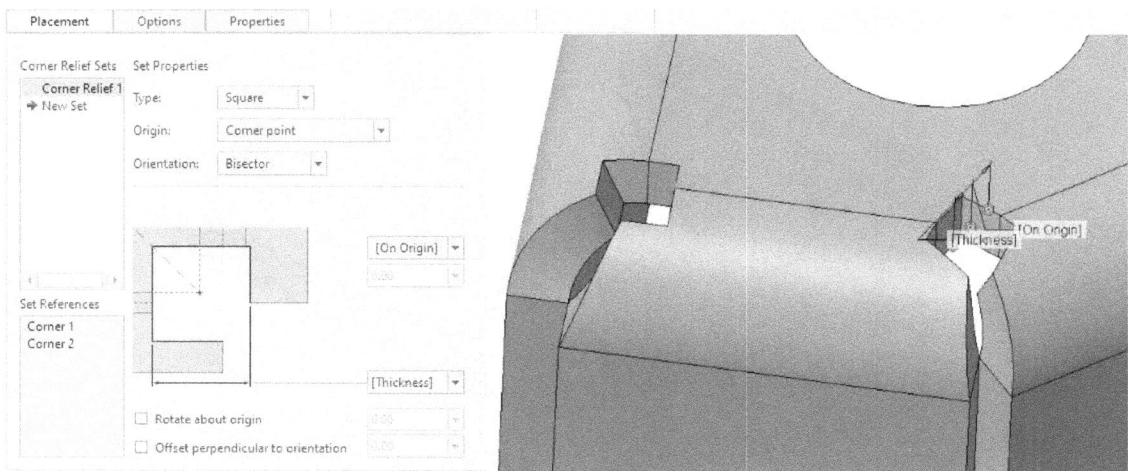

Figure 5–42

5. In the Origin drop-down list, select **Bend Line Intersection**.

6. In the Orientation drop-down list, select **Diagonal**.

7. Enable **Rotate about origin** and set the angle to **45** degrees.

8. Edit the width to **0.125**. Note that the drag handles are now available, as shown in Figure 5−43.

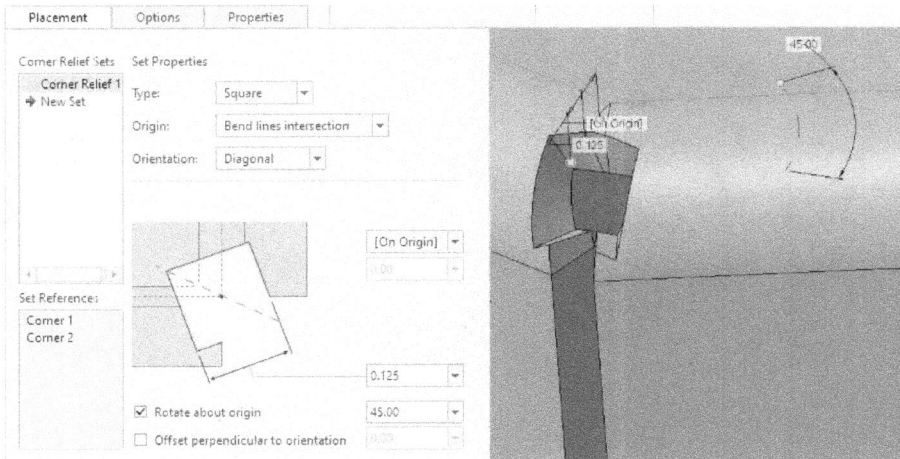

Figure 5−43

9. In the dashboard, click ✔ (OK). The model displays as shown in Figure 5−44, and two new 3D notes named **No Relief** are shown.

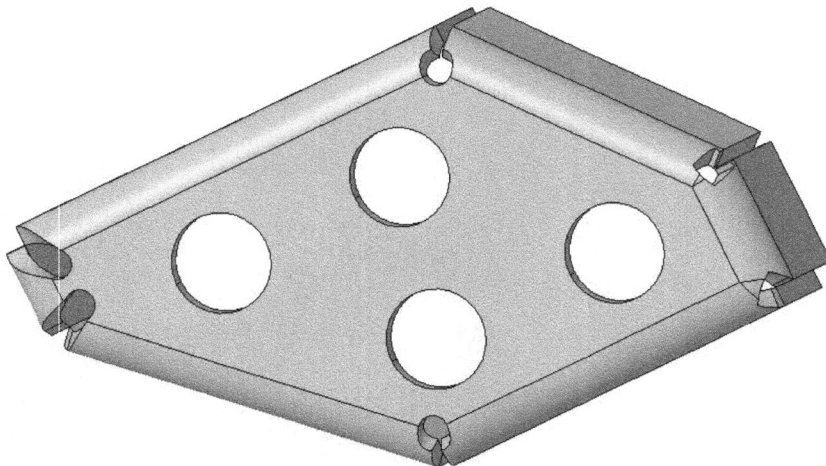

Figure 5−44

Task 5: Define a flat pattern.

Design Considerations

In this task, you will create a flat pattern to check the unbent geometry. The corner relief is only displayed as geometry in the unbent state of model.

1. Click 🔳 (Flat Pattern) in the *Sheetmetal* tab. The top surface shown in Figure 5–45 is the default surface selected to remain fixed while in unbend.

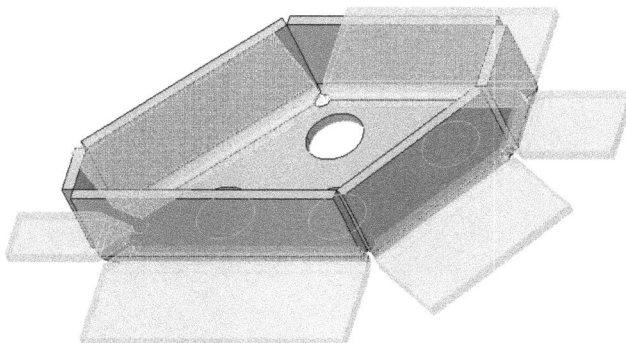

Figure 5–45

2. Complete the feature. In the In-graphics toolbar, enable 🔳 (Bend Notes).

3. Set the model orientation to **BOTTOM**. The finished model displays as shown in Figure 5–46.

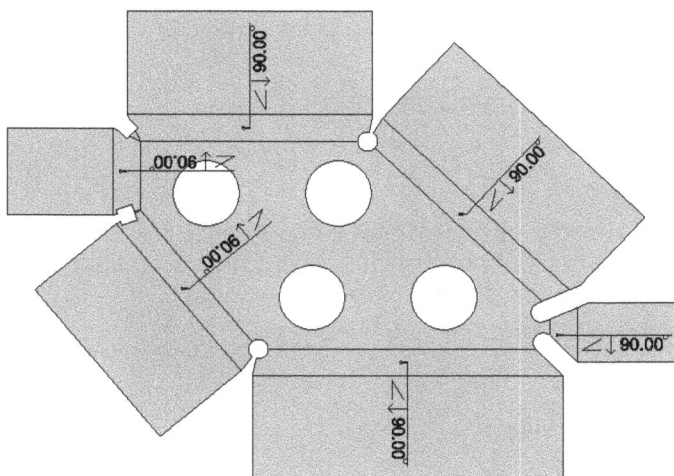

Figure 5–46

4. Save the part and erase it from memory.

End of practice

Practice 5b
Create a Notch for Bend Relief I

Practice Objective

- Create and place a notch UDF.

In this practice, you will create a notch UDF and use it to create a bend relief on another part, as shown in Figure 5–47.

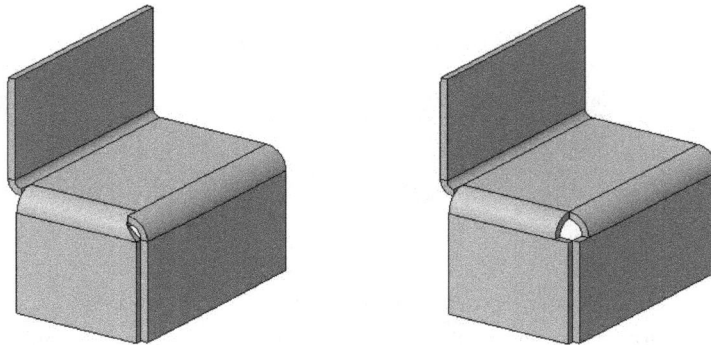

Figure 5–47

Note: Minimize the number of references established during the creation of the cut on the reference part. If the UDF is too complicated to place, this method loses efficiency.

Task 1: Open the reference part and create a cut.

Design Considerations

Notch features are often used for bend relief at corners, since obround and rectangular relief cannot cross the bend geometry of another wall. In this task, you will create a sheet metal cut feature that is going to be used for the definition of the notch UDF.

1. Set the working directory to the *Notch_Relief_I* folder.
2. Open **ref_part.prt**.
3. Set the model display as follows:

    - ⚔ *(Datum Display Filters)*: None
    - ⚓ *(Spin Center)*: Off
    - ⬚ *(Display Style)*: ⬚ (Shading With Edges)

4. Click ⬏ (Unbend).

5. Remove the default fixed surface, and select the surface shown in Figure 5−48 to remain fixed.

   *Note: You can also right-click and select **Clear**.*

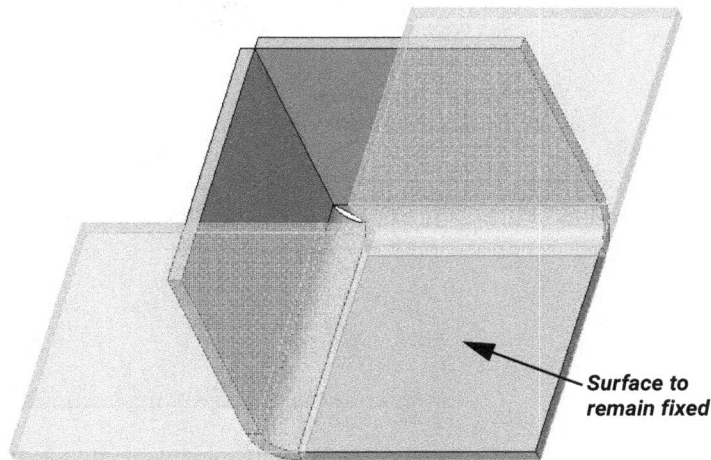

Surface to remain fixed

Figure 5−48

6. Click ✓ (OK) to complete the feature. The unbent reference part displays as shown in Figure 5−49.

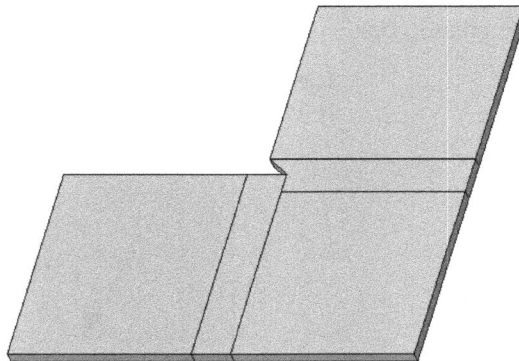

Figure 5−49

7. Display the datum axes and their tags.

8. Click ⬛ (Extruded Cut) in the *Sheetmetal* tab.

9. Click on the screen and select ✐ (Define Internal Sketch) from the mini toolbar.

10. Select the bend surface as the sketching plane, as shown in Figure 5–50.

11. Select the hidden surface of the bend surface shown in Figure 5–50 as the **Bottom** orientation plane. Remember that these references are selected when placing the UDF and it is important that you do not select unnecessary references.

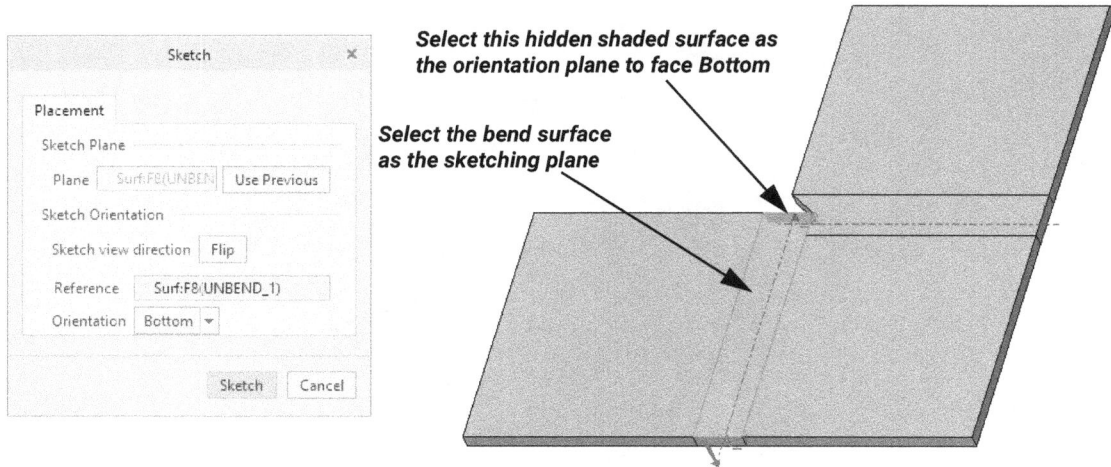

Figure 5–50

12. Click **Sketch**.

13. Click ⬚ (References) in the *Sketch* tab.

14. Remove the selected references and select the three sketching references shown in Figure 5–51: the vertex and the two bend axes. Ensure that only these three are selected and close the References dialog box.

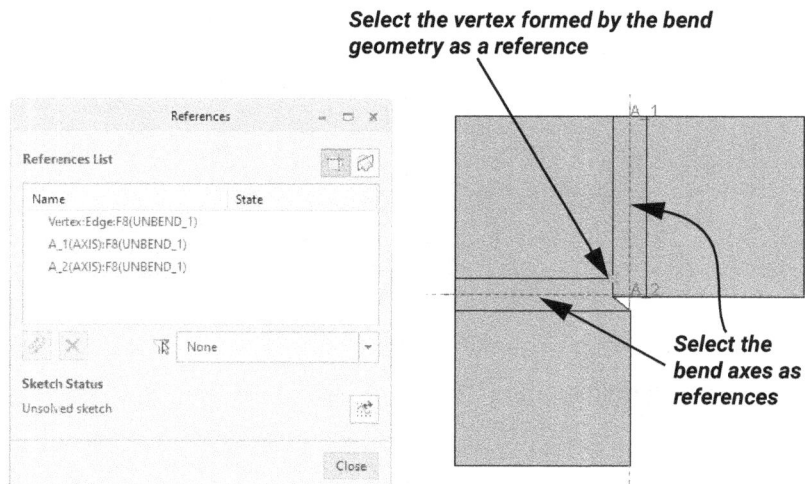

Figure 5–51

15. Click **Close**.

16. Create two centerlines to be used for symmetry in the sketch. The centerlines should be created on top of both the horizontal and vertical bend axes.

17. Click ⟁ (Coordinate System) in the Sketching group in the *Sketch* tab and select the intersection of the two sketched centerlines.

18. Sketch the rectangle as shown in Figure 5–52. DO NOT add constraints to align the entities to the edges of the existing geometry. The symmetry constraint enables you to capture the intent. Dimensions are not required for this section.

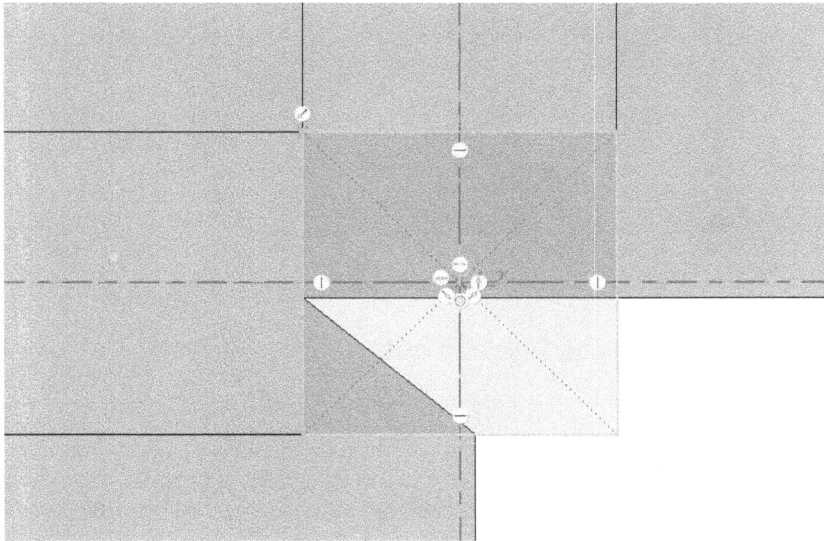

Figure 5–52

Note: *You could also use* ▢ *(Centered Rectangle) instead of using centerlines and the symmetry constraint.*

19. Complete the sketch. To remove material from the inside of the sketch, ensure that the purple arrow points toward the interior of the model. If required, click on the arrow to flip its direction.

20. Click ⊒ ⊑ (Through All) for the **depth** option.

21. Click ✔ (OK) in the *Extruded Cut* dashboard. The part displays in the default view, as shown in Figure 5–53.

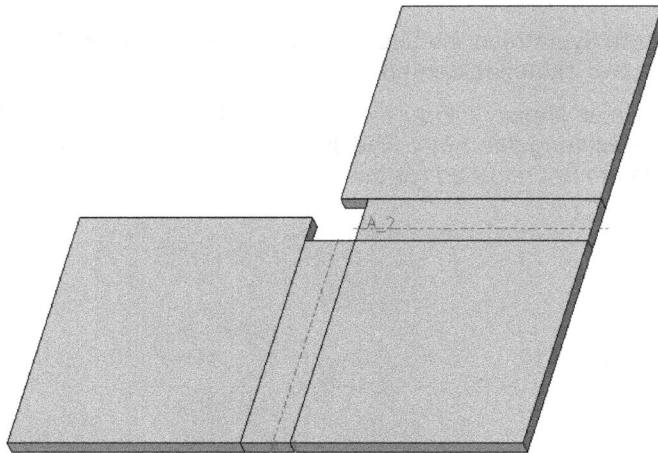

Figure 5–53

Task 2: Define a UDF from the finished cut.

Design Considerations

In this task, you will create a notch UDF feature using the cut you created as a reference. UDFs enable the geometry to be created once and then reused as required on other models.

1. Select the *Tools* tab and click 🔧 (UDF Library)**>Create**.

2. Enter **corner_notch** as the name.

3. Select **Stand Alone>Done**.

4. Click **Yes** in the dialog box to include the reference part.

5. When prompted to select features to add to the UDF, select the square cut (**Extruded Cut 1**) you just created.

6. Select **Done>Done/Return**.

7. Click **Yes** in the dialog box to indicate that you are creating this UDF to define a notch.

8. Set the tool *Name* to **corner**.

9. Select **Both** when prompted for symmetry.

10. Specify prompts for the references shown in Figure 5–54. Verify that the correct entity is highlighted on screen before entering the prompt.

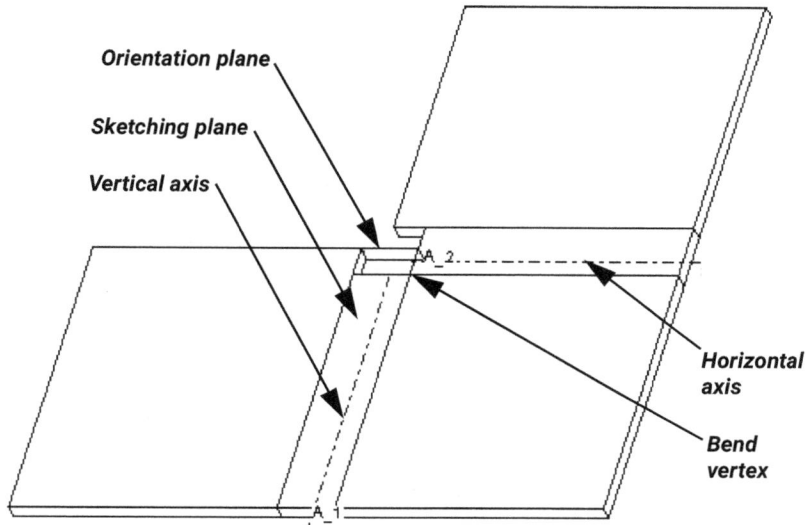

Figure 5–54

11. Select **Done/Return** and click **OK** in the UDF dialog box.

12. Select **Done/Return**.

13. Save the part.

Task 3: Create a notch feature using this UDF on another part.

Design Considerations

In this task, you will create a notch feature by placing the UDF you created in Task 2 on another part. This technique enables you to create the requested geometry easily and quickly.

1. Open **corner_relief.prt** and return the model to the default view.

2. Create an unbend feature so that the part displays as shown in Figure 5–55.

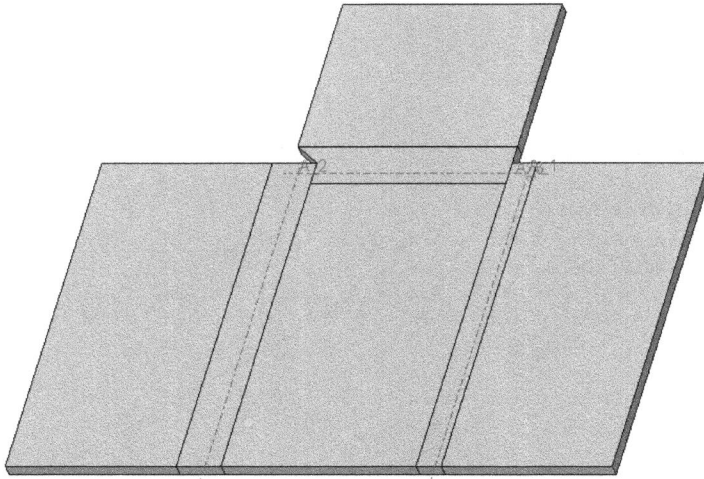

Figure 5–55

3. Select **Engineering>Notch** in the *Sheetmetal* tab to create a notch feature.

4. Select **corner_notch.gph** and click **Open**. The Insert User-Defined Feature dialog box opens as shown in Figure 5–56.

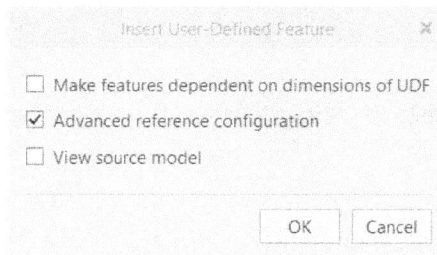

Figure 5–56

Note: The sub-window containing the reference part might open behind the main window.

5. Enable **View source model**.

6. Click **OK**.

7. The User Defined Feature Placement dialog box opens, as shown in Figure 5–57.

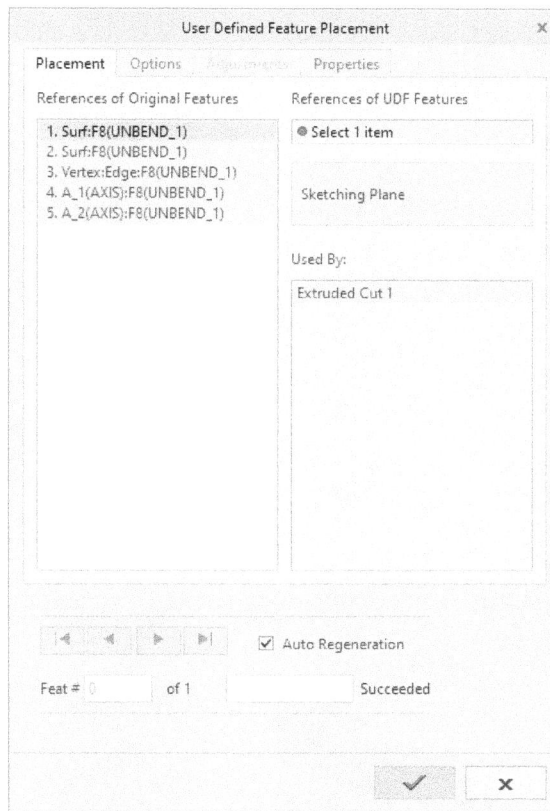

Figure 5–57

Note: If required, move the window containing the reference part so that you can see the prompts in the message window.

8. Select the corresponding references to those highlighted on the reference part as shown in Figure 5−58.

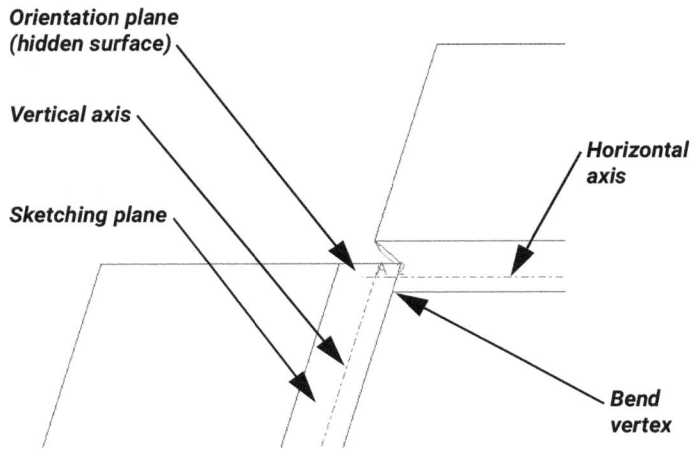

Figure 5−58

9. Click ✓ (OK) to complete the placement.

10. Create a bend back feature to restore the model to the bent condition. The part displays as shown in Figure 5−59.

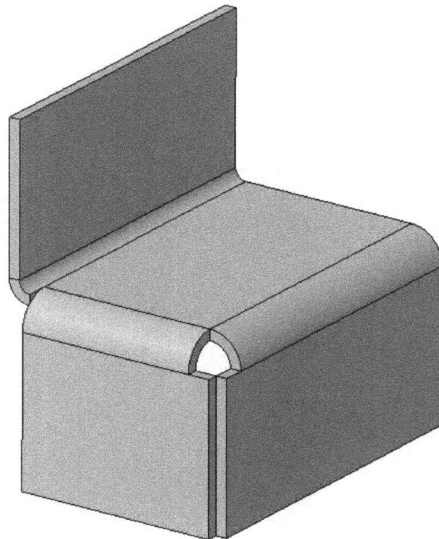

Figure 5−59

11. Save the part and erase it from memory.

End of practice

Practice 5c
Create a Punch Feature

Practice Objective

- Create a punch feature.

In this practice, you will use the punch UDF to create the punch feature shown in Figure 5–60.

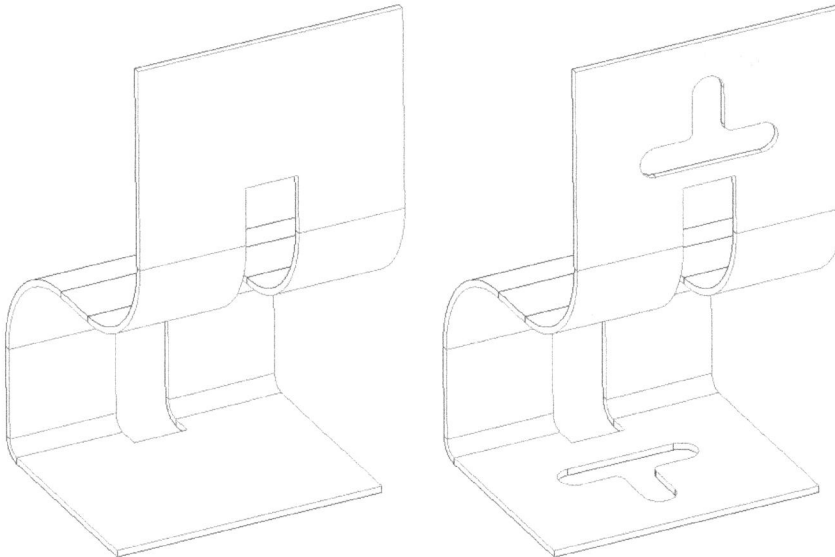

Figure 5–60

Task 1: Open a part and create two punch features.

Design Considerations

Punches are specific closed-profile shapes that remove material. Using punches in conjunction with UDFs enables you to create the requested geometry easily and quickly on multiple models. The process of creating and placing punches is similar to the process of creating and placing notches. You can create a number of punch UDF features, place them in a library, and reuse them on different models. For the purpose of this practice, the punch UDF feature is already created and placed in the common library. In this task, you will use this UDF to remove material on your part.

1. Set the working directory to the *Punch_Feature* folder.

2. Open **punch.prt**.

3. Set the model display as follows:

- *(Datum Display Filters)*: None
- *(Spin Center)*: Off
- *(Display Style)*: (No Hidden)

4. Examine how the model was created. You are going to add a punch to the upper and lower portions of this part.

5. Select **Engineering>Punch** in the *Sheetmetal* tab.

6. Select **t_punch.gph** in the working directory and click **Open**. The Insert User-Defined dialog box opens.

7. Select **View source model**.

8. Click **OK**. The User Defined Feature Placement dialog box opens, as shown in Figure 5−61.

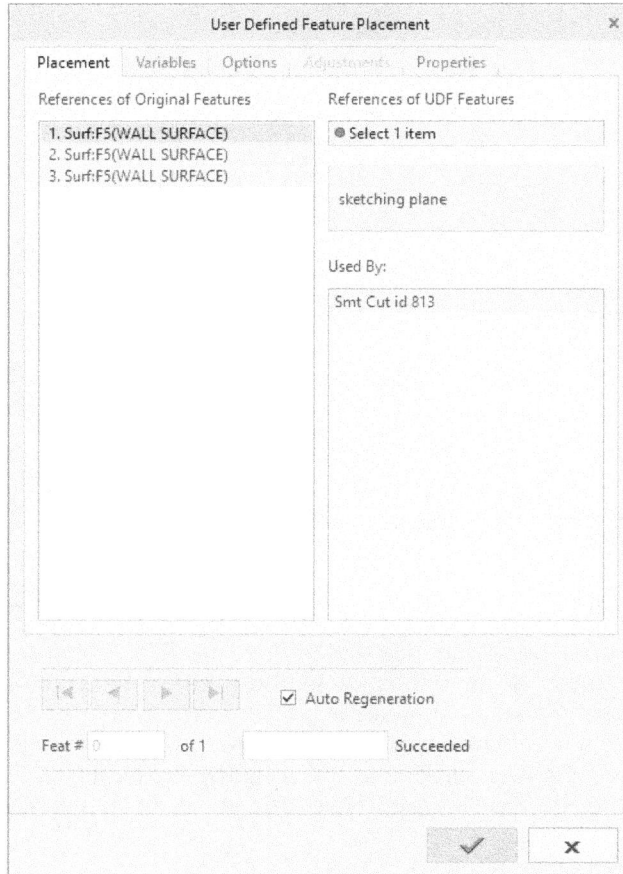

Figure 5−61

9. Select the corresponding references to those highlighted on the reference part, as shown in Figure 5–62.

   • Depending on the design intent, you can select a different option for the display of non-variable dimensions.

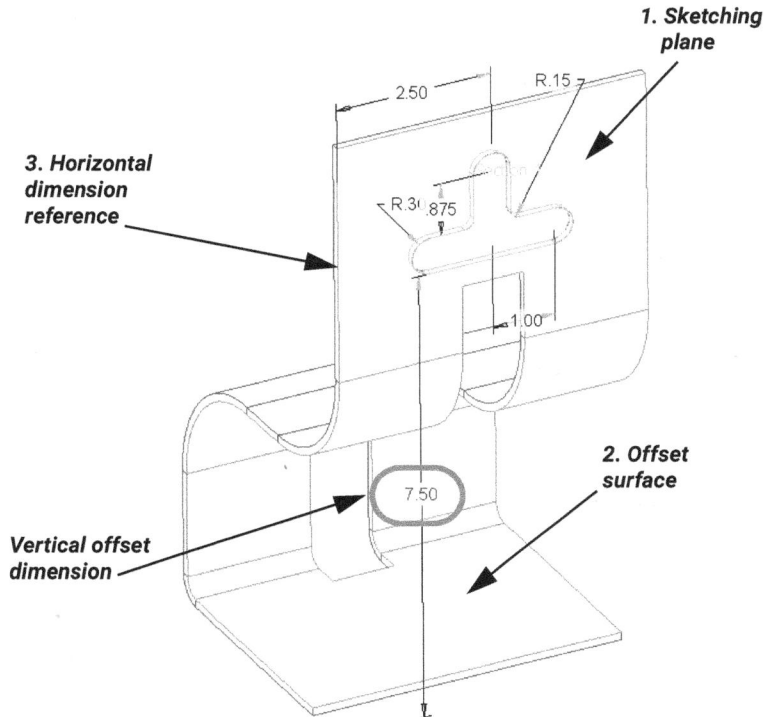

Figure 5–62

10. Select the *Variables* tab and specify a value for the vertical offset dimension (d31). This dimension locates the cut with respect to one of the reference surfaces, and can vary from model to model. When the punch UDF was created, the dimension was designated variable. Enter **7.5**.

11. Click ✓ (OK) to complete the placement of the punch UDF.

12. Place an additional punch so that the finished part displays as shown in Figure 5–63. The vertical offset dimension is **1.5** this time.

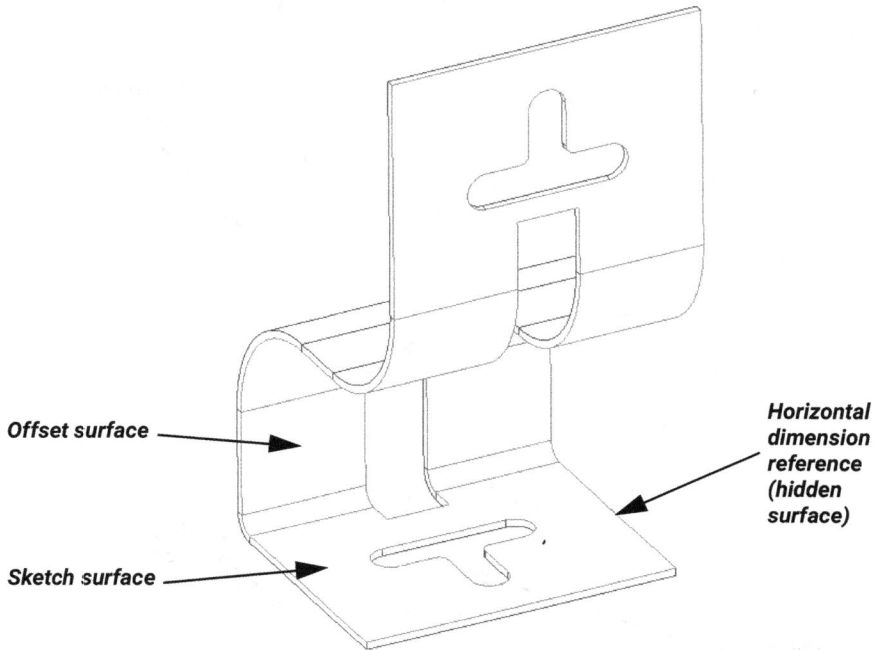

Offset surface

Horizontal dimension reference (hidden surface)

Sketch surface

Figure 5–63

13. Save the part and erase it from memory.

End of practice

Practice 5d
Create a Notch for Bend Relief II

Practice Objective

* Create and place a notch UDF.

In this practice, you will create a notch UDF and use it to create a bend relief on another part, as shown in Figure 5-64.

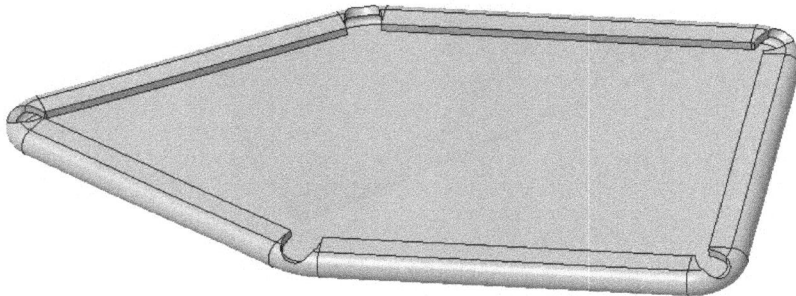

Figure 5-64

Note: Minimize the number of references established during the creation of the cut on the reference part. If the UDF is too complicated to place, this method loses efficiency.

Task 1: Open the reference part and create a cut.

Design Considerations

Notch features are often used for bend relief at corners, because obround and rectangular relief cannot cross the bend geometry of another wall. In this task, you will create a sheet metal cut feature that is going to be used for the definition of the notch UDF.

1. Set the working directory to the *Notch_Relief_II* folder.
2. Open **iron_gp.prt**.
3. Set the model display as follows:

   * *(Datum Display Filters)*: None

   * *(Spin Center)*: Off

   * *(Display Style)*: ☐ (Shading With Edges)

4. Click ▵ (Unbend) in the *Sheetmetal* tab.

5. Maintain the default fixed surface.

6. Click ✔ (OK) to complete the feature. The unbent reference part displays as shown in Figure 5−65.

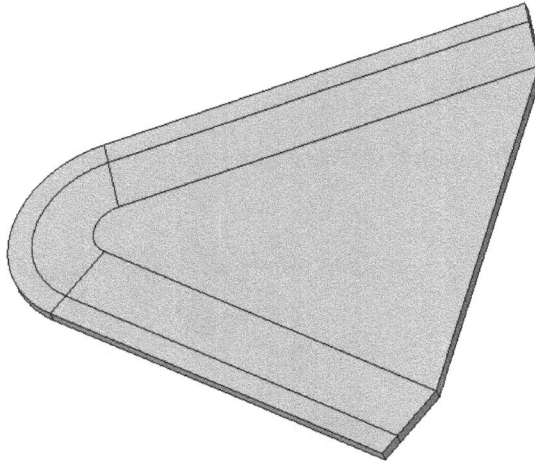

Figure 5−65

7. Click ▱ (Extruded Cut) in the *Sheetmetal* tab.

8. Click in the graphics area and select ✎ (Define Internal Sketch) from the mini toolbar.

9. Select the fixed surface as the sketching plane, as shown in Figure 5−66.

10. Select the hidden surface of the bend, as shown in Figure 5−66, as the **Top** orientation plane. Note that these references are selected when placing the UDF and it is important that you do not select unnecessary references.

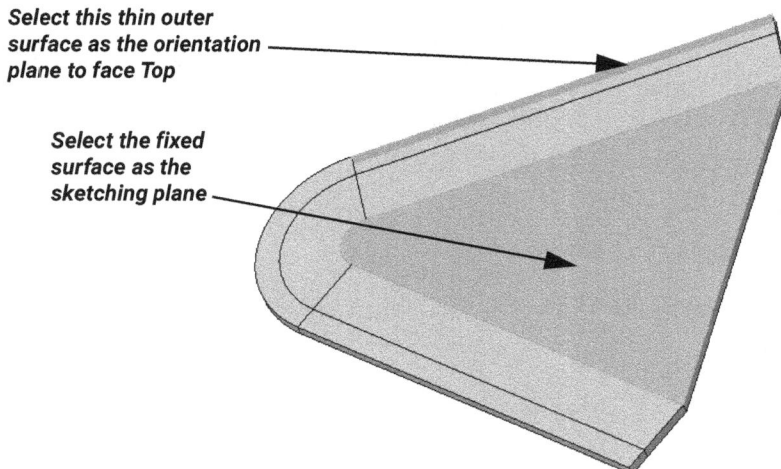

Select this thin outer surface as the orientation plane to face Top

Select the fixed surface as the sketching plane

Figure 5−66

11. Select the three sketching references shown in Figure 5–67. Ensure that only these three are selected and close the References dialog box.

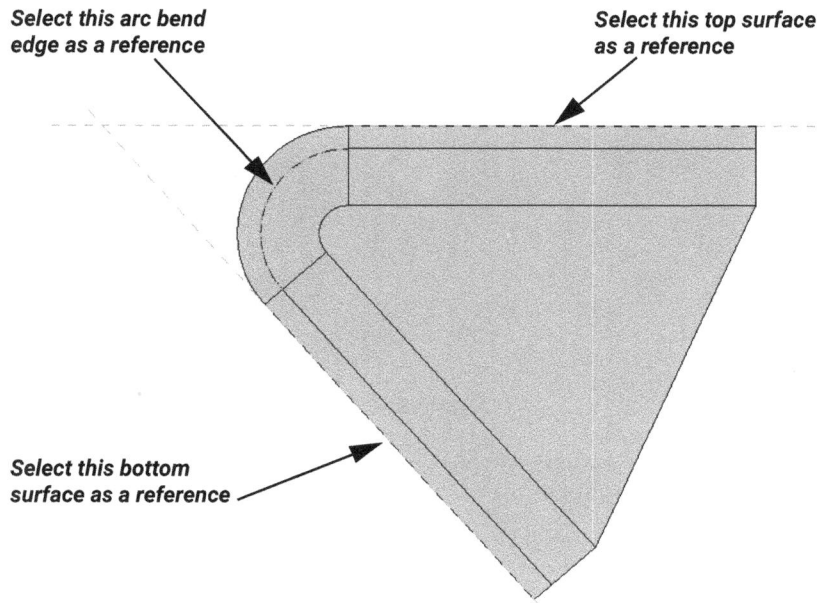

Select this arc bend edge as a reference

Select this top surface as a reference

Select this bottom surface as a reference

Figure 5–67

12. Sketch a construction circle to be used for offset dimensioning in the sketch. Create the center of the circle at the intersection of the top and bottom edges and make the circle tangent to the arc bend edge, as shown in Figure 5–68.

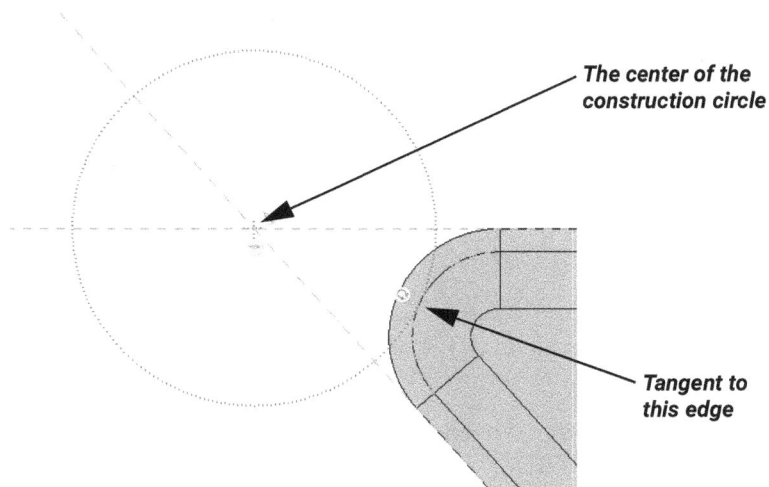

The center of the construction circle

Tangent to this edge

Figure 5–68

13. Sketch a concentric offset circle as shown in Figure 5–69. Set the value to **0.05**.

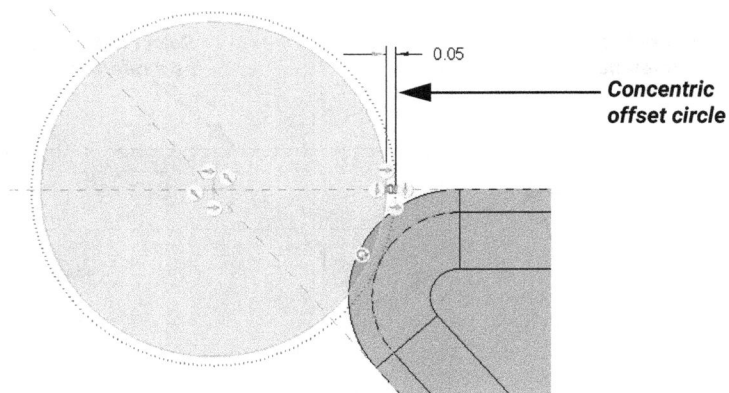

0.05

Concentric
offset circle

Figure 5–69

14. Click ⌖ (Coordinate System) in the Sketching group of the *Sketch* tab and select the center of the two circles, as shown in Figure 5–70.

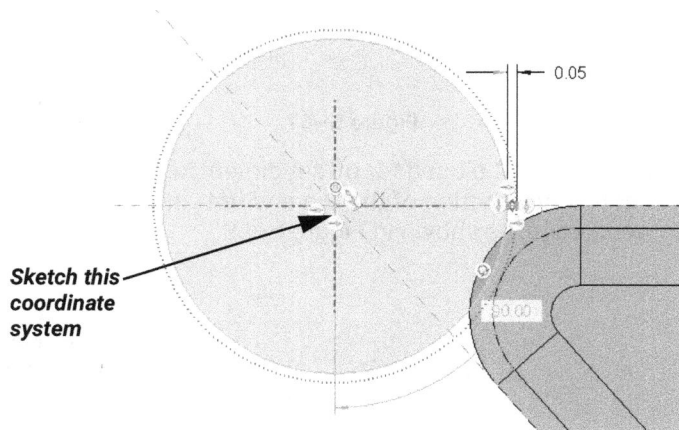

0.05

Sketch this
coordinate
system

90.00

Figure 5–70

Note: You might have to set the Y-axis to ⊥ *(Vertical) if an angular dimension displays.*

15. Complete the sketch. Verify that the arrow points toward the interior of the model, so that material is removed from the inside of the sketch. If required, click on the arrow to flip its direction.

16. Click ⊒⊟ (Through All) to specify the **depth** option.

17. Click ✔ (OK) in the *Extruded Cut* dashboard. The part displays in the default view, as shown in Figure 5–71.

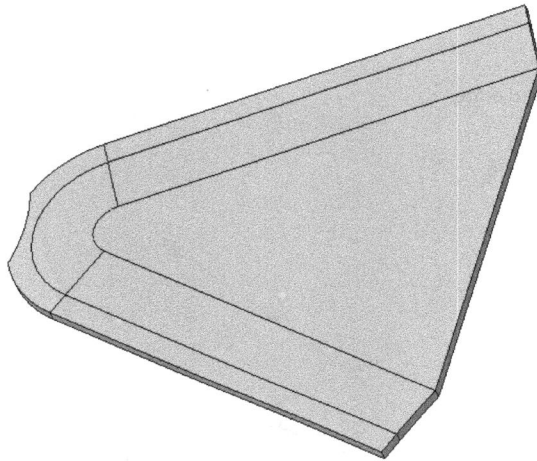

Figure 5–71

Task 2: Define a UDF from the finished cut.

Design Considerations

In this task, you will create a notch UDF feature using the cut you created as a reference. UDFs enable the geometry to be created once and then reused as required on other models.

1. Select the *Tools* tab and click 🗋 (UDF Library).

2. Select **Create** and enter **iron_corner_notch** as the name.

3. Select **Stand Alone>Done**.

4. Click **Yes** in the dialog box to include the reference part.

5. When prompted to select features to add to the UDF, select the **Extruded Cut** that you just created.

6. Select **Done>Done/Return**.

7. Click **Yes** in the dialog box to indicate that you are creating this UDF to define a notch.

8. Set the tool *Name* to **iron_corner**.

9. Select **Both** when prompted for symmetry.

10. Specify prompts for the references shown in Figure 5–72. Verify that the correct entity is highlighted on screen before entering the prompt.

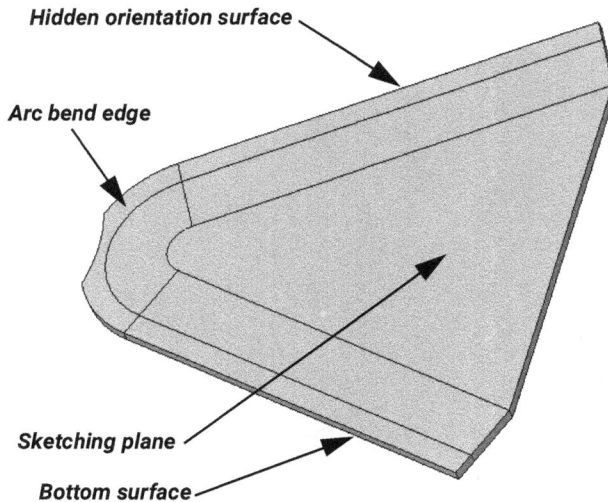

Figure 5–72

Note: The order in which the prompts display might differ depending on how your references were originally selected.

11. Select **Done/Return** and then click **OK** in the UDF dialog box.

12. Select **Done/Return**.

13. Save the part.

Task 3: Create a notch feature using this UDF on another part.

Design Considerations

In this task, you will create a notch feature by placing the UDF you created in Task 2 on another part. This technique enables you to create the requested geometry quickly and easily.

1. Open **iron_desk.prt** and orient the model as shown in Figure 5–73.

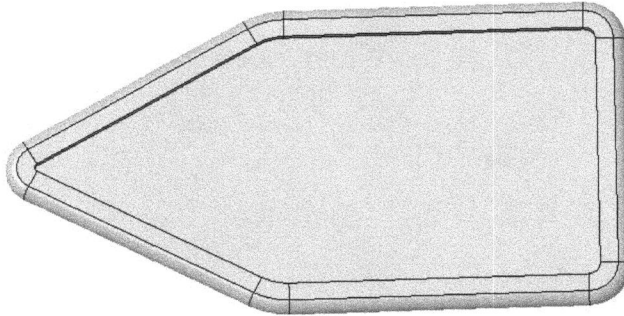

Figure 5–73

2. Create an unbend feature so that the part displays as shown in Figure 5–74.

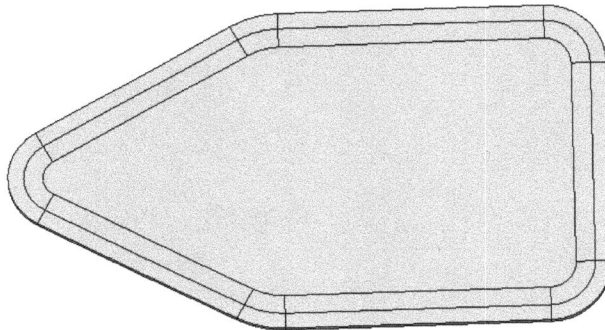

Figure 5–74

3. Select **Engineering>Notch** in the *Sheetmetal* tab to create a notch feature.

4. Select **iron_corner_notch.gph** and click **Open**. The Insert User-Defined Feature dialog box opens, as shown in Figure 5–75.

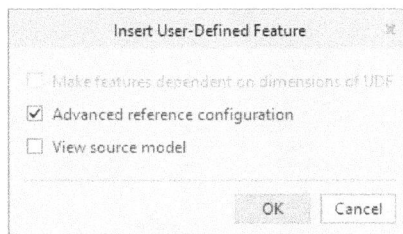

Figure 5–75

Note: The sub-window containing the reference part might open behind the main window.

5.   Select **View source model**.

6.   Click **OK**. The User Defined Feature Placement dialog box opens, as shown in Figure 5–76.

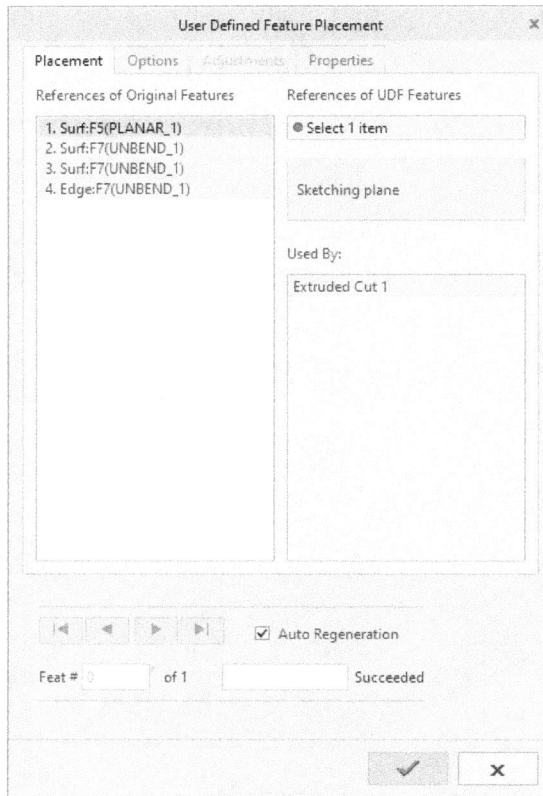

Figure 5–76

7.   The original sketching plane reference highlights on the reference part. Select the new sketching plane reference, as shown in Figure 5–77.

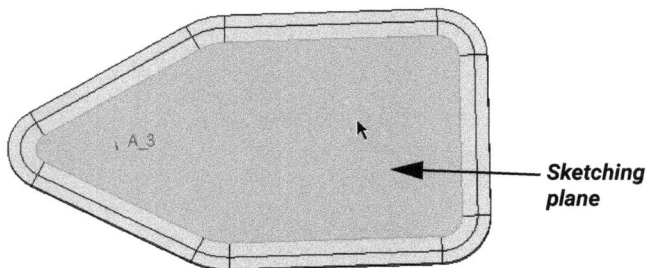

Figure 5–77

Note: If required, move the window containing the reference part so that you can see the prompts in the message window.

8. The second row in the *References of Original Features* area highlights, as shown in Figure 5–78.

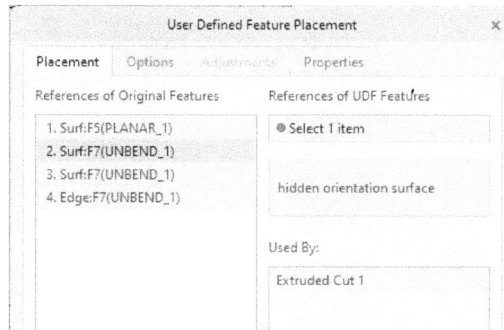

Figure 5–78

9. The original orientation surface reference highlights on the reference part. Select the new orientation surface, as shown in Figure 5–79.

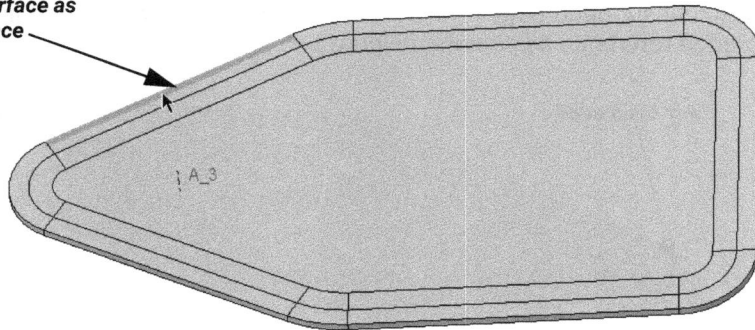

Figure 5–79

10. The third row in the *References of Original Features* area highlights, as shown in Figure 5–80.

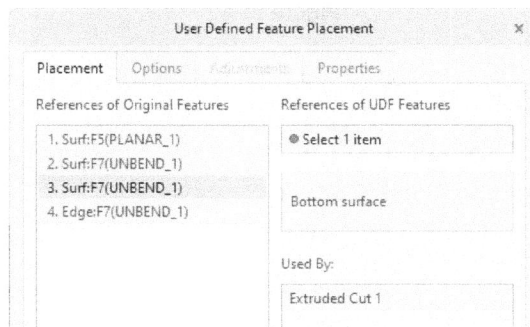

Figure 5–80

11. The original bottom surface reference highlights in the reference part. Select the new bottom surface reference, as shown in Figure 5–81.

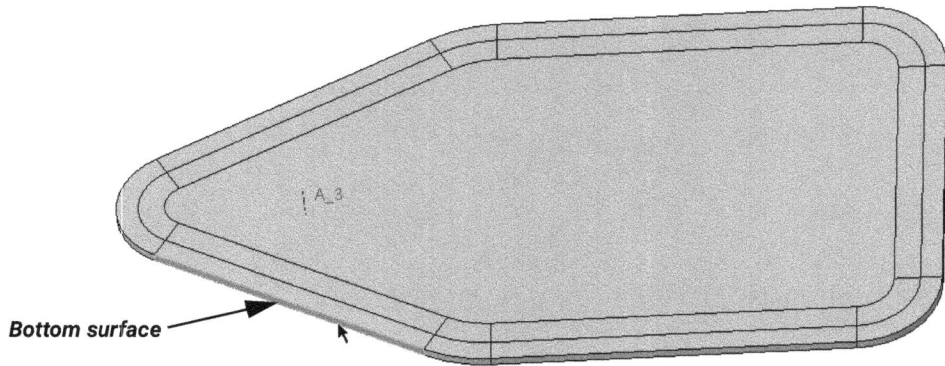

Figure 5–81

12. The fourth row in the *References of Original Features highlights*.

13. The original arc bend edge reference highlights on the reference part. Select the new arc bend edge reference as shown in Figure 5–82.

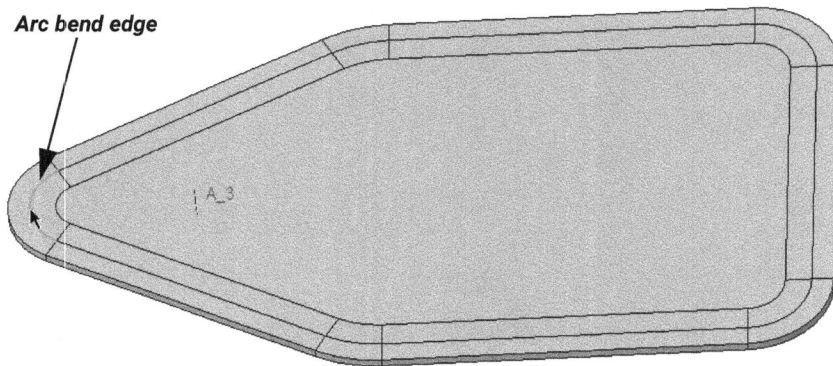

Figure 5–82

14. Click ✔ (OK) to complete the placement. The model displays as shown in Figure 5–83.

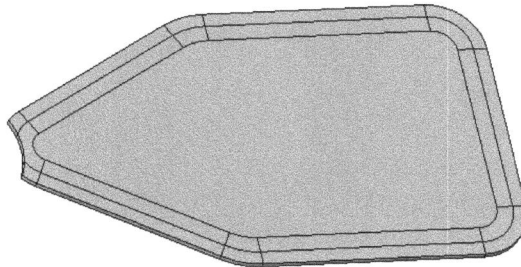

Figure 5–83

Task 4: Place another notch feature.

1. Select **Engineering>Notch** in the *Sheetmetal* tab to create another notch feature.

2. Select **iron_corner_notch.gph** and click **Open**.

3. Select **View source model**.

4. Click **OK**. If required, move the window containing the reference part so that you can see the prompts in the message window.

   Note: The sub-window containing the reference part might open behind the main window.

5. Select the new references as shown in Figure 5–84. Refer to the reference part and User Defined Feature Placement dialog box to help determine the required reference.

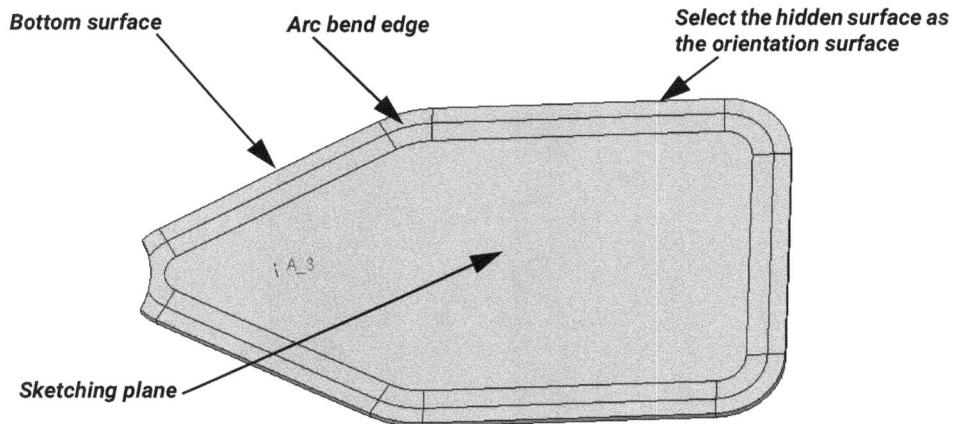

Figure 5–84

6. Click ✔ (OK) and select **Done** to complete the placement. The model displays as shown in Figure 5–85.

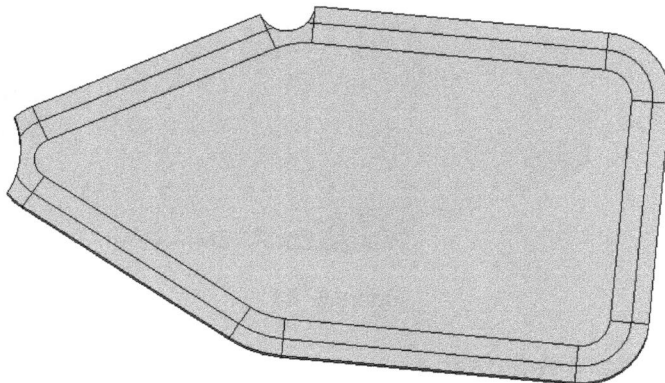

Figure 5–85

Task 5: Create another notch feature.

1. Select **Engineering>Notch** in the *Sheetmetal* tab to create another notch feature.

2. Select **iron_corner_notch.gph** and click **Open**.

3. Select **View source model**.

4. Click **OK** and the User Defined Feature Placement dialog box opens.

   Note: The sub-window containing the reference part might open behind the main window. If required, move the window containing the reference part so that you can see the prompts in the message window.

5. Select the new references as shown in Figure 5–86. Refer to the reference part and the User Defined Feature Placement dialog box to help determine the required reference.

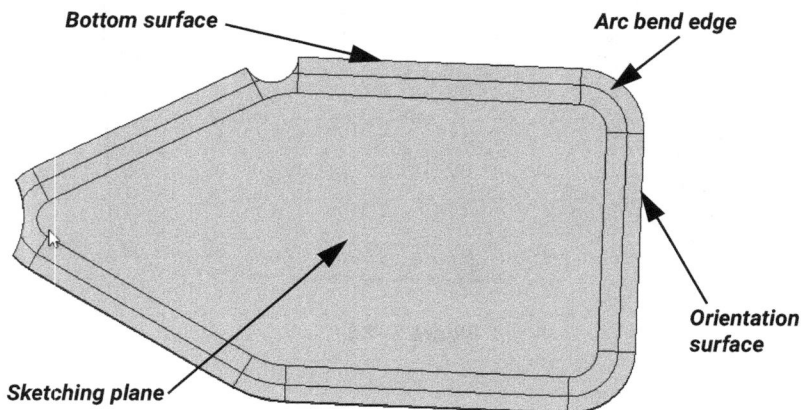

Figure 5–86

6. Click ✔ (OK) and select **Done** to complete the placement. The model displays as shown in Figure 5−87.

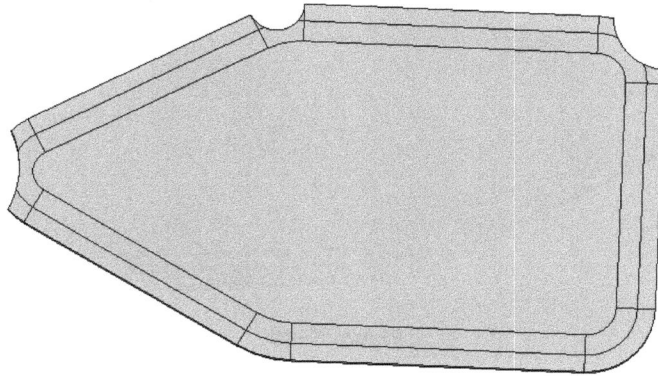

Figure 5−87

Task 6: Mirror the UDFs.

1. Select both groups to mirror, as shown in Figure 5−88.

2. Select ⬙⬘ (Mirror) in the mini toolbar.

3. Select datum plane **FRONT** as the mirror plane, as shown in Figure 5−88.

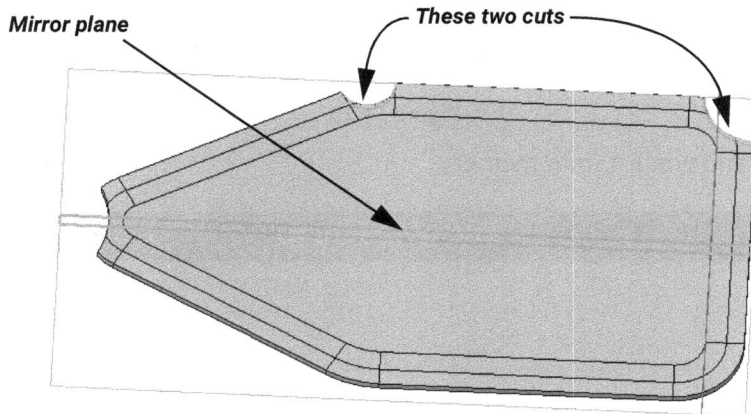

Figure 5−88

4. Click ✓ (OK) to the complete mirror. The model displays as shown in Figure 5–89.

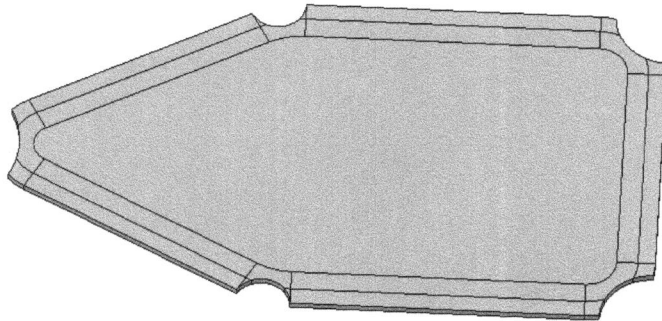

Figure 5–89

5. Create a bend back feature to restore the model to the bent condition. The model displays as shown in Figure 5–90.

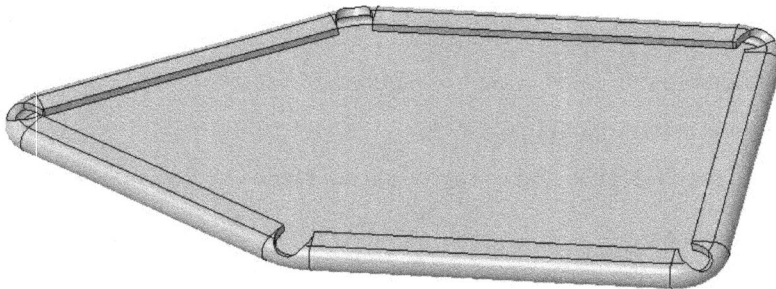

Figure 5–90

6. Save the part and erase it from memory.

End of practice

Chapter Review Questions

1. Subordinate UDFs automatically generate a reference model.

    a. True

    b. False

2. Which of the following is not an optional element in the UDF dialog box?

    a. Var Dims

    b. Feat Name

    c. Units

    d. Var Elements

3. Corner relief is used to prevent unwanted deformations. Which of the following methods can be used to create a corner relief? (Select all that apply.)

    a. Define the corner relief as a feature.

    b. Define the corner relief as part of a flange feature.

    c. Create a default corner relief automatically while unbending by selecting File>Prepare>Model Properties. Select change next to *Relief*.

    d. Define the corner relief in the conversion feature when converting a solid part into a sheet metal part.

    e. To apply a corner relief you must have at least one ripped edge in the model.

4. What features are generally created in a sheet metal model using sheet metal cuts and user-defined features (UDFs) to create geometry? (Select all that apply.)

    a. Notch

    b. Punch

    c. Flat walls

    d. Flange walls

5. Which of the following features are often used for bend relief at corners?

    a. Notch

    b. Punch

6. Which of the following features tend to be closed-profile shapes that remove material?

    a. Notch

    b. Punch

Bend Features

Although bends can be created in the context of sketched walls, you can also work in the flat state and add bends, as required, by using bend features. To create the appropriate geometry, you may also have to add relief where bends occur.

Learning Objectives

- Learn the three types of bend features and how they are used in a sheet metal part.
- Understand how to use the **Transition** and **Bend** relief options when creating a bend feature.
- Learn to create a bend feature by specifying or sketching a bend line using the appropriate references.
- Define the direction and bend angle in the *Bend* dashboard.
- Understand how the position of the bend line and the direction can result in different geometry.
- Learn how to adjust the bend line position to meet the design intent using relations.
- Understand the bend line notes, how to display them on the sheet metal model, and how they can be oriented.
- Consider the best practice statements for creating bend features in a sheet metal part.

6.1 Bend Features

Three types of bend features are available in Creo Parametric and are as follows: Bend, Edge Bend, and Planar Bend.

Bend

The Bend feature adds bend geometry to the flat area of a wall on a sheet metal part. The feature consists of a line on the flat face of a wall that is dimensioned for the required placement. You can create two types of bends: ⋈ (Angle Bend) and ⌒ (Rolled Bend). Figure 6−1 shows a bend line sketch on the top and the resulting **Angle** or **Rolled** bend on the bottom.

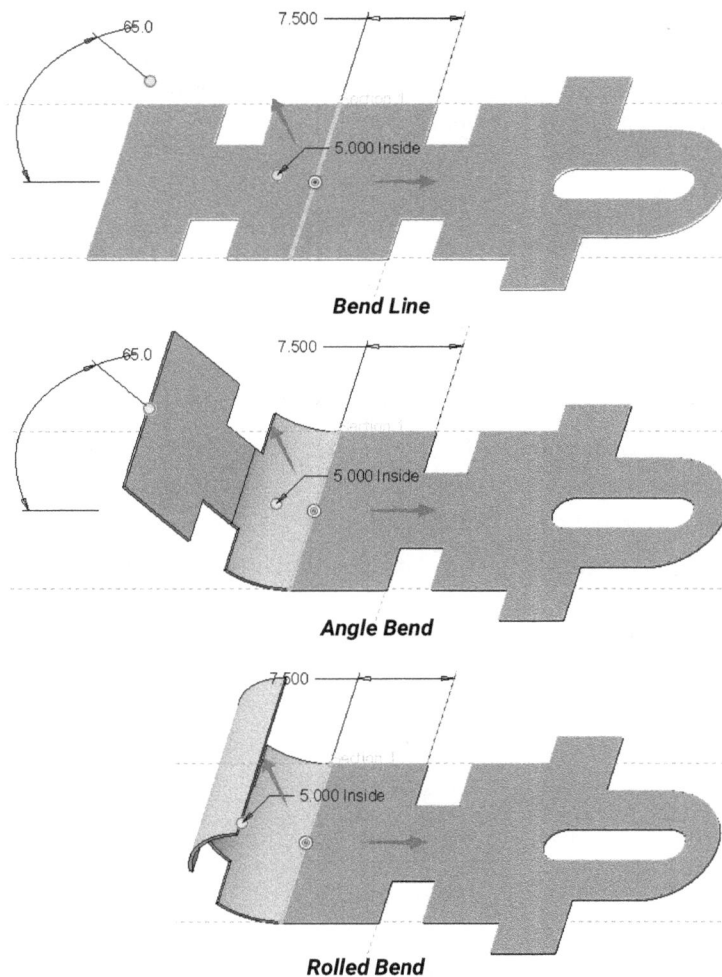

Bend Line

Angle Bend

Rolled Bend

Figure 6−1

Note: Click ⋈ (Bend) in the Sheetmetal tab.

Angle

Angle bends bend the material adjacent to a sketched bend line through a specified radius and angle. The angle refers to the angle at which the wall segment travels as it is bent. Figure 6-2 shows a bend line in the top image and the resulting bend in the bottom image.

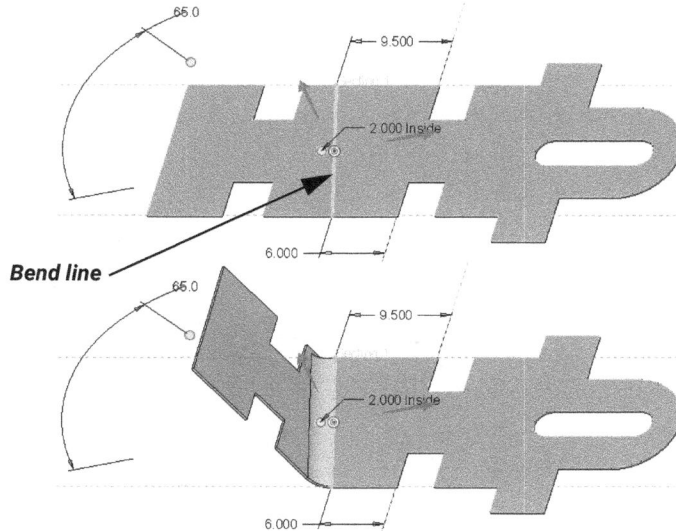

Figure 6-2

Rolled

Rolled bends bend the material adjacent to the sketched bend line through a specified radius. The included angle of the bend is defined by the amount of material available to bend. Figure 6-3 shows a bend line sketch on the left and the resulting bend on the right. Material on both sides of the bend line has been bent.

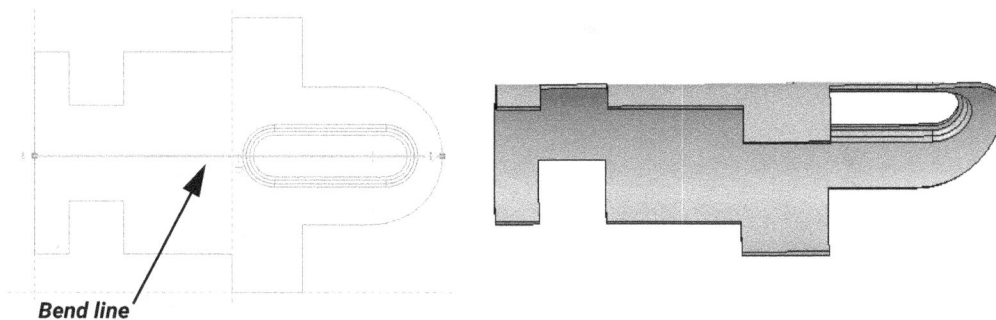

Figure 6-3

Edge Bend

The Edge Bend feature is used to bend sharp corners. You can create the edge bend similar to the round feature when creating a solid model. Multiple edges and multiple sets can be added to the create the bends, as shown in Figure 6-4.

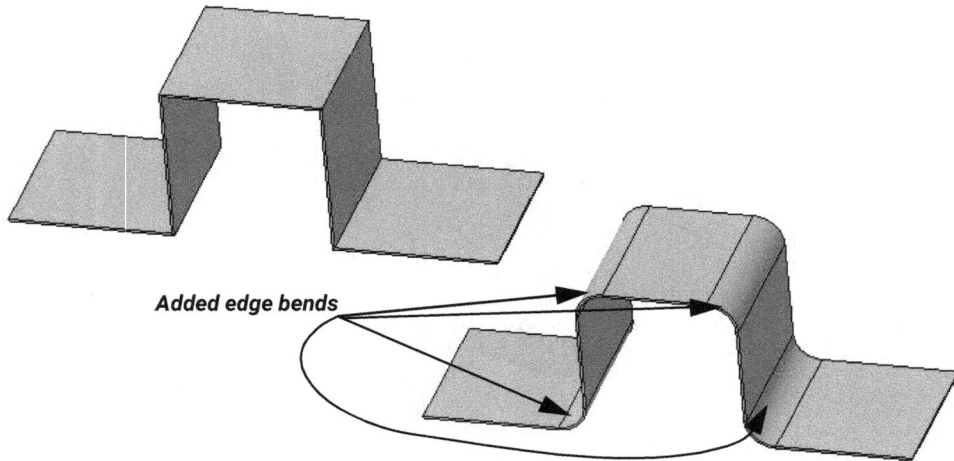

Added edge bends

Figure 6-4

Note: *Expand* ※ *(Bend) and select* ⌐ *(Edge Bend) in the Sheetmetal tab.*

Relief can be added to edge bend features, as shown in Figure 6-5.

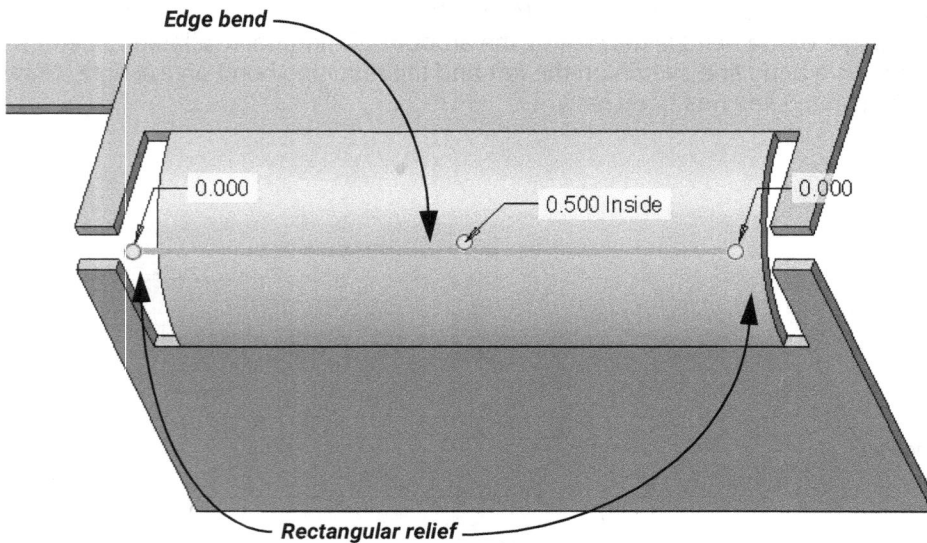

Edge bend

0.000

0.500 Inside

0.000

Rectangular relief

Figure 6-5

To create an edge bend, click ⌐ (Edge Bend) and select an edge. In the Relief panel, you can select relief types such as **No Relief**, **Rip**, **Stretch**, **Rectangular**, or **Obround**, as shown in Figure 6–6.

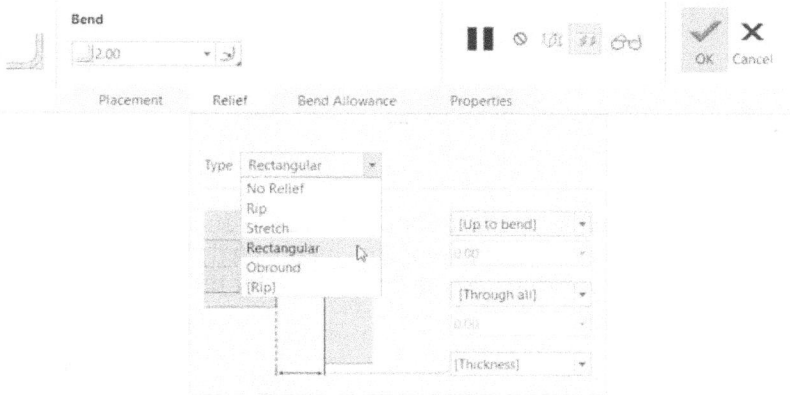

Figure 6–6

Planar Bend

A Planar Bend feature bends the material around an axis that is perpendicular to the wall. They are sketched features that consist of a sketched line on the flat surface that is dimensioned for the required placement. You can create two types of bends: **Angle** and **Rolled**. Figure 6–7 shows a planar angular bend.

*   In the *Sheetmetal* tab, expand 🌿 (Bend) and select 🍃 (Planar Bend).

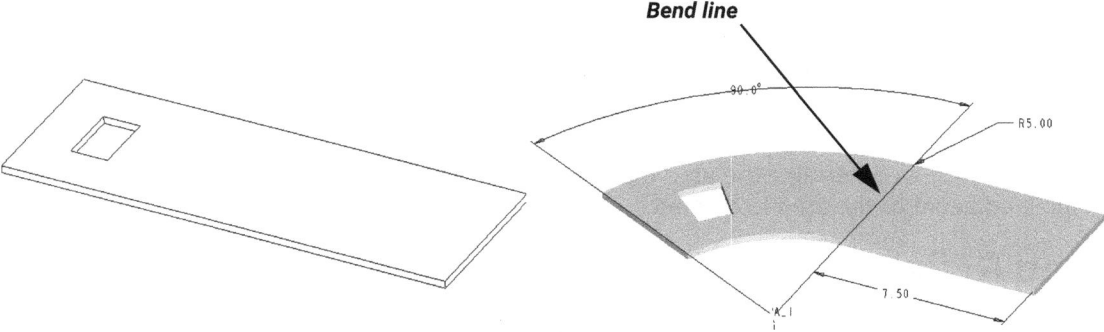

Figure 6–7

6.2 Creating a Bend Feature

When creating a bend feature, the following additional options are available to help control the bend:

- Transition

- Relief

Transition

Adding a transition in the Transition panel defines an area to accommodate any deformation from the bent area to a flat area. Once the bend line has been defined, you can add a transition and open the *Sketch* tab to start sketching the boundaries for the transition area, as shown in Figure 6–8.

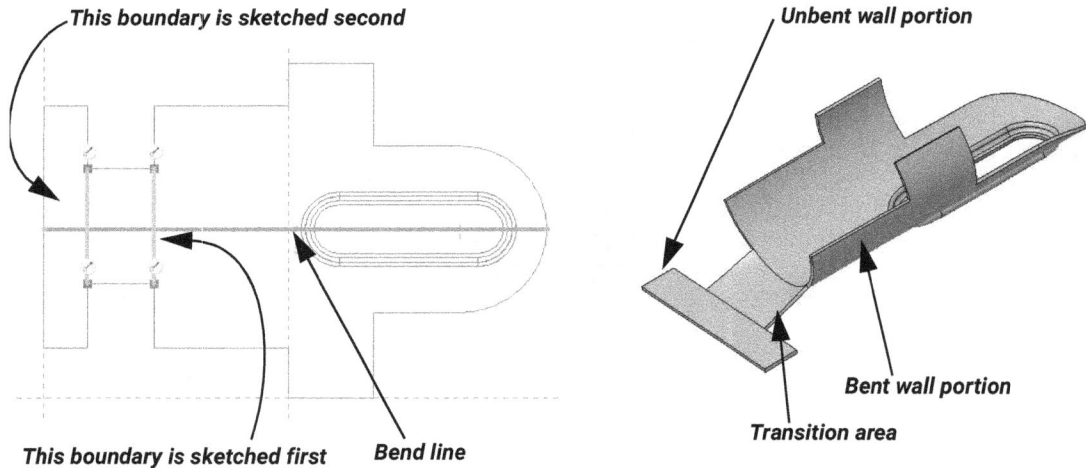

This boundary is sketched second

Unbent wall portion

This boundary is sketched first *Bend line*

Bent wall portion

Transition area

Figure 6–8

The sketched lines determine the area that transitions from bent to flat (unbent). Sketch the first line adjacent to the area to be bent.

Bend Relief

You might need to add a bend relief when bending a part. The *Relief* dashboard creates a bend relief at the end points of a bend feature. Select the required relief option after you have defined the bend line (**No Relief**, **Stretch**, **Rip**, **Rectangular**, and **Obround**). Figure 6–9 shows a bend feature with obround relief applied.

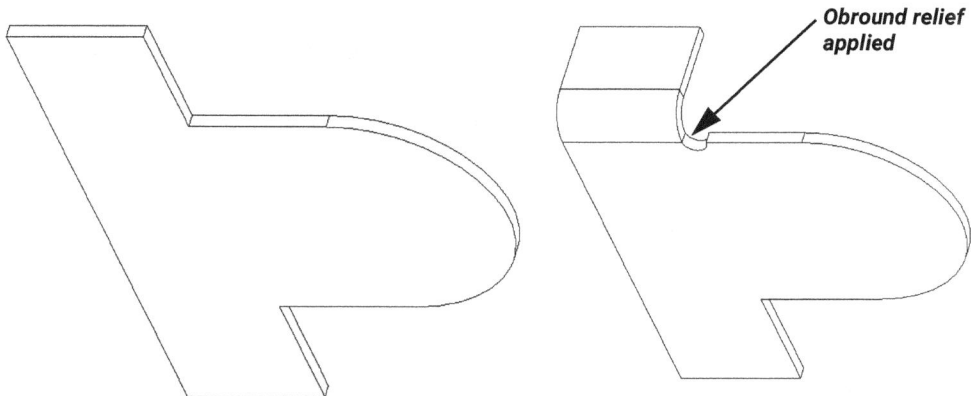

Obround relief
applied

Figure 6–9

How To: Create a Bend Feature

1. Select the surface to bend and click ⚒ (Bend) in the mini toolbar. The *Bend* dashboard opens as shown in Figure 6–10.

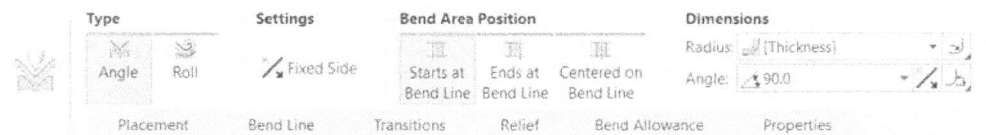

Figure 6–10

2. Specify the type of bend in the *Bend* dashboard, as shown in Figure 6–11. There are two general types of bends. Click ⚒ (Angle Bend) or ⚒ (Rolled Bend).

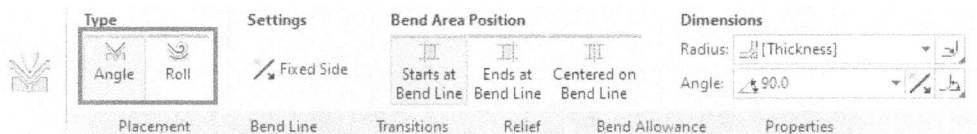

Figure 6–11

*Note: You can also right-click and select **Angle Bend** or **Rolled Bend**.*

3. Drag the handles of the bend line to the appropriate references, or click and select 🖉 (Define/Edit Internal Bend Line) in the mini toolbar.

   Creo Parametric uses the bend line as a reference for calculating the developed length when creating bend geometry. The bend line must reach from one edge of the sheet metal part to the other.

4. Define additional options (such as bend placement, transitions, reliefs, etc.), if required.

5. Specify the side of the bend line on which to create the bend feature and the side of the bend line that is to remain fixed, as shown in Figure 6-12.

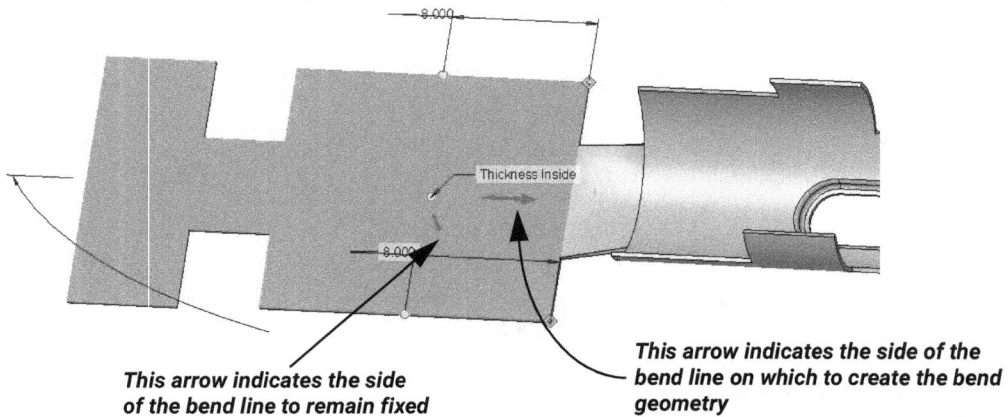

This arrow indicates the side
of the bend line to remain fixed

This arrow indicates the side of the
bend line on which to create the bend
geometry

Figure 6-12

6. Click ✎ (Change Fixed Side) or ✎ (Change Bending Direction), as shown in Figure 6-13, or select on the arrow to flip the direction.

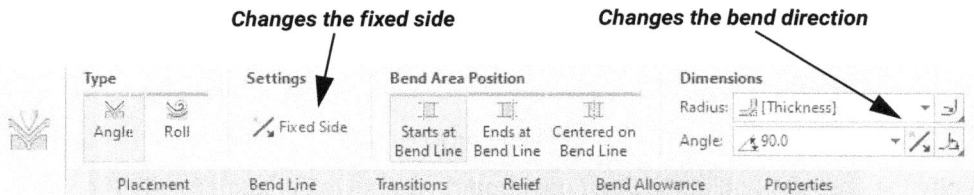

Changes the fixed side

Changes the bend direction

Figure 6-13

Note: Alternatively, right-click to flip the fixed area or bend direction.

7. Specify the bend angle and radius in the *Bend* dashboard, as shown in Figure 6-14. Several default values are available or you can enter a value.

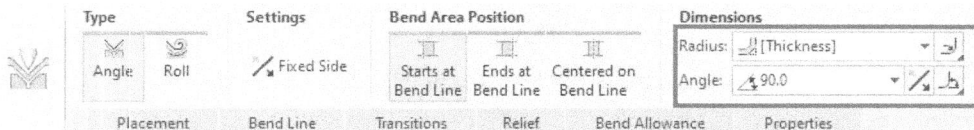

Figure 6-14

8. Click ✔ (OK) in the *Bend* dashboard. The completed feature is shown in Figure 6–15.

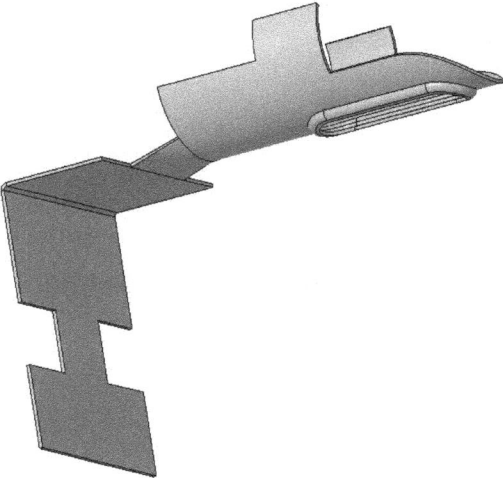

Figure 6–15

Bend Line

The bend line can consist of an edge or curve. When a bend line is selected, the offset option becomes available to offset from the existing curve or edge, as shown in Figure 6–16.

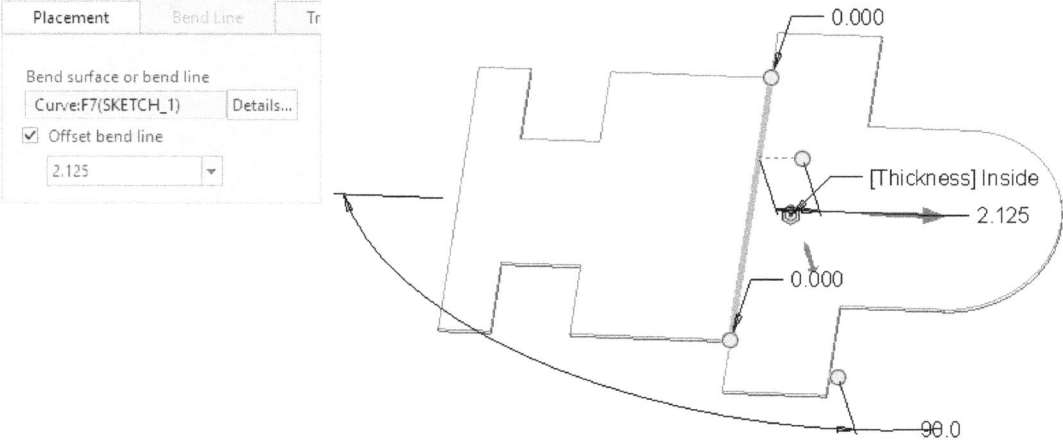

Figure 6–16

Bend Surface

Once a surface is selected, the *Bend Line* dashboard becomes available to create a bend line by sketching or by specifying references.

Bend Line References

Select the *Bend line end 1 Reference* collector and select an edge, surface, or vertex. Select the *Offset* reference collector to locate the bend line end 1 reference, as shown in Figure 6–17. Alternatively, you can also specify the references by using the drag handles.

- You can also right-click and select **Bend Line End 1 Placement** or **Bend Line End 2 Placement**.

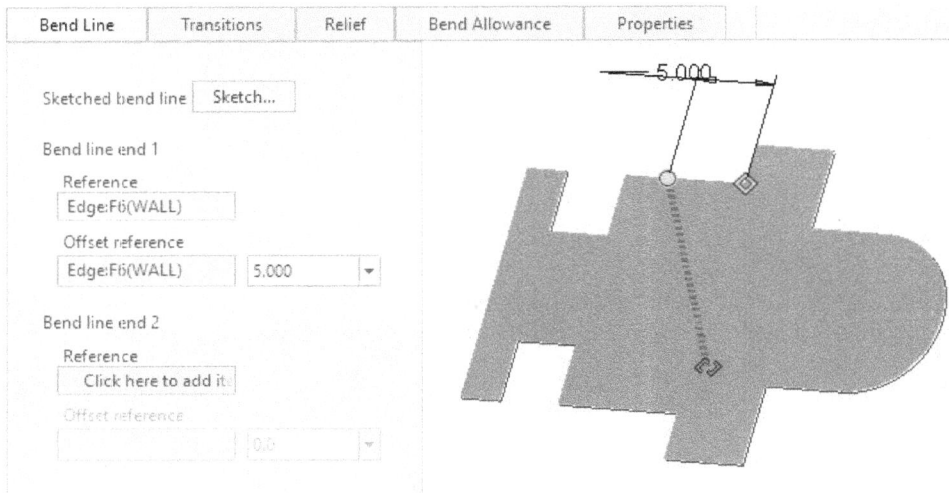

Figure 6–17

- Select or use the drag handles to locate the **Bend line end 2** references. This locates one end of the bend line.

Sketched Bend Line

Sketching a bend line enables you to create dimensions and constraints to locate the bend line. To specify a user defined bend line, click **Sketch** in the Bend Line panel or click on the screen and select ✎ (Define/Edit Internal Bend Line) from the mini toolbar. Define the sketching and orientation planes to open the *Sketch* tab and create the bend line, as shown in Figure 6–18.

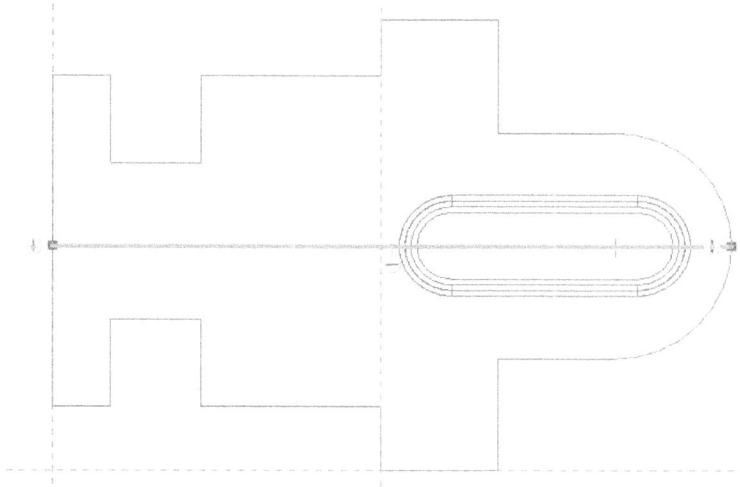

Figure 6–18

Bend Placement

Three bend placement options are available in the *Bend* dashboard or mini toolbar and are described as follows:

Option	Description
⫿	The bend area starts at the bend line.
⫿	The bend area ends at the bend line.
⫿	The bend line is in the middle of the bend area.

Transitions

Click **Transitions** and sketch a transitional area for the bend, as shown in Figure 6–19. Verify that the first line sketched is adjacent to the bend line.

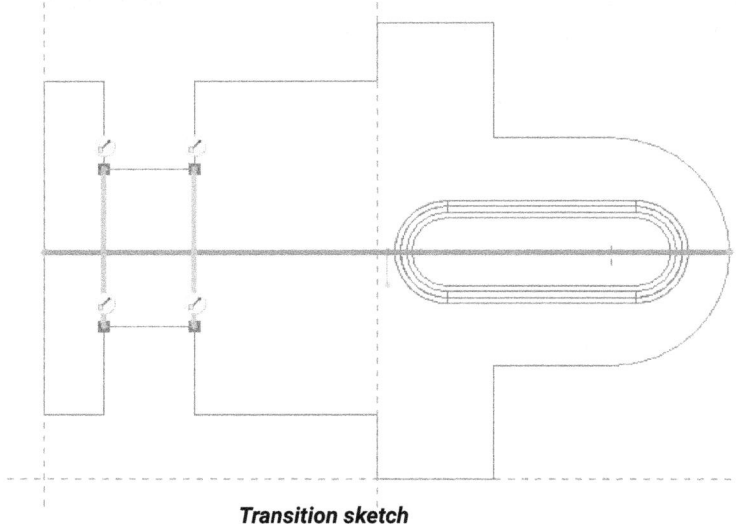

Transition sketch

Figure 6–19

Relief

If required, add a bend relief by selecting the Relief panel, as shown in Figure 6–20.

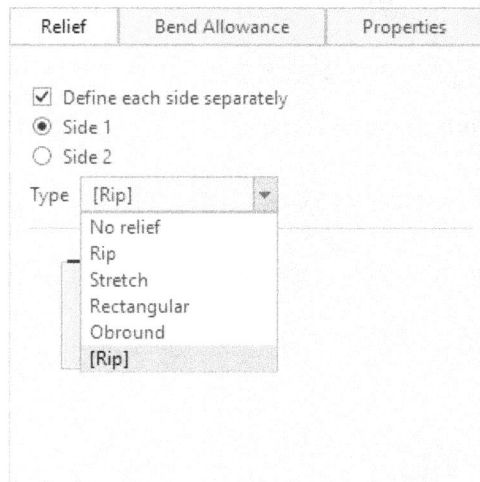

Figure 6–20

Alternatively, a relief can be specified by clicking on the screen and selecting ✐ (Edit Relief) from the mini toolbar. Then, select on the screen again and, expand ✐ (Bend Relief Type) and select the appropriate relief type, as shown in Figure 6–21.

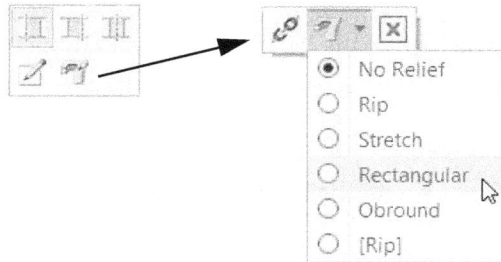

Figure 6–21

The following types of reliefs are available:

*   No Relief
*   Rip
*   Stretch
*   Rectangular
*   Obround

6.3 Position of the Bend Line

Creo Parametric uses the bend line as a reference for calculating the developed length when creating bend geometry. The bend line must reach from one edge of the sheet metal part to another, unless a relief is defined. You must also specify the side of the bend line on which to create the bend feature and the side of the bend line that is to remain fixed.

Depending on the position of the bend line and the side of the part that is bent, the resulting geometry could display differently. To capture the design intent you must understand how these two factors could affect the part you are creating.

Figure 6–22 shows a bend feature with the bend created below the bend line.

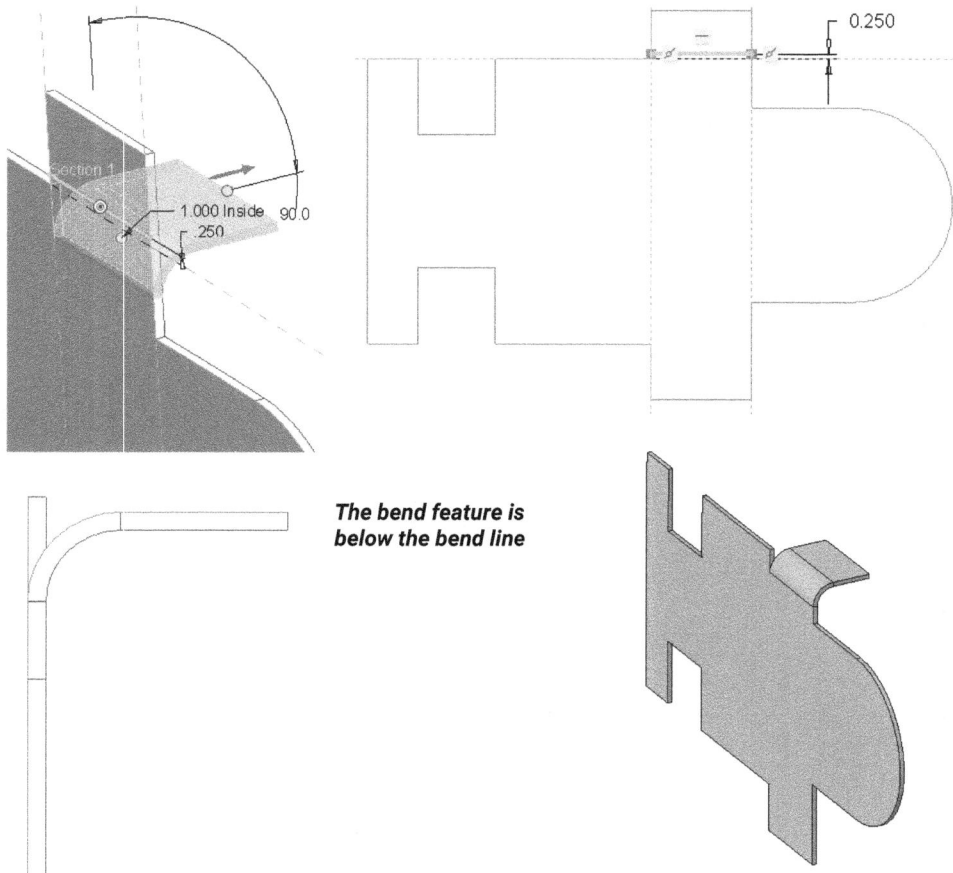

The bend feature is below the bend line

Figure 6–22

Figure 6−23 shows a bend feature with the bend created above the bend line.

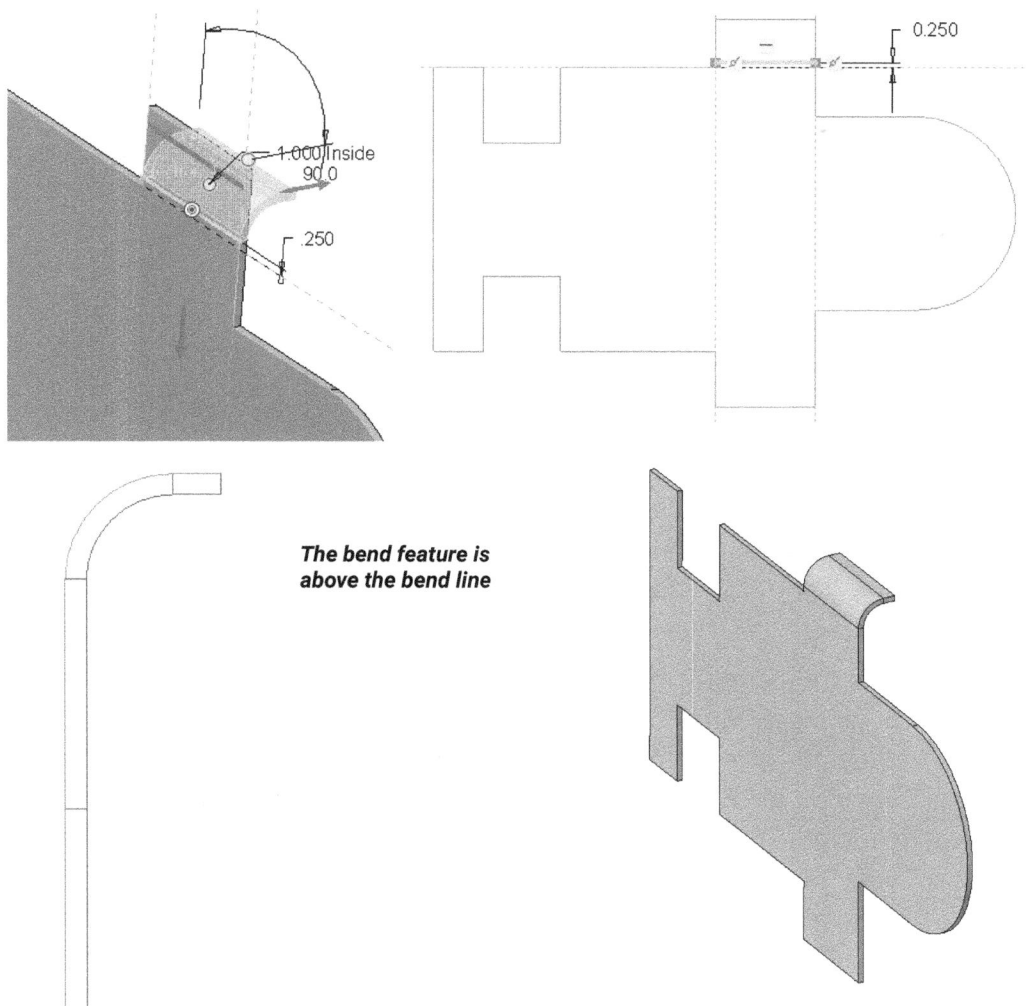

1.000 Inside
90.0

.250

0.250

*The bend feature is
above the bend line*

Figure 6−23

Figure 6-24 shows a bend feature with the bend created on both sides of the bend line.

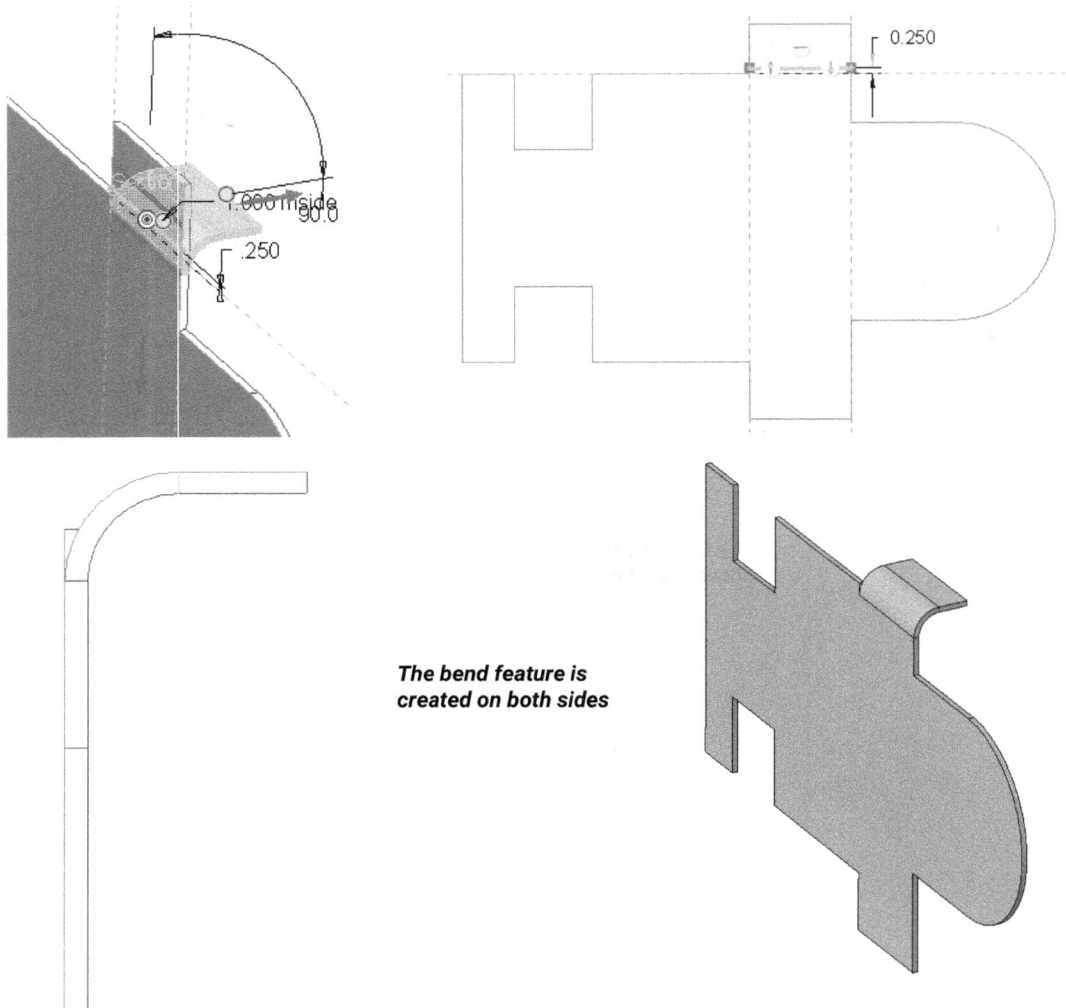

0.250

.250

1.000 Inside
90.0

*The bend feature is
created on both sides*

Figure 6-24

6.4 Bend Line Adjustment

In some cases when creating the bend feature, an adjustment to the position of the bend line might be required to meet the design intent. In the example shown in Figure 6−25, the design intent requires that the top surface of the bent wall is coplanar to the thin edge surface of the adjacent wall.

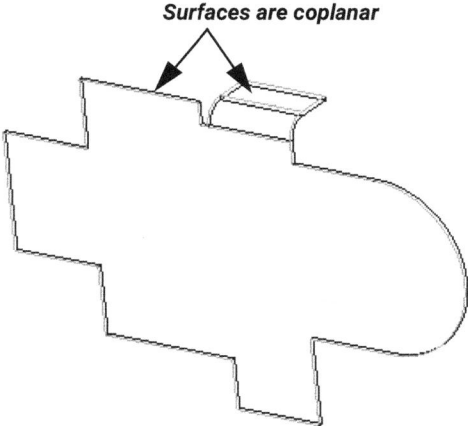

Figure 6−25

This criteria can be met by modifying the location of the bend line or controlling it with a relation. Using a relation produces more accurate results than modifying the location of the bend line directly on the model.

You can add relations when creating the bend line by using the offset distances in the Bend Line panel or using dimensions in the sketch to locate the bend line, as shown in Figure 6−26.

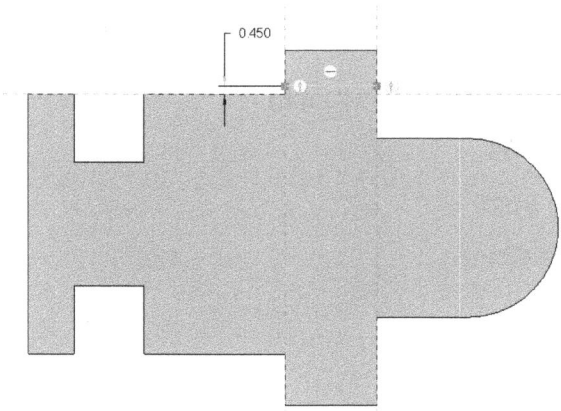

Figure 6−26

If offset references are selected in the Bend Line panel, you must create a relation for each of the offset dimensions.

This dimension is referred to as the bend line adjustment (BLA) dimension. It can be modified to control the placement of the bend using relations.

The dimensions used in a relation to control the value of the BLA dimension ensure that the design criteria is met, as shown in Figure 6−27. These dimensions include material thickness (T), inside bend radius (R), and the developed length of the bend (L).

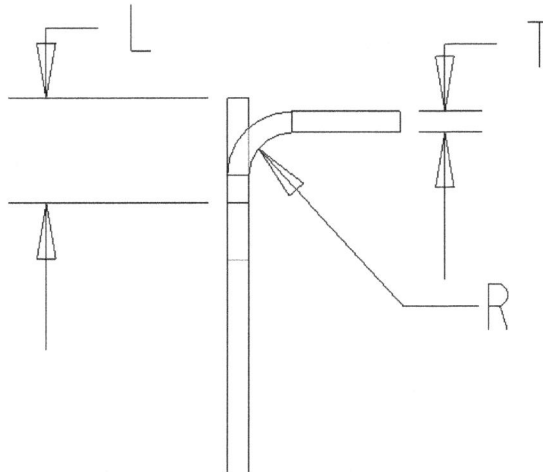

Figure 6−27

To ensure that the top surface of the bent wall is coplanar with the thin edge surface of the adjacent wall, use the following relation format:

BLA = L - (R + T)

Consider the model shown in Figure 6−28. The following dimensions are used to create a relation:

- Dimension locating the bend line (BLA) = d40

- Material thickness (T) = d5

- Inside bend radius (R) = d25

- Developed length (L) = d26

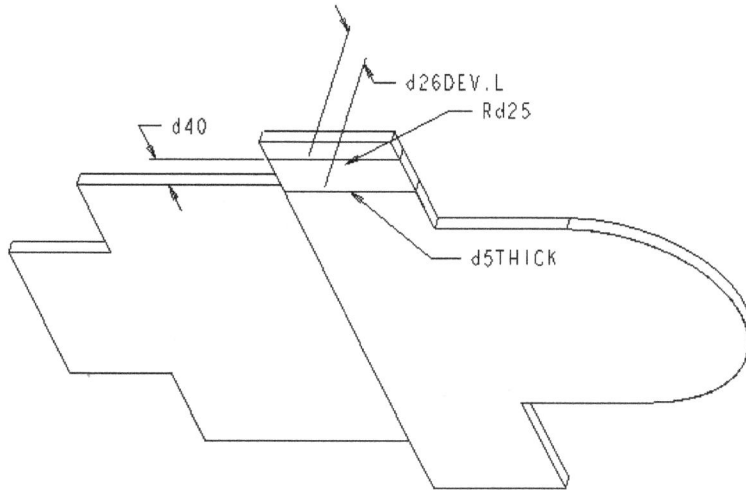

Figure 6–28

The relation takes the form of d40 = d26 - (d25 + d5). With this relation, the bend surface remains coplanar with the thin edge surface, as shown in Figure 6–29, regardless of changes to the values of L, R, and T.

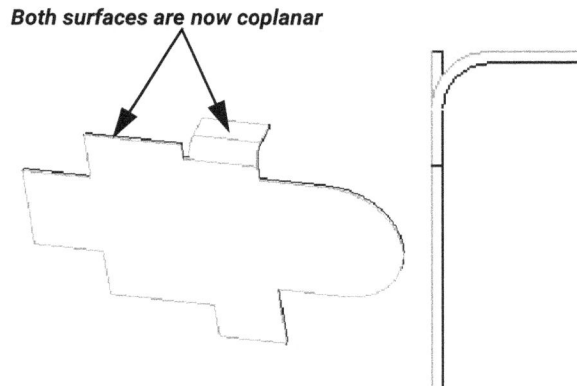

Both surfaces are now coplanar

Figure 6–29

6.5 Bend Line Notes

Bend line notes display on the sheet metal model when it is flattened using the Flat Pattern feature, as shown in Figure 6-30. These notes help you understand the design intent of the model.

The bend line notes describe how the model should display when bent

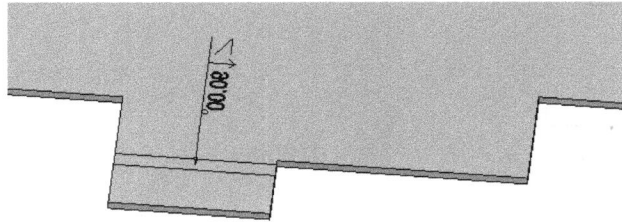

Figure 6-30

The symbols used in the bend line notes describe how the bend was created and include bend type, bend direction, and bend angle. The symbols are described as follows:

Bend Description		Symbol	Description
Bend Type	**Angle**	∠	Identifies the bend as angular.
	Roll	∩	Identifies the bend as rolled.
Bend Direction	**Up**	↑	Inside radius is on the sheet metal model's green surface.
	Down	↓	Inside radius is on the sheet metal model's white surface.
Bend Angle		**45°**	Identifies the inside bend angle. It displays based on the format set in the **ang_units** config option.

The following conditions must be met to display the bend line notes in a model:

- Bend Notes must be enabled. Select **File>Options>Sheetmetal** and select **Show bend notes**, as shown in Figure 6-31.

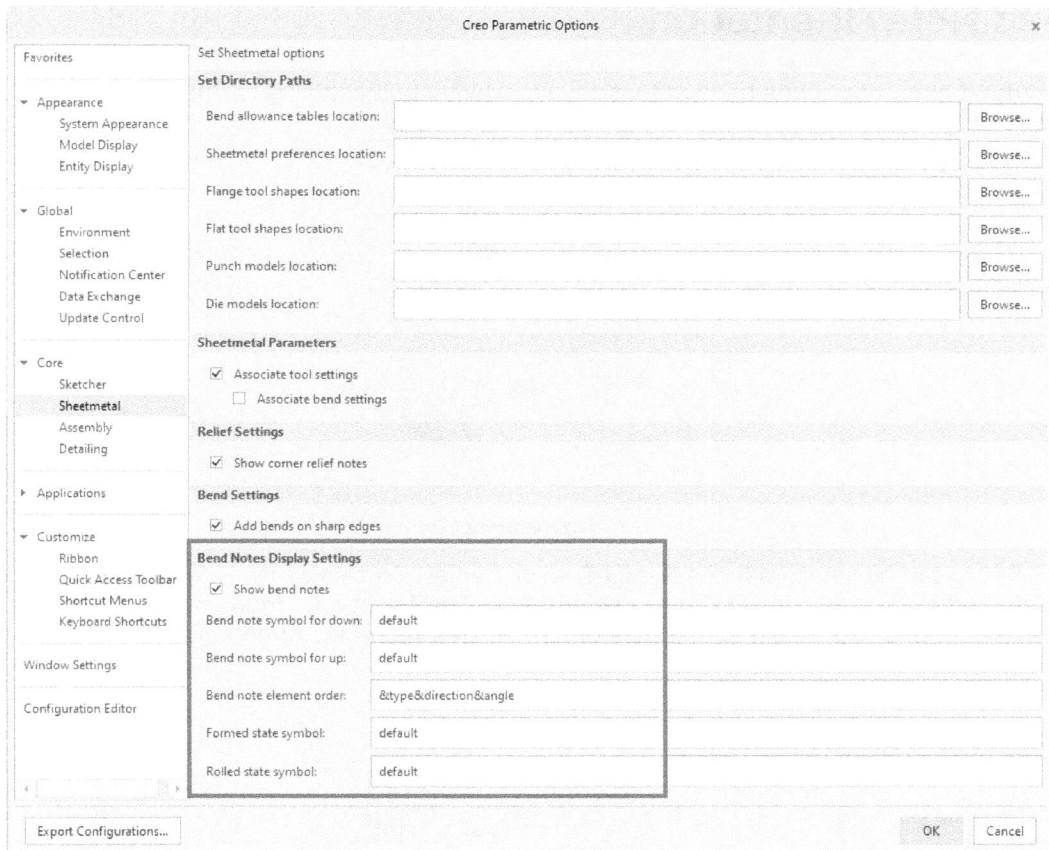

Figure 6–31

Note: *To display the bend line notes in the Model Tree, click* 🔽 *(Tree Filters)>General> Annotations.*

- In the In-graphics toolbar, expand 🗐 (Annotation Display Filters) and click ⊰ (Bend Notes) to toggle the bend note display on and off.

- The **smt_bend_notes_dflt_display** config.pro option is set to **yes** (default).

Bend Note Orientation

The default orientation for a bend note is always relative to the driving surface. The bend note shown in Figure 6–32 is parallel to the green driving surface.

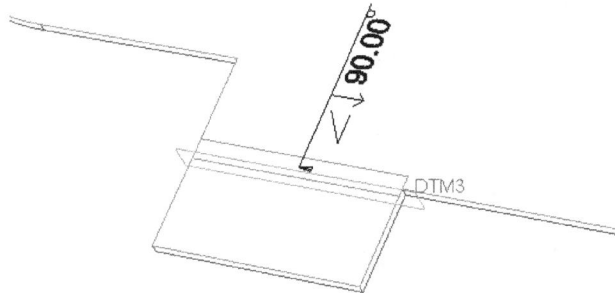

Figure 6–32

A bend note can be selected in the Model Tree or display. To change the orientation of a bend note, right-click on it and select **Change Orientation**. The Annotation Plane dialog box opens as shown in Figure 6–33. Select a reference or named view to set the orientation.

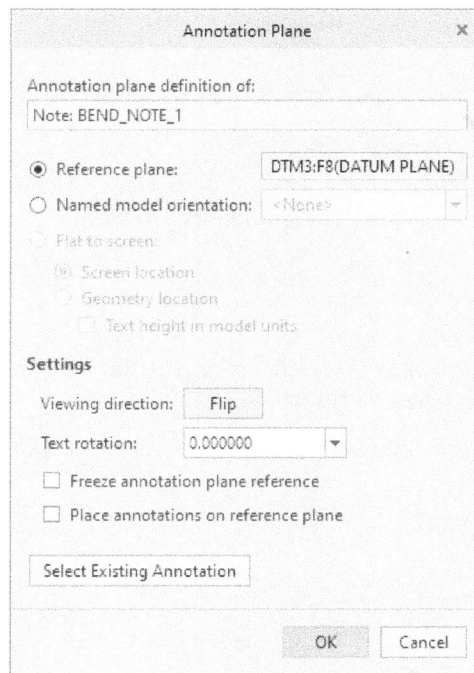

Figure 6–33

Datum plane **DTM3** was selected as the Reference Plane for the bend note shown in Figure 6−34.

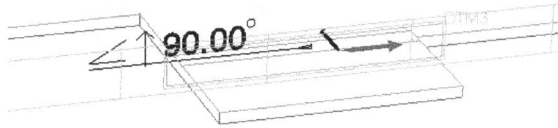

Figure 6−34

Best Practices for Bend Features

Consider the following points when working with the unbend and bend back features:

- Do not add unnecessary unbend/bend back features. They add unnecessary features to the part and increase its file size. They can also cause regeneration problems.

- If you create an unbend feature to display the flattened model, delete the unbend feature before proceeding with the design.

- Do not delete an unbend feature if you have created features specifically in the flattened state. The feature might fail if you delete the unbend feature.

- Create a projected datum curve after creating an unbend feature. The curve follows the sheet metal surface when it is bent back.

Practice 6a
Bend Flat Geometry

Practice Objectives

- Create roll bends with transition.
- Create angle bends.

In this practice, you will begin with a flat part and create bend features to obtain the final geometry, as shown in Figure 6-35.

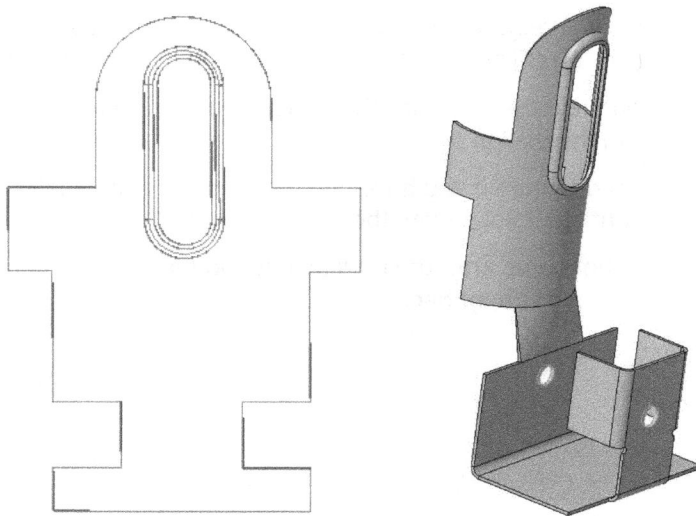

Figure 6-35

Note: Be consistent when selecting the bend side and fixed side of the wall when creating the bend features.

Task 1: Open a part and create a roll bend feature with transition.

Design Considerations

Wall_mount.prt was created in the flat condition. It consists of two wall features, a cut, and a form feature. In this task, you will create a roll bend. This bends the material adjacent to the sketched bend line through a specified radius. The design intent requires that only one side of the sheet metal part be bent. To achieve that, you will need to create transition geometry enabling you to split the existing geometry into two parts, one to be bent and the other to remain flat.

1. Set the working directory to the *Bend_From_Flat* folder.

2. Open **wall_mount.prt**.

3. Set the model display as follows:

   - *(Datum Display Filters)*: None

   - *(Spin Center)*: Off

   - *(Display Style)*: (No Hidden)

4. Select the surface shown in Figure 6−36 for the bend surface.

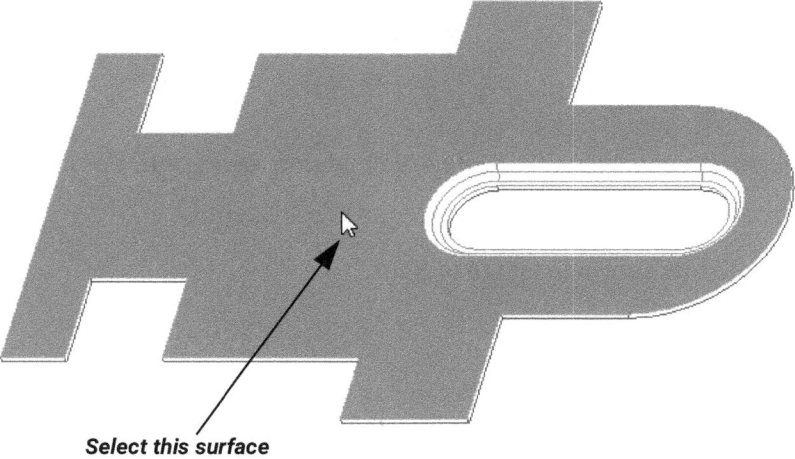

Select this surface

Figure 6−36

5. Click (Bend) in the mini toolbar.

6. The *Bend* dashboard displays as shown in Figure 6−37.

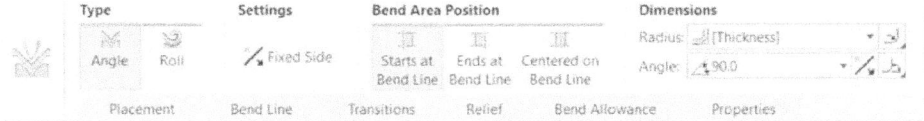

Figure 6−37

7. Right-click and select **Rolled Bend**, as shown in Figure 6–38.

Figure 6–38

Note: You can also click 🦢 *(Rolled Bend) in the Bend dashboard.*

8. Click on the screen and select 📝 (Define/Edit Internal Bend Line) from the mini toolbar.

   *Note: You can also click the Bend Line panel and click **Sketch**.*

9. Sketch the profile, as shown in Figure 6–39.

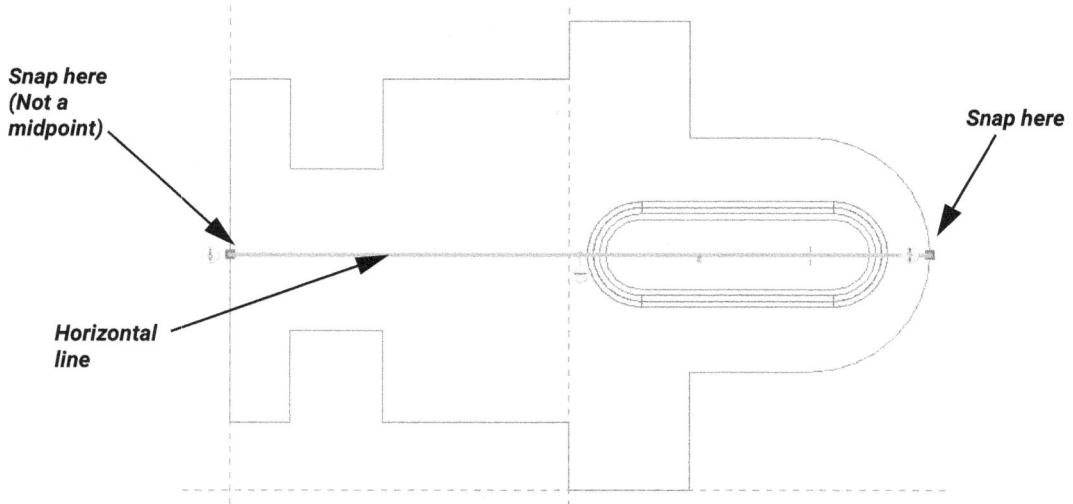

Figure 6–39

10. Complete the sketch.

11. The arrow displays, indicating the side of the entity on which to create the feature. Click on the screen and select 🔲 (Centered on Bend Line) from the mini toolbar to create the bend feature on both sides of the bend line.

12. If necessary, flip the bend direction arrow to match the image shown in Figure 6−40.

13. An arrow displays indicating the area to be fixed. If required, flip the arrow to keep the fixed area below the bend line, as shown in Figure 6−40.

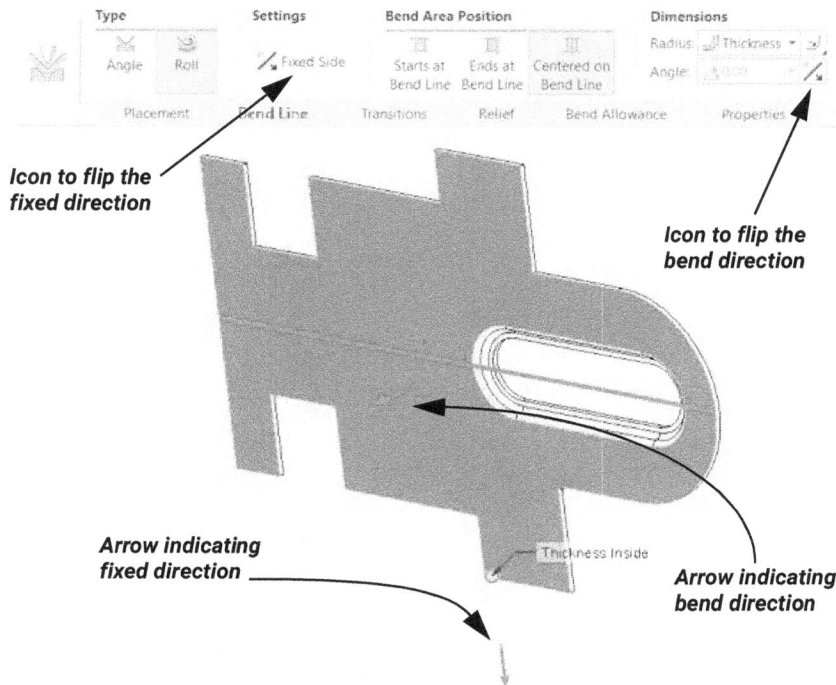

Figure 6−40

14. Verify that ⤵ (Dimension Inner Surface) is selected in the *Bend* dashboard and set the bend *Radius* to **5.00**, as shown in Figure 6−41.

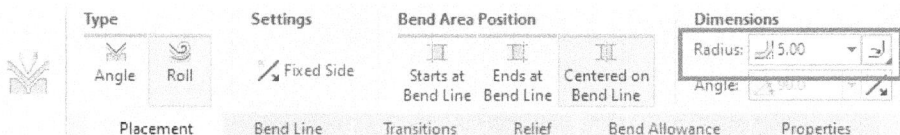

Figure 6−41

15. You are now ready to define an area to accommodate the deformation from the bent area to the flat area. Select the Transitions panel.

16. Select **Add Transitions** in the Transitions panel.

17. Click **Sketch**. Sketch the transition area, as shown in Figure 6−42. The vertical line on the right side must be sketched first because it is adjacent to the region to be bent.

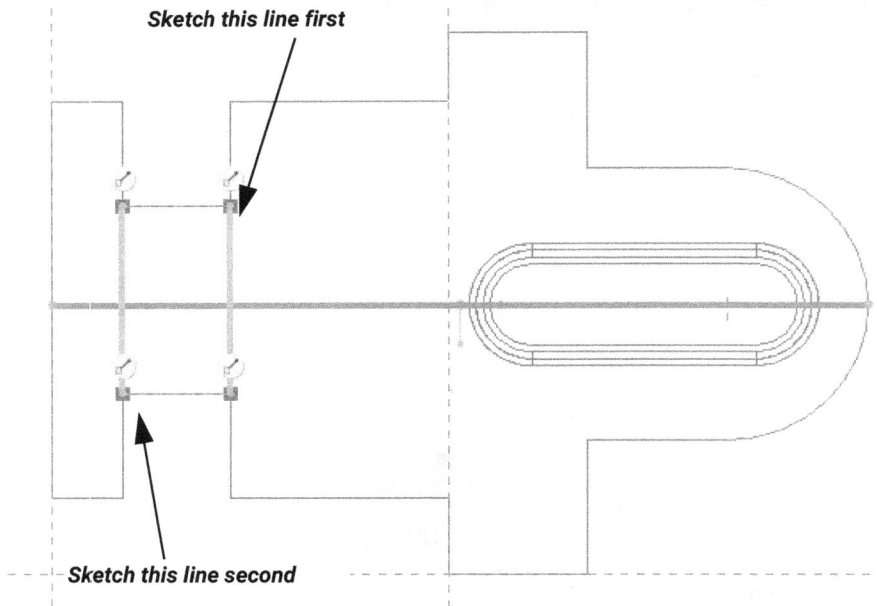

Figure 6−42

18. Complete the sketch.

19. Click ✔ (OK) to complete the feature.

20. Set the display to ⬜ (Shading With Edges) and set the model to the default orientation, as shown in Figure 6−43.

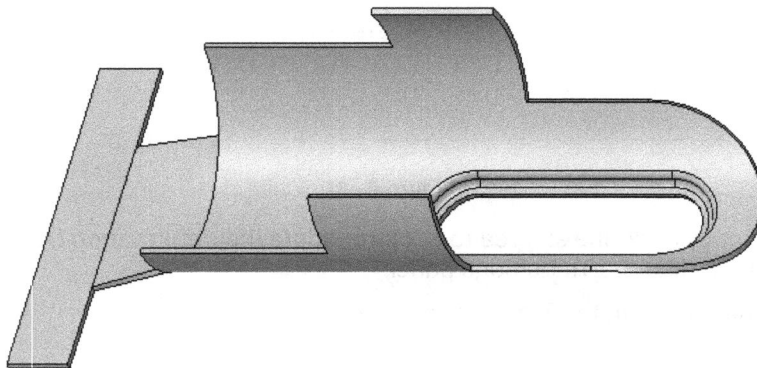

Figure 6−43

Task 2: Create another flat wall to define the remaining geometry.

Design Considerations

In this task, you will create a flat wall by sketching its shape. The roll bend feature created in Task 1 changed the geometry location of the part in respect to the three default datum planes. To be able to use the datum planes as references when creating the flat wall, unbend the part before creating it.

1. Create an unbend feature by clicking ⌐⊒ (Unbend) in the *Sheetmetal* tab. Select the fixed edge shown in Figure 6−44 to remain fixed while the unbending takes place.

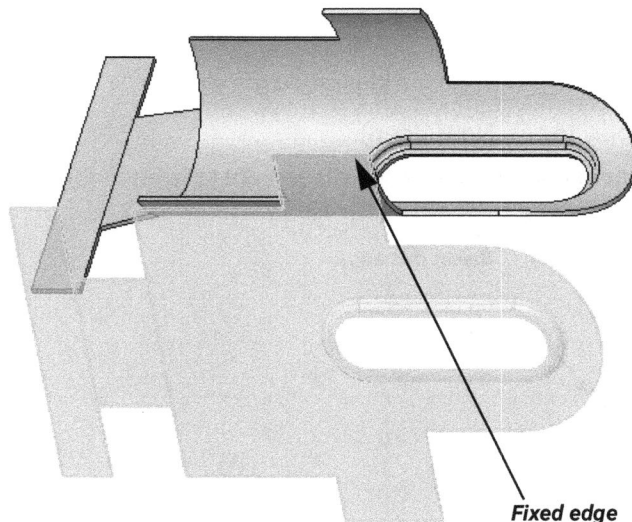

Fixed edge

Figure 6−44

2. Complete the Unbend feature.

3. In the In-graphics toolbar, expand ⌐⧈ (Annotation Display Filters) and click ⌐⧍ (Bend Notes) to toggle off bend notes.

4. Orient the model so it displays approximately as shown in Figure 6–45.

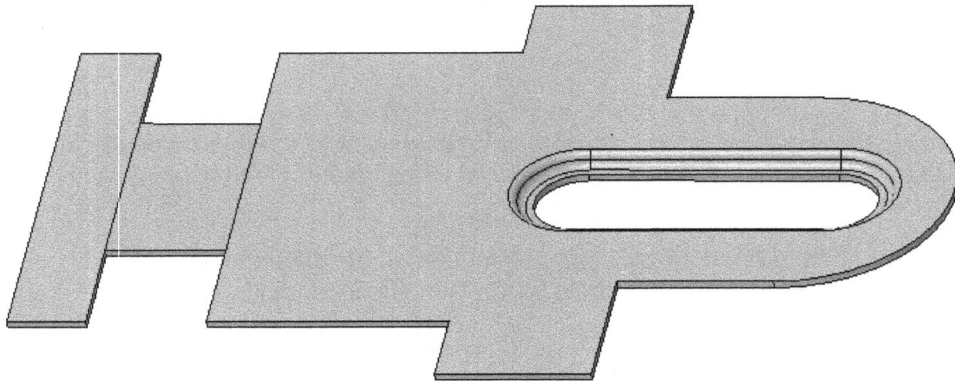

Figure 6–45

5. Set the model display to ⬚ (No Hidden).

6. Select the attachment edge to define the placement reference for the flat wall, as shown in Figure 6–46.

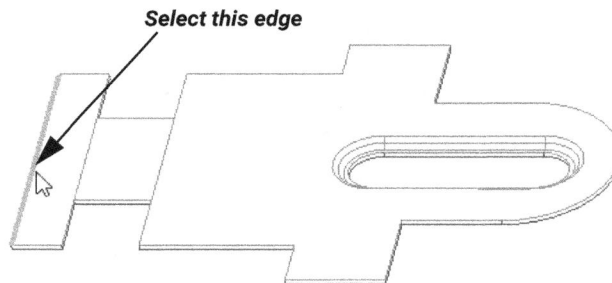

Select this edge

Figure 6–46

7. Click ✎ (Flat) in the mini toolbar.

8. Select **Flat** in the Angle drop-down list, as shown in Figure 6–47.

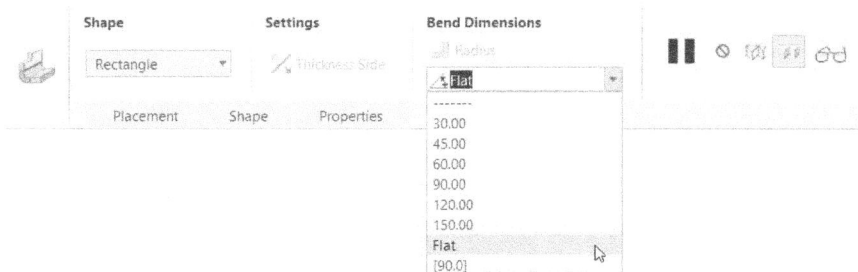

Figure 6–47

9. The geometry previews as shown in Figure 6–48.

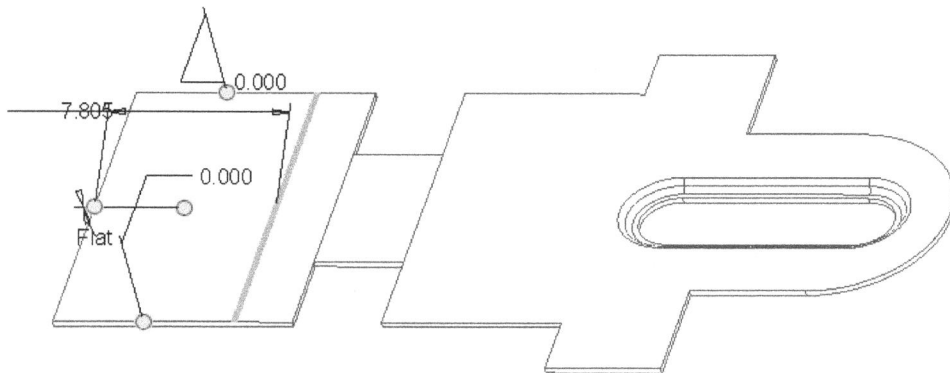

Figure 6–48

10. Select **User Defined** in the Type drop-down list in the dashboard, as shown in Figure 6–49.

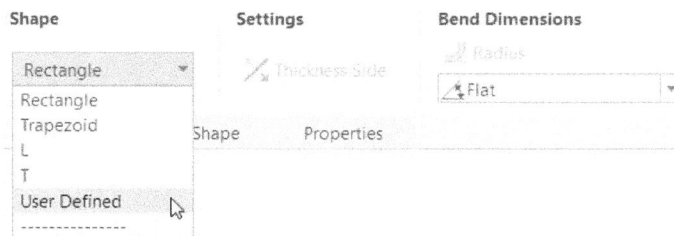

Figure 6–49

11. Open the Shape panel and click **Sketch**.

12. In the model, click the purple arrow to flip its direction. This enables you to see the green surface while in Sketcher.

13. In the Sketch dialog box, select **Bottom** as the direction for the orientation reference, and click **Sketch** to open the *Sketch* tab.

14. Sketch the section for the flat wall as shown in Figure 6−50.

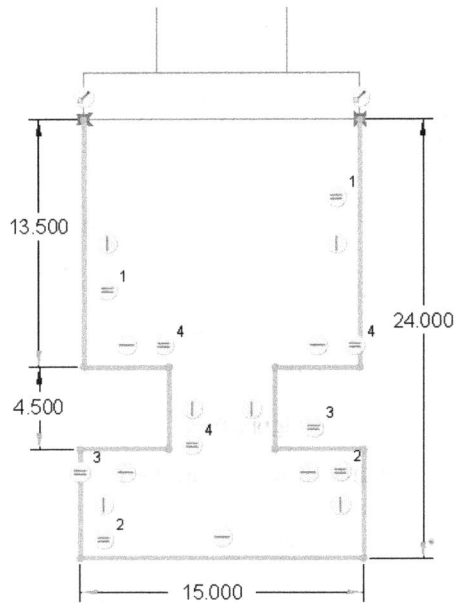

Figure 6−50

Note: Be careful to create equal lengths L1, L2, and L3 on the section.

15. Complete the sketch and the feature.

16. Orient the model, as shown in Figure 6−51.

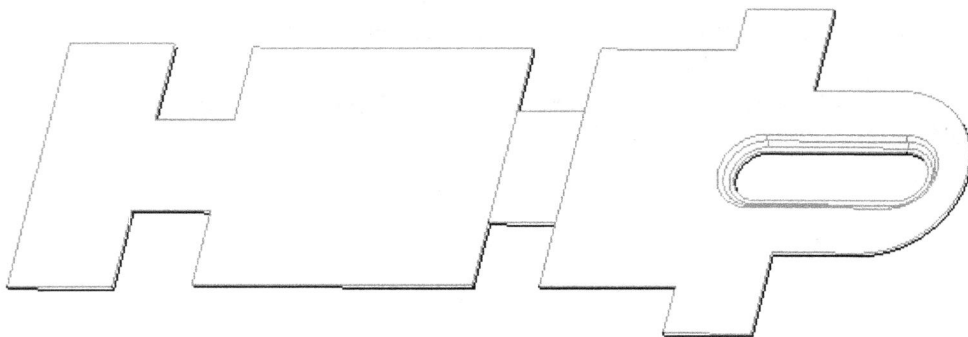

Figure 6−51

17. Click (Bend Back) in the *Sheetmetal* tab to bend back the part.

18. Select the edge shown in Figure 6–52 to remain fixed.

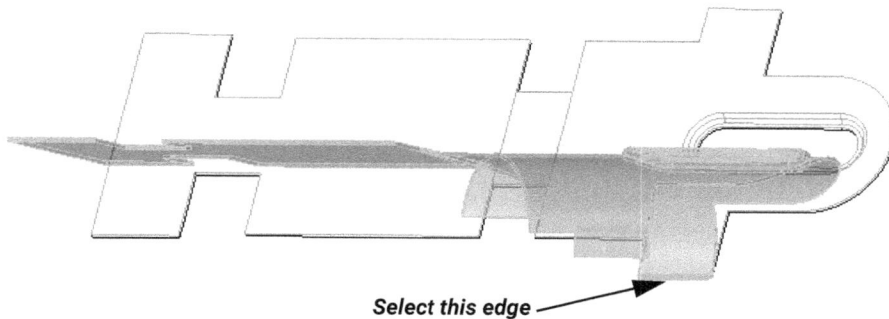

Select this edge

Figure 6–52

19. Complete the feature.

20. Set the display to ⬚ (Shading With Edges) and set the model to the default orientation, as shown in Figure 6–53.

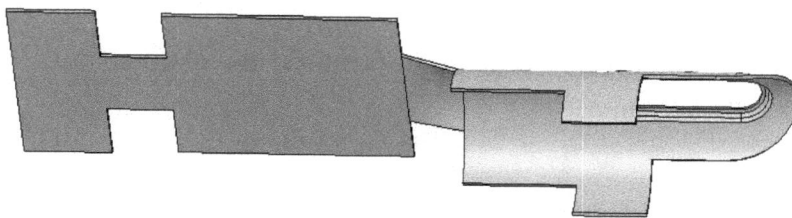

Figure 6–53

Task 3: Create four additional angle bend features.

Design Considerations

In this task, you will create the remaining four angle bends. For each, bend you will select the correct references to achieve the required dimensioning schemes.

1. Select the flat surface shown in Figure 6–54 as the Bend surface and select ※ (Bend) in the mini toolbar.

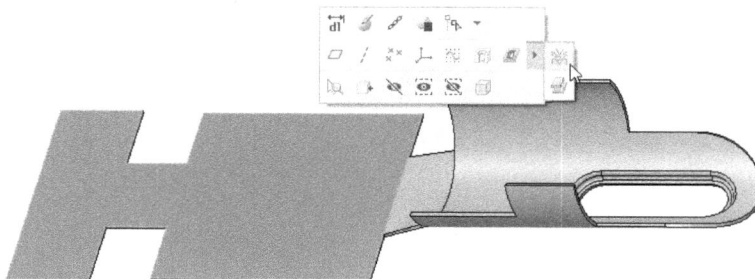

Figure 6–54

2. Right-click and select **Bend Line End 1 Placement**, as shown in Figure 6–55.

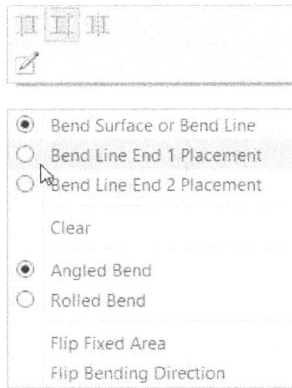

Figure 6–55

*Note: You can also select the Bend Line panel and click in the reference collector for **Bend line end 1**.*

3. Select the edge shown in Figure 6–56 as the first bend line reference.

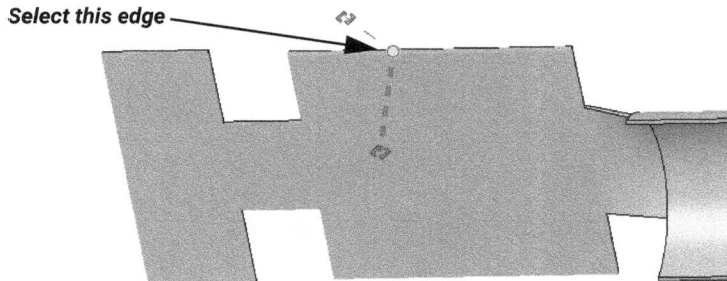

Figure 6–56

4. Drag the *Offset reference* handle to the edge shown in Figure 6–57 and set the value to **8.00**.

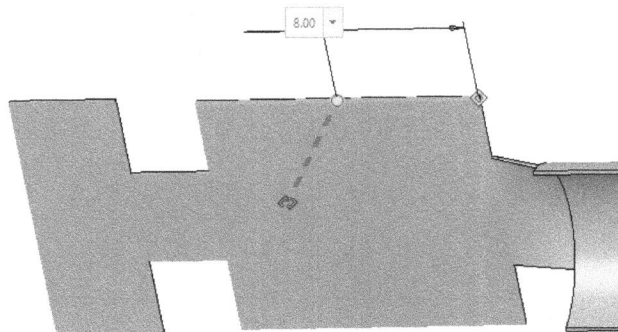

Figure 6–57

*Note: You can also right-click and select **Bend Line End 1 Offset**.*

5. Right-click and select **Bend Line End 2 Placement**.

6. Select the edge shown in Figure 6−58.

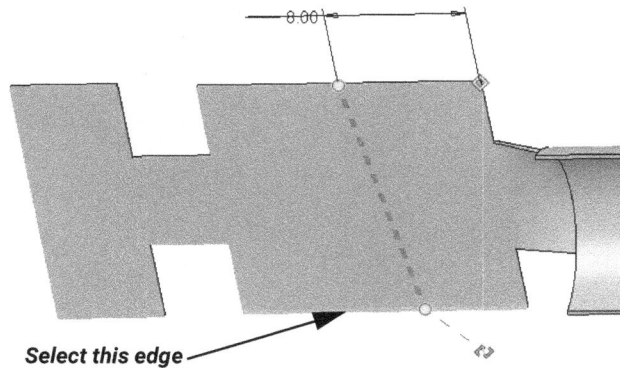

Figure 6−58

7. Select the same *Offset reference* used in Step 4 and set the value to **8.00** for the second bend line, as shown in Figure 6−59.

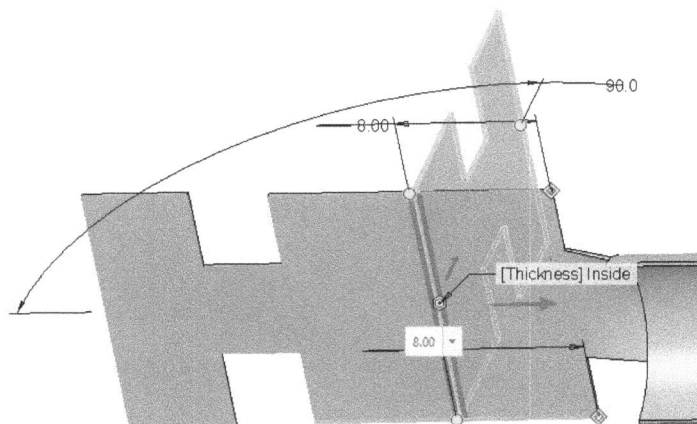

Figure 6−59

8. Verify that the arrows point in the direction, as shown in Figure 6–60. Specify a **90°** bend *Angle*.

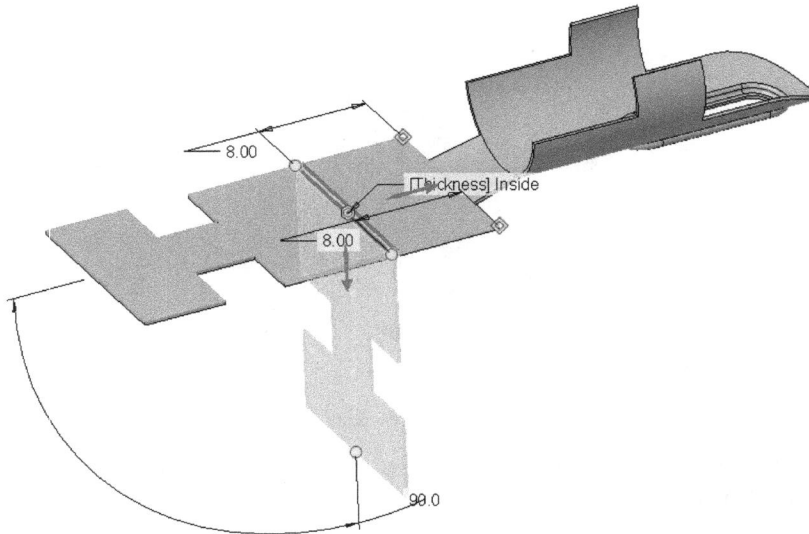

Figure 6–60

9. Set the bend *Radius* to **2 *Thickness**. Click ✔ (OK) to complete the Bend. The part displays as shown in Figure 6–61.

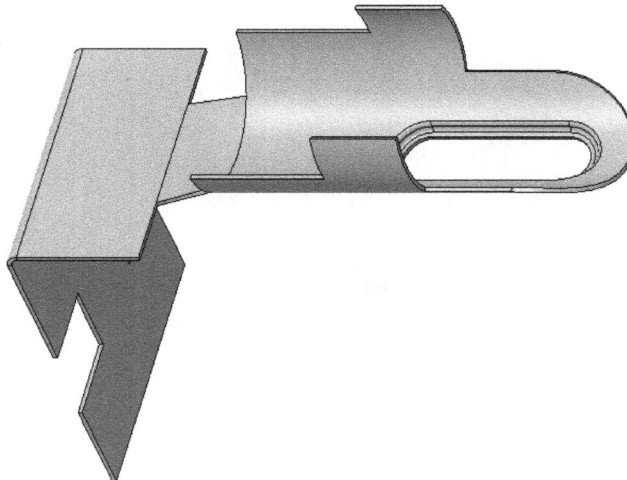

Figure 6–61

10. Set the model display to ▱ (No Hidden).

11. Select the surface shown in Figure 6–62 and click ☀ (Bend) in the mini toolbar.

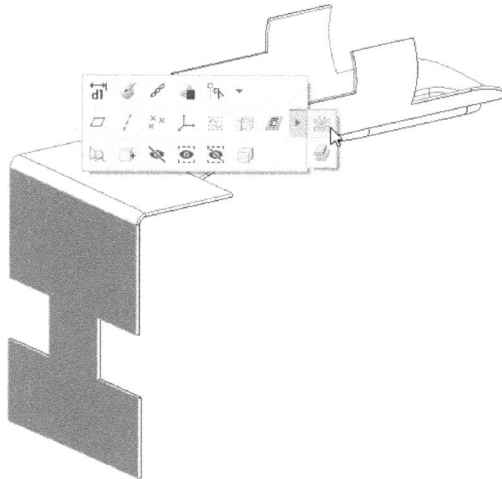

Figure 6–62

12. Expand the Bend Line panel and select the appropriate references to create the bend line, as shown in Figure 6–63.

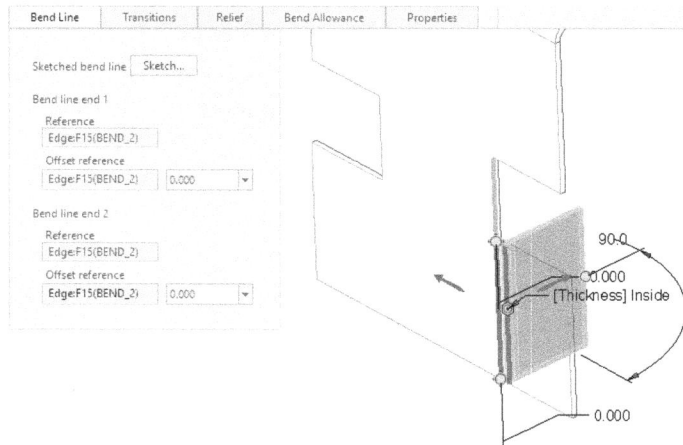

Figure 6–63

13. Select the Relief panel and select **Define each side separately**.

14. Create an **Obround** relief on the side shown in Figure 6–64. Set the *Width* to **2.0*Thickness** and the *Depth* of the obround relief to **Tangent to Bend**.

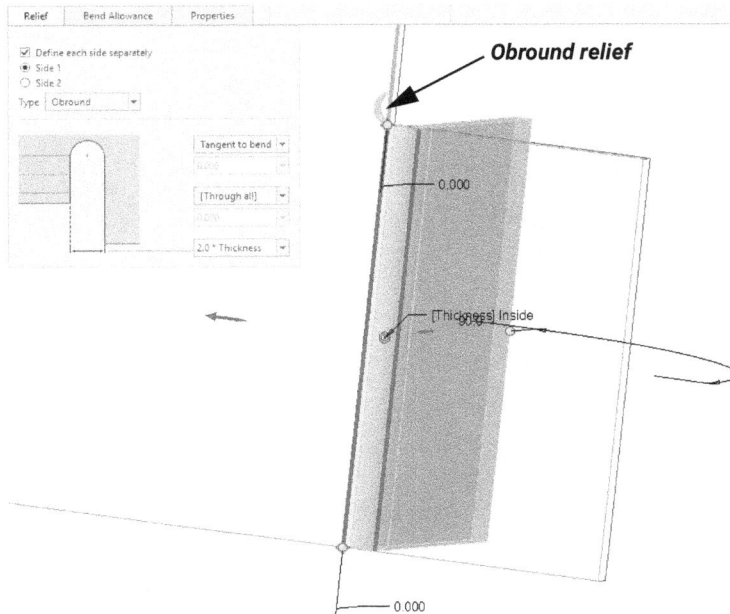

Figure 6–64

15. Specify a **90°** bend *Angle* and set the *Radius* of the bend to **2.0*Thickness**. The part displays as shown in Figure 6–65. Flip the angle direction, if required.

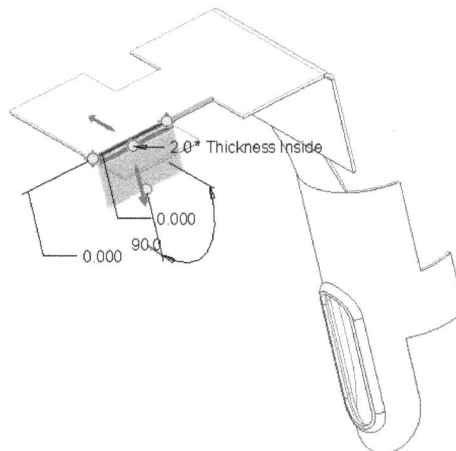

Figure 6–65

16. Complete the feature and set the display to ⬜ (Shading With Edges).

17. Create another bend like the one just created. The model displays as shown in Figure 6–66.

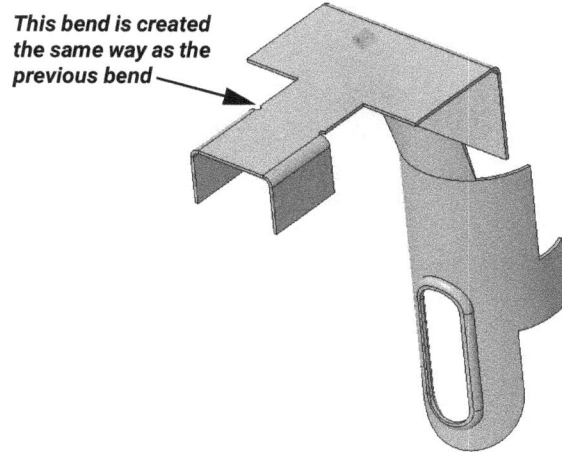

This bend is created the same way as the previous bend

Figure 6–66

18. Set the model display to ⬚ (No Hidden).

19. Create the final regular angle bend feature with an inside radius. Select the surface for the bend feature as shown in Figure 6–67 and click ⚒ (Bend) in the mini toolbar.

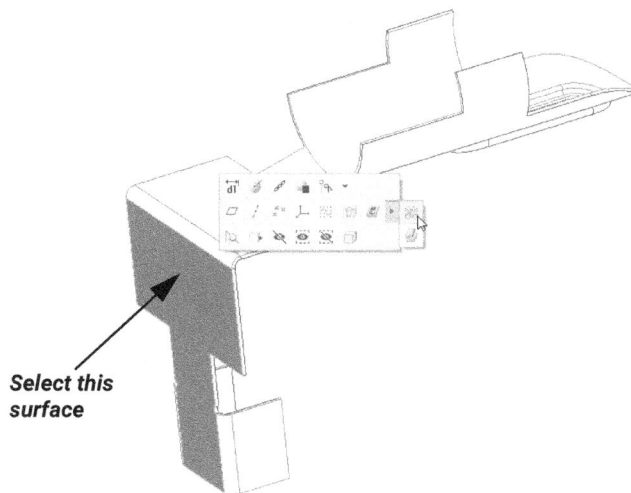

Select this surface

Figure 6–67

20. Select the appropriate references (select the vertices on the existing walls) and keep the geometry on the right side of the bend line fixed, as shown in Figure 6−68.

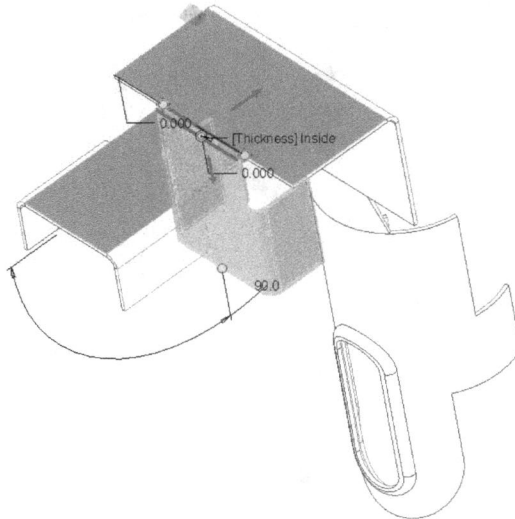

Figure 6−68

21. Select the default bend *Angle* of **90°**.

22. Set the bend *Radius* to **2.0*Thickness**.

23. Complete the feature and set the display to ⬛ (Shading With Edges). The part displays as shown in Figure 6−69.

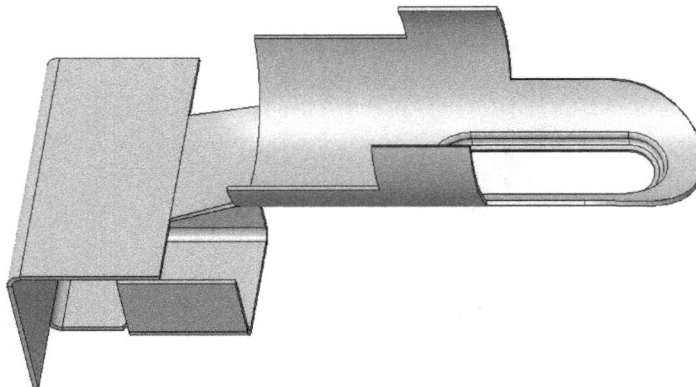

Figure 6−69

Task 4: Create a hole for the mounting hardware.

1. Select the surface shown in Figure 6–70 and select 🔲 (Hole) in the mini toolbar. Use the dimensioning scheme shown and set the depth to ⧉ ⧉ (Through All).

   - Create the hole using the dimensions shown on the right.

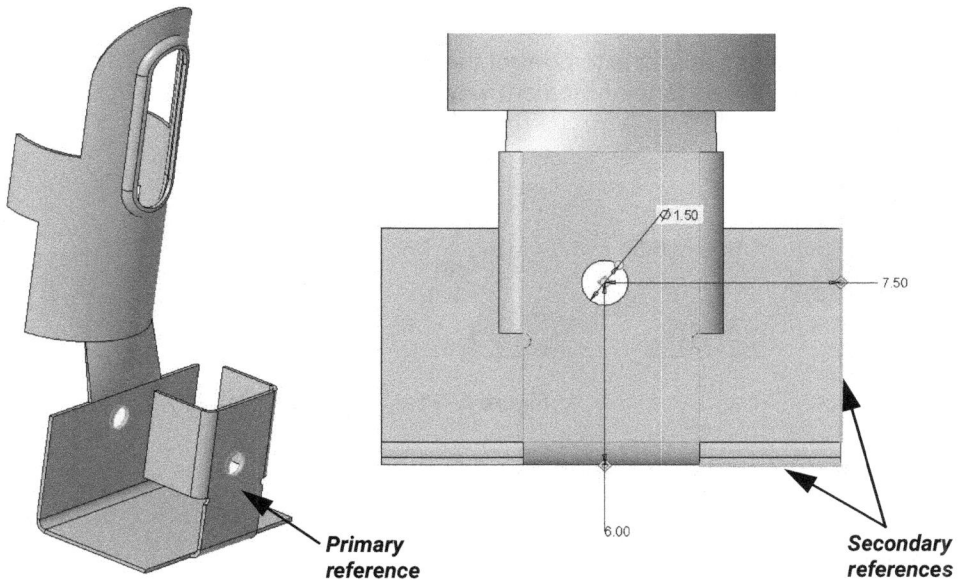

Figure 6–70

2. Save the part and erase it from memory.

End of practice

Practice 6b
Create a Bend Line Adjustment

Practice Objective

*   Use relations to control the position of the bend line.

In this practice, you will use relations to control the location of the bend lines of two bends, as shown in Figure 6–71. The surface of the bent walls should be coplanar with the thin edge or surface of the adjacent wall.

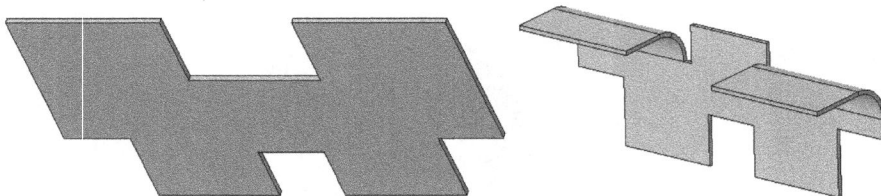

Figure 6–71

Task 1: Open a part and create two bend features.

Design Considerations

In this task, you will practice creating bend features again. Additionally, you will learn how to use relations to control the position of the bend line in accordance with your design intent. A relation to control the position of the bend can be created for both a sketched bend or a bend created from selected references. If a bend is created by selecting references, two relations are required to be added for each offset value. A sketch bend is created in this task so that only one relation is required to control the bend position.

1. Set the working directory to the *Bend_Line_Adjustment* folder.

2. Open **bend_line_adj.prt**.

3. Set the model display as follows:

    *   ⁎⁄⌐ *(Datum Display Filters)*: None

    *   ⋟ *(Spin Center)*: Off

    *   ◻ *(Display Style)*: ◻ (No Hidden)

4. Select the surface shown in Figure 6–72 and click ※ (Bend) in the mini toolbar.

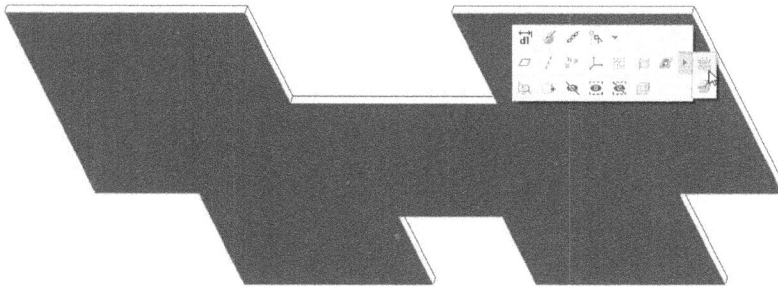

Figure 6–72

5. Click on the screen and select 🎟 (Up To Bend Line) from the mini toolbar.

6. Edit the bend radius to **1.00**.

7. Click on the screen and select 📝 (Define/Edit Internal Bend Line) from the mini toolbar.

8. Sketch the bend line as shown in Figure 6–73.

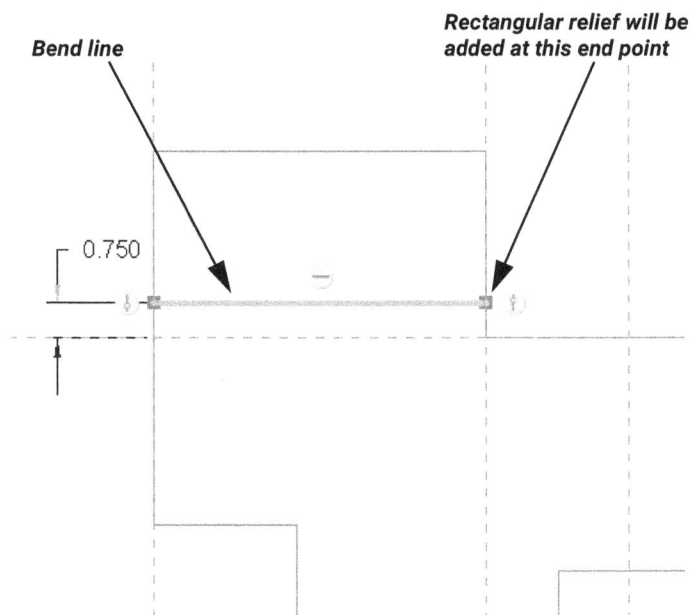

Figure 6–73

9. Complete the sketch.

10. The fixed side arrow should both point below the bend line as shown in Figure 6−74. Click ⚹ (Change Fixed Side) for the fixed side arrow, if required. Click ⚹ (Change Bending Direction) if the wall bends in the wrong direction.

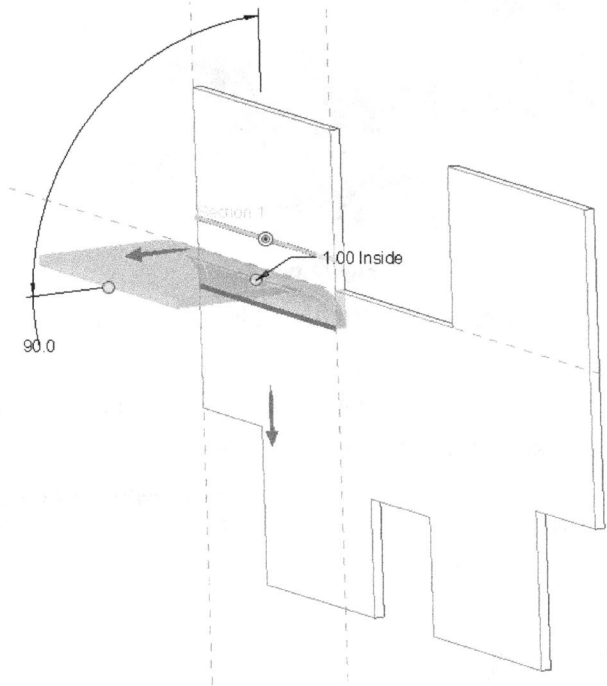

Figure 6−74

11. Define a rectangular relief for the right end point of the bend line and **No Relief** for the left end point. Set the *Width* to **0.5** and the *Depth* to **Up To Bend**.

12. Set the bend *Angle* to **90°** and complete the feature. The part displays as shown in Figure 6−75.

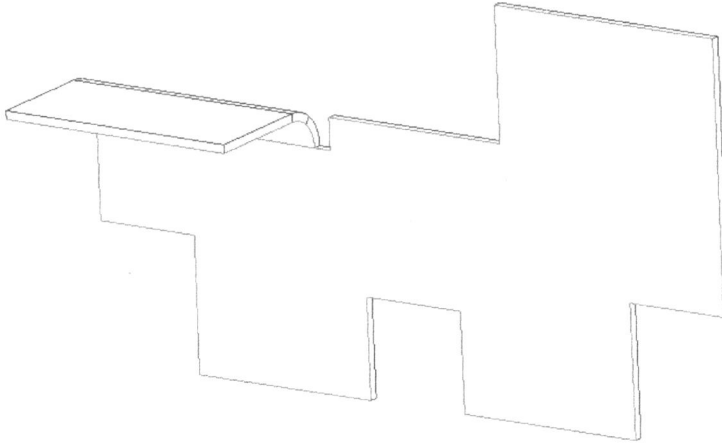

Figure 6−75

13. Use the same specifications to create another bend on the other side of the part as shown in Figure 6−76.

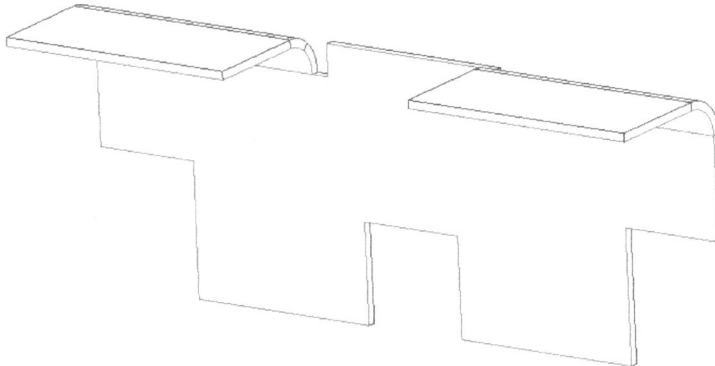

Figure 6−76

Task 2: Check the locations of the bent walls.

1. Select the *Analysis* tab, expand (Measure), and select (Distance).

2. Expand the *Setup* and *Results* areas in the Measure: Distance dialog box, as shown in Figure 6–77.

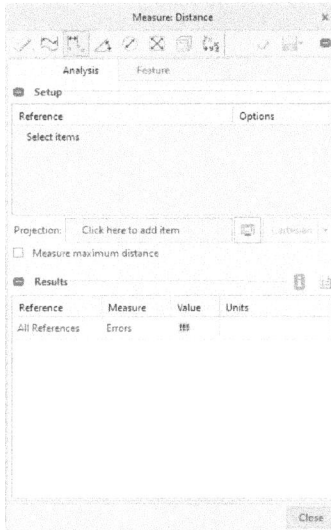

Figure 6–77

3. Hold <Ctrl> and select the surfaces shown in Figure 6–78 as the references.

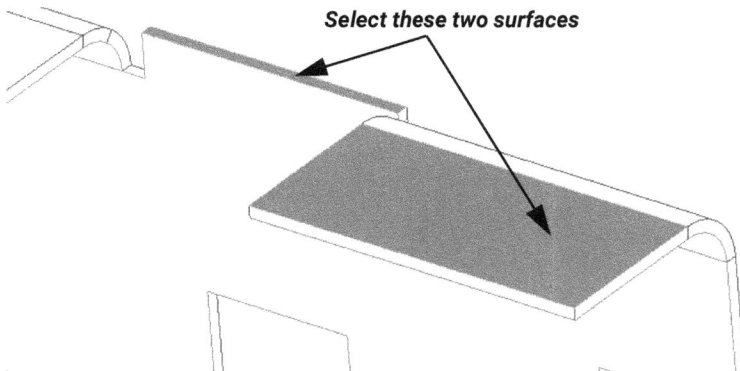

Select these two surfaces

Figure 6–78

4. The distance analysis displays with a value of **0.304**, as shown in Figure 6−79.

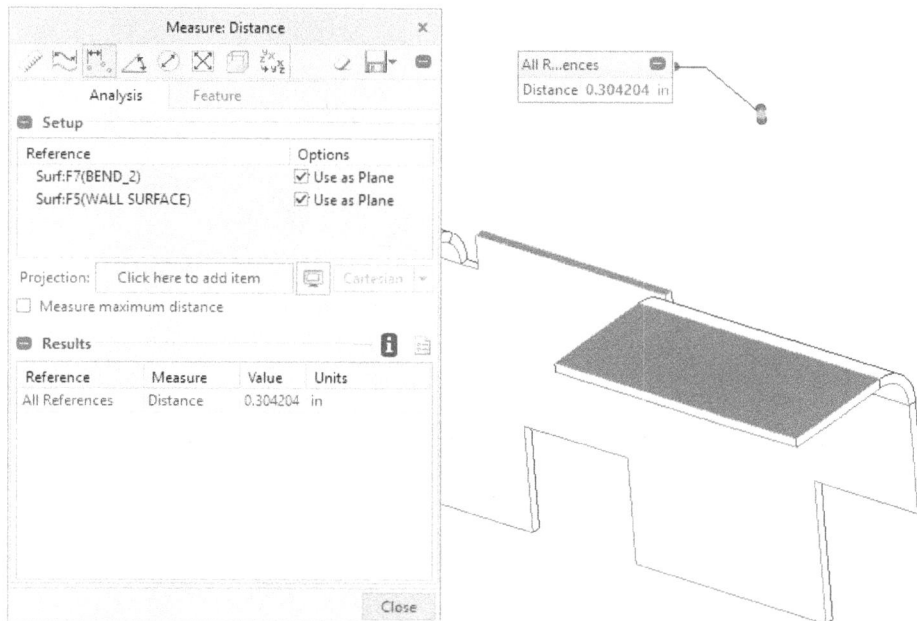

Figure 6−79

5. Expand ⊟▾ (Save Analysis) in the Measure: Distance dialog box and ensure that **Make Feature** is selected.

6. Click **OK** to create the feature.

Design Considerations

These two surfaces are not coplanar because the linear dimension locating the sketched bend line has not been adjusted. You can write a relation for bend line adjustment to make the wall coplanar.

7. Close the Measure: Distance dialog box.

Task 3: Write a relation to control the position of the bend line.

Design Considerations

In this task, you will create a relation based on the BLA formula. This relation will ensure that your design intent is maintained when the dimension values of the affected features are changed.

Note: The formula for BLA is BLA = L - (R+T). L is the developed length of the bend, R is the inside radius, and T is the wall thickness.

1. Select the *Sheetmetal* tab and select **Model Intent>Relations**.

   Note: You can also select the Tools tab and click **d=** *(Relations).*

2. Scroll to the bottom of the relation editor to type in the relation on an empty line.

3. Select the first wall and second bend in the graphics window or Model Tree. The system displays the dimensions of these features using dimension symbols, as shown in Figure 6−80.

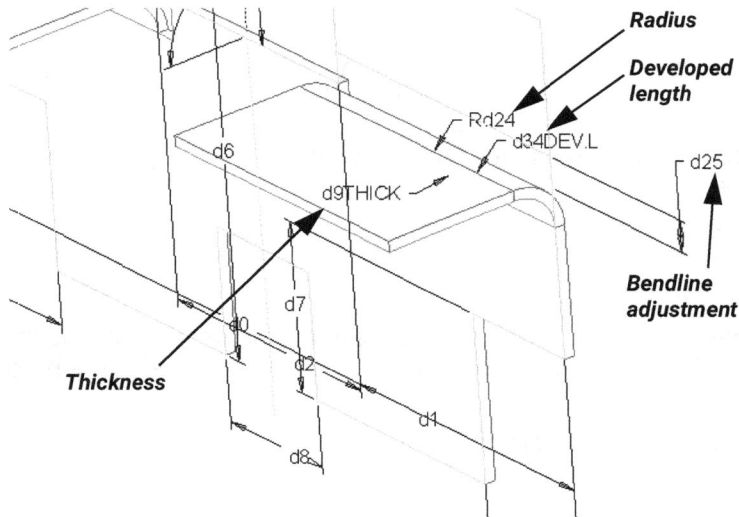

Figure 6−80

4. Locate the symbolic dimension that corresponds to the developed length (**d#DEV.L**), inside radius (**Rd#**), material thickness (**d#THICK**), and BLA dimension (**d#**), as shown in Figure 6−80.

5. Enter the formula **BLA = L - (R+T)** in the Relations dialog box as shown in Figure 6–81. (Example: **d25 = d34 - (d24 + d9)** based on Figure 6–80.)

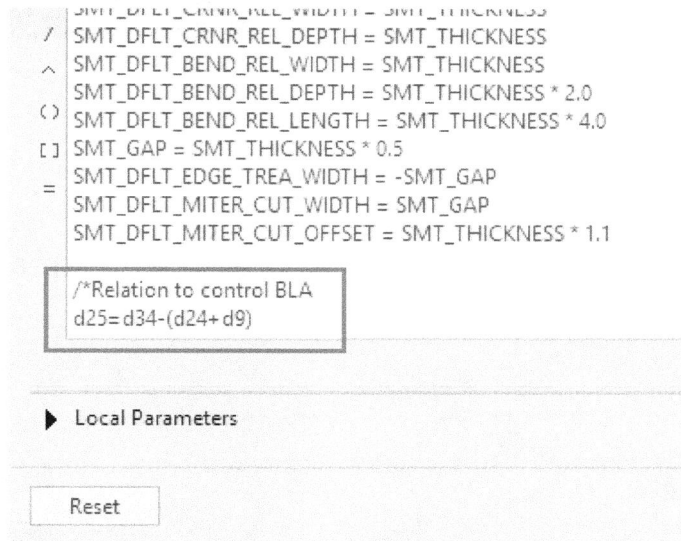

SMT_DFLT_CRNR_REL_WIDTH = SMT_THICKNESS
/ SMT_DFLT_CRNR_REL_DEPTH = SMT_THICKNESS
^ SMT_DFLT_BEND_REL_WIDTH = SMT_THICKNESS
SMT_DFLT_BEND_REL_DEPTH = SMT_THICKNESS * 2.0
( ) SMT_DFLT_BEND_REL_LENGTH = SMT_THICKNESS * 4.0
[ ] SMT_GAP = SMT_THICKNESS * 0.5
= SMT_DFLT_EDGE_TREA_WIDTH = -SMT_GAP
SMT_DFLT_MITER_CUT_WIDTH = SMT_GAP
SMT_DFLT_MITER_CUT_OFFSET = SMT_THICKNESS * 1.1

/*Relation to control BLA
d25=d34-(d24+d9)

▶ Local Parameters

Reset

Figure 6–81

Note: Formula for BLA: BLA = L - (R+T).

6. Click ✓ (Verify) to verify the relation and click **OK**.
7. Regenerate the model.
8. Measure the distance between the surfaces again to see if they are coplanar.
9. Create a similar relation for the other bend feature.
10. To test the relations, modify the bend radius to **2.00**.
11. Regenerate the model twice.
12. Measure the distance between the two surfaces to see if they are still coplanar.
13. Save the part and erase it from memory.

End of practice

Practice 6c
Edge Bends

Practice Objectives

- Create a bend on a sharp edge.
- Add relief to the edge bend.

In this practice, you will create edge bend with relief, as shown in Figure 6–82.

Figure 6–82

Note: Ensure that you are consistent when selecting the bend side and fixed side of the wall when creating the bend features.

Task 1: Open a sheet metal part.

1. Set the working directory to the *Edge_Bends* folder.
2. Open **edge_bend.prt**.
3. Set the model display as follows:

- ⚒ *(Datum Display Filters)*: None
- ⊱ *(Spin Center)*: Off
- ⬜ *(Display Style)*: ⬜ (Shading With Edges)

The model displays as shown in Figure 6–83.

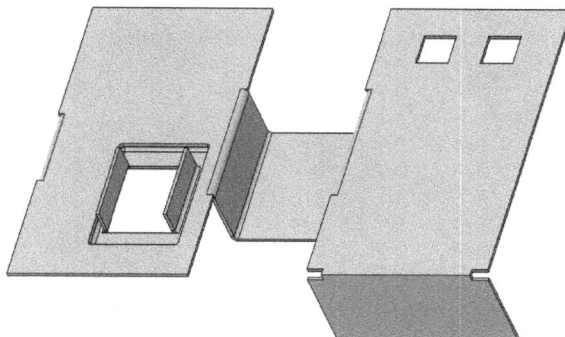

Figure 6–83

Task 2: Create an edge bend and add relief.

1. Select the edge shown in Figure 6–84 and select ⌐ (Edge Bend) in the mini toolbar.

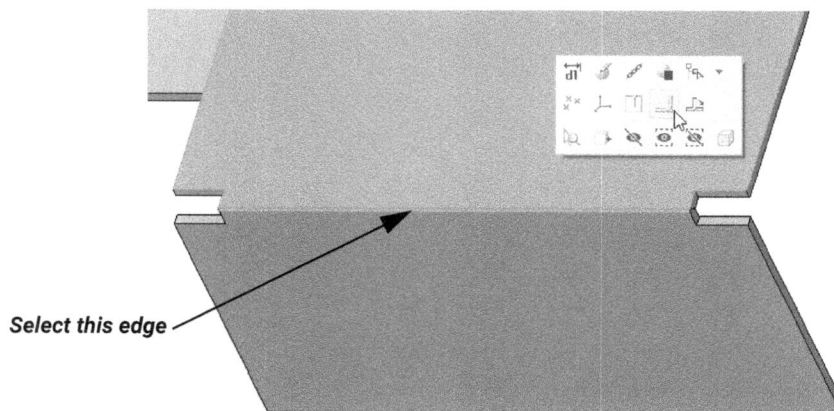

Select this edge

Figure 6–84

2. In the dashboard, set the thickness to **0.2**.

3. Zoom in on the model, as shown in Figure 6–85. Note that there is rip relief between the edge bend and adjacent wall.

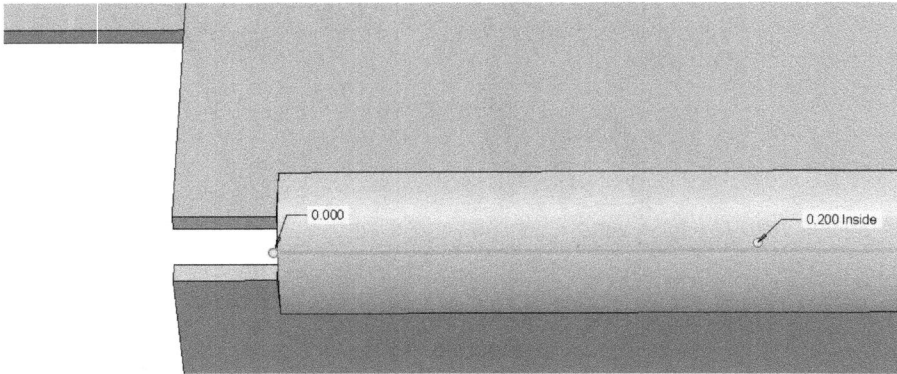

Figure 6–85

4. In the *Edge Bend* dashboard, expand the Relief panel and select **Rectangular** from the Type drop-down list, as shown in Figure 6–86.

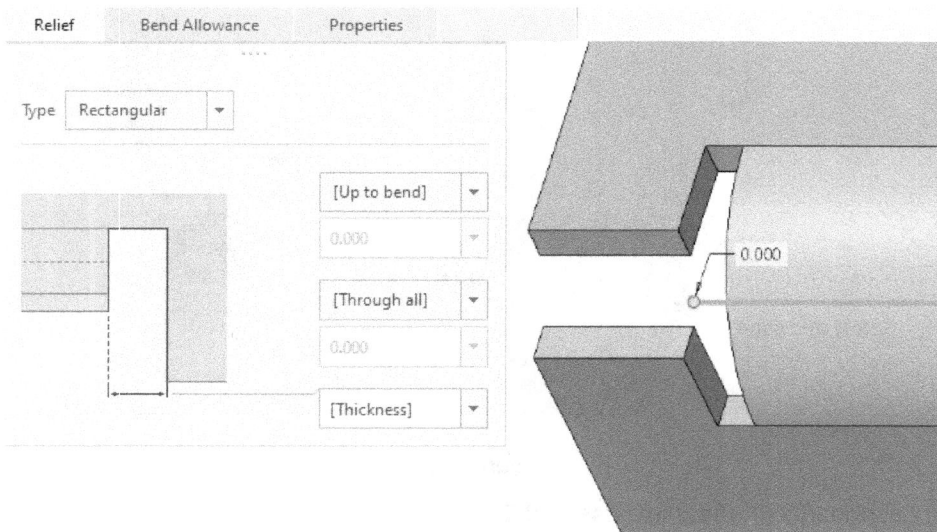

Figure 6–86

Note: *The rip relief updates to rectangular.*

5. Select **Obround** from the Type drop-down list. The relief updates as shown in Figure 6–87.

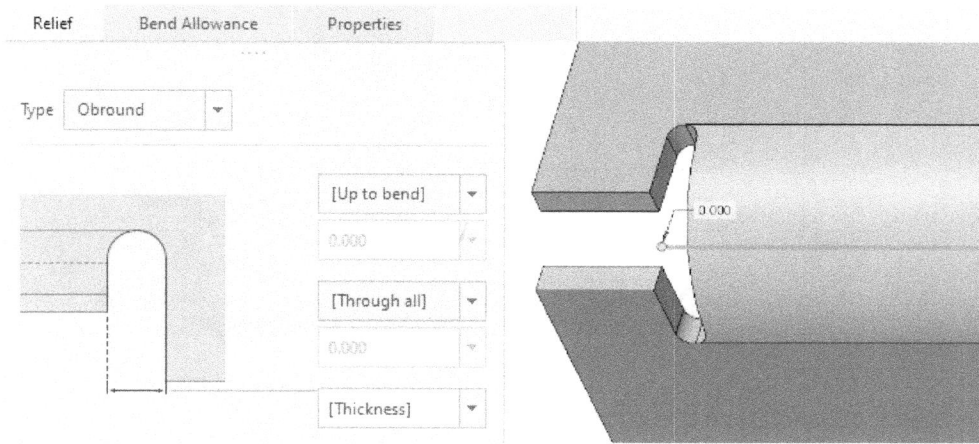

Figure 6–87

6. Edit the bend depth from *Up to bend* to **Tangent to bend**. The relief updates as shown in Figure 6–88.

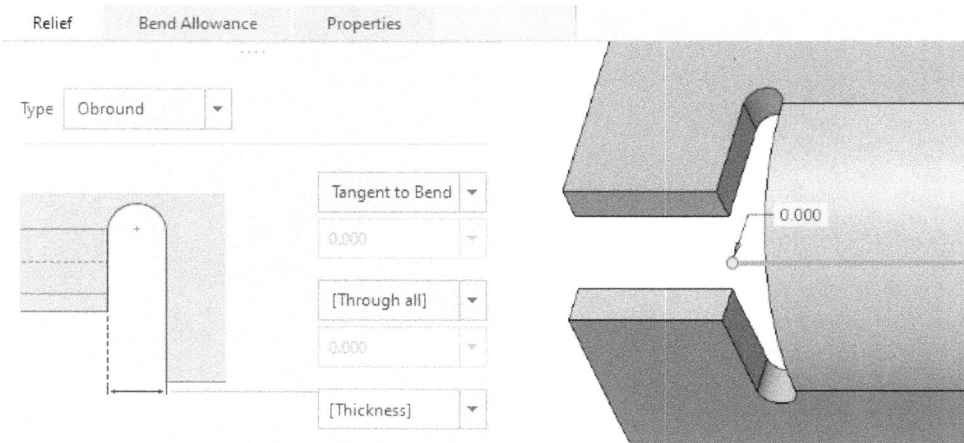

Figure 6–88

7. Click ✓ (OK) to complete the change. The model displays as shown in Figure 6–89.

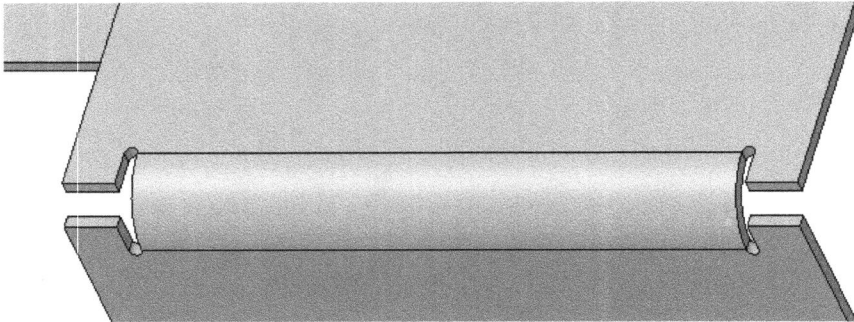

Figure 6–89

8. Save the model and erase it from memory.

End of practice

Chapter Review Questions

1. The bend line can consist of an edge or curve.

   a. True

   b. False

2. Which of the following are true statements using a bend line? (Select all that apply.)

   a. The bend line is used as a reference for calculating the developed length when creating bend geometry.

   b. The bend line must always reach from one edge of the sheet metal part to another.

   c. You must specify the side of the bend line on which to create the bend feature.

   d. You must specify the side of the bend line that is to remain fixed.

3. Which of the following statements should you consider when working with unbend and bend back features? (Select all that apply.)

   a. Do not add unnecessary unbend/bend back features.

   b. If you create an unbend feature to display the flattened model, delete the unbend feature before proceeding with the design.

   c. Do not delete an unbend feature if you have created features specifically in the flattened state.

   d. Create a projected datum curve after creating an unbend feature. The curve follows the sheet metal surface when it is bent back.

Answers: 1a, 2acd, 3abcd

Unbending Complex Geometry

When bend geometry is complex, more advanced techniques are required to flatten it. This enables you to rip or deform the geometry, as required.

Learning Objectives

- Understand the differences between ruled and non-ruled geometry.
- Understand how unbending geometry in sheet metal depends on the methods used to create the geometry.
- Use the deformation control options to select additional geometry to deform or change the sketch to reflect the required result.
- Use the split area feature to control the deformed areas of the model during unbending.
- Create a cross-section driven unbend feature to select an edge or create a sketch to control the unbend geometry.
- Learn the different types of rip features that can be created to unbend a model.

7.1 Ruled and Non-Ruled Geometry

Ruled Geometry

Ruled geometry is geometry that only has curvature in one direction, such as cylindrical or conical geometry, as shown in Figure 7-1 and Figure 7-2.

- Planar geometry is also considered ruled, but it does not have curvature to unbend.

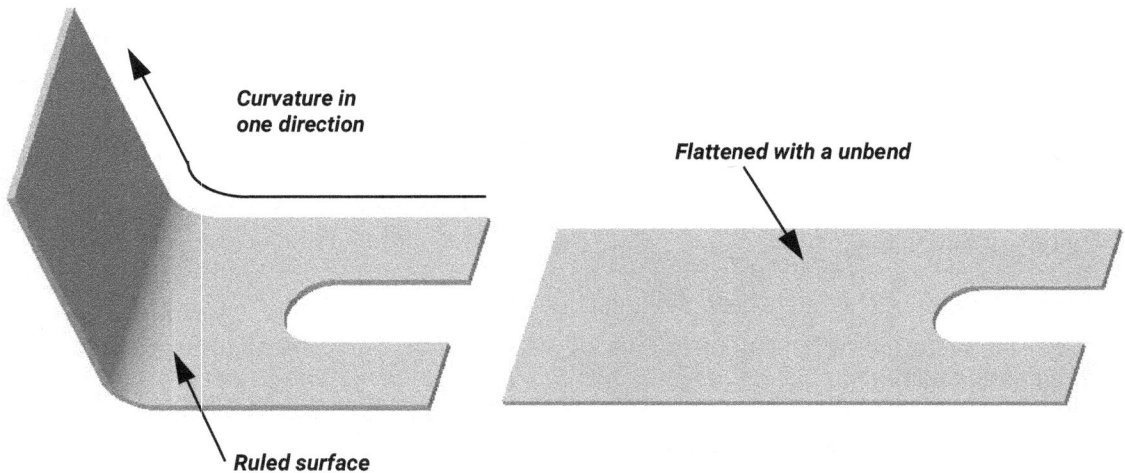

Curvature in one direction

Flattened with a unbend

Ruled surface

Figure 7-1

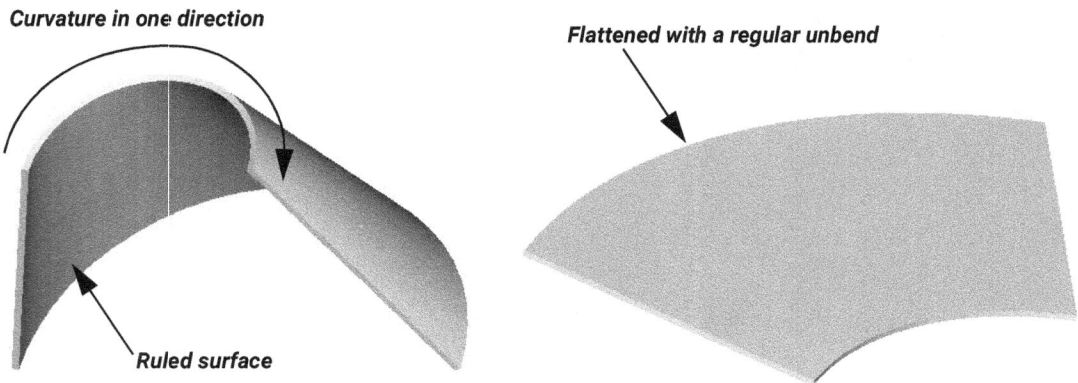

Curvature in one direction

Flattened with a regular unbend

Ruled surface

Figure 7-2

Non-Ruled Geometry

Non-ruled surfaces have curvature in two directions, as shown in Figure 7–3.

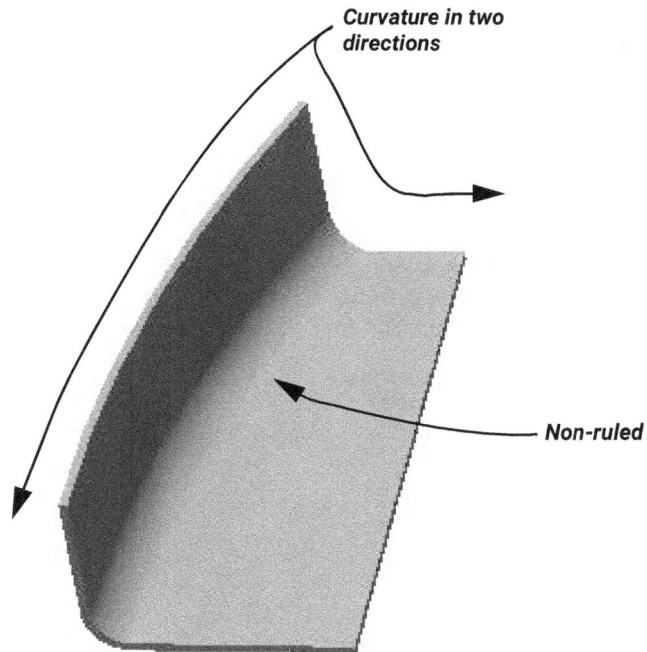

Figure 7–3

7.2 Unbending Non-Ruled Geometry

The ability to develop or unbend sheet metal geometry depends on the methods used to create the model. Some features, such as flange walls result in simple bend geometry, which is easy to develop. However, features such as swept walls or converted solid models can produce geometry that is not as easy to develop.

You have already used the unbend feature to unbend some of your models without deformation control. This method works with ruled geometry and geometry that only has curvature in one direction.

When creating an unbend feature, Creo Parametric might highlight areas that are deformed when it creates the unbend feature. This typically happens with non-ruled geometry that does not extend to one of the outside boundary edges of the part. For the system to flatten those types of surfaces, you must select an additional surface to deform. The surface you select must have edges that reach the outside boundary of the model, as shown in Figure 7–4.

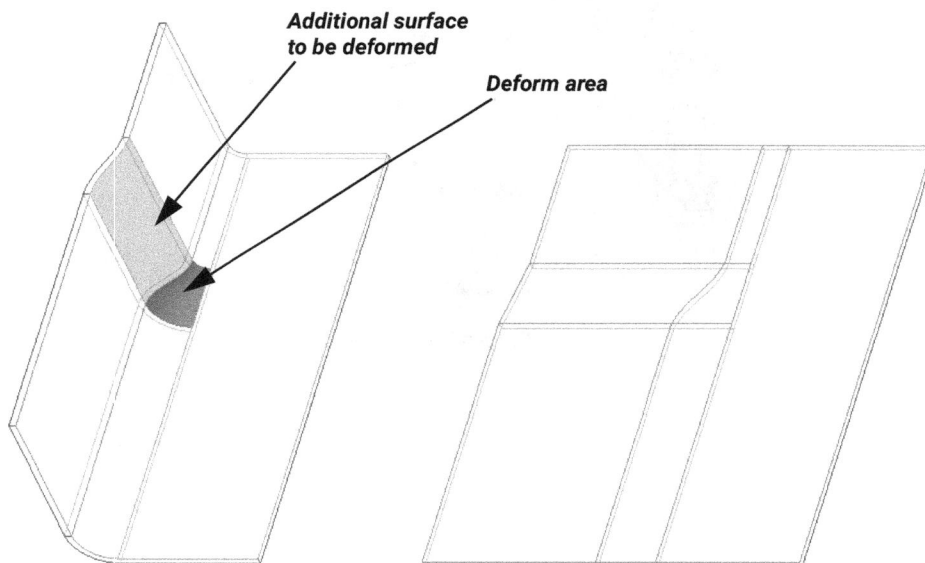

Additional surface to be deformed

Deform area

Figure 7–4

This additional surface acts as a channel through which the material deformation can travel to reach the outside boundaries of the model. If you have multiple surfaces to be deformed, you can also break up a surface into multiple patches that can be used as the channel surfaces.

When Creo Parametric needs to deform a certain portion of the model to unbend it, the system makes an approximation of the final outline of the flat pattern by connecting vertices in the deform area with line segments. The degree of approximation depends on the amount of deformation, meaning that some surfaces have more deformation than others.

Creo Parametric enables you to define the deform area with a sketch. When creating the Unbend feature, the following two elements in the *Bend* dashboard help you confine the deformation to a more specific area:

- The Deformation panel enables you to select additional surfaces to deform.

- The Deformations Control panel enables you to more accurately reflect the flattened geometry by editing the automatic sketched profile of the deform area.

Figure 7-5 shows a bent sheet metal part. After unbending, a certain amount of deformation occurs in the area surrounding the cut feature. To remove some of this deformation, you can edit the automatic deform profile to sketch one that more accurately reflects your final geometry.

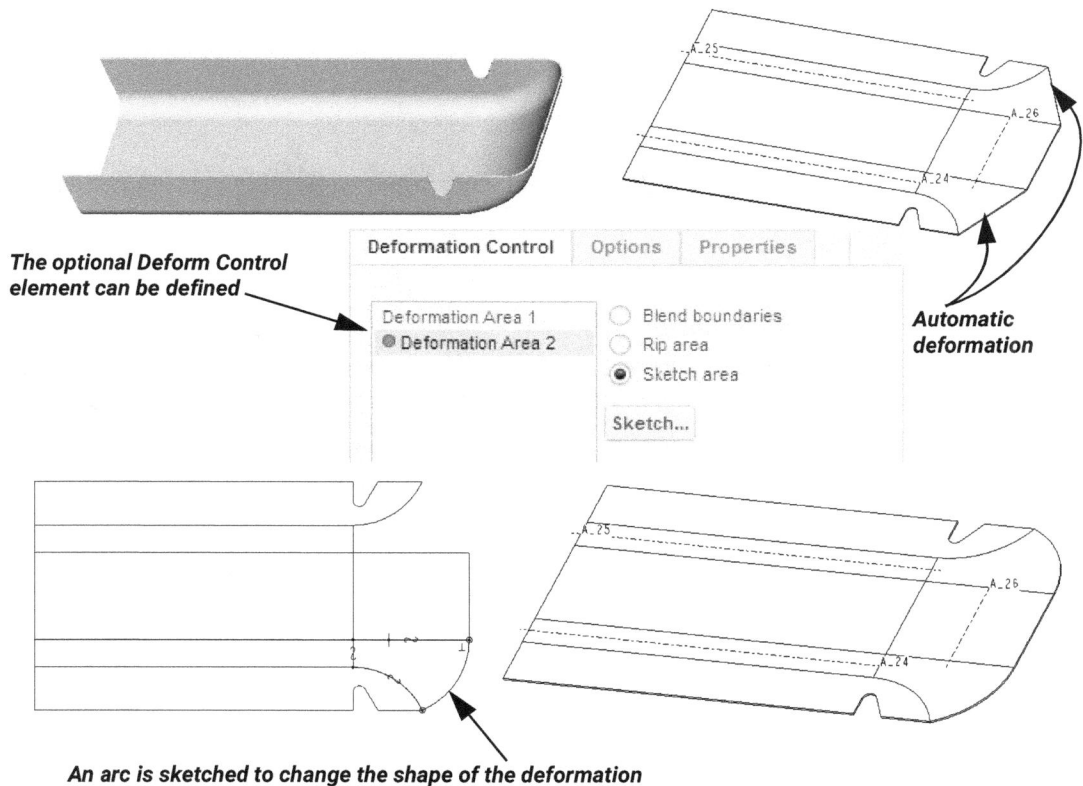

Figure 7-5

7.3 Split Area Feature

The split area feature enables you to further control the areas of the model that are deformed during unbending. This feature isolates a region of a surface to be deformed during unbending. A model can be unbent by selecting the surfaces to be deformed, resulting in unbent geometry, as shown in Figure 7−6.

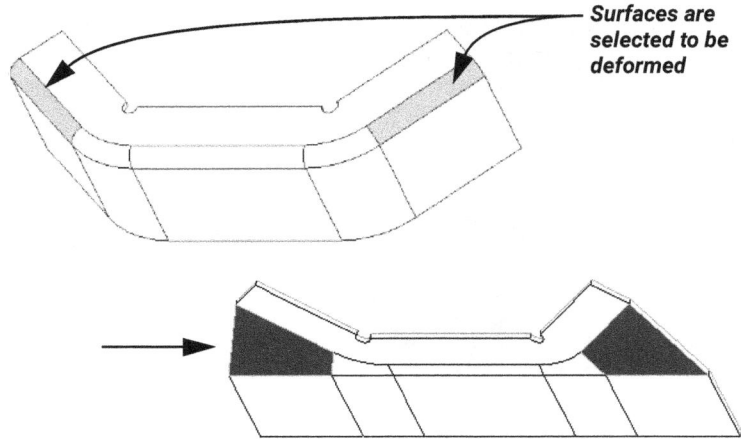

Figure 7−6

Split area features can also be created by sketching sections on adjacent surfaces, as shown in Figure 7−7. When unbending the geometry, these areas can be selected for deformation.

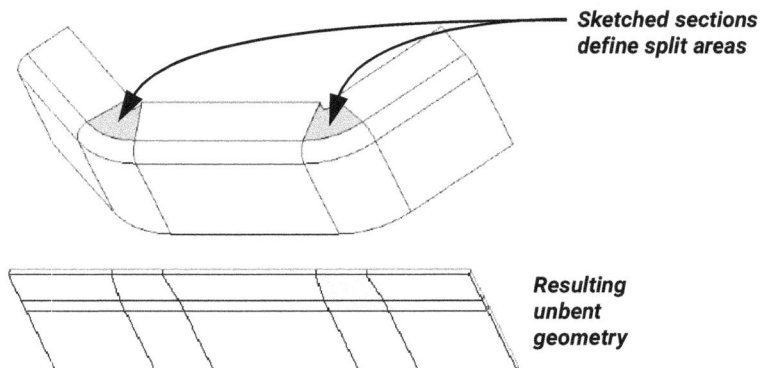

Figure 7−7

7.4 Cross-Section Driven Unbends

With non-ruled surfaces, you can use a cross-section driven unbend feature, as shown in Figure 7–8. A cross-section driven unbend feature uses an edge or sketched entity to influence the shape of the unbent geometry.

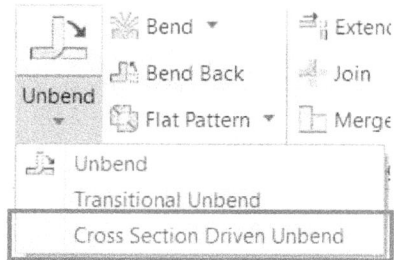

Figure 7–8

A cross-section driven unbend feature requires you to select an edge of the bend to remain fixed, select or sketch the cross-section of the unbend, and select a surface to remain fixed.

In Figure 7–9, the cross-section driven unbend feature is created by selecting an edge to influence the unbend geometry.

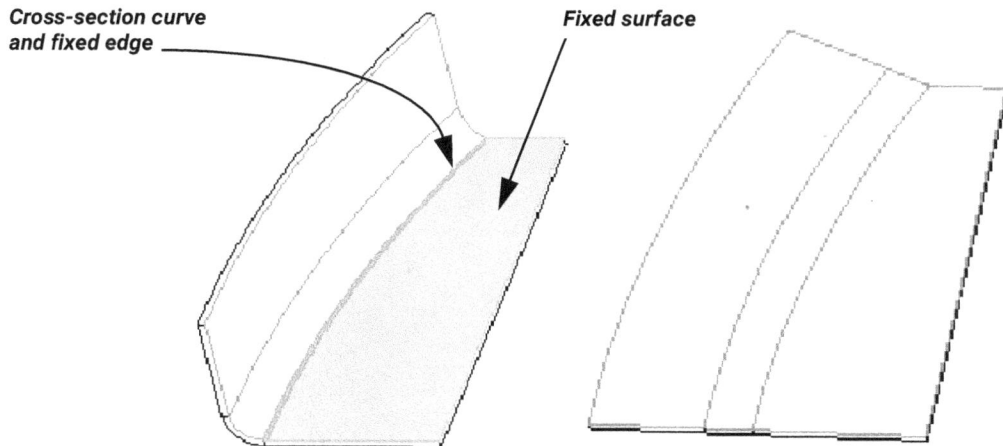

Figure 7–9

In Figure 7–10, the cross-section driven unbend feature is created by sketching an entity to influence the unbent geometry.

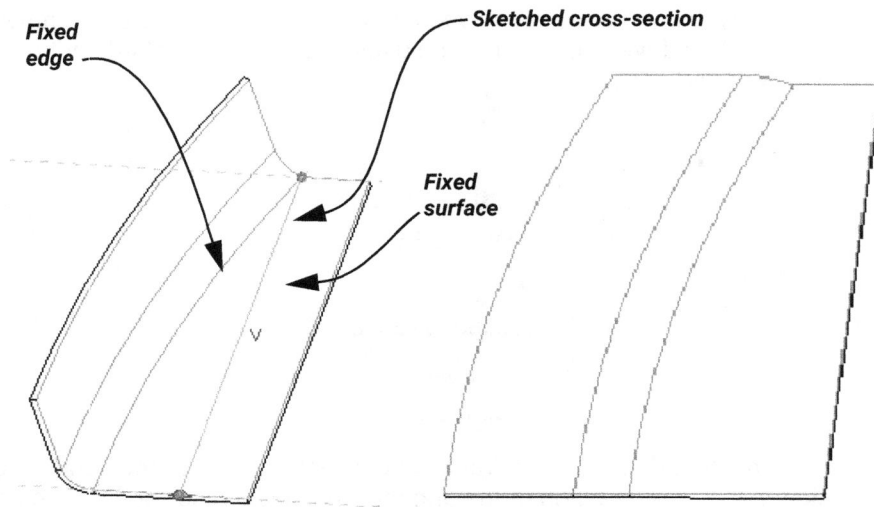

Figure 7–10

7.5 Rip Features

Depending on the types of parts you design, you might need to create additional features to unbend a model. Most sheet metal parts tend to have open edges, but some parts, such as transition pieces in HVAC environments, have closed profiles, as shown in Figure 7–11. These closed profile parts cannot be flattened without the use of a rip feature.

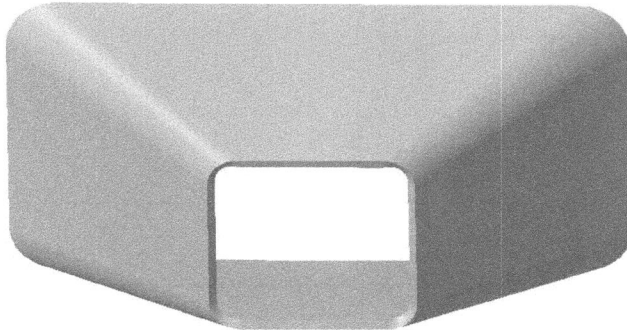

Figure 7–11

When creating a Rip feature, Creo Parametric creates a tear in the sheet metal geometry, similar to rip relief. Rip features can be created as an edge rip, surface rip, sketched rip, and rip connect, as shown in Figure 7–12.

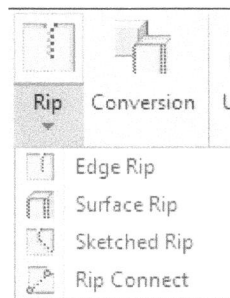

Figure 7–12

Sketch Rip

For a sketch rip, sketch a section to define the rip line, as shown in Figure 7–13.

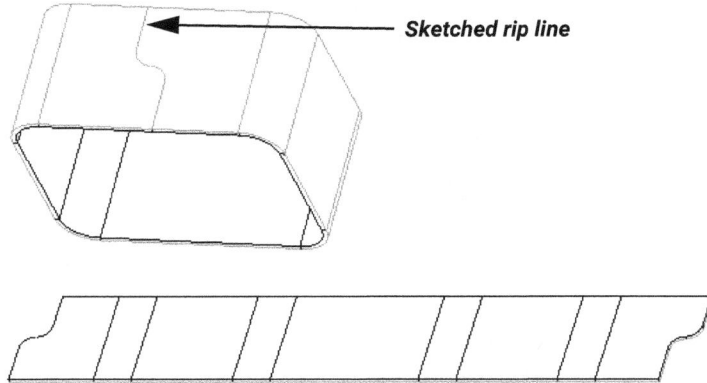

Sketched rip line

Figure 7–13

Edge Rip

For an edge rip, select an existing edge as the reference. The system creates a zero-volume cut at that location, as shown in Figure 7–14.

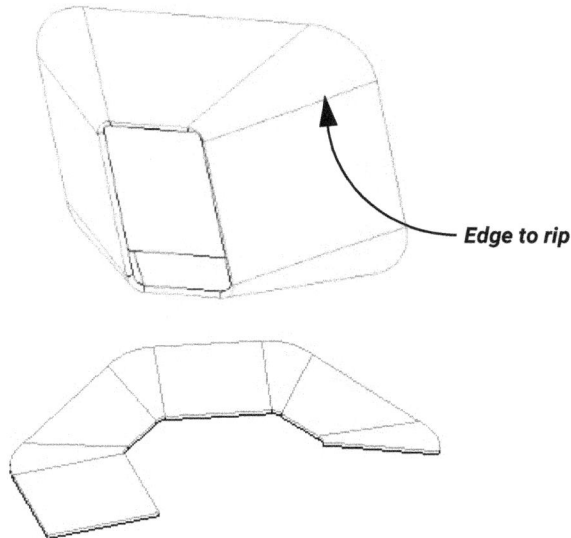

Edge to rip

Figure 7–14

Surface Rip

For a surface rip, select a surface. The system creates a cut by removing an entire surface patch, as shown in Figure 7–15.

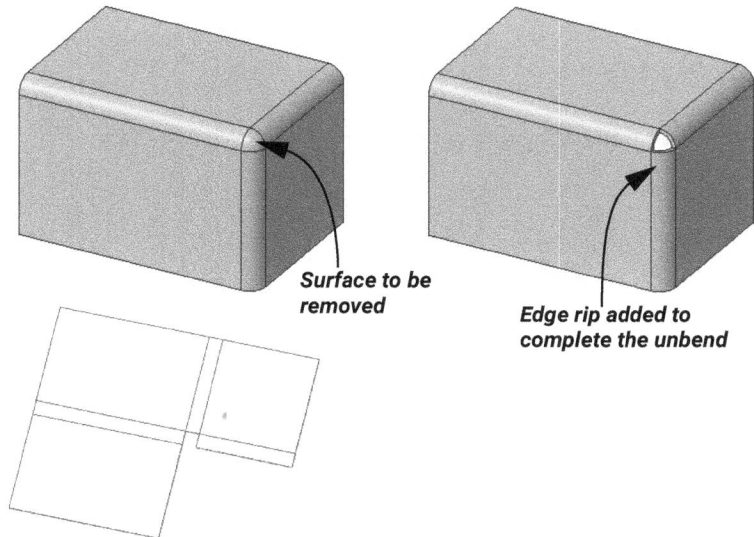

Surface to be
removed

Edge rip added to
complete the unbend

Figure 7–15

Rip Connect

The rip connect element is similar to the edge rip. However, instead of selecting an existing edge, you select two points or vertices between which to create the rip as shown in Figure 7–16. This enables some flexibility when you are deciding where to rip the sheet metal wall.

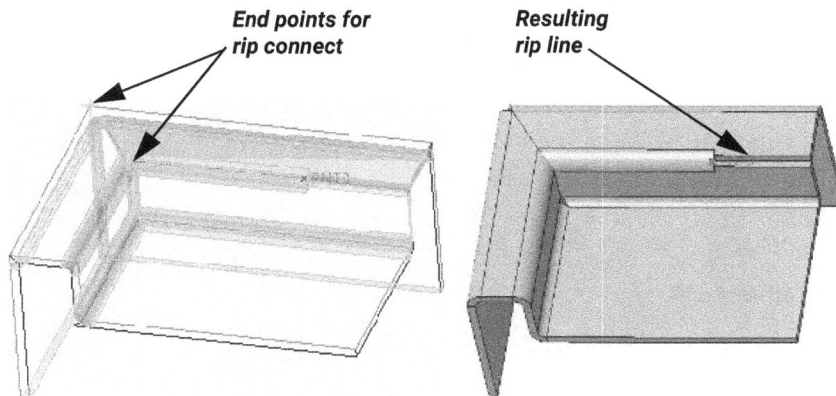

End points for
rip connect

Resulting
rip line

Figure 7–16

Practice 7a
Deform Surfaces

Practice Objective

- Use a deform surface to unbend non-ruled.

In this practice, you will unbend a feature by selecting a surface to deform. The feature displays as shown in Figure 7−17.

Figure 7−17

Design Considerations

In this exercise, you will unbend the part. You must select an additional surface to deform to complete the unbend. This surface acts as the channel through which the deformation can reach the outside boundary of the model.

1. Set the working directory to the *Deform_Surfaces* folder.

2. Open **unbend_deform_surface.prt**.

3. Set the model display as follows:

   - ⚓ *(Datum Display Filters)*: None

   - ⤳ *(Spin Center)*: Off

   - ⬜ *(Display Style)*: ⬜ (Hidden Line)

4. In the *Sheetmetal* tab, click ⬛ (Unbend).

5. The surface, shown in Figure 7–18, is selected by default to remain fixed.

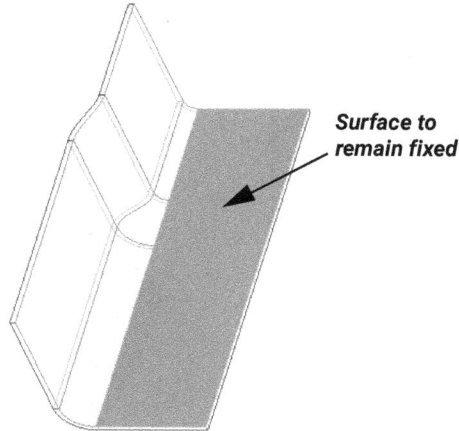

Surface to remain fixed

Figure 7–18

6. Note that the Deformations panel is highlighted. The bend feature cannot be completed without adding a deformation surface. Click **Deformations** in the *Unbend* dashboard.

7. A surface is already selected by default. Select the surface in the Automatic detected deformation surfaces collector as shown in Figure 7–19. Note that the surface highlights in the model.

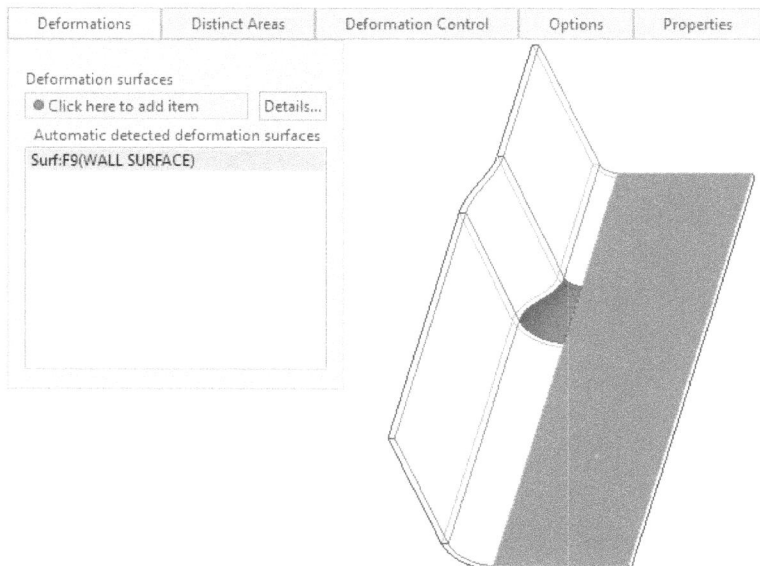

Figure 7–19

8. You must select an additional surface to deform; it acts as the channel through which the deformation can reach the outside boundary of the model. Select the *Deformation surfaces* collector and select the additional surface to be deformed, as shown in Figure 7–20.

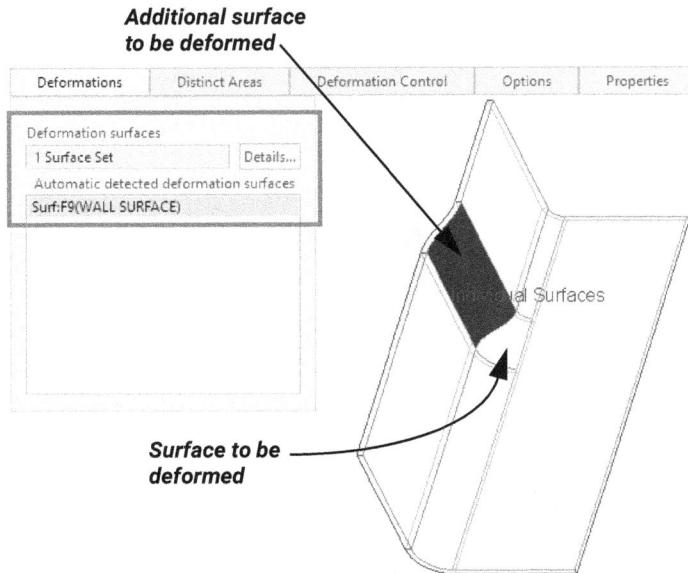

Figure 7–20

9. Complete the unbend feature. The flattened part displays as shown in Figure 7–21.

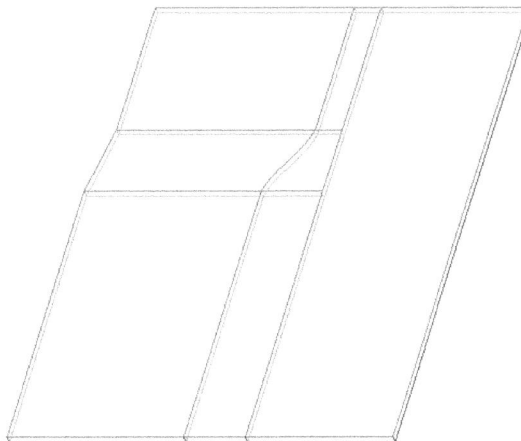

Figure 7–21

10. Save the file and erase it from memory.

End of practice

Practice 7b
Cross-Section Driven Unbend

Practice Objective

- Create a cross-section driven unbend.

In this practice, you will create two cross-section driven unbend features. One unbend is influenced by a selected edge and the other unbend is influenced by a sketched edge. The feature displays as shown in Figure 7–22.

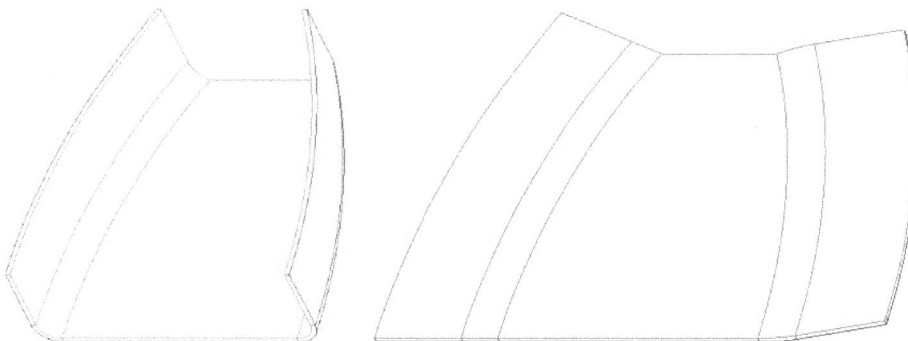

Figure 7–22

Task 1: Open a part and create a cross-section driven unbend using a selected edge.

Design Considerations

In this task, you will create a cross-section driven unbend using a selected edge. The resulting outside edges will be perpendicular to the cross-section curve reference.

1. Set the working directory the *Cross_Section_Unbend* folder.

2. Open **unbend_xsec.prt**.

3. Set the model display as follows:

- *(Datum Display Filters)*: None

- *(Spin Center)*: Off

- *(Display Style)*: (No Hidden)

4. Expand ⬚ (Unbend) and select **Cross Section Driven Unbend,** as shown in Figure 7‒23.

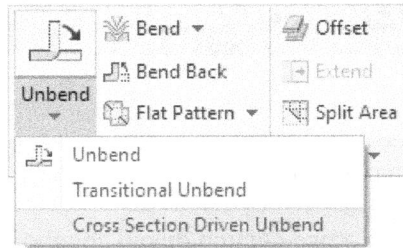

Figure 7‒23

5. The Xsec Driven Type dialog box opens, as shown in Figure 7‒24.

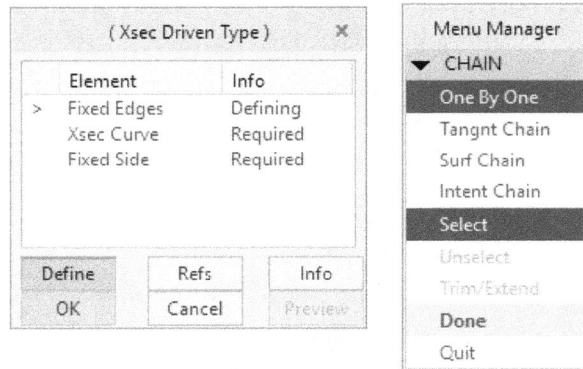

Figure 7‒24

6. Maintain the default options and select the edge to remain fixed, as shown in Figure 7‒25.

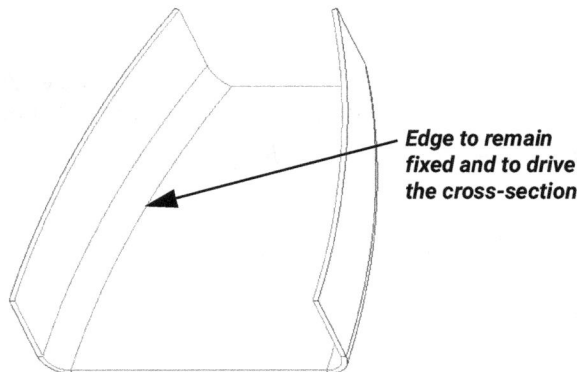

*Edge to remain
fixed and to drive
the cross-section*

Figure 7‒25

7. Select **Done**.

8. Select **Select Curve>Done**. Select the same edge as the curve to control the cross-section.

9. Select **Done**.

10. Select **Okay** to specify the side to remain fixed as shown in Figure 7–26. If required, select **Flip**.

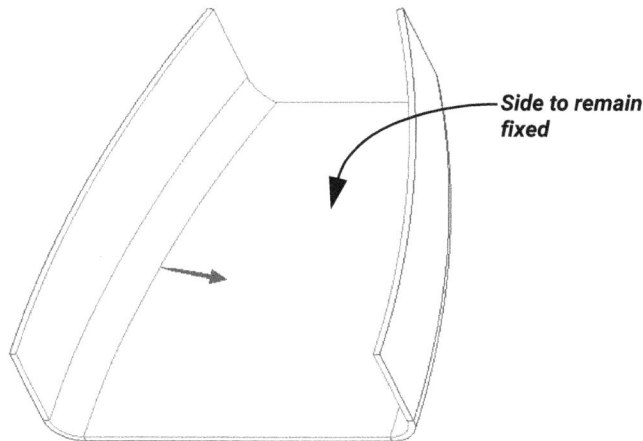

Figure 7–26

11. Click **OK** in the Xsec Driven Type dialog box. The final flattened condition of the model is shown in Figure 7–27. The resulting outside edges are perpendicular to the cross-section curve reference.

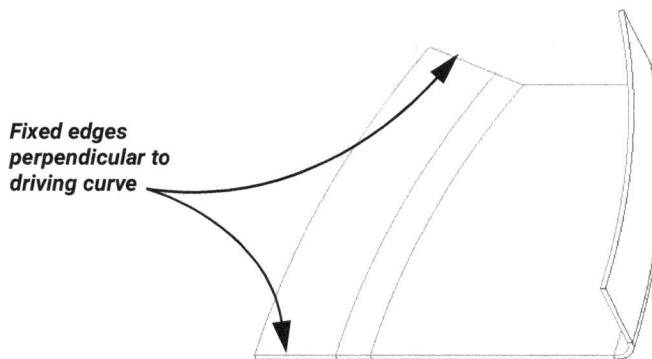

Figure 7–27

Task 2: Create a cross-section drive unbend feature using a sketched curve.

Design Considerations

In this task, you will create a cross-section drive unbend feature using a sketched curve. The resulting outside edges will be perpendicular to the cross-section curve reference.

1. Expand ⌐ (Unbend) and select **Cross Section Driven Unbend**.
2. Select the fixed edge as shown in Figure 7–28.

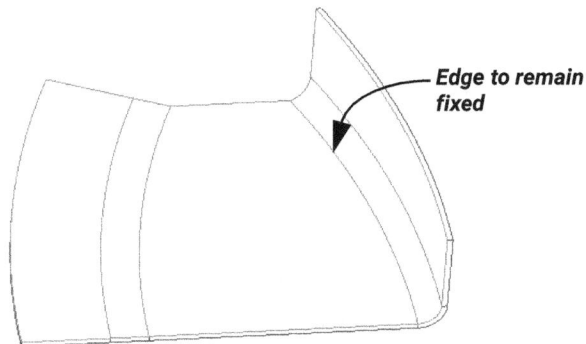

Edge to remain fixed

Figure 7–28

3. Select **Done**.
4. Select **Sketch Curve>Done**.
5. Select the sketching plane shown in Figure 7–29.
6. Select Bottom and select the edge shown in Figure 7–29 as the orientation reference.

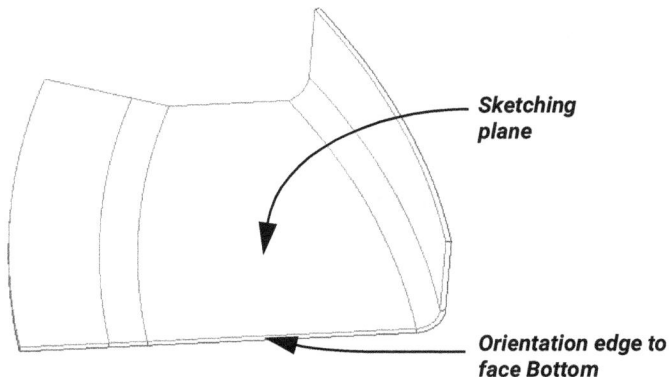

Sketching plane

Orientation edge to face Bottom

Figure 7–29

7. Select two vertices as Sketcher references and sketch the line shown in Figure 7–30.

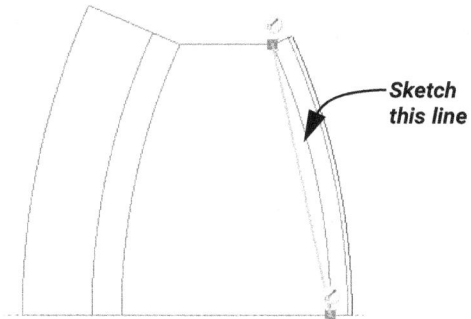

Figure 7–30

8. Complete the sketch.

9. Select the side of the curve to remain fixed, as shown in Figure 7–31 and select **Okay**.

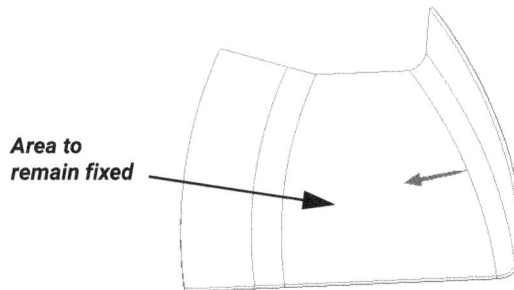

Figure 7–31

10. Click **OK** in the dialog box. The finished unbend feature is shown in Figure 7–32.

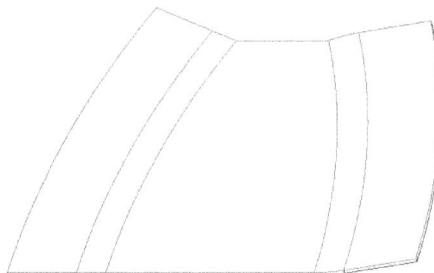

Figure 7–32

11. Save the part and erase it from memory.

End of practice

Practice 7c
Rip Features and Deformation Control

Practice Objectives

- Create a rip feature.
- Use the deform control element to alter the unbent geometry.

In this practice, you will use an edge rip to unbend a part. The resulting deformation area is adjusted by sketching a new outline, as shown in Figure 7–33.

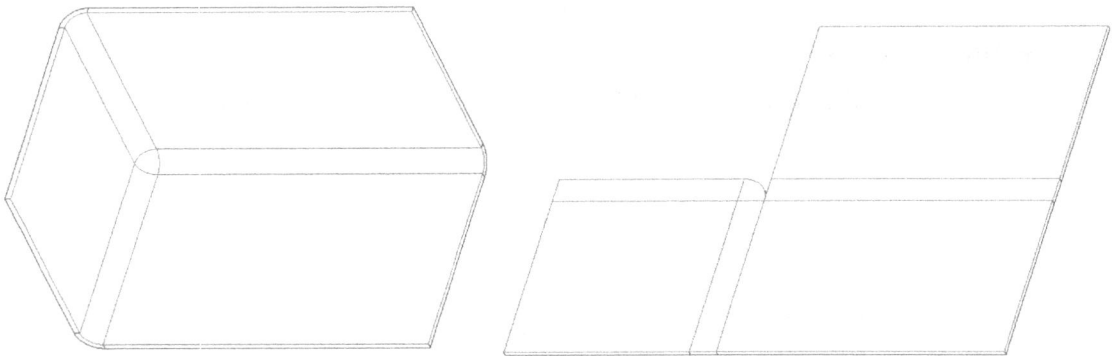

Figure 7–33

Task 1: Open a part and create an edge rip.

Design Considerations

In this task, you will create an edge rip to create a zero-volume cut. This edge rip makes an unbend feature possible in the next task.

1. Set the working directory to the *Deform_Control* folder.

2. Open **deform_control.prt**.

3. Set the model display as follows:

    - *⚒ (Datum Display Filters)*: None

    - *➤ (Spin Center)*: Off

    - *▱ (Display Style)*: ▱ (No Hidden)

4. Expand ⬚ (Rip) and select ⬚ (Edge Rip) in the Engineering group in the *Engineering* tab to tear the model along an edge. The *Edge Rip* dashboard opens as shown in Figure 7−34.

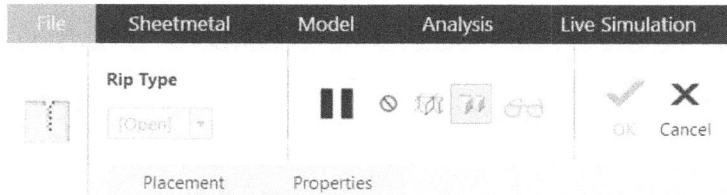

Figure 7−34

5. Select the two edges along which to create the rip feature, as shown in Figure 7−35.

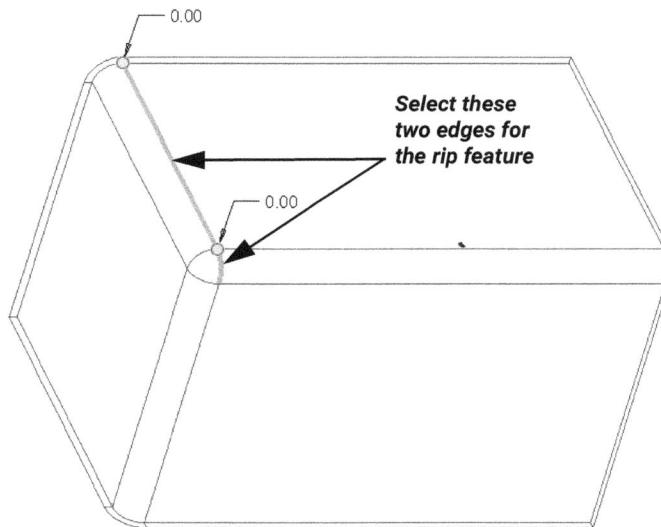

Figure 7−35

6. Click ✔ (OK) in the *Edge Rip* dashboard. A zero-volume cut has been created along the selected edges.

Task 2: Unbend the geometry.

Design Considerations

In this task, you will create an unbend feature facilitated by the edge rip created in Task 1. The geometry of the resulting deform area is examined.

1. Click ⬚ (Unbend).

2. Right-click and select **Clear** to remove the default fixed surface. Select the surface to remain fixed as shown in Figure 7-36.

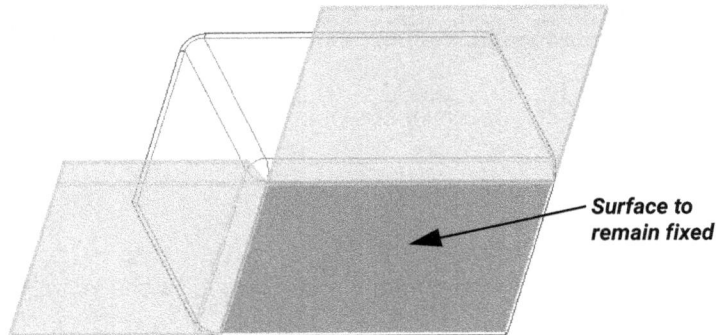

Surface to
remain fixed

Figure 7-36

3. Click 𝄐 (Verify Mode) to preview the model. Note the bend area where the corner of the model was located. Verify that the deformation that has occurred as shown in Figure 7-37.

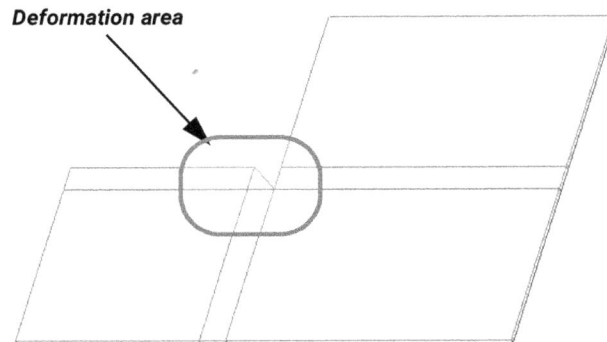

Deformation area

Figure 7-37

Task 3: Define the Deform Control element.

Design Considerations

In this task, you will edit the profile of the deform area to a shape that could be more consistent with the forming operations.

1. Click ▶ (Resume). Select the Deformation Control panel.

2. Select the Deformation Control panel and select **Sketch area**, as shown in Figure 7–38.

Figure 7–38

3. Click **Sketch** in the Deformation Control panel.

4. The *Sketch* tab opens. You can now edit the profile of the deformed area.

5. Sketch a 3-point arc to connect the end points of the current deform area profile, as shown in Figure 7–39. No additional dimensions or references are required.

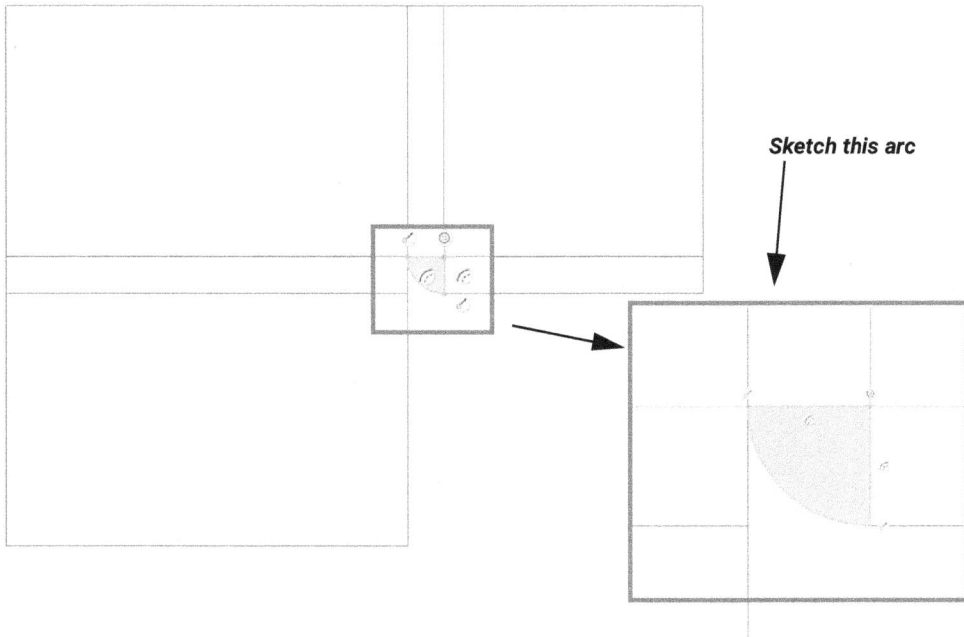

Sketch this arc

Figure 7–39

6. Complete the sketch.

7. Click ✔ (OK) in the *Unbend* dashboard.

8. The finished Unbend feature is shown in Figure 7–40.

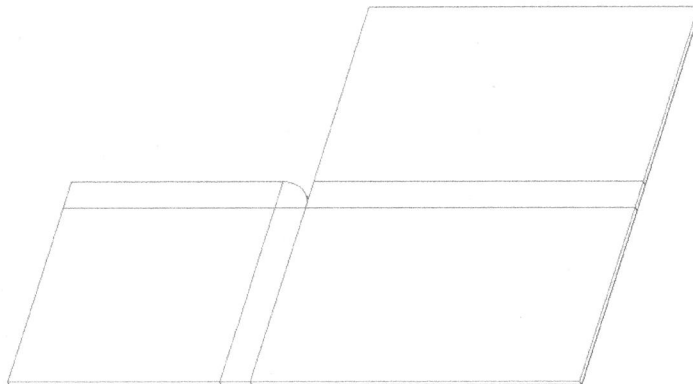

Figure 7–40

9. Save the file and erase it from memory.

End of practice

Practice 7d
Split Area Feature

Practice Objective

*   Create a split area feature.

In this practice, you will unbend a part using split area features to isolate deformation to specific regions, as shown in Figure 7–41.

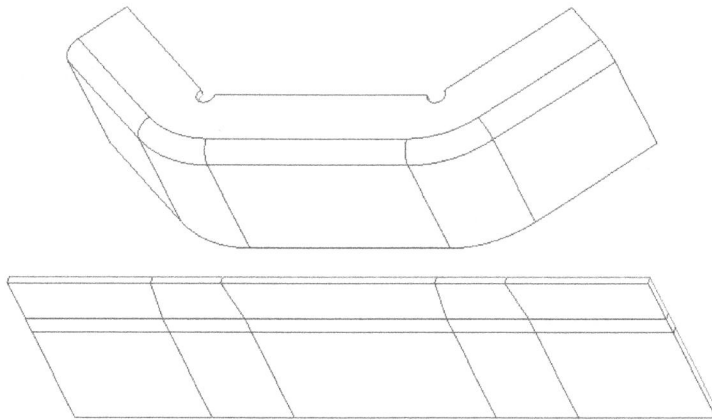

Figure 7–41

Task 1: Open a part and unbend the geometry.

Design Considerations

In this task, you will unbend the geometry by selecting available surfaces as deformation areas.

1. Set the working directory to the *Split_Area* folder.
2. Open **deform_area.prt**.
3. Set the model display as follows:

    *   ⁙ *(Datum Display Filters)*: None
    *   ⋙ *(Spin Center)*: Off
    *   ◻ *(Display Style)*: ◻ (No Hidden)

4. Click ⟂ (Unbend). Select the surface shown in Figure 7–42 as the surface to remain fixed.

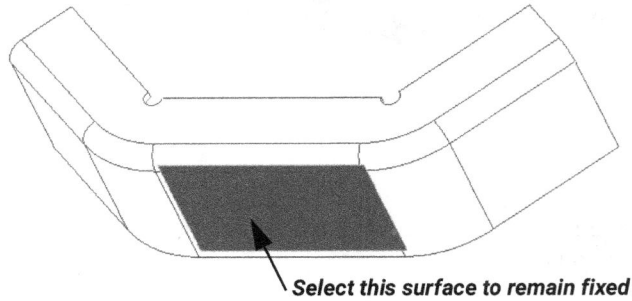

Select this surface to remain fixed

Figure 7–42

5. Select the Deformations panel. The shaded surfaces in Figure 7–43 are automatically selected to deform. The deformation surfaces do not reach the outside of the part. You must select additional surfaces to be deformed. Select the *Deformation surfaces* collector and select the surfaces shown in Figure 7–43.

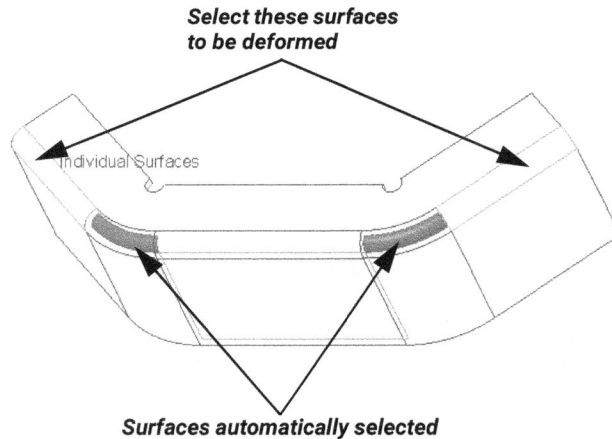

Select these surfaces to be deformed

Individual Surfaces

Surfaces automatically selected

Figure 7–43

Note: Press *<Ctrl>* to select the two surfaces.

6. Complete the feature. The deformation occurs in the surfaces you selected, as shown in Figure 7−44.

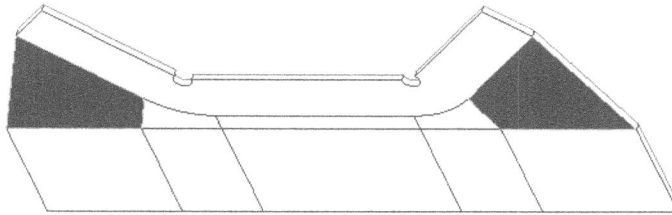

Figure 7−44

7. Since this deformation model is not acceptable, delete the unbend feature.

Task 2: Create split areas to isolate the deformation during unbending.

Design Considerations

In this task, you will create split areas to isolate the deformation. These split areas are then selected to facilitate the unbending of the part.

1. Click ▧ (Split Area) in the Editing group from the *Engineering* tab.

2. Select the plane shown in Figure 7−45 as the sketching plane.

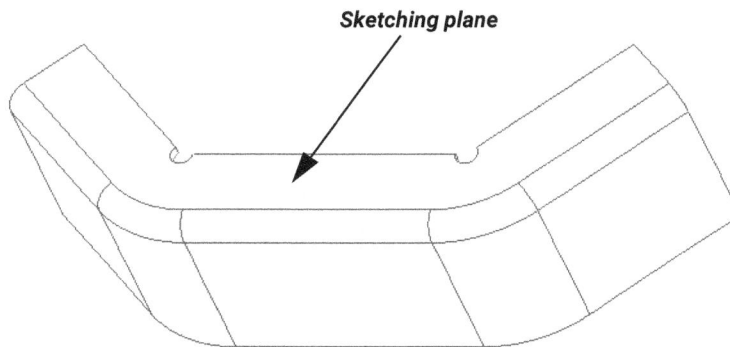

Figure 7−45

3. Sketch the section shown in Figure 7−46. Connect the end points of the arcs with line segments.

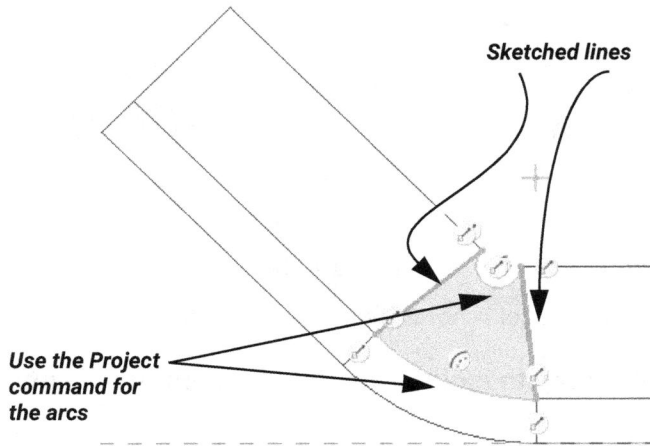

Sketched lines

Use the Project command for the arcs

Figure 7−46

4. The completed split area displays as shown in Figure 7−47.

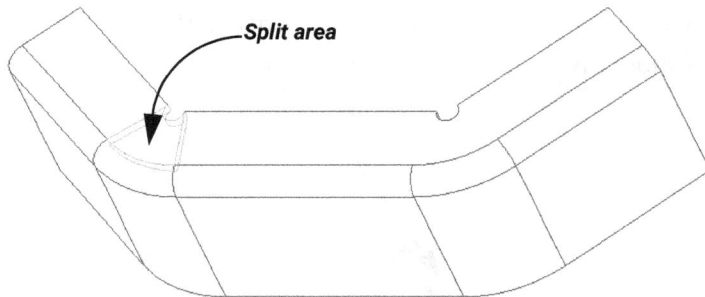

Split area

Figure 7−47

5. Create a second split area feature, as shown in Figure 7−48.

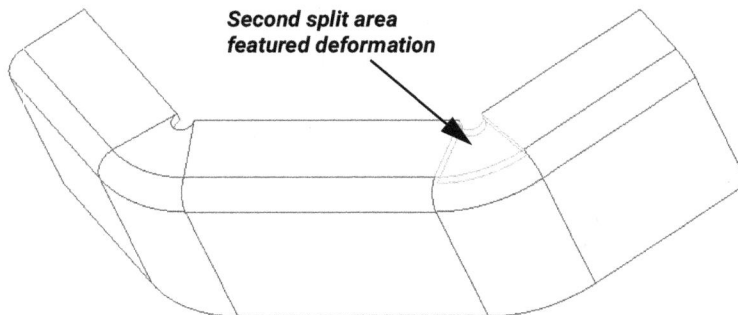

Second split area featured deformation

Figure 7−48

Task 3: Create an unbend feature using the deform areas.

Design Considerations

In this task, you will use the split areas created in Task 2 to unbend the part. The shapes of the split areas can be sketched to represent results from different process and materials.

1. Unbend the entire part. If required, select the surface shown in Figure 7–49 as the surface to remain fixed.

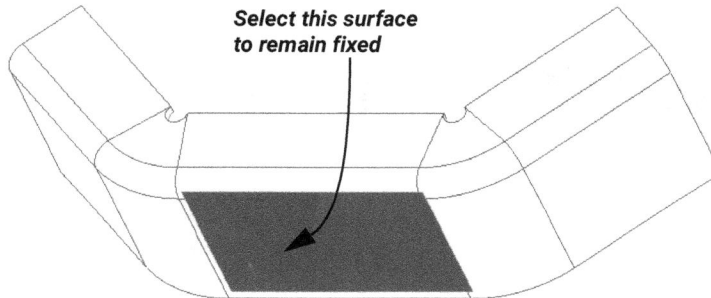

Select this surface to remain fixed

Figure 7–49

2. Select the Deformations panel.

3. Note the there are two surfaces already selected for deformation. Ensure the first surface in the automatic detected deformation surface collector is highlighted. Select in the Deformation surfaces collection field and select the split area feature adjacent to the highlighted surface, as shown in Figure 7–50.

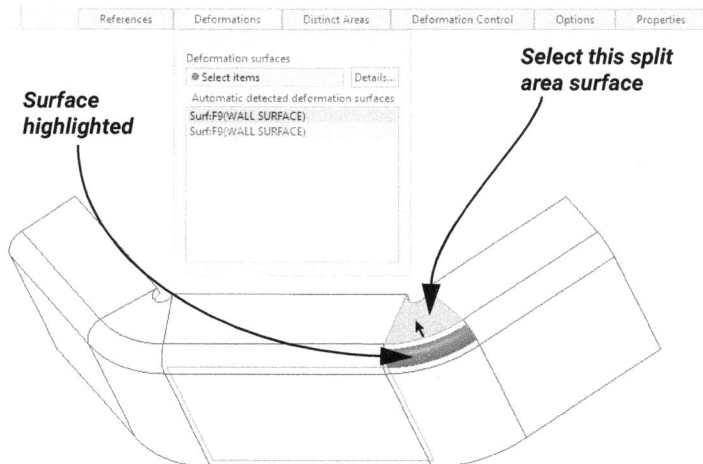

Surface highlighted

Select this split area surface

Figure 7–50

4. Repeat Step 3, hold <Ctrl>, and select the other split area surface.

5. Complete the feature. The deformation now occurs in the split areas you selected, as shown in Figure 7-51.

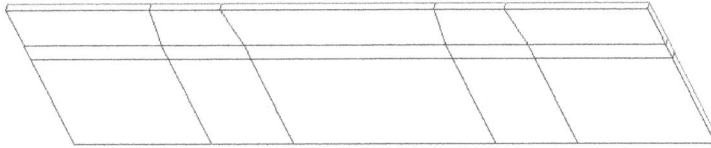

Figure 7-51

6. Save the part and erase it from memory.

End of practice

Chapter Review Questions

1. Which of the following options describes geometry that only has curvature in one direction, such as cylindrical or conical geometry?

   a. Ruled geometry

   b. Non-ruled geometry

2. To flatten non-ruled geometry, you must typically select additional geometry to deform that reaches to the outside boundary of the model.

   a. True

   b. False

3. If you have multiple surfaces to be deformed, you can also divide a surface into multiple patches that can be used as the channel surfaces.

   a. True

   b. False

4. Which of the following features enables you to further control the areas of the model that are deformed during unbending? This feature isolates a region of a surface to be deformed during unbending.

   a. Offset

   b. Bend Back

   c. Rip

   d. Split Area

5. Which of the following features enables you to use an edge or sketched entity to influence the shape of the unbent geometry?

   a. Offset

   b. Bend Back

   c. Rip

   d. Cross Section Driven Unbend

6. A closed profile part cannot be flattened without the use of a rip feature.

   a. True

   b. False

Answers: 1a, 2a, 3a, 4d, 5d, 6a

Sheet Metal Forms

Creo Parametric provides several tools, such as punches and dies, for forming your sheet metal model using external features to adjust the shape.

Learning Objectives

- Understand how a die or punch form feature is created and their differences.
- Understand the general steps to place an existing form feature using constraints.
- Learn the process used to start and place a Punch Form feature using assembly constraints.
- Learn the process used to start and place a Die Form feature using assembly constraints.
- Learn the general steps used to flatten form geometry that spreads over single or multiple surfaces.
- Use the Unstamp Edges feature to flatten selected rounded and chamfered edges.
- Understand the restrictions that apply when using form features on a sheet metal part.

8.1 Introduction to Form Features

Creo Parametric provides you with the ability to emulate forming operations in sheet metal fabrication with form features. Form features use external reference parts to define the shape to be impressed into the sheet metal part. They can be created using die or punch forms.

Die

A die form is a model that contains features that create a negative shape to be formed on a sheet metal part. A base plane or surface is used as a reference for locating it against a sheet metal wall.

A die form reference part is shown on the left in Figure 8–1. A sheet metal part with the resulting form feature is shown on the right.

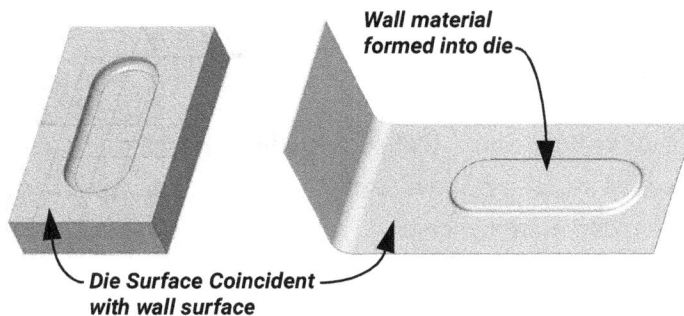

Figure 8–1

Note: *The geometry of multiple die forms can be defined on the same die form reference part.*

Punch

A punch form is a model that contains features that create a positive shape to be formed on a sheet metal part. While these features can take on any shape, try to keep them as simple as possible. As with die forms, you can create multiple punch forms on a single reference model. To differentiate between them, Creo Parametric prompts you with an arrow that specifies which side of the form is affected.

Figure 8−2 shows a punch form reference part containing geometry for two different punch forms. The adjacent sheet metal parts have two different form features created using the same reference part.

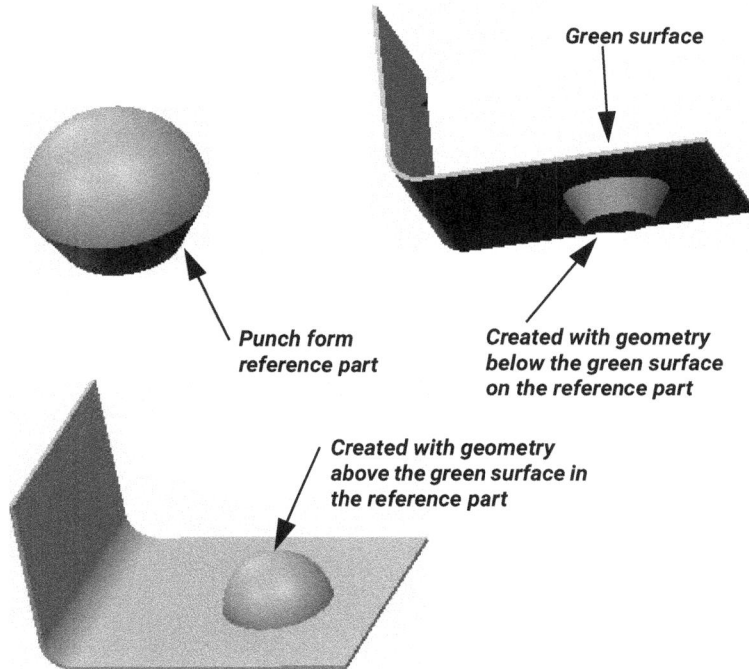

Green surface

Punch form reference part

Created with geometry below the green surface on the reference part

Created with geometry above the green surface in the reference part

Figure 8−2

Note: *You can create die and punch form reference parts as solid or sheet metal parts. If created as a sheet metal part, the green surface corresponds to the form geometry.*

8.2 Placing a Punch or Die Form Feature

The placement of punch and die features is almost identical. The main difference is in the real-world operation these features are representing: punches are positive shapes over which the sheet metal is formed and dies are negative shapes into which the sheet metal is formed.

How To: Place a Punch or Die Form Feature

1. In the *Sheetmetal* tab, expand ⬇ (Form) and select ⬇ (Die Form) or ⬇ (Punch Form) to open the form dashboard. For example, the *Punch Form* dashboard is shown in Figure 8–3.

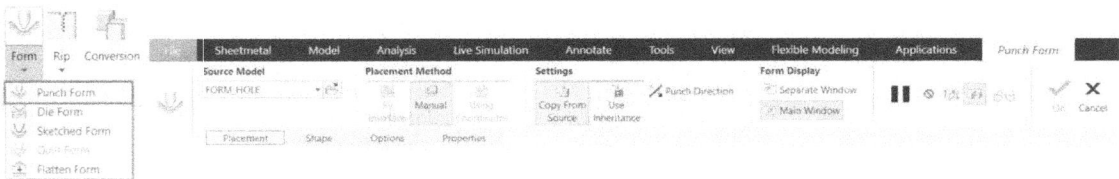

Figure 8–3

2. Click ⬜ (Open) and select the required form part in the Open dialog box.

   Note: This example assumes that the form part has already been created.

   Several options are available for adding the form feature:

   - ⬜ (Place Using Interface): Place a form using Interface.

   - ⬜ (Place Manually): Place a form using Standard Assembly Placement.

   - ⬜ (Place Using Coordinate System): Place a form using a Coordinate System.

   Note: It is recommended that you always create your form reference parts with the default datum planes. This ensures that you always have references for assembling the form part to the sheet metal part.

3. When manually placing a form, you add assembly placement constraints to position the form feature on the sheet metal part, as shown in the Die form example in Figure 8–4.

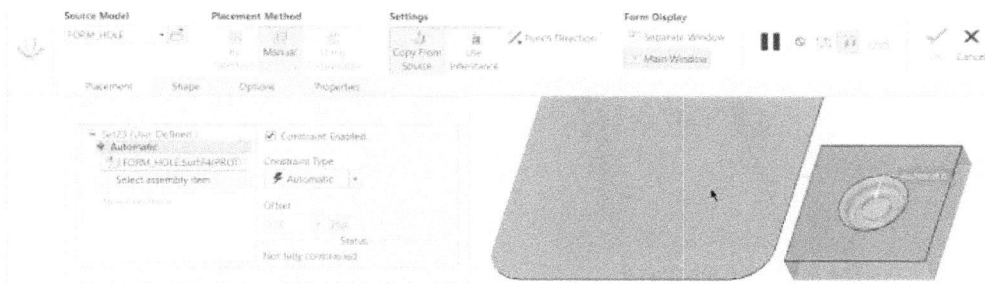

Figure 8–4

Additional icon options are described as follows:

- (Copy Dependant Merge): Creates a dependent relationship between the form feature and sheet metal part when the form feature is placed. If the form feature is modified, the sheet metal part updates with the changes. If the form feature is moved or deleted, Creo Parametric freezes the form geometry on the sheet metal part.

- (Copy Independent Inheritance): Places the form feature on the sheet metal part without establishing a dependent relationship. If the form part is modified, the sheet metal part does not update with the changes.

- (Flip Punching Direction): Used to flip the form direction.

When a form is an independent inheritance, you can change it locally and save it as a new form tool. You can right-click on the form feature and select **Save Source Model**, as shown in Figure 8–5, to save the form with a new name.

Figure 8–5

Form geometry can contain openings or holes as shown in Figure 8–6. The opening cannot extend below the base plane and any opening must be able to accommodate at least two times the material thickness of the sheet metal wall.

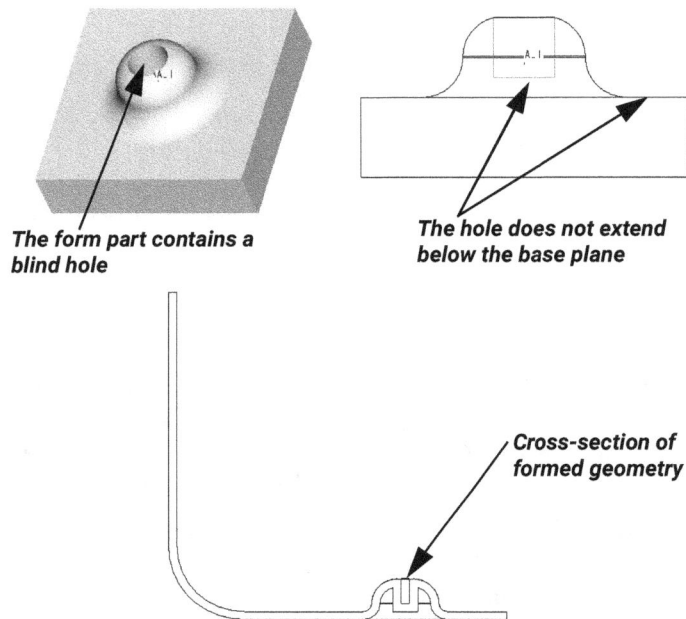

The form part contains a blind hole

The hole does not extend below the base plane

Cross-section of formed geometry

Figure 8–6

The Options panel shown in Figure 8–7, enables you to select the types of edges that are to be rounded and enables you to enter the inside or outside radius. The image shown is for a punch, but the panel for the die is identical. The tool's manufacturing information can be entered in the *Tool Name* and *Coordinate System* fields.

Figure 8–7

4. The *Excluded punch (die) model surfaces* collector to define an opening. When you select a surface on the form reference part, the corresponding surface on the formed sheet metal geometry is removed, as shown in Figure 8–8.

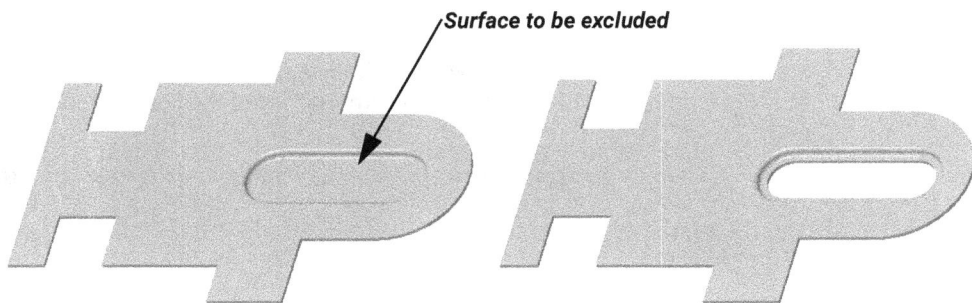

Figure 8–8

5. Click ✓ (OK) in the Form dialog box to complete the feature.

Dependency Options

The dependency options for ⩔ (Punch Form) and ⩕ (Die Form) features are the same as merge and inheritance features. In the dashboard, click ⊞ (Copy Independent), expand the Shape panel, and select **Automatic Update**, **Manual Update**, or **No Dependency**, as shown in Figure 8–9.

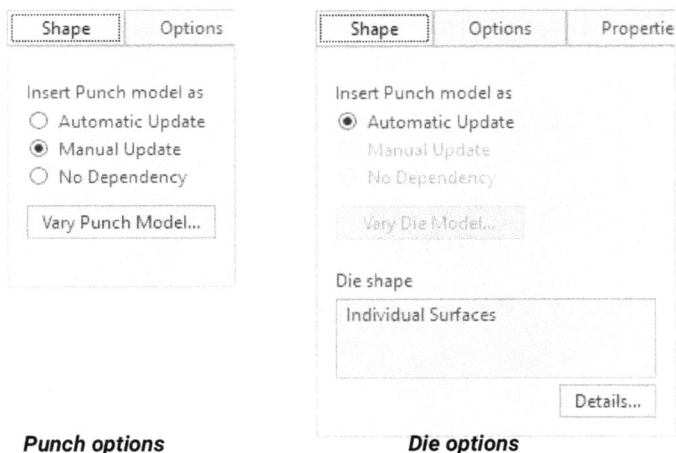

Shape	Options		Shape	Options	Propertie

Insert Punch model as
○ Automatic Update
◉ Manual Update
○ No Dependency

Vary Punch Model...

Insert Punch model as
◉ Automatic Update
○ Manual Update
○ No Dependency

Vary Die Model...

Die shape

Individual Surfaces

Details...

Punch options　　　　　　　**Die options**

Figure 8–9

The options in the Shape panel are as follows:

Option	Description
Automatic Update	The feature is automatically updated when the source model is modified and in session.
Manual Update	The feature is not updated when the source geometry is modified. You can update the feature at any time, provided the source geometry is available.
No Dependency	There is no dependency between the feature and the source model.

Assembly Considerations

Consider how different assembly techniques affect the resulting geometry. On the left in Figure 8–10, the base plane of the reference part is constrained to the top surface of the sheet metal part. On the right, the base plane of the reference part is constrained with the underside of the sheet metal part. This difference affects the depth to which the form geometry is pressed into the sheet metal material.

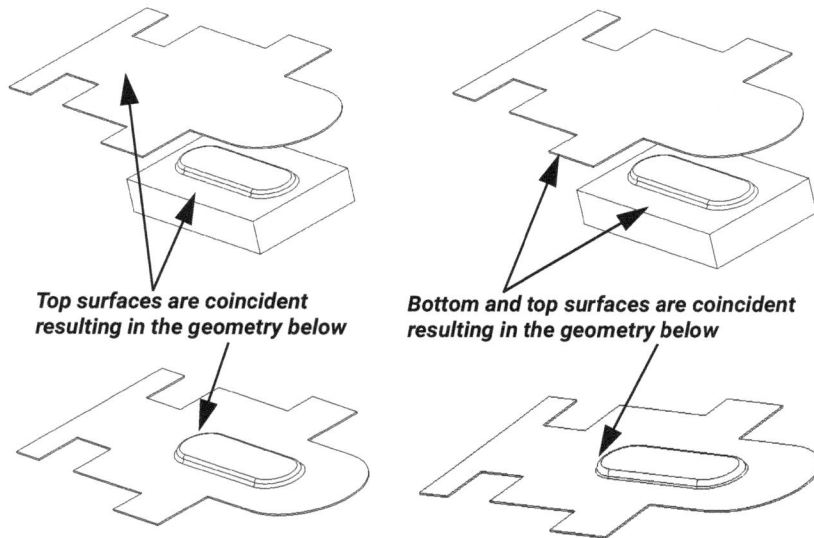

Top surfaces are coincident resulting in the geometry below

Bottom and top surfaces are coincident resulting in the geometry below

Figure 8–10

Radius Considerations

Consider the magnitude of the radius values on the form part. For example, to align the surfaces in the sheet metal and punch form reference part shown in Figure 8–11, the large radius on the form must have a magnitude greater than the sheet metal thickness. The resulting formed geometry has an inside radius equal to (R-T).

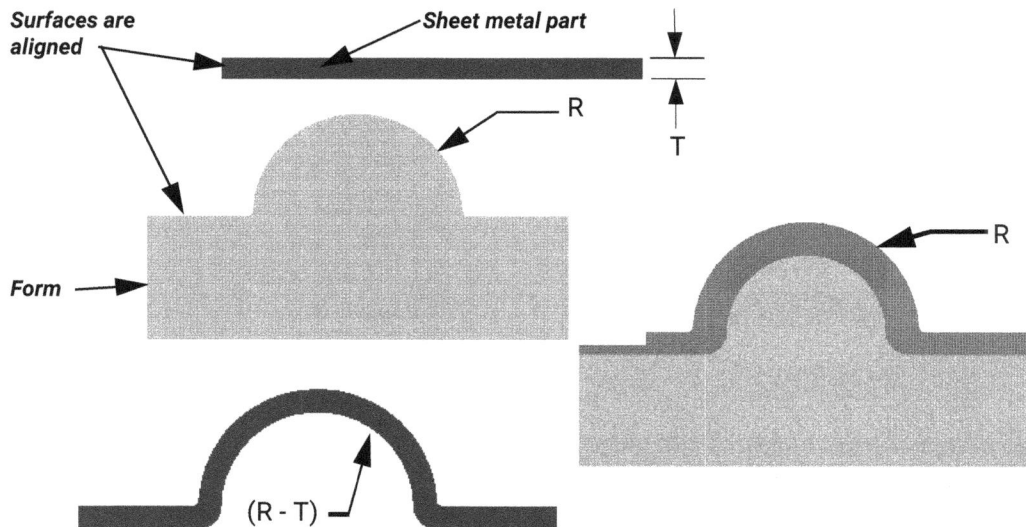

Surfaces are aligned

Sheet metal part

R

T

Form

R

(R - T)

Figure 8–11

Bending

Bend and unbend features can be created across form geometry, as shown in Figure 8–12.

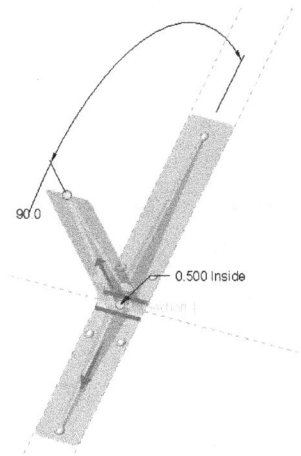

Figure 8–12

8.3 Flattening Form Geometry

You might need to return the model to the flat condition after you have placed the form features. Formed geometry cannot be unbent using the Unbend feature. To flatten formed geometry, you must create a flatten form feature. The flatten form can be used for forms that spread over single or multiple surfaces.

Creo Parametric does not develop the form surfaces. Instead, the flatten form feature adds a surface to the model in the shape of the form feature to hold its place, as shown in Figure 8–13.

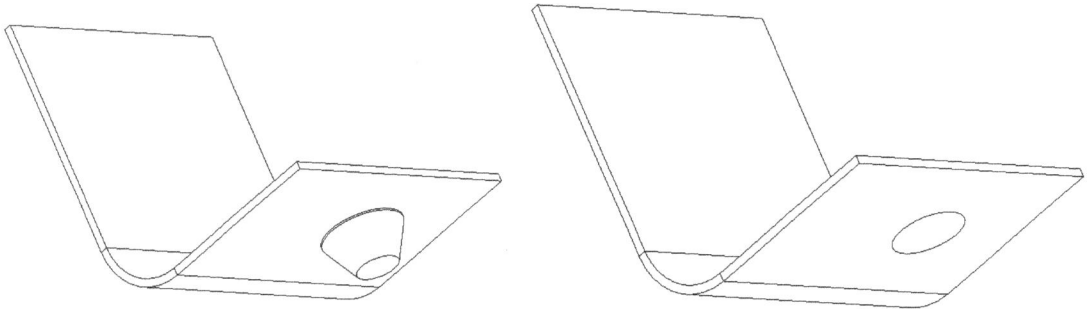

Figure 8–13

If you need to remove the form features from the model to reduce regeneration times, it is better to suppress them than to use the **Flatten Form** feature option.

How To: Flatten Form Geometry

1. Expand ⩗ (Form) and select ⬆ (Flatten Form) in the *Sheetmetal* tab. The *Flatten Form* dashboard opens, as shown as in Figure 8–14.

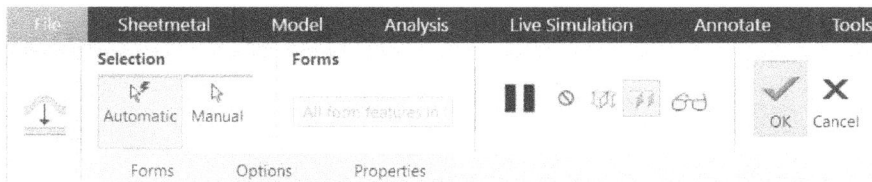

Figure 8–14

2. Select the form geometry in the model shown in Figure 8–15.

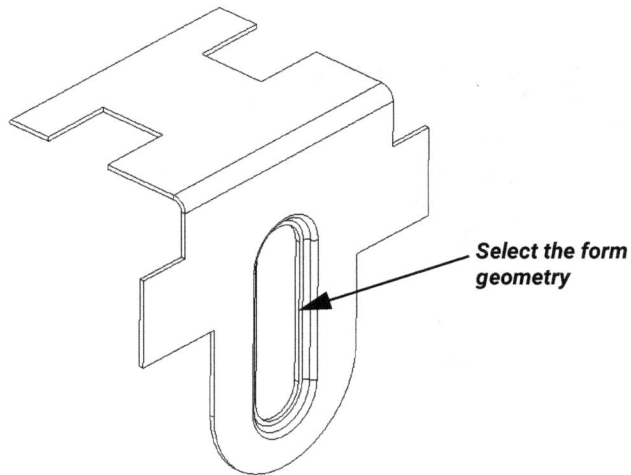

Select the form geometry

Figure 8–15

3. Click ✓ (OK) in the *Flatten* dashboard to complete the operation.

8.4 Flat Patterns

Using flat patterns, the entire form can be flattened, as shown in Figure 8–16.

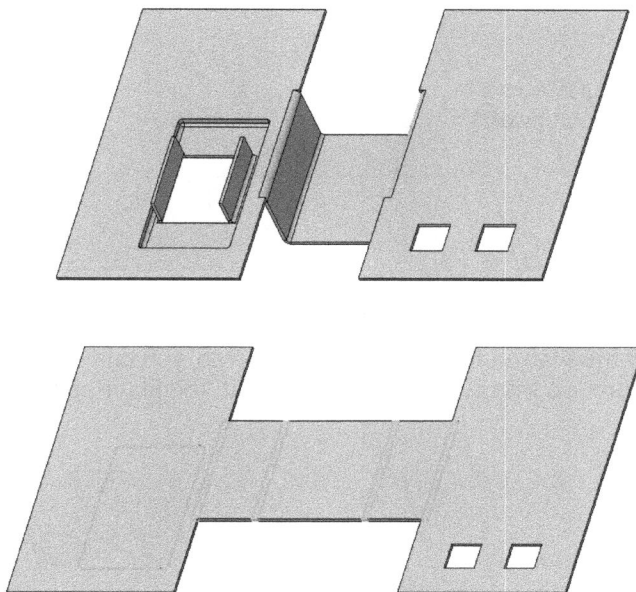

Figure 8–16

To flatten a model, click 🔲 (Flat Pattern) and the *Flat Pattern* dashboard opens. Expand the Options panel and ensure that the **Flatten forms** option is selected, as shown in Figure 8–17.

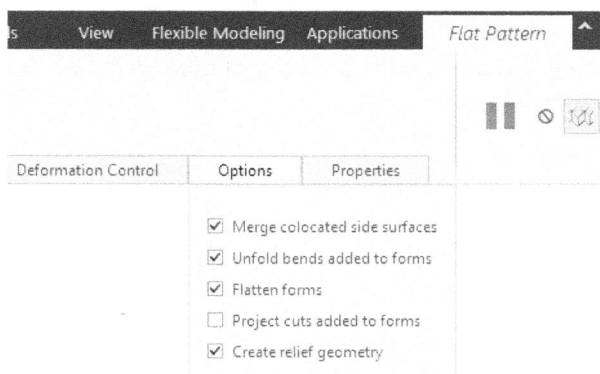

Figure 8–17

If you clear the **Flatten forms** checkbox, forms remain in their formed state, as shown in Figure 8–18.

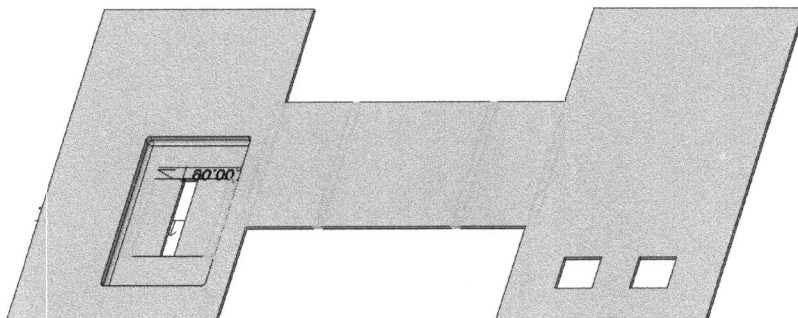

Figure 8–18

In the Options panel, if the **Flatten forms** option is selected, you can select the **Project cuts added to forms** checkbox, so that cuts are projected with the Flat Pattern feature, as shown in Figure 8–19.

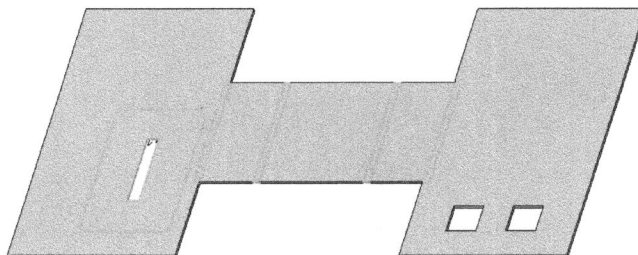

Figure 8–19

The ⬇ (Flatten Form) feature also contains the **Project cuts and holes** checkbox in the Options panel, as shown in Figure 8–20.

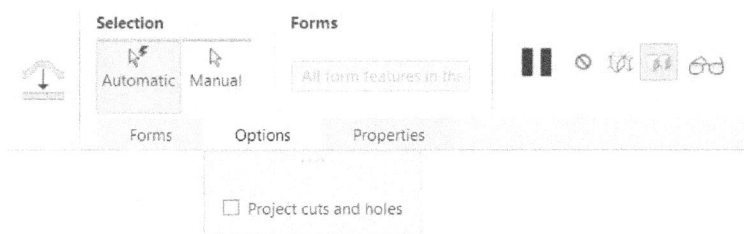

Figure 8–20

If selected, cuts are projected with the Flatten Form feature.

8.5 Flattened Representation

You can create a simplified representation of a sheet metal model where the formed model is the master representation, and the flat state is another representation.

To display the flattened geometry in a new window, in the In-graphics toolbar, click 🖼 (Flat Pattern Preview), as shown in Figure 8–21.

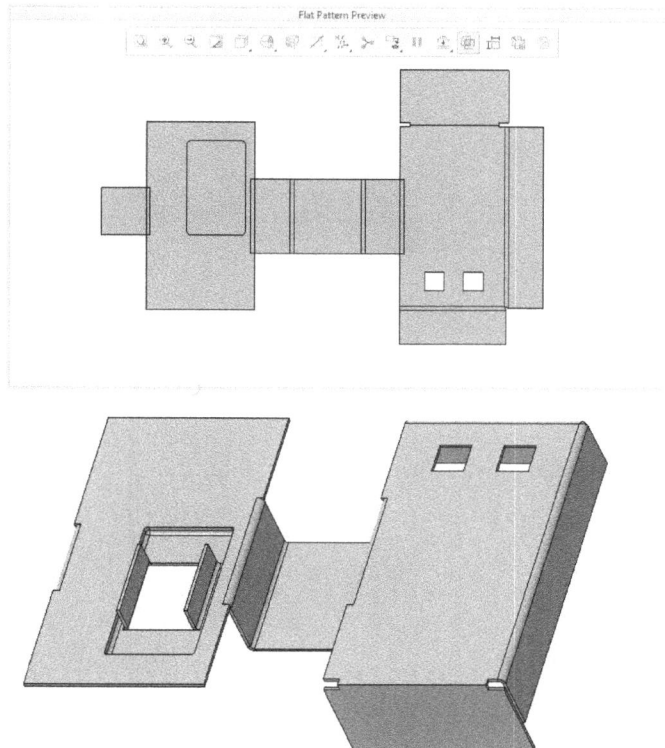

Figure 8–21

In the In-graphics toolbar, in the Flat Pattern Preview window, click 🖼 (Create Representation), and then enter a name in the Make Flat Representation dialog box, as shown in Figure 8–22.

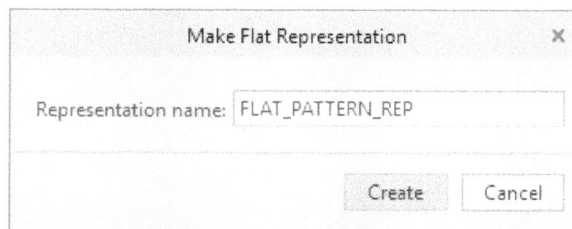

Figure 8–22

Click **Create** to create the simplified representation.

To access the simplified representation, in the In-graphics toolbar, click ![icon] (View Manager). In the View Manager, note that **Master Rep** is the formed model, as shown in Figure 8–23.

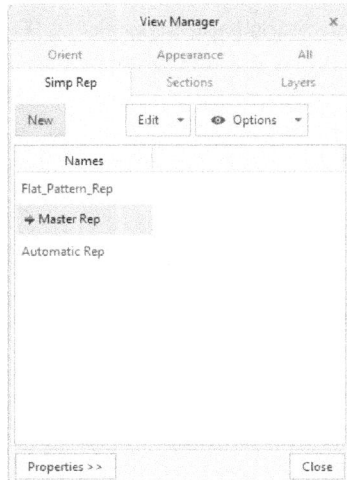

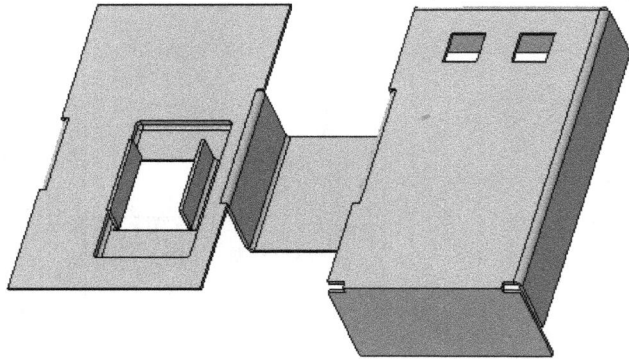

Figure 8–23

Double-click on the flat state to activate it, as shown in Figure 8–24.

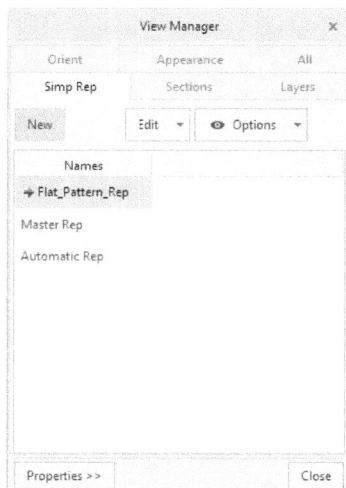

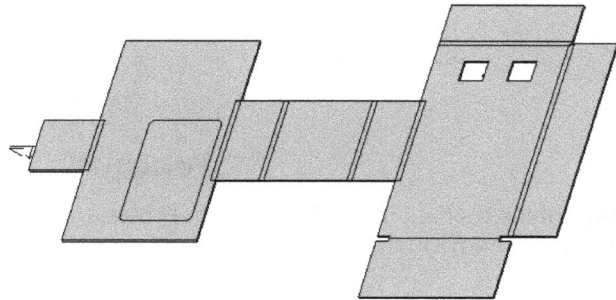

Figure 8–24

8.6 Unstamp Edges Feature

Rounds and chamfers can be created on sheet metal parts to represent edge treatments. Using the Unstamp Edges feature, you can flatten selected rounded and chamfered edges. As a result, the length of the model could change to conserve the volume of material. Consider the parts shown in Figure 8-25. The length of the part decreases when the chamfer is flattened, but the volume and thickness remain constant.

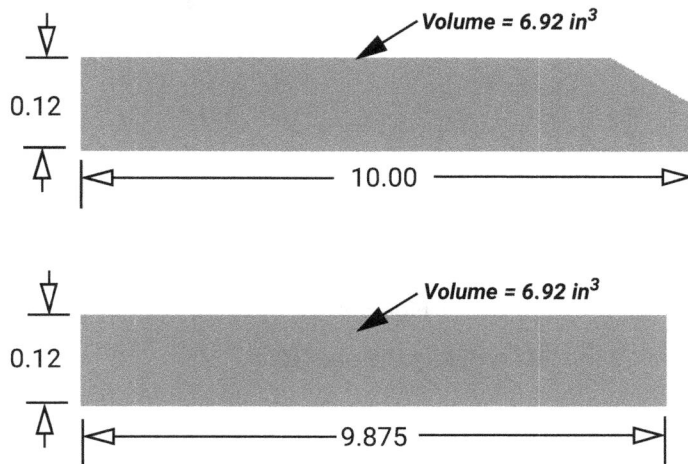

Figure 8-25

How To: Create an Unstamp Edges Feature

1. Select **Editing>Unstamp Edge** in the *Sheetmetal* tab. The Unstamp dialog box and Menu Manager open, as shown in Figure 8-26.

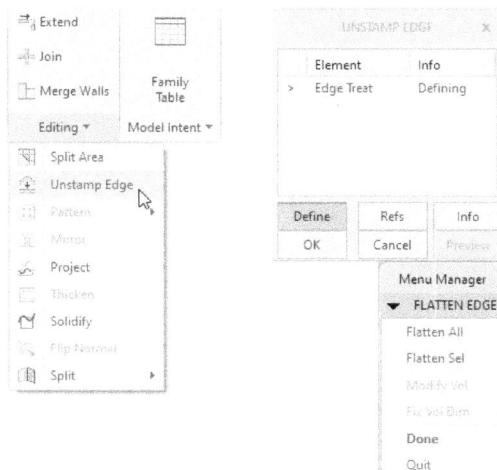

Figure 8-26

2. Select **Flatten All** or **Flatten Sel** and select the geometry in the model shown in Figure 8–27.

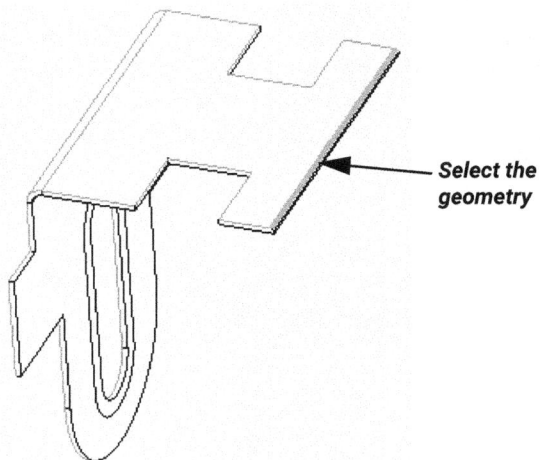

Select the
geometry

Figure 8–27

3. Select **OK** in the dialog box to complete the operation.

8.7 Form Feature Restrictions

The following restrictions apply when using form features on a sheet metal part:

- The form geometry does not yield a thinner wall thickness in the area where the form was placed as it would during actual sheet metal fabrication.

- The mass properties of the model are affected by the extra material that is present. You can overcome this using the **Flatten** form feature option.

- Creo Parametric does not check whether the form geometry is valid.

Practice 8a
Punch Form

Practice Objectives

- Create a form feature.
- Save the form changes to a new tool.

In this practice, you will create a form using a punch, as shown in Figure 8–28.

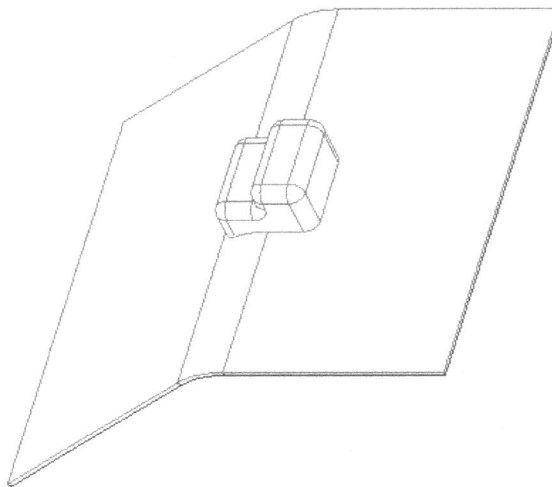

Figure 8–28

Task 1: Create a form feature.

Design Considerations

In this task, you will use a die reference part to create the center stiffener geometry on the bracket using a form feature. Some surfaces on the reference part are excluded as you create the form to generate the holes at the ends of the stiffener geometry.

1. Set the working directory to the *Punch_Form* folder.

2. Open **sheetform.prt**.

3. Set the model display as follows:

    *   ×/. *(Datum Display Filters)*: None

    *   ⌐ *(Spin Center)*: Off

    *   ⬚. *(Display Style)*: ⬚ (No Hidden)

4. Expand ⩔ (Form) and select ⩔ (Punch Form), as shown in Figure 8-29.

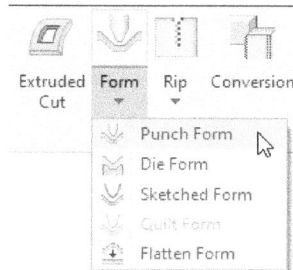

Figure 8-29

5. In the *Punch form* dashboard, click 📁 (Opens a punch model) and select **form.prt**. Click **Open**.

6. In the In-graphics toolbar, enable ⌖ (Csys Display).

7. Select the Placement panel and select the coordinate systems of each part, as shown in Figure 8-30.

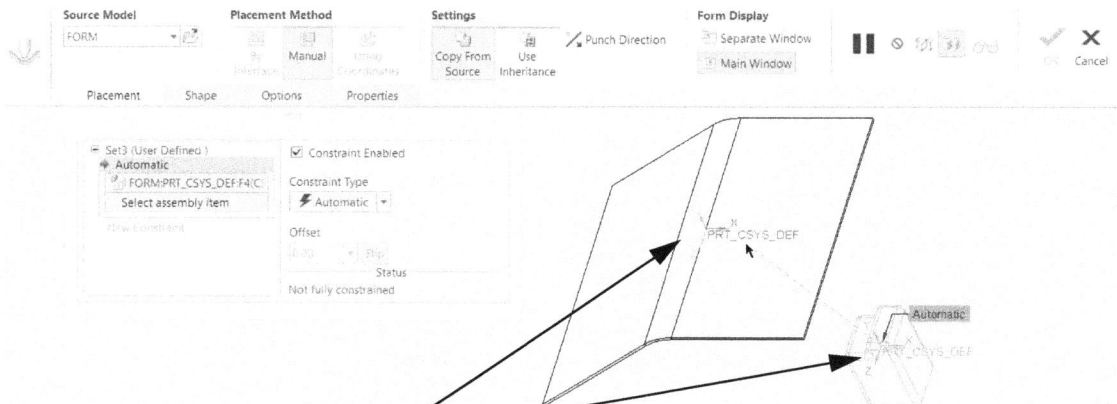

Select the two coordinate systems

Figure 8-30

8. Click ✓ (OK) and save the model.

9. In the In-graphics toolbar, disable ⌖ (Csys Display).

Task 2: Unbend and flatten form.

1. Click ⬚ (Unbend) to unbend the geometry.

2. Maintain the default surface to remain fixed and complete the unbend feature.

3. Expand ⬚ (Form) and select ⬚ (Flatten Form). The *Flatten Form* dashboard opens, as shown in Figure 8–31.

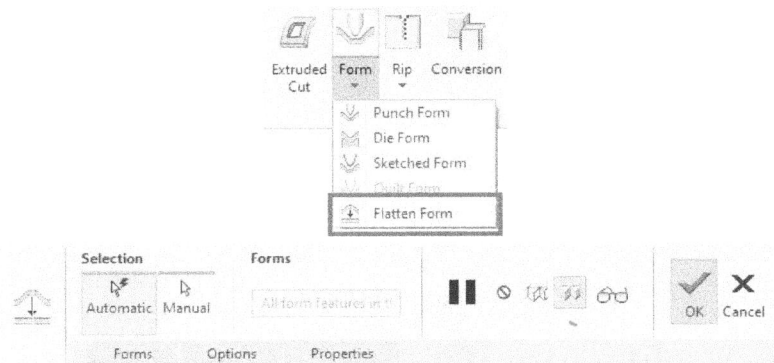

Figure 8–31

4. Expand the Forms panel in the dashboard and note that the *Forms* field reads **All form features in the model**.

5. Click ✓ (OK) to complete the feature. The model displays as shown in Figure 8–32.

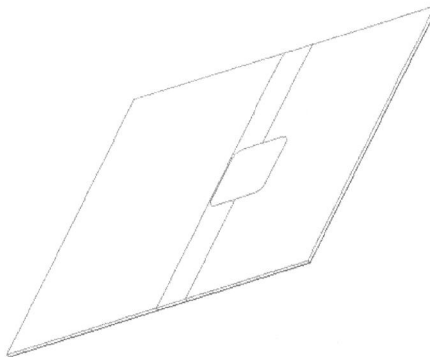

Figure 8–32

Task 3: Modify a form and save to a new form tool.

1. In the Model Tree, select **Form 1** and select ✍ (Edit Definition) in the mini toolbar. The *Punch Form* dashboard opens.

2. Click ▦ (Use Inheritance) to change to Independent inheritance.

3. In the dashboard, open the Shape panel and click **Vary Punch Model**, as shown in Figure 8–33.

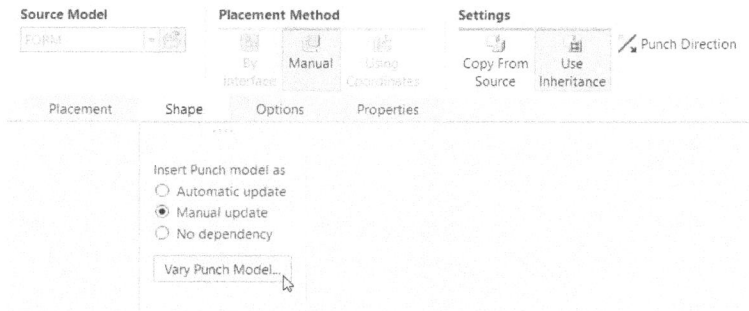

Figure 8–33

4. The Varied Items dialog box opens. Select **Round2** of the model. The radius dimension displays, as shown in Figure 8–34.

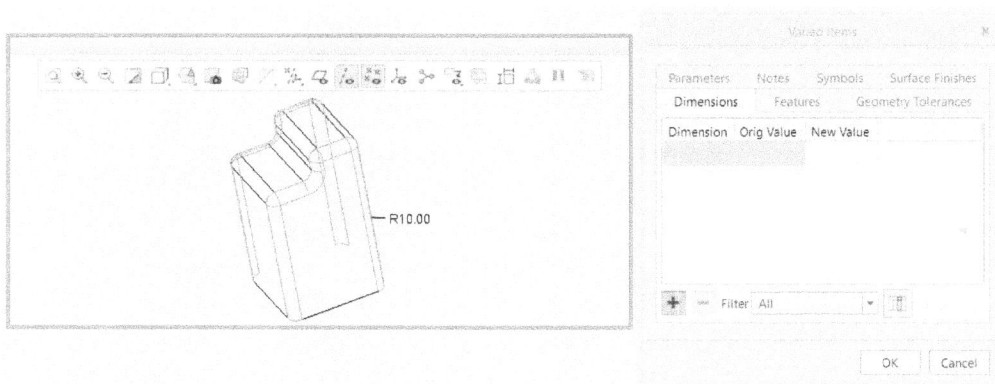

Figure 8–34

5. Click ✚ (Add Dimension). Select the radius dimension to add it to the Varied Items dialog box.

6. In the Varied Items dialog box, set the *New Value* to **5**, as shown in Figure 8–35, and click **OK**.

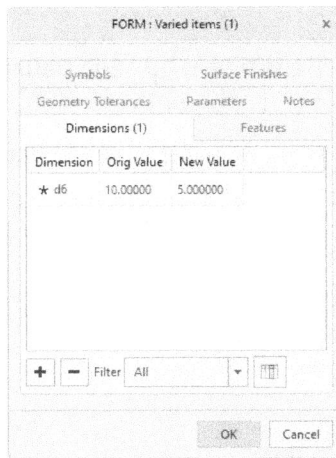

Figure 8–35

7. Click ✔ (OK) to complete the form with the changes.

8. In the Model Tree, right-click on **Form1** and select **Save Source Model**, as shown in Figure 8–36.

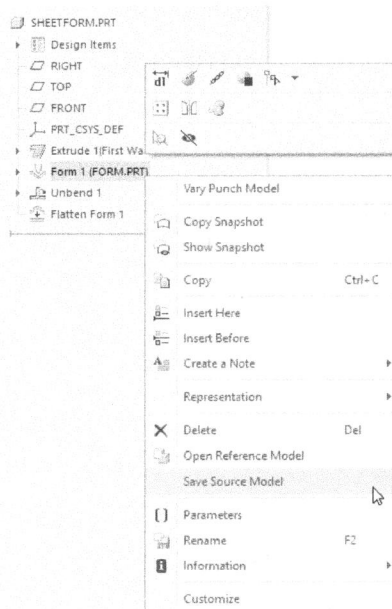

Figure 8–36

9. Set the *New Name* to **Form_1** and click **OK**. The new form tool is created.

10. Save and erase the files.

End of practice

Practice 8b
Die Form

Practice Objectives

- Create form features.
- Create a bend across a form feature.

In this practice, you will create several punch and die form features on the bracket part and create a bend across one of the forms. The completed feature is shown in Figure 8–37.

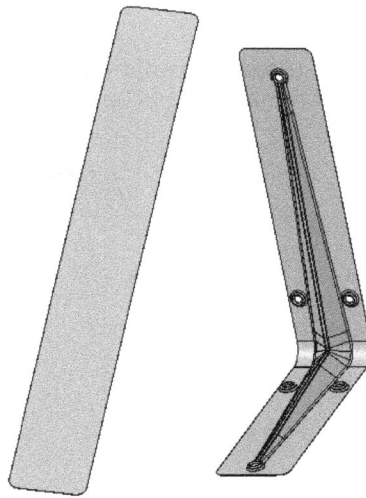

Figure 8–37

Task 1: Open a part and create the center rib structure as a form feature.

Design Considerations

In this task, you will use a punch reference part to create the center stiffener geometry on the bracket using a form feature. Some surfaces on the reference part are excluded as you create the form to generate the holes at the ends of the stiffener geometry.

1. Set the working directory to the *Die_Form* folder.
2. Open **bracket.prt**.

3. Set the model display as follows:

   - %. *(Datum Display Filters)*: ⅃₆ (Csys Display)

   - ⤳ *(Spin Center)*: Off

   - ⬚. *(Display Style)*: ⬚ (No Hidden)

4. Expand ⬇ (Form) and select ⋈ (Die Form) in the *Sheetmetal* tab to add a form to the model.

5. Click ⬚ (Opens a punch model).

6. Double-click on **form_middle-die.prt** in the Open dialog box.

7. In the Model Tree, select **PRT_CSYS_DEF**.

8. Select **CSO** in the form part.

9. In the In-graphics toolbar click ⬚. (Saved Orientations)> **FRONT**. Note the form is a negative shape that the flat sheet metal wall will be formed into, as shown in Figure 8−38.

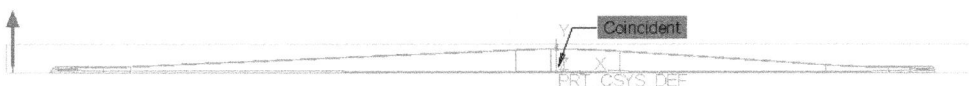

Figure 8−38

10. Press <Ctrl>+<D> to return to the default orientation.

11. In the In-graphics toolbar, disable ⅃₆ (Csys Display).

12. The model display as shown in Figure 8−39.

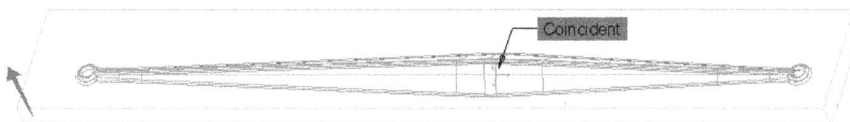

Figure 8−39

13. Select the **Options** panel and select in the *Exclude die model surfaces* collector, as shown in Figure 8−40.

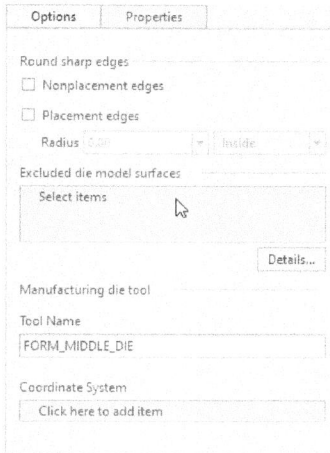

Figure 8–40

14. Select the surfaces to exclude, as shown in Figure 8–41.

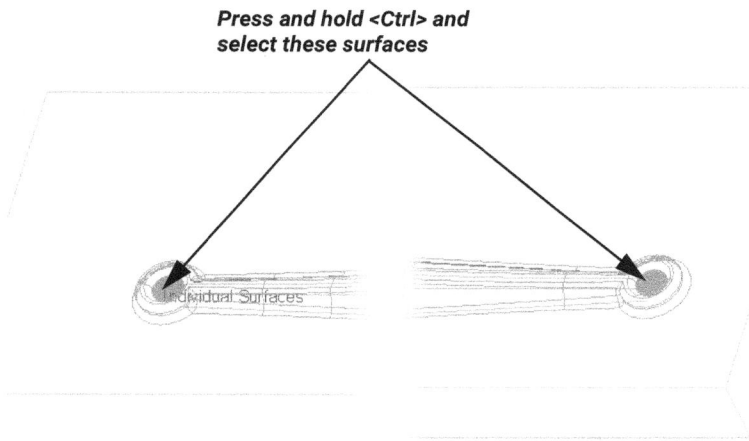

Press and hold <Ctrl> and select these surfaces

Figure 8–41

Note: These openings created in the sheet metal part act as holes for fasteners.

15. Click ✔ (OK) to complete the form.

16. Shade the display. The resulting geometry is shown in Figure 8–42.

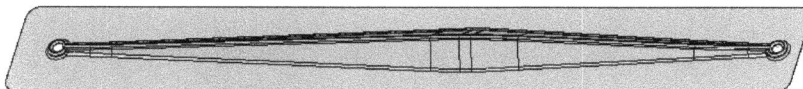

Figure 8–42

Task 2: Add additional forms for fasteners.

Design Considerations

In this task, you will use a die reference part to create the remaining mounting holes in the bracket. You will create one form feature and use a pattern table to create a total of four fastener holes.

1. Enable 🛠 (Plane Display) and disable 🛠 (Csys Display) in the In-graphics toolbar.

2. Expand ⟱ (Form) and select ▨ (Die Form) in the *Sheetmetal* tab to add a form to the model.

3. Click 🗁 (Opens a punch model).

4. Double-click on **form_hole.prt** in the Open dialog box.

5. Expand the **Placement** panel in the dashboard.

6. Select the surface of the bracket and surface of the form shown in Figure 8–43. Ensure that the constraint is **Coincident**.

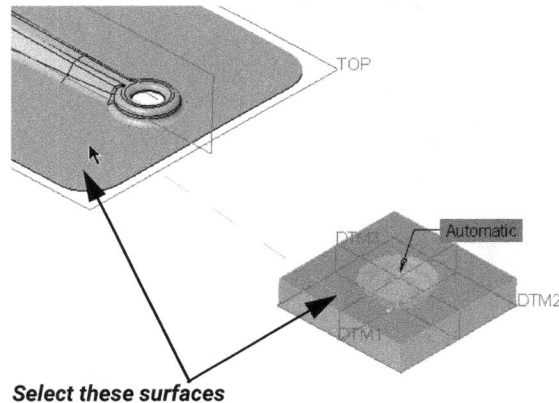

Select these surfaces

Figure 8–43

Note: Datum plane tags are displayed for reference.

7. In the Placement panel, click **Flip** to reorient the form correctly.

8. Click **New Constraint**.

9. Create a **Distance** constraint between **DTM3** and **FRONT**. Set the Distance to **0.7**, as shown in Figure 8–44.

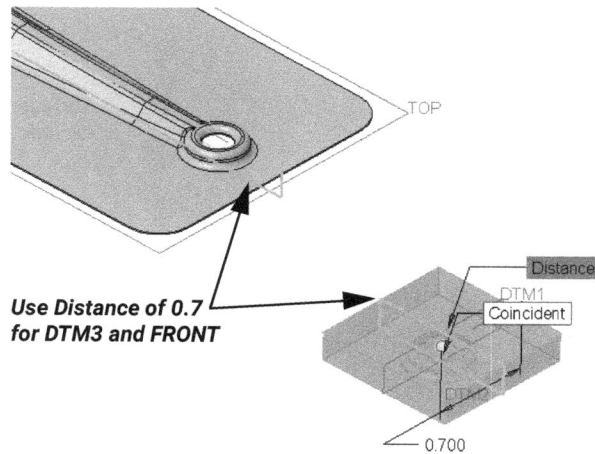

Use Distance of 0.7
for DTM3 and FRONT

Figure 8–44

10. Create a **Distance** constraint between **DTM1** and **RIGHT**. Set the Distance to **1.6**, as shown in Figure 8–45.

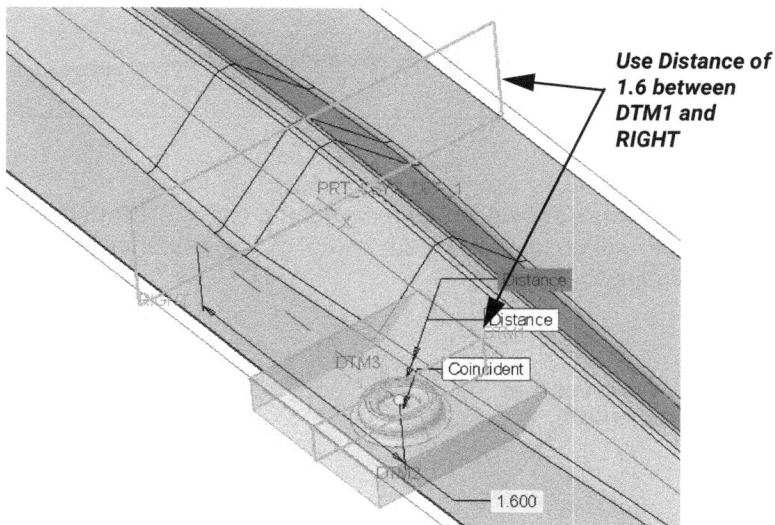

Use Distance of
1.6 between
DTM1 and
RIGHT

Figure 8–45

11. Select the **Options** panel and select in the *Excluded die model surfaces* collector.

12. Select the surface shown in Figure 8–46 to be excluded.

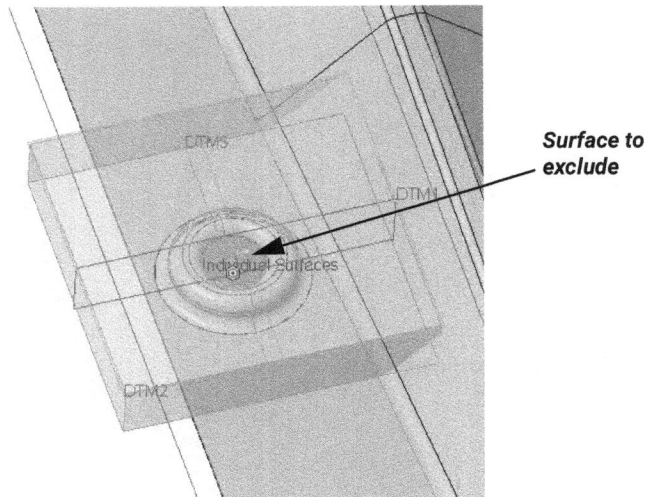

Figure 8–46

13. Complete the feature and return to the default orientation.

14. Disable ⬛ (Plane Display). The finished fastener form displays as shown in Figure 8–47.

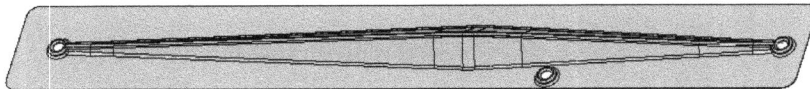

Figure 8–47

15. Select the Hole Form feature shown in Figure 8–48 and click ⬛ (Pattern) in the mini toolbar. A pattern table will be used to create a total of four fastener forms. The tab for feature patterning displays.

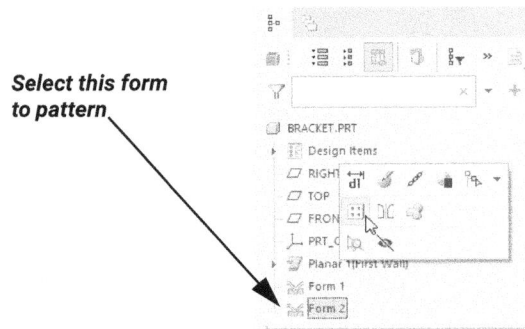

Figure 8–48

Note: You can also select the Hole Form feature on the model and select ⬛ *(Pattern).*

16. Select **Table** in the drop-down list in the *Pattern* dashboard to create a pattern that is driven by a table.

17. Press and hold <Ctrl> and select the two dimensions in the order shown in Figure 8−49 to drive the pattern.

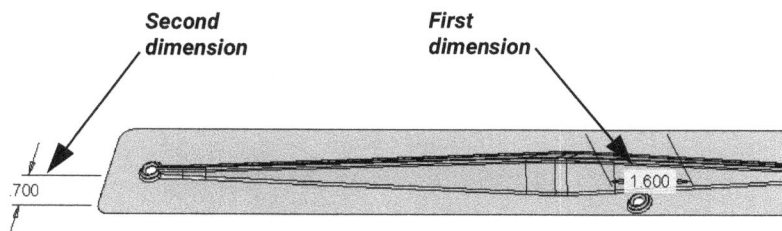

Figure 8−49

18. Select the Tables panel and select the Name cell for the active table. Set the new table *Name* to **hole_forms**.

19. Right-click in the *Index* field and select **Edit**, as shown in Figure 8−50.

Figure 8−50

20. Edit the table to reflect the values shown in Figure 8−51. Remember to add values in the *idx* (index) column.

	C1	C2	C3	C4	C5
R1	!				
R2	! Input placement dimensions and model name for each pattern member.				
R3	! The model name is that of the pattern leader or any of its family table instances.				
R4	! Indices start from 1. Each index has to be unique,				
R5	! but not necessarily sequential.				
R6	! Use '*' for default value equal to the leader dimension and model name.				
R7	! Rows beginning with '@' will be saved as comments.				
R8	!				
R9	!	Table name TABLE1.			
R10	!				
R11	! idx	d8(1.60)	d7(0.70)		
R12		2	-1.6	0.7	
R13		3	1.6	-0.7	
R14		4	-1.6	-0.7	

Figure 8−51

Note: *The symbolic forms of the dimensions (d7 and d8 in Figure 8−51) could be different in your models.*

21. Select **File>Exit** to close and save the table.

22. Click ✔ (OK) to complete the pattern. The finished form features display as shown in Figure 8−52.

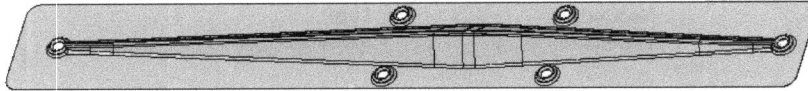

Figure 8−52

Task 3: Create a bend feature to finish the part.

Design Considerations

In this task, you will create the final bend feature. The bend feature will bend the first wall and form geometry.

1. Select the surface shown in Figure 8−53 and click ※ (Bend) in the mini toolbar.

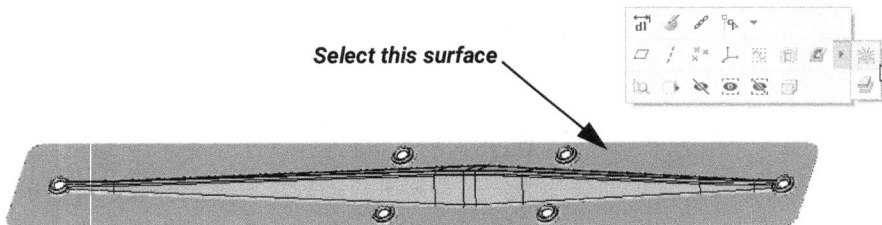

Select this surface

Figure 8−53

2. Click on the screen and select 🖉 (Define/Edit Internal Bend Line). Sketch a single line aligned to datum plane **FRONT**, as shown in Figure 8−54.

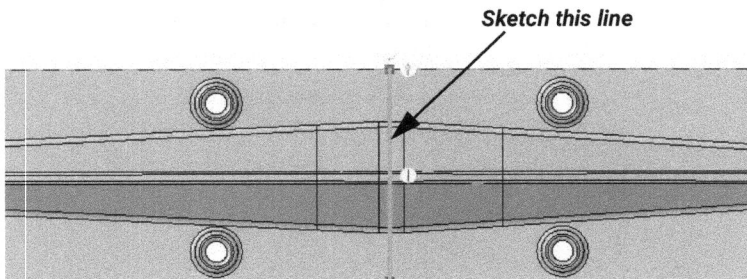

Sketch this line

Figure 8−54

3. Complete the sketch.

4. Set the inside bend *Radius* to **0.50**.

5. Use the default bend *Angle* of **90°**. If required, flip the fixed surface and bend direction arrows, as shown in Figure 8–55.

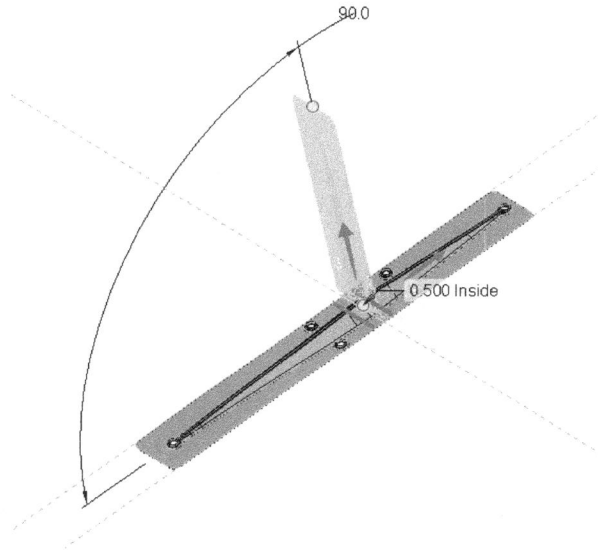

Figure 8–55

6. Complete the feature. The part displays as shown in Figure 8–56.

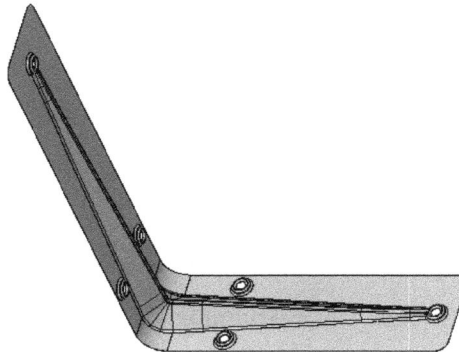

Figure 8–56

7. Save the part and erase it from memory.

End of practice

Practice 8c
Flatten Form Geometry

Practice Objective

- Flatten a form feature.

In this practice, you will use the flatten form feature with the Edge Treatment element to simulate the unbending of features. The part contains form geometry and a chamfer to simulate a rolling process, as shown in Figure 8–57.

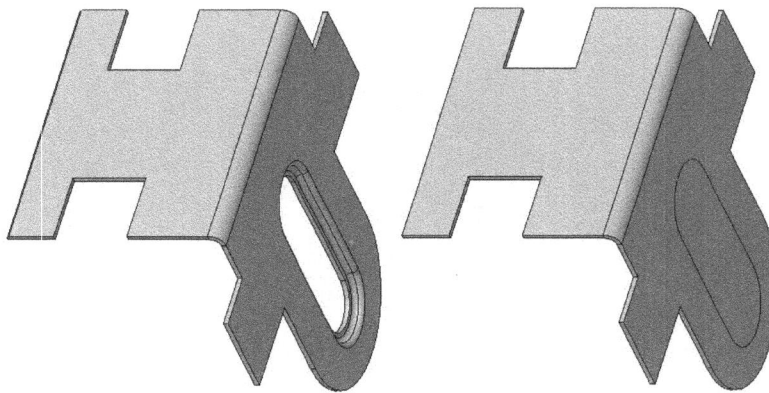

Figure 8–57

Task 1: Open a part and create a flatten form feature.

Design Considerations

In this task, you will create a flatten form feature. The flatten form feature adds a surface to the model in the shape of the form feature to hold its place.

1. Set the working directory to the *Flatten_Form* folder.

2. Open **flatten_form.prt**.

3. Set the model display as follows:

    - ⁑ *(Datum Display Filters)*: None

    - ⋋ *(Spin Center)*: Off

    - ▢ *(Display Style)*: ▢ (Shading With Edges)

4. Expand ⩙ (Form) and select ⬆ (Flatten Form) in the *Sheetmetal* tab.

5. The form geometry is selected and flattened in the model as shown in Figure 8–58.

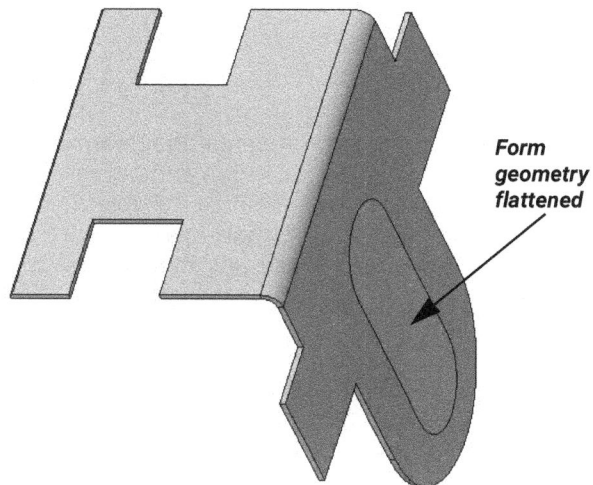

Form geometry flattened

Figure 8–58

6. Click ✔ (OK). The completed flatten form is shown in Figure 8–59.

Figure 8–59

The opening caused by the Excluded Surface in the form geometry is filled when the form feature is flattened. The only remaining geometry is a *footprint* surface of the form feature.

Task 2: Create an unstamp edge feature to address the chamfer on the end of the part.

Design Considerations

Chamfers are created on sheet metal parts to represent edge treatments. During fabrication, the chamfer material is displaced by the rolling operation and not removed from the part. The Edge Treatment element accounts for this by maintaining the volume of the part. In this task, you will use the optional Edge Treatment element to flatten the chamfered edge. As a result, the length of the model changes to conserve the volume and thickness of material.

1. Select **Editing>Unstamp Edge** in the *Sheetmetal* tab. The Unstamp dialog box opens, as shown in Figure 8–60.

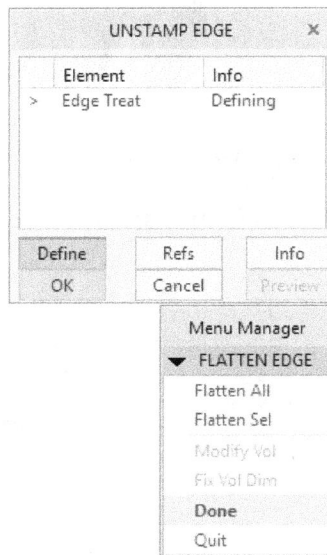

Figure 8–60

2. Select **Flatten Sel** in the Menu Manager.

3. Select the edge of the chamfer at the end of the model, as shown in Figure 8−61.

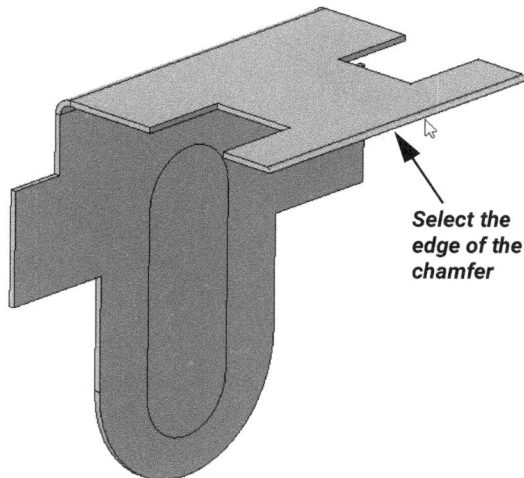

Select the edge of the chamfer

Figure 8−61

4. Select **Done Refs**.

5. Select **Modify Vol** and select the dimension for the chamfer length, as shown in Figure 8−62. Enter **0.125**.

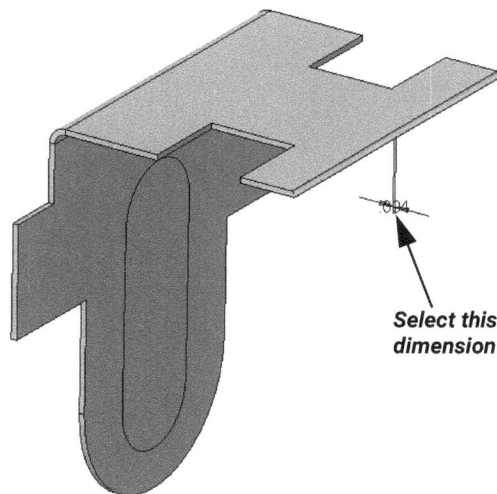

Select this dimension

Figure 8−62

*Note: The **Modify Vol** option enables you to modify the edge offset that occurs when the chamfer is flattened.*

6. Select **Done>Done** and click **OK**. The final flatten form feature displays as shown in Figure 8–63.

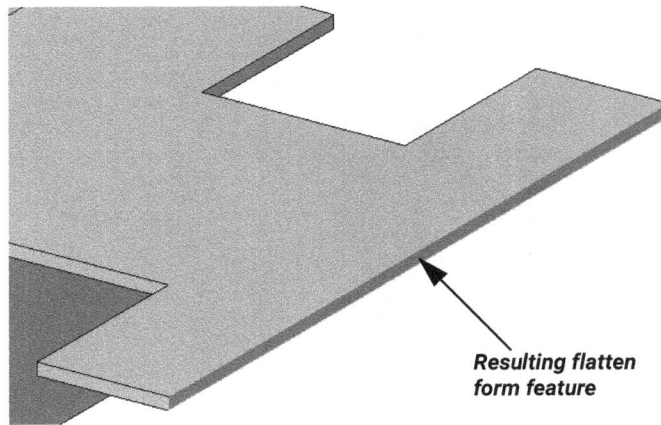

Resulting flatten
form feature

Figure 8–63

7. Save the part and erase it from memory.

End of practice

Practice 8d
Flat Patterns

Practice Objectives

- Modify a part used as a die form.
- Create a flat pattern to flatten the model.

In this practice, you will modify a die part to see the impact on the model. You will also create a flat pattern to flatten the entire model. The original model is shown in Figure 8–64.

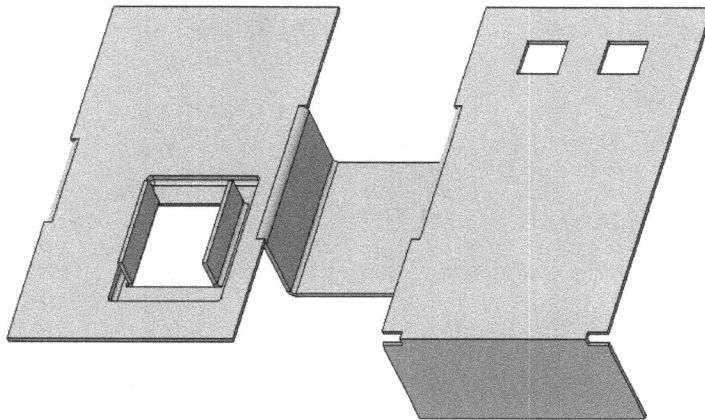

Figure 8–64

Task 1: Open a part.

Design Considerations

In this task, you will open a fully formed model that uses a die form.

1. Set the working directory to the *Flat_Pattern* folder.
2. Open **flat_pattern.prt**.
3. Set the model display as follows:

    - ⚌ *(Datum Display Filters)*: None

    - ⤙ *(Spin Center)*: Off

    - ▱ *(Display Style)*: ▱ (Shading With Edges)

Task 2: Modify the form part used to create the formed opening and review the effect on the sheet metal part.

1. In the Model Tree, select **Form 1 (DIE.PRT)**, right-click and select **Open Reference Model**. The form model opens as shown in Figure 8−65.

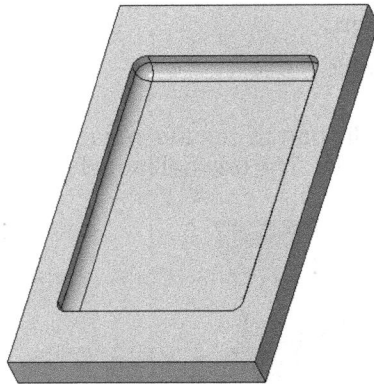

Figure 8−65

2. Select the recessed surface and select ⃡d1 (Edit Dimensions).
3. Edit the length to **3**, as shown in Figure 8−66.

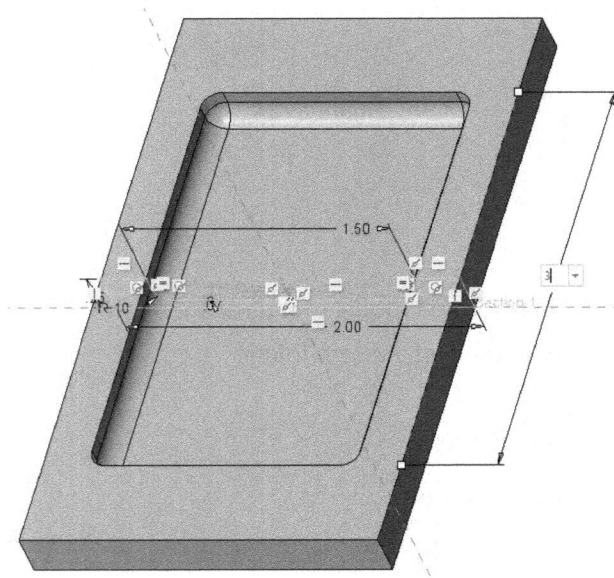

Figure 8−66

4. Regenerate the model and close the **DIE.PRT** window.

5. Note that the form has not updated to reflect the change.

6. In the Model Tree, select **Form 1(DIE.PRT)** and select 🖌 (Edit Definition).

7. Expand the *Shape* tab and note that the model was defined using the **Manual Update** option, as shown in Figure 8–67.

Figure 8–67

8. Select **Automatic Update** and note the form immediately updates, as shown in Figure 8–68.

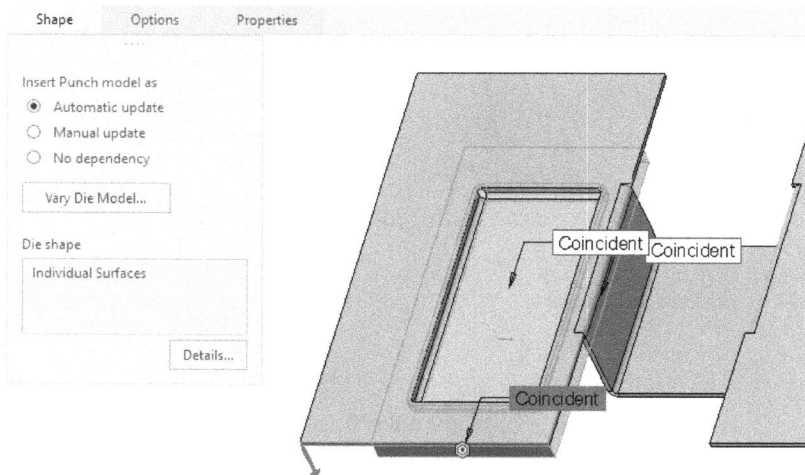

Figure 8–68

9. Click ✓ (OK) to complete the change. The model displays as shown in Figure 8–69.

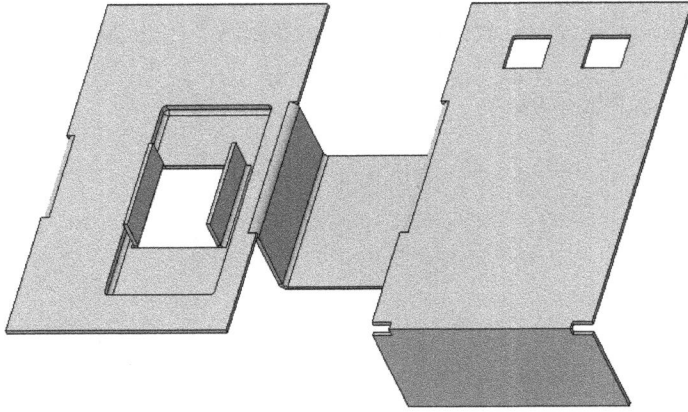

Figure 8–69

Task 3: Create a flat pattern to flatten the model.

1. In the Bends group in the ribbon, click 🔲 (Flat Pattern).

2. Click ✓ (OK) to complete the change. The model updates as shown in Figure 8–70.

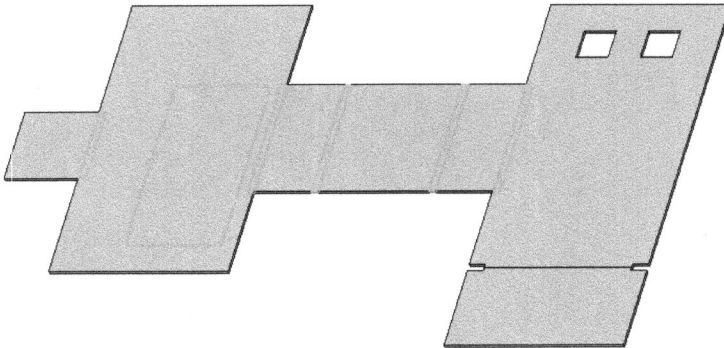

Figure 8–70

3. In the Model Tree, select **Flat Pattern 1** and select 🥄 (Edit Definition) in the mini toolbar.

4. In the Options panel, clear the checkmark for **Flatten Forms**.

5. Click ✔ (OK) to complete the change. The model updates as shown in Figure 8–71.

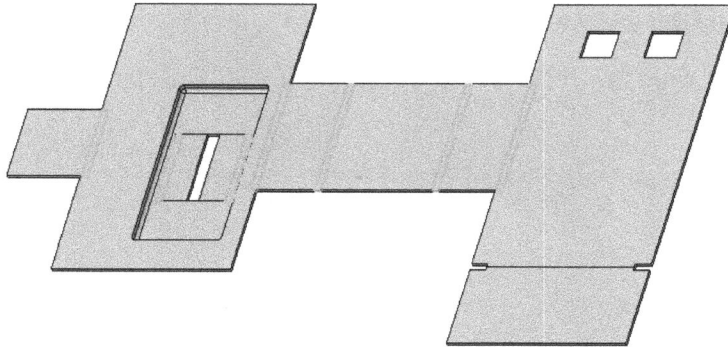

Figure 8–71

Note: In this case, the form is not flattened along with the rest of the model, enabling you to visualize how the form will look when pressed.

6. In the Model Tree, select **Flat Pattern 1** and select 🖌 (Edit Definition) in the mini toolbar.

7. In the Options panel, select **Flatten Forms**, then select **Project cuts added to forms**.

8. Click ✔ (OK) to complete the change. The model updates as shown in Figure 8–72.

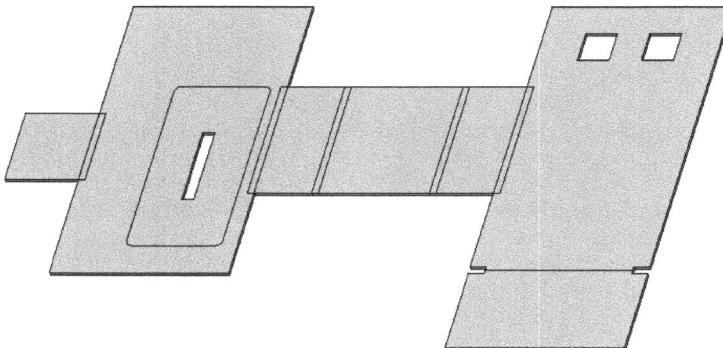

Figure 8–72

Note: In this case, the form is flattened, but the cut is projected onto the flat surface.

Task 4: Create a flat state representation of the model.

1.   Select **Flat Pattern 1** in the Model Tree and delete it.

2.   In the In-graphics toolbar, click 🖼️ (Flat Pattern Preview). The Flat Pattern Preview window opens, as shown in Figure 8–73.

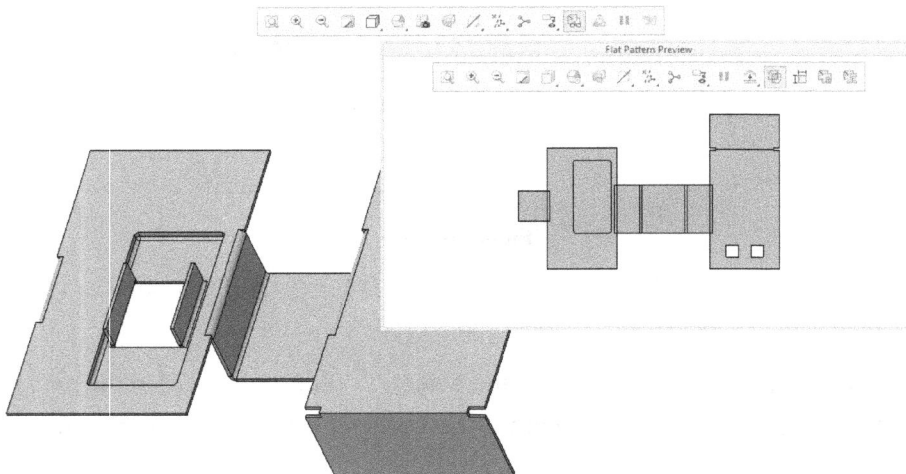

Figure 8–73

Note: You could create flat pattern representation manually, but this process demonstrates a quicker way to accomplish it.

3.   In the In-graphics toolbar in the Flat Pattern Preview window, click 🖼️ (Create Representation).

4.   The Make Flat Representation dialog box opens. Edit the name to **PANEL_FLAT_REP**, as shown in Figure 8–74.

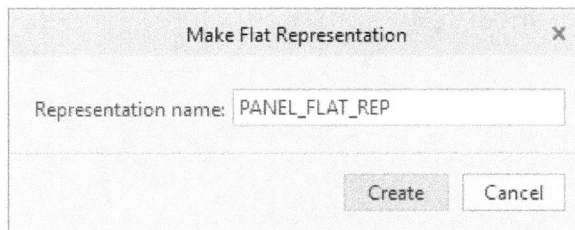

Figure 8–74

5.   Click **Create**.

6.   In the In-graphics toolbar, click 🖼️ (View Manager).

7. In the View Manager, select the *Simp Rep* tab.

8. To activate the flat representation, double-click on **Panel_Flat_Rep**, as shown in Figure 8−75.

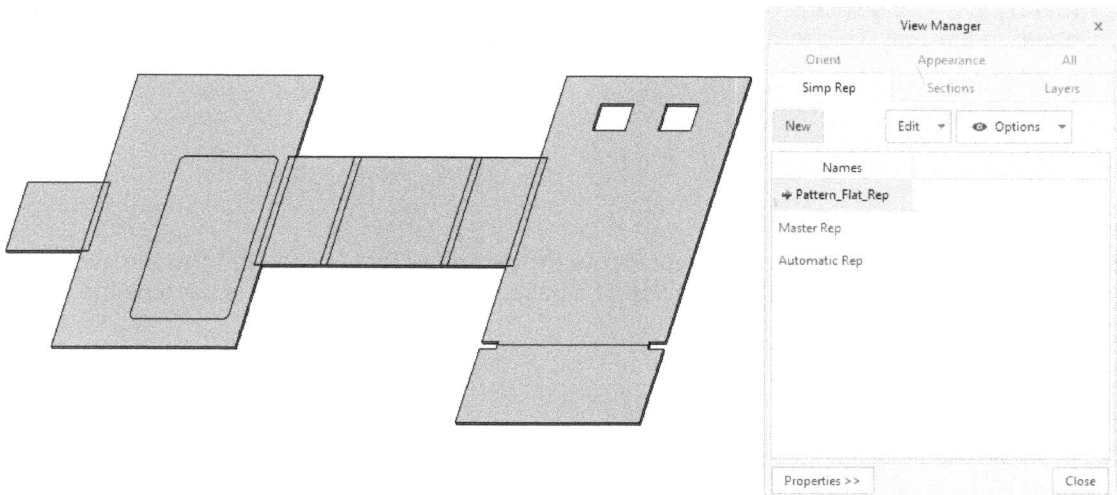

Figure 8−75

9. Double-click on **Master Rep** to activate the formed representation.

10. Click **Close**.

11. Close the model and erase it from memory.

End of practice

Chapter Review Questions

1. Which type of form feature is a model that contains feature(s) to be formed on a sheet metal part? A base plane or boundary surface is used as a reference for locating it against a sheet metal wall. This form also requires you to select a seed surface.

   a. Die form

   b. Punch form

   c. Quilt form

   d. Flatten form

2. Which type of form feature only represents the geometry that is used to form the sheet metal part? It does not require the use of a base plane. The entire part is used as the basis for the form geometry.

   a. Die form

   b. Punch form

   c. Quilt form

   d. Flatten form

3. Which of the following icons enables you to place a punch using standard assembly placement?

   a.

   b.

   c.

4. Which of the following icons enables you place the punch form as an independent inheritance feature?

   a.

   b.

   c.

   d.

5. The (Copy Dependant Merge) option places the form feature on the sheet metal part without establishing a dependent relationship. If the form part is modified, the sheet metal part does not update with the changes.

   a. True

   b. False

6. If you need to remove the form features from the model to reduce regeneration times, it is better to suppress them than to use the **Flatten Form** feature option.

    a. True

    b. False

7. The length of the part decreases when a chamfer is flattened, but the volume and thickness remain constant.

    a. True

    b. False

8. Which of the following statements describes restrictions when using form features on a sheet metal part? (Select all that apply.)

    a. The form geometry does not yield a thinner wall thickness in the area where the form was placed as it would during actual sheet metal fabrication.

    b. The mass properties of the model are affected by the extra material that is present. You can overcome this using the Flatten form feature option.

    c. Creo Parametric does not check whether the form geometry is valid.

Documenting a Sheet Metal Part

You can create flat states of your model for use on drawings. To further document the drawing, you can add bend order tables, which document the bends, bend radii, and bend sequence in a tabular format.

Learning Objectives

- Display the sheet metal model in its flat and formed conditions using a family table.
- Change the model properties to display the flatten state in the sheet metal model.
- Use the general steps and learn to create the fully formed and fully flat states using the family table.
- Learn to open the flat state instance using a variety of options.
- Understand the process of documenting the sheet metal flat state in a drawing by adding a drawing model.
- Create a bend order table by defining a sequence of bends.

9.1 Flat States

A flat state enables you to display a part in its flattened and formed conditions on the same drawing. Figure 9–1 shows a model in its flattened and formed conditions.

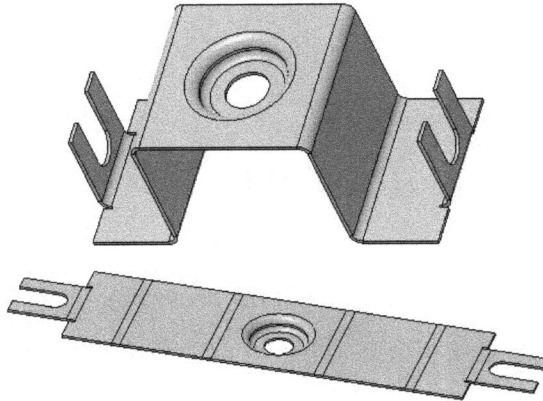

Figure 9–1

The flat state is based on a family table. Family tables enable you to define multiple instances of the same part. An example of a family table using this process is shown in Figure 9–2.

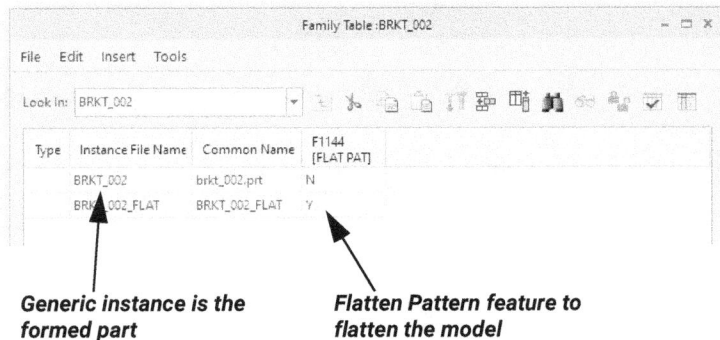

Generic instance is the formed part

Flatten Pattern feature to flatten the model

Figure 9–2

The instances are created automatically without having to edit the part's family table. Creating a flat state enables you to do the following:

- Store multiple similar models in the same file.

- Simulate different steps of the sheet metal fabrication process.

- Store a developed flat pattern inside a bent generic model.

9.2 Creating Flat States

A flat state is created using the 🖼 (Flat Pattern Preview) option in the In-graphics toolbar.

How To: Create a Flat State

1. In the In-graphics toolbar, click 🖼 (Flat Pattern Preview) and the Flat Pattern Preview window opens, as shown in Figure 9-3.

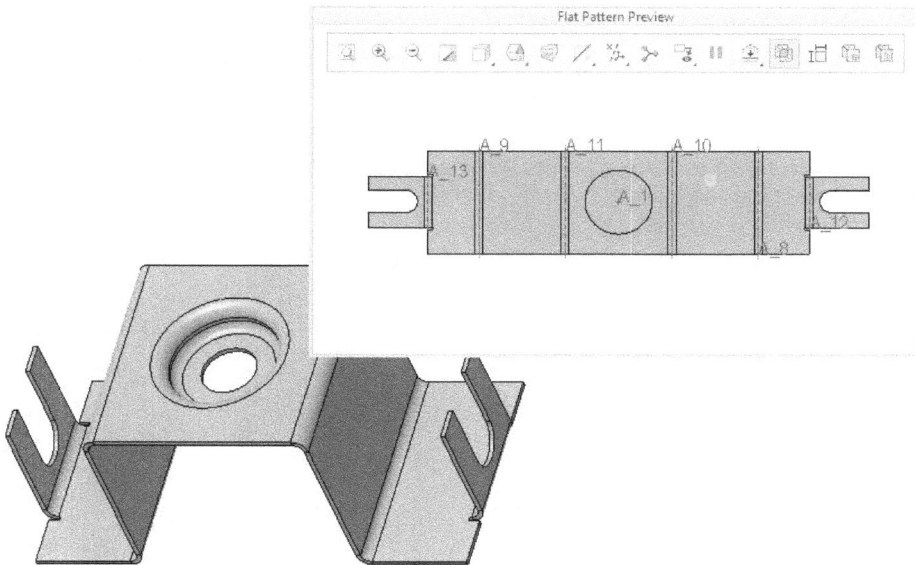

Figure 9-3

2. In the In-graphics toolbar inside the Flat Pattern Preview window, click 🖼 (Create Instance), as shown in Figure 9-4.

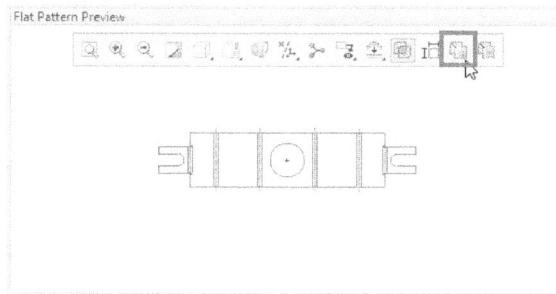

Figure 9-4

- The Make Flat Instance dialog box displays, as shown in Figure 9–5.

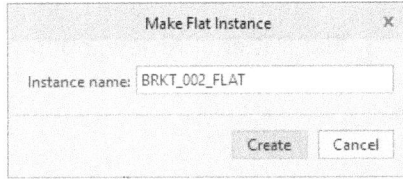

Figure 9–5

3. Edit the Instance name or accept the default and click **Create**.

4. In the *Sheetmetal* tab of the ribbon, click ▦ (Family Table). Note that a family table is added and a column displays for the unbend feature.

   The family table is located in the generic part and contains the new instance and a new column for an unbend feature. The Unbend feature is suppressed in the generic model and resumed in the instance, as shown in Figure 9–6.

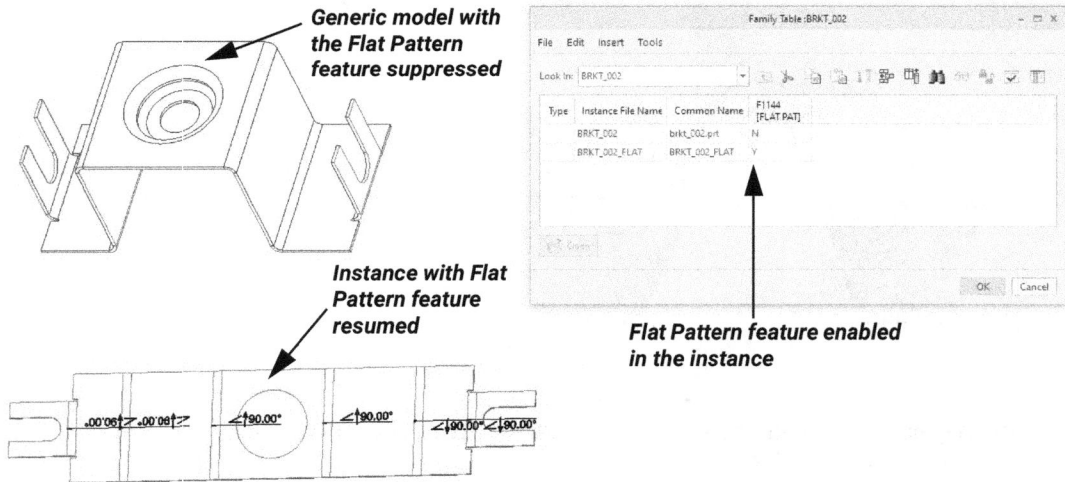

Generic model with the Flat Pattern feature suppressed

Instance with Flat Pattern feature resumed

Flat Pattern feature enabled in the instance

Figure 9–6

5. To open the flat state instance, select **the flat state instance** and click 📂 (Open) in the Family Table dialog box. It displays as shown in Figure 9−7.

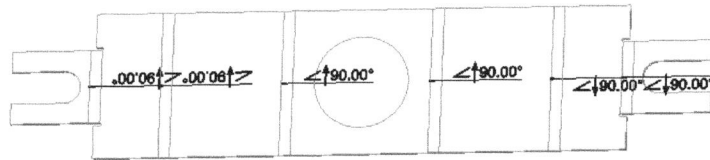

Instance:BRKT_002_FLAT.PRT

Figure 9−7

Note that any additional features you add to the instances behave exactly like those created in regular family table instances.

9.3 Opening Flat State Instances

After you have created a family table using the **Flat State** option, you can open the flat instance using any of the following methods:

- Highlight the instance in the Family Table dialog box and click **Open**.

- Open the generic model. You can then select an instance in the list or open the generic model.

- Open the instance directly if an instance index file has been created.

9.4 Adding a Flat State Instance to a Drawing

A sheet metal flat state can be used in the documentation of a design in a detail drawing. Since the creation of a family table yields two separate models, you can display both models on the drawing at the same time, as shown in the drawing in Figure 9-8.

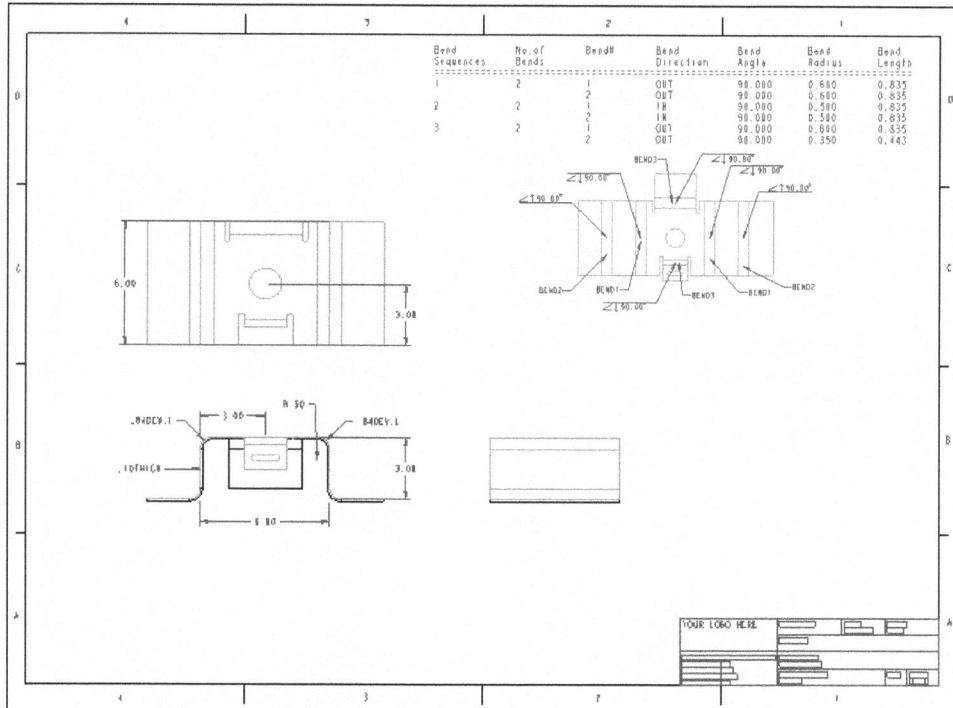

Figure 9-8

How To: Add a Flat State Instance to a Drawing

1. Click ⬚ (Drawing Models) in the *Layout* tab and select **Add Model**. Select a sheet metal part in the Open dialog box and click **Open**. The Instance dialog box opens listing the family table instances that have been created. Select the Flat State instance in the Instance dialog box. You need to associate this instance of the part to the drawing to display a view of the flat pattern.

2. Click ⬚ (General View) to add a General view of the flat instance to the drawing and orient the view as required.

Deformed Areas

In some cases, the flat pattern is not entirely accurate due to deformed areas in a model, as shown in Figure 9–9. You might need to edit these areas.

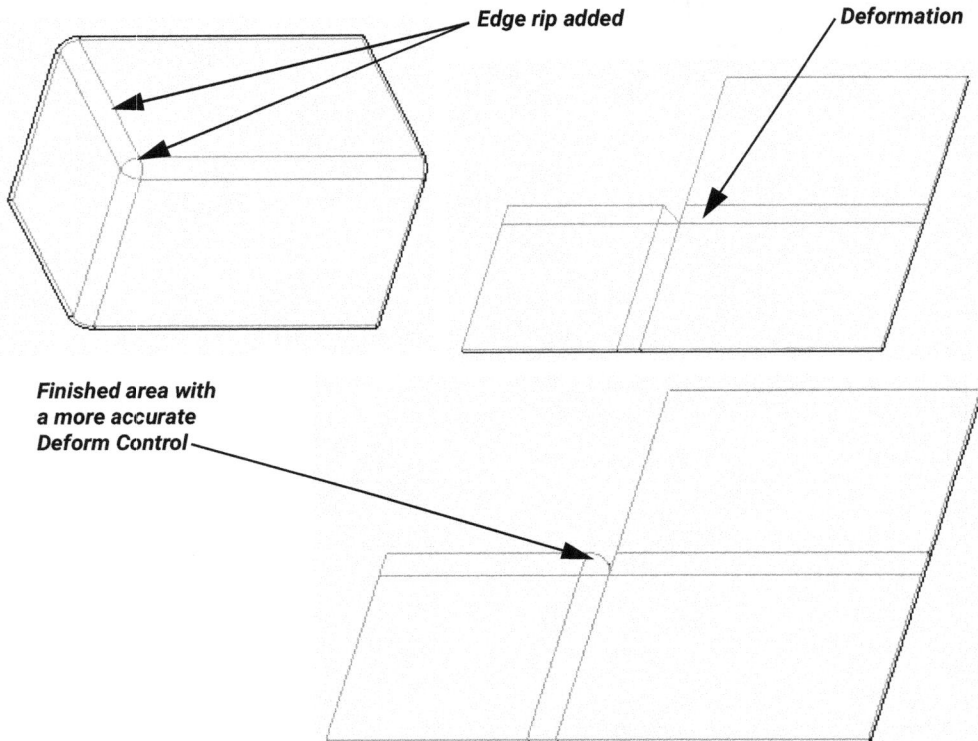

Figure 9–9

- When showing a flat pattern of a sheet metal part in a drawing, Creo Parametric can automate the creation of ordinate dimensions.

How To: Create Ordinate Dimensions

1. Select the *Annotate* tab.
2. Expand $\equiv_{12}^{8}$ (Ordinate Dimension) and select $\equiv_{12}^{4}$ (Auto Ordinate Dimension).
3. Select the surfaces in the flat pattern view for which you want to display ordinate dimensions.
4. Select a first edge reference as the first base line for the dimensions.
5. Select a second edge reference as the second base line for the dimensions.

- The resulting ordinate dimensions display as shown in Figure 9–10.

Select this horizontal edge as the second base line ————

Select this vertical edge as the first base line ————

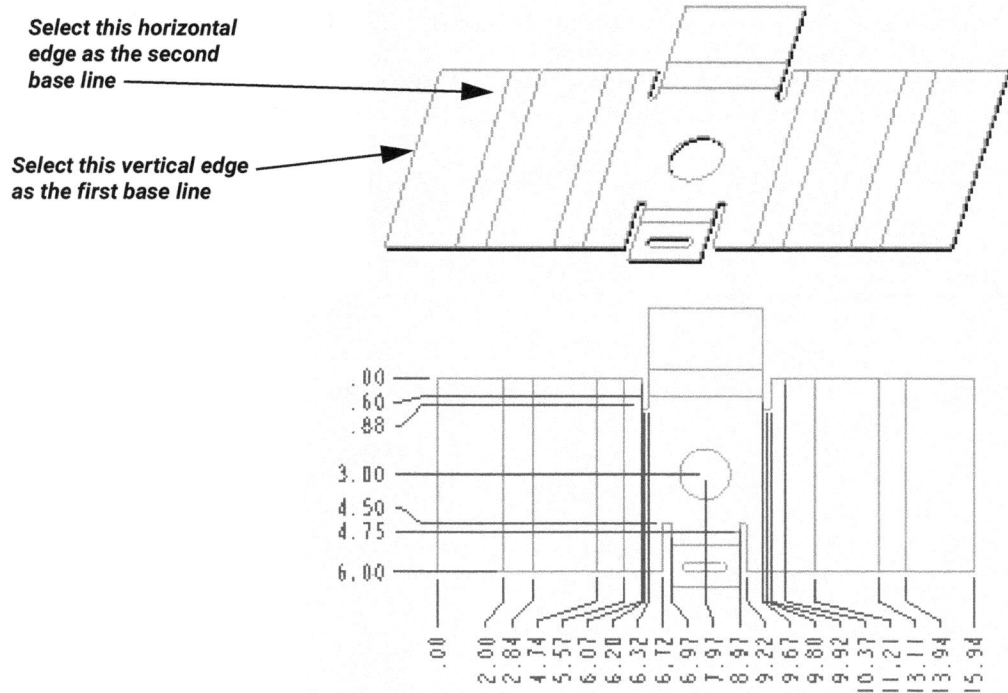

Figure 9–10

9.5 Documenting the Bend Order

To support the fabrication and manufacturing processes, Creo Parametric enables you to create a bend order table. The bend order table includes information such as bend sequence, radius, and angle. With the model completely flat, you can select the bend or a group of bends in a specific sequence and save that sequence to a file, as shown in Figure 9−11.

| | | | | | Bend Order | | − □ ✕ |

Bend Sequences	No.of Bends	Bend#	Bend Direction	Bend Angle	Inside Bend Radius	Bend Length
1	2	1	OUT	90.000	0.253	0.460
		2	OUT	90.000	0.253	0.460
2	2	1	IN	90.000	0.253	0.460
		2	IN	90.000	0.253	0.460
3	2	1	IN	90.000	0.250	0.455
		2	IN	90.000	0.250	0.455

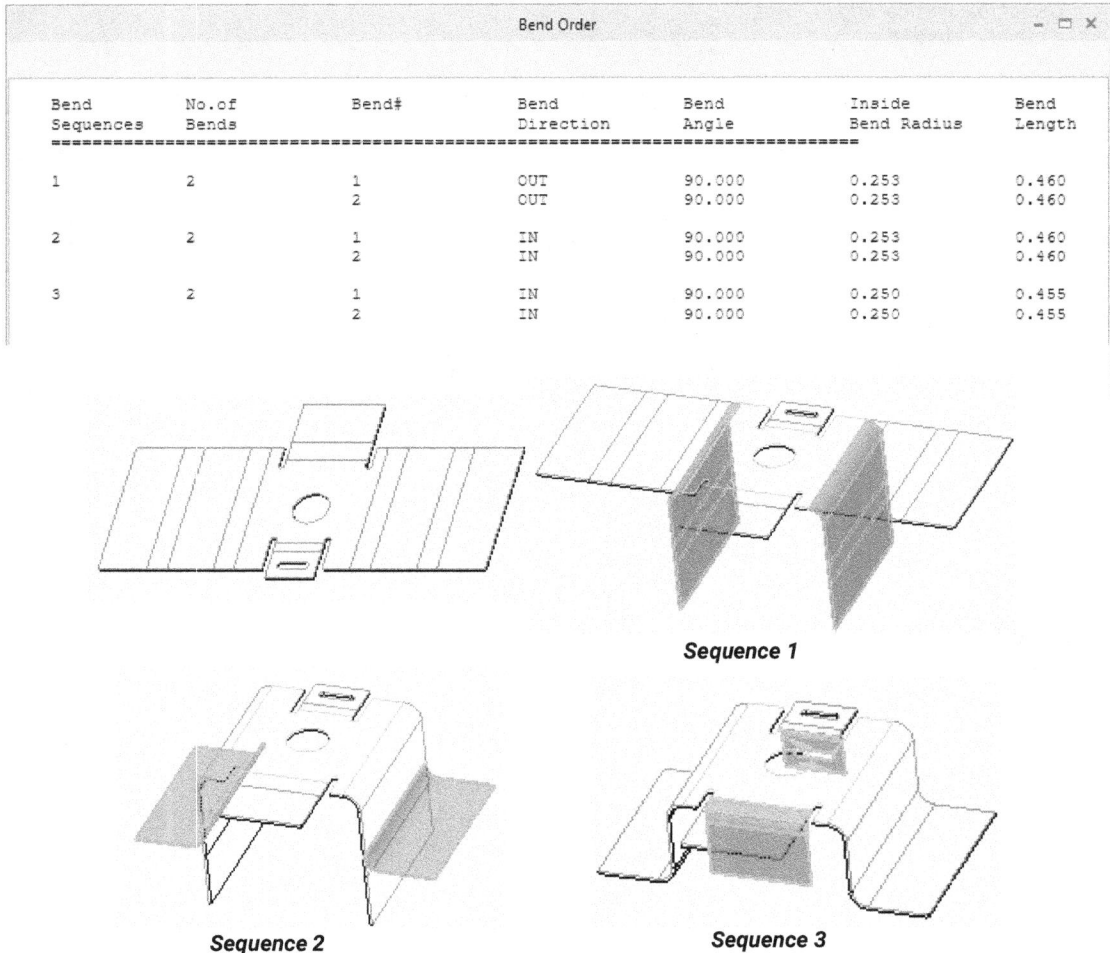

Sequence 1

Sequence 2

Sequence 3

Figure 9−11

The table can then be displayed as a note on a detail drawing. The values for the bend radius and developed length in the table update automatically on the drawing when the part is changed in Sheetmetal mode. However, you must add any new bends to the table manually.

How To: Create a Bend Order Table and Display the Table in the Drawing

1. Select **Bends>Bend Order** in the *Sheetmetal* tab. The Bend Order Table dialog box opens, as shown in Figure 9–12.

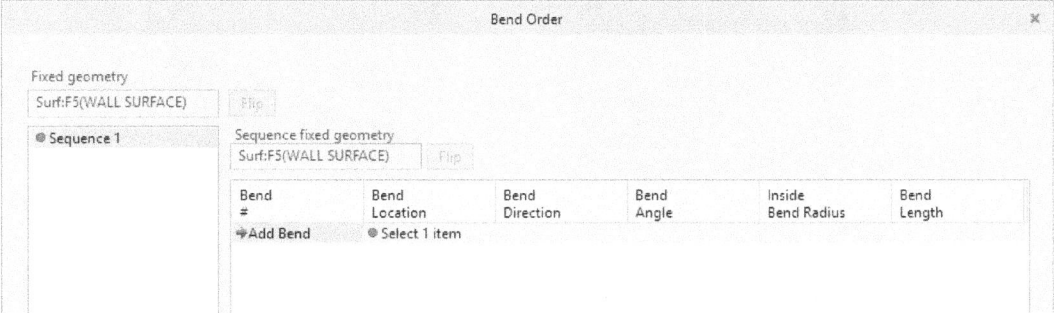

Figure 9–12

By default, a fixed surface is selected. Select a different fixed surface, if required.

2. Select one or more bends to add to the table as shown in Figure 9–13.

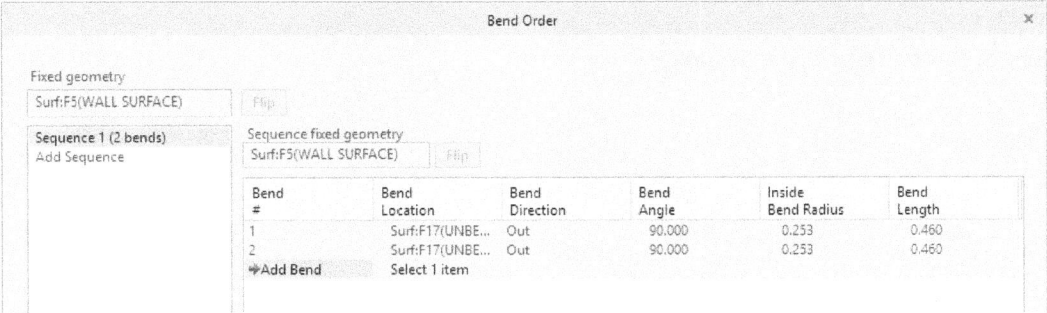

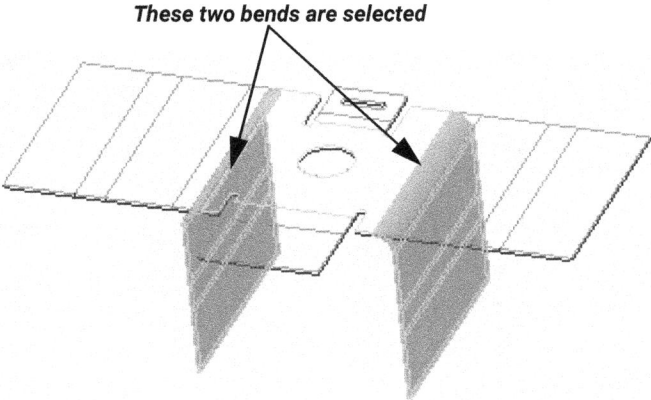

These two bends are selected

Figure 9–13

3. Select **Add Sequence** to add an additional set of bends, as shown in Figure 9-14.

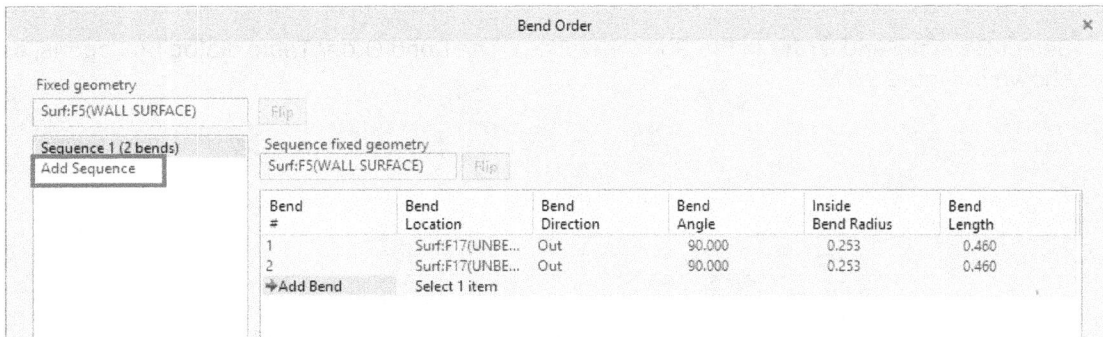

Figure 9-14

4. Click **OK** in the Bend Order dialog box to complete the table.

The bend order table can be viewed or changed by selecting one of the following:

* Select **File>Prepare>Model Properties** and select **change** next to Bend Order.

* Select **File>Prepare>Model Properties** and click ⚙. Click **Change** to edit the bend order table.

* Select **Bend>Bend Order Table**.

Practice 9a
Sheet Metal Drawing

Practice Objectives

- Create and display a bend order table.
- Create a flat state.
- Display the fully formed and flat state instances on the same drawing.
- Add ordinate dimensions to the flat state view.

In this practice, you will create a drawing of a sheet metal part containing both the formed and flat states, as shown in Figure 9–15.

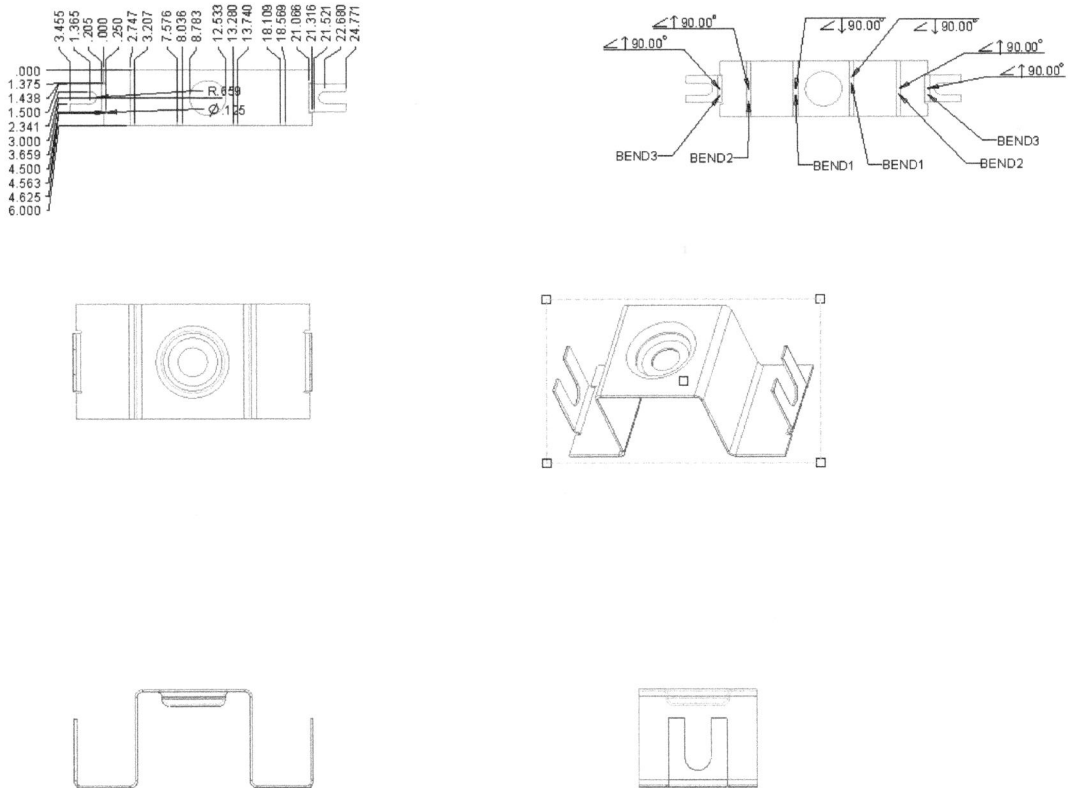

Figure 9–15

Task 1: Open a part and create a bend order table to document the bending process.

Design Considerations

In this task, you will create a bend order table. You will select a group of bends in a specific sequence and save that sequence to a file.

1. Set the working directory to the *Sheetmetal_Drawing* folder.

2. Open **brkt_002.prt**.

3. Set the model display as follows:

   - ⁕ *(Datum Display Filters)*: None

   - ⚬ *(Spin Center)*: Off

   - ▱ *(Display Style)*: ▱ (No Hidden)

4. Select **Bends>Bend Order** in the *Sheetmetal* tab.

5. The Bend Order dialog box opens and the part returns to the flat condition. Select the *Sequence fixed geometry* collector as shown in Figure 9–16.

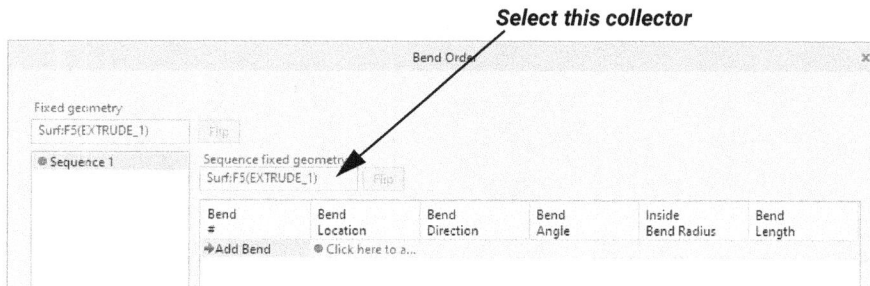

Figure 9–16

6. Change the fixed surface by selecting the surface shown in Figure 9–17 (the same surface is used throughout the bend order table creation).

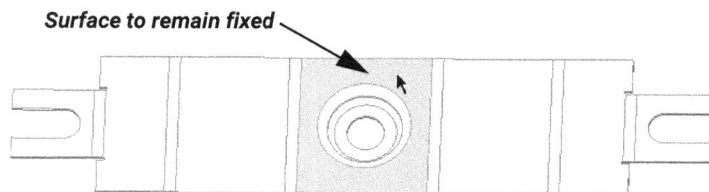

Figure 9–17

7. Select the *Bend Location* collector field, as shown in Figure 9–18, to select a bend for adding it to the current sequence.

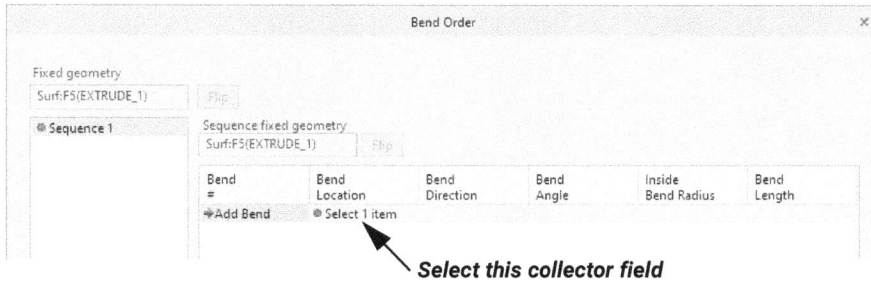

Figure 9–18

8. Select the bends as shown in Figure 9–19. Note that both of the bends are added to **Sequence 1**.

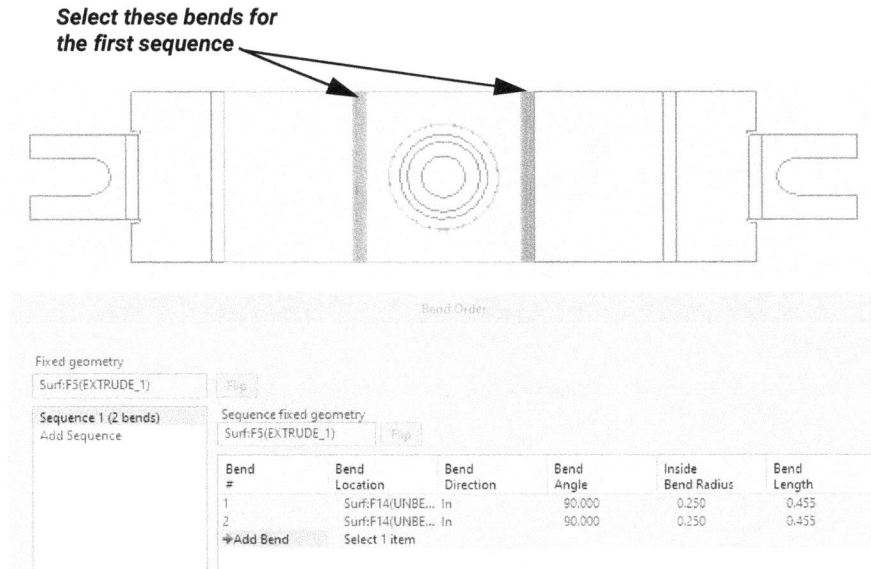

Figure 9–19

9. Select **Add Sequence** on the left side of the Bend Order dialog box, as shown in Figure 9–20.

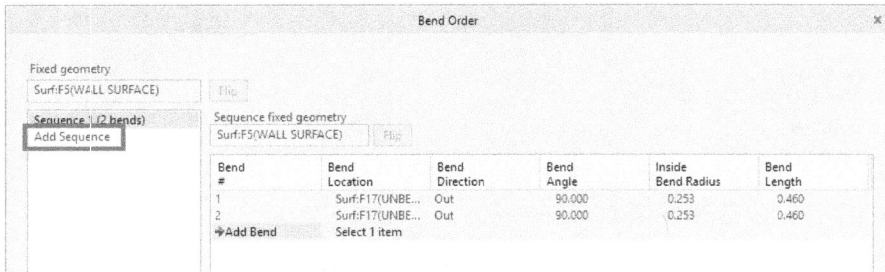

Figure 9–20

10. A new sequence is added to the dialog box and the model displays in a semi-bent condition, as shown in Figure 9–21.

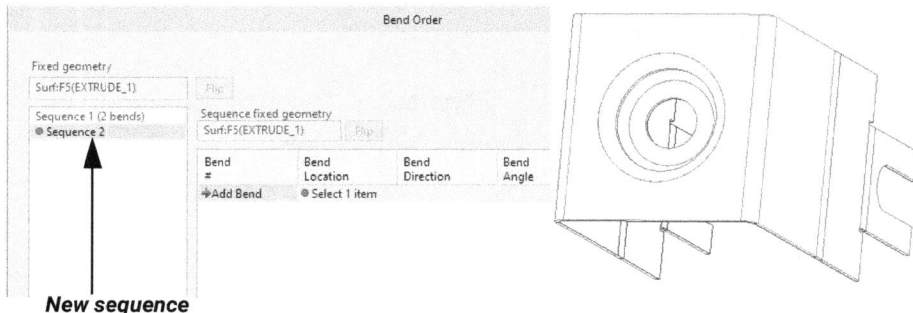

New sequence

Figure 9–21

11. Select the bends for the next sequence as shown in Figure 9–22.

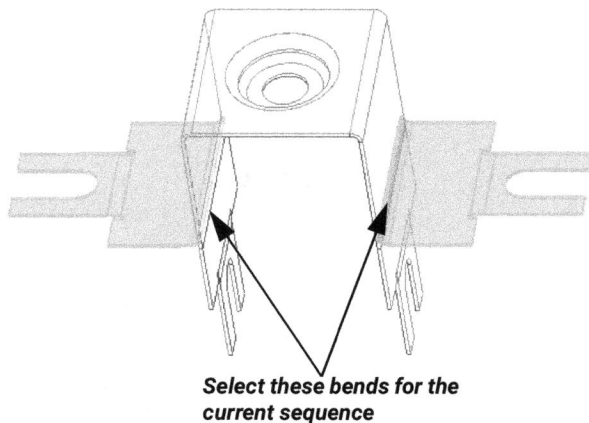

Select these bends for the current sequence

Figure 9–22

12. Select **Add Sequence** in the dialog box.

13. The part again displays in a semi-bent condition. Select the bends for the final sequence, as shown in Figure 9−23.

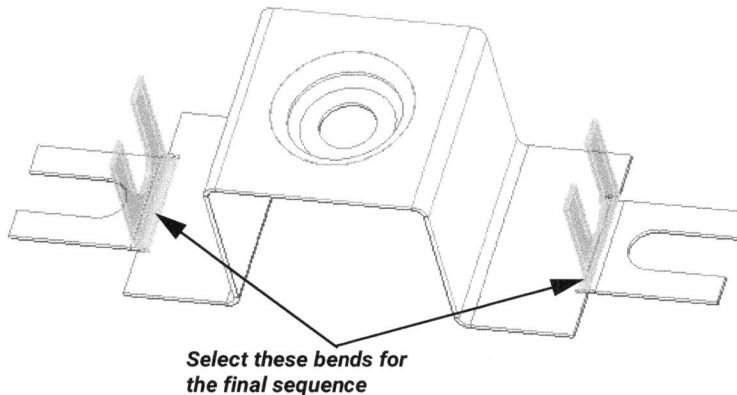

Select these bends for the final sequence

Figure 9−23

14. Click **Save** and save the table to the current working directory with the current name.

15. Click **OK**.

16. Select **File>Prepare>Model Properties** and click ⚙ next to Bend Order, as shown in Figure 9−24.

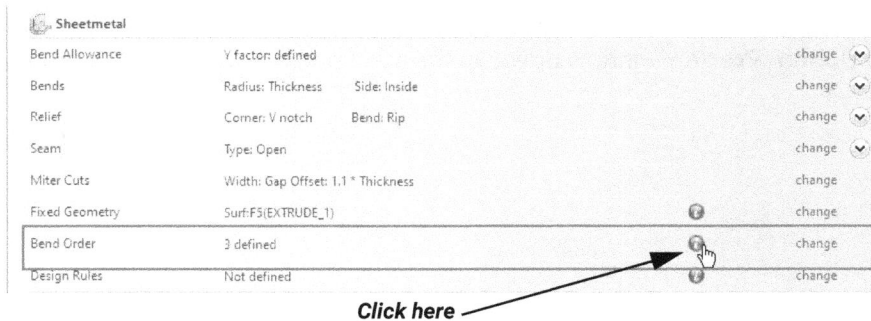

Click here

Figure 9−24

*Note: You can also select **change** next to Bend Order in the Model Properties dialog box to change the bend sequence.*

17. The Bend Order table displays to examine the bend sequence shown in Figure 9-25.

Bend Sequences	No.of Bends	Bend#	Bend Direction	Bend Angle	Inside Bend Radius	Bend Length
1	2	1	IN	90.000	0.250	0.455
		2	IN	90.000	0.250	0.455
2	2	1	OUT	90.000	0.250	0.455
		2	OUT	90.000	0.250	0.455
3	2	1	OUT	90.000	0.250	0.455
		2	OUT	90.000	0.250	0.455

Figure 9-25

Note: In the Bend Direction column, IN and OUT refer to the facing direction of the green side of the model.

18. Close the information window and Model Properties dialog box.

Task 2: Create a flat state.

Design Considerations

In this task, you will create a flat state to display a part in the flattened and formed conditions. These two states will be displayed on the same drawing in the following tasks.

1.   In the In-graphics toolbar, click 🔲 (Flat Pattern Preview).

2.   **The Flat Pattern Preview** window opens in the main graphics area, as shown in Figure 9-26.

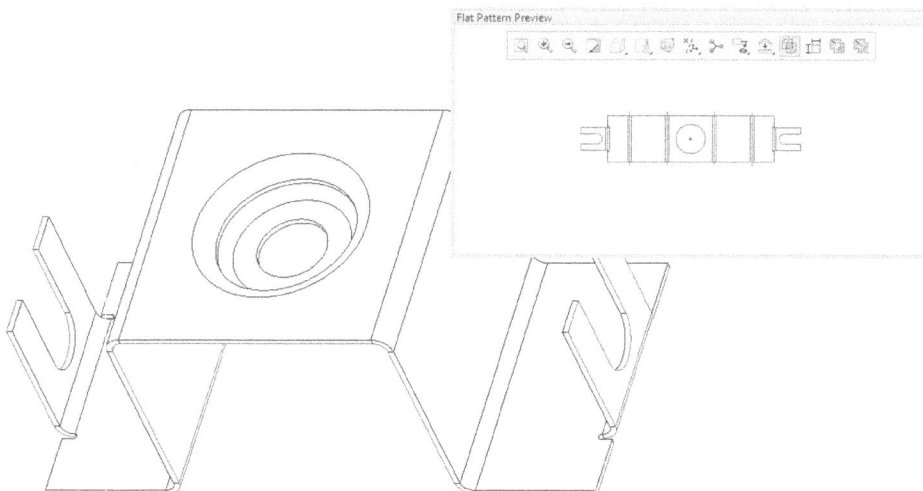

Figure 9-26

3. In the In-graphics toolbar inside the Flat Pattern Preview window, click ⬚ (Create Instance), as shown in Figure 9–27.

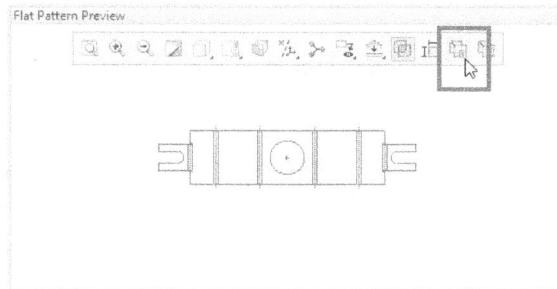

Figure 9–27

4. The Make Flat Instance dialog box displays, as shown in Figure 9–28.

Figure 9–28

5. Click **Create** to accept **BRKT_002_FLAT** as the default name of the flat state instance.

6. In the *Sheetmetal* tab of the ribbon, click ⬚ (Family Table). Note that a family table has been added. A column displays for the Flat Pattern feature.

7. Select **BRKT_002_FLAT** and click ⬚ (Open) in the Family Table dialog box to open the flat instance file. It displays as shown in Figure 9–29.

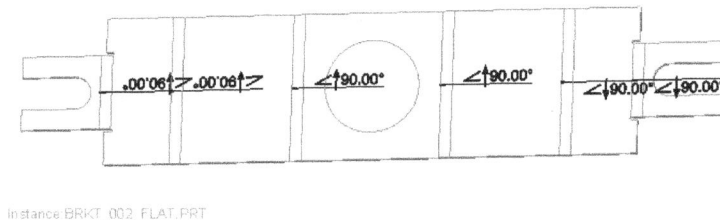

Figure 9–29

8. Close the window containing the instance. The **BRKT_002** part window should now be active.

Task 3: Create a drawing of the sheet metal part.

Design Considerations

In this task, you will create a new drawing to display a part in the formed conditions.

1. In the Quick Access toolbar, click ☐ (New).
2. Select **Drawing, enable the Use drawing model file name option**.
3. Click **OK**.
4. Select the options shown in Figure 9–30 to create the new drawing and then click **OK**.

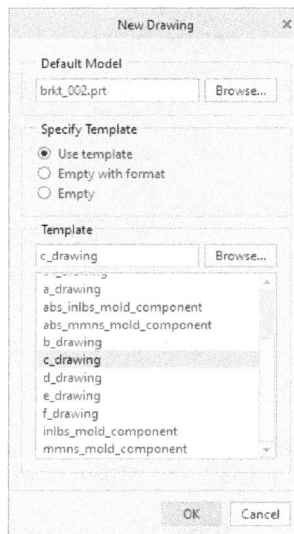

Figure 9–30

5. When prompted to select the instance to use for the drawing, select **The generic** and click **Open** in the dialog box.

6. Arrange the default template views as shown in Figure 9–31. Click ⊟ (General View) to add a General view to the drawing. Select **No Combine State** and click **OK**. Do not use cross-section or scaling. Leave the General view in the default orientation.

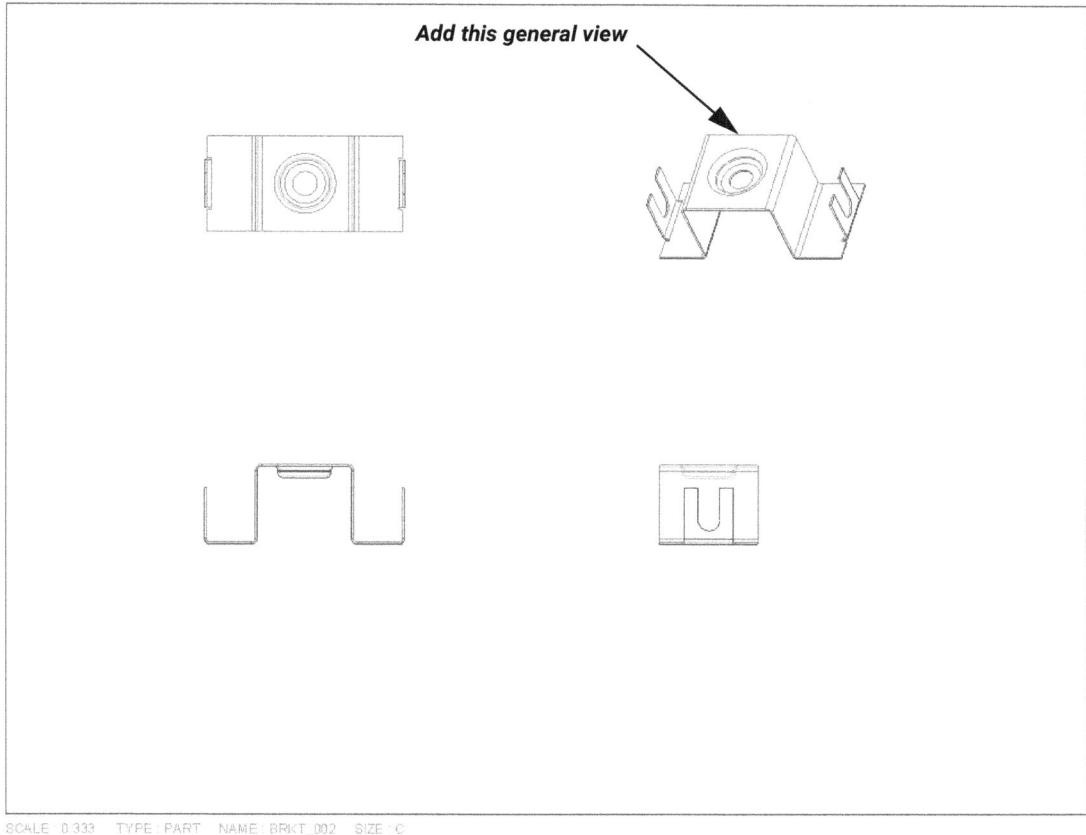

Add this general view

SCALE : 0.333   TYPE : PART   NAME : BRKT_002   SIZE : C

Figure 9–31

Task 4: Display the flat pattern and the bend order table.

Design Considerations

In this task, you will create a drawing view to display the part in the flat state on the same drawing and you will display the bend order table. Bend order labels will be applied to the flat state view.

1. Click ✎ (Drawing Models).

2. Select **Add Model** and select **brkt_002.prt** in the Open dialog box and click **Open**.

3. Double-click on **BRKT_002_FLAT** in the Select Instance dialog box.

4. Select **Done/Return**.

5. Click ▱ (General View) to add a General view of the flat instance to the drawing.

6. In the Drawing Views dialog box, select **Geometry references**.

7. Select **Back** from the Reference 1 drop-down list, and in the Model Tree, select datum plane **RIGHT**.

8. Select **Bottom** from the Reference 2 drop-down list, and in the Model Tree, select datum plane **FRONT**.

9. Click **OK**. The model orients as shown in Figure 9–32.

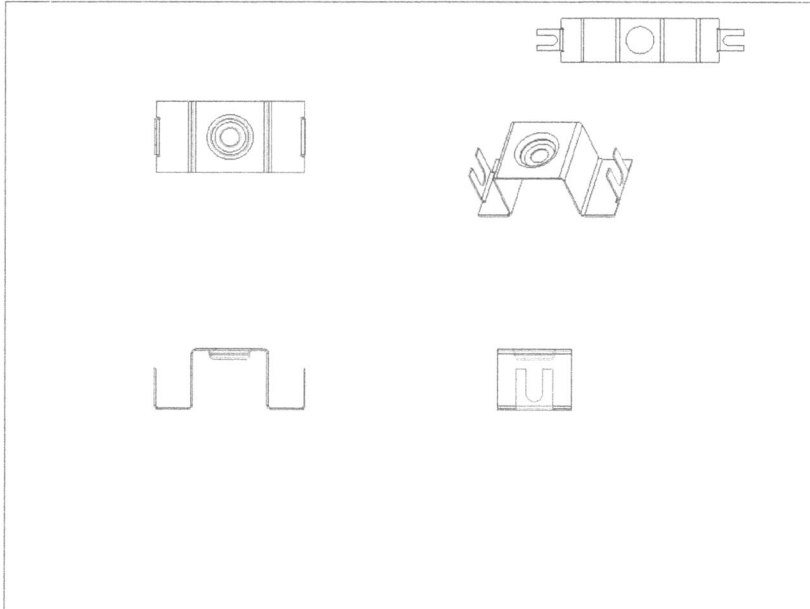

Figure 9–32

10. Select *Annotate* tab. Click ▦ (Show Model Annotations). The Show Model Annotations dialog box opens.

11. In the Show Model Annotations dialog box, click the ▦ (Show Model Notes) tab.

12. In the Model Tree, select the **BKT_002_FLAT <BRKT_002>.prt**. The notes display in the dialog box and in the view window. Place a check next to each note in the dialog box or click ⸝ (Select All) as shown in Figure 9–33.

Figure 9–33

13. Click **OK** in the Show Model Annotations dialog box. The bend order table and bend order labels display as shown in Figure 9–34.

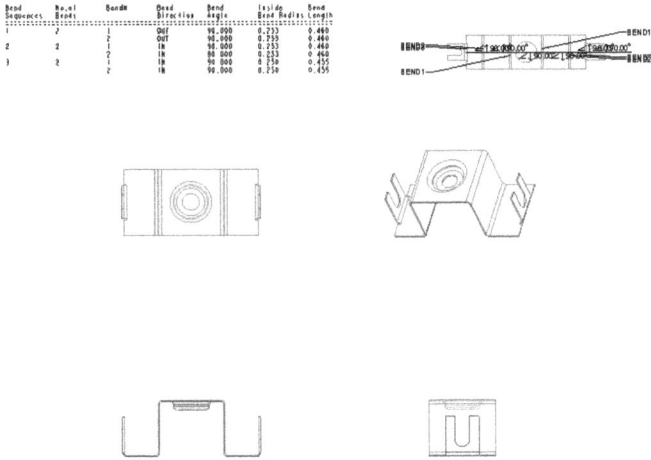

Figure 9–34

14. Erase all unnecessary bend notes and tables, the bend order table, and the bend order labels.

15. Arrange the bend order labels as shown in Figure 9–35.

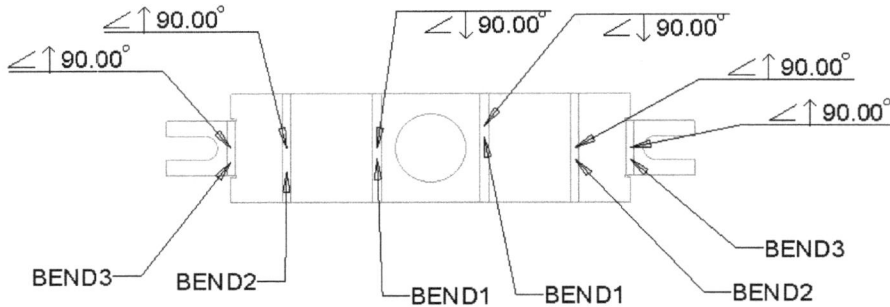

Figure 9–35

Task 5: Add ordinate dimensions to the flat state view.

Design Considerations

In this task, you will create ordinate dimensions to display dimensions in the flattened conditions. As ordinate dimensions are common in sheet metal part drawings, an **Auto Ordinate** option is available to create these dimensions quickly.

1. Insert another General view of the flat pattern.

2. In the Drawing Views dialog box, select **Geometry references**.

3. Select **Back** from the Reference 1 drop-down list, and in the Model Tree, select datum plane **RIGHT**.

4. Select **Bottom** from the Reference 2 drop-down list, and in the Model Tree, select datum plane **FRONT**.

5. Click **OK**.

6. Select the *Annotate* tab.

7. Expand ⁼ᵢ° (Ordinate Dimension) and select **Auto Ordinate Dimension**.

8. Hold <Ctrl> and select the seven parallel surfaces shown in Figure 9–36.

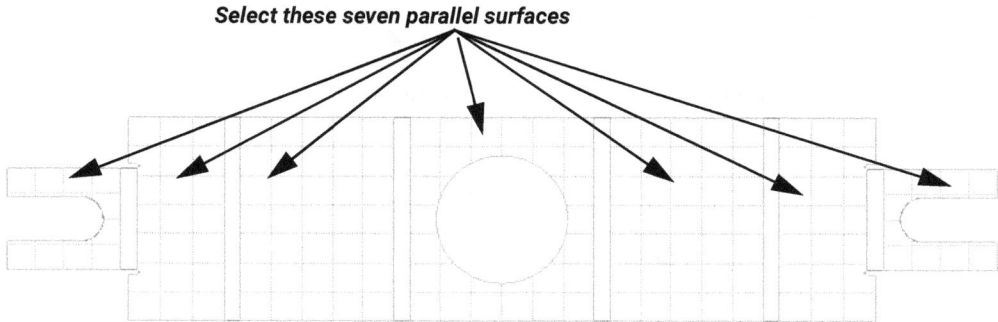

Select these seven parallel surfaces

Figure 9–36

9. Click **OK** in the Select dialog box, or middle-click.

10. Select **Select Base Line** in the **AUTO ORDINATE** menu to specify the first base line.

11. Select the edge shown in Figure 9–37 to define the horizontal base line in the flat state instance.

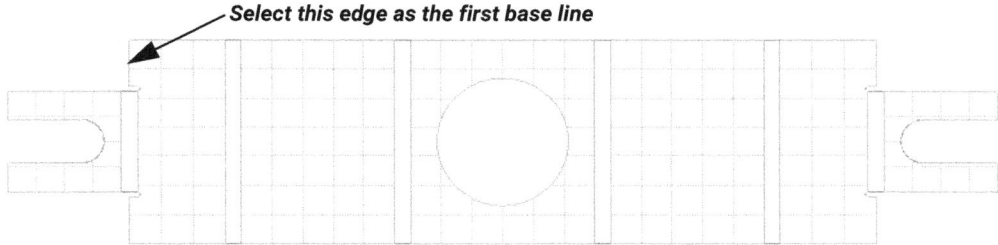

Select this edge as the first base line

Figure 9–37

- The ordinate dimensions are automatically created as driven dimensions, as shown in Figure 9–38.

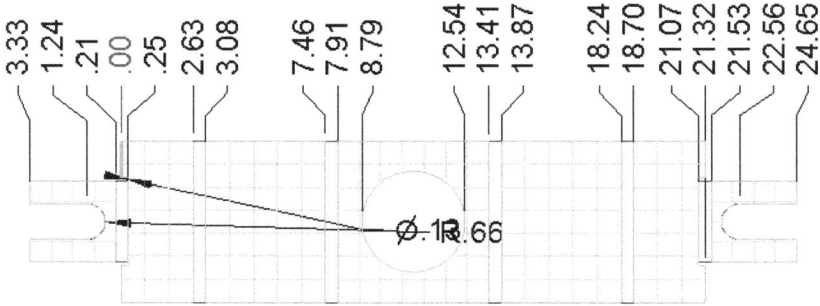

Ø-1R.66

Figure 9–38

12. Select **Select Base Line** in the **AUTO ORDINATE** menu to specify the second base line.

13. Select the edge shown in Figure 9–39 to define the second base line in the flat state instance.

Select this edge as the second base line

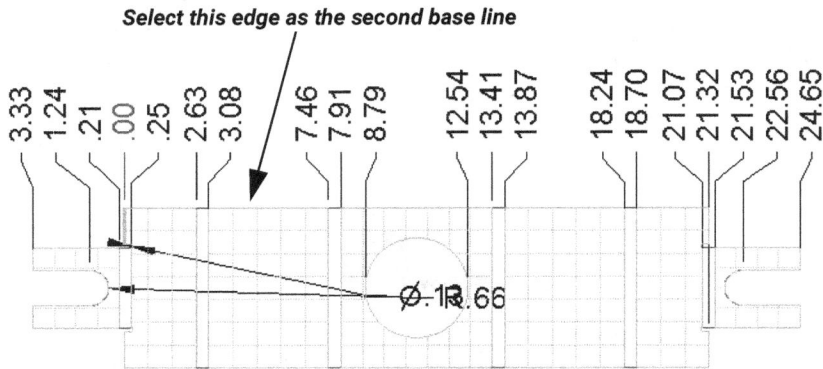

Figure 9–39

- The ordinate dimensions are automatically created as driven dimensions, as shown in Figure 9–40.

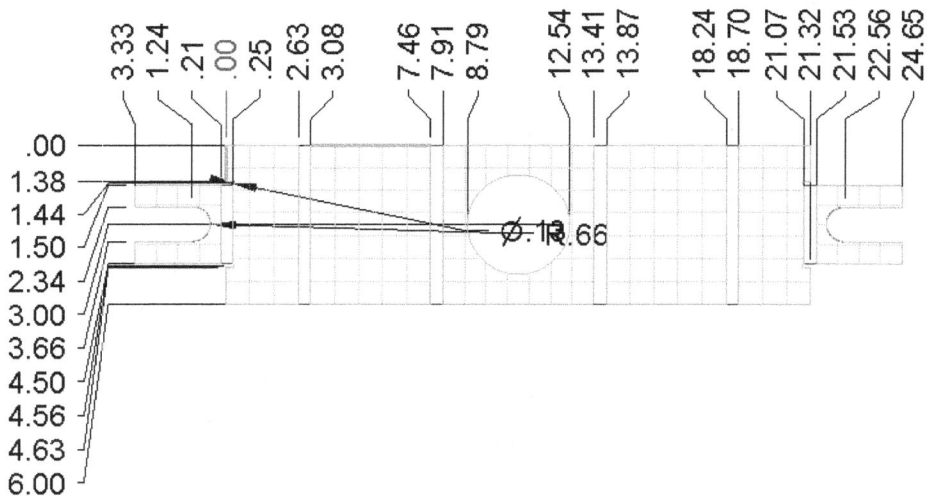

Figure 9–40

14. Select **Done/Return**.

15. Rearrange dimensions as required.

16. Save the drawing and close the window.

End of practice

Practice 9b
Bend Tables in Drawings

Practice Objective

- Create a flat state and a bend table with minimal instruction.

In this practice, you will create a flat state and a bend order for the Project part. You will then create a drawing of the part.

1. Set the working directory to *Drawing_Bend_Tables*.
2. Open **project_ex4.prt**.
3. Set the model display as follows:

   - ⚲ *(Datum Display Filters)*: None
   - ⚙ *(Spin Center)*: Off
   - ⬜ *(Display Style)*: ⬜ (No Hidden)

4. Create a bend order table.
5. Create a flat state.
6. Create a drawing with the views shown in Figure 9−41.
7. Display the bend order table and bend order labels, as shown in Figure 9−41.

Bend Sequences	No. of Bends	Bend#	Bend Direction	Bend Angle	Inside Bend Radius	Bend Length
1	2	1	OUT	90.000	1.870	3.002
		2	IN	90.000	2.000	3.207
2	1	1	IN	90.000	0.250	0.458
3	1	1	IN	120.000	0.250	0.610
4	2	1	OUT	90.000	0.250	0.458
		2	OUT	90.000	0.250	0.458

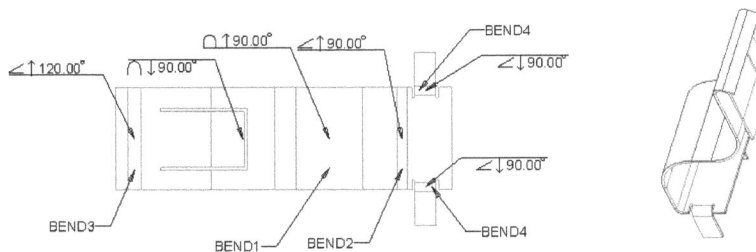

Figure 9−41

8. Save the drawing and erase it from memory.

End of practice

Chapter Review Questions

1. Creating a flat state enables you to do which of the following? (Select all that apply.)

   a. Store multiple similar models in the same file.

   b. Automatically create ordinate dimensions in the drawing.

   c. Simulate different steps of the sheet metal fabrication process.

   d. Store a developed flat pattern inside a bent generic model.

2. After you have created a flat pattern instance in a family table, you can open the instance using which of the following methods? (Select all that apply.)

   a. Highlight the instance in the Family Table dialog box and click Open.

   b. Open the generic model. You can then select an instance in the list or open the generic model

   c. Open the instance directly if an instance index file has been created

   d. Click ⬛⇄ and select the instance.

3. Since the creation of a family table yields two separate models, you can display both models on the drawing at the same time.

   a. True

   b. False

4. Which of the following icons in the *Layout* tab enables you to add a model in the drawing?

   a. ▭

   b. ⬛⇄

   c. ⤢

   d. ⊙d

5. What information does the bend order table include? (Select all that apply.)

   a. Bend sequence

   b. Ordinate dimensions

   c. Angle

   d. Radius

6. The bend table displays as a note on a detail drawing. The values for the bend radius and developed length in the table update automatically on the drawing when the part is modified.

   a. True

   b. False

7. You must manually add new bends to a bend table.

   a. True

   b. False

Converting Solid Parts

If you have an existing solid or surface model that needs to be a sheet metal part, you do not have to recreate it as such. Instead, you can convert the sheet metal part to a solid.

Learning Objectives

- Learn to convert a solid part into a sheet metal part with a uniform thickness by selecting a driving surface or by shelling the part.
- Learn how to start the conversion operation and define, if required, the edge rip, rip connect, bends, and corner relief options.

10.1 Converting Solid Parts

Creo Parametric enables you to convert a solid part into a sheet metal part. For solid parts with a uniform thickness, you can convert the part by selecting a driving surface, which becomes the green surface in the sheet metal part. For parts with non-uniform wall thickness, you could be able to convert by shelling.

How To: Convert a Solid Part

1. With the solid model active, select **Operations>Convert to Sheet Metal** to start the conversion. The *Convert* dashboard displays, as shown in Figure 10−1.

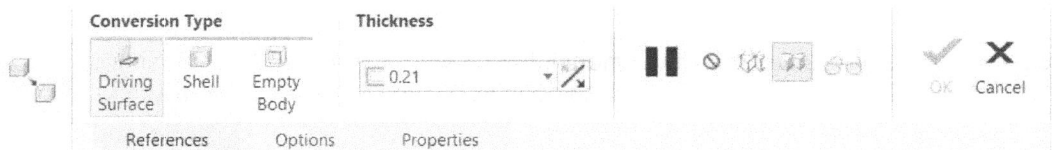

Figure 10−1

2. You can convert the part using one of the following options:

- (Driving Surface)
- (Shell)
- (Empty)

Driving Surface

To use (Driving Surface), select an existing model surface as the green side of the new sheet metal wall, as shown in Figure 10−2.

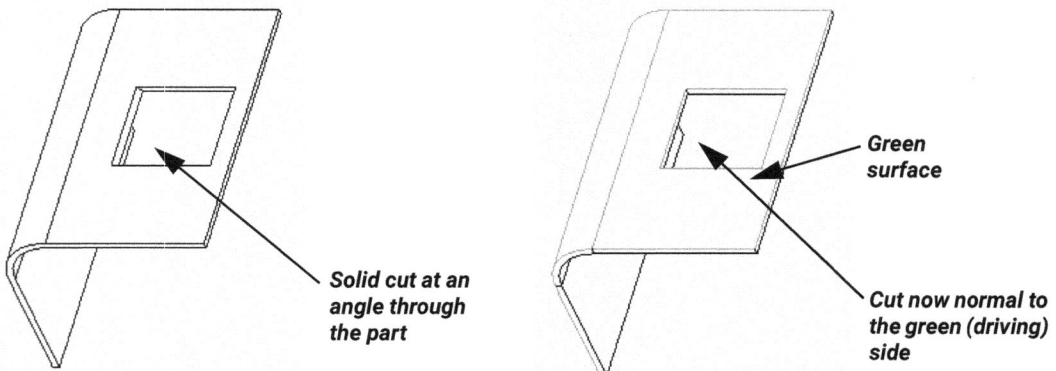

Solid cut at an angle through the part

Green surface

Cut now normal to the green (driving) side

Figure 10−2

The part shown on the left in Figure 10–2 is a solid part created with a thin extrude. It can easily be converted to a sheet metal part using ⬦ (Driving Surface) because it has a constant wall thickness. The top surface is selected as the driving surface and becomes the green surface. Thin geometry with non-uniform thickness is covered later in this chapter.

The solid cut in the part shown on the left in Figure 10–2 was created at an angle to the top surface. When the part is converted to a sheet metal part, the cut automatically takes on the properties of a sheet metal cut. The part shown on the right now displays the cut surfaces perpendicular to the sheet metal wall.

Shell

To use the ▭ (Shell) option, select one or more surfaces to be removed. The system hollows the part to the required thickness, as shown in Figure 10–3.

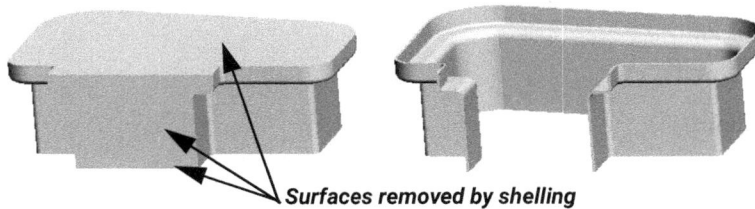

Surfaces removed by shelling

Figure 10–3

Once a solid model has been converted to a sheet metal part, all of the existing geometry is listed as the **Convert(First Wall)** feature in the Model Tree, as shown in Figure 10–4.

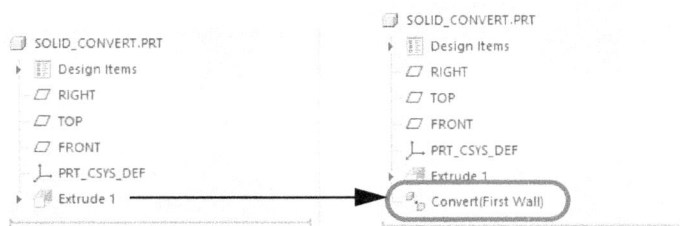

Figure 10–4

*Note: You can also select **Operations>Switch to Solid Part** to convert the sheet metal part back to a solid part.*

Additional walls and sheet metal features are built from that point. To convert the sheet metal part back to a solid part, delete the Convert(First wall) feature and any other sheet metal features that you have added after the original conversion.

Empty

To use the ▭ (Empty) option, nothing has to be selected other than the icon itself, then select ✓ (OK). This will convert an empty solid body into an empty sheet metal body.

10.2 Conversion Feature

Once a solid part has been converted, you still might not be able to unbend it. Complex surfaces, such as rounds or blended features, might need to be modified; closed profiles might need rips applied so that they can be unbent; or sharp corners might need a bend radius to be functional. All of these situations can be addressed using the conversion feature.

How To: Use the Conversion Feature

1. Click 🔧 (Conversion) in the *Sheetmetal* tab to start the conversion operation.

2. The conversion feature has a number of optional elements that can be defined as required to develop the part:

   - ▢ (Edge Rip)

   - ◲ (Rip Connect)

   - ◢ (Edge Bend)

   - 🔧 (Corner Relief)

3. Once the elements have been correctly defined, click ✓ (OK) to complete the operation.

Edge Rip

The Edge Rip element creates rip geometry along an existing edge, similar to the rip feature. The edge is then converted from a sharp edge to three adjacent walls that meet at their inside surfaces, as shown in Figure 10−5.

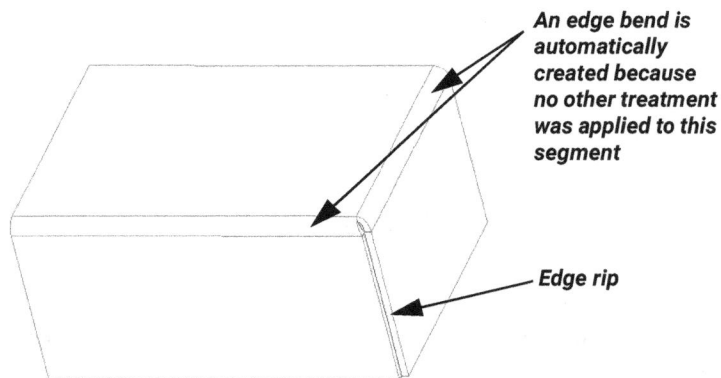

An edge bend is automatically created because no other treatment was applied to this segment

Edge rip

Figure 10−5

By default, the edge rip is created using an Open corner type. You can change this if required to an entered value (**Blind**), **Gap**, or an **Overlap**. This is done by selecting the Placement panel and selecting the appropriate option in the flyout, as shown in Figure 10–6. You can also select the *Edge treatment* option in the tab flyout.

Figure 10–6

As with Flange walls, the **Close corner** option is available here for the **Open** edge treatment type, as shown in Figure 10–7.

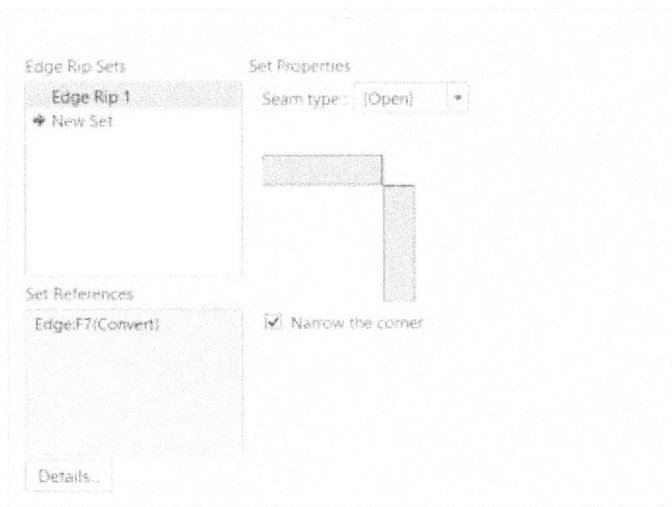

Figure 10–7

A point can be created before the conversion feature. This enables you to divide existing edges into multiple segments, which can then be treated individually, as shown in Figure 10–8.

An edge bend is automatically created because no other treatment was applied to this segment

Edge rip

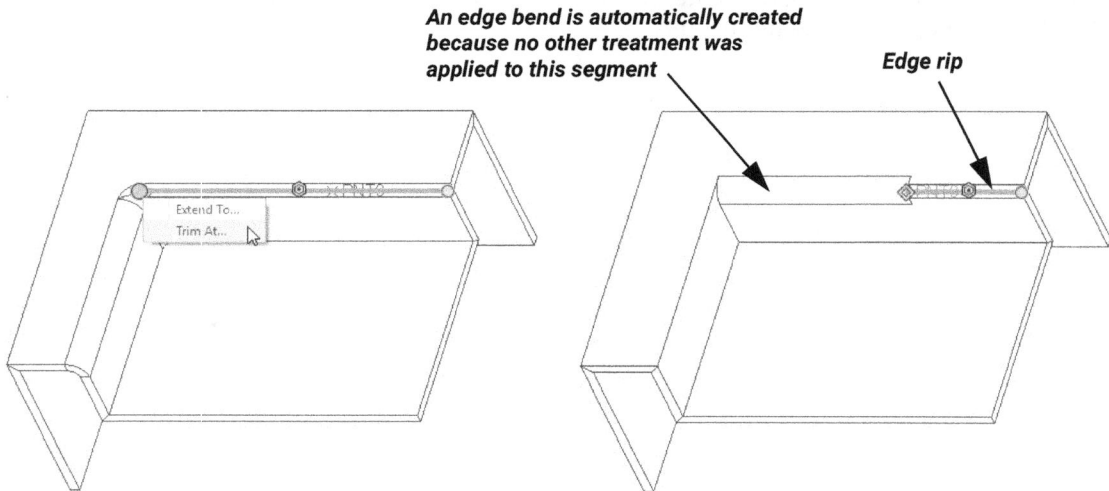

Figure 10–8

Rip Connect

The Rip Connect element is similar to the edge rip. However, instead of selecting an existing edge, you select two points or vertices between which to create the rip as shown in Figure 10–9. This enables some flexibility when you are deciding where to rip the sheet metal wall.

End points for rip connect

Resulting rip line

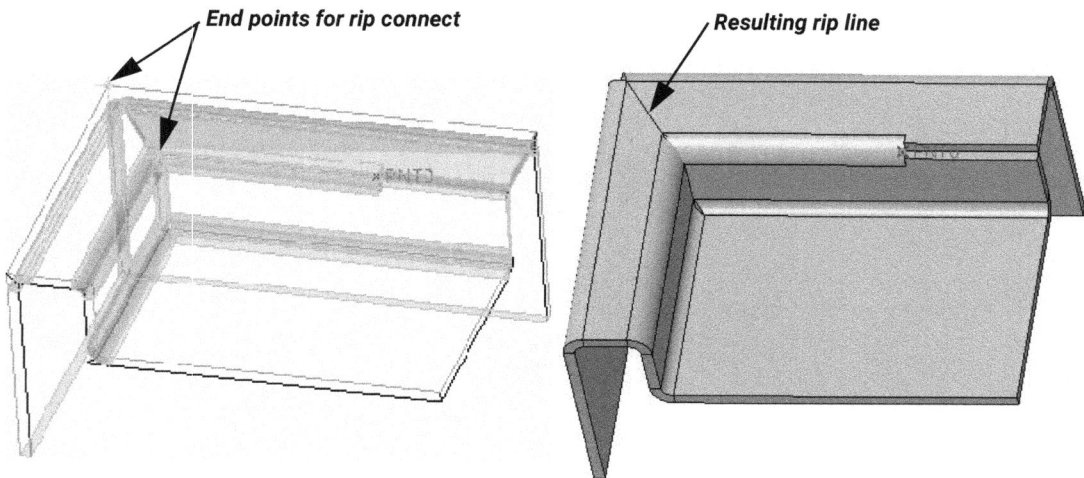

Figure 10–9

Edge Bends

The Edge Bends element specifies non-tangent edges along which to create an edge bend. The element creates an inside and outside radius, as shown in Figure 10-10. It is applied to all non-tangent edges by default if another conversion treatment has not been applied to them.

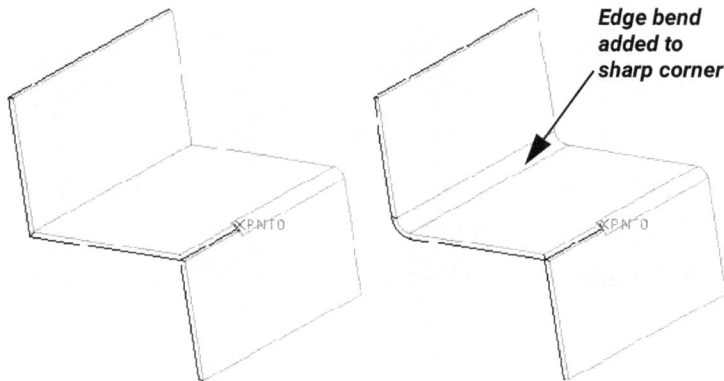

Edge bend added to sharp corner

Figure 10-10

Corner Relief

The Corner Relief element creates relief at specific corners, as shown in Figure 10-11. Similar to the corner relief option when creating walls, selected vertices are highlighted with specific symbols that indicate the particular relief or conversion feature that has been applied.

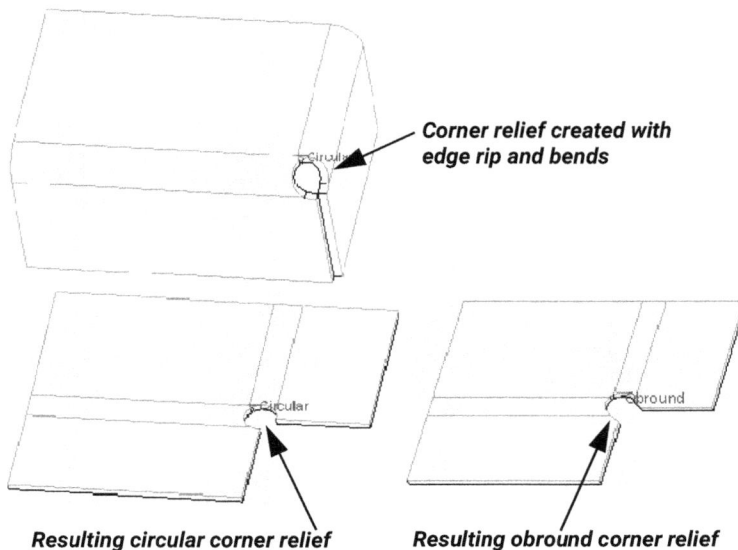

Corner relief created with edge rip and bends

Resulting circular corner relief

Resulting obround corner relief

Figure 10-11

A corner relief can be created as a separate feature. The options for this element are described as follows:

Symbol	Corner Relief Results
[V Notch]	The SMT_DFLT_CRNR_REL_TYPE corner is created as the type.
V Notch	V Notch corner is created
Obround	Obround corner is created.
Circular	Circular corner is created.
No relief	No relief is applied. The default V-notch is applied.
Normal	Create cut from the corner up to and normal to the bend end to provided relief.
Square	Square corner is created.
Rectangular	Rectangular corner is created.

10.3 Additional Conversion Options

Creo Parametric provides you with additional control over the conversion by enabling the following actions:

- Overwrite the calculated thickness by entering a value manually.

- Include additional surfaces or exclude surfaces.

- Keep, remove, or ignore the adjacent rounds and chamfers, as shown in Figure 10-12.

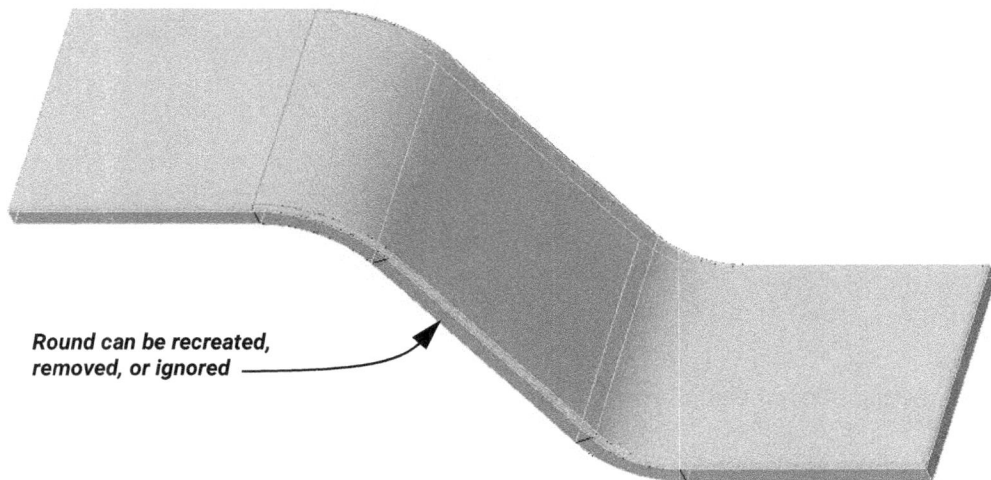

Round can be recreated, removed, or ignored

Figure 10-12

- Keep non-classified surfaces as separate quilts.

- Troubleshoot errors.

In the example shown in Figure 10–13, the indicated surface was selected as the *Driving surface*. The adjacent surfaces have a different thickness, and so are not included by default.

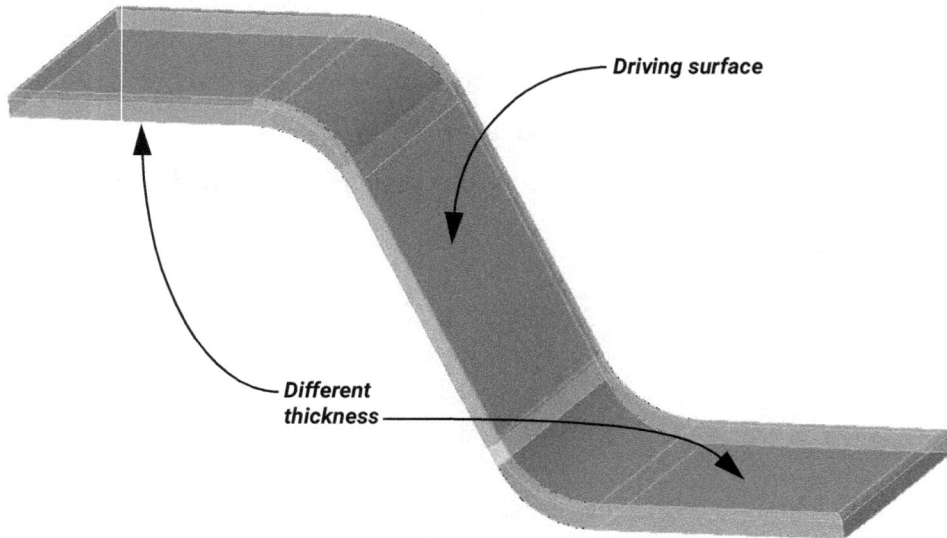

Figure 10–13

You can manually select the adjacent surfaces, and the system will alter the geometry so that a constant thickness is applied. To add additional surfaces, either expand the references panel and select surfaces in the **Include surfaces** collector, or right-click and select **Include surfaces**, as shown in Figure 10–14.

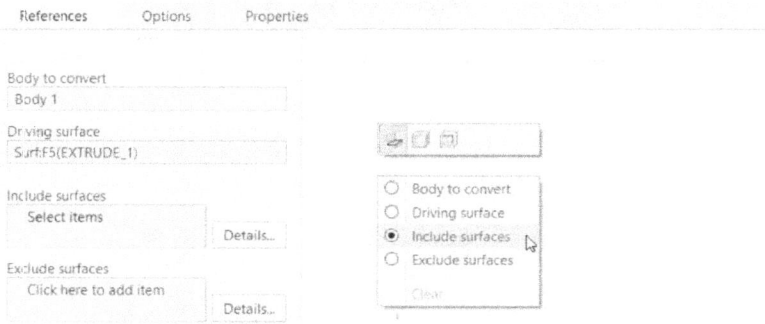

Figure 10–14

Select additional surfaces to include in the sheet metal part. Note that the system creates the solid geometry with a constant thickness, and leaves unclassified surfaces where the original thickness was greater, as shown in Figure 10-15.

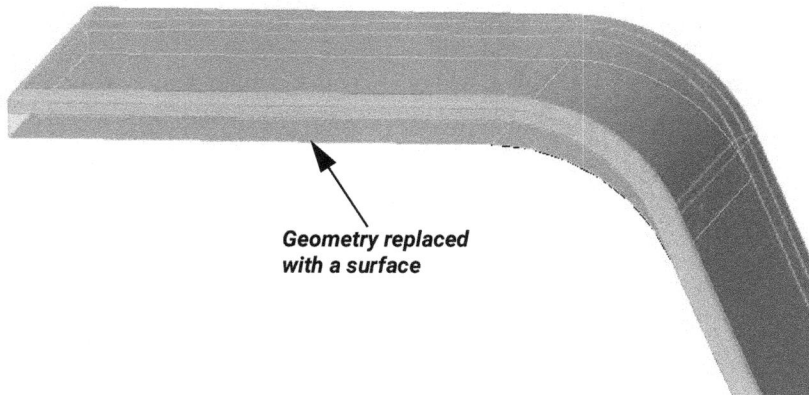

**Geometry replaced
with a surface**

Figure 10-15

If you complete the feature, the Troubleshooter might open, indicating the that there are potential problems with the geometry, as shown in Figure 10-16.

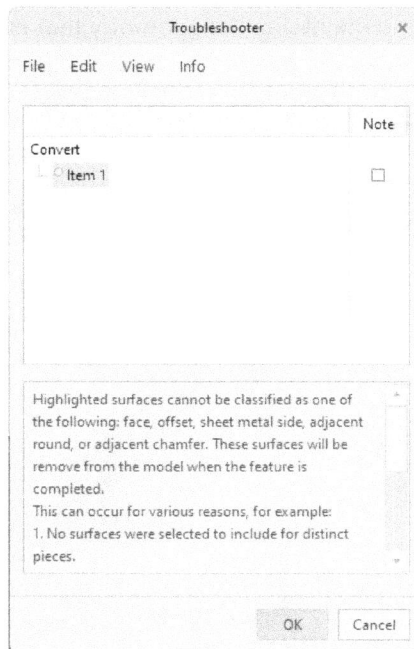

Figure 10-16

If you click **OK**, you can still complete the feature, as shown in Figure 10−17.

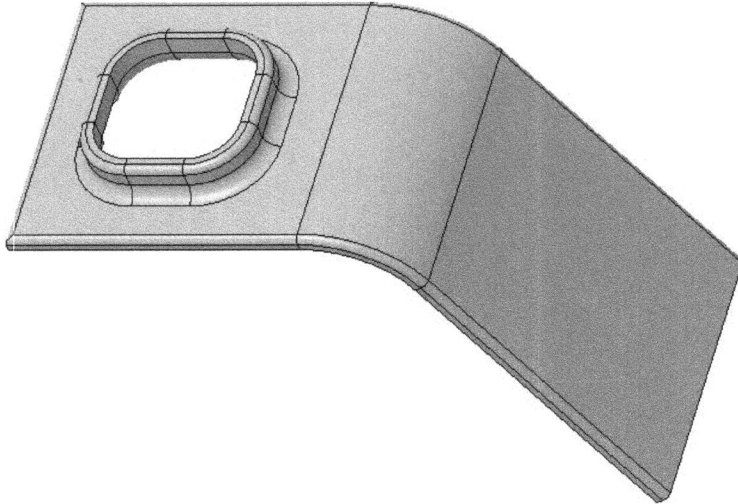

Figure 10−17

In the Options panel, you can enable the **Keeps not classified surfaces as a quilt** option. When using this option, Creo Parametric maintains the geometry that is not specifically included, as shown in Figure 10−18.

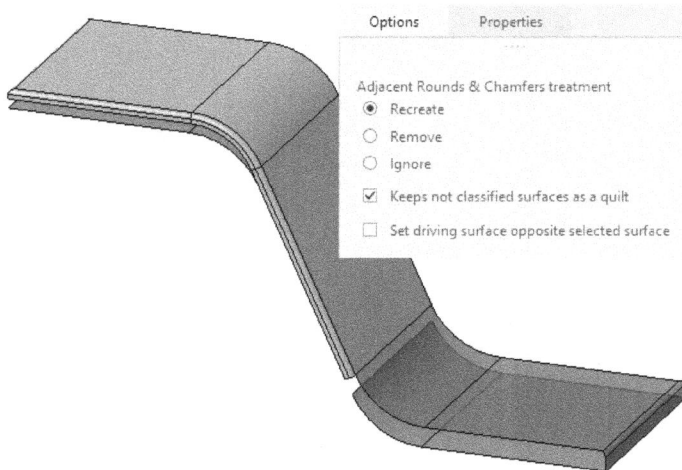

Figure 10−18

You can also decide how to handle rounds in the original model. You can **Recreate**, **Remove** or **Ignore** the rounds when the sheet metal model is created.

Practice 10a
Convert a Solid Part

Practice Objectives

- Convert a solid part into a sheet metal part using the shell method.
- Create conversion features with an edge rip relief and a corner relief.

In this practice, you will convert a rectangular solid part into a sheet metal part and unbend it, as shown in Figure 10–19.

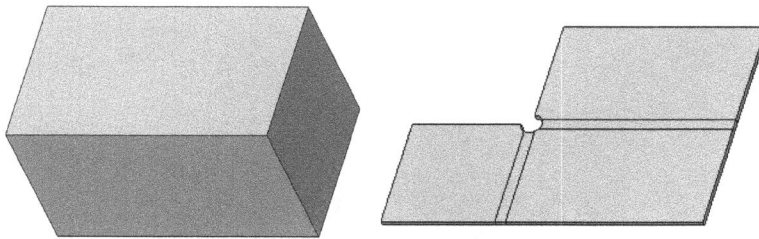

Figure 10–19

Task 1: Open a solid part and convert it to a sheet metal part.

Design Considerations

A part created as a solid has to be converted to a sheet metal part. The part has non-uniform wall thickness, and you will convert it by shelling the part and removing three surfaces. Once a solid model has been converted to a sheet metal part, all of the existing geometry is listed as the First Wall feature in the Model Tree.

1. Set the working directory to the *Convert_Solid* folder.
2. Open **solid_convert.prt**.
3. Set the model display as follows:

   - (Datum Display Filters): None
   - (Spin Center): Off
   - (Display Style): (Shading With Edges)

4. Select **Operations>Convert to Sheet Metal** in the *Model* tab. The *Convert* dashboard opens, as shown in Figure 10−20.

Figure 10−20

5. Under *Settings*, click ☐ (Shell) and select the surfaces shown in Figure 10−21 to be removed.

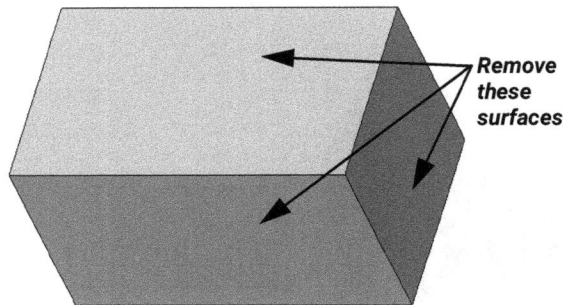

Figure 10−21

6. Set the shell *Thickness* to **0.125**, as shown in Figure 10−22.

Figure 10−22

7. Complete the feature. The part has been converted to a sheet metal part, as shown in Figure 10–23.

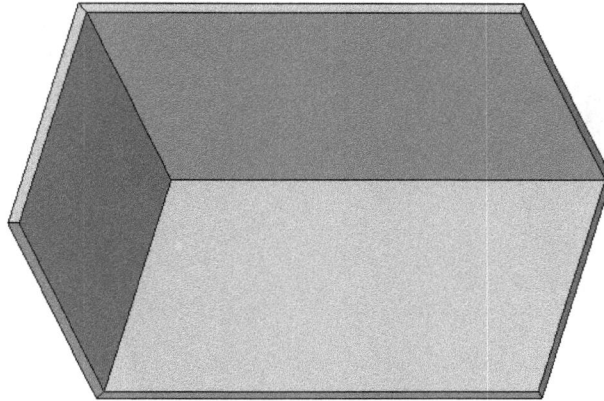

Figure 10–23

The Model Tree now lists the First Wall feature and the outside surface of the model represents the green side of the sheet metal part.

Task 2: Create a conversion feature.

Design Considerations

To create the required documentation, you need to unbend the converted geometry. To do this, you will use the Conversion feature and apply edge rip and corner relief to the part.

1. Click ⚒ (Conversion) in the *Sheetmetal* tab. The *Conversion* dashboard opens, as shown in Figure 10–24.

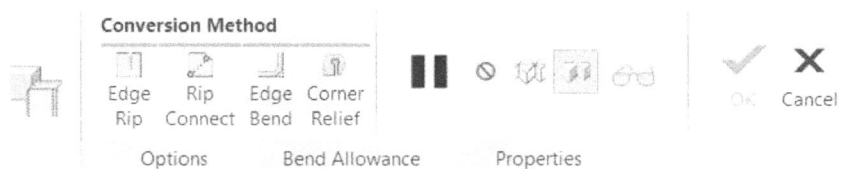

Figure 10–24

2. Click ⬚ (Edge Rip) in the *Conversion* dashboard.

3. The *Edge Rip* dashboard opens. Select the edge shown in Figure 10–25 as a reference for the rip feature.

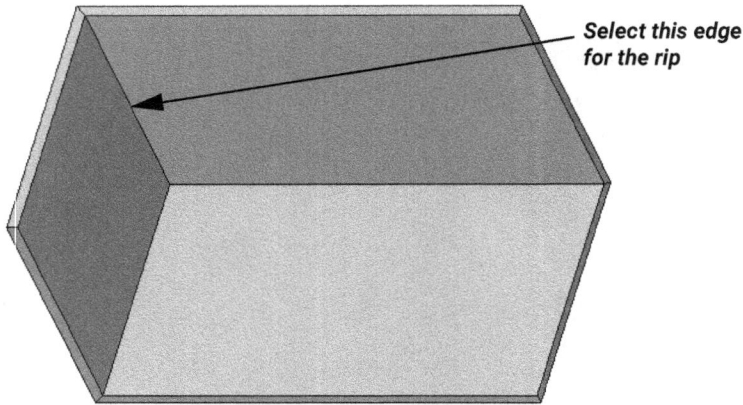

Select this edge for the rip

Figure 10–25

4. The preview displays as shown in Figure 10–26. The system automatically applies edge bends to the remaining internal edges.

Figure 10–26

5. Click ✔ (OK) in the *Edge Rip* dashboard.

6. Click ⬚ (Corner Relief) in the *Conversion* dashboard.

7. Select **Circular** in the *Corner Relief* dashboard.

8. Expand the Placement panel.

9. Select **Bend lines intersection** and then enter **0.5** for the thickness, as shown in Figure 10−27.

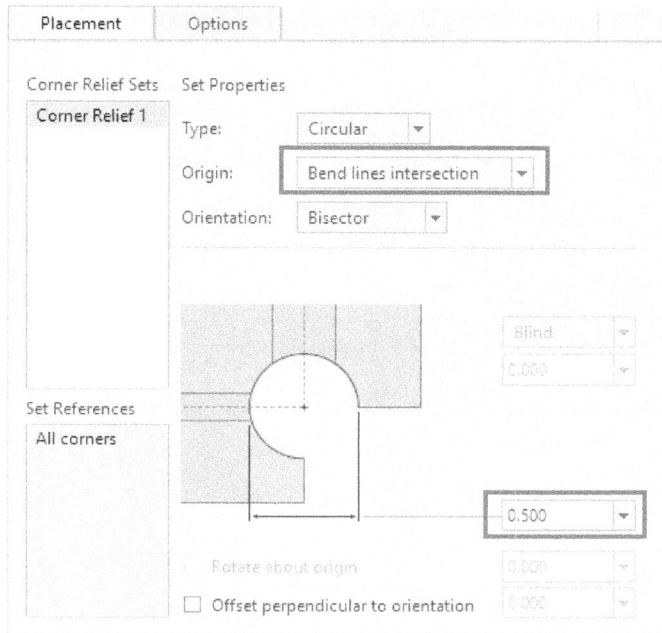

Figure 10−27

10. Click ✔ (OK) in the *Corner Relief* dashboard. The model displays as shown Figure 10−28.

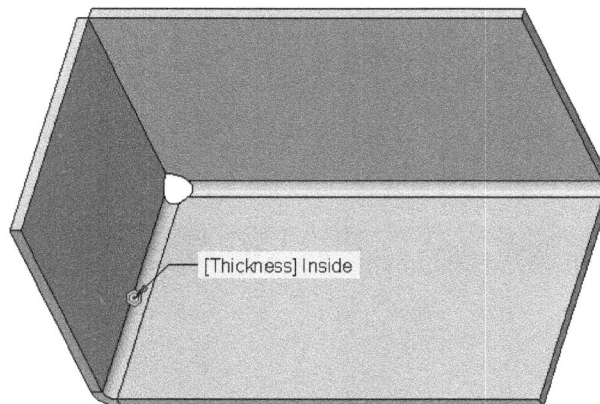

Figure 10−28

11. Click ✔ (OK) in the *Conversion* dashboard.

Task 3: Unbend the model.

1. Unbend the entire part. Select the surface shown in Figure 10–29 to remain fixed.

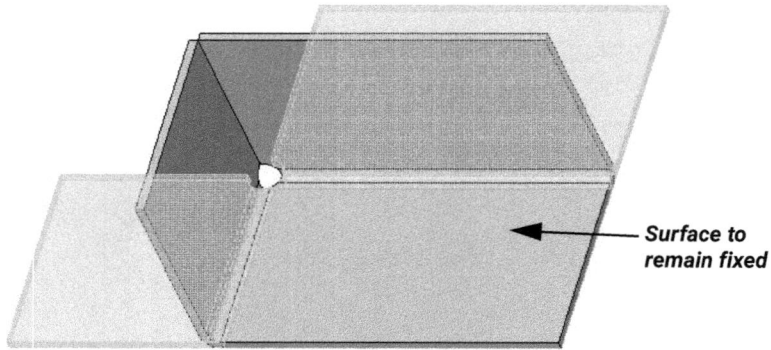

Surface to remain fixed

Figure 10–29

2. Complete the feature. The finished flat pattern is shown in Figure 10–30.

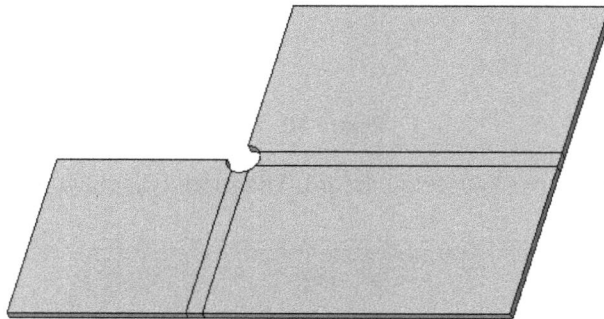

Figure 10–30

3. Save the part and erase it from memory.

End of practice

Practice 10b
Conversion Feature

Practice Objective

- Create conversion features with point relief and rip connect relief.

In this practice, you will convert a solid part and use various elements of the conversion feature to develop the part. The model is shown in Figure 10-31.

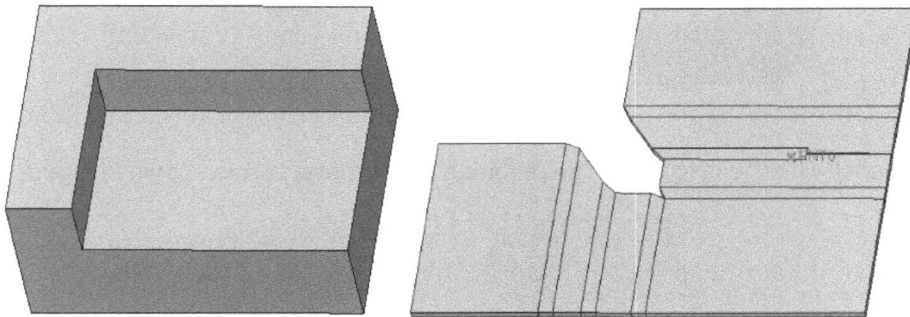

Figure 10-31

Task 1: Open a solid part and convert it into a sheet metal model.

Design Considerations

A part with non-uniform wall thickness was created as a solid and has to be converted into a sheet metal part. In this task, you will convert the solid part by shelling it and removing required surfaces. Once a solid model has been converted to a sheet metal part, all of the existing geometry is listed as the First Wall feature in the Model Tree. After you convert the part, add the Conversion feature (Edge Rip and Rip Connect) to enable the part to unbend.

1. Set the working directory to the *Conversion_Feature* folder.
2. Open **conversion_feat.prt**.
3. Set the model display as follows:

    - *(Datum Display Filters)*: None
    - *(Spin Center)*: Off
    - *(Display Style)*: (Shading With Edges)

4. Select **Operations>Convert to Sheet Metal** in the *Model* tab.

5. Under *Settings*, click ⬚ (Shell) and select the three surfaces shown in Figure 10–32 to be removed.

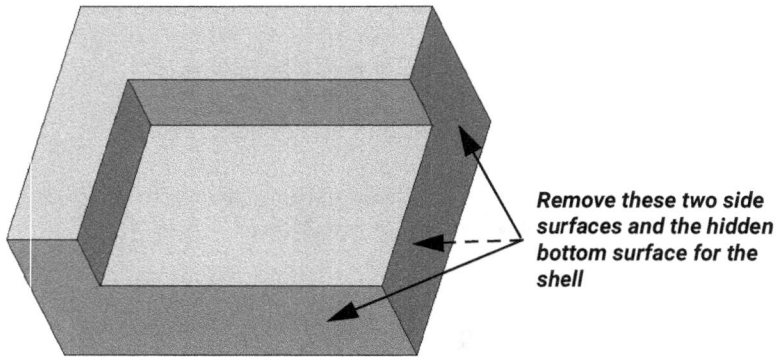

Remove these two side surfaces and the hidden bottom surface for the shell

Figure 10–32

6. Set the shell *Thickness* to **0.25**. The resulting sheet metal part is shown in Figure 10–33.

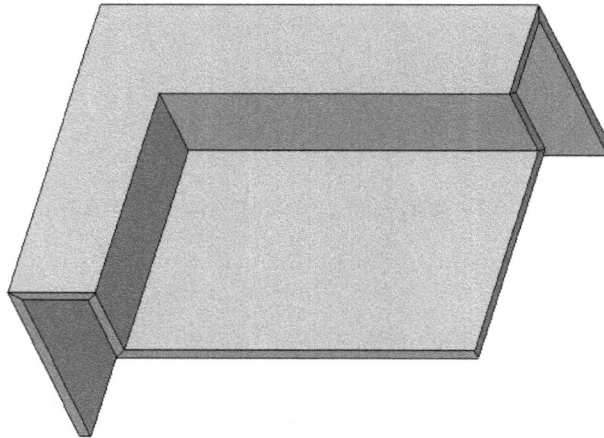

Figure 10–33

7. Select **Datum>Point>Point** in the *Sheetmetal* tab to create a datum point. Select the edge shown in Figure 10–34.

8. Select **Reference** in the Datum Point dialog box and select the surface shown in Figure 10–34. Create the point so that it is *Offset* by **5**.

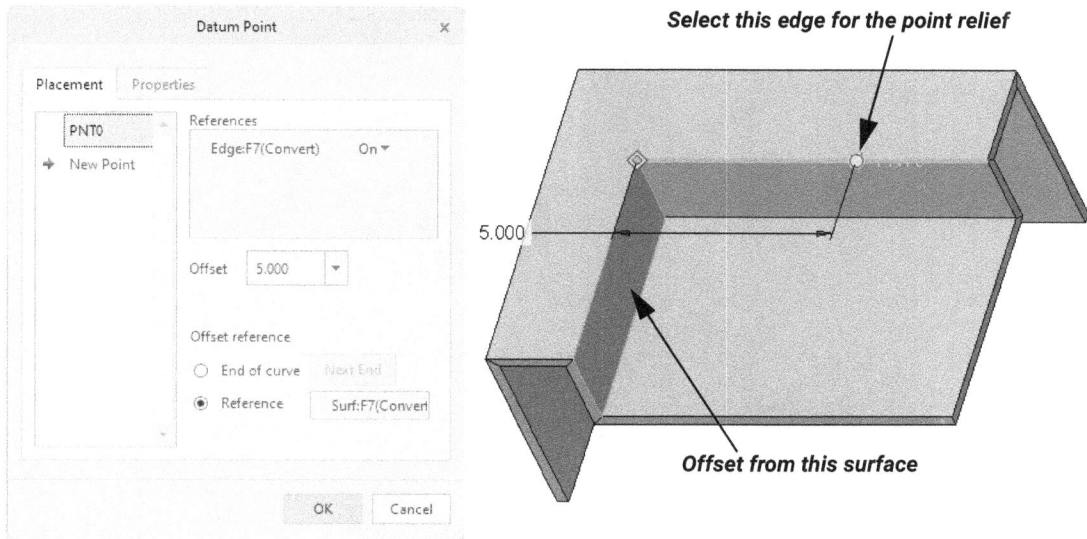

Figure 10–34

9. Click **OK** to complete the datum point.

10. Ensure datum points and their tags are toggled on.

11. Click 🪑 (Conversion) in the *Sheetmetal* tab to create a conversion feature.

12. Click ⬚ (Edge Rip) in the *Conversion* dashboard and select the edge shown in Figure 10–35.

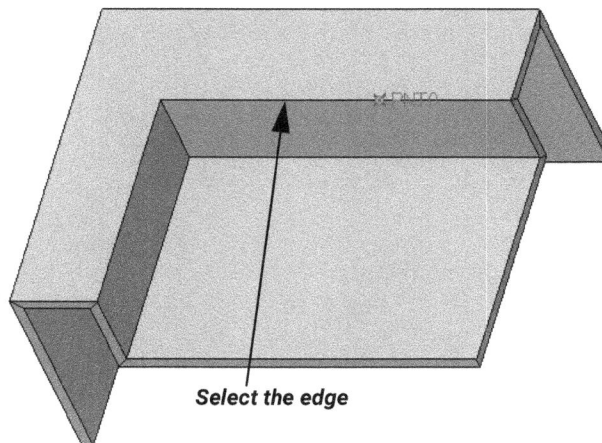

Figure 10–35

13. Right-click on the left side drag handle and select **Trim At**, as shown in Figure 10−36.

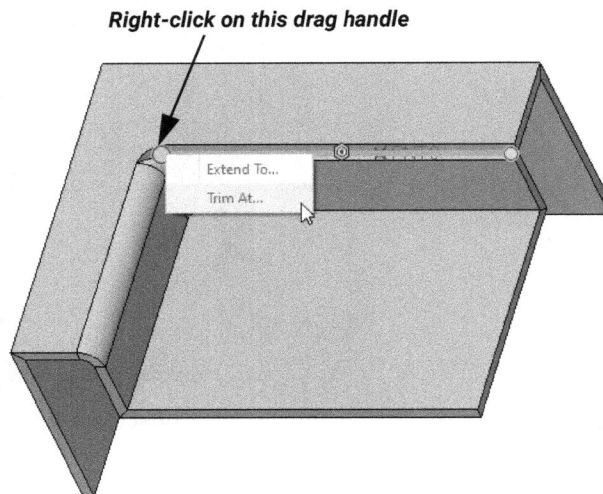

Figure 10−36

14. Select the newly created point (**PNT0**). The part displays as shown in Figure 10−37.

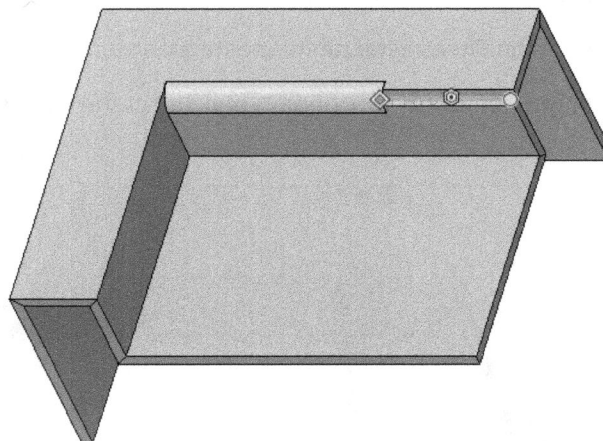

Figure 10−37

15. Hold <Ctrl> and select the additional edges shown in Figure 10−38.

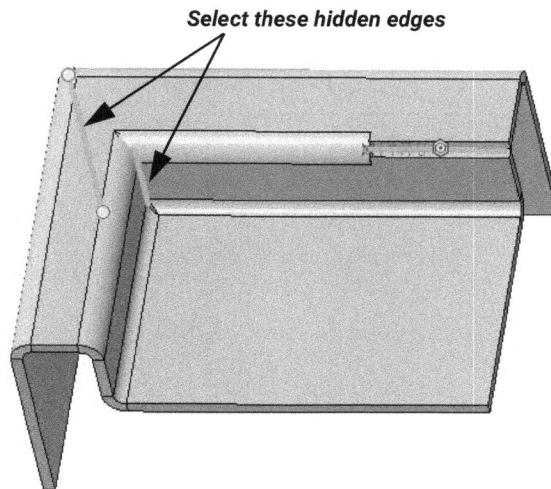

Select these hidden edges

Figure 10−38

16. Click ✓ (OK) to complete the Edge Rip. The part displays as shown in Figure 10−39.

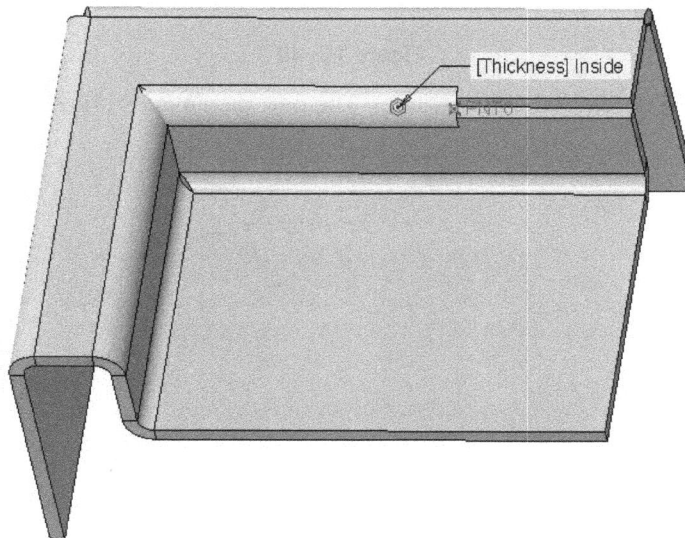

[Thickness] Inside

Figure 10−39

17. Click ▨ (Rip Connect) in the *Conversion* dashboard. Hold <Ctrl> and connect the vertices shown in Figure 10−40.

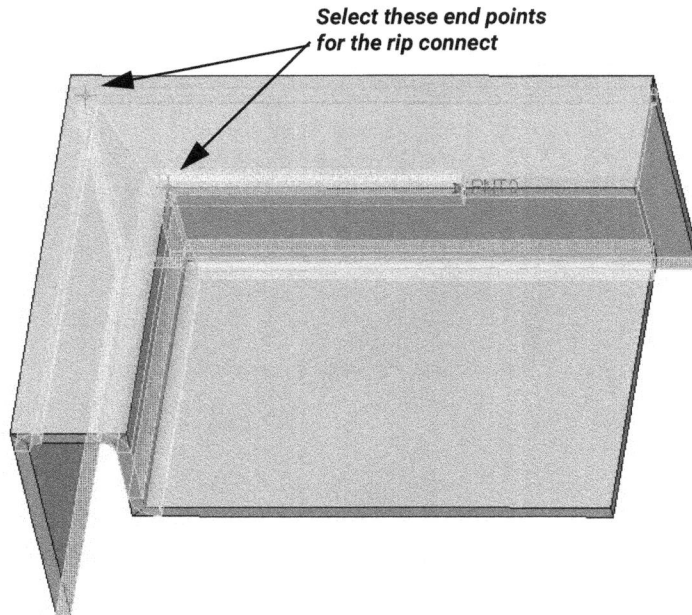

Figure 10−40

18. Click ✓ (OK) to complete the rip connect. The part displays as shown in Figure 10−41.

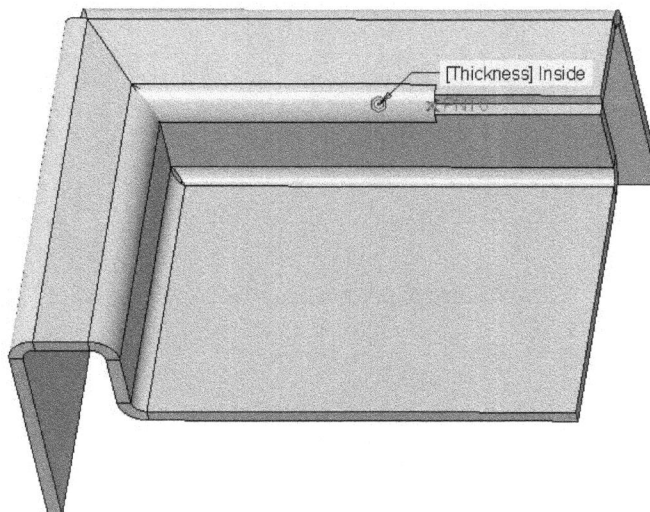

Figure 10−41

Note: Creo Parametric has added edge bends on all non-tangent edges that have not been assigned a conversion element.

19. Click ✔ (OK) in the *Conversion* dashboard. The finished conversion feature is shown in Figure 10−42.

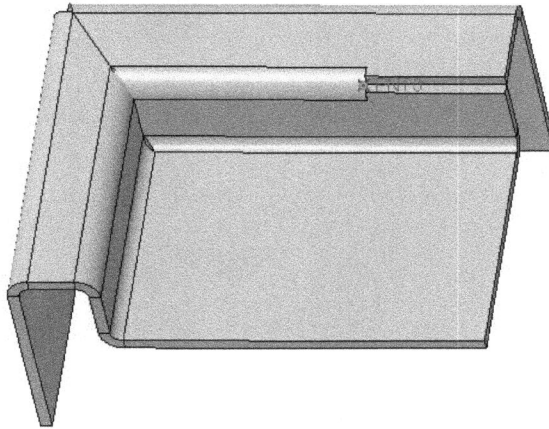

Figure 10−42

Task 2: Unbend the model.

1. Unbend all of the geometry in the part. Select the surface shown in Figure 10−43 to remain fixed.

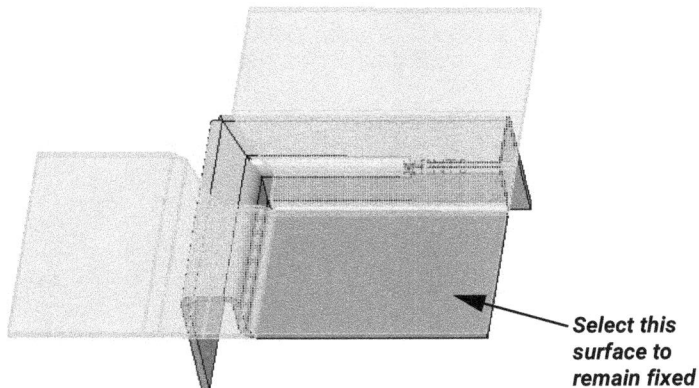

Select this
surface to
remain fixed

Figure 10−43

2. The finished flat pattern is shown in Figure 10−44.

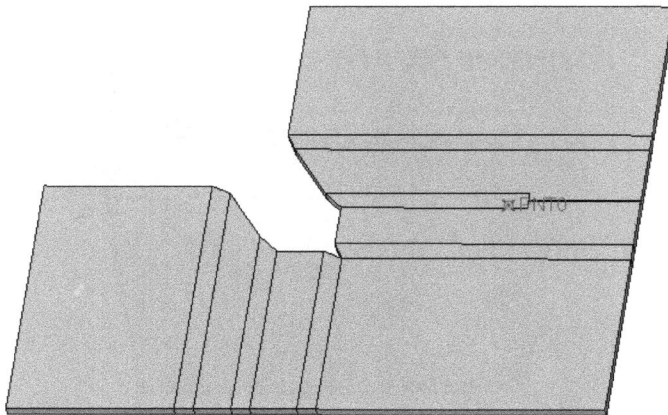

Figure 10−44

3. Save the part and erase it from memory.

End of practice

Practice 10c
Convert Walls with Non-Uniform Thickness

Practice Objective

* Create a sheet metal part from a solid part that has a non-uniform thickness.

In this practice, you will convert a solid model to a sheet metal model and investigate the tools for handling non-uniform thickness.

Task 1: Open the flat_pattern.prt model.

1. Set the working directory to *Convert_Non_Uniform*.
2. Open **bracket.prt**.
3. Set the model display as follows:

   * ⅍ *(Datum Display Filters)*: All Off
   * ⋗ *(Spin Center)*: Off
   * ▱ *(Display Style)*: ▱ (Shading With Edges)

   The model displays as shown in Figure 10−45.

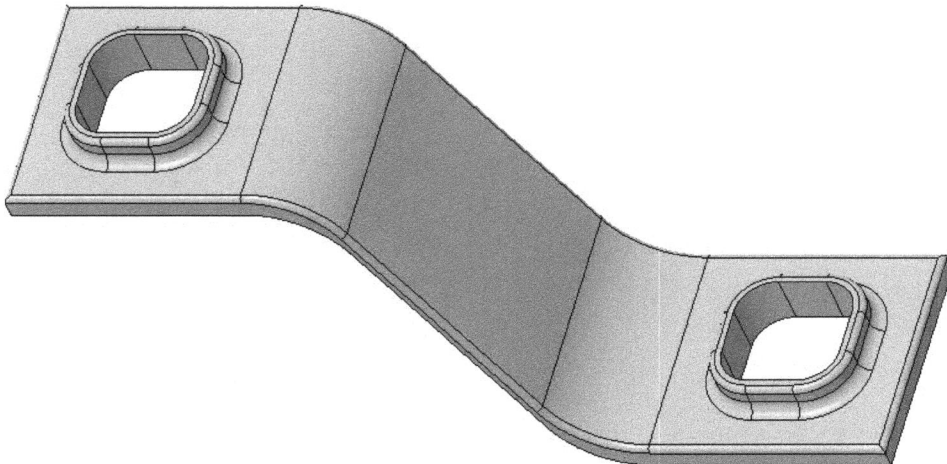

Figure 10−45

Task 2: Add a conversion feature to convert the model to sheet metal.

1. In the *Model* tab, expand the **Operations** group, and then select **Convert to Sheet Metal**.

2. In the *Convert* dashboard, click ⬦ (Driving Surface).

3. Select the flat surface shown in Figure 10−46.

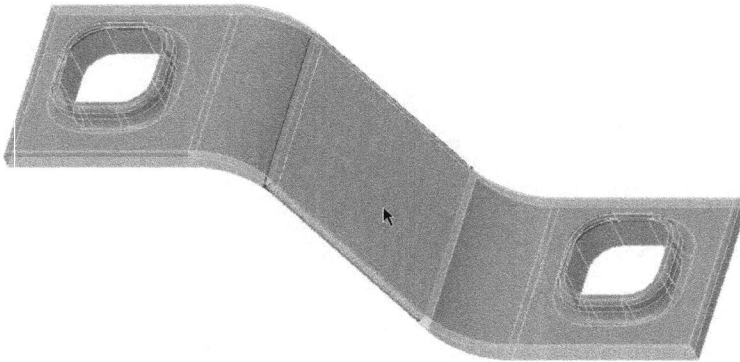

Figure 10−46

4. In the In-graphics toolbar, expand ⬜ (Saved Orientations) and select **FRONT**. The model displays as shown in Figure 10−47.

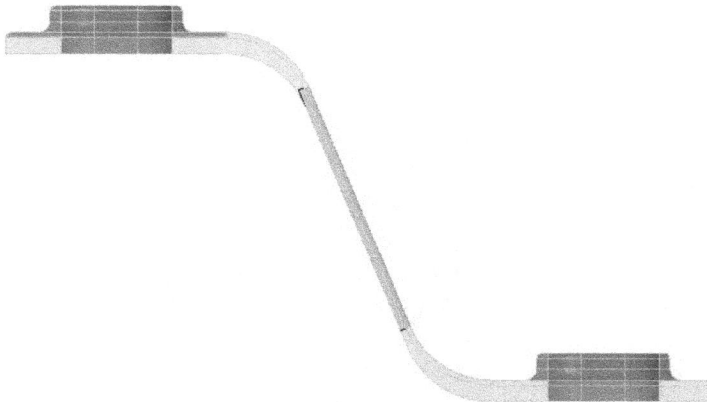

Figure 10−47

Note: Areas with a thickness that is different than the thickness from the driving surface are automatically excluded.

5. Press <Ctrl>+<D> to return to the default orientation.

6. Right-click and select **Include surfaces**.

7. Hold <Ctrl> and then select the two adjacent surfaces shown in Figure 10–48.

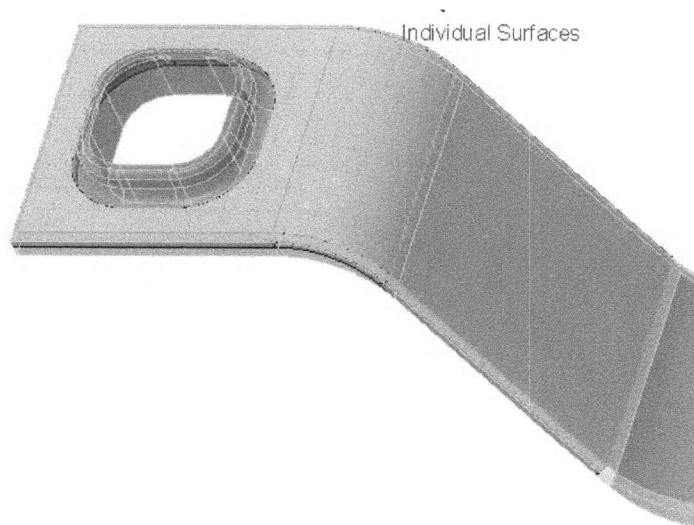

Figure 10–48

8. Return to the **FRONT** orientation and note that the preview of the solid geometry extends to the newly selected surfaces, with the unused material displayed as surface geometry, as shown in Figure 10–49.

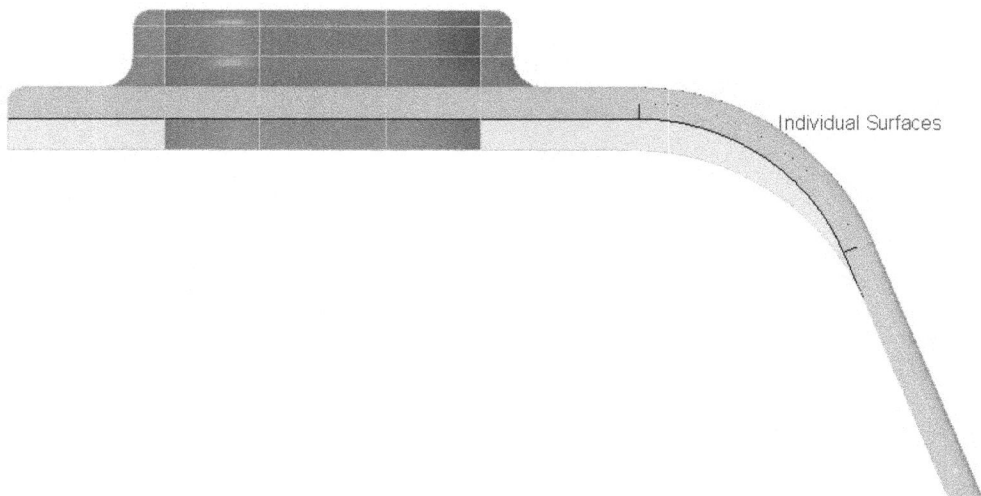

Figure 10–49

9. Return to the default orientation.

10. Hold <Ctrl> and select the surface shown in Figure 10−50.

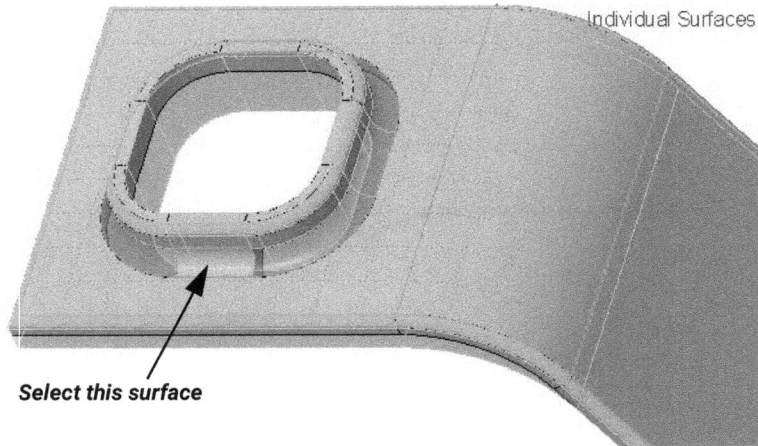

Figure 10−50

11. Select the remaining seven surfaces comprising the round. The model updates as shown in Figure 10−51.

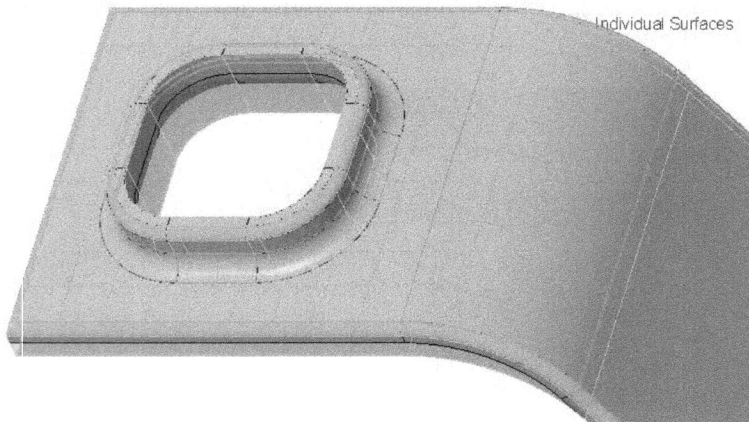

Figure 10−51

12. In the dashboard, click ✓ (OK). The Troubleshooter opens, as shown in Figure 10−52.

Figure 10−52

13. In the Troubleshooter, click **Item 1**. A description of the potential issue displays, indicating that the surfaces cannot be classified, as shown in Figure 10−53.

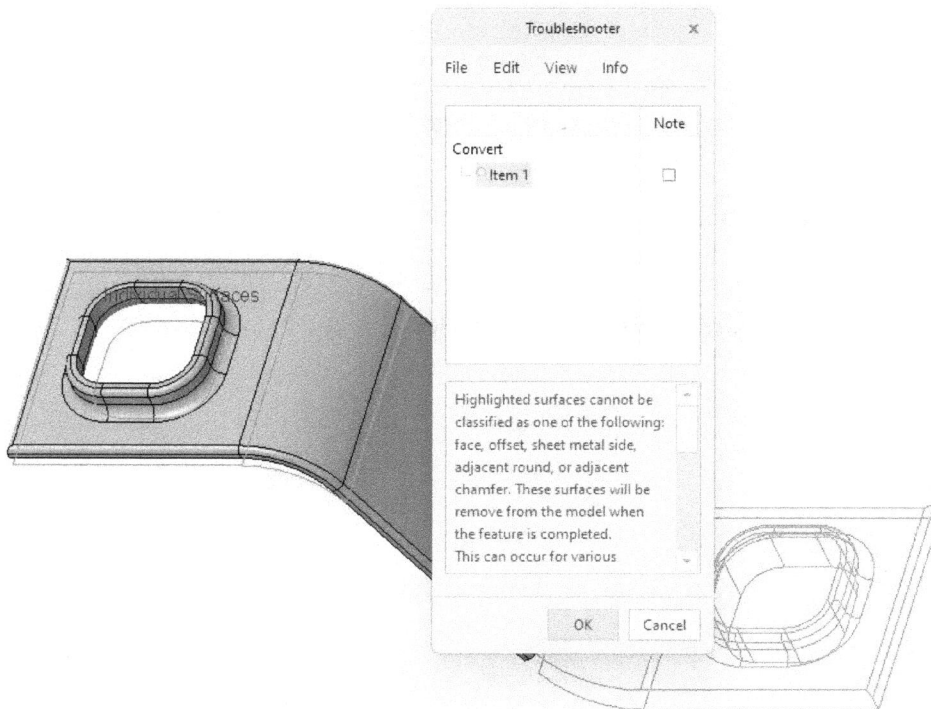

Figure 10−53

14. Select **OK**, and note that the geometry displays as a constant thickness, as shown in Figure 10–54.

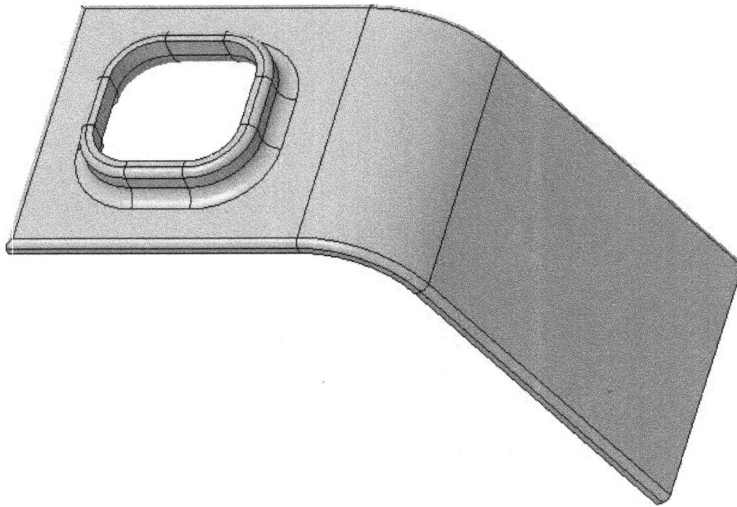

Figure 10–54

15. Modify the geometry by selecting **Convert(First Wall)** from the tree and selecting ✍ (Edit Definition).

Task 3: Include the unclassified surfaces in the resulting model.

1. Expand the Options panel.

2. Enable **Keeps not classified surfaces as a quilt**.

3. Click ✔ (OK).

4. In the Troubleshooter, select **OK**. Note that the unclassified surfaces are included as quilts, as shown in Figure 10−55.

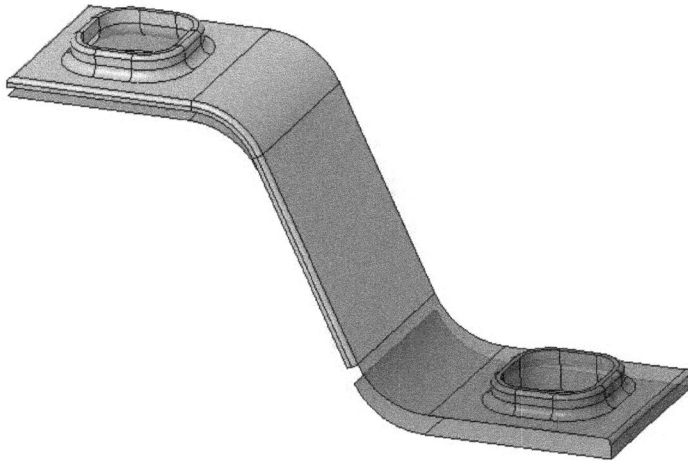

Figure 10−55

5. Modify the geometry by selecting **Convert(First Wall)** from the tree and selecting 🖌 (Edit Definition).

6. In the Options panel, disable **Keeps not classified surfaces as a separate quilt**.

Task 4: Add additional surfaces.

1. Right-click and select **Include surfaces**.

2. Hold <Ctrl> and select the two adjacent surfaces shown in Figure 10−56.

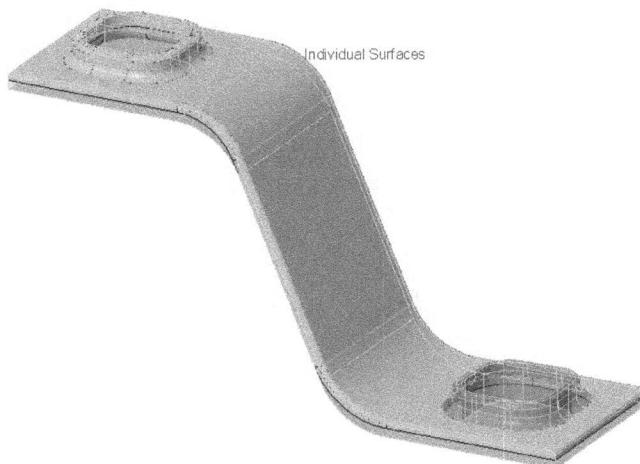

Figure 10−56

3. Click ✔ (OK).

4. In the Troubleshooter, click **OK**. Note that the unclassified surfaces are included as quilts, as shown in Figure 10–57.

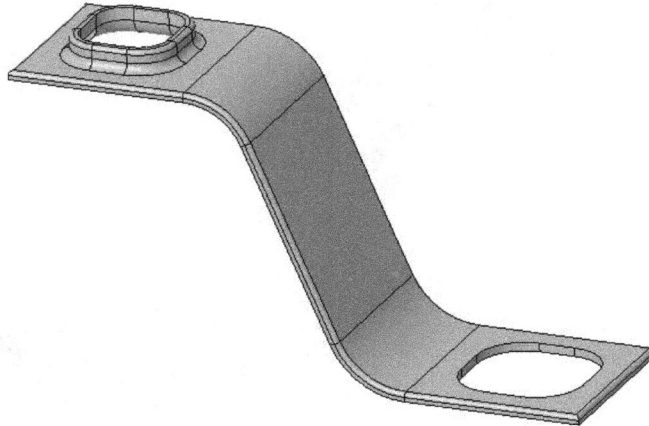

Figure 10–57

5. Modify the geometry by selecting **Convert(First Wall)** from the tree and selecting ✎ (Edit Definition).

6. Expand the Options panel, and in the *Adjacent Rounds & Chamfers treatment* area, select **Remove**.

7. Click ✔ (OK).

8. In the Troubleshooter, click **OK**. The model displays as shown in Figure 10–58.

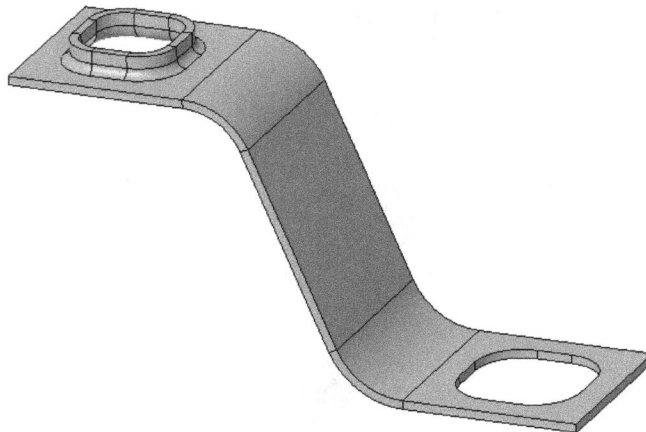

Figure 10–58

9. Close the model and erase it from memory.

End of practice

Chapter Review Questions

1. For solid parts that are already of uniform thickness, which option in the *Conversion* dashboard can you use to convert the part?

    a. Driving surface

    b. Shell

2. When the part is converted to a sheet metal part, any cuts automatically take on the properties of a sheet metal cut and displays perpendicular to the sheet metal wall.

    a. True

    b. False

3. Once a solid model has been converted to a sheet metal part, all of the existing geometry is listed as the First Wall feature in the Model Tree.

    a. True

    b. False

4. You can also select **Operations>Switch to Solid** to convert the sheet metal part back to a solid part.

    a. True

    b. False

5. Once a solid part has been converted, it can always be unbent.

    a. True

    b. False

6. Which element in the *Conversion* dashboard creates rip geometry by selecting two points or vertices?

    a. Edge Rip

    b. Rip Connect

    c. Edge Bend

    d. Corner Relief

Answers: *1a, 2a, 3a, 4a, 5b, 6b*

Sheet Metal Setup

The geometry of sheet metal models is controlled by several parameters, including bend allowance and the developed length. The developed length can be controlled by bend tables for known materials or calculated. Setting these parameters can save you time when modeling.

Learning Objectives

- Understand how you can control the developed length of the model using different methods.
- Learn how to use the default formula to calculate the developed length of the sheet metal model.
- Use the Model Properties dialog box to change the bend allowance or use bend tables to calculate the developed length.
- Use relations and sheet metal parameters to predefine a number of feature definition options and skip some menu selections.
- Learn to set the fixed surface for bent geometry using the Model Properties dialog box.

11.1 Calculating the Developed Length

When you create sheet metal geometry, it is good practice to check the model's ability to be flattened. When you unbend a sheet metal part, Creo Parametric uses a formula to determine the developed length. However, this formula might not be appropriate for the fabrication methods you use. It is important to understand how Creo Parametric makes these calculations to be able to modify them to suit your particular process.

You can control the developed length of the model using the following methods:

- Adjust the Y-factor, which works in conjunction with a formula to control the position of the neutral bend line.

- Modify the developed length dimension on the model. This method overrides the formula used by Creo Parametric. With this method, you can reset this value at any time.

- Use a bend table to control the developed length of the part. The bend table includes a table of developed length values, which correspond to a bend radius and a material thickness that varies incrementally.

Factors that determine the most accurate developed length of a sheet metal part include the sheet metal material and fabrication process being used. You should determine how Creo Parametric addresses these issues before you start so that changes to the default configuration can be made if required.

11.2 Y-Factor and the Default Formula

Creo Parametric uses a default formula to calculate the developed length of the sheet metal model. This formula has the following format:

$$L = \left(\frac{\pi}{2} \times R + \text{yfactor} \times T\right)\frac{\Theta}{90}$$

where:

L = developed length

R = inside bend radius

T = material thickness

Θ = bend angle

A unique parameter in this formula is the Y-factor. The Y-factor is a ratio based on the position of the neutral bend line with respect to the wall thickness of the material, as shown in Figure 11−1.

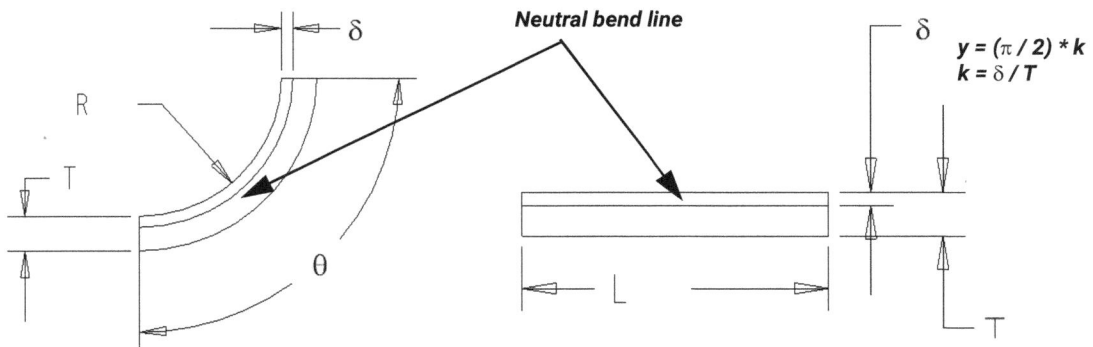

Figure 11−1

*Note: The **initial_bend_y_factor** config.pro option only affects new parts.*

The default Y-factor value is **.50**, but it can be changed in the part setup. You can also use the **initial_bend_y_factor** config.pro option to control the Y-factor value.

Consider the bend shown in Figure 11−2. If the Y-factor value is **0.5**, the following calculation is made:

$$y = \frac{\pi k}{2}$$

$$y = \frac{\pi \delta}{2T}$$

$$0.5 = \frac{\pi \delta}{2T}$$

$$\delta = \frac{T}{\pi}$$

$$\delta = \frac{T}{3.14\ldots}$$

When the Y-factor value is **0.5**, the neutral bend line is approximately one third of the way through the thickness.

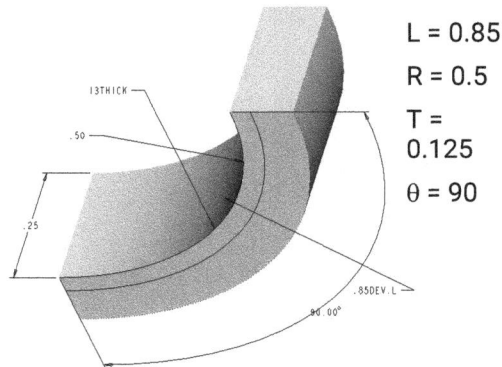

L = 0.85

R = 0.5

T = 0.125

θ = 90

Figure 11−2

If the neutral bend line is approximately one third of the way through the material thickness, how long is a developed bend using the default Y-factor? The following example uses a simple wall with a 90° bend. The inside bend radius is **0.50** and the material thickness is **0.125**.

$$L = \left(\frac{\pi}{2} \times R + y factor \times T\right)\frac{\Theta}{90}$$

$$L = \left(\frac{\pi}{2} \times 0.5 + 0.5 \times 0.125\right)\frac{90}{90}$$

$$L = 0.8479$$

$$L \approx 0.85$$

11.3 Bend Tables

Select **File>Prepare>Model Properties** and select **change** next to **Bend Allowance** in the Model Properties dialog box. The Preferences dialog box opens as shown in Figure 11–3, and enables you to set the Y-factor or change the bend table.

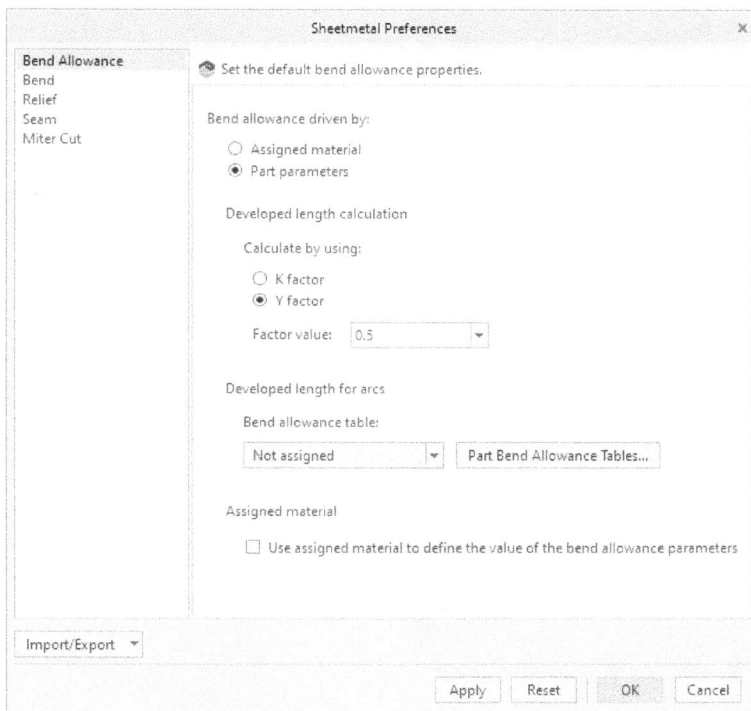

Figure 11–3

You can use a bend table rather than the default formula to calculate the developed length of the bend, as shown in Figure 11−4.

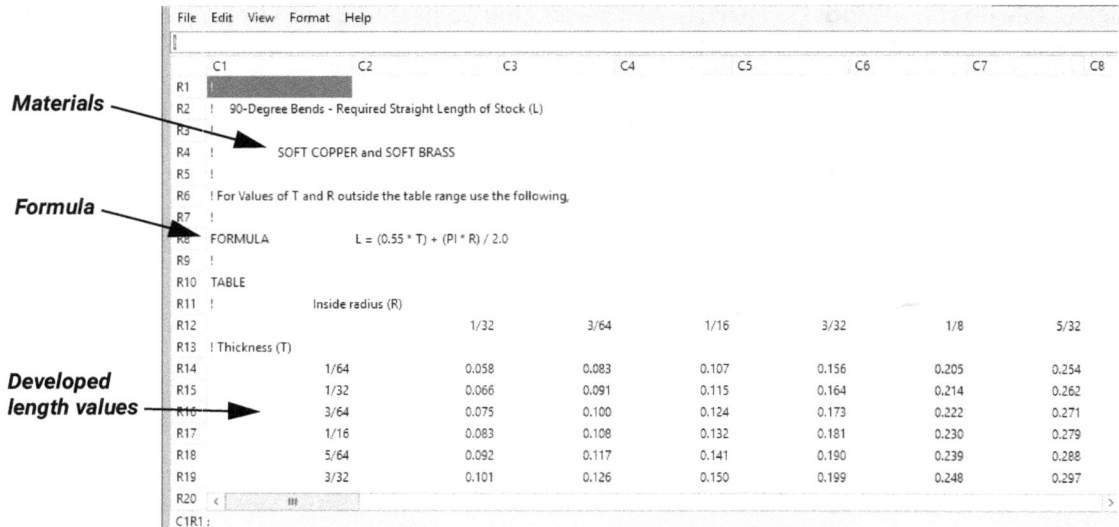

Figure 11−4

A bend table displays an organized collection of data that represents the material thickness and bend radii, and the corresponding developed lengths. The body of a bend table displays the developed length information. The bend radii display in columns across the top and the material thickness values display in rows down the left side, as shown in Figure 11−5.

! Inside radius (R)				
	1/32	3/64	1/16	3/32
! Thickness (T)				
1/64	0.058	0.083	0.107	0.156
1/32	0.066	0.091	0.115	0.164
3/64	0.075	0.100	0.124	0.173
1/16	0.083	0.108	0.132	0.181
5/64	0.092	0.117	0.141	0.190
3/32	0.101	0.126	0.150	0.199
1/8	0.118	0.143	0.167	0.216
5/32	0.135	0.160	0.184	0.233
3/16	0.152	0.177	0.201	0.250
7/32	0.169	0.194	0.218	0.267

Figure 11−5

Bend tables use the following rules:

- If the values for the bend radius and material thickness match those in the table, Creo Parametric uses the values from the table.
- If the value falls between two of the values in the table, Creo Parametric linearly interpolates the developed length value.
- If the value falls outside the table, Creo Parametric uses the table's formula. If the table does not have a formula, the system uses the default formula and Y-factor.

Creo Parametric provides three default bend tables. You can edit them to include values that suit your specific materials and processes. The default bend tables are developed for the following materials:

- **TABLE1:** Soft Brass and Copper.
- **TABLE2:** Hard Brass, Copper, Soft Steel, and Aluminum.
- **TABLE3:** Hard Copper, Bronze, Cold Rolled Steel, and Spring Steel, as shown in Figure 11–6.

File Edit View Format Help

	C1	C2	C3	C4	C5	C6
R1	!					
R2	! 90-Degree Bends - Required Straight Length of Stock (L)					
R3	!					
R4	! HARD COPPER, BRONZE, COLD-ROLLED STEEL, and SPRING STEEL					
R5	!					
R6	! For Values of T and R outside the table range use the following,					
R7	!					
R8	FORMULA	L = (0.71 * T) + (PI * R) / 2.0				
R9	!					
R10	TABLE					
R11	!	Inside radius (R)				
R12		1/32	3/64	1/16	3/32	
R13	! Thickness (T)					
R14	1/64	0.060	0.085	0.109	0.158	
R15	1/32	0.071	0.096	0.120	0.169	
R16	3/64	0.082	0.107	0.131	0.180	
R17	1/16	0.093	0.118	0.142	0.191	
R18	5/64	0.104	0.129	0.153	0.202	
R19	3/32	0.116	0.141	0.165	0.214	
R20	1/8	0.138	0.163	0.187	0.236	
R21						

C1R1 :

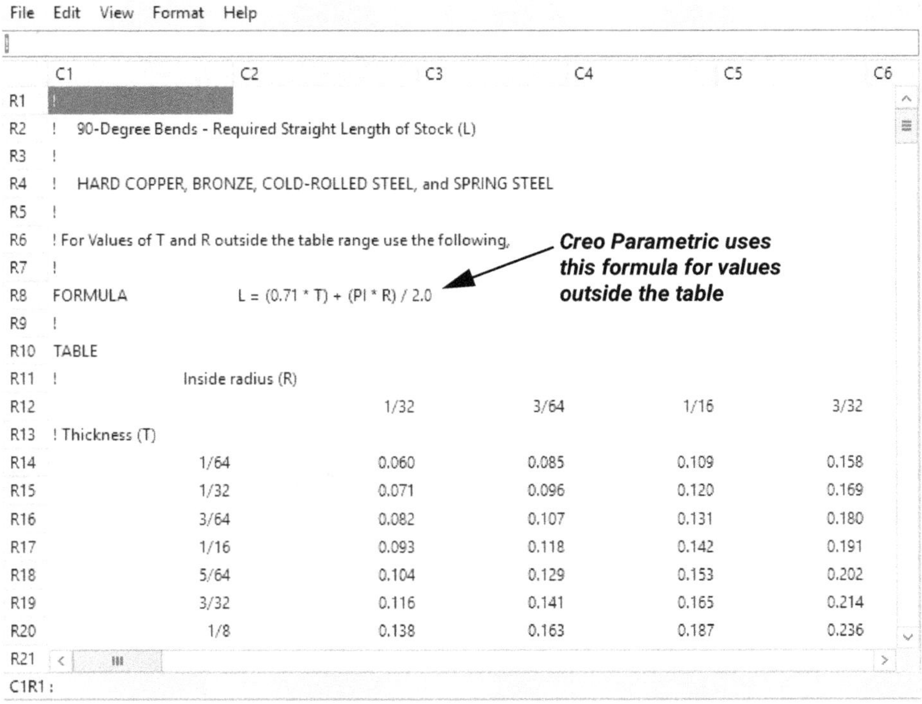

Figure 11–6

You can create custom bend tables to reflect your fabrication processes. Figure 11−7 shows a customized bend table.

```
!
!    90-Degree Bends - Required Straight Length of Stock (L)

!

!              SOFT COPPER and SOFT BRASS

!

! For Values of T and R outside the table range use the following.

!

FORMULA          L = (0.55 * T) + (PI * R) / 2.0

!

TABLE

!              Inside radius (R)

                    .031250      .046875     .062500      .093750

! Thickness (T)

      .015625       .058000      0.083       0.107        0.156

      .031250       0.066        0.091       0.115        0.164

      .046875       0.075        0.100       0.124        0.173

      .062500       0.083        0.108       0.132        0.181

      .078125       0.092        0.117       0.141        0.190
```

Figure 11−7

Note: To ensure that the bend table uses the materials that you have created, you can specify material in the bend table.

The following information is added to a custom bend table:

- Logic statements accommodate variability in the process.

- A CONVERSION line sets the values in the body of the table equal to the "A" term in the conversion formula.

- A formula is specified for values outside the table instead of relying on the default formula.

- Materials are added to correspond to those defined in the part file.

11.4 Sheet Metal Parameters and Relations

To simplify your work in Sheetmetal mode, menu selections for adding and modifying sheet metal parameters and relations can be grouped together. This enables you to predefine a number of feature definition options and parameters. You can then skip some menu selections when a feature is created using a preset value.

> *Note: To drive a sheet metal part using parameters, select **File>Options> Configuration Editor**. Change the value of the **smt_drive_bend_by_ parameters** to **yes**.*

Select **Model Intent>Parameters** in the *Sheetmetal* tab. The sheet metal Parameters dialog box opens as shown in Figure 11−8.

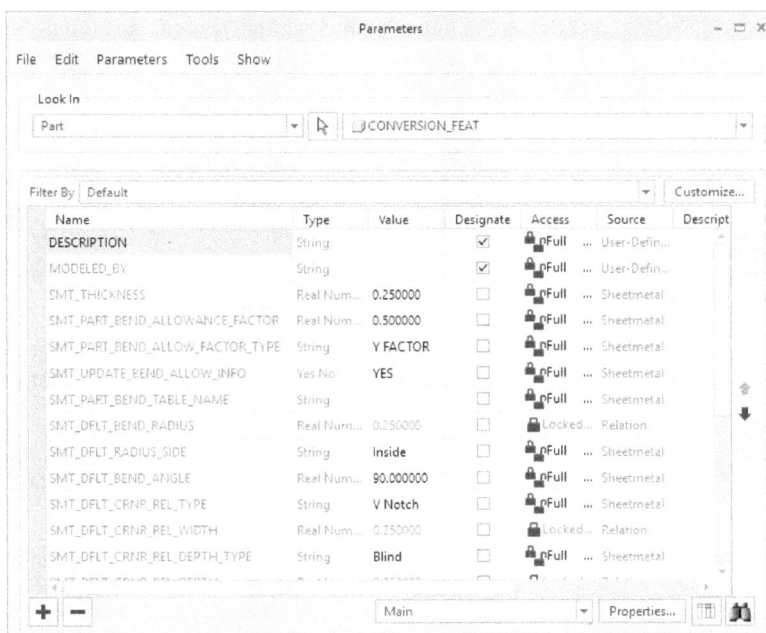

Figure 11−8

> *Note: Some of the Parameters are locked and need to be changed in the Relations Editor.*

The parameters and icons available in the sheet metal Parameters dialog box are as follows:

Option	Functionality
Reset	Reset the parameters.
+	Adds a parameter.
−	Removes a parameter.

Option	Functionality
SMT_THICKNESS	Defines the sheet metal thickness.
SMT_PART_BEND_ALLOWANCE_FACTOR	Set the **Part Bend Allowance** as the default.
SMT_PART_BEND_ALLOW_FACTOR_TYPE	Defines to use the K-factor or Y-factor.
SMT_UPDATE_BEND_ALLOW_INFO	Sets the other bend allowance parameters depending on the material assigned when set to Yes.
SMT_PART_BEND_TABLE_NAME	Defines the table name.
SMT_DFLT_BEND_RADIUS	Defines the default bend radius. You can set the default radius to **Thickness** or **2*Thickness**. This parameter is locked and must be defined in the Relations Editor.
SMT_DFLT_RADIUS_SIDE	Defines the default bend radius side. You can set the default radius side to **Inside** or **Outside**.
SMT_DFLT_BEND_ANGLE	Defines the default bend angle. You can set the default bend angle to any value between 0 and 360.
SMT_DFLT_CRNR_REL_TYPE	Defines the default corner relief type. You can set the default relief type to **No Relief**, **None**, **Circular**, or **Obround**.
SMT_DFLT_CRNR_REL_WIDTH	Defines the default corner relief width (diameter for circular relief). You can set the default corner relief width to **Thickness** or **2*Thickness**. This parameter is locked and must be defined in the Relations Editor.
SMT_DFLT_CRNR_REL_DEPTH_TYPE	Defines the default depth type. You can set the default depth type to **Blind**, **Tangent to Bend**, or **Up to Bend**.
SMT_DFLT_CRNR_REL_DEPTH	Defines the default corner relief depth (Obround relief only). You can set the default corner relief depth to **Thickness** or **2*Thickness**. This parameter is locked and must be defined in the Relations Editor.
SMT_DFLT_BEND_REL_TYPE	Defines the default bend relief type. You can set the default bend relief type to **No Relief**, **Rip**, **Stretch**, **Rectangular**, or **Obround**.
SMT_DFLT_BEND_REL_DEPTH	Defines the default bend relief depth. You can set the default bend relief depth to **Up to Bend** or **Tan to Bend** (**Tan to bend** for Obround relief only). This parameter is locked and must be defined in the Relations Editor.
SMT_DFLT_BEND_REL_WIDTH	Defines the default bend relief width. You can set the default bend relief width to **Thickness** or **2*Thickness**. This parameter is locked and must be defined in the Relations Editor.
SMT_DFLT_BEND_REL_ANGLE	Defines the default bend relief angle for stretch relief. You can set the default bend relief angle for stretch relief to any value between 0 and 360.

Option	Functionality
SMT_GAP	Defines the gap for overlaping edges, edge treatment, and miter cuts.
SMT_DFLT_EDGE_TREA_TYPE	Defines the default edge treatment type. You can set the default edge treatment to **Blind**, **Gap**, **Open**, or **Overlap**.
SMT_DFLT_EDGE_TREA_WIDTH	Defines the default edge treatment width. This parameter is locked and must be defined in the Relations Editor.
SMT_DFLT_MITER_CUT_WIDTH	Defines the default miter cut width. This parameter is locked and must be defined in the Relations Editor.
SMT_DFLT_MITER_CUT_OFFSET	Defines the default miter cut offset value. This parameter is locked and must be defined in the Relations Editor.

The columns available in the sheet metal Parameters dialog box are as follows:

Column Headings	Description
Name	Parameter name.
Value	Values can be entered or selected for each parameter in the menu that displays when you select one of these cells.
Attribute	Some parameters can be set to **Auto** or **Manual** (default). If set to **Manual**, you are prompted for the parameter or option, or it displays in a menu during feature definition. The default value is defined in the *Value* column. If set to **Auto**, the parameter is automatically applied during feature definition without prompting.
Add Relation	If set to **Yes**, a relation between the parameter and resulting dimension is created (e.g., a relation for the default corner relief width would be added as d3=SMT_DFLT_CRNR_REL_WIDTH).
Status	The status displays with a symbol that is added to each row for which values have been changed from the default.

After you have set the parameters to the required values, the values can be exported to a file and imported to set parameters in other sheet metal parts. The file is exported with a .TXT or .CVS extension.

Presetting parameters and options significantly improves your workflow by reducing the number of selections required to create some features.

Select **Model Intent>Relations** in the *Sheetmetal* tab. The sheet metal Relations dialog box opens as shown in Figure 11–9.

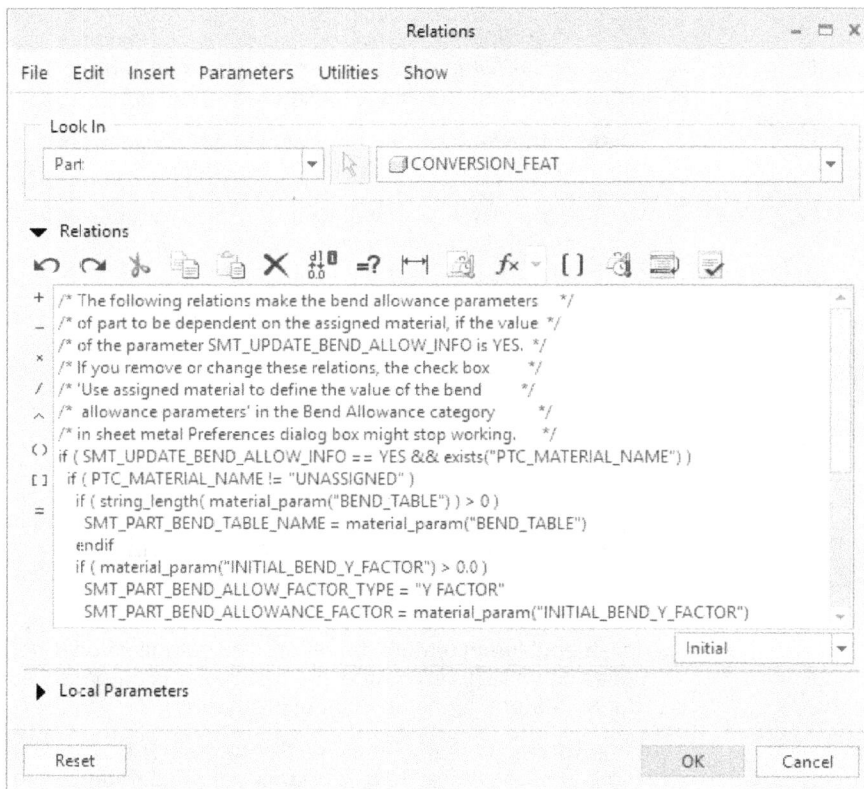

Figure 11–9

The parameters available in the sheet metal Relations dialog box are as follows:

Option	Functionality
SMT_DFLT_BEND_RADIUS = smt_thickness()	Defines the default bend radius.
SMT_DFLT_CRNR_REL_WIDTH = smt_thickness()	Defines the default corner relief width (diameter for circular relief).
SMT_DFLT_CRNR_REL_DEPTH = smt_thickness()	Defines the default corner relief depth.
SMT_DFLT_BEND_REL_WIDTH = smt_thickness()	Defines the default bend relief width.
SMT_DFLT_BEND_REL_DEPTH = smt_thickness()	Defines the default bend relief depth.
SMT_GAP = smt_thickness () * 0.5	Defines the gap value for overlaping edges, edge treatment, and miter cuts.
SMT_DFLT_EDGE_TREA_WIDTH = -SMT_GAP	Defines the default edge treatment width.
SMT_DFLT_MITER_CUT_WIDTH = SMT_GAP	Defines the default miter cut width.
SMT_DFLT_MITER_CUT_OFFSET = smt_thickness() * 1.1	Defines the default miter cut offset value.

11.5 Default Fixed Geometry

When working on a complex model, you might forget which surface or edge you selected to remain fixed during unbends and bend backs. To avoid shifting your model orientation when bending and unbending the model, you should select the same surface or edge to remain fixed. Select **File>Prepare>Model Properties** and select **change** next to Fixed Geometry. The Fixed Geometry option can be used to automatically specify that the same entity remain fixed each time. The dialog box is shown in Figure 11–10.

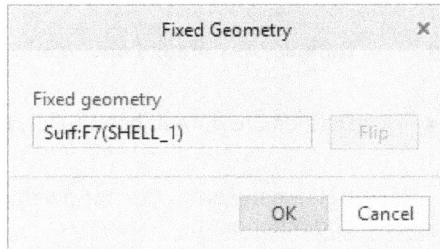

Figure 11–10

Practice 11a
Calculate Developed Length

Practice Objectives

- Adjust the developed length of bends by modifying the Y-factor.
- Adjust the developed length of bends using bend tables.

In this practice, you will examine the effect of the Y-factor and bend tables on the developed lengths of bends.

Task 1: Open the part and create an unbend feature.

Design Considerations

In this task, you will unbend the wall so you can examine how changes to the developed length of the bend affect the overall length of the flattened part.

1. Set the working directory to the *Developed_Length* folder.
2. Open **developed_length.prt**.
3. Set the model display as follows:

    - ⁝⟋. *(Datum Display Filters)*: None

    - ⊱ *(Spin Center)*: Off

    - ⬚. *(Display Style)*: ⬚ (Shading With Edges)

4. Create a regular unbend feature using the fixed surface shown in Figure 11−11.

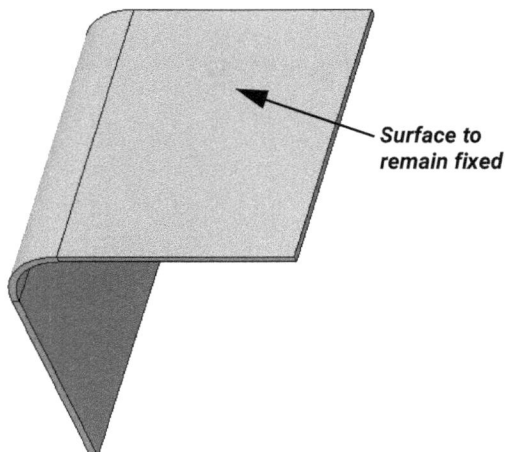

Surface to
remain fixed

Figure 11−11

Task 2: Measure the length of the unbent part and save the measurement.

Design Considerations

In this task, you will create and save the analysis measurement so you can retrieve it after making changes to the developed length of the bend in upcoming tasks.

1. Select the *Analysis* tab, expand ✏ (Measure), and select ⊓ (Distance). Expand the Measure: Distance dialog box, as shown in Figure 11−12.

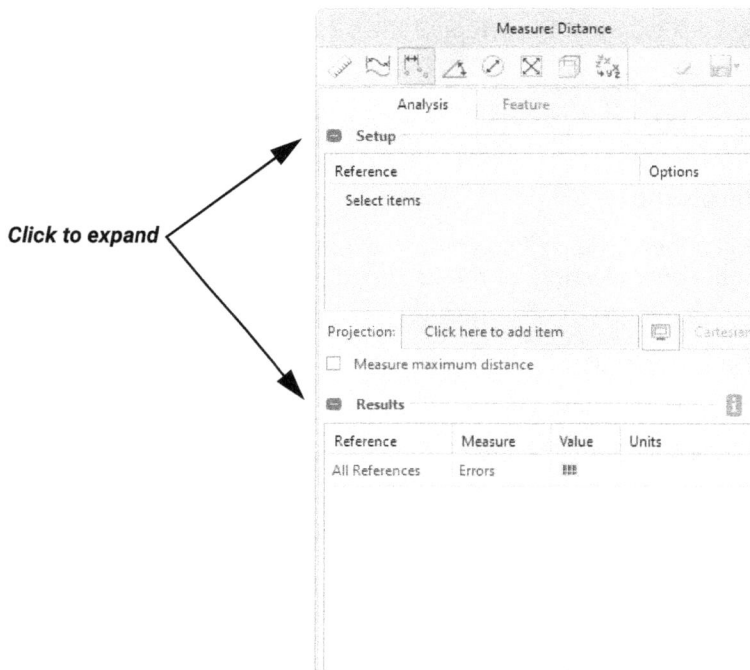

Figure 11−12

2. Hold <Ctrl> and select the two thin end surfaces for the references, as shown in Figure 11–13. The system calculates the result to be **9.63330**.

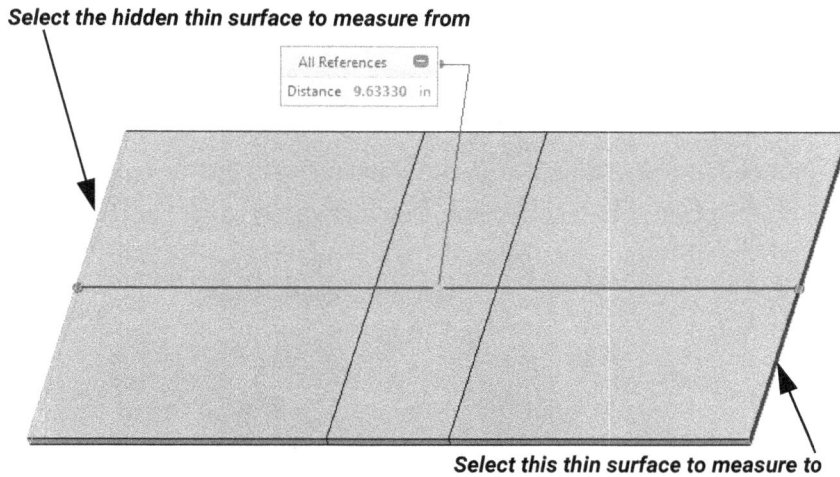

Select the hidden thin surface to measure from

Select this thin surface to measure to

Figure 11–13

3. Expand ⊟▾ (Save Analysis) and select **Save Analysis**, as shown in Figure 11–14.

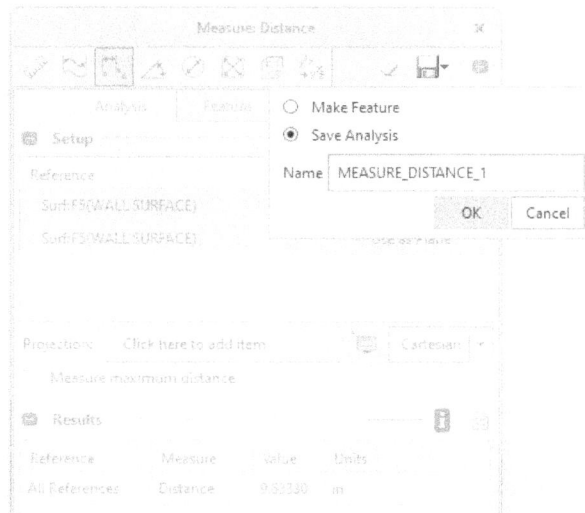

Figure 11–14

4. Set the measurement Name to **length** and press <Enter>.

5. Click **Close** to close the dialog box.

Task 3: Modify the developed length of the bend.

Design Considerations

You can modify the developed length of individual bends by modifying the developed length dimension directly on the part. This has no impact on other bends in the part.

1. Select the flattened wall and select ⟻⟼ (Edit Dimensions) in the mini toolbar.

2. Double-click on the developed length dimension shown in Figure 11−15. Change the dimension value to **2.00**.

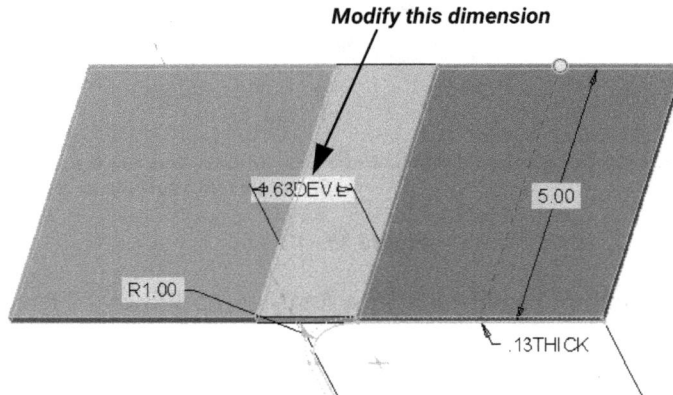

Figure 11−15

Note: The developed length of the bend is modified independent of the default formula.

3. Regenerate the model. In the Model Tree, select **LENGTH** and click ⟋ (Edit Definition) in the mini toolbar. Note that the distance is now **10.0000**.

Task 4: Return the developed length dimension to a driven state and modify the Y-factor.

Design Considerations

By default, Creo Parametric uses the following formula to calculate the developed length of all bends in a sheet metal part:

$$L = \left(\frac{\pi}{2} \times R + yfactor \times T \right) \frac{\Theta}{90}$$

If you modify the value of the Y-factor, all bends using this formula are affected.

1. Select the flattened wall and select ⟻⟼ (Edit Dimensions) in the mini toolbar.

2. Double-click on the developed length dimension. Expand the arrow and select **Return to Driven** in the drop-down list, as shown in Figure 11−16.

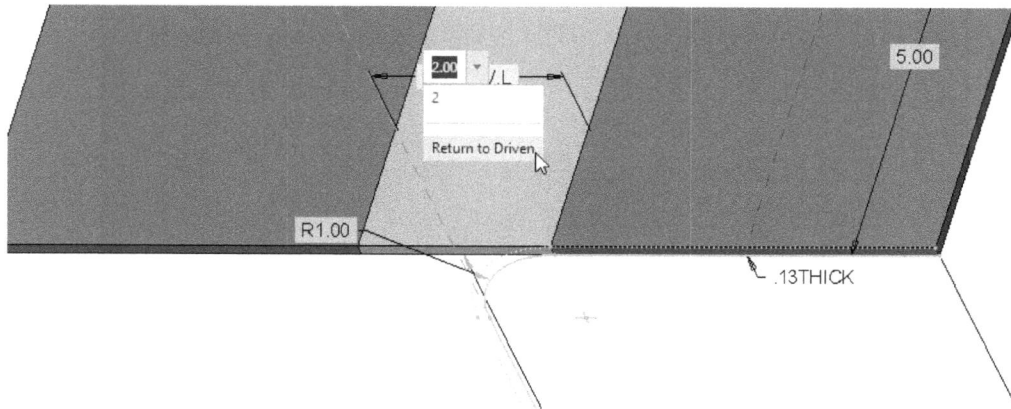

Figure 11−16

3. Regenerate the model.

4. Select **File>Prepare>Model Properties**. Select **change** next to **Bend Allowance**, as shown in Figure 11−17. This enables you enter a different Y-factor to be used in the default formula.

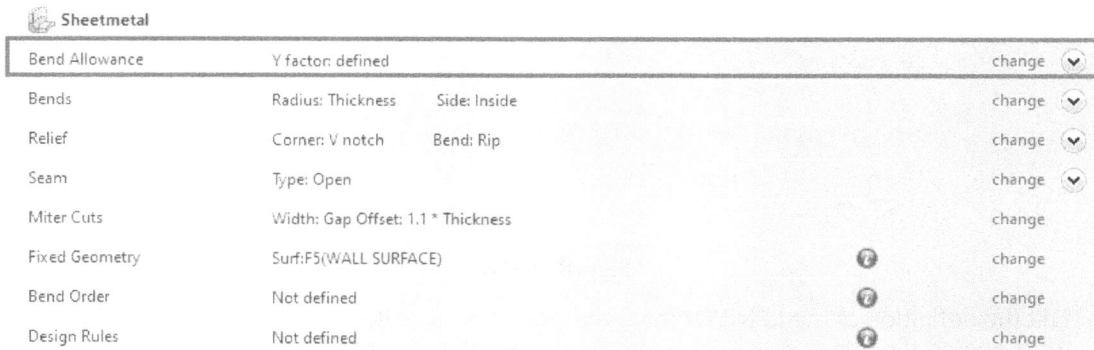

Figure 11−17

5. The Sheetmetal Preferences dialog box opens and enables you to enter a different Y-factor to be used in the default formula. Enter **0.25** as shown in Figure 11–18 and click **Apply**.

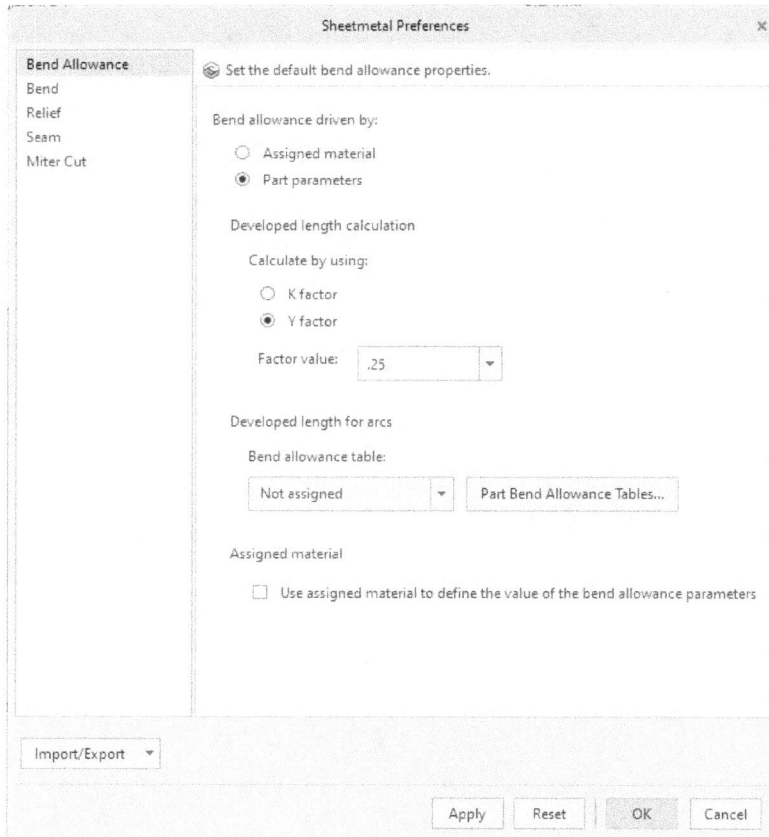

Figure 11–18

6. Edit the definition of the **LENGTH** measurement, and note that the distance is now **9.60205**. By changing the Y-factor, you have altered the developed length of the part.

Task 5: Assign and edit a bend table to drive the developed length of the bend.

Design Considerations

When you assign a bend table, you override the calculation of developed lengths made with the default formula.

1. Open the Sheetmetal Preferences dialog box again.

    Note: Select **change** *next to* **Bend Allowance** *to open the Preferences dialog box.*

2. Click **Part Bend Allowance Tables** in the Preferences dialog box. This option enables you to apply a bend table that has been saved in the part file.

3. Double-click on **table1.bnd** to add TABLE1 to the model, as shown in Figure 11–19.

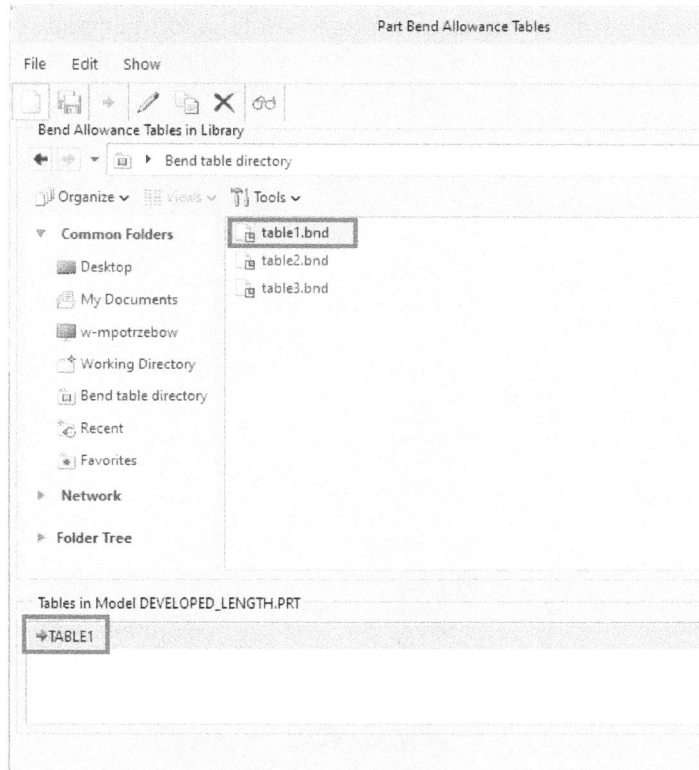

Figure 11–19

Note: TABLE1 is a predefined bend table for soft brass and copper.

4. Click 🖉 (Edit) to edit the bend table and change the developed length of the model.

5. The editor window opens displaying the bend table as shown in Figure 11–20. Find the cell that corresponds to a material thickness of **0.125** and a bend radius of **1.000** (row R22, column C26). The value in the table is the same as the current developed length dimension of **1.640**.

    *   By assigning a bend table, you can override the default formula and use specific values that correspond to your company's processes and standards. By changing the Y-factor, you are using the default formula to control your model.

	C22	C23	C24	C25	C26	C27	C28	C29	C30
R4									
R5									
R6									
R7									
R8									
R9									
R10									
R11									
R12									
R13									
R14 00	0.750000	0.812500	0.875000	0.937500	1.000000	1.062500	1.125000	1.187500	1.250000
R15									
R16 00	1.187000	1.286000	1.384000	1.481000	1.580000	1.678000	1.777000	1.875000	1.972000
R17 00	1.195000	1.294000	1.392000	1.489000	1.588000	1.686000	1.785000	1.883000	1.980000
R18 00	1.204000	1.303000	1.401000	1.498000	1.597000	1.695000	1.794000	1.892000	1.989000
R19 00	1.212000	1.311000	1.409000	1.506000	1.605000	1.703000	1.802000	1.900000	1.997000
R20 00	1.221000	1.320000	1.418000	1.515000	1.614000	1.712000	1.811000	1.909000	2.006000
R21 00	1.230000	1.329000	1.427000	1.524000	1.623000	1.721000	1.820000	1.918000	2.015000
R22 00	1.247000	1.346000	1.444000	1.541000	1.640000	1.738000	1.837000	1.935000	2.032000
R23 00	1.264000	1.363000	1.461000	1.558000	1.657000	1.755000	1.854000	1.952000	2.049000
R24 00	1.281000	1.380000	1.478000	1.575000	1.674000	1.772000	1.871000	1.969000	2.066000
R25 00	1.298000	1.397000	1.495000	1.592000	1.691000	1.789000	1.888000	1.986000	2.083000
R26 00	1.316000	1.415000	1.513000	1.610000	1.709000	1.807000	1.906000	2.004000	2.101000
R27 00	1.333000	1.432000	1.530000	1.627000	1.726000	1.824000	1.923000	2.021000	2.118000
R28 00	1.350000	1.449000	1.547000	1.644000	1.743000	1.841000	1.940000	2.038000	2.135000
R29									

Value to be modified

Figure 11–20

6. Highlight the correct cell and enter **1.675**. Select **File>Exit** in the editor window.

7. Click **OK**.

8. Click 📋 (Regenerate) and close the Model Properties dialog box.

9. The distance is now **9.67500**.

10. Save the part and erase it from memory.

End of practice

Practice 11b
Sheet Metal Parameters and Relations

Practice Objective

- Set default parameters in sheet metal.

In this practice, you will predefine some options and parameters to reduce the number of options required to create features.

Task 1: Create a new sheet metal part and set up default parameters and relations for the model.

Design Considerations

In this task, you will modify the default sheet metal parameters and relations. This can automate tasks, such as applying bend relief and specifying bend radius. It can also help to ensure consistency.

1. Set the working directory to the *Sheetmetal_Parameters* folder.

2. Create a sheet metal part called **sheet_params** using the default template.

3. Set the model display as follows:

    - *(Datum Display Filters)*: None

    - *(Spin Center)*: Off

    - *(Display Style)*: (No Hidden)

4. Select **File>Options>Configuration Editor**. Change the value of the **smt_drive_bend_by_parameters** to **yes**. Save the change.

5. Select **Model Intent>[ ]** (Parameters) in the *Sheetmetal* tab.

    *Note: Many parameter values can also be set by selecting **File>Prepare>Model Properties** and selecting **change** beside **Bend Allowance**.*

6. The Parameters dialog box opens as shown in Figure 11–21.

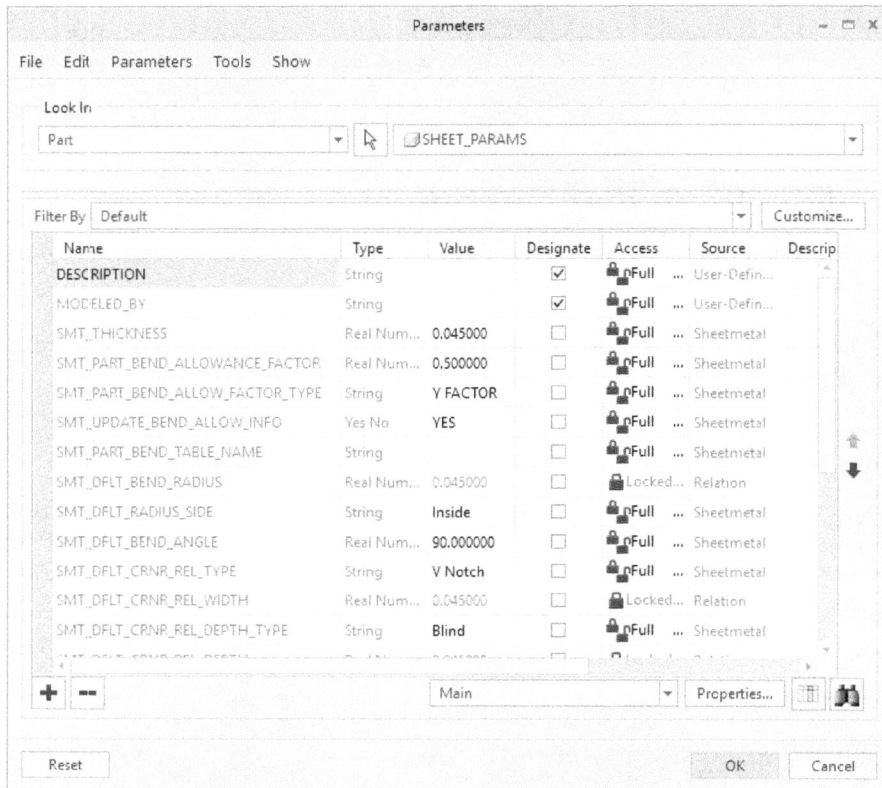

Figure 11–21

7. Verify or make the changes to the parameters as follows.

Parameter	Value
SMT_DFLT_RADIUS_SIDE	Inside
SMT_DFLT_BEND_REL_TYPE	Obround
SMT_DFLT_BEND_REL_DEPTH_TYPE	Up to Bend

Note that **SMT_DFLT_BEND_RADIUS** and **SMT_DFT_BEND_REL_WIDTH** values are locked. These values must be changed in the Relation Editor.

8. Select **File>Export Data>in * .csv format** in the Sheetmetal Parameters dialog box.

9. Save the **param_table.csv** file in your current working directory. These parameter settings can now be retrieved if required.

10. Click **OK** to close the Parameter dialog box.

11. Select **Model Intent>Relations**. The Relations Editor dialog box opens as shown in Figure 11-22.

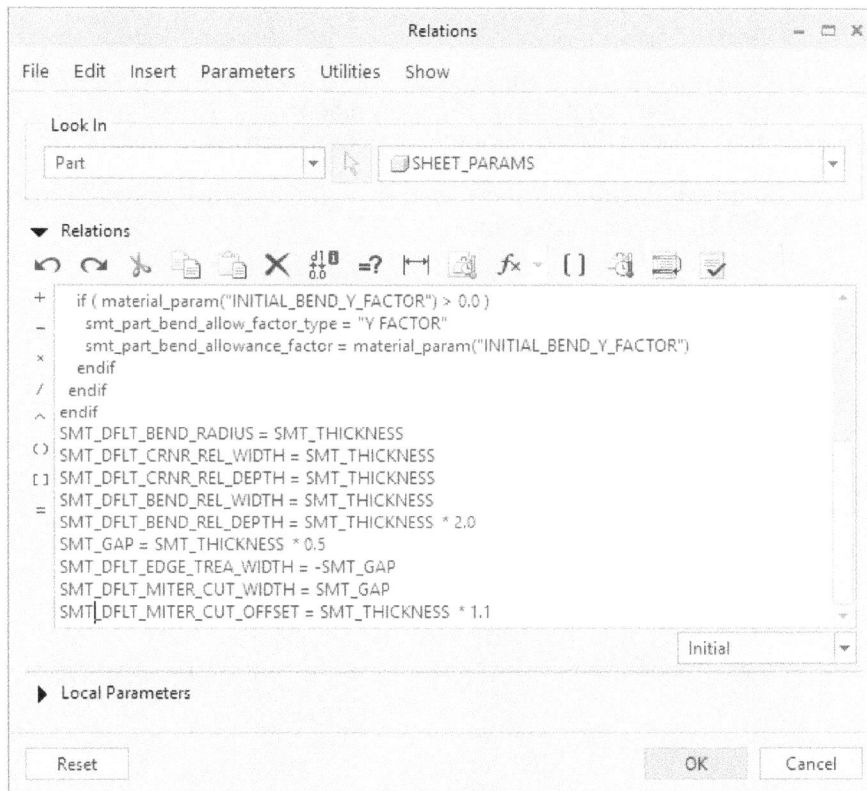

Figure 11-22

12. Change the **SMT_DFLT_BEND_RADIUS = SMT_THICKNESS** relation to **SMT_DFLT_BEND_RADIUS = SMT_THICKNESS*2.0**.

13. Select **File>Export Relations** in the Sheetmetal Relations dialog box.

14. Change the name to **practice11a_rel.txt** and save the file.

15. Click **Reset**. All the relation values are returned to their original settings.

16. Since you just saved the relation settings to a file, they can be retrieved. Select **File>Import Relations**. All of the relation values return to those you set.

Task 2: Create an extruded primary wall.

Design Considerations

In this task, you will create an extruded primary wall with a sharp corner in the sketch. You will use the SharpsToBend element to automatically apply a bend at the sharp corner. This element enables you to sketch cross-sections without the need to sketch every bend.

1. Click (Extrude) to create an extruded wall. Set the *Depth* to **Symmetric**, and enter **8**. Set the *Thickness* to **0.125**, as shown in Figure 11–23.

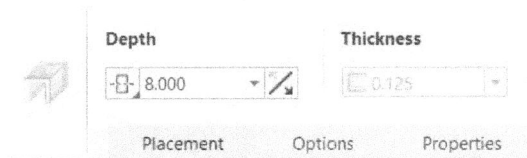

Figure 11–23

2. Select datum plane **FRONT** as the sketching plane.
3. Sketch the section with a sharp corner, as shown in Figure 11–24.

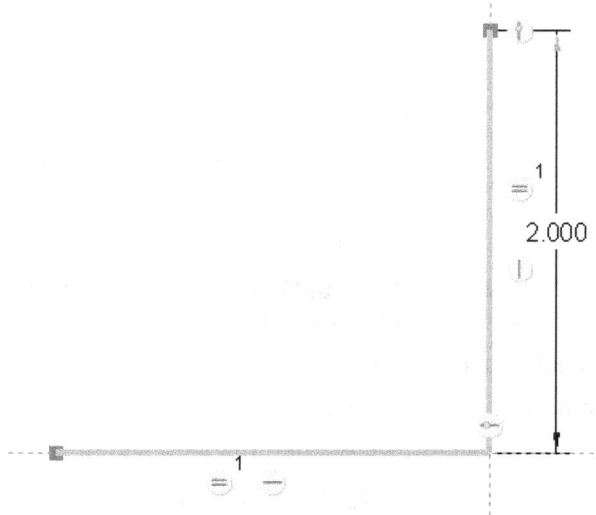

Figure 11–24

4. Complete the sketch.
5. Ensure that the arrow points toward the interior of the model as shown in Figure 11–25. If required, click on the arrow to flip its direction.

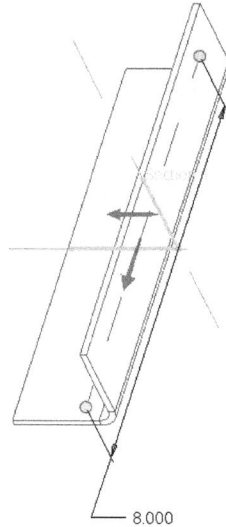

Figure 11–25

Note: The sharp edge automatically has a bend applied.

6. Click the Options panel and note that **Add bends on sharp edges** is selected by default, as shown in Figure 11–26.

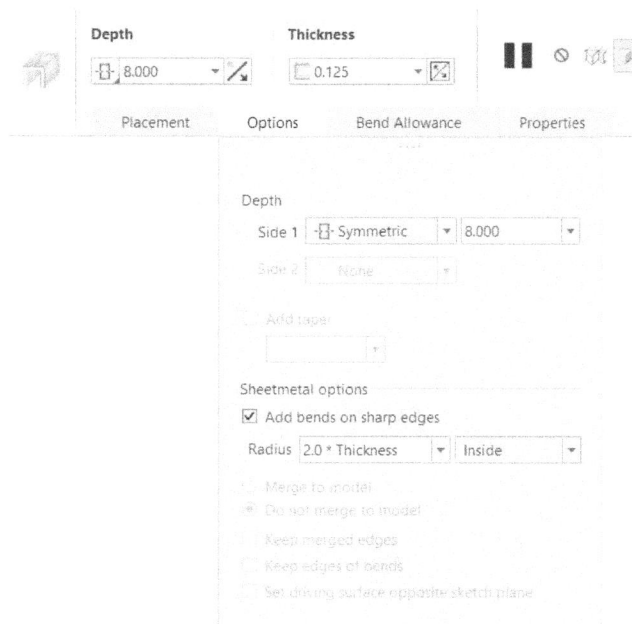

Figure 11–26

Design Considerations

The **Add bends on sharp edges** option causes the radius to be applied to all sharp corners in the section. The bend *Radius* is automatically set to **2.0 * Thickness** and **[Inside]**.

In the Sheetmetal Parameters dialog box, the value for the **SMT_DFLT_RADIUS_SIDE** (sheet metal default radius side) parameter is set to **Inside**.

7. Complete the feature. The part displays as shown in Figure 11−27.

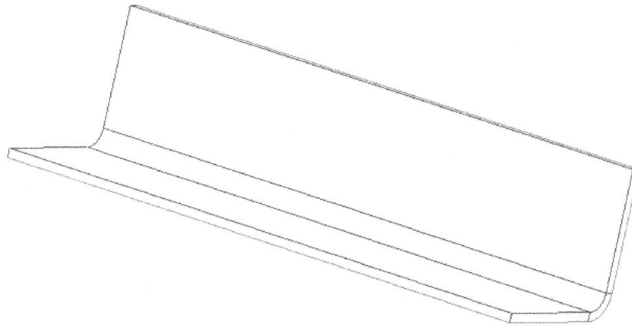

Figure 11−27

Task 3: Create a sheet metal cut.

1. Click ☐ (Extruded Cut) in the *Sheetmetal* tab to create a sheet metal cut.

2. Create the cut shown in Figure 11−28 using ≝ (To Next) for the depth option.

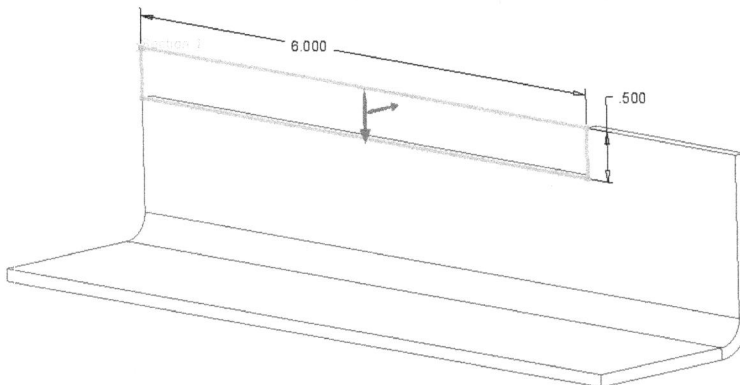

Figure 11−28

Task 4: Create a flange wall with an obround relief.

Design Considerations

In this task, you will create a flange wall and have the system automatically apply a bend relief as a result of the sheet metal parameters you set in Task 1.

1. Select the front edge shown in Figure 11–29 and click 🖐 (Flange) in the mini toolbar.

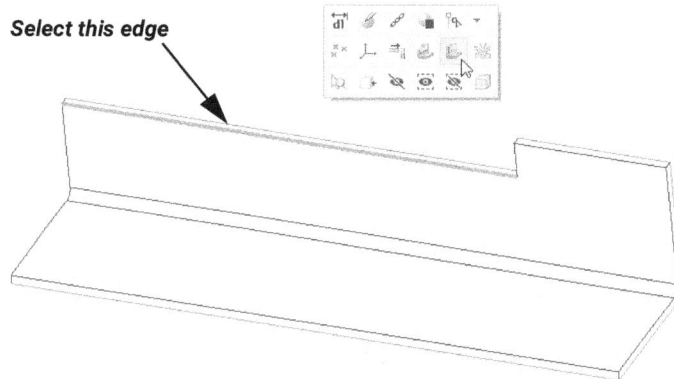

Select this edge

Figure 11–29

2. Edit the length to **4** and angle to **90**, as shown in Figure 11–30.

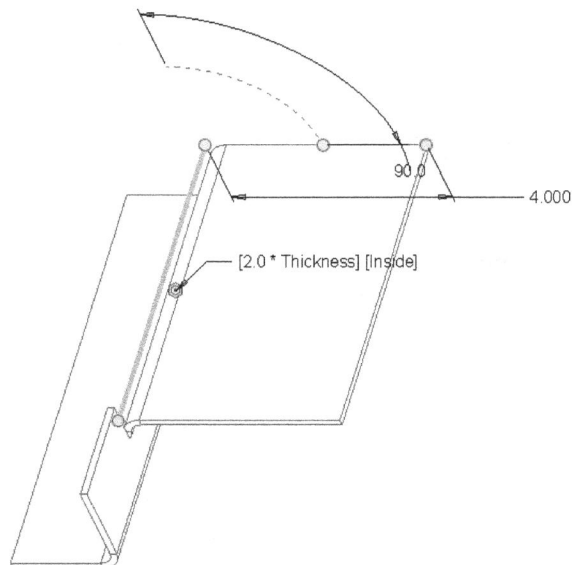

90.0

4.000

[2.0 * Thickness] [Inside]

Figure 11–30

3. Complete the feature by clicking ✔ (OK) in the dashboard. The part displays as shown in Figure 11–31.

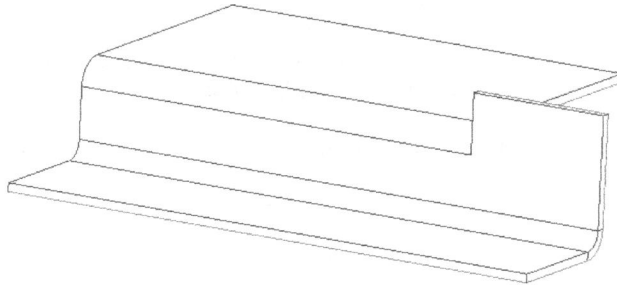

Figure 11–31

Design Considerations

The bend *Radius* is automatically set to **2.0*Thickness**.

The obround relief is automatically applied to the flange wall. The parameters defined in Task 1 decrease the time required to create features, such as this swept wall. In this case, **SMT_DFLT_BEND_RADIUS** and **SMT_DFLT_BEND_REL_TYPE** automated several steps in the process of creating this feature.

4. Select **Model Intent>Relations** to open the Sheetmetal Relations dialog box.

5. Change the value of the **SMT_DFLT_BEND_RADIUS** parameter to **Thickness** by deleting the ***2.0** and click **OK** to close the dialog box.

6. The part regenerates. The radii of the two bends has changed. The dimensions for these bend radii are controlled through relations by the parameter you just changed.

Task 5: Create a blind depth cut.

Design Considerations

In this task, you will create a sheet metal cut that is defined with a blind depth. Using a blind depth eliminates the need to flatten the part to create the cut geometry.

1. Select the surface shown in Figure 11–32 and click ⬚ (Extruded Cut) in the mini toolbar.

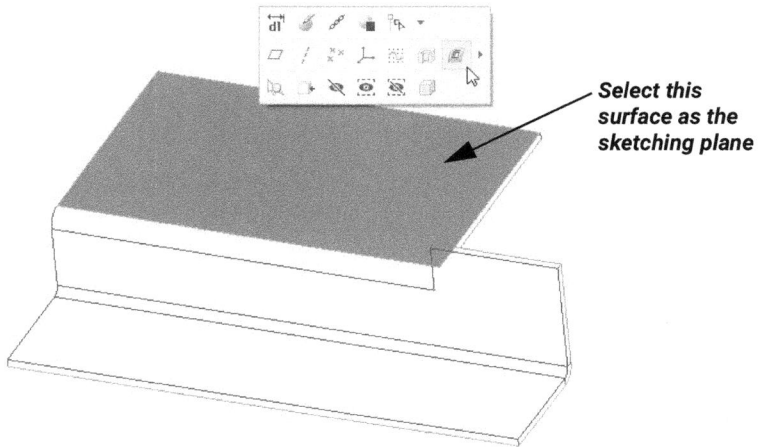

Select this surface as the sketching plane

Figure 11–32

2. Sketch the section shown in Figure 11–33.

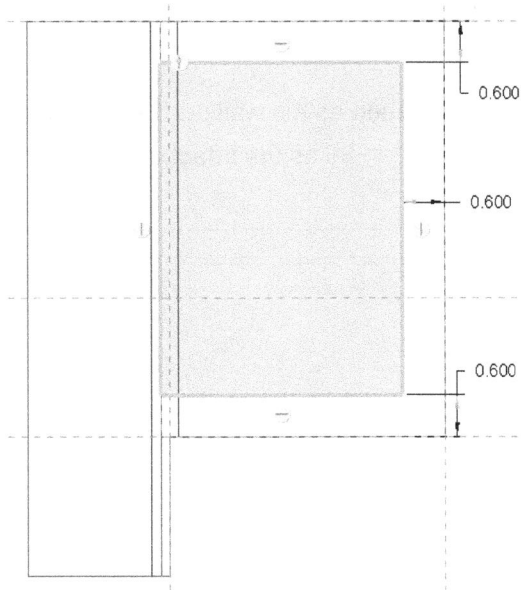

0.600

0.600

0.600

Figure 11–33

3. Complete the sketch.

4. Set the blind *Depth* to **0.75**. The cut displays as shown in Figure 11–34. Specifying a blind depth for a sheet metal cut eliminates the need to create this cut in an unbent state.

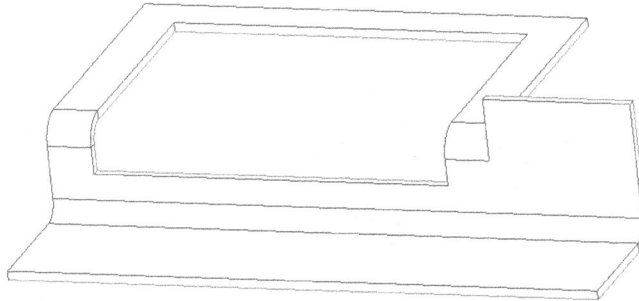

Figure 11–34

Task 6: Create flange walls with the flushed profile.

Design Considerations

In this task, you will create hems using the flange wall with the flushed profile. The predefined wall shapes enable you to quickly create and modify wall geometry.

1. Click ⬚ (Flange).
2. In the *Flange* dashboard, set **Flushed** as the wall profile to create a flushed hem.
3. Select the edge shown in Figure 11–35 as the attachment edge.

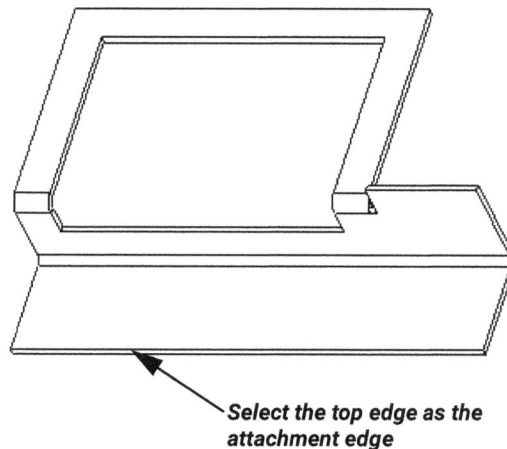

Select the top edge as the attachment edge

Figure 11–35

4. Edit the hem length to **0.45,** as shown in Figure 11–36.

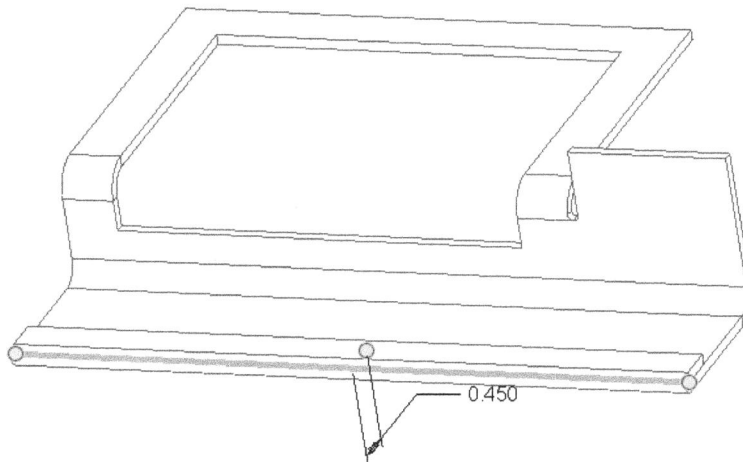

Figure 11–36

5. Complete the feature by clicking ✓ (OK) in the *Flange* dashboard.

6. Click ⬤ (Flange).

7. In the dashboard, set **Flushed** as the wall profile.

8. Select the edge shown in Figure 11–37 as the attachment edge for the second hem.

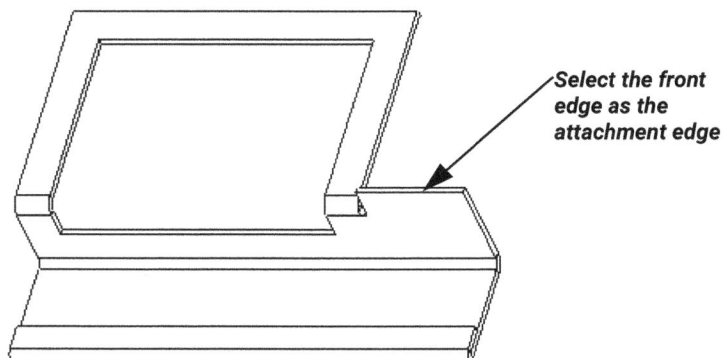

Select the front edge as the attachment edge

Figure 11–37

9. Click ✔ (OK) to complete the feature. The completed feature displays as shown in Figure 11–38.

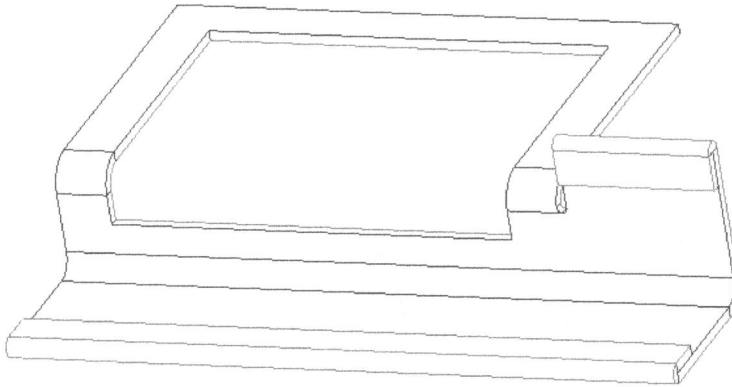

Figure 11–38

10. Save the model and erase it from memory.

End of practice

Chapter Review Questions

1. You can control the developed length of the model using which of the following methods? (Select all that apply.)

    a. Adjust the Y-factor, which works in conjunction with a formula to control the position of the neutral bend line.

    b. Modify the developed length dimension on the model. This method overrides the formula used by Creo Parametric.

    c. Use a bend table to control the developed length of the part.

    d. You cannot control the developed length of the model.

2. The Y-factor is a ratio based on the position of the neutral bend line with respect to the wall thickness of the material.

    a. True

    b. False

3. Bend tables use which of the following rules? (Select all that apply.)

    a. If the table does not have a formula, the system uses the default formula and Y-factor.

    b. If the values for the bend radius and material thickness match those in the table, Creo Parametric uses the values from the table.

    c. If the value falls between two of the values in the table, Creo Parametric linearly interpolates the developed length value.

    d. If the value falls outside the table, Creo Parametric uses the table's formula.

4. The **Fixed Geometry** option can be used to automatically specify that the same entity remains fixed each time.

    a. True

    b. False

Answers: 1abc, 2a, 3abcd, 4a

Investigating a Sheet Metal Part

Creo Parametric provides several tools for investigating the geometry of your sheet metal parts. You can also generate reports to find detailed information on the various features and parameters in the model.

Learning Objectives

- Learn to use the *Analysis* tab tools to check, measure, and analyze the sheet metal model.
- Understand the steps used to generate and save a report that provides information on the sheet metal part.
- Create design rules in the Model Properties dialog box to control individual models and processes.

12.1 Investigation Tools

Creo Parametric provides several tools for checking your models. You can use the measurement analysis options to check the developed length of the bend feature after modification. You can also use the **Angle** option to determine the angle between surfaces and the **Length** option to determine the length of an attachment edge.

In addition to measurement, you can analyze the curvature of surfaces on your sheet metal model. One of the most common problems when modeling sheet metal parts is the inability to flatten them when they are finished. In many cases, this is due to complex surfaces that require deformation. By using surface analysis tools, you can anticipate where you could have trouble later.

Surfaces with curvature in two directions (non-ruled) have a large amount of deformation in them to generate that shape in sheet metal. However, Creo Parametric cannot capture this condition by creating a deformation. Instead, you can determine which surfaces require such deformations by using the **Shaded curvature** tool. It calculates the product of maximum and minimum curvature at all points on a surface.

The Shaded analysis displays a fringe plot with various colors that denote the differences in curvature on a surface, as shown in Figure 12–1.

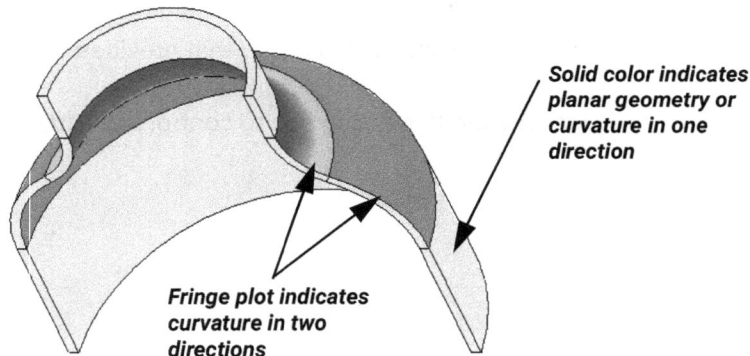

Solid color indicates planar geometry or curvature in one direction

Fringe plot indicates curvature in two directions

Figure 12–1

Solid colors represent planar geometry or ruled geometry (cylinders and cones). When a surface has multiple color variations, it is considered to have curvature in two directions. This means the surface has non-ruled geometry and deformation.

12.2 Sheet Metal Reports

Reports provide information about the sheet metal part. The report enables you to investigate your design and ensures that it adheres to company standards. Reports are typically required before manufacturing the part.

By default, sheet metal reports are generated in HTML. They provide information on the following items related to your sheet metal part:

- Thickness of part
- K-factor and Y-factor
- Part bend tables
- Feature bend tables
- Bend allowance
- Bend radii
- Violations of design rules

How To: Create a Sheet Metal Report

1. Select an entity in the Model Tree or graphics area, then right-click on it and select **Information>Model Information**. The report displays in the Creo Parametric browser window.

   Note: *Alternatively, you can select the Tools tab, expand* ⬚ *(Model), and select* ⬚ *(Model Information).*

2. The sheet metal report displays in the Creo Parametric browser window. The report is divided into sections.

   The *Model Info* area, shown in Figure 12−2, provides a summary of the model.

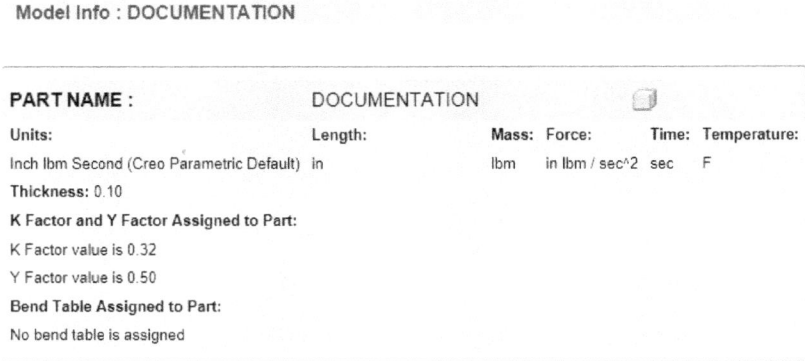

Model Info : DOCUMENTATION

PART NAME :	DOCUMENTATION				
Units:	Length:	Mass:	Force:	Time:	Temperature:
Inch lbm Second (Creo Parametric Default)	in	lbm	in lbm / sec^2	sec	F
Thickness: 0.10					
K Factor and Y Factor Assigned to Part:					
K Factor value is 0.32					
Y Factor value is 0.50					
Bend Table Assigned to Part:					
No bend table is assigned					

Figure 12−2

After the summary, the report provides detailed information on the sheet metal model, as shown in Figure 12−3 and Figure 12−4. This information can be useful to quickly determine the K- and Y-factors used by the part, the bend tables used by the part or by a specific feature, and the bend allowance information.

Used K and Y Factors by Part

K-factor		Y-factor		Type		Actions	
0.318		0.500		Part Assignment		⚠	🖹

Bend Tables Associated with Part

There are no associated Bend Tables with the model.

Feature List

No.		ID		Name		Type		Actions		Sup Order
1		1		DTM1		DATUM PLANE		⚠	📄	---
2		3		DTM2		DATUM PLANE		⚠	📄	---
3		5		DTM3		DATUM PLANE		⚠	📄	---
4		7		---		Wall Surface(First Wall)		⚠	📄	---
5		511		---		WALL		⚠	📄	---
6		584				WALL		⚠	📄	

Figure 12−3

12	882	---	FORM		⚠		
13	1441	DTM12	DATUM PLANE		⚠	📄	---

Bends Containing Feature Bend Table

There are no assigned Bend Tables to feature.

Bends Allowance

Feature Name		Feature ID		Equation	Bend Radius	Variables	Bend Allowance	Actions	
Wall id 511		511		L=(PI/2*R + Y Factor*T)*ANGLE/90 Y FACTOR = 0.50	rd53=0.500	ANGLE=90.00	0.835	⚠	📄
Wall id 584		584		L=(PI/2*R + Y Factor*T)*ANGLE/90 Y FACTOR = 0.50	rd58=0.500	ANGLE=90.00	0.835	⚠	📄
Wall id 657		657		L=(PI/2*R + Y Factor*T)*ANGLE/90 Y FACTOR = 0.50	rd70=0.500	ANGLE=90.00	0.835	⚠	📄
Wall id 385		385		L=(PI/2*R + Y Factor*T)*ANGLE/90 Y FACTOR = 0.50	rd45=0.250	ANGLE=90.00	0.443	⚠	📄

Figure 12−4

The *Bend Radii* area enables you to examine the bend radii used to create the model, including feature ID, dimension name, radius value, radius type, and inside radius value as shown in Figure 12–5. This information enables you to quickly determine whether or not the model was built according to corporate or industry standards.

○ Display all bend radii
○ Display suggested bend radii only
○ Display non suggested bend radii only

Bend Radii

Feature Name	Feature ID	Bend Radius	Radius Type	Inside Bend Radius
Wall id 511	511	rd53=0.500 ()	Inside	0.500
Wall id 584	584	rd58=0.500 ()	Inside	0.500
Wall id 657	657	rd70=0.500 ()	Inside	0.500
Wall id 385	385	rd45=0.250 ()	Inside	0.250

Design Rule Violations Check

Rule Name	Rule Formula	Rule Value	Current Value	ID of Ref#1	ID of Ref#2
MIN_CUT_TO_BEND	2*T+R	0.7000	0.5250	732	1027
MIN_WALL_HEIGHT	1.75*T+R	0.6750	0.5000	31	864
MIN_WALL_HEIGHT	1.75*T+R	0.6750	0.4500	29	827
MIN_SLOT_TAB_LENGTH	0.7	0.7000	0.2500	456	456
MIN_SLOT_TAB_LENGTH	0.7	0.7000	0.4000	865	865

Figure 12–5

If design rules have been established, you can use them to check whether your model adheres to the defined standards. When conflicts occur between your model and the established rules they display in the *Design Rules - Violations Check* area, as shown in Figure 12–5. When a violation occurs, this area displays the rule name and formula along with dimensional values. This enables you to determine why the design did not fulfill the rule criteria.

3. You can save the report into an HTML file by clicking ⊟ (Save to File) in the Browser toolbar.

Text Reports

You can also obtain a text report, if required. Text reports are not consolidated, instead each report displays in separate window. You can view, edit, or save each report to a file.

To output a text report, set the **info_output_format** config.pro option to **text**.

> **Note:** *By default, reports are generated in HTML.*

Once the configuration option has been changed, expand Model and select **Sheetmetal** in the *Tools* tab and select one of the following types of reports:

* Bend Reports
* Radii Reports
* Design Check

12.3 Design Rules

To address the variability in materials and processes during sheet metal fabrication, you can create design rules to govern a variety of situations. To create design rules for a model, select change by **Design Rules** in the Model Properties dialog box.

To set up design rules, you must create a design rule table and assign it to the model. You can create as many tables as required to control individual models and processes. You can use a table to establish rules for minimum wall height, minimum distance between cuts, minimum slot widths and heights, etc., as shown in Figure 12−6.

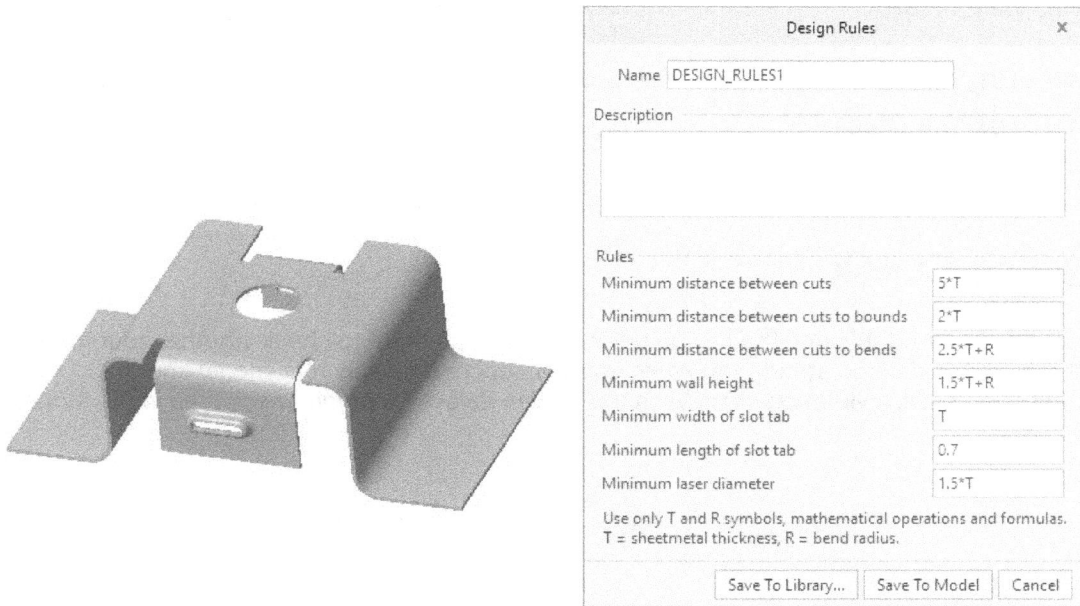

Figure 12−6

The design rules are described as follows:

Rule	Description
MIN_DIST_BTWN_CUTS	Checks the distance between two cuts or punches. The default value is 5T.
MIN_CUT_TO_BOUND	Checks the distance from the edge of the part to a cut or punch. The default value is 2T.
MIN_CUT_TO_BEND	Checks the distance from a bend-line to a cut or punch. The default value is 2.5*T+R.
MIN_WALL_HEIGHT	Checks the minimum bend height of formed walls. The default value is 1.5*T+R.
MIN_SLOT_TAB_WIDTH	Checks the minimum width of tabs. The default value is T.
MIN_SLOT_TAB_LENGTH	Checks the minimum length of tabs. The default value is 0.7.
MIN_LASER_DIM	Checks the minimum distance between features that are to be laser cut. The default value is 1.5*T.

Design Check

Once you have established the design rules, you can use them to check whether your model adheres to the defined standards. When conflicts occur between your model and the established rules, a violation displays in the *Design Rules - Violation Check* area in the Model Info report.

Practice 12a
Sheet Metal Information Tools

Practice Objectives

- Perform a Gaussian surface analysis.
- Generate a bend and a radii report.
- Establish design rules and perform a design check.

In this practice, you will investigate a sheet metal part using the investigation tools discussed in this chapter.

Task 1: Open a part and examine the model's surface curvature.

Design Considerations

In this task, you will open the part and perform a Gaussian surface curvature analysis. This form of analysis helps you to quickly identify any non-ruled surfaces on the sheet metal part.

1. Set the working directory to the *Sheetmetal_Information* folder.

2. Open **documentation.prt**.

3. Set the model display as follows:

    - (*Datum Display Filters*): None

    - (*Spin Center*): Off

    - (*Display Style*): (Shading With Edges)

4. Select the *Analysis* tab.

5. Expand (Curvature) and select (Shaded Curvature). The Shaded Curvature dialog box opens.

6. Set the selection filter, located at the bottom right corner of the main window, to **Solid Geometry**. This enables you to select the entire part when you perform the analysis.

7. Select any surface on the part. The entire part is selected. The result displays as shown in Figure 12–7.

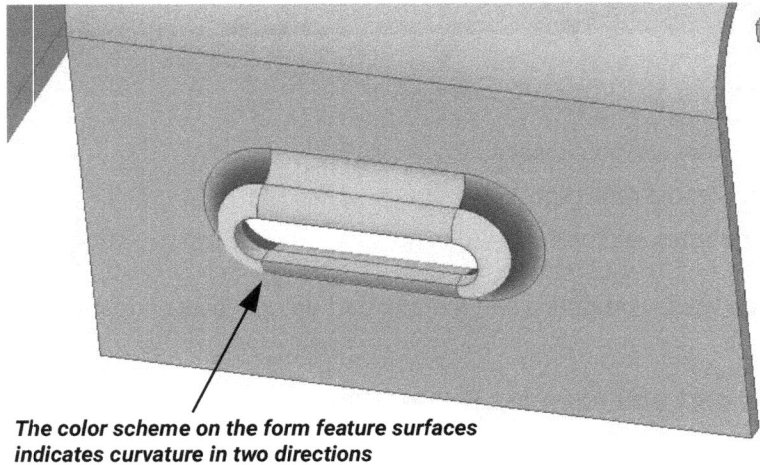

The color scheme on the form feature surfaces indicates curvature in two directions

Figure 12–7

The fringe plot area on the form feature on the back of the part has deformation during bending and unbending.

8. Close the dialog box and return the model to the default orientation.

Task 2: Examine the bend report for the model.

Design Considerations

In this task, you will generate a report on the sheet metal part. You will use this report to identify:

*   Bends for which a feature bend table has been used.
*   Bends that have angles other than 90°.

1. Select the *Sheetmetal* tab.

2. Select any object in the Model Tree, right-click and select **Information>Model Information**, as shown in Figure 12–8.

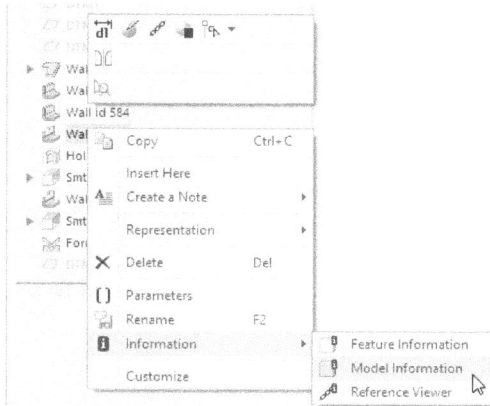

Figure 12–8

3. The sheet metal report displays in the Creo Parametric browser window. Scroll to the *Bend Allowance* area of the report, as shown in Figure 12–9.

	Bends Allowance						
Feature Name ▸	Feature ID ▸	Equation	Bend Radius	Variables	Bend Allowance	Actions	
Wall id 511	511	L=(PI/2*R + Y Factor*T)*ANGLE/90 Y FACTOR = 0.50	rd53=0.500	ANGLE=90.00	0.835	⊿⁺	🗈
Wall id 584	584	L=(PI/2*R + Y Factor*T)*ANGLE/90 Y FACTOR = 0.50	rd58=0.500	ANGLE=90.00	0.835	⊿⁺	🗈
Wall id 657	657	L=(PI/2*R + Y Factor*T)*ANGLE/90 Y FACTOR = 0.50	rd70=0.500	ANGLE=90.00	0.835	⊿⁺	🗈
Wall id 385	385	L=(PI/2*R + Y Factor*T)*ANGLE/90 Y FACTOR = 0.50	rd45=0.250	ANGLE=90.00	0.443	⊿⁺	🗈

Figure 12–9

4. Scroll to the *Bend Radii* area of the report (below the *Bend allowance* area), as shown in Figure 12–10. The *Bend radii* area identifies bends with radii for which a value has been entered, instead of using the *Thickness* or **2.0 * Thickness** option.

◉ Display all bend radii
○ Display suggested bend radii only
○ Display non suggested bend radii only

	Bend Radii							
Feature Name	▸	Feature ID	▸	Bend Radius	▸	Radius Type	▸	Inside Bend Radius	▸
Wall id 511		511		rd53=0.500 ()		Inside		0.500	
Wall id 584		584		rd58=0.500 ()		Inside		0.500	
Wall id 657		657		rd70=0.500 ()		Inside		0.500	
Wall id 385		385		rd45=0.250 ()		Inside		0.250	

Figure 12–10

5. Click the **Feature ID** of a bend to highlight it in the model.

6. Close the browser.

Task 3: Establish design rules.

Design Considerations

In this task, you will define design rules and generate a report to determine whether the part violates any of these rules. This product data quality tool can assist in preparation for manufacturing.

1. Select **File>Prepare>Model Properties**. Select **change** next to Design Rules as shown in Figure 12–11.

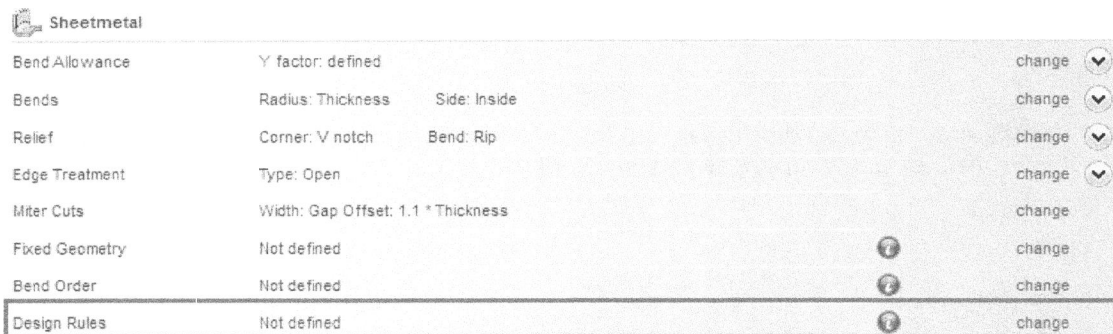

Sheetmetal				
Bend Allowance	Y factor: defined		change	⌄
Bends	Radius: Thickness	Side: Inside	change	⌄
Relief	Corner: V notch	Bend: Rip	change	⌄
Edge Treatment	Type: Open		change	⌄
Miter Cuts	Width: Gap Offset: 1.1 * Thickness		change	
Fixed Geometry	Not defined	ⓘ	change	
Bend Order	Not defined	ⓘ	change	
Design Rules	Not defined	ⓘ	change	

Figure 12–11

2. In the Design Rules dialog box, click ▢ (New).

3. The Design Rules dialog box opens displaying the default sheet metal parameters and values. Set the *Name* to **design_rules1**, as shown in Figure 12–12.

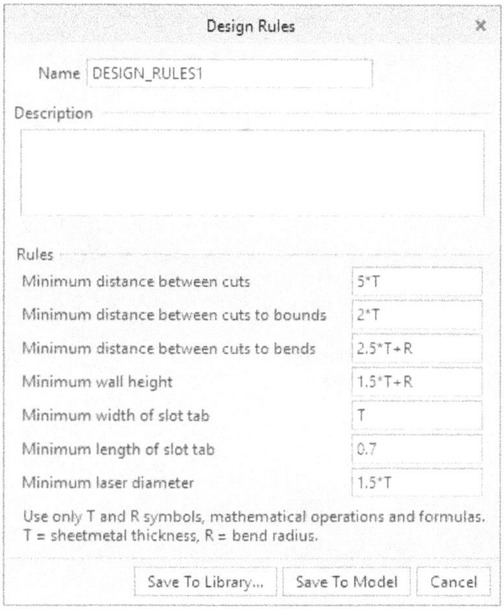

Figure 12-12

4. Edit the table to reflect the values shown in Figure 12-13. Select the appropriate cells in column *C2* to enter the new values.

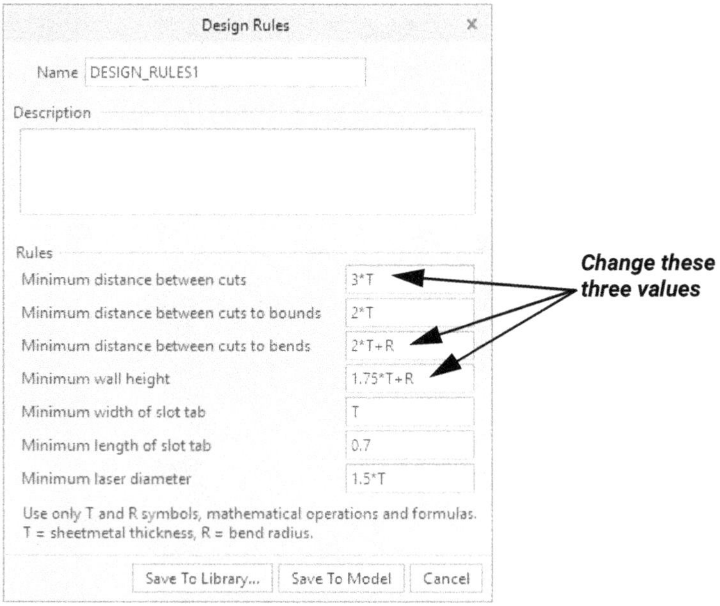

Figure 12-13

5. Click **Save To Model**. Click **OK** and close the Model Properties dialog box.

6. This assigns the rule table to the part and means the rules table is stored with the model.

   *Note: To save the table to disk, click **Save To Library**.... This option saves the file to your current working directory as **design_rules1.rul**.*

7. Select any entity, right-click and select **Information>Model Information**. Scroll down to the *Design Rules - Violations Check* area in the information window. A list of violations to the recently established design rules as listed, as shown in Figure 12−14.

Design Rule Violations Check

Rule Name	Rule Formula	Rule Value	Current Value	ID of Ref#1	ID of Ref#2
MIN_CUT_TO_BEND	2*T+R	0.7000	0.5250	732	1027
MIN_WALL_HEIGHT	1.75*T+R	0.6750	0.5000	31	864
MIN_WALL_HEIGHT	1.75*T+R	0.6750	0.4500	29	827
MIN_SLOT_TAB_LENGTH	0.7	0.7000	0.2500	456	456
MIN_SLOT_TAB_LENGTH	0.7	0.7000	0.4000	865	865

Figure 12−14

8. Select each line in the box to highlight the corresponding violation on the model. Once you have reviewed the violations, close the information window.

9. Save the model and erase it from memory.

Chapter Review Questions

1. Which tool calculates the product of maximum and minimum curvature at all of the points on a surface?

   a. Mesh Surface

   b. Sections

   c. Shaded curvature

   d. Measure

2. Which of the following items is not reported in a sheet metal Model Information report?

   a. Thickness of part

   b. K-factor and Y-factor

   c. Part bend tables

   d. Part density

   e. Bend radii

   f. Violations of design rules

3. To address the variability in materials and processes during sheet metal fabrication, you can create design rules to govern a variety of situations.

   a. True

   b. False

4. The mechanism for establishing design rules is to create a design rule table and assign it to the model.

   a. True

   b. False

Answers: 1c, 2d, 3a, 4a

www.ingramcontent.com/pod-product-compliance
Lightning Source LLC
Chambersburg PA
CBHW080124220326
41598CB00032B/4946